INTELLECTUAL LIFE AND LITERATURE AT SOLOVKI 1923–1930
THE PARIS OF THE NORTHERN CONCENTRATION CAMPS

LEGENDA

LEGENDA is the Modern Humanities Research Association's book imprint for new research in the Humanities. Founded in 1995 by Malcolm Bowie and others within the University of Oxford, Legenda has always been a collaborative publishing enterprise, directly governed by scholars. The Modern Humanities Research Association (MHRA) joined this collaboration in 1998, became half-owner in 2004, in partnership with Maney Publishing and then Routledge, and has since 2016 been sole owner. Titles range from medieval texts to contemporary cinema and form a widely comparative view of the modern humanities, including works on Arabic, Catalan, English, French, German, Greek, Italian, Portuguese, Russian, Spanish, and Yiddish literature. Editorial boards and committees of more than 60 leading academic specialists work in collaboration with bodies such as the Society for French Studies, the British Comparative Literature Association and the Association of Hispanists of Great Britain & Ireland.

The MHRA encourages and promotes advanced study and research in the field of the modern humanities, especially modern European languages and literature, including English, and also cinema. It aims to break down the barriers between scholars working in different disciplines and to maintain the unity of humanistic scholarship. The Association fulfils this purpose through the publication of journals, bibliographies, monographs, critical editions, and the MHRA Style Guide, and by making grants in support of research. Membership is open to all who work in the Humanities, whether independent or in a University post, and the participation of younger colleagues entering the field is especially welcomed.

ALSO PUBLISHED BY THE ASSOCIATION

Critical Texts
Tudor and Stuart Translations • *New Translations* • *European Translations*
MHRA Library of Medieval Welsh Literature

MHRA Bibliographies
Publications of the Modern Humanities Research Association

The Annual Bibliography of English Language & Literature
Austrian Studies
Modern Language Review
Portuguese Studies
The Slavonic and East European Review
Working Papers in the Humanities
The Yearbook of English Studies

www.mhra.org.uk
www.legendabooks.com

EDITORIAL BOARD

This book is dedicated to
Antonina Alekseevna Soshina

Intellectual Life and Literature at Solovki 1923–1930

The Paris of the Northern Concentration Camps

❖

ANDREA GULLOTTA

l

LEGENDA

Modern Humanities Research Association
2018

Published by Legenda
an imprint of the Modern Humanities Research Association
Salisbury House, Station Road, Cambridge CB1 2LA

ISBN 978-1-78188-691-5 (HB)
ISBN 978-1-78188-363-1 (PB)

First published 2018

Copy-Editor: Dr Nigel Hope

CONTENTS

❖

LIST OF ABBREVIATIONS

❖

Archives and Collections

AAS	Private Archive of Antonina Soshina, Solovki
ADRZ	Archive of the Dom Russkogo Zarubezh'ia im. Aleksandra Solzhenitsyna (Aleksandr Solzhenitsyn House of Russian Emigration), Moscow
AGFF	Archive of the Giangiacomo Feltrinelli Foundation, Milan
AG	Arkhiv Gor'kogo (The Gor'kii Archive), Moscow
AMM	Archive of the Historical, Educational, Human Rights and Charitable Society Memorial, Moscow
AMSPB	Archive of the Research and Information Centre Memorial, Saint Petersburg
APRF	Arkhiv Prezidenta Rossiiskoi Federatsii (Archive of the President of Russian Federation), Moscow
ASM	Archive of the Solovki State Historical, Architectural, and Natural Museum-Reserve
ATsM	Private Archive of Tsetsiliia Mel'nikova, Cologne
CBSB	Collection of the Bayerische Staatsbibliothek, Munich
CNLR	Collection of the National Library of Russia, Saint Petersburg
CPD	Collection of the Institute of Russian Literature of the Russian Academy of Sciences 'Pushkinskii dom', Saint Petersburg
CRSL	Collection of the Russian State Library, Moscow
GARF	Gosudarstvennyi Arkhiv Rossiiskoi Federatsii (State Archive of the Russian Federation), Moscow
ITs MVD RK	Informatsionnyi Tsentr, Ministerstvo Vnutrennykh Del Respubliki Karelii (Information Centre of the Ministry of Internal Affairs of the Republic of Karelia), Petrozavodsk
RGALI	Rossiiskii Gosudarstvennyi Arkhiv Literatury i Isskusstv (Russian State Archive of Literature and Art), Moscow
TsA FSB ROSSII	Tsentral'nyi Arkhiv Federal'noi Sluzhby Bezopasnosti (Central Archive of the Russian Federal Security Service), Moscow

Institutions

Glavlit	Glavnoe Upravlenie po Delam Literatury i Izdatel'stv (Main Administration for Literary and Publishing Affairs)
Gorardom	Gorodskoi Arestantnyi Dom (City District House of Detention)
GPU	Gosudarstvennoe Politicheskoe Upravlenie (State Political Directorate)
GULag	Glavnoe Upravlenie Lagerei (Chief Administration of Corrective Labour Camps)
GUMZ	Glavnoe Upravlenie Mestami Zakliucheniia (Main Administration for the Places of Detention)
Karlit	Karelian Glavlit
Ispravtruddom	Ispravitel'no-Trudovoi Dom (House of Corrective Labour)

MGB	Ministerstvo Gosudarstvennoi Bezopasnosti (Ministry for State Security)
NKVD	Narodnyi Komissariat Vnutrennikh Del (People's Commissariat for Internal Affairs)
OGPU	Ob"edinennoe Gosudarstvennoe Politicheskoe Upravlenie (Unified State Political Directorate)
Railit	Regional headquarters of the Glavlit
RKP	Rossiiskaia Kommunisticheskaia Partiia
RSFSR	Rossiiskaia Sovetskaia Federativnaia Sotsialisticheskaia Respublika (Russian Soviet Federative Socialist Republic)
SLON	Solovetskii Lager' Osobogo Naznacheniia (Solovki Special Purpose Prison Camp) or Severnye Lageria Osobogo Naznacheniia (Northern Special Purpose Prison Camp)
Sovnarkom	Sovet Narodnykh Komissarov (Council of People's Commissars)
STON	Solovetskaia Tiur'ma Osobogo Naznacheniia (Solovki Special Purpose Prison)
USIKMITL	Upravleniia Solovetskimi i Karelo-Murmanskimi Ispravitel'no Trudovymi Lageriami (Administrations of the Solovki and Karelian-Murmansk Forced Labour Camps)
USLON	Upravlenie Solovetskimi Lageriami Osobogo Naznacheniia (Administration of the Solovki Special Purpose Prison Camps)
VChK (Cheka)	Vserossiiskaia Chrezvychainaia Komissiia po Bor'be s Kontrrevoliutsiei i Sabotazhem (All-Russian Extraordinary Commission for Combating Counter-Revolution and Sabotage)
VTsIK	Verkhovnyi Tsentral'nyi Ispolnitel'nyi Komitet (Higher Central Executive Committee)

Other abbreviations

BAM	Baikalo-Amurskaia Magistral' (Baikal-Amur Main Line)
BBK or Belomorkanal	Belomorsko-Baltiiskii Kanal (White Sea-Baltic Canal)
Belbaltlag	Belomorsko-Baltiiiskii Lager' (White Sea-Baltic Canal Prison Camp)
CPSU	Communist Party of the Soviet Union
EKCh	Ekonomicheskaia Kommercheskaia Chast' (Economic Commercial Dept)
esery	sotsialist-revoliutsionery (socialist-revolutionaries)
kaery	kontr-revoliutsionery (counter-revolutionaries)
Kemperpunkt	Kemskii Peresyl'nyi Punkt (Kem' Transit Camp)
Komroty	Komandir Roty (commander of a company)
Krimkab	Kriminologicheskii Kabinet (Department of Criminology of the SLON)
KVCh	Kul'turno-Vospitatel'naia Chast' (Cultural and Educational Department)
lagkory	lagernye korrispondenty (camp correspondents)
likbez	likvidatsia bezgramotnosti (liquidation of illiteracy)
NS	*Novye Solovki* (One of the Journals of the SLON)
politiki or politzakliuchennye	Politicheskie Zakliuchennye (Political Prisoners)
RAPP	Rossiiskaia Assotsiatsiia Proletarskikh Pisatelei (Russian Association of Proletarian Writers)
seksot	Sekretnyi sotrudnik (secret collaborator, informer)
SO	*Solovetskie Ostrova* (One of the Journals of the SLON)
SOK	Solovetskoe Obshchestvo Kraevedeniia (Society of Ethnography of the Solovki)
Solteatr	Solovetskii Teatr (Theatre of the Solovki)
Sovpartshkola	Sovetskaia partiinaia shkola (Soviet Party School)
VOKhR	Voenizirovannaia Okhrana (Militarized Guards)

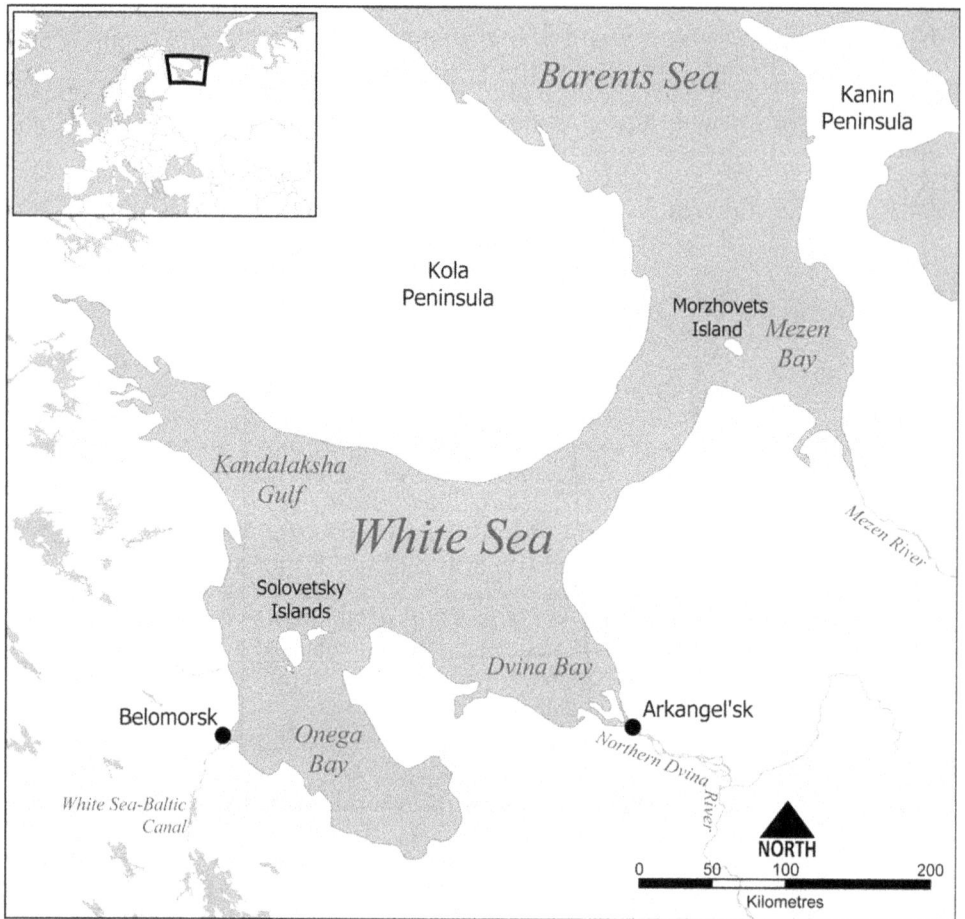

Map of the White Sea. The Solovki monastery is located on the west shore of the largest of the Solovetskii islands, which is around 25 × 16 km. Except for fragile sea-planes (see Fig. 4.6), the islands were accessible only by sea, and only from mid-May to mid-October: even today, the White Sea is frozen for six months of the year. (Credit: Norman Einstein, 2006)

INTRODUCTION

❖

> The SLON is the Paris of the Northern concentration camps.
> Ivan Ozerov[1]

Thirty years after the beginning of perestroika, it is finally possible to state that the Gulag has become a research theme that is thoroughly studied everywhere in the world, as testified by the many publications on the topic, which investigate many aspects of the history of the Soviet concentration camp system, and by the increasing number of conferences devoted to the Gulag. Surprisingly enough, the same cannot be said about Gulag literature.

Regardless of the many publications on authors who wrote about the Gulag (the most studied authors being Aleksandr Solzhenitsyn and Varlam Shalamov), it is impossible to speak of 'Gulag literature' as a defined object or as a fully defined research topic. In other words, using the most felicitous metaphor that has been applied to the Soviet camps, the many islands of the archipelago 'Gulag literature' have not yet been put on the map, and most of them remain totally unexplored to this day.

This fact in itself is rather surprising, considering both the quantity and the quality of the literary texts produced about the Gulag. The reasons for the lack of scholarly attention to this type of literature are many and complicated. One of the main ones is the fragmentariness of the corpus, which is comprised of literary texts published in different periods and, above all, in different and dispersed forms (see the case of Shalamov's *Kolyma Tales*, which appeared first in tamizdat and in samizdat, then in an abridged version during the perestroika period and, finally, in a definitive version in the 1990s).[2] Another major reason for such neglect can be found in the Russian socio-historical context, where the boom in the literature of the Gulag during Gorbachev's era produced a glut of material, with the consequence that the audience felt overfed and sated within a decade,[3] while under Putin the theme of Soviet state repression has been catalogued in the mainstream media as an unfortunate incident on the glorious path of Russia through the centuries.[4]

1   ['СЛОН — Париж северных лагерей']. Iurii Brodskii, *Solovki. Dvadtsat' let osobogo naznacheniia* (Moscow: Mir Iskusstv II, 2008), p. 15.
2   Varlam Šalamov, *I racconti di Kolyma* (Turin: Einaudi, 1999), I, pp. vii–xlii.
3   See the analysis of the phenomenon of the 'hypertrophy' of Gulag literature by Mauro Martini: *Oltre il disgelo: la letteratura russa dopo l'Urss* (Milan: Bruno Mondadori, 2002), pp. 47–63.
4   The government's attitude towards the past has had a strong impact on the memory of Soviet repression. The case of the history textbooks authorized by the Kremlin is just one of a series of actions which seem to be aimed at rehabilitating Stalin and, overall, the Soviet past by hiding the

The works devoted to Gulag literature usually provide an analysis of single literary works or single authors, leaving unanswered many questions about the specifics of Gulag literature. Most prominently, scholarly research on the aesthetic features of this peculiar type of literature has ignored some fundamental issues — such as, for instance, the impact of trauma on literary form, which seems to affect some structural stylistic features both in Gulag poetry and prose — focusing more on the witnessing function of these texts, on their genesis and their reception. Many other focal issues are still to be addressed, for instance the autobiographical substrate of the works generated from the Gulag, i.e. texts written by people who did not 'have the right to biography'[5] but were rather 'chosen by history' and, when putting down their recollections on paper, approached their role of 'active autobiography writers' in different ways.[6] Among other topics that have yet to be thoroughly investigated are the heritage of the literature of the Silver Age in the work of the numerous Gulag literature authors who grew up during this period and whose writing shows traces of that extraordinary time;[7] the connection between literary form and oral composition in relation to the question of the addressee of the poems composed orally within the camps; the impact of the socio-historical context on the literary works, which was the reason for the striking differences in literary form and stylistic choices between the texts written by former prisoners of Stalin's Gulag and those by Gulag prisoners under Khrushchev and Brezhnev; and so on.

Other than these, many questions remain unanswered, above all, questions about the scope and boundaries of the literary corpus. What is Gulag literature? Is it comprised only of works written by former Gulag detainees? Should only the

crimes perpetrated by the state. See, amongst the many articles devoted to the topic, the analysis by Vladimir Ryzhkov: Vladimir Ryzhkov, 'Putin's Distorted History', *The Moscow Times*, 18 November 2013 <http://www.themoscowtimes.com/opinion/article/putins-distorted-history/489799.html> [accessed 25 July 2014]. Over the last years we have witnessed a double-edged attitude towards the past: while a new Museum for the history of the Gulag was opened in the centre of Moscow on 30 October 2015, the NGOs and associations working on the preservation of the memory of Soviet repression are under pressure from the government, above all in relation to the 'Law on Foreign Agents' (see below, p. 33 n. 81). On the other hand, the events related to Perm'-36, i.e. the only museum based on a former Gulag site, where the management has been forcibly removed, shows another tendency, i.e. the state's attempt to take possession of the memory of repression also in relation to the spaces where it has been preserved by civil society for decades. Some of the latest initiatives by Memorial, e.g. the 'Topography of Terror' and 'The Last Address', i.e. the application of memorial plaques on the buildings where people were arrested during the years of the Great Terror, show how the fight for memory has now acquired also a geographical and material significance.

5   I am referring to a key concept in auto/biographical studies developed by Iurii Lotman; see Iurii Lotman, 'Literaturnaia biografiia v istoriko-kul'turnom kontekste (K tipologicheskomu sootnosheniiu teksta i lichnosti avtora)', *O russkoi literature* (St Petersburg: Isskustvo-SPB, 1997), pp. 804–16. As Claudia Criveller brilliantly shows, Lotman draws his theories from Tomashevskii's ideas; see Claudia Criveller, 'Gli studi sui generi auto-biografici e memorialistici in Russia', *Avtobiografija*, 1 (2012), 21–48.

6   John Paul Eakin, *Touching the World: Reference in Autobiography* (Princeton: Princeton University Press, 1992), p. 144.

7   Leonid Taganov, in his article on the 'hidden literature' (see below, p. 3 n. 11) does hint at the problem, although his analysis does not delve deep into the question. Throughout the present book I will use the term 'Silver Age', which although controversial is widely used. See Daniela Rizzi, 'L'inafferabile Età d'Argento', *Europa Orientalis*, 2 (1996), p. 78.

works that deal with the Gulag be included, or also those that deal with Soviet repression in general? Should therefore the later works by Vasilii Grossman, Anna Akhmatova's *Rekviem,* or Lidiia Chukovskaia's *Sof'ia Petrovna* be considered part of Gulag literature? Emblematic of the current situation is the lack of a commonly used name in Russia for this type of literature.

A first attempt to solve these questions was made by Leona Toker in *Return from the Archipelago. Narratives of Gulag Survivors.*[8] Toker provided a first reflection on the literary corpus, on some fundamental issues (such as the consideration of these works as aesthetic, and not only as texts that bear a witnessing function) and even on genre issues, as in the chapter devoted to Gulag memoirs as a genre, only to focus on an analysis of works by Shalamov and Solzhenitsyn in the main part of the book. What seemed to be the first step towards the opening up of a new field of research remained an isolated attempt to interpret such a vast corpus in a broader sense. Other studies confronted the theme of the literature of the Gulag,[9] but they were sporadic and dispersed and, for different reasons, did not have a significant impact on the field of Russian Studies. The topic never took root in the context of international academic research as did, for instance, the literature of the Holocaust. A new and detailed study of the literature of the Gulag would complete the vast panorama of Russian literature during the Soviet period, providing the missing piece of the puzzle in the picture of the different fronts where the literary *agon* was fought (official Soviet literature, underground literature, émigré literature).

The present book aims to shed light on one of the many islands which compose the vast archipelago of Gulag literature and which, to date, has remained mainly unexplored. As a matter of fact, almost no attention has been paid to the literary works produced within the Soviet camps. Apart from single articles devoted to literature written or composed in the camps[10] — where, however, the literary works were only quoted or described individually, but not set in a broader context[11]

---

8   Leona Toker, *Return from the Archipelago: Narratives of Gulag Survivors* (Bloomington: Indiana University Press, 2000).

9   Among the studies devoted to Gulag literature, three are particularly remarkable: Luba Jurgenson's *L'Expérience concentrationnaire est-elle indicible* (Monaco: Editions du rocher, 2003) is the only other attempt to analyse Gulag literature as a whole, although her work is limited to a specific topic, that of representation. Karoline Thaidigsmann analysed four writers and their literary works devoted to the Gulag: Karoline Thaidigsmann, *Lagererfahrung und Identität: Literarische Spiegelungen sowjetischer Lagerhaft in Texten von Varlam Šalamov, Lev Konson, Naum Nim und Andrej Sinjavskij* (Heidelberg: Universitätsverlag Winter, 2009). Recently, Alfred Gall's *Schreiben und Extremerfahrung: Die polnische Gulag-Literatur in komparatistischer Perspektive* (Berlin: Lit Verlag, 2012) presents an extensive panorama of Polish Gulag literature and offers a few lines of interpretation on the question of trauma and literature.

10   There are many articles devoted to the poems composed in the camps by Varlam Shalamov, Nina Gagen-Torn, and Anna Barkova, to quote just a few. Barkova can be considered the most-studied poet of the Gulag. See Catriona Kelly, 'Anna Barkova', in *Reference Guide to Russian Literature,* ed. by Neil Cornwell (London, Chicago: Fitzroy Dearborn, 1998), pp. 146–48.

11   An exception to this is Leonid Taganov's article on Gulag poetry as part of a 'hidden' Russian literature. Unfortunately, Taganov did not pursue this interesting line of research in recent years and focused mainly on Anna Barkova's poems. See: Leonid Taganov, 'Potaennaia literatura: poeziia GULaga', in *Voprosy ontologicheskoi poetiki. Potaennaia Literatura. Issledovaniia i materialy,* ed. by Leonid Bykov (Ivanovo: Ivanovskii Gosudarstvennyi Universitet, 1998), pp. 80–87.

— no attention has been paid to the nature, the scope, and the quality of the literary works produced within the Soviet camps. Again, this fact is rather surprising, considering the vast amount of texts kept in the archives and in the holdings of public libraries, both in Russia and in the West.[12]

The topic of the literary works produced within the Soviet camps is particularly stimulating. Firstly, it enables the study of literary texts produced in a repressive context, both those composed orally and circulated (and kept) clandestinely, and those published within the camps. Their features are very different, but they both — each in their own way — show how the individual responds to repression with creativity. Secondly, it helps to define the ways in which individuals express intellectual resistance at a textual level, by use of stylistic devices and images that are sometimes in themselves statements of dissent or individual freedom. Thirdly, the study of the literary texts published within the camps, as well as serving as an additional source for historical research, and regardless of their aesthetic quality, provides an in-depth view of the culture of the camps, of their mechanisms in terms of cultural initiatives and propaganda. It also makes it possible to study the different narrative strategies and stylistic choices implemented by the authors, who were usually forced to praise communist power but, at times, had the rare opportunity to express their feelings or recall their personal experience. More generally, the literature published within the Soviet camps has to be analysed in view of the capital importance that it had for every author, who had to take responsibility for his own words and risked being charged or punished for the thoughts expressed in his texts. What is more, the study of the literary texts published in the Soviet camp press can be extremely interesting when the censors, for some peculiar contingent reasons, allowed the publication of some texts that were free from Soviet ideology. It is to exceptions of this kind that this book is devoted. But there are also other reasons that have less to do with academic research.

At dawn on 22 December 1849, several alleged revolutionaries were taken to the Semenovskii Square in St Petersburg, where a firing squad, deployed and ready to fire, was waiting for them. Only after the first three condemned men had been blindfolded did an officer declare that Emperor Nicholas I had given his pardon to save them. The prisoners were then sent to Siberia to spend years in detention in faraway prisons. Among them was the young Fedor Dostoevskii. This experience had a significant impact on his personal life and especially on his writing. During his time in the fortress of St Peter and Paul, in anguished anticipation of a death sentence and isolated from the rest of the world, Dostoevskii began to revise his ideological positions. Four years in a penitentiary in Omsk and another five as a soldier in Semipalatinsk brought about radical changes, providing extraordinary insight which emerged in almost all his later works and is particularly noticeable in *Crime and Punishment*, *The Idiot*, and *The Brothers Karamazov*.[13]

---

12   An outstanding microform collection of Gulag publications, taken from the State Archive of the Russian Federation, was made by the International Institute for Social History in Amsterdam.
13   In this regard, see Cinzia De Lotto, 'Dostoevskij. Lettere dalla fortezza', in 'Le loro prigioni':

The experience of imprisonment, detention, or exile deeply affected the life and work of other writers of the Tsarist age, beginning with Aleksandr Radishchev. From the October Revolution onwards, the history of Russian literature was intertwined even more dramatically with the socio-political history of the country. The impact of the Bolshevik Revolution on culture was devastating. It abruptly redefined the dialectical relationship between intellectuals and the state to the exclusive benefit of the latter. The surgical removal of the Russian *intelligentsiia* from the body of the state, which began under Lenin and continued under Stalin, placed intellectuals at an inescapable crossroads: they were confronted with the choice between acceptance of the directives of the party-state, physical elimination, or, alternatively, emigration. From the shooting of Nikolai Gumilev to that of Isaak Babel', Boris Pil'niak, and Pavel Florenskii, from Osip Mandel'shtam's death in a transit camp to other deaths directly or indirectly caused by the contemporary socio-cultural context (those of Aleksandr Blok, Sergei Esenin, Vladimir Maiakovskii, and others), the path taken by post-revolutionary Russian literature was marked by state violence. Along with these famous personalities, who are known to the entire intellectual world, thousands of other lesser-known authors suffered threats, torture, arrests, and execution. As Roman Iakobson shrewdly said, an entire generation of poets of Russian literature was 'squandered'.[14] A whole galaxy of writers, whose only crime was to be born in an adverse context, was not given the opportunity that Dostoevskii had to develop his creative activity.

This study evolved from the impossible attempt to give an answer to two questions related to this discussion. How many 'potential Dostoevskiis' (i.e. promising writers whose experience of imprisonment decisively influenced the development of their work) did Russian literature lose? What would the great writers who died dramatically and prematurely in the Soviet era have written, if only they had been given the chance, and what impact would their suffering have had on their work? I have attempted to bring a naïve reader's curiosity into my work as a professional researcher in order to find the names and the works of authors who were expunged from the history of Russian literature because of their unlucky fate, with the aim of discovering, if not 'potential Dostoevskiis', at least good writers, authors who deserve to be given the attention of researchers and a place in cultural memory. I found many of them when I started to focus on the Solovki prison camp.

With this book, I intend to bring to the attention of the academic community a cultural episode that was unique in all respects. While the Soviet Union moved towards Stalinism and the Russian *intelligentsiia* was being eliminated, while the repressive system was being perfected and the socio-cultural context that would

scritture dal carcere, ed. by Anna Maria Babbi and Tobia Zanon (Verona: Edizioni Fiorini, 2007), pp. 257–74.At the trial, the writer pleaded not guilty, and if later he spoke of his 'guilt', it was an admission of moral responsibility, an internal examination of his intentions. It was similar to that which led Dmitrii Karamazov to assume the responsibility for his father's assassination, which he did not actually commit and that also weighed on his brother's Ivan's conscience, the ideologue of the crime. (ibid., p. 258)

14   I refer to the title of a text by Roman Iakobson, included in Roman Jakobson, 'O pokolenii, rastrativshem svoikh', in *Smert' Vladimira Maiakovskogo* (The Hague: Mouton, 1975), pp. 8–34.

FIG. I.1. Ivan Ozerov. ASM

define the artistic canons of Soviet literature and art was being formed, while the system of concentration camps was being created and the pre-revolutionary Russian culture was dying, a number of *intelligenty* created a small intellectual community in the place appointed for their elimination. It was a community whose aesthetic canons were drawn from pre-revolutionary or 'bourgeois' Russia. The 'Paris of the northern concentration camps' is what one detainee, Professor Ivan Ozerov, called the *Solovetskii Lager' Osobogo Naznacheniia* (Solovki Special Purpose Prison Camp), the so-called SLON.[15] At Solovki, site of the 'first Soviet Gulag',[16] while other

15   The same acronym also referred to the entire system of Northern Special Purpose Camps (Severnye Lageria Osobogo Naznacheniia), while the acronym USLON indicated the administration of the camps (Upravlenie Solovetskimi Lageriami Osobogo Naznacheniia, Administration of the Solovki Special Purpose Camps). After several administrative changes, in February 1937 the acronym was changed into STON (Solovetskaia Tiur'ma Osobogo Naznacheniia, Solovki Special Purpose Prison). In order to help the reader, throughout this book I will refer only to SLON whenever I mean to indicate the Solovki prison camp.

16   Although the Gulag institution was formed in 1930, most authors refer to the Solovki prison camp as the 'first Gulag', using the word as an antonomasia for all Soviet camps; see for example Anne Applebaum, whose chapter on the SLON in her history of the Gulag is called 'The first camp of the Gulag': *Gulag: A History* (New York: Doubleday, 2003), pp. 40–58. I will do the same when

prisoners perished by the hundreds or suffered terribly, a small number of inmates had the opportunity to continue the intellectual activity in which they had been involved before their imprisonment. In doing so, they opposed the system that wanted to crush them with a form of cultural resistance, a sort of peaceful protest, which was destined to be defeated from a material point of view, yet was still able to leave its mark and to send a message of great value to all humanity.[17]

The cultural resistance that occurred in the Solovki archipelago was absolutely unique. A key objective of the Soviet repressive system in the early years (and therefore also of the SLON) was the 're-education' process, i.e. the forced transformation of those who had different world-views into new Soviet citizens, faithful to the regime and 'religiously' devoted to the party. People connected to Tsarist Russia and to the White Army, the clergy, and representatives of other branches of the left, such as Socialist Revolutionaries and Anarchists, were especially targeted for 're-education'. In part, this re-educational process[18] was to be implemented through intellectual activity. For this reason, the camps published *zhurnaly* (journals) and *gazety* (newspapers) and allowed many other cultural activities. While in other camps ideological control over cultural activity was usually — but not always — strict, on the Solovki, thanks to some specific dynamics inside the camp administration, the *intelligenty* were able to work a miracle. In the midst of an attempt to destroy the old *intelligentsiia*, a remarkable 'cultural island' of the highest level, that largely ignored proletarian art and the aesthetic guidelines imposed by the central authorities,[19] was formed inside the Soviet Cocytus within the Solovki camp.[20] The renowned scholar Dmitrii Likhachev, then only one of the many prisoners of Solovki, later wrote in his memoirs: 'For me the discussions with A. A. Meier and with the Solovki *intelligentsiia* that revolved around him at the Krimkab were a second university (but first for importance)'.[21] This aspect — the uniqueness of the cultural life in the Gulag of Solovki — has never been considered in its full dimensions

this seems helpful to the reader.

17   Marián Húska, a Slovak economist who suffered persecution during the Communist occupation of Czechoslovakia and is also the creator of an original theory of Good and Evil, was particularly impressed by the history of the intellectual life of Solovki and by the cultural resistance of some of its prisoners. In an email exchange, he wrote: 'What was really brilliant from the point of view of the intellectual opponents in Solovki was that the prisoners created an informal "enclave" in the "Bolshevistic ghetto". It was a positive response to a negative challenge. [...] The behaviour of the prisoners of Solovki was an example of anti-catastrophic response. Cultural resistance was the best human (altruistic) response to the barbaric challenge they had. From this point of view, your research on the history of Solovki was very inspiring for me.' (e-mail dated 6 October 2010)

18   At the end of the period considered in my research, the term *perekovka* ('reforging') became a dominant slogan. During the construction of the White Sea-Baltic Canal, this term became a keyword. It also gave its name to a journal that was first published at the SLON. See chapter 3.

19   I refer to the aesthetic guidelines drafted by the GUMZ (Glavnoe Upravlenie Mestami Zakliucheniia, Main Administration of the Prisons), which are discussed in the third chapter.

20   In Greek mythology the Cocytus was one of the five rivers of Hades together with the Acheron, the Lethe, the Phlegethon, and the Styx. In Dante's *Divine Comedy* the Cocytus is a frozen lake.

21   'Для меня разговоры с А. А. Мейером в Кримкабе и со всей окружавшей его соловецкой интеллигенцией были вторым (но первым по значению) университетом'. See Dmitrii Likhachev, *Izbrannoe: Vospominaniia* (St Petersburg: Logos, 1995), p. 225.

FIG. I.2. Dmitrii Likhachev. AMM

and importance. Moreover, the literature produced in the Solovki prison camp presents some features which make it unique. One of the main aims of this study is to highlight those extraordinary features: an aspect that I consider fundamental is that even behind bars, even though isolated on that 'island of martyrdom',[22] even though frozen and terrified by torture and executions, the authors of the literature produced in the Solovki camps were still part of the world. The '*zona*' where they were confined shared common cultural and literary threads and very strong links with what has now become customary to define as the *bol'shaia zona*,[23] or the outside world, meaning the vast territory of the entire Soviet Union. As previously mentioned, these connections have not yet been studied.

22   It is under this title, *Solovki. The Islands of Martyrdom. From a Monastery to the First Soviet Camp*, that Iurii Brodskii's book (see note 1) was first published in Italy. See Jurij Brodskij, *Solovki. Le isole del martirio. Da monastero a primo lager sovietico* (Milan: La casa di Matriona, 1998).
23   Jacques Rossi in his *The Gulag Handbook* writes under the heading '*zona*': '2. Big zone — The Soviet Union, which was one big prison camp, in distinction to the 'small zone', i.e. the camps themselves ['2. Большая з. — Советский Союз (являющийся одним большим лагерем: в отличие от "маленькой з.", т. е. собственно лагеря)']'. See Zhak Rossi, *Spravochnik po GULAGu* (London: Overseas Publications Interchange, 1987), p. 132.

In addition to presenting this cultural-historical episode, this work will place it into a well-defined framework that will highlight not only the unique culture (and especially the literature) produced in the camp in the Northern Russian archipelago, but will also assess the significance of its cultural phenomena.

Before delving deeper into the topic, I have chosen to devote the first chapter to a literature review. In addition to a review of the publications devoted to the theme of the Solovki camp, I present a parallel diachronic overview of some of the publications dedicated to the Soviet camps and in particular to the Stalin-era ones, in order to underline the specificity of the SLON case. However, I have avoided an in-depth analysis of the quality of each publication and have only stressed key comments on a few relevant aspects.

The second chapter offers a reconstruction of the history of the Solovki prison camp. As the first camp entrusted entirely to the political police, the SLON served as a laboratory in which to solve the problem of the enormous number of prisoners, arrested by the chekists[24] in ever-increasing numbers since 1918. It was in the SLON that, piece by piece, the complex machinery of the Soviet concentration camps was forged, especially after the appearance of Naftalii Frenkel'.[25] This historical narrative of the camp is not the focus of this book; therefore this chapter draws primarily from secondary sources, although some unpublished archival documents have been utilized in order to shed more light on some events. Indeed, a major methodological concern faced in this chapter is the problematic nature of the material available for analysis. Both the ambiguity of archival documents, which are either missing or, if available, are sometimes partial and/or falsified, and the inevitable use by researchers of resources whose objectivity and scholarly value is dubious (principally memoirs, but also videos or interviews) generates concern.[26] For this reason, I decided to face the problem of researching the history of the SLON objectively by offering two

24   During the years of the camp's existence, the political police changed its name several times. Created in 1918 and first called Vserossiiskaia Chrezvychainaia Komissiia po Borb'e s Kontr-revoliutsiei i Sabotazhem (All-Russian Extraordinary Commission for Combating Counter-Revolution and Sabotage) or VChK, better known as the 'Cheka', in 1922 it became GPU (Gosudarstvennoe Politicheskoe Upravlenie, State Political Directorate), in 1923 OGPU (Ob''edi-nennoe Gosudarstvennoe Politicheskoe Upravlenie, Joint State Political Directorate), while later the role of political police passed to the NKVD (Narodnyi Komissariat Vnutrennikh Del, People's Commissariat for Internal Affairs). The latter had inherited the functions of the Tsarist Ministry of the Interior. During the years of the Great Terror, the NKVD took over the reins of the entire Soviet repressive system. Feliks Dzerzhinskii (1917–26), Viacheslav Menzhinskii (1926–34), Genrikh Iagoda (1934–36), Nikolai Ezhov (1936–38), and Lavrentii Beria (1938–45) served as the head of state repression during the years covered in this study. Despite all these changes, the officers were always called *chekisty* (in English chekists), the name deriving from the original name of the political police. See: *Lubianka: Organy VChK-OGPU-NKVD-NKGB-MGB-MVD-KGB. 1917–1991. Spravochnik*, ed. by Aleksandr Kokurin and Nikita Petrov (Moscow: Mezhdunarodnyi Fond Demokratiia, 2003), pp. 13–180.

25   A former prisoner of Solovki, Frenkel' had an impressive career in the security services thanks to his ideas about the exploitation of prisoners' labour. See chapter 2.

26   See the final chapter of Anne Applebaum's *Gulag*, pp. 515–22. The complexity and delicacy of the problem is compounded by the politicization which seemed to exist on both a local and a global level. For this reason, some publications have to be carefully considered because they do not have sufficient objectivity.

'versions' of the history of the camp: one provided by the official documents and the other based on memoirs by former prisoners of the SLON.[27] I have addressed the problem of memoirs as an historical source within the chapter, discussing a few methodological issues, but have subsequently provided the history of the camp through the eyes of witnesses, in order to give as broad a view as possible of the SLON. I decided to offer two different perspectives of these events, i.e. what in cinematic terms would be called a panoramic shot and a point of view shot.

The third chapter is devoted to the cultural activities which went on inside the camp of Solovki, with particular attention to the newspapers and journals published there. As many scholars have pointed out, the press was a fundamental tool in the hands of the Soviet government ever since its earliest days. Lenin's *Chto delat'* (What is to be done?)[28] discussed at length the importance of the press for the Russian revolutionary movement. Though Lenin's critics generally overlook this aspect and concentrate on questions that are more strictly relevant to Party organization,[29] the importance of the press is at the core of the fifth chapter[30] of the book ('Plan obshcherusskoi politicheskoi gazety' — a plan for an all-Russian political newspaper) and plays a crucial role in Lenin's thesis. *Chto delat'* marks a crucial stage in Lenin's reflections on the subversive use of the press and sheds light on the pragmatic use of the media which was fundamental to Lenin's regime and which Stalin, building on a well-founded tradition, would implement.[31] This gives the background to the phenomenon of the Soviet camp press. The press that operated inside the camps had other functions, as has been brilliantly demonstrated by Felicitas Fischer von Wiekersthal: it served mainly as an organizer, motivator, and as an instrument of re-education in the early years of the Soviet regime, and later became a means of propaganda.[32] Drawing on primary and secondary sources,

---

27   I chose to present only the information that I considered historically accurate after comparing it with information from other sources. When I decided to highlight information supplied from only one source, I did so in order to provide the widest possible spectrum of what life was like inside the camp. The utilization of memoirs is not innovative in itself; other books have already made extensive use of memoirs to expose the life of the SLON. My attempt aims to propose a more objective use of these texts, representing different points of view. Within the Solovki camp, in fact, different prisoners who were there at the same time often had very different experiences. This aspect has often not been reported, in favour of an instrumental use of memoirs by other authors.

28   Lenin, *Sochineniia*, 35 vols (Leningrad: Gosudarstvennoe Izdatel'stvo Politicheskoi Literatury, 1948–50), v.

29   See e.g. Robert Payne's book on Lenin (Robert Payne, *Lenin* (Milan: Della Volpe Editore, 1967), pp. 149–66), Robert Service's biography (Robert Service, *Lenin: A Biography* (London: Macmillan, 2000), pp. 137–43), and the introduction to the Italian edition of *Chto delat'*, written by Giuseppe Bedeschi (Lenin, *Che fare? Problemi scottanti del nostro movimento* (Rome: Newton Compton, 1976), pp. vii–xxv).

30   The position of the chapter is relevant: except for the conclusion, it is the last one of the book.

31   Recent research has investigated the dynamics that underlie the use of propaganda by considering elements other than the press and books. Gian Piero Piretto's book, for example, proposed an interpretation of visual culture under Stalin using a productive point of view, i.e. analysing how Stalin's insistent gaze on the people worked as a means of control and intimidation. See Gian Piero Piretto, *Gli occhi di Stalin. La cultura visuale nell'era staliniana* (Milan: Raffaello Cortina Editore, 2010).

32   Felicitas Fischer von Weikersthal, *Die 'inhaftierte' Presse: Das Pressewesen sowjetischer Zwangs-*

I present an overview of the many different types of publications produced in the Soviet camps. This is followed by an outline of the main features of the Soviet concentration camp press. I then analyse the publications of the SLON in order to draw attention to their unique features and to reconstruct the dynamics that made the 'intellectual miracle' of Solovki possible. Here, the discovery of unpublished archival documents was crucial. These documents shed light on specific aspects of the cultural policy of the camp, especially on the important role played by one of the most prominent administrators of the camp, Fedor Eikhmans.[33] Camp publications were interrupted in 1926 and began again in 1929 after Maksim Gor'kii's visit in June. It was impossible to reach any definite conclusions about the circumstances of Gor'kii's visit and, above all, about the possibility that the writer played a direct role in the decision to resume publishing activities. I therefore consider the contents of all the relevant sources at my disposal and propose a personal interpretation. After the description of SLON publications after 1929, I devote a few pages to the question of censorship and the organization of the press.

In the fourth chapter I analyse the literature produced in the SLON, accompanied by information concerning the main authors and the more significant works published in the camp. After presenting the authors of what I would call the 'first period of publications' (1924–26) and those of the 'second' (1929–30), it seemed necessary to provide a brief digression on other authors who did not publish in the SLON press but were active in these years. These authors' works were clandestine and were usually memorized and passed on orally or were kept hidden in private archives only to appear years later. By including some of these authors, I provide as comprehensive an overview as possible of the SLON literature. The chapter closes with some reflections on the features that made SLON literature unique in the bigger picture of the *lagernaia literatura* and of Russian literature in general. Those characteristics include not only stylistic and formal considerations, but also themes related to the contingency of the situation and to external literary influences. I provide an overview that aims to highlight the main themes, stylistic devices, and peculiarities of the texts published in the SLON press, and propose a few interpretations of specific questions, such as those of intellectual resistance. I then conclude by focusing on the 'literary enclave' of SLON and on its place in the history of Russian literature of the twentieth century.

The copious amount of material collected and its complexity informed my decision to provide appendices. The first appendix begins with an overview of the publications, which will help readers to orient themselves among the many different names and events. This is followed by a full contents list of the journal *SLON–Solovetskie Ostrova* (1923–26, 1929–30). It also contains an incomplete list of the contents of the *gazeta Novye Solovki* and of some of its supplements (1925–26, 1930), of which all literary publications (such as feuilletons and poems) have been

---

arbeitslager, 1923–1937 (Wiesbaden: Otto Harrassowitz, 2011).

33   A member of the Cheka and later of the OGPU, he was director and vice-director of the SLON at various times. See below, p. 45.

included, together with all the articles quoted in the main text. I hope these will be a useful research tool for those who might wish to study the cultural life of the SLON in the future.

The second appendix contains the biographies of the main authors discussed. The reconstruction of the lives and the literary careers of the authors before and after their Solovki experience was hindered by one of the many obstacles encountered during my research, i.e., the extremely limited availability of documents in the central Russian archives. Although the papers of many of the authors mentioned are held in the archives, I was not able to consult them even though a 2004 federal law allows access to personal archival documents seventy-five years after their creation.[34] Surprisingly, when coming back to the State Archive in Moscow in 2014 with the aim of working on the personal files of some of the prisoners that were not available in 2010 and that, I was told in 2010, I would be able to consult after 2012 (as most of the files were about people killed in 1937), I found out that these personal files had disappeared from the electronic catalogue. Similarly, the journals published within the camps, which had previously been stored in the *Zhurnal'nyi fond* of the GARF, had disappeared. A week of requests for an explanation did not produce any positive result. In view of these difficulties, I was forced to base my reconstruction on the information collected in other publications, on archival materials available elsewhere,[35] and on the recollections left by the many 'mediators of memory' of the SLON.[36]

The book is illustrated with images taken directly from the publications of the camp and from archive. The reproduction quality of these is inevitably imperfect, since in some cases only grainy or damaged photographs of the prisoners and their captors survive. All names have been transliterated using the modified Library of Congress system; and all translations are by myself, unless otherwise noted.

★   ★   ★   ★   ★

To conclude this introduction, I want to thank the many people who have contributed to this research and without whom this book would probably not have seen the light.

---

34 This prohibition can be circumvented if the researcher has written permission from the descendants of the victims. This is an almost impossible condition for the present work, since many of the protagonists died more than half a century ago. The search for any descendants is an enormous job, which I chose not to do. For the law in question, see The Federal Law 'About Archive Activity in Russian Federation' and its Differences from Legislative Acts earlier Regulating Legal Relations about Archive Activity of 22.10.2004, Article 25 [Федеральный закон «Об архивном деле в Российской Федерации» и его основные отличия от законодательных актов, ранее регулировавших правоотношения в сфере архивной деятельности от 22.10.2004, Ст. 25, see http://archives.ru/documents/fz/zakon-archivnoe-delo.shtml].

35 If the central archives proved to be at times inflexible, the local ones were often more cooperative. I was given all possible assistance by the Museum of Solovki. I also collected other materials in private archives and independent research centres such as Memorial and the Centre for the Recovered Names, where I was always helped in my research.

36 Aleida Assmann, *Erinnerungsräume: Formen und Wandlungen des kulturellen Gedächtnisses* (Munich: C. H. Beck, 1999).

Two fundamental moments in the genesis of this research should be mentioned. Firstly, a meeting in October 2007 with Irina Flige, director of the St Petersburg office of 'Memorial', thanks to whom I began to study the theme of repression in the Soviet era. Secondly, the tutoring by Professor Marialuisa Ferrazzi, who intuitively suggested the study of the literature and the cultural life of the Solovki Gulag between 1923 and 1930[37] as a topic, one which met my epistemological needs and my personal interests.

The work started when I began my PhD in Literary, Philological and Linguistics Science at the Department of Anglo-Germanic and Slavic Languages and Literatures of the University of Padua, was completed in the form of a dissertation at the end of my doctorate, and continued for almost six years.

Firstly, my deepest thanks go to the University of Padua, and in particular to the Slavic Studies Section of the Department of Anglo-Germanic and Slavic Languages and Literatures (now Department of Language and Literature Studies), which helped me in terms of facilities and support. Special thanks go to two people who over time have proven to be a fundamental source of invaluable advice and friendship, helping to ease the many difficulties encountered, Claudia Criveller and Alessandro Catalano.

The list of thanks for the help I was given during the search for materials in Russia is very long, so great was the support that I received both from individual researchers and from established institutions. First, I want to thank the St Petersburg Office of 'Memorial', especially the director Irina Flige, the archive director Tat'iana Morgacheva, Tat'iana Kosinova, and all the other people who have always offered me their assistance. The same gratitude goes to the employees of the Moscow Office of 'Memorial', in particular to the archivists Alena Kozlova and Irina Ostrovskaia. My most sincere gratitude for continued support and stimulating discussions also goes to Anatolii Razumov and the 'Vozvrashchennye imena' Centre, to the Museum of Solovki, and to Anna Balandina and Ol'ga Bochkareva who assisted me during the consultation of the archive. I am indebted to many other people: Mariia Belkina, Iurii Brodskii, Anastasiia Cherkasova, Iurii Dmitriev (who has been arrested recently and is currently in a Russian prison on the base of false accusations: I wish to express here my full support to him), Anton Demin and the 'Pushkinskii Dom', Semen Vilenskii (who passed away in the last months of work on this monograph: my thoughts are for him and his invaluable contribution to the preservation of the legacy and the literature of the Gulag), all the staff of the Gor'kii Archive at the IMLI RAN, Vitalii Shentalinskii, the Likhachev Fund, Sarah Gormady, and Dmitrii Balandin. Special thanks go to Nikolai Klepikov for his advice and for sending me a copy of his doctoral thesis and to Erin Alpert for allowing me to read her article while it was still being printed. I also thank Olga M. Cooke for sending me her article on Gennadii Andreev. I also would like to express my deepest gratitude to Felicitas Fischer von Weikersthal, Laura Piccolo, and Massimo Maurizio for the excellent advice they provided when asked to read part of this text.

---

37   These are the dates of the beginning and the end of the publishing activity inside the camp, and therefore the period under consideration in this work.

I must add to this already long list all the people who helped me during my stay in Germany (Tsetsiliia Mel'nikova and her family, Elena Dormann, Vera Ammer, Darek Balejko, Ryszard Makowski, and the Bayerische Staatsbibliothek), friends in the study group 'Giovani Europei' (especially Raluca Lazarovici-Mihalcu, Cinzia Mozzato, Marika Piva, and Marco Prandoni). Sincere thanks to all the scholars who listened to my doubts and gave me advice on my research. In addition to those already mentioned, my gratitude goes to Antonio Dell'Asta, Evgenii Dobrenko, Christa Ebert, Alla Gorcheva, Julie Hansen, Adalgisa Mingati, Gian Piero Piretto, Karl Schlögel, Maria Zalambani, and to an amazing scholar who unfortunately will not be able to read how grateful I am for his help and advice: Arlen Viktorovich Blium. They might be surprised to read this, but I also would like to thank Marco Clementi and Alda Giambelluca Kossova: it was thanks to them that I met Irina Flige and decided to research the Gulag. I express my gratitude to Father Viacheslav Umniagin, who involved me in the publication of the series of memoirs of former prisoners of the SLON and supported in these last three years my research activity on the Solovki prison camp. Sincere thanks goes also to Viktor Paaso of the Petrozavodsk office of 'Memorial' for helping me with research in the archives in Petrozavodsk, and my colleague and friend Massimo Tria for transcribing a document from the archives in Moscow. I would also like to express my thanks to all those who, in one way or another, have encouraged me with their appreciation and support: here I want to remember first of all my parents, but also Marina Balina, Duccio Basosi, Rodolphe Baudin, Manuel Boschiero, Christopher Butera, Ondřej Cinkajzl, Duccio Colombo, Cinzia De Lotto, Lazar Fleishman, Simone Francescato, Francesca Gori, Anna Grekova, Simone Guagnelli, Marián Húska, Maria Isola, Luba Jurgenson, Aleksei Kholikov, Oleg Kling, Elena Kostioukovitch, Il'ia Kukulin, Anna Labentz, Francesca Lazzarin, Anna Lesnevskaia, Igor' Loshchilov, Kristina Lytkina, Massimo Maurizio, Neira Merčep, Claudia Olivieri, Ioulia Podoroga, Konstantin Polivanov, Father Fiorenzo Reati, Salome Ruhadze, Marco Sabbatini, Susan Shean, Alexandra Smith, Bianca Sulpasso, Anja Tippner, Leona Toker, Pietro Tosco, Carlo Turrisi, Pavel Uspenskii, Andrei Ustinov, Mikhail Velizhev, Josephine von Zitzewitz, Iurii Zaretskii, and Claudia Zonghetti and my colleagues in Glasgow, especially Margaret Tejerizo, Shamil Khairov and all the staff of the Hunterian Museum. I would like to thank Daniela Rizzi, whose advice and support was crucial during the months in which I completed this book. A special thanks for her amazing work, advice, professional and even psychological support goes to my excellent editor Katharine Hodgson, and to Graham Nelson for granting me the best working conditions over these months of hard work.

Of all the above-mentioned people, special thanks go to Cinzia Mozzato and Amanda Swain, who helped me in the hard work of editing the first version of this text; to Julie Hansen, Karl Schlögel, and Leona Toker, whose advice has played a key role in the drafting of the final version of the present work; to Claudia Criveller, who gave me her constant advice throughout these years; and, above all, to Evgenii Dobrenko, who constantly and enthusiastically supported the publication of this book. Special thanks go to Antonina Alekseevna Soshina, an amazing researcher who worked for the Solovki museum for four decades and who has always been committed to the theme of the Solovki camp. Her total support and her complete willingness to help me understand the SLON and its many dark sides were absolutely decisive for me. Her premature death in the summer of 2013 gave me deep sorrow: I wish to dedicate this book to her memory, because it is thanks to people like Antonina Soshina that we are still able to know, research, and preserve the history and the culture of the Soviet camps, and of the people who lived and perished in them.

Most importantly, I want to thank my wife Lisa Gaye Crawshaw with all my heart, for managing to stay beside me in those years of enormous sacrifice and long separations, and for always giving me peace and security. This book would have never existed without her.

My last thought and my immense gratitude go to all the victims of SLON, to those who perished in it and to those who bore the scars for life, to those who had to go through atrocious suffering, and especially to those who held high the banner of the human spirit even in those conditions. My role obliged me to keep the maximum possible detachment from the material that I was investigating, and I tried hard to do so. I must confess that it was not easy. During these past few years, I became part of the destinies of many unfortunate people, to whom I could not help but feel close. In the hope of having returned to the scholarly community not only the names, but also the personalities of these representatives of the cultural and intellectual life of Russia, I make Anna Akhmatova's words mine: 'I'd like to name them all by name'.[38] I hope, however, that the attempt to arrive at this result will be sufficient to ensure forgiveness for any mistakes I have made in dealing with such a delicate subject.

---

38   ['Хотелось бы всех поименно назвать'] (Anna Akhmatova, 'Rekviem', *Sobranie sochinenii v shesti tomakh* (Moscow: Ellis Lak, 1998–2001), VI, 29).

CHAPTER 1

❖

The Solovki Camp and Its Literature

You have to invoke your memory, since there is no one else left who can remember the past of the Solovki.

DMITRII LIKHACHEV[1]

The history of the Solovki prison camp has been investigated by several scholars both in Russia and abroad. Far from breaking into completely unexplored territory, the present study — as already stated in the introduction — aims to shed light on a specific aspect of the SLON and its history, namely its publishing system and the literary works that were published there, in order to highlight its characteristics and to place it in a scholarly context.

Although some aspects of the history of the Solovki camp have already been investigated, research has often proved too fragmentary to provide a thorough assessment of the topic of the present work. Books, in particular anthologies, have pointed out the literary value of several protagonists of the 'SLON cultural season' but have held back from carefully assessing their specific achievements.[2] The history of the SLON publishing system did not receive adequate attention until Felicitas Fischer von Weikersthal's 2011 monograph; before that, only Dmitrii Driakhlitsyn's article in the journal *Sever* (September 1990) and, above all, Natal'ia Kuziakina's work[3] devoted some attention to the SLON publishing system. Yet there is a strong need for a proper evaluation of the peculiarity of the intellectual and literary life in the Solovki camp. This is evident from the fact that, unlike most Gulag memoirs, the majority of the SLON prisoners' memoirs (as well as the majority of monographs that refer to them) lend some insight into the publishing activities or the intellectual scene of the camp. Before making my own contribution to the long documentary tradition on SLON, I will review existing literature on the topic, putting it into a roughly diachronic perspective.[4]

---

1 'Надо призвать свою память, ибо помнить прошлое Соловков стало уже больше некому.' Dmitrii Likhachev, *Vospominaniia* (St Petersburg: Logos, 1995), p. 392.

2 See, for instance, *Poeziia uznikov Gulaga*, ed. by Semen Vilenskii (Moscow: Materik Rossia. XX vek, 2005), which includes several poems written by SLON prisoners. There are also a few articles in local magazines (above all in *Solovetskoe More*, see below, p. 32) and several anthologies published by the publisher-association 'Vozvrashchenie'. See below, p. 30.

3 See Dmitrii Driakhlitsyn, 'Periodicheskaia pechat' arkhipelaga', *Sever*, 9 (1990), 128–37, and Natalia Kuziakina, *Theatre in the Solovki Prison Camp* (Luxembourg: Harwood Academy Publishers, 1995). Apart from the above mentioned sources, see the introductory essay to the Arkhangel'sk library DVD-ROM. See the bibliography.

4 Sources are so numerous that it is impossible to quote directly from them. I will thus point out

In the 2003 preface to her remarkable bibliography of the Gulag,[5] Hélène Kaplan makes an interesting observation about the geographical and chronological imbalance evident in publications on this topic. She regards the perestroika years as a watershed between the period marked by the predominance of clandestine literature, memoirs, and books published outside Russia ('before') and the period when publications about the Gulag started to increase all over the world ('afterwards').

When addressing the literature of the Solovki camp, I will use a different chronology than the one proposed by Kaplan. To say that the perestroika years were a watershed reduces the seventy-year-long period that preceded Gorbachev to a seamless series of events, which inevitably eliminates or at least blurs crucial differences such as the enormous difference between the Stalin period and the Khrushchev era.[6] Historians agree that the long history of the Gulag should be divided into different periods and should take into account the significant differences that existed, for instance, between the camps of the immediate post-revolutionary period, the hell of the Kolyma camps, and the Gulag during the period of Soviet dissent. As a consequence, the chronology that underlies my bibliographical tour is comprised of three main periods:[7] October Revolution, Stalinization, Great Terror (1917–39); Second World War, Cold War, Samizdat era (1940–85); finally, Perestroika, the collapse of the Soviet Union and Post-Soviet period (1986–2017).

Revolution, Stalinization, and the Great Terror (1917–1939)

From its earliest days the Bolshevik regime was marked by strict press censorship.[8] Evidence of State violence and repression was either systematically erased from official publications or was ideologically justified. Except for a few government-authorized publications,[9] all books focusing on Bolshevik repression were printed abroad.

A sort of 'cage' was consequently created. Squeezed between Soviet Communism and 'the West', the very question of Soviet camps lay virtually buried for decades and

features that are relevant to my research; my remarks aim to emphasize the fact that limited attention has been paid to the cultural life in the Solovki camp.

5   Hélène Kaplan, 'The Bibliography of the Gulag today', in *Reflections on the Gulag*, ed. by Elena Dundovich, Francesca Gori, and Emanuela Guercetti (Milan: Feltrinelli, 2003), pp. 225–46.

6   This remark might be applied not only to Solovki camp literature but to Gulag literature in general.

7   The fact that the SLON was closed in 1939 is relevant to my choice of periodization of the bibliography of the Solovki prison camp, while a bibliography on the Gulag in my view should divide the Soviet era in pre- and post-Stalin.

8   One of the first Soviet decrees was aimed at limiting press freedom; see 'Dekret Soveta Narodnykh Komissarov o pechati ot 27-go okt. 1917 g.', in *Vlast' i khudozhestvennaia intelligentsiia. Dokumenty TsK RKP (B)–VKP (B), VChK-OGPU-NKVD o kul'turnoi politike. 1917–1953*, ed. by Andrei Artizov and Oleg Naumov (Moscow: Materik-Demokratiia, 2002), pp. 11–12.

9   This was especially the case of normative texts or, more generally, of jurists' publications in the Soviet Union. In *The Gulag Archipelago*, Solzhenitsyn focuses on the creation of legal measures to organise repression. See paragraphs 8 ('The Law as a Child'), 9 ('The Law Becomes a Man'), and 10 ('The Law Matures') in the first part ('The Prison Industry'), Aleksandr Solzhenitsyn, *Arkhipelag GULag, 1918–1956: opyt khudozhestvennogo issledovaniia* (Ekaterinburg: U-Faktoriia, 2006), I, 276–394.

could not resurface without being used instrumentally by either bloc. The problem was worsened by the fact that the West refused to recognize the Soviet regime for years, and regarded it as a dangerous destabilizing influence.[10] Soviet Russia, after all, was the very paradigm of a possible workers' utopia. In this context, while many writers tried to support the Soviet state (helped by Left-wing parties from all over the world, which looked towards the Soviet Union as a concrete example for their followers), others tried to discredit it, such as the Russian émigré authors of numerous books who flooded into Europe after the Revolution.[11] Unsurprisingly, the Soviet regime's internal repression was a leitmotif in the publications that opposed it; these anti-Soviet publications sometimes lacked restraint and ultimately proved to be a double-edged sword. Their urgent claims certainly contributed to a widespread distrust of Communist Russia's effective achievements, but they were so politically committed that the public started to distrust them and criticise their reliability.[12]

This type of literature often focused on the Solovki prison camp. The SLON was officially established on 13 October 1923;[13] by which time a few books about Soviet repression had already been published abroad.[14] That year, for example, Viktor Chernov, one of the founders of the Socialist Revolutionary Party (whose members were known as *Esery*), edited and published a book in Italy.[15] The Socialists were one of the most important communication channels between Russia and Europe in the post-Revolutionary years. As Kaplan suggests in her preface about the bibliography of the Gulag,[16] the journal *Sotsialisticheskii Vestnik* played a crucial role

10   The United States, for instance, officially recognized the Soviet regime as the legal government of Russia only in 1933.

11   Marcello Flores's *The Image of the USSR* explicitly addresses relations between the Soviet Union and the West at the time of Lenin and Stalin, see Marcello Flores, *L'immagine dell'URSS* (Milan: Il saggiatore, 1990). Although his book does not focus on the effects of camp-related news on Western public opinion, Flores tackles this subject in a later article, see Marcello Flores, 'L'Occidente e il Gulag', in *Gulag. Il sistema dei lager in URSS*, ed. by Marcello Flores and Francesca Gori (Milan: Mazzotta, 1999), pp. 95–101. Ludmila Stern's book mentions the operations made in the Soviet Union to 'combat the so-called "bourgeois lies" ', see Ludmila Stern, *Western Intellectuals and the Soviet Union, 1920–1940* (London: Routledge, 2007), pp. 40–41. For what concerns the UK, see Giles Udy, *Labour and the Gulag: Russia and the Seduction of the British Left* (London: Biteback Publishing, 2017).

12   This was at the base of a discussion within the ambient of Russian émigrés and in particular of former camp prisoners. Ivan Solonevich wrote an important text about it at the beginning of his *Rossiia v kontslagere*, see Ivan Solonevich, *Rossiia v kontslagere* (Sofia: Izd. Natsional'no-trudovogo soiuza novogo pokoleniia, 1936), p. 5. The book was soon translated in various languages (London, 1938; Paris 1938; Milan 1939).

13   See below, p. 44.

14   The first book about Soviet repression to be published abroad was: Andrei Kalpashnikov, *Prisoner of Trotsky's* (Garden City, NY: Doubleday, 1920). Jacques Rossi mentions six articles or memoranda published in the West between 1919 and 1923 in his *Gulag handbook* (Rossi, pp. 518–25).

15   Viktor Mikhailovich Chernov (1873–1952)'s book, which is mostly a collection of stories by Socialist Revolutionaries, was first published in Italy by the 'G. Oberdan Committee for the foundation of the Fascist Casa Marina', as a further proof of the political instrumentalization of the theme of repression. See *La Ce-ka: il terrore bolscevico. Raccolta di testimonianze a cura di Vittorio Cernov*, ed. by Vittorio Cernov (Milan: La Promotrice, 1923). The book does not directly tackle the question of the Solovki prison camp, but some of the contributors were eventually sent to the SLON.

16   Kaplan, pp. 232–33. Kaplan maintains that as many as 230 camps are accurately mapped out in

FIG. 1.1. A photo taken within the Solovki prison camp. ASM

in disseminating information about Bolshevik repression and the Soviet labour camps (SLON included) outside the Soviet Union. The shooting of six political prisoners at the Savvat'evo hermitage on the Solovki islands on 19 December 1923 sparked a European-wide response thanks mainly to the efforts of the journal.[17]

The Savvat'evo massacre was mentioned by various sources, among which was *Red Terror in Russia 1918–1923*, a book by Sergei Mel'gunov published in Berlin in 1924.[18] According to the writer's 'statement', the book represents 'a first attempt to

the journal's index, which the Bibliothèque Tourguenev wrote in 1992.

17   See below, p. 46. It is important to mention that political prisoners wrote a document that was eventually published in the *Sotsialisticheskii Vestnik*, raising a furore all over Europe, see 'Zaiavleniia politzakliuchennykh Petrominska i Solovkov. 1923–1924 gg.', ed. by Antonina Mel'nik, Antonina Soshina, *Zven'ia, Istoricheskii al'manakh*, 1 (1991), 245–51. Despite their attempts, most Western left-wing parties did not do enough to rally public opinion, as a prisoner suggests: 'When the events of 19 December occurred, it seemed subjectively to us that the "world would be convulsed" — our socialist world. But it appeared that it did not notice the Solovets events, and then a ring of laughter entered the tragedy.' Quoted from Isaac Don Levine's book (see below, p. 21) in Applebaum, p. 58. Translation by Anne Applebaum.

18   Sergei Mel'gunov, *'Krasnyi terror' v Rossii 1918–1923* (Berlin: Vataga, 1924). A former Kadet (representative of the Democratic Constitutional Party) who then converted to Socialism, Sergei Petrovich Mel'gunov (1879–1956) was a historian. He was exiled in 1922 and his book is still considered a valuable source, as testified by its recent translation into Italian, see Sergej Mel'gunov, *Il terrore rosso in Russia: 1918–1923* (Milan: Jaca Book, 2010). It was based upon first-hand accounts as well as articles that had appeared in the official Soviet press up until 1922 and in the Russian expatriate press later on. It is worthwhile quoting from a letter Iulii Martov sent to Boris Nikolaevskii on 12 December 1922 about the proposed expansion of the editorial board of *Letopis' revolutsii* (a Berlin-

provide a review, maybe far from being complete, of the material at our disposal. [...] Maybe it will encourage others to make a more extensive collection of similar material for publication'.[19] Mel'gunov's vision soon came true and not only in Europe. In 1925, a book written by the Russian-born American journalist Isaac Don Levine was published in New York. It was based on the letters of Soviet camp prisoners, amongst whom were several Socialist prisoners from the Solovki islands.[20] A former Soviet Union correspondent, Levine had a deep knowledge of the Soviet state. His book, which included prefaces written by intellectuals such as Karel Čapek, Albert Einstein, Gerhardt Hauptmann, Maurice Maeterlinck, Thomas Mann, Romain Rolland, Bertrand Russell, Arthur Schnitzler, H. G. Wells, and others, was commissioned by the International Committee for Political Prisoners.

In addition to these books, several well-known American and European newspapers contributed to the notoriety of the Solovki camp.[21] This, however, was mostly fuelled by 'first-hand' accounts of prisoners who had managed to escape from the Solovki islands and had finally arrived in Europe, or who had been released and sent into exile. In 1926, Sozerko Mal'sagov's *An Island Hell: A Soviet Prison in the Far North*, went to press in London, starting the 'tradition' of former SLON prisoners' narratives. In 1927, the French jurist Raymond Duguet collected details about the Solovki camp as told by these refugees in *A Prison in Red Russia. Solovki: The Island of Hunger, Torture and Death*.[22] Duguet's book delves rigorously into the question and

based journal), which offered representatives of both left and right political trends the opportunity to participate. This is what Martov says about Mel'gunov: 'Surely Mel'gunov is too right-wing to be summoned' [Мельгунов, конечно, слишком правый, чтоб его звать]. Cf. *Russkii Berlin 1921–1923*, ed. by Lazar' Fleishman, Robert Hughes, and Ol'ga Raevskaia-Hughes (Moscow: Russkii put', 2003), p. 330.

19   [...первая попытка сводки, далеко, быть может, неполной, имеющегося материала. [...] Может быть, она послужит побуждением для более широкого собрания и опубликования соответствующих материалов.] Mel'gunov, p. 9.

20   *Letters from Russian Prisons*, ed. by Isaac Don Levine (New York: Albert and Charles Boni, 1925). In his article about Levine, Eugene H. Methvin wrote: 'When Levine left Russia in 1924, he was not to return for forty years. The Stalinist turn toward unending terror and dictatorship turned him into an implacable enemy of the Soviet regime'. See Eugene H. Methvin, 'Isaac Don Levine: Herald of Free Russia', *Modern Age*, 37.3 (1995), p. 246.

21   Most of the articles that first appeared in these newspapers (especially those which were more reliable and detailed) were also published by *Sotsialisticheskii Vestnik*. Abraham Ascher wrote a well-researched article about the information channels used by SLON prisoners to smuggle news abroad. See Abraham Ascher, 'The Solovki Prisoners, the Mensheviks and the Socialist International', *Slavonic and East European Review*, 47.109 (1969), 423–35.

22   Raymond Duguet, *Un bagne en Russie rouge. Solovki: l'île de la faim, des supplices et de la mort* (Paris: J. Tallandier, 1927). The original version of the book was republished by Balland in 2004. I was not able to find reliable information about its author. We only know for certain that he was a jurist. Maybe he was using a pseudonym, though Nicolas Werth rejects this hypothesis in his preface to the 2004 edition. In an article, Jean-Jacques Marie highlights inaccuracies in the text and criticises Nicolas Werth for not having noticed them. But every text written about the Soviet camps during their existence has inaccuracies, and many of the claims made by Duguet can be confirmed by other sources or by archival research. I therefore do not accept Marie's case that the book is generally inaccurate; however, see Jean-Jacques Marie, 'Quand l'histoire tombe au niveau du dépotoir...', *Les Cahiers du mouvement ouvrier*, 23 (2004), 157–59.

An Island Hell:
A Soviet Prison in the Far North
By S. A. MALSAGOFF Translated by F. H. LYON

LONDON: A. M. PHILPOT LTD.
69, GREAT RUSSELL STREET, W.C.1
1926

FIG. 1.2. Sozerko Mal'sagov, author of *An Island Hell*. ASM

is well-documented. More books were published in the following years. In 1928, a Berlin-based press published Anton Klinger's *The Solovki Katorga*[23] and a Paris-based press issued Iuri Bezsonov's *My 26 Prisons and My Escape from Solovki*.[24]

It was then that Moscow intervened. Too many books about the Solovki and other camps had been published, creating such a worldwide uproar that several Western nations began to consider boycotting the Soviet Union's immensely profitable timber exports.[25] Much of this timber was harvested by prisoners in Soviet labour camps (including from the SLON). By this time, Soviet Russia had begun to use the question of prisons and camps as a propaganda tool in the international arena, showing how different Soviet prisons were from Tsarist and capitalist jails. Officially, communist prisons were not intended to punish prisoners but to re-educate them through labour; the Soviet authorities were generally silent about the real conditions of camp prisoners and about the brutal repression that was raging throughout the Soviet Union. Significantly enough, Soviet newspapers mentioned the Solovki camp only in order to underline its exemplary achievements.[26] The negative publicity from the West was radically changing the situation and the Soviet regime urgently needed to contain the worldwide notoriety of its prisons. The government's solution had a face and a signature, that of writer

23 *Katorga* is a word used in tsarist times to indicate forced labour. It comes from the Greek word 'katergòn'. See Applebaum, p. 16.

24 Sozerko Mal'sagov, *An Island Hell: A Soviet Prison in the Far North* (London: A. M. Philpot, 1926); Anton Klinger, *Solovetskaia katorga: Zapiski bezhavshego* (Berlin: Publ. po: Arkhiv russkoi revoliutsii, 1928); Youri Bezsonov, *Mes 26 prisons et mon évasion de Solovki* (Paris: Payot, 1928).

25 Echoes from the Solovki prison camp also reached Italy, see Edoardo Pantano, 'Boris Cederholm, au pays du Nep et de la Tchéka', *Bibliografia Fascista*, 5–6 (1929), 47–50.

26 See the *Izvestiia* articles which propose the Solovki camp as a model. See the reportage 'V Suzdal'skom i Solovetskom lageriakh: Zakliuchennye v Suzdale i Solovkakh o svoem rezhime', *Izvestiia*, 30 September 1924, and the following articles: Petr Krasikov, 'Solovki', *Izvestiia*, 15 October 1924; Ruben Katan'ian, 'V Solovkakh u politicheskikh', *Izvestiia*, 7 October 1924.

FIG. 1.3. Gor'kii surrounded by the main figures of SLON administration
during his visit in 1929. AMM

Maksim Gor'kii, the most influential left-wing Russian writer, who in 1929 visited
the Solovki prison camp and wrote a panegyric to Soviet power at the end of his
journey.[27] Gor'kii's book put some people's minds at ease in the West, but had an
indelible effect on his reputation, as shown by Solzhenitsyn's well-known invective
in *Arkhipelag Gulag*.[28]

The effect of Gor'kii's intervention did not completely assuage Europe's and
America's fears.[29] Between 1930 and 1938 memoirs and reports were still being
published all over the world, from Warsaw to Shanghai, from Helsinki to Sofia.[30]

27 Maksim Gor'kii, 'Po Soiuzu Sovetov: Solovki', in *Sobranie sochinenii v tridtsati tomakh* (Moscow:
Khudozhestvennaia literatura, 1952), XVII, 201–32. Gor'kii's visit will be addressed in the third
chapter.
28 About Gor'kii's alleged personal meeting with a teenager who — some memoirists say —
was later shot (see below, p. 148), Solzhenitsyn writes: 'Oh, great interpreter of the human heart!
Great connoisseur of human beings! How could he have failed to take the boy along with him?!'
['Сердцевед! знаток людей! — как мог он не забрать мальчика с собою?!'], see Solzhenitsyn, II, 51.
29 Some documents and memoirs of the Solovki prison camp inspired Western criticism towards
the Soviet Union, although in the following years Western nations' silence about the Soviet repression
and the Solovki camp gradually became harder to break through. Several articles, however, tried
to keep up awareness of the situation, but were unsuccessful. One of them was the *Memorandum on
the Russian Situation*, written by 'A group of London-based Russian Socialists and Democrats', see
'Memorandum on the Russian Situation', *Slavonic and East European Review*, 9 (1930/31), 497–503.
30 See bibliography.

However, international powers took no formal action against the Soviet Union. The escalation of Nazism, the outbreak of the Spanish Civil War, and a deep-seated fear that war would erupt at any moment raised international tension to a high level and took away any previous concern over the Soviet labour camps. The notorious Moscow Show Trials, which attracted worldwide attention, definitely undermined international interest in Soviet camps by refocusing attention on other news stories from the Soviet Union. Although books like Ivan Solonevich's *Russia in a Concentration Camp* were relatively successful on an international level, twenty years after the October Revolution the general public in the West had but a limited knowledge of the Soviet labour camp system and of Soviet repression. The actions aimed at raising awareness of Soviet camps in the West had mainly failed.

Second World War, Cold War, and Samizdat Era (1940–1985)

The Second World War coincided with a drastic drop in the number of publications about Soviet repression. However, the end of the war and the rapid escalation of the Cold War quickly changed the situation. Publishing flourished again, but it began to focus on other camps rather than on the SLON, which receded into the background. Two factors account for such a radical change. In 1939, the Solovki Gulag was dismantled and converted into a naval base.[31] Moreover, since the 1930s the SLON had lost its position as the camp that epitomized Soviet state repression: Stalin's camp system had spread throughout the Soviet Union, revealing its worst side in other places, such as in the camps in Kolyma. Nevertheless, important initiatives were still being launched. Between 1946 and 1954 several memoirs about the Solovki camp were published in the United States and in Germany. In 1954, Boris Shiriaev's book *The Inextinguishable Icon Lamp*[32] was published in New York. It was relatively successful among Russian expatriates.

After the war, many refugees from the Soviet Union decided to migrate to Germany, the nation that would soon become the very symbol of the Cold War. Some of them — mostly intellectuals who had survived the Gulag or repression — started editorial activities that consequently focused on those subjects. The most important Russian journals in Germany were *Grani* (which published in 1950 several short stories set in the SLON written by Gennadii Khomiakov-Andreev)[33] and *Posev*, which eventually started to publish books, becoming one of the most important Russian publisher in Western Europe.[34] In 1951, 'Posev' published *The Conquerors of the Blank Pages*,[35] the first memoirs by former SLON prisoner

---

31   See below, p. 58.

32   Boris Shiriaev, *Neugasimaia lampada* (New York: Izd-vo im. Chekhova, 1954). Shiriaev produced a literary reworking of his detention. In the catalogue of the Chekhov Publishing House the title is given as *The Unfading Light*. I would like to thank Leona Toker for this information.

33   Gennadii Andreev, *Gor'kie vody* (Frankfurt am Main: Posev, 1954).

34   Unfortunately, following my request to visit their archive I was told that, although the publishing house is still functioning today, 'Posev' no longer possesses the original manuscripts of the memoirs' authors, nor their correspondence (or any document that might be relevant to my research).

35   Mikhail Rozanov, *Zavoevateli belykh piaten* (Munich: Posev, 1951).

Mikhail Rozanov. After describing his detention, Rozanov self-published *Solovki Prison Camp in the Monastery, 1922–1939: Facts, Conjectures, 'Parashi': A Survey of the Memoirs of Solovki Prisoners by Solovki Prisoners*[36] in 1979. His second book compared all the memoirs that had been published abroad with the intention of ascertaining the historical truth. It is a valuable piece of research, and it can still be regarded, alongside archival documents, as the best source available for reconstructing the history of the SLON.

While the publishing house 'Posev' carried out its frenetic activity abroad, the Soviet Union was going through Stalin's last years and the Khrushchev Thaw. The era inaugurated by Khrushchev's well-known 'secret speech' at the Twentieth Congress of the Communist Party did not, however, lead to the dismantling of the camp system. The camps continued to take a heavy toll on the population and remained largely a taboo subject, even though Khrushchev authorized the publication of Aleksandr Solzhenitsyn's *One Day in the Life of Ivan Denisovich* in 1962. Solzhenitsyn's book is usually considered to be the first official attempt by the Soviet authorities to recognise the real conditions of camp prisoners, since the previous attempt — the 1933 book about the Belomorkanal[37] — was not written by former prisoners and was removed from the bookshop shelves during the purges.

In the 1960s, the *intelligentsiia* was refining its most powerful weapon: the alternative clandestine publishing system known as samizdat. Prohibited works and secret documents — amongst which were many concerning the repression and labour camps — began to be published in samizdat.[38] Some of these works raised the question of the SLON,[39] although most of the documents published either in

---

36   Mikhail Rozanov, *Solovetskii kontslager' v monastyre, 1922–1939 gody: fakty, domysly, 'parashi': obzor vospominanii solovchan solovchanami* (Printed in USA: Izdanie avtora, 1979). The word *parasha* is part of the Gulag lexicon: as well as the bucket used as a toilet in the prisons and barracks, it indicates also the fake news that circulated inside the camp. The *parashnik* was the prisoner who spread these rumours. See Vladimir Bykov, *Russkaia fenia* (Smolensk: Trast-Imakom, 1993), p. 147.

37   *Belomorsko-Baltiiskii Kanal imeni Stalina: Istoriia Stroitel'stva*, ed. by Maksim Gor'kii, Leopol'd Averbakh, and Semen Firin (Moscow: Gosudarstvennoe Izdatel'stvo 'Istoriia fabrik i zavodov', 1934). Thirty-six writers, under the guidance of Gor'kii, went on a cruise on the canal and, later, wrote essays and literary works that praised forced labour. Since many authors and two of the editors were repressed, during the Great Terror the volume was removed from public access and was kept in a *spetskhran* (i.e. the limited access holdings of the Soviet archives) up until recent years. Many researchers and writers have dealt with this episode, see, just to quote a few, Dariusz Tolczyk, *See No Evil: Literary Cover-ups and Discoveries of the Soviet Camp Experience* (New Haven: Yale University Press, 1999), pp. 150–80; Duccio Colombo, 'Sbornik o Belomorkanale: velikaia stroika stalinskoi literatury', *Slavica Tergestina*, 10 (2002), 231–43, and, by the same author, *Scrittori, in fabbrica! Una lettura del romanzo industriale sovietico* (Ospedaletto: Pacini, 2008); Frank Westerman, *Engineers of the Soul: In the Footsteps of Stalin's Writers* (London: Harvill Secker, 2010).

38   Samizdat documents included Lenin's testament and other political documents. Moreover, various narrative and poetic works by prohibited writers circulated. Most of them were or had been victims of Soviet repression, like Osip Mandel'shtam, Boris Pil'niak, and Isaak Babel.

39   Pavel Florenskii's works, Mikhail Frolovskii's and Iurii Chirkov's poems, Sergei Mel'gunov's book, and Ol'ga Adamova-Sliozberg's memoirs are just some of works about the SLON that circulated in samizdat. Antonina Soshina's personal archive included a rare copy of Vladimir Kemetskii's poems (Solovki, AAS, Vladimir Kemetskii, *Stikhi, Samizdatskaia kniga*), from which 'Vozvrashchenie' borrowed to publish a collection of Kemetskii's poems. See below, p. 30.

samizdat or in tamizdat[40] from the 1950s to the 1970s focused on Soviet intellectual dissent and the ordeal of Soviet dissidents in the Gulag, which at that time was attracting worldwide attention. Only a few documents brought up the question of the first camps,[41] such as Solovki, and they were consequently soon forgotten, although yet another clandestine mainstream, the circulation on audio tape of illegal music known as magnitizdat, kept on circulating Gulag songs, including those about the Solovki.

In 1973, at the end of remarkable efforts to gather oral testimony from former prisoners that lasted for around ten years, Solzhenitsyn published in Paris the first volume of *Arkhipelag Gulag*, thus paving the way for what might be regarded as a new stage in the public recognition of the Gulag. If the 1970 Nobel laureate gave the world the very first insight into the Soviet labour camps with *Ivan Denisovich*, in *Arkhipelag Gulag* he conjured up the entire world of Soviet repression, which the book chronicles almost encyclopaedically. Several chapters, in particular 'The Archipelago Rises from the Sea'[42] and 'The Archipelago Metastasizes',[43] are dedicated to the Solovki camp. Although Solzhenitsyn essentially borrowed from prisoners' memories and memoirs, his representation of the SLON is historically satisfactory: apart from some incorrect details and episodes, it faithfully depicts the prisoners' living and working conditions as we now know them. Solzhenitsyn, however, paid little attention to the camp press or cultural life. In his chapter 'The Muses in the Gulag',[44] for example, he focused instead on the most renowned White Sea–Baltic Canal camp newspaper, *Perekovka*, and on other artistic activities, rather than on works written by prisoners and published in the Solovki camp periodicals, which consequently continued to be ignored. Nevertheless, his focus on the tragedy of the SLON prisoners, which the title of the book charges with symbolic overtones, helped the camp to re-emerge from oblivion.

The first 1978 issue of the journal *Pamiat'* (published in samizdat and later republished in New York) included the memoirs of the former Solovki prisoner Ol'ga Vtorova-Iafa,[45] as well as an article by N. Stogov,[46] 'Prison Press 1921–1935',[47] which might be considered the first full-length study of the phenomenon of

---

40   The publication abroad (from Russian 'tam', there) of books that were either prohibited or censored.

41   These publications included the memoirs of Ekaterina Olitskaia, a revolutionary Socialist who was interned at the Solovki camp from 1922 to 1925. Ekaterina Olitskaia, *Moi vospominaniia* (Frankfurt am Main: Posev, 1971).

42   Solzhenitsyn, II, 22–57.

43   Ibid., pp. 58–92.

44   Ibid., pp. 377–404.

45   Ol'ga Vtorova-Iafa (Iasevich), 'Iz vospominanii', *Pamiat'*, 1 (1978), 93–158.

46   N. Stogov was Aleksandr Iosifovich Dobkin's pseudonym (1950–1998). One of the founders of the samizdat journal *Pamiat'*, he was a historian who devoted his career to the study of Aleksandr Meier's philosophical work and of the history of the Gulag based on material collected from private archives. His knowledge of the SLON (he also edited Nikolai Antsiferov's memoirs) and of private archives accounts for the competence he showed in the above-mentioned article. See the Aleksandr Iosifovich Dobkin entry in the *Encyclopedia of Saint Petersburg*, written by Irina Flige and Elena Rusakova: Elena Rusakova and Irina Flige, 'Dobkin Aleksandr Iosifovich' in *Entsiklopediia Sankt-Peterburga* <http://www.encspb.ru/article.php?kod=2805399823> [accessed 29 April 2015].

47   N. Stogov, 'Tiuremnaia pechat' 1921–1935 godov', *Pamiat'*, 1 (1978), 527–80.

internal publishing activity in Soviet labour camps. Reliable and accurate, Stogov's essay shed light on the subject by providing a striking reconstruction of the history of journals and newspapers (even wall-newspapers) that were run by Soviet camp labourers, including those of the Solovki camp. It also mentions authors and copy-editors and explains why the phenomenon of the labour camp press spread throughout the Gulag system. Finally, it provides a diachronic illustration of the development of the camp press itself.

After the publication of Stogov's essay, the history of the SLON and 'Solovki camp literature' fell back into oblivion. Only the rise of perestroika and the rapid collapse of the Soviet Union led to a radical turning point in the study of the Soviet Gulag.

Perestroika, Collapse of the Soviet Union, and Post-Soviet Period (1986–2017)

Mikhail Gorbachev's reforms opened a sort of 'Pandora's box'. The campaign for the liberalization of the Soviet Union launched in 1987 by the General Secretary of CPSU, whose grandfather had been a victim of Stalin's Great Terror,[48] had an immediate effect on the understanding and the recognition of the Gulag system. That same year the camp system was officially dismantled with the amnesty of political prisoners.[49] The climate of freedom and the hope for a better future made the need to reconstruct the past more urgent — in particular, the need to salvage from the abyss of history the millions of victims whom the regime had been hiding for years. Thanks to the contribution of 'Memorial'[50] and of similar associations or citizens' groups, a large number of memoirs and literary works were finally able to be published.

One of the first authors to be published was Pavel Florenskii, the 'Russian Leonardo', who had been a prisoner of the Solovki camp from 1934 to 8 December 1937, when he was shot at Levashovo. Florenskii's published works included not

---

48   See Michail Gorbačëv, *Riflessioni sulla rivoluzione d'Ottobre. Dal Palazzo d'Inverno alla perestrojka* (Rome: Editori riuniti, 1997), p. 39.
49   The amnesty had an immediate effect. Camps were abandoned and all political prisoners were released. Several photographic reports show the camps suddenly turned into ghastly ruins. These books were quite successful. See, for example, the Polish photographer Tomasz Kizny's book, Tomasz Kizny, *Gulag: Life and Death inside the Soviet Concentration Camps* (Buffalo: Richmond Hill, 2004).
50   In the last years of the Soviet Union, citizens founded spontaneous associations and committees to keep the memory of the Gulag victims alive. This was also the origin of 'Memorial', which gradually turned into a fully-fledged society and a leading research centre for studies on Soviet repression directed by the historian Arsenii Roginskii. Other than promoting research about the Soviet past, 'Memorial' has been monitoring human rights in post-Soviet Russia (especially in Chechnya), thus coming into conflict with the Kremlin. 'Memorial' is a universally recognized non-governmental organization. It has won many International awards and was nominated for the Nobel Peace Prize. 'Memorial''s office in St Petersburg, established by the former dissident Veniamin Iofe, has conducted research about the SLON for years. It has a specialized archive that is mostly based on former prisoners' letters and belongings, which the prisoners' families donated. Part of this archive is showed online on the site of a project headed by St Petersburg 'Memorial', 'The Virtual Museum of the Gulag' (http://gulagmuseum.org/start.do — Accessed 29 April 2015), which provides a very interesting source for research on the Gulag. It has also launched concrete initiatives, such as the 'Remembrance Days' when the prisoners' relatives and anyone who might be interested can visit the archipelago.

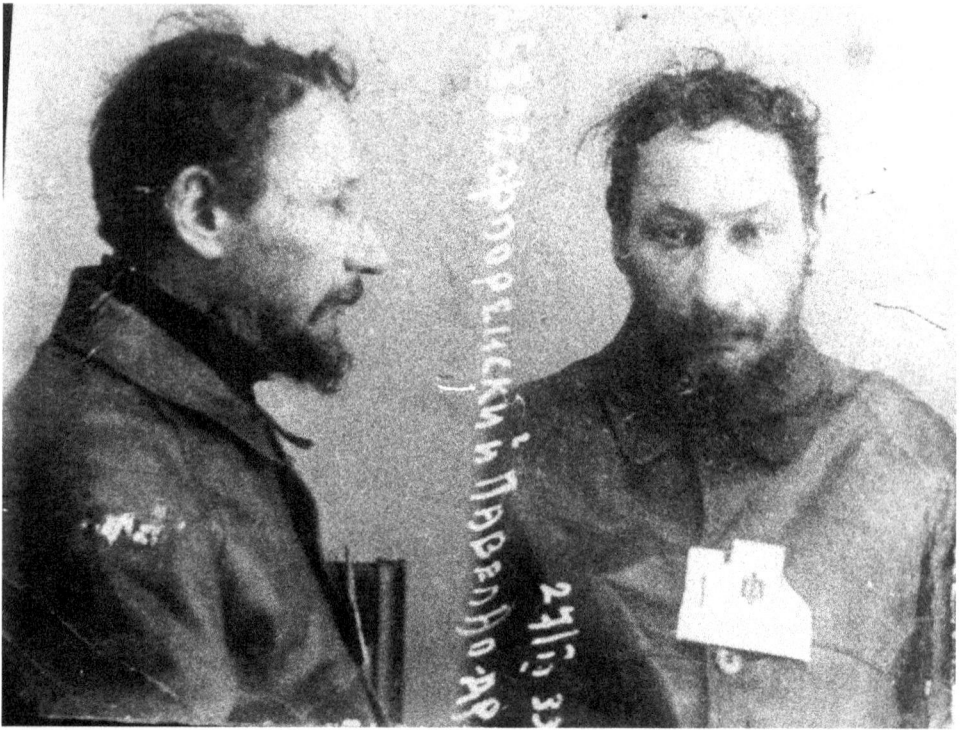

FIG. 1.4. Pavel Florenskii. ASM

only literary and philosophical books, but also the letters he sent to his family during his imprisonment (1988; 1990)[51] and the pedagogical epistles he sent to his children (1992).[52] Readers were deeply moved by Florenskii's touching letters,[53] as well as by memoirs and literary works published in those years by other former Solovki prisoners, such as Oleg Volkov (*Sinking into the Darkness*, 1989),[54] Iurii Chirkov (*And It Was all so…*, 1991),[55] Sergei Snegov (*The Noril'sk Tales*, 1991),[56] and above all Dmitrii Likhachev (*I Remember*, 1991).[57]

51   Pavel Florenskii, 'Pis'ma iz Solovkov [1934–1937gg.]', *Nashe nasledie*, 4 (1988), 115–28, and Pavel Florenskii, 'Pis'ma s Solovkov', *Vestnik Russkogo Khristianskogo Dvizheniia*, 160 (1990), 33–71, collected in Pavel Florenskii, *Pis'ma s Dal'nego Vostoka i Solovkov*, in *Sochineniia v chetyrekh tomakh* (Moscow: Mysl', 1998).

52   Pavel Florenskii, *Detiam moim: Vospominaniia proshlykh dnei* (Moscow: Moskovskii rabochii, 1992).

53   Because of his fame and the public impact of his work, Florenskii was (and still is) one of the authors whose work contributed the most to spreading the history of the Solovki camp both in the former Soviet Union and abroad.

54   Oleg Volkov, *Pogruzhenie vo t'mu* (Moscow: Molodaia gvardiia, 1989).

55   Iurii Chirkov, *A bylo vse tak…* (Moscow, Politizdat, 1991).

56   Sergei Snegov, *Noril'skie rasskazy* (Moscow: Sovetskii pisatel', 1991). Snegov (his real name was Shtein)'s works are mainly literary.

57   Likhachev, *Izbrannoe*. The first edition of the book, which contained fewer pages devoted to the Solovki, was published in 1991: Dmitrii Likhachev, *Ia vspominaiu* (Moscow: Progress, 1991). The

By 1991, Likhachev had become one of the most prominent figures in Russian culture. His extraordinary scholarly activity was supported by a fiercely courageous social commitment. For example, he protested on the front line in the campaign for press freedom and publicly defended Solzhenitsyn and Sakharov from attacks by the Politburo. The effect that his memoirs, which partly addressed the SLON years and delved deep into the intellectual life of the camp, had on his readers was tremendous.[58] As was the case with Florenskii, Likhachev's popularity contributed greatly to spreading knowledge about the Solovki camp.

While Gorbachev's perestroika enabled the reading public in both Moscow and Leningrad/St Petersburg to be informed about the SLON, things were also changing on the Solovki islands and more generally throughout the North-Western region of Russia. The relaxation of censorship allowed non-authorized information to flow. Many local journals and newspapers began to publish articles about the Northern territories and, consequently, about past repressions. The Karelian journal *Sever* (established in 1940) devoted several pages to the Solovki camp and its literature in the September 1990 issue,[59] partly using documents taken from the Petrozavodsk poet Iurii Linnik, who had been collecting them for years. Among the most important articles published in *Sever*, Dmitrii Driakhlitsyn's previously mentioned work, 'The Periodical Press of the Archipelago', is the most relevant to this research. Driakhlitsyn's article is a detailed analysis of the press system in the Solovki Gulag, and takes its cue from an article which had first appeared in 1927 in the camp journal *Solovetskie Ostrova*.[60] In Driakhlitsyn's article, the press system is shown in its developing stages. Driakhlitsyn provides much information regarding the different publications of the Solovki camp as well as literature produced within it.

Not only did perestroika allow research on Soviet repression, it also encouraged a revival in journalism. In 1990, a group of Solovki citizens founded the *Solovetskii Vestnik*, a newspaper which explicitly referred to the SLON periodical *Novye Solovki* in its layout. Although *Solovetskii Vestnik* lasted only five years, its weekly column 'Po sledam SLONa' (On the Trail of the SLON) contributed several articles on the question of Soviet camps.[61]

The increasing interest in the Gulag experience was not limited to the Northern regions. In the period between the beginning of perestroika and the subsequent collapse of the Soviet regime, the concurrence of various factors — in particular the gradual opening up of historical archives — resulted in a sudden publishing boom. Anthologies of historical documents, as well as studies of Russian history and of the

---

1995 edition has a longer section addressing the author's experience at the SLON.

58   Readers already knew about his experience as a *uznik*, as Likhachev never hid his past. In fact, he overtly addresses his experience at the camp in Marina Goldovskaia's 1988 documentary film on the Solovki prison camp (see below, p. 35 n. 87). For more on Likhachev's life, see Vladislav Zubok, *The Idea of Russia: The Life and Work of Dmitry Likhachev* (London: I.B. Tauris & Co. Ltd, 2017).

59   See *Sever*, 9 (1990).

60   Pavel Shenberg, 'Solovetskaia pechat'', *Materialy SOK*, 17 (1927), 65–91.

61   It is worth mentioning Antonina Mel'nik's articles as an important contribution to this line of research. In recent years another newspaper was set up on Solovki, *Sm. Vestnik*, a periodical of the Museum of the Solovki. At times, it deals with the theme of the SLON. The number of 3 August 2010 is entirely devoted to it.

camp system, censorship, the Gulag press, and Gulag literature and drama began to be published.[62] As far as SLON literature is concerned, it is worth mentioning the association (and publishing house) 'Vozvrashchenie', whose director, the former Gulag prisoner Semen Vilenskii, edited four books on the SLON writers in his 'Poety — uzniki Gulaga' (Poets — Prisoners of the Gulag) series. The first three books include poems by Vladimir Kemetskii, Mikhail Frolovskii, and Viktor Vasil'ev, whereas the fourth, *The Solovki Muse*, is an anthology of work by a number of poets, including some of those just named.[63] In the meantime, publishing was also gaining momentum outside Russia. In Luxembourg, Natal'ia Kuziakina published an outstanding monograph on the Solovki theatre[64] which reconstructs also the cultural life at the Solovki camp as well as devoting considerable attention to the development of its press system.

In the second half of the 1990s, the 'Gulag movement' was on the decline inside Russia. More than twenty years after the publication of *Arkhipelag Gulag*, by contrast, the world's interest in Soviet prison camps underwent a revival. A large number of monographs were published, especially in France, the United States, Great Britain, and Italy.[65]

---

62   See, in particular, the documentary series by the 'Mezhdunarodnyi Fond Demokratiia', which the former Russian president Boris El'tsyn founded in 1996, and which is mainly based on Aleksandr Iakovlev's personal archive, and the books published by 'ROSSPEN' (Rossiiskaia Politicheskaia Entsiklopediia). See bibliography for further details. A book that has also been relevant to my research is Alla Gorcheva's study on the Gulag press: Alla Gorcheva, *Pressa GULAGa (1918–1955)* (Moscow: Izd-vo MGU, 1996), together with its second, more detailed, edition: Alla Gorcheva, *Pressa GULAGa. Spiski E. P. Peshkovoi* (Moscow, Izd-vo MGU, 2009).

63   Vladimir Kemetskii (Sveshnikov), *Belaia noch'. Stikhi* (Moscow: Vozvrashchenie, 1998); Mikhail Frolovskii, *Severnaia vesna. Stikhi* (Moscow: Vozvrashchenie, 1992); Viktor Vasil'ev *Spolokhi. Stikhi* (Moscow: Vozvrashchenie, 1992); *Solovetskaia muza. Stikhi i pesni zakliuchennykh SLONa*, ed. by Vladimir Murav'ev (Moscow: Vozvrashchenie, 1992).

64   The book was published in Russia in 2009, in a very limited edition (500 copies), see Natal'ia Kuziakina, *Teatr' na Solovkakh* (St Petersburg: Dmitrii Bulanin, 2009). It was republished in 2014, see Natalia Kuziakina, *Theatre in the Solovki Prison Camp* (Hoboken: Taylor and Francis, 2014).

65   In Italy, where the Communist Party had for years covered up part of its past (above all, its active role in Soviet repression), years of guilty silence were finally followed by the first studies on the Gulag in the early 1990s. The first, remarkable contribution came in 1993 from Maria Ferretti, who addressed the question of memory in the 'new Russia' and included reflections on the Solovki camp, see Maria Ferretti, *La memoria mutilata: la Russia ricorda* (Milan: Corbaccio, 1993). References to the SLON would become a recurring theme in Italian Gulag historiography, which has typically been led by few specialists and by associations or research centres (including the above-mentioned 'Giangiacomo Feltrinelli Foundation'). Besides spreading knowledge of the Soviet Gulag in Italy, this line of research has also significantly contributed to the faithful depiction of the persecution that Italian prisoners experienced in the former Soviet Union. In 2003 the Giangiacomo Feltrinelli Foundation published *Reflections on the Gulag*, edited by Elena Dundovich, Francesca Gori, and Emanuela Guercetti. The book is well documented and boasts major contributors from all over the world who delve deep into different aspects of the history of the Gulag. The Italian contributors (who are members of Memorial Italia, which is modelled on the Russian association and which similarly aims to spread information about Soviet labour camps; see http://www.memorialitalia. it/ [accessed 25 July 2014]) provide an extensive dossier on the Italian victims, supplemented with original archival documents. See http://www.gulag-italia.it/ and the bibliography for a complete list. It is worth remembering how translations (especially Likhachev's memoirs and Florenskii's letters) helped to spark some interest in the subject.

In 2003, the American journalist Anne Applebaum published *Gulag: A History*, an outstanding historical reconstruction of the Soviet labour camps chronicling the history of the Gulag. Applebaum's book draws on a highly varied selection of sources and devotes an entire chapter, and part of her overall perspective on the Gulag system, to the history of the Solovki camp and crucial episodes in its development. Applebaum's meticulously documented research, which mentions the cultural life of the Solovki camp, gained her worldwide acclaim.[66] It won the 2004 Pulitzer Prize for General Non-Fiction Writing and it is currently regarded as one of the most important research sources on the topic.

In addition to Applebaum, other American scholars have addressed the history of the SLON. In 2004, Roy R. Robson published *Solovki: The Story of Russia Told through its Most Remarkable Islands*,[67] which traces the story of the Solovki islands back to prehistory. Robson's chapters on the Soviet camps and the SLON cultural life are detailed and well-documented, thanks to contributions from local experts and scholars. Unfortunately, the same cannot be said of the most recent monograph published in France, the sociologist Francine Dominique Liechtenhan's *The Laboratory of the Gulag*. Liechtenhan's book is often marred by moral commentary, and its depictions of cultural life and the publishing system of the camp are often inaccurate.[68]

It is no coincidence that the most important contributions to the study of the Gulag and Soviet repression over the last few decades have come from the West.[69] The political and cultural situation in Russia has worsened. Years after perestroika and the dismantling of the camps, the issue no longer seems interesting for Russians. Moreover, Putinism has made the assessment of the nation's 'problematic past' rather difficult. In fact, the darkest side of Russia's past seems to be a difficult subject: although many books are being published,[70] the campaign against the

---

66   As the author's website informs us, 'It [The book] has appeared or is due to appear in more than two dozen translations, including all major East and West European languages', see http://www.anneapplebaum.com/Gulag-a-history/ [accessed 25 July 2014].

67   Roy Robson, *Solovki: The Story of Russia Told through its Most Remarkable Islands* (New Haven: Yale University Press, 2004).

68   Francine D. Liechtenhan, *Le laboratoire du goulag 1918–1939* (Paris: Desclée de Brouwer, 2004). Quotes will be taken from the Italian version, Francine D. Liechtenhan, *Il laboratorio del Gulag* (Turin: Lindau, 2009). Some passages reveal inaccuracies: Liechtenhan, for instance, maintains that the *SLON* and the *Solovetskie Ostrova* were two different journals which had nothing in common, whereas the latter was a continuation of the former (see below, p. 104). Besides, her overall thesis is rather one-sided and aims to show how the SLON was basically 'hell on earth'. Liechtenhan deliberately ignores the experiences of witnesses who led a relatively decent life there. It is impossible to leave out the cultural vigour of the camp that emerges from the newspapers and journals which flourished there and which Liechtenhan mentions only to support her thesis — the SLON publications were, in her analysis, pure propaganda tools.

69   The list presented here does not include the whole range of publications related to Solovki and SLON, but only those which are relevant to my research. Works such as the books by Polish writer Mariusz Wilk, imbued with subjective reflections, are not included as they cannot be regarded as reliable sources. See, for instance, Mariusz Wilk, *Wilczy notes* [*Notebooks of a Wolf*] (Warsaw, Noir sur blanc, 2007).

70   See, for example Galina Ivanova, *Istoriia GULAGa, 1918–1958: Sotsial'no-ekonomicheskii i politiko-pravovoi aspekty* (Moscow: Nauka, 2006). Moreover, the publisher Rosspen launched in 2007 the series

NGOs who work on the memory of the Gulag and the contemporary inauguration of a new Museum of the Gulag in Moscow seem to prove that there currently is a different strategy by the Russian government aimed at taking ownership of the discourse on the memory of Soviet repression and suppressing all independent voices which try to put forward a different view of it. This seems to be the result of a long process: the editorial (mis)adventures of Iurii Brodskii's *Solovki: Twenty Years of Special Purpose Detention* is emblematic of how the situation has worsened over the last two decades. A photographer and writer who spent years collecting photographs and documents about the Solovki camp,[71] Brodskii had finally put together a unique collage of his own photographs and photographs dating back to the SLON years, as well as passages from former prisoners' memoirs. After repeated rejections from Russian publishers, an abridged version of the book was finally published in Italy in 1998. Brodskii's original and well-documented version was published in Russia only in 2002.[72]

It is worth mentioning that, as is often the case in Russia, there are huge differences between the two capitals and the provinces. This is true also of Gulag research studies, which are encouraged in the provinces by sympathetic and supportive local institutions such as museums and regionally funded societies. As far as the Solovki islands are concerned, the 'Solovki State Historical, Architectural and Natural Museum-Reserve' hosts a permanent exhibition on the history of the SLON and its archives include a range of documents and memoirs available to researchers. The publication of memoirs continues even today. Nikolai Kiselev-Gromov's *SLON: Special Purpose Forest of Solovki*,[73] which was republished in Arkhangel'sk in 2009, conjures up the memories of a former camp guard. In 2012 Shiriaev's *Neugasimaia lampada* was published in a new edition, with commentaries, by the Solovki monastery,[74] which has been undergoing a spiritual and economic rebirth in recent years. The monastery is currently issuing a series of SLON *vospominaniia*, which will provide a unique source for researchers.[75] Moreover, since 2002 the 'Comradeship of Northern Sailing', a section of the 'Marine Museum of the Solovki', has published an almanac, *Solovetskoe More*. So far, *Solovetskoe More* has

'Istoriia stalinizma', in which several books by both Russian and foreign scholars are published.

71   Brodskii's personal archive boasts more than 5,000 documents (including both photographs and negatives).

72   Iurii Brodskii, *Solovki. Dvadtsat' let osobogo naznacheniia* (Moscow: Rosspen, 2002). Quotes will be taken from the 2008 edition quoted in the introduction. Brodskii has written another book on Solovki which should be published in 2017.

73   Nikolai Kiselev-Gromov, *SLON: Solovetskii Les Osobogo Naznacheniia* (Arkhangel'sk: Tur, 2009). The book was first published in Shanghai in 1936, see Nikolai Kiselev-Gromov, *Lageria smerti v SSSR* (Shanghai: Knigoizdatel'stvo N. P. Malinovskogo, 1936). I cite the 2009 edition in this book.

74   Boris Shiriaev, *Neugasimaia lampada* (Solovki: Spaso-Preobrazhenskii Solovetskii Stavropigial'nyi Muzhskoi Monastyr', 2013).

75   In 2013 the first volume was published. It contains the memoirs of fifteen former Solovki prisoners, some of which were published for the first time. The board of the series is composed of historians, literary scholars, and religious figures such as Irina Flige, Lidiia Golovkova, and Mikhail Talalai. The chief editor is Viacheslav Umniagin, see *Vospominaniia Solovetskikh uznikov*, ed. by Viacheslav Umniagin, 5 vols (Solovki: Spaso-Preobrazhenskii Solovetskii Stavropigial'nyi Muzhskoi Monastyr', 2013–17).

published several articles on the SLON, some of which are devoted to its literature. Antonina Soshina's comprehensive and scholarly work played a major role in this line of research up until her death in 2013.[76]

An important tendency recorded in recent years is the attention devoted by literary scholars to some protagonists of the SLON literary scene whose work will be analysed in this book. Poems by Iurii Kazarnovskii have been published several times;[77] the scholarly community has been paying increasing attention to Aleksandr Iaroslavskii over the years,[78] including Vladimir Genis, who devoted a section of his book *Nevernye slugi rezhima* to the poet;[79] in 2014, Leonid Livak and Andrei Ustinov republished Vladimir Kemetskii's collection of poems *Kammennye tsvety*, while placing the poet within the context of the avant-garde literature of Russian émigrés in Paris.[80]

While Moscow is waging a none too quiet war on 'Memorial' and other activists in the field of memory,[81] in the West things are different. It is Italy that has launched the most surprising publishing initiative dedicated to the SLON with Maurizio Ciampa's *The Tremendous Era: Voices from the Solovki Gulag*.[82] Ciampa's book introduces a new negotiating perspective on the memory of the Gulag — a daring attempt to internalize and narrate other people's memories while adhering to historical truth and to the victims' real stories.

One publication which can be considered genuinely ground-breaking comes from Germany: it is Felicitas Fischer von Weikersthal's *The 'Imprisoned' Press: The Soviet Forced Labor Camp's Press, 1923–1937*, which shed light on many issues related to

76   In 2014 the Solovki Monastery published a posthumous collection of essays by Antonina Soshina. See Antonina Soshina, *Na Solovkakh protiv voli: sud'by i sroki 1923–1939* (Solovki: Spaso-Preobrazhenskii Solovetskii Stavropigial'nyi Muzhskoi Monastyr', 2014). All the numbers of *Solovetskoe More* are available online at the link: <http://www.solovki.info/?action=topic&id=299> [accessed 20 January 2015].

77   See, for instance, Ol'ga Kushlina, *Russkaia literatura XX veka v zerkale parodii* (Moscow: Vyschaia shkola, 1993), p. 236; Zoia Bogomolova, *Kak molniia v nochi: K. Gerd* (Izhevsk: Izd-vo Udmurtskogo universiteta, 1998), p. 123; Arkadii Arkanov, *Literaturnaia parodiia* (Moscow: Eskmo-Press, 2000), p. 192. The latest and most important contribution on Kazarnovskii is by Pavel Nerler, who has devoted a long chapter of his new monograph *Osip Mandel'shtam i ego solagerniki* to Iurii Kazarnovskii. See Pavel Nerler, *Osip Mandel'shtam i ego solagerniki* (Moscow: AST, 2015), pp. 213–60.

78   See, for instance, *Die Neue Menschheit. Biopolitische Utopien in Russland zu Beginn des 20. Jahrhunderts*, ed. by Boris Groys and Michael Hagemeister (Frankfurt am Main: Suhrkamp Verlag, 2005), pp. 412–14.

79   Vladimir Genis, *Nevernye slugi rezhima. Pervye sovetskie nevozvrashchentsy (1920–1933). Opyt dokumental'nogo issledovaniia v 2-kh knigakh* (Moscow: no pub., 2009), pp. 378–439.

80   Leonid Livak and Andrei Ustinov, *Literaturnyi avangard russkogo Parizha. Istoriia, Khronika, Antologiia. Dokumenty* (Moscow: OGI, 2014), pp. 731–48. For their book they used the anthology of poems *Kamennye tsvety. Stikhi*, a manuscript dated 1936 and first published in 2000 by Likhachev in the second edition of his memoirs.

81   Among the episodes of the silent war against Memorial are the 4 December 2008 raid on St Petersburg 'Memorial''s office and the subsequent confiscation of all the hard disks containing their digital archive (although the material was given back to 'Memorial') and the recent law on the 'Foreign Agents', which has created huge trouble for all civil society activists not under the control of the authorities. In December 2015, the St Petersburg office of 'Memorial' was declared a 'foreign agent', and the same happened to other offices of Memorial in the following years.

82   Maurizio Ciampa, *L'epoca tremenda. Voci dal Gulag delle Solovki* (Brescia: Morcelliana, 2010).

the press in the Soviet camps and, particularly, in the SLON. After an introductory chapter devoted to the history of the Soviet camps up until 1941, Fischer von Weikersthal's book delves deep into the question of re-educational activities within the camps and then focuses on the publications of the Solovki prison camp and of the Belbaltlag, the system of camps of the White Sea-Baltic canal building sites. It also sheds light on the question of censorship within the camp: together with Nikolai Klepikov's dissertation, it is the only study to do so.[83] In the final chapters of her book, Fischer von Weikersthal provides an analysis of the visual elements of camp publications and of the real purposes of the Gulag press. *Die 'inhaftierte' Presse: Das Pressewesen sowjetischer Zwangsarbeitslager, 1923–1937* is the ideal partner of the present book.[84]

Finally, Julie Draskoczy's recent book *Belomor: Criminality and Creativity in Stalin's Gulag*[85] has the merit of analysing the works published in the press of the Belomorkanal and bringing to light the surprising variety of texts and approaches, thus helping to pave the way for this book, which shares the same aim of providing a different narrative of the Gulag by looking at the works published by the prisoners during their detention.

Different kinds of material add to the wide range of available documentary sources. Societies and organizations that aim to keep memory alive continue to work and support researchers by opening up their archives. Many websites are devoted to the SLON, among which is the excellent site created by Iurii Serov and his Canadian team <http://www.solovki.ca> (or the 'Solovki encyclopaedia'). Another example of an outstanding resource is the DVD-ROM edited by the N. A. Dobroliubov Arkhangel'sk Public Library, which includes a large number of Solovki periodicals.[86] Film directors are also leading figures in contemporary

---

83   Nikolai Klepikov, 'Politicheskaia tsenzura na Evropeiskom Severe RSFSR/SSSR v 1920–1930-e gg.' (unpublished doctoral dissertation, Pomorskii Lomonosov University of Arkhangel'sk, 2005).

84   Also Olga M. Cooke has studied the Solovki camp literature since the 1990s. She has only published Gennadii Andreev's memoirs in the journal *Gulag Studies*, of which she is the editor. See Olga M. Cooke, 'Remembering Solovki: Gennady Andreev's *Solovetsky Islands*', *Gulag Studies*, 4 (2011), 91–120. Apart from Cooke's article, the literature of the Solovki prison camp has been analysed only by Claudia Pieralli in a 2013 article which followed my article on Gulag press as a first step of a joint project on Gulag poetry which was not taken forward. See: Claudia Pieralli, 'The Poetry of Soviet Political Prisoners (1921–1939): An Historical-Typological Framework', in *Contributi italiani al XV Congresso Internazionale degli Slavisti*, ed. by Marcello Garzaniti, Alberto Alberti, Monica Perotto, and Bianca Sulpasso (Florence: Firenze University Press, 2013), pp. 387–412; Andrea Gullotta, 'A New Perspective for Gulag Literature Studies: The Gulag Press', *Studi Slavistici*, 8 (2011), 95–111. An article by Pieralli on poems in volume 5 of the Solovki monastery series is forthcoming, it only makes some general considerations of the theme: see Claudia Pieralli, 'Poeziia uznikov Solovetskikh lagerei: neskol'ko zamechanii k teme', in *Vospominaniia Solovetskikh Uznikov*, 5 (forthcoming).

85   Julie Draskoczy, *Belomor: Criminality and Creativity in Stalin's Gulag* (Brighton, MA: Academic Studies Press, 2014).

86   See *Solovetskaia pechat' (1924–1930)* (Arkhangel'sk: Arkhangel'skaia oblastnaia nauchnaia biblioteka imeni N. A. Dobroliubova, 2007) [DVD-ROM]. The journals have all been scanned and uploaded. They can be browsed through a specific, functional program. Moreover, the website of the St Petersburg State Library shows on free display many numbers of SLON periodicals (http://leb.nlr.ru/ — accessed 25 July 2014).

research. Thanks to their contributions to the 'Solovki cinematic tradition',[87] they have helped to maintain a steadfast focus on the camp.

As is revealed by the foregoing, the history of the SLON still attracts readers, publishers, film directors, and scholars — and, eventually, even writers.[88] It also demonstrates how, despite being one of the most extensive lines of research about the camps, important aspects have not yet received a thorough assessment. Most probably, some of them will never be assessed: although several documents have already surfaced, most of them still need to be discovered. Some[89] think that the 'Solovki archive' was destroyed or that it lies buried in a secret place. The discovery of such an archive may bring new research perspectives.

Bibliography is a further obstacle to researchers' attempts to address the history of the camp. As the beginning of the present chapter clearly states, the 'Gulag' theme — the Solovki camp being no exception — has always been liable to ideological manipulation. Several studies, in particular early studies, are therefore not reliable from a scholarly point of view. For the same reasons, memoirs are also problematic, as we shall see. Moreover, some of the most important publications may not be entirely reliable as scholarly sources because they had radically different purposes (personal disclosures, information, and emotional release). This indeed is the case with Brodskii's book, which was very important for the spreading of knowledge about the Solovki camp but lacked objectivity.

Considering the scope and aim of the present study, research so far on the SLON has been doubly flawed. Either it does not regard the SLON intellectual scene as fundamental and unique (as is the case, for instance, with Liechtenhan's book) or is too fragmentary and lacks a more comprehensive background (as is the case with

---

87   In 1928, a documentary film on the Solovki prison camp was shot and released as a piece of Soviet propaganda (see chapter 2). In 1988, the director and MGU professor Marina Goldovskaia shot the documentary film *Vlast' Solovetskaia*, which — aiming to adhere to historical truth — is based on the stories of surviving prisoners who took part in the film, among whom was Likhachev. In 2006 the St Petersburg director Anastasiia Cherkasova shot the documentary film *Krepko tseluiu i liubliu*, which is based on the 'Remembrance Days' organized by St Petersburg 'Memorial'. About Goldovskaia's film, see Erin Alpert, 'Reinventing Soviet Visual Memory: A Case Study of Marina Goldovskaia's Documentary *Solovki Power*', *Studies in Russian and Soviet Cinema*, 7/2 (2013), 207–26. Finally, the French director Olivier Rolin is the author of the 2014 documentary film *Solovki — la Bibliothèque disparue*, devoted to the library collection of the camp, which was found in the library of Ertsevo. At the conference *Geschichte(n) des Gulag — Realitaet und Fiktion* (Heidelberg, 20–22 March 2012) Oksana Bulgakowa read a paper in which Goldovskaia's documentary was analysed. The proceedings of that conference include her paper, and also a paper from Zuzanna Bogumil on memory about the Solovki. See Oksana Bulgakowa, 'Die filmische Darstellung von Körperlichkeit in extremen Situationen', in *(Hi-)Stories of the Gulag: Fiction and Reality*, ed. by Felicitas Fischer von Weikersthal and Karoline Thaidigsmann (Heidelberg: Universitätsverlag Winter, 2016), pp. 303–22, and Zuzanna Bogumil, 'The Solovetski Islands and Butovo as two "Russian Golgothas". New Martyrdom as a Means to Understand Soviet Repression', ibid., pp. 133–54.

88   In 2014 the Russian writer Zakhar Prilepin set his novel *Obitel'* in the Solovki prison camp, as did Evgenii Vodolazkin in 2016 (see p. 281). Zakhar Prilepin, *Obitel'* (Moscow: AST, 2014).

89   Interviews with Anatolii Razumov (Saint Pietersburg, July 2008), Irina Flige (St Petersburg, June 2009), and Iurii Dmitriev (Petrozavodsk, July 2009).

Soshina's brilliant articles, which have never cohered into a single monograph). There is still a gap in both Russian and non-Russian literary criticism, as SLON literature has not been thoroughly analysed: this book is intended to fill it.

CHAPTER 2

❖

The SLON between History and Historiography

On the White Sea there's a red elephant
Camp song[1]

The History of the Camp as Recounted in Documents

The First Gulag

The SLON — which was founded by Lenin's decree and which flourished under Stalin's regime — is universally regarded as the 'very first Gulag'. Although scholars typically argue[2] that other prison camps were fully operational by the time the Solovki camp was set up, it is hard to deny the SLON's crucial role in the establishment of the entire camp system, which prospered in the Soviet Union until shortly before its fall.

In many regards, the Solovki camp was an exception. As stated above, it was the first camp entirely run by the political police, which gradually created a theoretically efficient, profitable system that exploited prisoners as forced labourers. It was the first 'special purpose camp', where specific groups of prisoners were interned.[3] Finally, it was the 'laboratory' where criteria and strategies that would later become crucial to the whole Gulag system were first experimented with and developed. These include the differentiation between 'ordinary' and 'political' prisoners, the exploitation of forced labourers outside the camp, and the nourishment scale, by which the allocation of food rations was related to job performance. Additionally, archival materials show that the *organy* (i.e. Soviet security agencies) were particularly interested in the SLON.[4]

---

1   'На белом море красный слон'. Quoted in many sources, amongst which is: Nikolai Antsiferov, *Iz dum o bylom: vospominaniia* (Moscow: Feniks, Kul'turnaia initsiativa, 1992), p. 337.
2   For instance, Applebaum (pp. 31–34) and Liechtenhan (pp. 30–35). It is interesting to mention Jehanne M. Gheith's and Katherine R. Jolluck's definition of the SLON as a 'proto-Gulag camp', see Jehanne M. Gheith and Katherine R. Jolluck, *Gulag Voices: Oral Histories of Soviet Incarceration and Exile* (New York: Palgrave Macmillan, 2011), p. 223.
3   So-called 'special purpose' jails already existed: for example, those in Petrominsk, Kholmogory, in the Arkhangel'sk region, where political prisoners were sent. From 1923 onwards, all were sent to the Solovki islands, as we shall soon see.
4   In the first years Feliks Dzerzhinskii asked for information about the camp conditions as testified by the documents published in: *F. E. Dzerzhinskii — predesedatel' VChK-OGPU. 1917–1926,*

The decision to set up a special-purpose camp was partly a natural consequence of the dramatic increase of prisoners in the newly established Soviet state. Beginning with the October Revolution, the Bolshevik regime's terror and violence resulted in a seamless wave of arrests. The wealthy bourgeoisie and aristocrats, the clergy and representatives of political factions opposed to the Bolsheviks were the first to be arrested. Two other categories of prisoners were then added to the first, obvious ones. Factory workers and peasants — the very social classes represented by Communist emblems of hammer and sickle, those classes for whom the Russian Revolution was theoretically fought — were also arrested.[5] The revolutionary violence increased after the creation of the Cheka, in 1918. The Cheka acquired virtually unlimited power. Its objective was to do away with anything that might thwart, directly or indirectly, the survival of Soviet power. The Cheka drew heavily on its extraordinary power. Many documents dating from those years remind us how ordinary gestures or naive utterances could lead to imprisonment or even capital punishment.[6] Thousands of peasants were purged in those years. In 1918, peasants protested against grain requisitions and thus became the first victims of the 'peasant war against the Soviet State', which, as Graziosi argues, 'continued under profoundly different conditions the peasant revolution against the Tsarist regime'.[7] The Red Terror and the subsequent Civil War added to the number of victims.

The dramatic increase in arrests inevitably led to a crisis in the Soviet prison system. Originally built to house a limited number of prisoners, Tsarist prisons suddenly became unbearably overcrowded. Makeshift prisons were set up to house the prisoners. Basements, deserted palaces, prison camps originally built for German prisoners but left empty after the Brest-Litovsk treaty — anything would suffice. The *organy*, however, generally opted for monasteries. Here again, their choice was deliberate. Structurally sound and enclosed by walls, with cells in which the monks lived and well-established supply systems, monasteries could be converted easily into jails. Therefore, they served as prisons long before the Soviet seizure of all Church properties and possessions.[8] Monasteries thus rapidly turned from places of prayer to places of suffering.

This trend also affected the Solovki monastery, although the peripheral position of the archipelago spared the monastery from most of the ravages that hit

ed. by Andrei Plekhanov and Aleksandr Plekhanov (Moscow: Mezhdunarodnyi Fond Demokratiia, 2007).

5   Andrea Graziosi delves deep into the question in his 1996 book: Andrea Graziosi, *The Great Soviet Peasant War: Bolsheviks and Peasants, 1917–1933* (Cambridge, MA: Harvard University Press, 1996) and in the chapter 'Revolution and War', see Andrea Graziosi, *L'Urss di Lenin e Stalin. Storia dell'Unione Sovietica. 1914–1945* (Bologna: Il Mulino, 2007), pp. 89–132. On the repression of workers' see, for instance, Leopold H. Haimson, Ziva Galili y Garcia, and Richard Wortman, *The Making of Three Russian Revolutionaries* (Cambridge: Cambridge University Press, 1987), p. 513.

6   Some are mentioned in Applebaum, p. 29.

7   Graziosi, *L'Urss*, p. 106.

8   It was a decree by the Soviet Central Committee published on 23 February 1922 that officially sanctioned the seizure of Church properties. The whole set of documents related to the seizure of Church properties has been published in *Arkhivy Kremlia*, ed. by Nikolai Pokrovskii and Stanislav Petrov (Moscow-Novosibirsk: ROSSPEN-Sibirskii khronograf, 1997), pp. 111–94.

FIG. 2.1. The tannery of the SLON. ASM

other places of worship in the first few months following Red October.[9] Yet the winds of revolution slowly arrived at the White Sea. On 28 December 1918, the former Solovki monk Nicodemus, then bishop of Belgorod, was martyred by the Bolsheviks.[10] Stunned by events, in August 1919 the monks of the Solovki monastery sent a letter to the Archbishop of Canterbury, begging him to intercede with the captains of the British Army so that they would not have to leave the region.[11] In that letter, the monks explicitly asked the Head of the Anglican Church to protect the Russian Orthodox Church from the Bolsheviks. Their fears were not unfounded. It was quite likely the monastery would attract Bolshevik attention not only because of its economic value, but also because of its symbolic significance. Russian believers considered it as one of the most sacred places of prayer. Moreover, over the centuries it had established sound relations with the Tsarist regime.

9   See Irina Reznikova, *Pravoslavie na Solovkakh: Materialy po istorii Solovetskogo lageria* (St Petersburg: Memorial, 1994), and Fiorenzo Reati, *Dio dirà l'ultima parola. La persecuzione della Chiesa cattolica in Russia in epoca sovietica* (Lavis: Arca, 2003).

10   See *Solovetskie ostrova: dukhovnoe, kul'turnoe i prirodnoe nasledie*, ed. by Petr Boiarskii, Aleksandr Liutyi, and Viacheslav Stoliarov (Moscow: Rossiiskii NII prirodnogo i kul'turnogo nasledia, 2005), p. 611.

11   Ibid. The British Army was present in the area as part of the British military intervention in Russia between 1918 and 1920, in what has recently been defined as 'Churchill's crusade'. See Clifford Kinvig, *Churchill's Crusade: The British Invasion of Russia 1918–1920* (London: Hambledon Continuum, 2006).

The Solovetskii Monastery

Two monks, Savvatii and German, founded the Solovki Monastery in 1429,[12] during their quest to discover a spiritual retreat for prayer. After three days at sea, the monks arrived at the main island of the archipelago and settled there. In 1436, another hermit, Zosima, joined them. In just a few years, the three monks established the monastery and created a strong community, despite the harsh climatic conditions. The community also initiated various activities, such as fishing and breeding livestock. As a result, the monastery was flourishing economically within a few decades. In the meantime, they set up hermitages and churches throughout the territory of the archipelago, erecting *skity* [hermitages] on the Main Isle, the island of Anzer, Muksalma, and on the Zaiatskie islands.[13]

In 1566, the monastery had its official consecration. At that time, its economic and spiritual growth peaked. The hegumen of the Solovki monastery, who was largely responsible for its architectural development, was elevated to the rank of Metropolitan of Moscow, under the name of Philip II.[14] His life as Metropolitan was, however, short-lived and tormented. Elected while the *oprichnina* was raging, Philip II took sides with the boyars and with other victims of the *oprichniki*, thus provoking Ivan IV ('the Terrible'), who deposed him from office and eventually had him murdered by Maliuta Skuratov. Ivan's rage did not directly affect the monastery, which by the end of the sixteenth century was thriving and able to carry out the monk Tikhon's new architectural plans. High, substantial walls connected by flanking towers were raised at that time, lending the monastery its current shape. It was during Ivan IV's reign that the monastery was first used as a prison, thus starting a tradition that was to develop in the following centuries.[15] Its peripheral position naturally exposed the monastery to attacks from foreign armies. In the second half of the sixteenth century, during the Livonian War, Swedish troops made an unsuccessful attempt to seize the monastery.[16]

A second peak of tension in the history of the Solovki monastery coincided with the *raskol* (schism). Taking sides against Nikon's Reformation, the monks experienced

12   A complete and comprehensive history of the Monastery is in Robson's book. A short chronology is available on the Solovki monastery's official website, see http://solovki-monastyr.ru/abbey/history/ [accessed 25 July 2014].

13   The Solovki archipelago is formed by six islands, the largest being the Great Isle (*Bol'shoi ostrov*), where the monastery and the Savvat'evo and Sekirnaia gora hermitages are. The other islands are Anzer, where the so-called 'Golgotha' (*Golgofskii skit*) was erected, the Bol'shaia and the Malaia Muksalma, the Bol'shoi and the Malyi Zaiatskii. The wind-blown landscape of the Zaiatskie islands makes them bare and atypical compared to other islands with their abundant woods.

14   Philip II, or Fedor Kolychev (1507–69), was born to influential boyar parents but preferred to serve as a monk. He was ordained at the Solovki monastery in 1538 and, after being appointed as hegumen in 1548, he stayed there until he was enthroned as Metropolitan in Moscow.

15   The first prisoner, the hegumen of Sergiev Posad Artemii, was sent there in 1554 by Ivan the Terrible. The monastery prisons subsequently housed a number of representatives of both the nobility and the clergy, amongst whom was Silvan, Maksim Grek's main disciple, who died on the Solovki islands at the end of the sixteenth century. Skopin, p. 30.

16   See Vladimir Skopin, *Na Solovetskikh ostrovakh* (Moscow: Iskusstvo, 1991), p. 17. The episode is also mentioned in Georgii Frumenkov, *Solovetskii monastyr' i oborona Belomoria v XVI–XIX vv.* (Arkhangel'sk: Severo-Zapadnoe Knizhnoe Izdatelstvo, 1975), p. 11.

an eight-year siege (1668–76) that resulted in the seizure of the monastery and in their subsequent mass murder at the hands of the *strel'tsy*. The Solovki monastery, however, began to flourish again and the Tsars began to pay visits. The first Tsar to visit was Peter the Great,[17] in 1694 and again in 1702.[18]

After the first, internecine assault of the *strel'tsy* in the seventeenth century, a second great assault paralysed the monastery in 1854 (which in 1765 had been declared a *stauropegion*, that is, a monastery which is not subject to the local church, but is directly subject to the Synod of Bishops, i.e. is controlled directly by Moscow). At the height of the Crimean War, the British Navy surrounded and bombarded the monastery for nine hours. Unable to penetrate the walls erected by the monks, whose defence was strategically organized by the Archimandrite Aleksandr, the British vessels eventually withdrew. The event contributed to the monks' increasing fame. The monastery became a popular pilgrimage destination[19] and began to host temporary labourers. In December 1915, its community consisted of 213 monks and 137 labourers.[20]

However, peace did not last for long: the rise of Communism changed the situation radically.

The Slow Decay of the Solovetskii Monastery

The first, radical changes took place at the time of the Red Army's seizure of Arkhangel'sk on 21 February 1920. Until then, hostilities between the White Guard and the Red Army had resulted in the White Guard's supremacy throughout the northern regions, which were also defended by British troops, whose support had proved crucial. The gradual withdrawal of its foreign allies weakened the White Guard, leading to its eventual defeat.

Since their first settlement in the Arkhangel'sk province, the Bolsheviks had shown interest in the Solovki archipelago. The monastery, in particular, attracted them. On 29 April 1920, a Cheka commission led by Mikhail Kedrov was formally

17   After Peter, several members of the royal family went to the *Solovetskii Monastyr'* throughout the centuries. Princess Elizaveta's pilgrimage in 1913 is still legendary, see Robson, p. 195.
18   During Peter the Great's reign, the number of prisoners in the monastery increased rather dramatically. They were mostly members of the nobility. Soon after Peter's death, some of his acolytes underwent the same fate. Other than the above mentioned, the most famous monastery *plenniki* under the Tsars were the diplomat Petr Alekseevich Tolstoi (1645–1729), an ancestor of the novelist Lev Nikolaevich Tolstoi, and Prince Vasilii Lukich Dolgorukii (1670–1739). Among the prisoners of the monastery is the legendary figure of Petr Ivanovich Kalnyshevskii (1691–1803), the last Ataman Koshevoi of the Zaporozhskii Sich: he was 84 when he was sent there, and he was condemned to a lifelong imprisonment. In 1801, when he was almost 110 and totally blind, he was finally pardoned. He died shortly after, aged 112. Although his tomb has never been identified, Ol'ga Adamova-Sliozberg writes in her memoirs about her visit to the Ataman Koshevoi's tomb during her detention. See Skopin, pp. 30–31 and Ol'ga Adamova-Sliozberg, *Put'* (Moscow: Vozvrashchenie, 1993), p. 49.
19   Amongst the numerous visitors were the poet Sergei Esenin and Vasilii Nemirovich-Danchenko, whose book about the journey has been recently republished. See Vasilii Nemirovich-Danchenko, *Belomor'e i Solovki: vospominaniia i rasskazy* (Moscow: Izd. Gosudarstvennaia publichnaia istoricheskaia biblioteka Rossii, 2009).
20   *Solovetskie ostrova: dukhovnoe, kul'turnoe i prirodnoe nasledie*, p. 611.

asked to assess its condition.[21] After some months, a second commission carried out an inventory and reported the subsequent seizure of the monastery's goods. The monastery was now under the administration of the Soviet authorities, which, amongst other things, decided to use it as a camp for White Army prisoners.[22]

As darker and darker clouds gathered over the monastery and its community, Zosima the Hermit, by then bedridden, uttered this prophecy: "The times that will come will be such that we must pray to God we don't live to see them'. When he was asked about what exactly would happen, he said with a sigh that they would conquer all Russia'.[23]

In September, the Prior of the monastery, Archimandrite Veniamin, was arrested.[24] While repression was raging throughout the Soviet Union, the Bolsheviks continued to send commissions to the Solovki in order to carry out the confiscation of the monastery's goods. These operations resulted in outright pillaging, during which a large number of treasures were plundered, as contemporary witnesses report.[25] Simultaneously, the Bolsheviks launched a press campaign. By then, the Soviet state's real intentions had become crystal clear. The author of an article in the Arkhangel'sk region *Izvestiia* suggested that 'the severe weather conditions, the working regime and the struggle against nature will be a good school for every vicious element!'.[26]

Some Communists, however, did not take part in the raids. Gerasim Alekseevich Alekseev, the head of one of the many commissions sent to the Solovki, wrote a report in which he explicitly defended the monks and praised the religious community's

21   In her book, Kuziakina (pp. 10–14) writes extensively about the commissions.

22   A number of books document this episode. In Brodskii's book, in particular, two photographs of the documents which testify the arrival of prisoners in 1920 are included (Brodskii, p. 39). Liechtenhan suggests instead that the prisoners never reached the islands, following a shipwreck (Liechtenhan, p. 272). However, the only source for this is Shiriaev's memoirs (Shiriaev, p. 47): no further documentation verifies it.

23   ['Настанет такое время, что не дай Бог нам до него дожить'. Когда же его спрашивали, что именно случится, то он со вздохом говорил, что всю Россию победят]. See *Solovetskie ostrova: dukhovnoe, kul'turnoe i prirodnoe nasledie*, p. 612. See also Manuil (Lemeshevskii), 'Solovetskii tsvetnik', Dvkhovnyi Sobesednik, 2.22 (2000), pp. 51–69.

24   After spending many years in jail, Veniamin was murdered in 1928. Brodskii, p. 41.

25   References to ravages and pillaging can be found in Brodskii's, Liechtenhan's and Kuziakina's books.

26   [Суровая климатическая обстановка, трудовой режим и борьба с природой будут хорошей школой для всяких порочных элементов!]. Quoted in Brodskii, p. 13. The Arkhangel'sk *Izvestiia* also took part in the correspondence over the administrative seizure of the islands, which suggests that the article was written on commission. See: Moscow, GARF, f. 1235, op. 95, d. 155, 'Perepiska s Narodnym komissariatom finansov RSFSR, redaktsiei gazety *Izvestiia*, Arkhangel'skoi gubernskim i Suzdal'skim uezdnym ispol'nitelnymi komitetami ob opublikovanii teksta privetstviia Suzdal'skogo uezdno-gorodskogo ispolkoma Vladimirskoi gubernii VTsIK v sviazi s postanovleniem o zamene prodovol'stvennoi razverstki prodnalogom, o peredache tsennosti Solovetskogo monastyria (30.12.20–8.4.21)'. In the same period, the Bolsheviks started many research activities on the islands, such as its hydrobiological station, see: Moscow, GARF, f. 2307(a), op. 2, d. 74, 'Delo o sozdanii gidrobiologicheskoi stantsii v Solovkakh (2.6.21–30.9.21)', and: Moscow, GARF, f. 2307 (a), op. 2, d. 302, 'Doklad zaveduiushchego Arkhangel'skim gubernskim otdelom narodnogo obrazovaniia, dokladnye zapiski professora Livanova o rabote ekspeditsii po issledovaniiu Belogo Moria i o neobkhodimosti organizatsii Solovetskoi biologicheskoi stantsii (28.7–1.9.21)'.

activity. Alekseev actually decided to resign from the commission after witnessing the ravages that were carried out without his formal authorization:

> A chaotic situation has developed on the Solovki islands, where numerous and diverse authorities arrive from every quarter and take control, and take this and that without my permission, one does not know whom to obey. [...] In view of all the above, and having no more strength to continue the struggle against this, I beg you to relieve me of my post immediately.[27]

Alekseev's concerns went unheeded. Ruthless pillaging continued and living conditions on the archipelago worsened.[28] After the decree imposing the seizure of Church property came into force in 1922, a third commission reached the Solovki islands, this time led by Nikolai Pomerantsev.[29] He informed the Soviet authorities in Moscow of his bewilderment at the ongoing looting and destruction and saved a large number of treasures by transferring them to Petrograd. In the meantime, however, the idea of turning the monastery into a labour camp was spreading, especially after the establishment of the *Severnye Lageria Osobogo Naznacheniia* [Northern Special Purpose Camps],[30] which initially included the Kholmogory and Petrominsk camps. The foundation of the Solovki Special Purpose camp began shortly after these events, in 1923, when Dzerzhinskii himself showed his willingness to organize a system of camps:

> The Republic cannot take pity on criminals and cannot spend significant resources on them. They have to cover their expenses by working. They have to be accommodated in isolated places — at Pechora, at Obdorsk etc. It will be soon necessary to work on the organization of forced work (*katorga* labour), on camps that will colonize uninhabited areas and with iron discipline. We have plenty of places and space.[31]

The undertaking began on 8 March, when the Arkhangel'sk Party Executive

---

27 [Хаотическое положение сложилось на Соловецких островах, куда съехались со всех сторон много разнообразной власти, и каждая власть контролирует, берет без разрешения то, другое и третье. Не знаешь, кому и как подчиняться. [...] Ввиду вышеизложенного, не имея более сил бороться с этим, прошу Вас немедленно меня освободить от занимаемого поста]. Kuziakina, p. 11 and Brodskii, p. 44. Enquiries about Alekseev have led to no further information on his biography. Even in Marina Osipenko's well-documented article on the years between 1920 and 1923 there are no biographical data on Alekseev: Marina Osipenko, 'Khraniteli very. Bratiia Solovetskogo monastyria posle Oktiabr'skogo perevorota 1917 g.', *Sever*, 3–4 (2013), 31–59.

28 The first typhus epidemic on the islands dates back to these years. See *Solovetskie ostrova: dukhovnoe, kul'turnoe i prirodnoe nasledie*, p. 613.

29 See Elena Morshakova, Tat'iana Tutova, 'Solovetskie sviatyni v Moskovskom Kremle', *Nashe nasledie*, 59–60 (2001), 108–21.

30 For an extensive description of the Northern Special Purpose Camps and other northern Russian camps, see *Sistema ispravitel'no-trudovykh lagerei v SSSR: 1923–1960. Spravochnik*, ed. by Mikhail Smirnov (Moscow: Zven'ia, 1998). It was translated into German and digitized: see *GULAG. Das Lagersystem in der UdSSR* (Berlin: Memorial Deutschland, 2006) [On DVD].

31 [Республика не может быть жалостлива к преступникам и не может на них тратить больших средств, — они должны покрывать своим трудом расходы на них, ими должны заселяться пустынные, бездорожные местности — на Печоре, в Обдорске и пр. Необходимо будет далее заняться действительно организацией принудительного труда (каторжных работ) — лагеря с колонизацией незаселенных мест и с железной дисциплиной. Мест и пространства у нас достаточно]. Graziosi, *L'Urss*, p. 181.

Committee imposed the annexation of the Solovetskii Monastery to the Northern Camps, thus paving the way for the establishment of the SLON. Moscow consequently decided to transfer the archipelago's jurisdiction from the local authorities to the OGPU. In June that year, a government-appointed commission reached the islands, together with the first convoy of prisoners.[32] For the very first time a place of detention was directly entrusted to the political police. On 13 October, the Sovnarkom approved a document giving the procedure for setting up the camp:

> The Council of People's Commissars of the USSR decrees:
>
> 1. To organize the Special Purpose Camp of compulsory work of Solovki and two transit-distributional points in Arkhangel'sk and Kem'.
>
> 2. To entrust the OGPU with the organization and administration of the camp and the transit-distributional points indicated in point 1.
>
> 3. To transfer without financial compensation to OGPU all the lands, buildings, live and dead inventory formerly belonging to the ex Solovki monastery, and to do the same with the Petrominsk camp and Arkhangel'sk transit-distributional point.
>
> 4. To transfer at the same time to the use of OGPU the radio station present on the Solovki islands.
>
> 5. To require OGPU to proceed immediately to the organization of the work of the prisoners in order to utilize the agricultural, fishery, timber etc. activities and enterprises, freeing them from the payment of State or local taxes and duties.[33]

---

32   Shiriaev arrived with the first convoy. A final assessment of the monastery properties was carried out in 1924, when the camp was fully operational, see Moscow, GARF, f. 393, op. 43a, d. 487, 'Postanovleniia i vypiski iz protokolv zasedanii Malogo Soveta Narodnykh Komissarov RSFSR o rezul'tatakh proverki tserkovnogo imushchestva byvshego Solovetskogo monastyria (20.5–2.11.1924)'.

33   [Совет Народных Комиссаров СССР постановляет: 1. Организовать Соловецкий лагерь принудительных работ особого назначения и два пересыльно-распределительных пункта в Архангельске и Кеми. 2. Организацию и управление указанными в ст. I лагерем и пересыльно-распределительными пунктами возложить на ОГПУ. 3. Все угодья, здания, живой и мертвый инвентарь, ранее принадлежавший бывшему Соловецкому монастырю, а равно Пертоминскому лагерю и Архангельскому пересыльно-распределительному пункту, передать безвозмездно ОГПУ. 4. Одновременно передать в пользование ОГПУ находящуюся на Соловецких островах радиостанцию. 5. Обязать ОГПУ немедленно приступить к организации труда заключенных для использования сельскохозяйственных, рыбных, лесных и пр. промыслов и предприятий, освободив таковые от уплаты государственных и местных налогов и сборов]. Moscow, GARF, f. 5446, op. 1, d. 2, l. 43, 'Postanovlenie SNK SSSR "Ob organizatsii Solovetskogo lageria prinuditel'nykh rabot" ot 13 oktiabria 1923 g.'. The idea to set up the SLON was not debated at Sovnarkom. Dzerzhinskii never mentioned it as an item on the agenda, as shown by the survey of 1923's Sovnarkom documents (included in: Moscow, GARF, f. 5446, op. 1; GARF, f. 5446, op. 1a; GARF, f. 5446, op. 2; GARF, f. 5446, op. 2a, 'Protokoly i postanovleniia Soveta Narodnykh Komissarov i Soveta Ministrov SSSR (podlinniki). 1923–1950 gg.)'. The related dossier features only the 13 October *postanovlenie*, which was actually ratified by the Sovnarkom after being separately considered by the OGPU. Although in his memoirs Anton Klinger writes about Dzerzhinskii's direct role in the creation of the Solovki camp (Klinger, p. 159), no documents seem to confirm this. We know that Dzerzhinskii was informed about the operations led by OGPU, which aimed to set up Northern camps (as confirmed by the 'Zapiska upolnomochennogo po organizatsii i ustroistvu lagerei VChK Predsedateliu VChK F.E. Dzerzhinskomu ob ustroistve Severnykh kolonii VChK' written on 24 January 1922, and included in the online documents of the Iakovlev Fund, available at http://www.alexanderyakovlev.org/almanah/inside/almanah-doc/1000692 [accessed 25

FIG. 2.2. Aleksandr Nogtev. ASM

The Early Years of the SLON

Setting up the camp proved extremely difficult. A few days before the arrival of the first convoy of prisoners, a huge fire — which broke out on 25 May 1923 and lasted three days — destroyed the monastery, reducing it to a heap of ash and blackened walls. The origins of the fire are still debated; however, as most scholars suggest,[34] the chekists themselves probably set the monastery on fire to disguise the more visible effects of pillaging.

Despite the disastrous condition of the monastery, the newly appointed director of the SLON, Aleksandr Nogtev (who held this position until 1925 and then again between May 1929 and May 1930), did not hesitate to start organizing the camp, whose headquarters were set up the Solovki Kremlin's charred walls. Nogtev and his subordinates (among whom was the head of administration and vice-director Fedor Eikhmans) were given the task of supervising and isolating dangerous individuals in order to ensure the stability of the Soviet state, as stated in the camp regulations which came into force in 1926:

> The Solovki Special Purpose camps for compulsory work are organized by the Unified State Political Directorate (OGPU) for the isolation of particularly harmful state convicts, both political and criminal, the actions of whom have caused or might cause material damage to the tranquillity and integrity of the Union of Soviet Socialist Republics.[35]

July 2014] and whose archive collocation is: Moscow, TsA FSB ROSSII, f. 1, op. 6, d. 28, ll. 3–6). As previously stated, we also know that Dzerzhinskii was interested in the camp, but we have no evidence about his actual involvement in its creation, although his intervention is presumable.

34   See, for instance, the Italian version of Brodskii's book (Brodskii, p. 30), while Francine Dominique Liechtenhan believes it was an accidental fire (Liechtenhan, p. 44).

35   [Соловецкие лагеря принудительных работ Особого Назначения организованы Объединенным Государственным Политическим Управлением для изоляции особо вредных государственных преступников, как уголовных, так и политических, деяния коих принесли или могут принести существенный ущерб спокойствию и целостности Союза Советских Социалистических Республик]. The 2 October 1924 regulation is included in: *Solovetskie lageria Osobogo Naznacheniia OGPU — Fotoletopis'* (St Petersburg: Gosudarstvennyi muzei istorii Sankt-Peterburga, Muzei S.M. Kirova, Solovetskii gosudarstvennyi istoriko-arkhitekturnyi i prirodnyi muzei-zapovednik, 2004), p. 9. The book signalled the cooperation between the three museums for the 65th anniversary of the closure of the SLON; it was part of an editorial project concerning an album which the camp administration gave to Sergei Kirov, probably in 1929. In the book,

The quote above shows also the peculiarity of the Soviet penal system, aimed not only at punishing the actual 'criminals' but also the potential ones.[36] Prisoners destined for the Solovki camp belonged to social classes or categories that were doomed to extinction, apart from the common criminals. All other prisoners (White Guard soldiers, priests, *intelligenty*, the lower-middle and middle class, traders, people connected with the Tsarist regime) were used in forced labour camps. They were strictly controlled by the security guards and had to endure frequent torture.[37]

Amongst the prisoners, only the *politiki* (i.e. the representatives of political factions that were not aligned with the Bolsheviks, such as the Socialist Revolutionaries and the Social Democrats)[38] were not subjected to forced labour as a matter of principle.[39] Unlike their fellow inmates, the *politiki* had developed a highly refined group organization during their decades of detention under the Tsarist regime.[40] It is not surprising, then, that the camp chiefs had difficulties coping with them. Tensions came to a climax on 19 December 1923, when Nogtev and his men killed six political prisoners. The reaction of the *politiki* to this was impassioned. They went on hunger strike and wrote a joint document in protest;[41] as seen above, they desperately tried and finally managed to get news about the murders to the world outside the camp. In 1925, camp authorities finally decided on a solution to the difficulties created by the *politiki*. All political prisoners were forced to pack up and evacuate in a few hours. They were boarded on boats to be scattered throughout the Northern camps.

In addition to the removal of the political prisoners, the camp registered a number of other sudden changes. First, the camp administration organized a series of cultural activities, giving the prisoners the possibility of creating a burgeoning and prolific cultural community. Among the activities were a theatre, museum, and library, and a unique publishing system, as we shall see in the following chapters. Simultaneously, the purpose of forced labour changed radically. It gradually became

photographs from the album are supported by documents and memories. Another copy is at the new Museum for the History of the Gulag in Moscow.

36   This is why Graziosi speaks of 'preventive social and categorical surgery' when dealing with Stalinist idea of repression, see Graziosi, *L'Urss*, p. 337. The 'preventive' side of the Soviet penal system is already evident in the passage quoted here from the 1926 SLON camp regulations.

37   Among the prisoners there were several foreigners. The files of the Italian prisoners of the SLON are kept at the archive of the Giangiacomo Feltrinelli Foundation in Milan, see: Milan, AGFF, 'Dante Serpo'; Milan, AGFF, 'Luciano Visintini'; Milan, AGFF, 'Giorgio Perosio'.

38   At the SLON political prisoners were referred to as '*politzakliuchennye*', or simply '*politiki*'. Prisoners belonging to the other categories mentioned above were known respectively as '*kaery*' ('*Kontr-revoliutsionery*', counter revolutionaries) and '*ugolovniki*' (ordinary criminals).

39   Memoirs written by political prisoners never mention forced labour, while they register tortures which the prisoners endured at the Sekirka (see below, p. 70), see Cologne, ATsM: Vladimir Rubinshtein, *Vospominaniia*, p. 21.

40   The political prisoners' experience and organization partly accounts for the establishment of special purpose camps. Applebaum writes extensively about the numerous complaints filed by the directors of ordinary prisons concerning disorders and difficulties which arose as they attempted to cope with the *politzakliuchennye*: see Applebaum, p. 39.

41   The following words are included in the document: 'We have the last and only way of fighting — to die' [По крайней мере теперь остается одно и последнее средство борьбы — смерть]. See 'Zaiavleniia politzakliuchennykh Petrominska i Solovkov. 1923–1924 gg.', p. 250.

FIG. 2.3. The brick factory of the SLON. ASM

more and more important that the prisoners perform useful activities. Initially the camp thrived mainly on a merely punitive use of forced labour, where prisoners performed superfluous or humiliating tasks. In following months, a completely different economic system took over, where prisoners' work was expected to be productive and profitable. The change was intended both to meet Dzerzhinskii's requirements as stated in 1923 and to respect the general philosophy underlying the expectations of the Moscow authorities. For the OGPU, it now seemed imperative to make prison camps completely autonomous as well as economically independent. In fact, the Soviet state spent millions of roubles on prisons in the post-revolutionary period.[42]

Once they had opted for the industrial exploitation of *katorga*, the camp commanders worked hard to carry out their mission to make a profit out of forced

---

42   The intention was of no consequence. In March 1925, a request for 600.000 roubles was forwarded to Moscow: the sum was meant to cover building costs, and after some hesitations, the Sovnarkom approved it (Moscow, GARF, f. 5446, op. 5a, d. 720, 'Ob uvelichenii smety OGPU na 2-e polugodie na 600.000 rublei na pokrytie defitsita po soderzhaniiu sollagprinrabosnaz (mart–aprel' 1925 g.)'). The request was repeated in May 1926 (Moscow, GARF, f. 5446, op. 7a, d. 537, 'Ob otpuske OGPU sredstv na pokrytie defitsita po soderzhaniiu Solovetskogo lageria prinuditel'nykh rabot osobogo naznacheniia i peresyl'no-raspredelitel'nogo punkta g. Kemi (May–iiul' 1926)'), in June 1927 (Moscow, GARF, f. 5446, op. 8a, d. 365, 'Ob otpuske OGPU sredstv na raskhody po soderzhaniiu USLONa (iiun'–iiul' 1927)') and in May 1928, when it was accompanied by a note expressing the hope that the question would be settled by June 1929 (Moscow, GARF, f. 5446, op. 9a, d. 444, 'Ob ustanovlenii defitsita po smete Solovetskogo lageria OGPU osobogo naznacheniia/ USLON/ s 1.VI.28 po iiun' 1929 g. (ma' 1928)'). In her book, Applebaum convincingly documents the failure of the economic plan underlying the creation of the Solovki camp and, in general, of the Gulag system.

labour. The camp also continued to perform traditional activities, as shown by the takeover and development of production activities started by the monks — above all fishing, breeding livestock, and manufacturing (small factories had been built there between the late nineteenth and the early twentieth century), but also small industrial activities, such as a brick factory and a tannery. However, the nascent SLON administration primarily pursued tree-felling for timber. The *lesorazrabotka* became the camp's leading activity, and it was certainly the most profitable one. The camp exported hundreds of tons of timber every year, thus providing the Soviet state with valuable profits.[43] Moreover, the discovery of peat deposits in the woods promptly turned them into a further economic resource for the camp.[44]

Ironically, the man who is usually indicated as the creator and implementer of these radical changes in the profit-making exploitation of labour was a former prisoner, an inmate whose ideas deeply affected the economic and industrial development not only on the Solovki islands, but throughout the now growing Gulag archipelago.

Naftalii Frenkel'

Naftalii Aronovich Frenkel' first appears in the documentation in 1924. An ordinary inmate at the Solovki prison camp, he soon embarked on a brilliant career. His insight into the repressive machine was so keen that he became one of its leaders. Many historians still regard the circumstances of his spectacular rise from prisoner to leader in the Soviet regime as mysterious.[45] There is no doubt that the particular legendary aura surrounding Frenkel' adds to the mystery. It lies at the core of the numerous versions of his biography,[46] which alternately depict him as a Turk, a Jew, and even a Ukrainian.[47] In the most popular 'parasha' (a Gulag slang term meaning a rumour) on Frenkel''s rise, his career began when he placed a letter in the camp's complaints box. In it, he described his plan to improve the camp's productivity. The letter is said to have earned him a journey to Moscow, where he was whisked off to meet Stalin.

---

43   The export of timber coming from the camps became one of the leitmotiv of Soviet propaganda. In the film *Solovki — Solovetskie lageria osobogo naznacheniia* directed by A. Cherkasov (USSR, 1928) one of the few textual references is about the export of wood processed by the prisoners.

44   In order to transport timber and peat, the management used the railway which had been built in the early months of the SLON and which was abandoned after the closure of the camp, leaving behind tracks which are still visible.

45   For instance, Applebaum, pp. 51–53.

46   See, amongst others, Solzhenitsyn, II, 61–65. The archive of the St Petersburg section of 'Memorial' holds a copy of Frenkel''s original *delo*, from which the story of the former SLON prisoner might be gathered. He was arrested in Moscow on 11 November 1923 for illegally crossing the borders from the Soviet Union. Sentenced to ten years, his sentence was reduced to five years as early as 1926. The camp chiefs' intercession on his behalf, documented by a note, resulted in his release, on 22 July 1927. Frenkel' was, however, promoted to the administration of economic affairs when still a prisoner. See St Petersburg, AMSPB, 'Lichnoe delo Naftalia Aronovicha Frenkelia'.

47   As Applebaum shows, and as testified by his original *delo*, he was born in 1883 in Haifa, Palestine, which at the time still belonged to the Ottoman Empire. A Jew, he lived in Odessa for many years. This explains the confusion about his nationality. See Applebaum, p. 53.

The Moscow archives of Memorial include the unpublished memoirs of Iakov Kuperman,[48] an accountant who became entangled in the maze of Soviet prisons in 1930 and later worked for Frenkel' for almost two decades. Kuperman's memoirs include detailed descriptions of Frenkel' and his personality, including what might be regarded as the truth about his impressive rise to power. The memoir's reliability is evident from the special conditions in which Kuperman acquired the information[49] and from the fact that his version mostly coincides with historical reconstructions of the episode included in other sources.[50] There is no reason to distrust Kuperman's reliability as a narrator.

In Kuperman's version, Frenkel' started to cooperate with the OGPU when he was a prisoner at the Solovki camp. Almost immediately, he became one of the *nadzirateli*, the supervisors chosen from among the prisoners,[51] and worked hard until he became the director of the commercial and economic department of the camp.[52] A natural-born businessman, Frenkel' was amazed at the unprofitable use of forced labour. He waited for the right opportunity — the arrival of one of the many control commissions in 1926 — to write down a detailed industrial plan aimed at the economic improvement of the camp. He then delivered his note to Gleb Bokii,

48   Moscow, AMM, f. 2, op. 1, d. 77, Iakov Kuperman, *Piatdesiat' let 1927–1977 — vospominaniia. Bez daty*. Moscow. Mashinopis', bez podpisi.

49   Frenkel' confided this to Kuperman during a private meeting, which took place when the former leader of the OGPU had already retired. Frenkel' was one of the few *apparatchiki* to avoid the purges of the Great Terror, even though, in Kuperman's view, Ezhov despised him and thought of denouncing him just before he was removed from his post as chief of the NKVD. See Moscow, AMM, op. 2, f. 1, d. 77, l. 24.

50   Alongside memoirists and researchers, also the writer Vasilii Grossman had his own version of Naftalii Frenkel''s life. In *Life and Fate*, Grossman described his rise, presumably borrowing from descriptions made by Party members: 'Frenkel', at the very beginning of NEP, had built a car factory in Odessa. In the mid-twenties he had been arrested and sent to Solovki. While at the Solovki camp, Frenkel' sent Stalin an ingenious project — the old Chekist used exactly that word, "ingenious". In considerable detail, with full economic and scientific substantiation, he had laid out the most efficient manner of exploiting the vast mass of prisoners in order to construct roads, dams, hydroelectric power stations and artificial reservoirs. The prisoner-'Nepman' became a lieutenant-general in the MGB — the boss appreciated his ideas.' [Френкель в начале нэпа построил в Одессе моторный завод. В середине двадцатых годов его арестовали и выслали в Соловки. Сидя в Соловецком лагере, Френкель подал Сталину гениальный проект, — старый чекист именно это слово и произнес: 'гениальный'. В проекте подробно, с экономическими и техническими обоснованиями, говорилось об использовании огромных масс заключенных для создания дорог, плотин, гидростанций, искусственных водоемов. Заключенный нэпман стал генерал-лейтенантом МГБ, — Хозяин оценил его мысль.]. See Vasilii Grossman, *Zhizn' i sud'ba* (Ekaterinburg: U-Faktoriia, 2005), pp. 945–46. The English translation is by Robert Chandler, although I made some minor changes in order to make it more literal.

51   The *nadziratel'stvo* was part of the mechanism for maintaining control within the camps. Ordinary criminals could take part in it, while the *kaery* could not. See the article on camp regulations, in *Solovetskie lageria osobogo naznacheniia OGPU — Fotoletopis'*, pp. 11–13. Surveillance was delegated not only to the *nadziratel'stvo*, but also to the VOKhR (Voenizirovannaia Okhrana), a special department of armed guards.

52   As the director of EKCh (*Ekonomicheskaia Kommercheskaia Chast'*) in the camp, Frenkel' wrote an article on the SLON press which already made some elements of his theory about the exploitation of forced labour explicit. See Naftalii Frenkel', 'Eksploatatsionno-kommercheskie perspektivy Solovetskogo khoziaistva', *NS*, 23 (1925), 2. From now onwards the *Novye Solovki* will be indicated as *NS*.

FIG. 2.4. A photograph of Naftalii Frenkel'
taken from Vladimir Zotov's diary. AMSPB

a member of the commission and a high-ranking OGPU bureaucrat. 'When Bokii was leaving, a prisoner ran towards him, gave him a big notebook, and yelled: 'Don't forget, this proposal was written by me, Frenkel''.[53] Subsequently, the camp administration summoned him and sent him to Moscow to meet with Viacheslav Menzhinskii, the head of OGPU.[54]

After some time, in 1927, Frenkel' was released from imprisonment and given full powers to reorganize the camp's economic management. While production improved under Frenkel''s management, and fewer prisoners were tortured because Frenkel' regarded torture as counterproductive, hundreds of prisoners died as a consequence. He divided prisoners into groups according to their ability to work. They were forced to cope with unbearable work schedules and tasks. It is unsure whether it was Frenkel' himself who established the system of allocating food rations that varied according to the task performed, but it is a matter of fact that they were implemented by the camp administration when Frenkel' was in charge, and that this system was later adopted throughout the Soviet Union. The changes to the food rations worked the weakest prisoners to death.[55] Finally, following

53   [Когда он уезжал, к нему подбежал заключенный, передал ему большую тетрадь и крикнул: 'Не забудьте, это предложение написал я — Френкель']. Moscow, AMM, op. 2, f. 1, d. 77, l. 17.

54   Ibid. Menzhinskii had a thick moustache: here probably lies the reason why the legend of Frenkel''s meeting with Stalin was born. Nevertheless, Frenkel' and Stalin met afterwards, as stated again by Kuperman. See Moscow, AMM, op. 2, f. 1, d. 77, ll. 25–26.

55   Three different food rations corresponded to the categories mentioned above. The first group included those deemed capable of heavy work, who received a daily ration of 800 gr. of bread and 80 gr. of meat. The second group received 500 gr. of bread and 40 gr. of meat. The third group, that of the 'invalids', only received 400 gr. of bread and 40 gr. of meat. Those who were not included

Frenkel''s plan, all cultural activities were reduced. The commander considered culture unprofitable and, therefore, useless.

While Frenkel''s system was changing the history of the SLON and laying the foundations for the future Gulag system, protests were growing throughout Europe against the living conditions of prisoners in the Soviet Union. Publications by SLON escapees inflamed these protests. Not surprisingly, the Soviet authorities always denied these accusations and decided instead to provide tangible evidence of the prisoners' living conditions. In 1928, they made and released a documentary film directed by Aleksei Cherkasov entitled *Solovki — Solovetskie lageria osobogo naznacheniia*. The film showed all the activities that prisoners were said to perform at the camp, including cultural activities. Prisoners could thus be seen working and smiling, displaying their toned bodies.[56] Upon its release, the film received mixed reactions. In fact, Cherkasov's extremely positive depiction of life at the prison camp attracted bitter criticism from Moscow.[57]

The international protests did not change Frenkel''s plan, whose main goal, however, was the extension of camp activities to the mainland. If, on the one hand, this prompted a general increase in profits, then, on the other hand, it created tension between the camp administration and Karelian Party representatives.[58] Having objected to the creation and the autonomy of the camp, the Karelian Party representatives regarded the SLON's expansion plans on the mainland and its economic success as a threat. The camp, after all, was completely independent of Karelia, though it performed a number of activities there. Moreover, the SLON had a significant advantage over local competitors because it had an unpaid workforce at its disposal. Local Karelian businesses began to lose all competitive bids to the SLON (especially those related to the building of the railway between Kem'[59] and Ukhta).[60] In order to reduce such tensions, Moscow promoted the annexation of the SLON to the Autonomous Republic of Karelia in 1930, and the creation of the USIKMITL, i.e. the Administration of the Solovki and Karelian-Murmansk Forced Labour Camps (Upravleniia Solovetskimi i Karelo-Murmanskimi Ispravitel'no-

---

in the first category were therefore inexorably bound to get weaker and weaker, until they became *dokhodiagi* (in camp jargon, 'moribunds'). See Applebaum, p. 56.

56   The film circulated abroad: the family of a prisoner, Zinaida Iakovlevna Gol'dgoer, recognized her while watching the movie and finally got news about her: see Aleksandr Goldgoer, 'Toska razluki', *Solovetskii vestnik*, 13 [78] (1993), p. 3. Zinaida Gol'dgoer survived the SLON and was later sent to Siberia, see *Vospominaniia Solovetskikh uznikov*, p. 736.

57   Kuziakina, p. 21.

58   On the difficult relations between Soviet Karelia and the SLON, see Nick Baron, *Soviet Karelia: Politics, Planning and Terror in Stalin's Russia, 1920–1939* (London and New York: Routledge, 2009), pp. 83–88, 119–36.

59   The transit camp to the SLON was built in this little Karelian town. All the prisoners destined for the Solovki camp passed through it. It was known as 'Kemperpunkt'.

60   The question first arose in 1925, when the Central Committee of the Karelian party asked the Central Committee to prevent the use of forced labour from the Solovki camp on the mainland. See Moscow, GARF, f. 3316, op. 64, d. 86, 'Vypiska iz protokola zasedaniia Prezidiuma TsIK SSSR ob otmene postanovleniia TsIK Karel'skoi SSR po voprosu o nedopushchenii ispol'zovaniia rabochei sily Solovetskikh lagerei pri postroike mostov na territorii Karel'skoi SSR i perepiska po etomu voprosu, (21.4–11.5.25)'.

Trudovymi Lageriami).[61] It was one of many significant changes imposed by Moscow in those years.

Three Years of Change

The period between 1929 and 1931 proved crucial for the history of the SLON camp and the Soviet labour camp system as a whole. In fact, after the camp's 'frenkelizatsiia', the Solovki model — as it had first been forged by Frenkel' in its economic and operational aspects — was extended to the entire territory of the Soviet Union. Expeditions sought out potential sites for labour camps[62] and within a few years many new *lageria* were set up. Coordination of the system of labour camps depended on the GULag ('Glavnoe Upravlenie Lagerei', Chief Administration of Corrective Labour Camps) leadership. The GULag was officially created on 25 April 1930 as a new institutional body meant to supervise this unprecedented expansion. Its first director was Eikhmans, who had already moved to Moscow in May 1929 as the head of the third OGPU *spetsotdel*.[63] All the SLON headquarters moved to Kem'. The SLON was now one of twelve sectors which made up a new complex of camps, the above-mentioned USIKMITL, which extended much further than the archipelago to include a vast area from the Kola Peninsula to the Urals.

These changes had disastrous effects upon the Solovki islands. Dmitrii Uspenskii's rise to the post of director of the camp in 1930 played a particularly important role in the violent turn of events during this period. Both a pitiless man and a zealous officer, Uspenskii promoted and carried out a series of executions that wiped out many prisoners from 1929 onwards.[64] His first exploit was that of the 'Kremlevskii zagovor' (Kremlin conspiracy), when many prisoners allegedly attempted to revolt and escape from the camp. Uspenskii executed thirty-six prisoners, some of whom had executive duties in the camp. Later, he sentenced to death eight members of the

---

61   The decision (see Moscow, GARF, f. 1235, op. 125, d. 290, 'Delo po khodataistvu TsIK Karel'skoi ASSR o peredache Solovetskikh ostrovov iz Severnogo Kraia v sostav Karel'skoi ASSR (17.2–3.10.1930)') met an old aspiration of the Karelian leadership and, surprisingly, also of the *Arkhangel'skaia guberniia*. In fact, in 1927 the Karelian administration and the governor of Arkhangel'sk issued a joined request for the transfer of jurisdiction from the latter to the former. The request was rejected (see Moscow, GARF, f. 1235, op. 71, d. 43, 'Delo o rassmotrenii i otklonenii khodataistva Arkhangel'skogo gubernskogo ispolnitel'nogo komiteta o peredache territorii Solovetskikh Ostrovov iz sostava Arkhangel'skoi gubernii v sostav Karel'skoi SSR (16.12.26–22.3.27)').
62   A large number of Solovki prisoners took part, for example, in the expedition to Vaigach, which Eikhmans organized and supervised. Amongst them was Konstantin Gurskii, who describes it vividly in his mainly unpublished memoirs, included in the Moscow Memorial archives, See Moscow, AMM, f. 2, op. 3, dd. 15–18, Konstantin Gurskii, *Po dorogam gulaga. Moi Vaigach. Mashinopis'*.
63   It was the Special Section of the OGPU that headed the SLON since its creation in 1923.
64   In his memoirs, Likhachev writes that Uspenskii was personally involved in the 1929 shooting (see Likhachev, *Izbrannoe: Vospominaniia*, p. 198). Besides, the SLON director was responsible for the murder of the Iaroslavskie (Aleksandr Iaroslavskii and his wife Evgeniia) and proved particularly sadistic when killing the woman: see Evgeniia Iaroslavskaia-Markon, '"Klianus' otomstit' slovom i krov'iu..." (publikatsia i primechaniia Iriny Flige)', *Zvezda*, 1 (2008), 127–59. Because most of these repressive acts took place in the year when Maksim Gor'kii went to the Solovki, memoirists connected the two events. It is instead likely that the increase of executions was provoked by Uspenskii's rise.

medical staff for negligence in patient care.[65] In 1930, a special Moscow commission led by Aleksandr Shanin resulted in the indictment and shooting of many prisoners who were a part of the surveillance staff and who had inflicted torture and violence on fellow prisoners — among them the notorious executioner Igor' Kurilko. The document Shanin wrote for Iagoda mentions almost all the cases of abuse that the guards had inflicted:

> The interrogation of a series of members of the surveillance staff and of prisoners brought to light an established system of despotism and total corruption at the USLON. Prisoners have been subject to demands for bribes and extortion on a large scale, and in addition the theft of food rations and of clothing equipment destined for the prisoners has developed. The tendency towards personal enrichment on the backs of the prisoners developed on the base of illegal abuse and terrorization of prisoners at the USLON. The guards are mainly composed of declassed and even counterrevolutionary elements, who have full freedom of action. Their methods of terrorization of prisoners are:
>
> 1. Beating with sticks, clubs, ramrods, whips and so on.
> 2. During the winter, keeping the prisoners 'on the rocks' dressed only in underwear standing 'at attention' for 3–4 hours.
> 3. During the summer, leaving the prisoners 'on the mosquitoes', i.e. naked standing 'at attention'.
> 4. Putting the prisoners in the so-called 'kibitki', i.e. a punishment blocks made up of cold little boarded extensions where prisoners during the winter are left for many hours wearing only their underwear. There have been instances of prisoners freezing to death.
> 5. Putting the prisoners on the so-called 'zherdochki', i.e. narrow benches on which the prisoners are in a squatting position and, subject to a complete ban on movement and talking, are kept in that same position from early morning to late evening.
> 6. Homicides masked as escapes.
> 7. Sexual abuse of women and forced cohabitation of woman prisoners with surveillants.
> 8. The so-called 'seagulls', i.e. during the winter the prisoner is taken dressed only in underwear on to a pole set up on the pier on which has been carved a wooden seagull. The prisoner is forced to count: 'One seagull, two seagulls' up to two thousand times, i.e. practically to total exhaustion.
> 9. Prisoners are forced to transfer water from one hole to another using their hands.
> 10. Prisoners dressed only in underwear put in a punishment cell made up of a one-metre high pit, the ceiling and floor of which are made up of thorny branches. One prisoner held out no more than 3 days and then died.

65   I attribute the responsibility for the 'Kremlevskii zagovor' to Uspenskii because previous investigations and reports about the violent methods of the overseers did not lead to any consequences. In a document dated 1928, many violent situations (including the killings and torture at the Sekira mountain and in the forests of the archipelago) are described by the prisoners and compiled by an unidentified person. The document was sent to the OGPU and was registered and stored. See Moscow, RGALI, f. 1185, op. 3, ed. khr. 83, 'Vypiski neustanovlennogo litsa iz pis'ma zakliuchennykh Solovetskikh lagerei v OGPU ob usloviiakh zhizni (26.9.1927–9.6.1928)'. I wish to thank Massimo Tria for transcribing the document for me.

11. The so-called 'dolphins', i.e. while prisoners walk over a bridge, guards yell 'dolphin' after pointing at one prisoner or another, who is obliged to dive into the water. If he doesn't, he is beaten and thrown in the water; and other forms of torture and abuse of prisoners.[66]

Uspenskii was appointed director of the SLON after the transfer of Nogtev and Eikhmans. Most probably, he supported the elimination of Kurilko, even though a witness identified Eikhmans as the promoter of the *chistka*.[67] If Uspenskii's early executions earned him the attention of OGPU chiefs, the second series of executions he carried out swept away his potential rival Kurilko and thus secured his promotion.

66   [Допросами ряда лиц из надзора и заключенных выявлена установившаяся в УСЛОНе система произвола и полного разложения. В широких размерах развито взяточничество и вымогательство с заключенных, а также расхищение вещевого и продовольственного пайка, предназначенного для заключенных. Тенденция личного обогащения за счет заключенных развилась на базе легализованного в УСЛОНе издевательства и терроризирования заключенных. Формирование надзора производится из наиболее деклассированных, а подчас и к.-р. элементов, которым предоставляется полная свобода действий. Способы терроризирования заключенных применяются следующие: 1. Избиение палками, прикладами, шомполами, плеткой и т.п. 2. Зимой постановка заключенных в так называемые «на камни» в одном белье в положении «смирно» на срок до 3–4 часов. 3. Летом постановка заключенных так назыв. «на комары», т.е. раздетого в положении «смирно». 4. Заключение в так назыв. «кибитки», т.е. карцера, представляющие из себя холодны[е] небольшие дощатые пристройки, в которых заключенные в зимнее время в одном белье выдерживались по несколько часов. Есть случаи смерти от замерзания. 5. Посадка на так назыв. «жердочки», т.е. узкие скамьи, на которые заключенных усаживали на корточки и, абсолютно запрещая шевелиться и разговаривать, выдерживали в таком положении с раннего утра до позднего вечера. 6. Убийства под видом побега. 7. Изнасилование женщин и принуждение к сожительству заключенных женщин с надзором. 8. Так назыв. «чайки», т.е. заключенного зимой в одном белье выводили к устроенному шесту возле пристани, на котором сделана деревянная чайка, и заставляли считать: «чайка раз, чайка два» — до 2 тыс. раз, т.е. фактически до состояния полного изнеможения. 9. Заставляли заключенных переливать руками воду из проруби в прорубь. 10. Посадка заключенных одном белье в карцер, представляющий собой яму высотой не более метра, потолок и пол которой выстланы колючими сучьями. Заключенный выдерживал не более 3 дней и умирал. 11. Так назыв. «дельфины», т.е. при проходе заключенных через мост лица из надзора, указывая на того или иного заключенного, кричали «дельфин». Заключенный обязан был бросаться в воду, за неисполнение подвергался избиению и сбрасыванию в воду и т.п. виды истязаний и издевательств над заключенными.] See: Moscow, TsA FSB ROSSII, f. 2, op. 8, d. 120, ll. 154–60, 'Iz materialov doklada zam. nachal'nika Administrativno-organizatsionnogo upravleniia OGPU A.M. Shanina zamestiteliu predsedatelia OGPU G.G. Iagode o proizvole i izdevatel'stvakh nad zakliuchennymi v Solovetskikh lageriakh (12.5.1930)' (http://www.alexanderyakovlev.org/almanah/inside/almanah-doc/1000720) [accessed 24 November 2014]. The documents produced by the Shanin commission were published in the *Istoricheskii arkhiv* journal, see Dmitrii Pavlov, '"Vyiavlena sistema proizvola i polnogo razlozheniia". Materialy komissii OGPU ob usloviiakh soderzhaniia zakliuchennykh v Solovetskom lagere osobogo naznacheniia. 1930 g.', *Istoricheskii arkhiv*, 5 (2005), 65–82.

67   The witness is Gurskii, whose memoirs include this reference to Eikhmans, see Gurskii, p. 20. Lidiia Spiridonova, instead, connects the SLON 1930 internal purges with Gor'kii's visit, suggesting that the writer might have interceded on behalf of the prisoners to improve their living conditions. Spiridonova's theory does not seem to be supported by documents, and neither is Gurskii's. See Lidiia Spiridonova, *Gor'kii: dialog s istoriei* (Moscow: Nasledie — Nauka, 1994), p. 225.

FIG. 2.5. The camp entrance on the Muksalma island. AMM

While bloody conflict was raging throughout the camp, the spread of a typhus epidemic led to the deaths of thousands of victims. Nevertheless, the number of Solovki prisoners increased quite dramatically. Hundreds of peasants arrived at Solovki from the Ukraine and from other agricultural areas of the Soviet Union, as a disastrous effect of dekulakization.

Major Change: The Belomorsko–Baltiiskii Kanal

The most significant event in the history of the SLON and of the Gulag at that time was the launch of the first Five-Year Plan and, more specifically, the decision to build major infrastructure projects by exploiting the forced labour of Gulag inmates. The SLON was particularly affected by the construction of the Belomorsko-Baltiiskii Kanal (White Sea-Baltic Canal).[68] The undertaking was, in itself, titanic. Working conditions were brutal. Nevertheless, Stalin demanded quick completion and, in order to meet his requests, the GULag administration sent thousands of prisoners from all over the Soviet Union to Medvezh'egorsk, which became the operational centre of the huge building site. The SLON provided the largest number of prisoners to the project, not only because it was logistically the closest camp, but also because

---

68   Much has been written about the exploitation of labour on the building-site. Cynthia Ruder's outstanding monograph was one of the first and deals also with the (in)famous collective book issued under the guidance of Gor'kii, Leopol'd Averbakh and Semen Firin quoted above (p. 25 n. 37): see Cynthia A. Ruder, *Making History for Stalin: The Story of the Belomor Canal* (Gainesville, FL: University Press of Florida, 1998). Iurii Dmitriev's book includes a large number of documents and shows how, although operations started late in 1931, plans to create the Canal developed between 1929 and 1930, see Iurii Dmitriev, *Belomorsko-Baltiiskii vodnyi put'. Ot zamyslov do voploshcheniia* (Petrozavodsk: self-published, 2003). Amongst the authors who visited the Belomorkanal was Viktor Shklovskii, whose brother, a former SLON prisoner, had been transferred to the BBK. In a recent publication, Serena Vitale revealed the details of Shklovskii's encounter with his brother. See Serena Vitale, *A Mosca! A Mosca!* (Milan: Mondadori, 2010), pp. 109–11.

of the number of prisoners available. Thus, Karelia now housed newcomers from the Solovki prison camp, as well as several members of its former administration,[69] its theatre companies (except for one), and its printing equipment. The last two were used to promote the new imagery of the Five Year Plan inside labour camps, which turned theatre and journals into mere propaganda means and changed its educational keyword into 'perekovka' (reforging), thus abandoning the idea of re-education for a more repressive management of prisoners, who were asked to be physically 'reforged' through work and not only educated anew.

The prisoners' migration to Karelia marks a turning point in the history of the SLON, which becomes rather obscure. There are three possible reasons for our current lack of information. First, historians have almost invariably focused on the Belomorsko-Baltiiskii Kanal,[70] viewing it as the natural development of the ideas that originated on the Solovki islands. Secondly, the transfer of many prisoners from the camps to the Belomorkanal[71] meant that many potential writers of memoirs were dispersed, so there are fewer accounts of Solovki from prisoners who were there during this period than there were accounts about previous years. Thirdly, the number of sources for researchers was dramatically reduced because in the period between 1931 and 1939 the SLON was no longer in the foreground, having lost both its leading role in the penitentiary system and its internal press, which up until then had achieved much more visibility than publications in other camps.[72] Moreover, fewer documents were produced in this period than in earlier stages in the history of the SLON.

Consequently, deciphering what actually happened in the Solovki camp between 1931 and 1937 is extremely difficult. We now know that cultural activities were gradually suppressed. We know that production slowed down, too, though to a lesser extent, following the complete deforestation of the islands, which by then looked like a wasteland of tree stumps. We also know that thousands of Ukrainians and many intellectuals ended up at the Solovki, amongst them Pavel Florenskii, who continued his research in a camp laboratory. Finally, we know that representatives of foreign countries, who were allowed to visit other Soviet camps, were not allowed to visit the Solovki.[73] This suggests that the regime had become even more repressive, as the few memoirs dating from those years maintain.

---

69   Amongst them, Frenkel' was appointed director.

70   BBK is the abbreviation for the canal.

71   Camps were scattered all along the ship canal (227 km) running through the Karelian woods. The camps formed the *lager'* known as BelBaltLag, which Uspenskii started to direct in July 1933. Operations took no longer than twenty months, as the canal was opened in August 1933. Thousands of prisoners lost their lives there.

72   Re-established in 1929, the Solovki press ceased in 1930.

73   Liechtenhan includes reports of the Thompson commission in her book (see Liechtenhan, p. 234) together with the story of the Finnish Communist Arvo Tuominen (Liechtenhan, pp. 221–24), which can also be found in other sources. Her reports about Nazi emissary Wolfgang Mund's supposed visit to Belomorkanal (Liechtenhan, p. 226) are indeed not very convincing. As the only source is Mund's own memoir, which was published at the beginning of the operation Barbarossa, his reports cannot be regarded as reliable: probably, Mund possessed a copy of some of Belomorkanal reports, including Tuominen's bulletins.

The Last Years of the Camp

The violent detention regime at SLON reached its peak after 1937, as largely testified to by documents. The wave of mass arrests during the Great Terror and, more specifically, the violent repression imposed after Ezhov's 00447 order (30 July 1937)[74] sent a mass of prisoners to the Solovki camp.

By 1937, the SLON had become a fully-fledged detention camp. While it still contained prisons, it had completely lost its status as a concentration camp, as well as any related productive labour. The acronym was changed to STON (Solovetskaia Tiur'ma Osobogo Naznacheniia, Solovki Special Purpose Prison). Cultural and non-cultural activities alike were suppressed. The museum was shut down, as was the theatre. Only the library survived. The unmistakable logic of the Great Terror, whereby the NKVD gave orders for the execution of a large number of prisoners,[75] took a heavy toll on the Solovki prisoners. Ezhov himself forwarded those lists to the STON:

> In relationship to my decree n. 00447 I ORDER:
> [...]
> 3. 1200 people from the Solovki prison have to be approved for repression.[76]

Several executions were carried out by the Kremlin walls of the archipelago. However, former Solovki prisoners were mostly killed after being transferred to the mainland. One of the harshest of all such 'social cleansing' operations took place between 27 October and 4 November 1937, in the Sandormokh forest, Karelia.[77] In roughly one week, 1,111 STON prisoners were executed. The Levashovo forest at the gates of Leningrad was also filled with mass graves. Among the victims who

---

74   See: Moscow, APRF, f. 3, op. 58, d. 212, ll. 55–78, 'Operativnyi prikaz narodnogo komissara vnutrennykh del soiuza S.S.R. № 00447 ob operatsii po repressirovaniiu byvshikh kulakov, ugolovnikov i dr. antisovetskikh elementov (30.7.1937)'. The full text is available on the Memorial website, in the collection of documents related to Soviet repression. See <http://www.memo.ru/history/document/0447.htm> [accessed 29 April 2015].

75   See Robert Conquest, *The Great Terror: A Reassessment* (Oxford and New York: Oxford University Press, 2008) and Oleg Khlevniuk, *1937-i: Stalin, NKVD i sovetskoe obshchestvo* (Moscow: Izdat. Respublika, 1992); idem, *The History of the Gulag: From Collectivization to the Great Terror* (New Haven: Yale University Press, 2004).

76   [В соответствии с моим приказом №00447 ПРИКАЗЫВАЮ [...] 3. Вам для Соловецкой тюрьмы утверждено для репрессирования 1200 лиц.] See: Solovki, ASM, copy, 'Plan na rasstrel dlia Solovetskoi tiur'my, utverzhdennyi v Moskve 16 avgusta 1937 g.'. Not only was the quota proposed by Ezhov met, but it was even exceeded: 1818 prisoners were shot during the operations. See Olga Bochkareva, *Solovetskie lageria i tiur'ma 1920–1939. Materialy k istorii, Chapter 13*, online publication on the website www.solovki.ca: <http://www.solovki.ca/gulag_solovki/turma_na_solovkah.php> [accessed 29 April 2015].

77   Veniamin Iofe, who made an outstanding contribution to research on the history of the Solovki camp, provided a detailed description of all the events related to the Sandormokh massacre. See Veniamin Iofe, 'Solovetskii rasstrel 1937 goda', in *Memorial'noe kladbishche Sandormokh. 1937, 27 oktiabria–4 noiabria (Solovetskii etap)*, ed. by Irina Flige (Reznikova) (St Petersburg: Izdanie NITs 'Memorial', 1997), pp. 160–63. The toponym Sandormokh is sometimes written Sandarmokh. The burial site was discovered by Iofe, Flige, and Dmitriev in 1997. See Alexander Etkind, *Warped Mourning: Stories of the Undead in the Land of the Unburied* (Stanford: Stanford University Press, 2013), p. 172.

ended up in Levashovo was Pavel Florenskii, who was shot on 8 December 1937.[78]

Executions continued on the Solovki islands in the years that followed. A major change, however, was soon to happen. The GULag directors decided to evacuate the camp due to the imminent war with Finland and the peripheral position of the archipelago, which was too close to the Finnish border. All the prisoners were sent to other camps and the STON was officially shut down with a secret *prikaz* № 001335 (2 November 1939):

> The Council of People's Commissar of the USSR decrees:
> 1. To allow the NKVD of the USSR to close from 1 December 1939 the Solovki prison and to transfer the prisoners to other prisons.
> 2. To advise the NKVD of the USSR to transfer to the People's Commissariat for the Navy from the date indicated above the Solovki islands and all the buildings and subsidiary enterprises.
> The transfer has to be implemented following the steps included in the Disposition of the Council of People's Commissar of the USSR of 15 February 1936 'About the steps of the transfer of state enterprises, buildings and structures' (S.Z. SSSR 1936 g. № 11, art. 93).[79]

All residual activities ceased; the library closed and its collection was lost until 2013, when the French film director Olivier Rolin found it in the public library of Ertsevo. The museum collection was, as far as we know, lost forever. In a few months, a naval base to train the *Iunkers* (Navy volunteers) was set up. And so, in 1939, the history of the Solovki camp came to a sudden end.

The History of the Camp as Told by Memoirs

Methodological Preface

The preceding section investigated the documentary history of the Solovki camp. There is, however, a different set of narratives about the life and experiences of SLON prisoners, handed down to us in the memoirs they wrote by the dozen.

As is well known, there is an intense and extremely active debate within the international academic community about life writing. One of the core points of this debate, born at the beginning of the century in different nations but developed on a truly international scale over the last four or five decades, relates to the question of

---

78   Several associations have collected list-related documents, among them the Centre for Recovered Names (Tsentr Vozvrashchennye Imena). The documents have been included in most martyrologies. The Solovki Museum has a copy of the *protokoly* related to the STON prisoners who were shot in 1937. See Solovki, ASM, copy, 'Protokoly rasstreliannykh zakliuchennykh'.

79   [Совет Народных Комиссаров Союза ССР постановляет: 1. Разрешить НКВД СССР к 1 декабря 1939 года закрыть Соловецкую тюрьму и заключенных перевести в другие тюрьмы. 2. Предложить НКВД СССР передать к указанному сроку Соловецкие острова с находящимися на них строениями и подсобным хозяйством в ведение Народного Комиссариата Военно-Морского Флота. Передачу произвести в порядке, установленном Постановлением СНК СССР от 15 февраля 1936 года «О порядке передачи государственных предприятий, зданий и сооружений» (С. З. СССР 1936 г. № 11, ст. 93).] See Solovki, ASM, copy, 'Postanovlenie № 1953–539ss SNK SSSR "O zakrytii Solovetskoi tiur'my i peredache Solovetskikh ostrovov v vedenie narkomvoenmorflota" (25.11.1939)'.

trustworthiness, which was put into sharp focus by Philippe Lejeune in his theory of the autobiographical pact between autobiographer and reader.[80] This question is extremely relevant when applied to the use of memoirs in historical research.

Technically speaking, memoirs are 'unreliable documents'. Memoir writing is temporally removed from the experience recorded and recollection typically brings about a degree of reticence. Conscious or unconscious obstacles widen the space between the narrator and the character, the writing self and the living self, thus creating a distortion of 'historical truth'.[81] Two seminal questions raised by Andrei Tartakovskii ('to what is the text devoted?' and 'for whom is it written?'),[82] as well as the subjective rendering of facts, which tends to blunt narratives, have to be carefully weighed. Of course, the very precariousness of the sources, primarily based on personal feelings or on second-hand reports, adds to the difficulty of carrying out an 'objective' assessment.[83] Misgivings about the status of memoirs as reliable historical sources are therefore well-founded.

Distortion turns out to be a major factor in some camp-related memoirs,[84] which, like autobiographies, are 'an artefact, a construct wrought from words' because 'autobiography is not a recollection of one's life [...] Memories do not make an autobiography', as Mandell states. As Gusdorf puts it, 'Every autobiography [...] does not show us the individual seen from outside in his visible actions but [...] as he believes and wishes himself to be and to have been'.[85] Nevertheless, it is undeniable that a straightforward assessment of the documentary value of memoirs can give more reliability to the information contained in them. In some cases, for instance, the cross-referencing of episodes mentioned in different memoirs provides readers with objective criteria against which the depiction of life in the camp can be assessed.[86] As was the case with Kuperman's version of Frenkel's story analysed

80   Philippe Lejeune, *Le pacte autobiographique* (Paris: Seuil, 1975).

81   In their memoirs, Shiriaev and Kiselev-Gromov were silent about the darkest episodes of their experience. A successful writer, Shiriaev did not refuse to cooperate with the camp propaganda, as shown by some documents included in official publications (see below, p. 187); a former guard, Kiselev-Gromov is silent about his crimes for which, considering his role, he was personally responsible.

82   Andrei Tartakovskii, *Russkaia memuaristika i istoricheskoe soznanie XIX veka* (Moscow: Nauka, 1991), pp. 20–22.

83   On the theoretical issues of writing memoirs, see Jean-Louis Jeannelle, *Écrire ses Mémoires au XXe siècle: déclin et renouveau d'une tradition* (Paris: Gallimard, 2008). On the tradition of memoir writing in Russian culture, see *The Russian Memoir: History and Literature*, ed. by Beth Holmgren (Evanston: Northwestern University Press, 2007).

84   It is Irina Flige who suggested this idea to me, during our interview in Faenza (September 2010). In connection with this point, as previously stated, Mikhail Rozanov (see p. 25) wrote *Solovetskii kontslager' v monastyre* by comparing all the memoirs written until then, and managed to work out the most reliable version of events recounted by different memoirists on several occasions.

85   Barret J. Mandell, 'Full of life now', in *Autobiography: Theoretical and Critical*, ed. by James Olney (Princeton: Princeton University Press, 1980), p. 49; Georges Gusdorf, 'Conditions and Limits of Autobiography', ibid., p. 45. Although Gusdorf and Mandell referred to autobiography, I believe that their statement may be applied to memoirs too.

86   Distinctions are imperative: Kuziakina has brilliantly dismissed the 'notorious' story of Georgii Osorgin and of his wife's visit to the camp, which appears in many memoirs, according to which Osorgin, sentenced to death, prefers not to tell his wife the truth to spare her bad memories during her last visit to Solovki. As we know now, several months separated his wife's visit from Osorgin's

previously, in other cases specific details can either testify to or deny reliability. The prisoners' private letters, for example, are almost 'live recordings' of events, even though they are obviously qualified by their authors' reticence due to censorship, by self-censorship prompted by their need to reassure their families, as well as by the inevitable hiatus between the writing self and the living self.[87]

The memoirs written on Solovki consequently need to be analysed thoroughly — where possible — in order to assess the veracity of the facts recounted. They can give only a partial account of life within the camp, and only for some categories of prisoner: SLON memoirists are almost all intellectuals, so we only have their recollections. Such an assessment, however, is difficult, as other sources besides memoirs may also be unreliable. The analysis of archival documents might prove misleading, especially in the case of Soviet labour camps. The camp administration was typically responsible for fabricating evidence, such as fake death certificates. For example, death certificates for prisoners who were shot often cited natural causes of death, or prisoners whom the guards shot in the woods were said to be attempting escape. Considering the SLON in more detail, we know that the administration never reported the typhus epidemics, which were mentioned neither in official documents nor in the camp press. These deaths were generally attributed to less contagious illnesses or to scurvy.

When addressing the question of the Gulag, it is extremely difficult to investigate the prisoners' narrative reliability. Despite this, memoirs are crucial to any research into Soviet repression.[88] As Egidijus Aleksandravicius maintains, 'history and memory are unreliable narrators':[89] if the researcher's task is to lay bare all the facts, trying to ignore the layers of misinformation, speculation, and other obstacles to get to the information beneath, it is therefore imperative to draw upon prisoners' memoirs and to compare them with the archival documents in order to avoid uncertainty.

The Solovki memoirs are a special case because they are often radically different from one another.[90] The bulk of SLON memoirs is unique in its variety of witness and undermines a certain uniformity that the narrative of camp memoirs which date back to other times (such as, for instance, the Great Terror or the post-Second

death sentence. See Kuziakina, p. xvi. Osorgin's story is an example of the reconstruction of camp-related collective memory. I discuss this episode in detail in a forthcoming article (written with Claudia Criveller) with the provisional title of 'Russkie avtobiograficheskie teksty: vzgliad s Zapada'.

87   On theoretical issues linked to letter writing and self, see, among others, *Exil et épistolaire aux XVIIIe et XIXe siècles*, ed. by Rodolphe Baudin, Simone Bernard-Griffiths, Christian Croisille, and Elena Gretchanaia (Clermont Ferrand: Presses Universitaires Blaise Pascal, 2007).

88   Applebaum, for example, draws widely upon Gulag memoirs in her research. At the end of her book, she also provides an essay about the numbers of inmates in the Soviet labour camps compiling all the different and contradictory statistics at her disposal, thus providing readers with a valuable exploration of the difficulties faced by researchers when working with official archive documents which are reticent and contain lacunae. See Applebaum, pp. 515–22.

89   Interview with Egidijus Aleksandravicius (Faenza, March 2010).

90   In order to suggest the variety of SLON memoirs, Antonina Soshina mentioned the famous tale of the blind men who all give contradictory descriptions of an elephant. See interview with Antonina Alekseevna Soshina (Solovki, July 2009).

World War period) can have.

The Political Prisoners

The political prisoners had only a brief experience in the Solovki prison camp, where they gathered as a movement for the last time. Arrested and deprived of their leaders after the October Revolution, political prisoners were sent first to various jails and then to special purpose camps in Petrominsk and Kholmogory. When the Solovki prison camp was set up, all of them were transferred there without notice.[91] Their memoirs are the last trace of the life of some Russian political movements which had considerable importance in the history of Russian thought.

The young Social Democrat Vladimir Osipovich Rubinshtein, who was arrested and sentenced to imprisonment in Petrominsk, never made it to that camp. Instead, in the summer of 1923, he arrived at the Solovki islands, together with the political prisoners who were with him at the time.[92] The group included different political factions, such as Social Democrats, Socialist Revolutionaries, Anarchists, and Left Social Revolutionaries. Upon their arrival on the islands, the political prisoners were sent to a hermitage on the main island, Savvat'evo. Surrounded by woods and near a beautiful lake, located 11 kilometres from the Kremlin, and entirely built of red brick, the Savvat'evo hermitage was the OGPU's first solution to the problem of political prisoners. Once they reached the hermitage, the prisoners immediately established their own social structures. Each faction elected its *starosta*, who was the only one entitled to speak with the administration on behalf of his group. They then chose their representatives in order to form a joint organizational committee. The prisoners gradually created a highly organized commune. Food was rationed among its members; every faction had its own cook who provided meals for the whole community; and labourers worked hard to fix every leak in the hermitage building. The joint committee settled all organizational questions during long meetings at the Church of Saint Mary of Smolensk. It was in this same place that the political prisoners founded their cultural centre. The church hosted concerts and plays, seminars, chess tournaments, lessons in English, mathematics, and social sciences.[93] Lessons typically ended up in debates and lengthy discussions about political issues, which were eventually printed. From the very beginning, prisoners created a journal, *Spolokhi*. Only three copies were typewritten and passed around.[94]

---

91   The 'Gleb Bokii' boat picked them up at Arkhangel'sk. During the journey, prisoners planned to take command of the ship and to head for the Scandinavian coasts. The leaders of the different groups, however, could not agree about the plan which consequently failed. See Rubinshtein, p. 24.
92   Rubinshtein was part of the very first group of political prisoners sent to Solovki. I have consulted a typescript kept in Tsetsiliia Mel'nikova's private archive in Cologne. His memoirs have partially been published in the first of the four volumes of memoirs by former SLON prisoners published by the Solovki monastery, see Umniagin, I, 184–93.
93   Prisoners also founded a little orchestra, with a guitar, a mandolin, or a balalaika and cigarette paper used as a sort of trumpet, which helped them evoke the sound of sacred music. Rubinshtein, p. 33.
94   Unfortunately, all the copies of *Spolokhi* were lost.

Moreover, the Political Red Cross[95] provided the *politiki* with magazines, books, and journals, which they collected to create their own library and an archive.

The camp administration suddenly disrupted the *politiki*'s peaceful, almost idyllic, existence[96] in this politically and culturally stimulating setting in December 1923. The administrators' intolerance was probably fuelled by the fact that all political prisoners, as previously stated, firmly rejected forced labour. Tensions first erupted when some of the prisoners were sent to the Muksalma Island to avoid overcrowding. Nogtev, who was in charge of the operation, did not warn the *politiki* about their transfer nor, more importantly, did he consult with the *starostas*. On 16 December, Nogtev went to talk to the *starostas*, who denied him access and refused to confer with him. As a result, Eikhmans handed the political prisoners a note, which imposed a 6 p.m.–6 a.m. curfew beginning on 19 December. Most likely, this was an attempt to provoke them. The administration knew that the prisoners would never obey this diktat, which clearly foreshadowed a change in the detention regime. On the day the curfew was to begin, Nogtev appeared, backed by an armed commando of VOKhR.[97] His strategy worked. Many prisoners, especially the Anarchists and the Socialist Revolutionaries, started to walk around the backyard, as if to defy the commanders. Nogtev gave orders to open fire on them. Several prisoners died in the first burst of gunfire. When those who had previously sought refuge in the building ran to help the wounded, Nogtev ordered the guards to open fire for the second time. The platoon went back to the Kremlin leaving five prisoners dead and three wounded. One of the wounded died after a week of agony.[98]

The next day, Eikhmans went to Savvat'evo and told the *starostas* that he had ordered a formal investigation and that Nogtev would be immediately removed from office. He also allowed the prisoners to organize funerals for their fellow

95   The Political Red Cross was an organization that helped political prisoners. Created under the Tsars, it was active also in Soviet times, when it was directed by Gor'kii's second wife, Ekaterina Peshkova. The Political Red Cross was a significant source of support for the detainees: it saved many lives by sending money and medicines, or by interceding with the state security services for the release of some inmates or, even, for their emigration. It was dismantled in 1936. Many of its workers were arrested and executed. Much has been written on the *Politicheskii Krasnyi Krest*: among other sources, other than the second part of Gorcheva's quoted book (Gorcheva, *Pressa GULAGa. Spiski E. P. Peshkovoi*, pp. 171–220) see: Iaroslav Leont'ev, 'Politicheskii krasnyi krest v strane serpa i molota', *Obshchaia gazeta*, 42 (1996), available online at the link: http://socialist.memo.ru/books/html/leont09.htm#y1 [accessed 19 October 2014]; Maria Cristina Galmarini, 'Defending the Rights of Gulag Prisoners: The Story of the Political Red Cross, 1918–38', *The Russian Review*, 71.1 (2012), 6–29.

96   The political prisoners were also allowed to meet with family members: this way Tsetsiliia Mel'nikova, then a three-year-old child, lived in Savvat'evo with her parents, Socialist Revolutionaries. See interview with Tsetsiliia Moiseevna Mel'nikova (Cologne, December 2009).

97   VOKhR guards had large-calibre rifles, as was clear when the *politiki* examined the bodies of fellow prisoners. As Rubinshtein points out, these weapons were not commonly used by VOKhR guards. It therefore seems likely that Nogtev's operations were deliberately planned as a massacre. Rubinshtein, p. 39.

98   Reconstruction was made possible by comparing Rubinshtein's and Olitskaia's versions, which present slight and altogether irrelevant differences. See Olitskaia, pp. 216–24 and Rubinshtein, pp. 35–43.

inmates. After the ceremony, the prisoners launched an uncompromising battle against the administration. They first wrote to Moscow, then to the Socialist International. Distributed by the Political Red Cross, their reports reached an international arena, as already mentioned above. Moscow responded by appointing a new commission, led by Ruben Katanian, who went to Savvat'evo that summer. However, the whole affair came to nothing. In the following months, the camp guards started to ignore the political prisoners, who recommenced their everyday life in the hermitage.

A new convoy of political prisoners arrived that summer. Ekaterina Olitskaia, a young woman who had been arrested some months before and charged with conspiracy with the Socialist Revolutionaries was among them. While in jail, Olitskaia had learned information about the then legendary camp of Solovki and of the Savvat'evo commune through coded exchanges[99] with a fellow inmate, Sima (Serafima) Iudicheva. Iudicheva, who had once been a prisoner there, looked forward to going back to the Solovki and being reunited with her friends. She wanted to immerse herself again in its culturally and politically active world. Other prisoners did not, however, share her enthusiasm: Aleksandra Shchesnevskaia was afraid to return to the Solovki, especially after the 19 December incident. Iudicheva herself had personally witnessed the burst of gunfire that killed two of her friends. Despite this experience, her enthusiasm was so contagious that Olitskaia too started to be curious about the Solovki islands.

When Olitskaia arrived there, she was amazed at the relatively lenient treatment of political prisoners. Her march to the Savvat'evo hermitage together with other *politiki* was 'like a stroll', and she happened to meet the *starosta* Ivanitskii, who cheered her up and made her feel comfortable.

> So now I was going with my transfer group to Savvat'evo. The road passed through a forest. In some places it was rounded by lakes, all connected, which had been carved out at some point by glaciers. It was the end of August. The forest lived an untroubled life. Neither the animals nor the birds were afraid of people. The monks did not hunt, and neither did the hermits who arrived at the hermitage. There was no-one else living on Solovki.
>
> [...]
>
> Our transfer — the transfer of prisoners to Savvat'evo — did not resemble at all a transfer of prisoners. The security guards walked tranquilly, they did not straighten the formation, they did not hurry. We went without being shouted at, without being made to walk in formation. There was no-one we might have met on the secluded road. There was nowhere for the prisoners to escape to.[100]

---

99   It was a communicative code, similar to that of the telegraph. In fact, it was based on the tapping of fingers on the walls. In this way the prisoners could speak through walls.

100   [А пока я шла этапной группой от кремля к Савватию. Дорога шла лесом. Кое-где огибала она озера, цепью смыкающиеся, вырытые когда-то ледником. Был конец августа. Лес жил непотревоженной жизнью. Ни звери, ни птицы не боялись людей. Монахи не занимались охотой. Богомольцы, приезжавшие в обитель, тоже. Другого населения на Соловках не было. [...] Наш переход — этап к Савватию — ничем не напоминал этап. Конвоиры шли спокойно, они не равняли строй, не торопили. Мы шли без окриков, без соблюдения строя. Никто не

FIG. 2.6. Ekaterina Olitskaia. ASM

Once the group arrived in Savvat'evo, they were welcomed with tears of joy by their old friends. Olitskaia, a new inmate, was overwhelmed with amazement at the comfort, cleanliness, and light in the rooms.

The winter of 1924, however, was harsher than the previous year. As happened every year, ice prevented boats from reaching the island[101] and the Political Red Cross could not deliver goods to the isolated prisoners, whose number had increased consistently since the winter of 1923. Food soon grew scarce, as did medicines and newspapers. Declaring a state of emergency, the *starostas* requested that the prisoners be sent back to the mainland. In reaction to Eikhmans's repeated refusal, about 230 prisoners went on hunger strike.[102] On the fifteenth day without food, the *starosta* Bogdanov[103] could no longer bear the suffering of his fellow inmates and went to Eikhmans with a formal request. He asked Eikhmans to ship the political prisoners to the mainland once boat travel was possible again so that they could live

мог встретиться на этой уединенной дороге. Некуда было бежать арестантам]. Olitskaia, pp. 235–36. Olitskaia refers to the canals that connect the lakes, which had been created by the monks throughout the centuries.

101   It was impossible to reach the archipelago from October to May because the White Sea froze in winter.

102   Only the Social Democrats did not take part in the hunger strike.

103   Boris Osipovich Bogdanov was a leader of the Mensheviks. He was a prominent figure in the February Revolution and was one of the few political prisoners to survive the camps, where he spent most of his life. Much has been written on Bogdanov, see Natal'ia Bogdanova, *Moi otets — Men'shevik* (St Petersburg: NITs Memorial, 1994); Irina Flige, 'Sud'ba men'shevika', in Umniagin, I, 150–58; Boris Sapir, 'Nash solovetskii starosta', ibid., pp. 159–62.

in the same conditions as in Savvat'evo's detention camp. The pact, which formally signalled the end of the hunger strike, was hailed as a victory, though some regarded it as a Pyrrhic victory. David Batser, who had reached the island in September, certainly thought so: 'Formally it is a victory. But straight away we found ourselves wondering whether it had been a Pyrrhic victory, and whether they might take us to a place which was even worse than Solovki.'[104]

For some time, life went on as usual. The *politiki* were finally transferred to the mainland in the summer of 1925, but the experience was far worse than they had expected.

> I woke up really early, maybe it was still dark. Maybe I was awakened by the unusual movements and the voices on the courtyard. Looking out of the window [...] I saw many guards in a uniform that was new and unknown to me. [...] The group of guards started coming towards us in the block. I took a quick look and saw that both of our buildings were surrounded by soldiers in that same uniform.[105]

Once orders were given to pack up, the *starostas* had their fellow prisoners prepare themselves and dismantle the library and the archive. The convoy finally set out for the mainland. The guards, however, turned out to be unexpectedly brutal. Ekaterina Olitskaia realized how different everything was from her first 'stroll' to the hermitage the previous year:

> At last the guards had finished assembling the prisoners. A general command was given: ... '...The least insubordination to the guards... one step to the side... will be considered as an attempt to escape... shooting on the spot... Forward march!' It was not even one year before that I was walking along that same path towards the Savvat'evo hermitage. We then walked freely, without guards, chatting tranquilly. Now, on both sides of the road, the guards were walking with their loaded rifles. At the front and at the end we had guards on horseback. There were harsh shouts.[106]

At the Kremlin, the prisoners waited for their friends from Muksalma and Anzer. After they gathered together, the almost four hundred political prisoners left the Solovki monastery for good. They were dispersed to different prisons. In less than three decades, almost all of them would be killed by the Bolsheviks. Their battles

---

104 [Формально это победа. И тут же невольно вставал вопрос — не пиррова ли это победа, не везут ли нас на еще худшее, чем Соловки.]. See Dmitrii Batser, 'Solovetskii iskhod', *Zven'ia*, I (1991), 288–8 (p. 291).

105 [Я проснулся очень рано, быть может это было еще ночь. Возможно что меня разбудило необычное движение и голоса на дворе. Взглянув в окно [...] я увидел много надзирателей в новенькой еще не знакомой мне форме. [...] Группа надзирателей направлялась к нам в корпус. Приглядевшись, я заметил, что оба наших здания окружены солдатами в такой же форме.] Rubinshtein, p. 80.

106 [Наконец, прием зэков конвоем был закончен. Раздалась общая команда... «...Малейшее неподчинение конвою... Шаг в сторону... рассматривается как попытка к бегству... Расстрел на месте... Шагом марш! Не прошло и года, как я шла по этой же тропинке в Савватьевский скит. Тогда мы шли свободно, без конвоя, спокойно беседуя. Теперь по обе стороны дороги с ружьями наперевес шагали конвоиры. Впереди и позади ехал конный конвой. Грубые окрики.] Olitskaia, p. 276.

became legendary for other prisoners. In years following, some political prisoners would occasionally be sent to the Solovki. Once there, they would organize hunger strikes and try to resist, but their efforts were fruitless.[107]

A Real Nightmare: General Work

While political prisoners were living in the Savvat'evo commune, most of the other prisoners endured nightmarish suffering. Hardship and torture were part of the daily routine for those who worked in the forests of the main islands. Felling timber was the job of most of the non-political prisoners and all those inmates who were not employed by the camp administration and therefore had lighter work. Going through prisoners' memoirs, we realize that the chekists felt particular satisfaction at sending the representatives of the former nobility or the White Guard to forced labour.

From their initial arrival at the transit camp in Kem', those prisoners' trajectory through the SLON was diametrically opposed to that of the *politiki*. They were immediately introduced to camp routine. Physical abuse and beatings were the common penalty for any lack of attention or complaint. These prisoners were continually exposed to insults and humiliation. They personally experienced the arbitrariness of power summed up in the words used by commanders to welcome new prisoners: 'Here we don't have Soviet power, we have "Soloviet" power'.[108] Mal'sagov mentions an episode that dates back to his stay at Kemperpunkt and sheds light on the total amorality of the SLON guards:

> One such Pavlov (Nikolai Ivanovich) rules the affairs of the camp. He is a real racketeer. He takes bribes on an 'auction' principle: the one who offers most has a free day. Here's an example. On the Popov island[109] there is no water, it is necessary to fetch it from Kem'. Two carts with water tanks are made for the purpose. Since transporting water is far easier than uprooting pine trees, prisoners compete desperately for this work. Pavlov openly asked who would offer more for that work. There were three prisoners who managed to bring with them large sums of money. They offered more than the others (150 roubles altogether) and transported water until the day I escaped.[110]

107 Iurii Chirkov's memoirs mention Viktor Kharodchinskii (see below, p. 265) and Anatolii Groisman, young political prisoners who in 1935 went on a hunger strike to protest against the ban on reading newspapers. They were both executed two years later. See Chirkov, pp. 53–58.

108 [У нас здесь власть не советская, а соловецкая]. Many memoirs include the quote. It was usually Nogtev or Kurilko who welcomed new prisoners in this way.

109 Popov island is a little island just outside the Kem' harbour. It is famous for having provided the set of the world-renown movie *Ostrov* [The Island] by Pavel Lungin (Pavel Lungin's Studio, 2006).

110 [Делами лагеря управляет некий Павлов (Николай Иванович), продажный мошенник. Он берет взятки по аукционному принципу: тот, кто предлагает больше всего денег, высвобождает себе день. Приведу такой пример. На Поповом острове нет воды — ее необходимо доставлять из Кеми. Для этой цели предназначены две телеги с цистернами. Поскольку возить воду — самая легкая работа по сравнению с выкорчевыванием пней, за такой труд заключенные отчаянно соревнуются. И Павлов открыто спрашивал, кто больше заплатит за эту работу. Были трое арестантов, которые ухитрились провезти с собой крупные суммы денег. Они и предложили больше остальных (в складчину 150 рублей), и возили воду до самого моего побега.] Sozerko Mal'sagov, *Adskie ostrova: Sovetskaia tiur'ma na*

FIG. 2.7. Timber felling at SLON. ASM

First the inmates were taken on boats so crowded that some prisoners did not survive the journey,[111] then they docked on the Solovki and were kept in rooms in the Kremlin or in barracks which were built for the newcomers. After a period of 'quarantine', they were each assigned to forced labour and to their respective brigades. Of all the brigades, the *obshchie raboty* (general work) notorious 12th company was the most frightening. Mikhail Nikonov–Smorodin wrote about the brigades in 1928:

> The Solovki prison camp was divided into fifteen companies, populated following the 'class principle' of the camp.
>
> First company. Prisoners coming from the top of the camp administration: *starostas*, bosses, helpers of the bosses in different activities on the Solovki.
>
> Second company. Specialists in positions of responsibility, professional people employed in accordance with their skills.
>
> Third company. Chekists of high rank, workers of the ISO.[112]
>
> Fourth company. Musicians of the Solovki orchestra.
>
> Fifth company. Firemen of the Solovki fire brigade.
>
> Sixth company (watchmen). Formed almost exclusively of about a thousand clergymen.
>
> Seventh company. Doctors (some of whom are also allocated to the Tenth company).

Dal'nem Severe (Nal'chik: Izdat. tsentr 'El-fa', 1996), p. 48. For the original edition of the book in English, see Chapter 1, n. 25.

111   This happened in the summer. Prisoners who arrived at Kemperpunkt at other times normally stayed there until navigation started again.

112   *Informatsionno-sledstvennyi otdel* (Informative and Investigative Section).

Eighth company. Inveterate hooligans, 'leopards'.

Ninth company. Rank and file chekists.

Tenth company. Office workers and some specialists.

Eleventh company (negative elements). Jail.

Twelfth company (workers). Workers sent for heavy 'general work'.

Thirteenth company (quarantine). This is where all the newcomers to Solovki are sent. The twelfth and thirteenth company are the 'bottom' of the camp.

Fourteenth company (the prohibited). The prohibited, prisoners under special surveillance who work only inside the Kremlin walls.

Fifteenth company. Craftsmen.[113]

Camp folklore found one more brigade to join the list:

Camp humorists call the cemetery 'the sixteenth company'.[114]

An ordinary day for a forced labour prisoner started in the same way as for any other Kremlin prisoner: morning muster and roll call. After receiving a meagre breakfast and rations for the day, the inmates went to the woods with their brigade. Isolated in the midst of the forest, prisoners had to endure strenuous physical work and their commanders' constant abuse. Their job was to fell trees and transport heavy logs, usually in severe weather conditions. The timber was then exported to Europe. Both guards and prisoners were well aware of this trade, as Major General Zaitsev points out in his memoirs, giving vent to his anger at those who bought the blood-stained goods.[115] Another inmate, Arnold Schaufelberger (born into a family of porcelain workers who used to supply their products to the Tsar), is one of the memoirists who wrote about the timber-producing labour camp in some detail:

When we arrived in the forest, the squad was divided into groups of three people each, and every one of these groups had to saw down, remove the branches and trim and stack in a day one cubic *sazhen*[116] of wood. Often the

---

113 [Соловецкий лагерь делился на пятнадцать рот, населенных по лагерному «классовому принципу». Первая рота. Заключенные из верхов лагерной администрации: староста, завы, помощники завов разными соловецкими предприятиями. Вторая рота. Специалисты на ответственных должностях, лица свободных профессий, используемые по прямому назначению. Третья рота. Чекисты высокой марки, служащие ИСО. Четвертая рота. Музыканты соловецкого оркестра. Пятая рота. Пожарники соловецкой пожарной дружины. Шестая сторожевая рота. Населена почти исключительно духовенством, численностью около тысячи. Седьмая рота. Медицинский персонал (частью помещается еще и в десятой роте). Восьмая рота. Отпетая шпана, «леопарды». Девятая рота. Рядовые чекисты. Десятая рота. Канцелярские работники и некоторые спецы. Одиннадцатая рота отрицательного элемента — карцер. Двенадцатая рабочая рота. Рабочие на физических «общих» работах. Тринадцатая карантинная рота. Сюда попадают все прибывающие на Соловки. Двенадцатая и тринадцатая рота являются «дном» лагеря. Четырнадцатая запретная рота. Запретники — заключенные, находящиеся под особым наблюдением, работающие только в стенах кремля. Пятнадцатая рота. Мастеровые.] Mikhail Nikonov-Smorodin, *Krasnaia katorga* (Sofia: Izd-vo N.T.S.N.P., 1938), p. 108.

114 [Шестнадцатой ротою соловецкие шутники называют кладбище]. Ibid.

115 Ivan Zaitsev, *Solovki. Kommunisticheskaia katorga ili mesto pytok i smerti. Iz lichnykh stradanii, perezhivanii, nabliudenii i vpechatlenii* (Shanghai: Slovo, 1931), p. 118–31.

116 1 sazhen = 2.1336 metres.

cutting and sawing happened in one place, and the stacking of the *balany*[117] happened somewhere a hundred steps away from the working place. The work was made harder by the fact that Solovki is a hilly place in general and to carry on your shoulders *balany* weighing 2–3 poods[118] (and sometimes more) was unbelievably hard.[119]

As mentioned above, camp guards (usually former prisoners who had begun to cooperate with the administration) contributed significantly to this desolate scenario. Many witnesses maintain that guards earned the commanders' esteem by behaving pitilessly towards fellow prisoners, putting them through unspeakable torture.[120]

Even outside the forest, prisoners had to endure work that was utterly pointless and extremely demanding. As Nikonov-Smorodin says:

> Our group worked all night cleaning up the Kremlin: they dragged all kinds of metal junk and lumber from one place to another, they swept and cleaned the cobbled floors inside the fortress. And the next day, and the day after that they dragged the lumber and all the junk back to its previous place. That is one of the most revolting and irritating peculiarities of the Solovki *katorga* system: even if there's no real work to do, they won't leave your hands unused, they would make you even beat the air rather than let you 'indulge in rest'.[121]

These were not, however, the only risks camp prisoners ran. A greater danger came from common criminals who habitually tyrannized them. Bezsonov conjures up the scheme of camp hierarchies vividly:

> Twelve o'clock. The bell rings for lunch. The servers have left a long time ago. From the kitchen, directed to their barracks, go the 'chekists' with their little barrels filled with fish. After them, asserting their rights with constant abuse and sometimes even with fights, the '*shpana*' receive their lunch. Then they serve soup even for us.[122]

---

117 *Balany* is the word for trimmed logs. Measures were established by the administration.

118 1 pood = 16.38 kilograms.

119 [Партия, прибывшая в лес, делилась на группы по 3 человека каждая, и такая группа обязана была спилить, обсучить, расчистить и сложить за один день одну кубическую сажень дров. [...] Зачастую рубка и пилка производились в одном месте, а складывать баланы приходилось за несколько сотен шагов от места работы. [...] Затрудняло работу еще и то, что Соловки вообще гористые и таскать на плече баланы весом по 2–3 пуда, а иногда и больше, было неимоверно тяжело.] Arnol'd Shaufel'berger, 'Solovki — Vospominaniia', in *Leonard Shaufel'berger (10.1.1839–19.2.1894)*, ed. by Elena Tarkhanova and Marcus Schütz (St Petersburg: Izd-vo Politekhnicheskogo Universiteta, 2009), p. 88. Schaufelberger's book is thoroughly pervaded by his hatred of the *politiki*, clearly nourished by the author's anti-Semitism.

120 Other than those listed in the Shanin commission's document quoted above, tortures frequently included the practice of having the prisoner sit a few metres from the ground with loads on his/her legs, after which the prisoner was left crippled.

121 [Наш этап всю ночь работал по уборке Кремля: перетаскивали всякий железный хлам и бревна на другое место, мели и чистили мощенную камнем внутренность крепости. А на завтра и послезавтра опять перетаскивали бревна и всякий хлам на прежнее место. Это одна из самых возмутительных и раздражающих особенностей соловецкой каторжной системы: если нет настоящей работы, все равно, не оставлять руки праздными, занимать людей хоть водотолчениемъ в ступе, — лишь бы не «баловать отдыхом».] Nikonov-Smorodin, p. 116.

122 [12 часов. Колокол на обед. Раздатчики ушли уже давно... От кухни по направлению к

FIG. 2.8. Iurii Bezsonov. ASM

There were other difficulties for prisoners. They hardly ever received adequate clothing, and most of them arrived on Solovki wearing the same clothes they wore when arrested. Malnutrition generally turned vigorous individuals into skeletons, who were left to become emaciated and die in the camp.[123] Informers were a common threat, and there were many of them even amongst the *intelligenty*[124] as Schaufelberger maintains. Additionally, prisoners were terrified of punishment and especially of the notorious 'Sekirka'.

The *Sekirnaia gora*, or 'hatchet mountain', was home to a former sanctuary on a small mountain.[125] The guards used it as an isolation block, from which prisoners rarely returned. The chekists sadistically abused their many victims, although their

баракам идут «чекисты» с маленькими бочками, наполненными рыбой. За ними, отстаивая свои права, с руганью, а иногда и дракой получает свой обед «шпана». Затем, наливают суп и нам.] Iurii Bezsonov, *Dvadtsat' shest' tiurem i pobeg s Solovkov* (Paris: Impr. de Navarre, 1928), p. 164. For the original edition of the book in French, see previous chapter. The term 'shpana' refers to common criminals.

123   Kiselev-Gromov, p. 30.

124   Shaufel'berger, p. 70.

125   The toponym comes indeed from the verb 'to flog' (*sech'*, past: *sek*) and it is linked to a miracle that entailed the flogging of a Karelian woman who wanted to settle there. However, over the centuries, most people have referred its name to the Russian word 'sekira' (hatchet). See <http://solovki-monastyr.ru/spp/svyato-voznesenskij-skit/> [accessed 20 June 2016].

numbers have probably been exaggerated, as Rozanov shows.[126] Nevertheless, memoir writers unanimously regard the Sekirka as the bleakest feature of the camp, as can be seen from the following passage from Volkov's book:

> For anyone who was imprisoned on the Solovki, there was no word more terrifying than that. It was there that Dzerzhinskii's worthy disciples invented and put in action a whole range of tortures and refined torments, starting from the 'zherdochki' — those thin wooden bars on which you were forced to sit for days maintaining equilibrium without sleep and food, in terror of a brutal beating; to the pushing of tortured, bound prisoners down the icy stone steps of a hundred-metre long flight of stairs: at the bottom, they would gather up lacerated bodies, with broken bones and fractured skulls. Mass shootings were also organized on the Sekirnaia mountain.[127]

The Sekirka was not, however, the only place where camp prisoners endured suffering. They were also exposed to torture of all kinds on the so-called 'Golgotha' on Anzer Island, where those deemed as invalids (the ill, old, and disabled) were sent to die, and on the Zaiatskii islands, where the *zhenskii shtrafizoliator* (women's isolation unit) was built.

The Difficult Life of Women

The women's isolation unit on the Zaiatskii islands was another desolate place in the prison camp, though women's living conditions everywhere within the SLON were usually dire. In the camp, women were often forced to satisfy the commanders' sexual desires. Although many refused to submit, the chekists managed to persuade even the most obstinate among them. Forced prostitution was such a widespread practice that in the 1920s one prisoner, Ol'ga Sidorova, ran the sex slave trade for the commanders.[128] Many prisoners wrote about the humiliating conditions women suffered in the Solovki camp, but none can match Emel'ian Solov'ev's detailed description:

> Coercive cohabitation was a common phenomenon. Every member of the chief administration has the right to have a 'cook' or a 'domestic'. For this role, a former chekist chooses for himself a girl that he likes.
>
> Many, pinched with hunger and worn out by general work, go for cohabitation immediately, but at first some, above all young ones with characters not yet destroyed by the Solovki, refuse. If so, through the 'Work office' and then, through the crew dispatcher of the *zhenkorpus*, the former chekists or the collaborators of the guards — all people experienced in these affairs — send

---

126 Rozanov, *Solovetskii kontslager'*, p. 127.
127 [Для тех же, кто сидел на острове, не было страшнее слова. Именно там, в церкви на Секирной горе, достойные выученики Дзержинского изобретательно применяли целую гамму пыток и изощренных мучительств, начиная от «жердочки» — то ненькой перекладины, на которой надо было сидеть сутками, удерживая равновесие, без сна и без пищи, под страхом зверского избиения, до спуска связанного истязуемого по обледенелым каменным ступеням стометровой лестницы: внизу подбирали искалеченные тела, с перебитыми костями и проломленной головой. Массовые расстрелы также устраивались на Секирной.] Volkov, p. 88.
128 Brodskii, p. 223 and p. 428.

FIG. 2.9. Women's barracks at SLON. AMM

them to carry out such heavy work that sooner or later the exhausted and starving girl will herself turn to her protector, who from time to time shows himself to his chosen object. The most inaccessible ones are sent to Zaichiki, i.e. Zaiatskie islands, to be broken, seven versts away from the Kremlin. Life on the Zaichiki is so hard and depressing that time after time the proudest girls resign themselves to accepting their lot.[129]

129 [Принуждение к сожительству — обычное явление. Всякий занимающий начальственную должность получает право иметь в своей квартире 'кухарку' или 'прислугу'. В качестве таковой бывший чекист выбирает себе приглянувшуюся девушку. Многие, изголодавшись и измучившись на общих работах, идут на сожительство с начальством сразу же, но некоторые, особенно молодые девушки, с еще не сломленным Соловками характером, сначала отказываются. Тогда их, через Отдел Труда, а последний, через нарядчиц женкорпуса, бывших чекистов или сотрудниц милиции, опытных в таких делах, посылают на такие тяжелые работы, что раньше или позже измученная и голодная девушка сама обратится к покровителю, который периодически появляется перед глазами избранницы. Самых неприступных отправляют ломать в командировку на 'Зайчики', то есть Заяцкие острова в семи верстах от Кремля. На 'Зайчиках' настолько тяжело и грустно жить, что постепенно самые гордые девушки смиряются со своей участью.] Solov'ev's memoirs are quoted in Brodskii, p. 160. Memorial has published online the letters Emel'ian Solov'ev and his wife Agapiia Ivanovna sent to the Political Red Cross. The letters are kept at GARF and can be read at the following link: <http://pkk.memo.ru/letters_pdf/002496.pdf> [accessed 25 July 2014]. The term 'zhenkorpus' refers to the women' corpus.

Not every woman had to endure such atrocious violence. Years later, in 1937, upon Ol'ga Adamova-Sliozberg's arrival at the SLON, she spent many peaceful months there. The prison director at that time, Monakhov, suggested that women prisoners be divided in groups of four and that they should choose their fellow inmates. This is how Sliozberg's group managed to organize themselves:

> We decided on this plan: we would wake up at 8 and for one hour we would do physical exercise with the window open. Then we would have breakfast and start our lessons: for two hours a day, Zhenia would practice English language with us; for two hours, Zina used to teach us mathematics. For one hour I would practise French with Zhenia and for one hour Russian with Lida, then I would read French books. There were 250 of them in the camp library, and they were all good books.[130]

This practice was completely abandoned once Monakhov was arrested.[131] The detention regime became harsher and harsher for women, as it did throughout the camp system from 1937 onwards. Many of them were shot in the 1937 massacres.

The Camp Guards

Monakhov's case was quite an exception.[132] The chekists typically enlisted extremely cruel, sadistic people. Physical and sexual violence together with murder are recurring themes in SLON memoirs. Even those who did not personally commit crimes turned out to be extremely influential:

> One of the representatives was the Head of the forest division of the Volgostroi,[133] Seletskii. I knew him from the Solovki: he was a former officer who was sent to Solovki as a prisoner and worked as head of tree-felling companies. His name would provoke terror amongst the prisoners: to end up in tree-felling companies often meant to die. Seletskii himself never beat and never killed anyone, but out of desperation or for other reasons he used to get drunk, he used to become depraved and connived with guards and helpers (mainly common criminals) when they pitilessly beat and kill prisoners in tree-felling companies. If by chance he happened to be sober, he was a gallant, handsome man.[134]

130 [Мы установили такой порядок: вставали в 8 часов и час делали гимнастику при открытом окне. Потом завтракали и садились за учебу. 2 часа в день Женя занималась с нами английским языком, 2 часа Зина учила нас математике. Час я занималась с Женей французским и час с Лидой русским, потом я читала французские книги, которых в библиотеке было 250 томов, и все очень хорошие.] Adamova-Sliozberg, p. 48.

131 Adamova-Sliozberg recalled Monakhov as follows: 'He made one year of our lives in prison easier. He was a very good man' [Он скрасил нам год жизни в тюрьме. Это был очень хороший человек]. Ibid., p. 49.

132 Gurskii too hints at some kind-hearted chekists. See Gurskii, p. 216.

133 The Volgostroi was a special administration of the NKVD whose main work was related to the construction of the Moscow-Volga canal.

134 [Одним из представителей был Начальник лесного отдела Волгостроя Селецкий. Я когда-то знал его по Соловкам: бывший офицер, он был заключенным и в Соловках работал начальником лесозаготовок. Одно его имя приводило заключенных в ужас: попасть на лесозаготовки часто означало гибель. Сам Селецкий не бил и не убивал, но с отчаяния,

FIG. 2.10. The train at the SLON. ASM

As suggested above, Frenkel' softened the harshest aspects of camp terror, because he believed that continuous torture and murder were counterproductive in terms of economic development. It was during the years of 'frenkelizatsiia' that Nikolai Kiselev (whose pseudonym was 'Gromov') planned his escape from the prison camp. After spending several years at the camp, where he worked side by side with the chekists, Kiselev did not want to collaborate in their violence any more. He eventually managed to escape and, once abroad, he wrote his memoirs, in which he described in detail all the agonies that guards imposed on prisoners, from his point of view as a former guard.

Kiselev wrote extensively about timber-producing labour camps, evoking the difficult existence prisoners led there,[135] as well as the guards' typical behaviour. We are told that, after a day's work, the chekists would go to their club where they exchanged views on the cruelties and violence they had inflicted upon their prisoners. We also learn how they would cover up for one another by obfuscating facts in their reports.[136]

или почему другому, он пьянствовал, развратничал и попустительствовал охранникам и десятникам, по большинству из уголовников, нещадно избивать и убивать на лесозаготовках заключенных. Если его тогда удавалось видеть трезвым, это был бравый цветущий мужчина.] Andreev, p. 144.

135 The author insists especially on the darkness, which was a major obstacle to work. See Kiselev-Gromov, p. 33.

136 Ibid., p. 31.

Van'ka Potapov emerges in Kiselev's book as one of the most ferocious overseers. It is striking that Kiselev described him as a 'beast in human form, not only morally but also in his appearance'.[137] When frustrated prisoners undertook self-mutilation, Kiselev maintains, Potapov did not excuse them from work. On the contrary, he would punish or even shoot them (he boasted that he had shot four hundred prisoners). What is more, he kept amputated limbs as trophies.

Apart from providing an insider's point of view of the torture inflicted on the prisoners, Kiselev's memoirs include striking descriptions of his 'colleagues' — whom he repeatedly called 'sadistic' and '*psikhicheskii bol'noi*' (mentally ill). Most significantly, they unmask one of the greatest propaganda operations ever attempted by the SLON leadership. He reveals how exceptional measures were taken during the shooting of the documentary film *Solovki*. Women wore the clothes of prisoners who had been shot in Moscow and whose personal property had been transported to Kem' in special railway trucks. Prisoners were forced to smile and seem happy but, whenever the camera was turned off, they were beaten on their backs. Some of the brigades were given sheets, blankets, and pillows for their barracks, but soon afterwards they went back to sleeping as usual on wooden planks, the *sploshnye nary*.[138] The film showed men and women talking to each other, while the penalty for unauthorized conversation between men and women was typically 14 to 30 days of punishment. As Kiselev suggests, the film was not bad, but the blood and tears were not there.[139]

The Clergy between Tolerance and Repression

Despite their frightening sadism, the chekists would at times make unexpected concessions. For example, their initial tolerance towards Orthodox monks was surprising. From the establishment of the camp in 1923, some monks had been given permission to stay at the monastery, working in the camp administration but also taking part in productive activities.[140] As time went by, the religious community grew bigger and bigger. Many high-ranking representatives of the Orthodox Church, clergymen, and representatives of other religions who had been sent to the Solovki islands soon joined the monks' original community. Initially, at least, the camp directors responded favourably to their requests. Easter and Christmas celebrations were permitted in those early years.[141] The clergy also benefited from

---

137 [Зверь в образе человека — не только морально, но и в наружности] Ibid., p. 62.

138 Bunks on which the prisoners normally slept. See Rossi, pp. 230–31.

139 [Фильм сделан не плохо. [...] Вообще там нет слез, крови]. Kiselev-Gromov, pp. 105–08.

140 The religious community usually performed important tasks such as the delivery of parcels and food rationing, as they were the only ones who did not steal. Besides, their fishing experience was useful for the administration. The most interesting work about the Solovki religious community is Irina Reznikova (Flige)'s quoted book.

141 Aleksandr Bulygin's mainly unpublished memoirs, now included in the Memorial archives in Moscow, reveal that some priests were allowed to conduct services and that prisoners, among them Bulygin himself, were sometimes allowed to go to mass. See Moscow, AMM, f. 2, op. 1, d. 31, Aleksandr Bulygin, *Solovetskaia byl'* — *vospominaniia*, 1981, mashinopis', bez podpisi, l. 56. The text has been partially published in Umniagin, III.

FIG. 2.11. The post office at the SLON. ASM

some privileges, which they would use to help fellow prisoners.[142]

These privileges, however, gradually ceased. The clergy were soon treated like the rest of the prisoners, although they sometimes managed to organize clandestine events. Father Nikolai Chekhranov writes that in 1926, together with two prelates, he managed to celebrate a clandestine Easter mass at Kemperpunkt. The celebration was much more religiously poignant for him than the celebration which took place at the same time in Rostov-on-Don cathedral:

> Yes, the circumstances of Easter 1926 were unusual. When the three of us were celebrating it in a partially built bakery, at that same moment in Rostov the city's clergy were also celebrating the Easter mass in the cathedral church suffused with electric light, with the participation of the amazing choir led by I. F. Kovalev. But... we came to think that our Kem' Easter with archbishop Ilarion in the bakery without windows and doors under the illumination of the stars, without mitres and brocade robes, was dearer to God than the magnificently furnished Rostov one...[143]

142 Likhachev, for instance, was helped by Father Nikolai Piskanovskii, see Likhachev, *Izbrannoe: Vospominaniia*, pp. 147–49.

143 [Да, обстановка пасхи 26-го года необычайна. Когда мы втроем ее справляли в недостроенной пекарне, в это время там, в Ростове, в залитом электрическим светом

In the end, the clergy at the Solovki prison camp had to endure the same fate as other prisoners; almost all of its members were eliminated between the 1920s and the 1930s and became martyrs in their respective religious communities.

It is worth underlining the fact that a great number of believers lived in the camp. Among them was the *intelligentsiia* representative Ol'ga Vtorova-Iafa, who had been arrested at the age of 52 and charged with cooperating with others arrested in connection with the Meier case.[144] Her faith helped her to cope with imprisonment and gave her the ability to live quite peacefully. Having already visited the Solovki islands on a pilgrimage, Vtorova-Iafa regarded her second visit as a 'tour'.[145] When she arrived in 1929, she overcame her initial shock and managed to find some sort of happiness there, despite the typhus epidemic that was raging at the time. Her memoirs depict quite vividly the suffering of her fellow inmates,[146] while at the same time providing interesting portraits of people she met there. The book includes a striking evocation of one peculiar 'witches' Sabbath' that the women prisoners spontaneously organized after a forced anti-typhus disinfection (a disease which had claimed some sixteen victims a day, as Vtorova-Iafa wrote):[147]

> I now remember that night as a delirium full of nightmares. Under the blinking light of the dim kerosene lamp, barely burning because of lack of oxygen, which had been used up by the previous group of prisoners, in the smoky, steamy and stinking atmosphere of the utterly dirty place, between the dark wooden walls of the old monastery *bania*, under the low and similarly dark boarded ceiling, naked women's bodies abounded — some young, well-made, others old, dried up or shapeless, with pendulous breasts and stomachs, and even equally variegated tattooed ones as is the custom in the criminal environment. To pass the time somehow, we started singing folk songs and then we broke into dance. A circle dance of naked women started whirling round with laughter and whoops in the middle of the *bania*, and other naked women were jumping and squatting inside the circle on the dirty floor. It was a sort of frantic pandemonium, a real Sabbath of witches from Bald Mountain, a demoniac rejoicing, Walpurgis Night.[148]

кафедральном соборе, при участии чудного хора И.Ф. Ковалева городское духовенство совершало тоже пасхальное торжественное богослужение. Но!.. думается нам, наша Кемская Пасха с владыкой Иларионом в пекарне без окон и дверей, при звездном освещении, без митр и парчовых риз, дороже была для Господа, чем великолепно обставленная Ростовская...] Moscow, AMM, f. 2, op. 1, d. 127, Pavel Chekhranov, *Paskha 1926 goda. Vospominaniia*, Mashinopis', l. 13. The text has been partially published in Umniagin, 1.

144 In 1929 many people, either closely or loosely connected with Aleksandr Meier and with his philosophical-religious circle *Voskresenie* [Resurrection], were arrested and sent to the Solovki islands. They eventually became the core of local *intelligentsiia*, they started to be part of the camp's administration and rapidly became some of the leaders of the flourishing cultural scene at the SLON in the late 1920s.

145 Vtorova-Iafa, p. 133. Iafa's memoirs were published in 1976 by the *Pamiat'* almanac under a pseudonym, Ol'ga Iasevich. The manuscript is in the archives of St Petersburg's Memorial, see St Petersburg, AMSPB, Ol'ga Vtorova-Iafa, *Vospominaniia*.

146 'Solovki is the state of the unfortunate people' [Соловки — государство несчастных]: this phrase denoted the prisoners' different nationalities. Ibid., p. 141.

147 Ibid., p. 143.

148 [Эта ночь вспоминается мне сейчас как полный кошмаров горячечный бред. При

A similar case to that of Vtorova-Iafa, i.e. a case where a religious faith was strong enough to enable believers to endure their existence, can be found in another episode, which dates back to 1935. The fifteen-year-old student Iurii Chirkov heard a man crying during his first night at Kem'. Drawing himself up close to the man, he discovered the nature of those tears:

> Father Vasilii, a priest from Riazan', with a beard that looked greenish from age, was kneeling in a corner, praying and crying. I could not bear it and went down to console the old man. It turned out that he was crying for joy, since he was going to die not anywhere in the taiga, but on the land made holy by Zosima and Savvatii.[149]

The Very Different Stories of Two Underage Inmates

Chirkov's story opens a new chapter in the story of SLON prisoners, that of underage inmates. Iurii Chirkov was arrested on 5 May 1935 and charged with participation in an anti-Stalin conspiracy along with some of his classmates. For this reason, he was sent to the Solovki islands. Chirkov's memoirs are uniquely imbued with a teenager's attempt to catch a first glimpse of life through barred windows and barbed wire.

In his book, Chirkov recounts how he adapted easily to the camp *byt* because he was constantly protected by his fellow prisoners. His childlike kindness attracted general sympathy — especially that of Father Ofen, who guided him through the routines during his first days at the camp, telling him the history of the monastery and talking about the achievements of its religious community. Other than Father Ofen, the inmates with whom he shared a *barak* also liked the young student and helped him during his detention. At one stage, he fell ill and a nurse helped him to get work as an assistant at the hospital, which spared him potentially fatal hard labour.[150] At the hospital, his life was a succession of bright and bleak days. However, he managed to make his dream of continuing to study for school exams even inside the camp come true. In the camp library he found all the necessary books. What is more, the building proved to be a peaceful haven for the young student.

мигающем свете тусклой керосиновой лампы, еле горевшей вследствие отсутствия кислорода, выдышанного предыдущей партией, в прокуренной парной и смрадной атмосфере донельзя загрязненного помещения, среди темных бревенчатых стен старой монастырской бани, под низким и таким же темным дощатым потолком кишели голые женские тела — одни молодые, хорошо сложенные, другие старые, высохшие или расплывшиеся, с отвислыми грудями и животами, при этом одинаково пестро растатуированные, как это принято в уголовной среде. Чтобы как-нибудь скоротать время, затянули хоровые песни, потом пустились в пляс. Хоровод из голых женщин с хохотом и гиканьем кружился посреди бани, а внутри его на грязном полу такие же голые женщины прыгали вприсядку — это была какая-то бешеная свистопляска, сущий шабаш ведьм с Лысой Горы, бесовское радение, Вальпургиева ночь.] Ibid., p. 146.

149 [Отец Василий, священник из Рязани, с зеленоватой от старости бородой, стоял в углу на коленях, молился и плакал. Я не мог вынести и спустился утешить старика. Оказалось, он плакал от радости, что умрет не где-нибудь в тайге, а на земле, Зосимой и Савватием освященной.]. Chirkov, pp. 12–13.

150 Ibid., p. 33.

FIG. 2.12. Iurii Chirkov. ASM

His experience of working as a medical assistant was actually both vital and traumatic. Chirkov cried so much that at times his superiors whisked him off to a different ward to spare him further suffering. In the end, Chirkov asked them if he could resign: 'I would rather freeze in the forest than spend one day more working here'.[151] His superiors sent him to work as an assistant to the surgeon Arkadii Aleksandrovich Oshman. When a commission inspected the place and found Chirkov sleeping, Leonid Timofeevich Titov, a prisoner and one of the hospital directors, asked the commissioner Mikhailov to spare the young man. Chirkov was thus saved for the second time. Later, his experience became more and more unique, thanks to his work in the camp library, where he found a way to study and to meet renowned professors who did their best to stimulate the young student with *blitsekzameny*, i.e. quick exams on several different topics.[152] Among those professors was Pavel Florenskii, of whom Chirkov paints a long narrative portrait, composed during the last years of the great philosopher's life.[153]

---

151   [Лучше я в лесу замерзну, чем еще день проработаю здесь]. Ibid., p. 43.

152   Ibid., pp. 70–79.

153   The author managed to see Florenskii while he was leaving for Levashovo to be murdered. 'Among the lines of people who were walking, the face of Professor Florenskii could be glimpsed, and Professor Litvinov was keeping his silver-bearded head high. They were both from the Project Administration Office. Kotliarevskii (in his new leather hat) and Vangengeim (in a black coat and in a deer-skin cap) appeared. They saw me. They nodded, their hands were busy with the luggage. Kotliarevskii gave me a wink and smiled, but it was an unhappy smile. The former head of the hospital L. T. Tatov arrived rolling down like a ball. I waved at him. He turned his head, smiled confusedly, recognized me, shook his head. And the lines kept on going and going' [В рядах проходящих мелькнуло лицо профессора Флоренского, вот высоко несет голову седобородый профессор Литвинов (оба из ПСБ). Показались Котляревский (в новой кожаной ушанке) и Вангенгейм (в черном пальто и пыжиковой шапке). Увидели меня. Кивают головами, а руки заняты чемоданами. Котляревский подмигнул и улыбнулся, но улыбка вышла невеселая. Шариком покатился бывший заведующий лазаретом Л. Т. Татов. Я его окликнул. Он повернул голову, улыбнулся растерянно, узнал меня, затряс головой. И мимо, мимо идут ряды]. Ibid., pp. 173–74. There is a misspelling in the original: 'Tatov' is 'Titov' and his full name is Leonid Timofeevich (1883–1938).

FIG. 2.13. The SLON library. AMM

Chirkov's fate was ultimately as dramatic as that of most prisoners. The sort of kindness that helped him through his first years at the camp was an exception, especially considering that those years corresponded to a violent climax in the history of the Soviet machinery of repression.[154]

The experience of another underage inmate, Sergei Shchegol'kov, was indeed completely different.[155] Shchegol'kov, too, arrived at the Solovki as a teenager (he was seventeen at the time of his arrest), having been accused of involvement in an anti-Stalin conspiracy. The similarities with Chirkov's case, however, stop there. The very circumstances of his arrest were different from Chirkov's: he was tortured and savagely beaten, and forced to admit his supposed guilt.[156] His life at the camp was nightmarish. Subjected to forced labour, terrified by hearing

154 Chirkov spent three years on the Solovki islands, from 1935 to 1938.
155 Shchegol'kov arrived at the Solovki in 1933 and remained there until 1938.
156 Other minors involved in the Shchegol'kov affair were the alleged leader of the group, Vladimir Kon'kov, who was shot in prison, and Evgenii Perfilov, who was executed in a camp. Some 'members' of this group did not even know one another when they were arrested, see Solovki, AAS, Sergei Shchegol'kov, *Nebol'shoe povestvovanie o tom, kak sovetskaia vlast' i partiia VKP(b) sdelali menia 'gosudarstvennym prestupnikom-terroristom', kotoryi gotovil pokushenie na zhizn' tovarishcha Stalina, Mashinopis'* s fotografiami i avtografami avtora, pp. 15–17.

FIG. 2.14. Sergei Shchegol'kov. ASM

about the countless shootings that took place at the camp, Shchegol'kov suffered dramatically from starvation in years when hunger was more extreme than usual. In fact, after the Holodomor, the SLON had less food and was soon overcrowded with Ukrainian peasants. The author recalls the presence at the Solovki camp of some Ukrainian women, employed in the breeding of livestock, who were charged with cannibalism. Shchegol'kov's short memoirs are a series of bitter remarks[157]and of spine-chilling reports:

> The destiny of the prisoners was the same. Most of the prisoners were sent to die, some were sent to perish in other camps. [...] In the camp many people died even without being shot, from malnutrition (above all the criminals). They were defeated by the already meagre rations, then they would 'feed' from the refuse dumps, which led to dysentery and inevitable death. They died of exhaustion from work and the northern climate (scurvy).[158]

Shchegol'kov's unhappy fate reminds us of Dmitrii Likhachev's frightening words

157 'Here there's no thought of spiritual life' ['Здесь уже не до духовной жизни']. Shchegol'kov, p. 10.
158 [Судьба заключенных в тюрьме была та же. Большую часть людей послали на смерть, часть отправили погибать в другие лагеря. [...] В лагере много людей умирало и без расстрелов, от истощения (особенно уголовников). Ими проигрывалось и без того скудное питание, далее «питались» из мусорных свалок, в результате дизентерия и неминуемая смерть. Умирали от непосильной работы и северного климата (цинга).] Ibid., p. 11.

on the *besprizorniki*, children who were abandoned in towns or were orphans of the 'enemies of the People'. They were sent to labour camps to die of hunger and cold, the administration did not feed them and they survived only thanks to the help of other inmates.[159] In his memoirs, Likhachev states that he founded a special section for them and managed to improve their living conditions. Due to this activity, he was allowed to take walks on the main island, which he recounts at some length.

The Lucky and the Privileged

Having arrived at the Solovki islands after receiving his university degree, Likhachev managed to be excused from general work[160] almost immediately and entered the camp administration because of his connections with high-ranking employees, mainly with the *kruzhok* of Professor Aleksander Meier. Likhachev's memoirs are striking both because of his brilliantly elegant evocation of the camp's cultural life and because of the incredible luck that helped him during his stay at the SLON, saving his life on many occasions.[161]

Likhachev's life in the camp was that of a young student surrounded by brilliant intellectuals who, spared from hard labour, was able to grow up in an extraordinarily fertile cultural setting. Likhachev's privileged position is similar to that of Boris Shiriaev, whose fate (and a slight degree of flattery) earned him an important place among the intellectual élite which flourished in the first years of the SLON (1924–26) when almost all the 're-educational' activities were introduced. In his book *Neugasimaia lampada*, Shiriaev conjures up his memories of the experience as a camp prisoner. There is a compellingly poetic and spiritual edge to his memoirs, which lends his book its literary significance but also contributes to its distortion of historical facts.[162]

159 In the years following the Revolution, the *besprizorniki* represented one of the major social problems in the Soviet Union. They wandered through the cities, formed gangs, took drugs, engaged in robbery and committed all kinds of crimes. The Bolsheviks soon had them regularly arrested and sent to labour camps. In 1928 the Soviet government decided to intensify their action against *besprizornost'*, and in a few years 'liquidated' the problem. On the topic, see *Deti GULAGa. 1918–1956. Dokumenty*, ed. by Semen Vilenskii (Moscow: Rosspen, 2002).

160 Amongst the general work Likhachev had to endure was the 'Vridlo', i.e. 'Temporarily fulfilling a horse's activity' [Временно исполняющий должность лошади]. Prisoners were actually used as pack horses.

161 Gurskii repeatedly expresses some misgivings about Likhachev's reliability, and about his image. For instance, Likhachev recalls how, being on a list of prisoners to be shot, he was warned by a friend and managed to avoid death by hiding behind some logs. Likhachev's fortuitous escape, however, can hardly be compared with other memoirs, as pointed out by Gurskii: as far as we know, no one could avoid capital punishment once they were on a death list. Moreover, Likhachev's hiding overnight would have certainly led to the death penalty for attempted escape. Gurskii's innuendos about Likhachev's family connections with OGPU members is likewise debatable, even though some of the student's privileges are indeed surprising — especially the fact that his parents lived in facilities reserved for OGPU members. See Gurskii, pp. 233–35 and Likhachev, *Vospominaniia*, pp. 196–99.

162 For example, the book initially records the execution, as an example to others, of General Daller. Neither archival documents nor memoirs record such an execution, which certainly calls into question the assumed reliability of the episode. The cross on Daller's tomb, moreover, is sheer imagination. See Shiriaev, pp. 35–44 and p. 388. In an article in the journal *Solovetskie Ostrova* (from now onwards *SO*), the same Shiriaev recalled the episode of the finding of Daller's tomb. The date of

Pavel Florenskii is another intellectual who became a privileged prisoner for a brief time on the Solovki. After arriving on the islands in 1934, he was asked to conduct research for the 'Iodprom', a local firm that extracted iodine from seaweed. Florenskii had his own special barrack, a long way from the *ugolovniki*, and could therefore use his time conducting scientific research (for instance, on ice), as he had done before becoming a prisoner. He also wrote his family a number of heartfelt letters in which, besides describing his imprisonment, he taught his children science, geography, and, more generally, 'life' lessons. When asked to give his opinion on a name for his nephew, Florenskii writes:

> I did not write about a name for Vasia and Natasha because I was not asked to, and I do not want to impose my opinion. It is very difficult to talk about this issue in general, not on a specific matter. After all, the name itself does not make a person good or bad; it is only a musical form on which you can write a good or a bad piece. The name can be compared with the Chreia, that is the way in which the basic parts and elements of a composition are distributed and coordinated, but it is not the name that creates the theme of the works or their quality.[163]

Aleksei Vangengeim's story is quite similar to that of Florenskii. An MGU meteorology lecturer and the last director of the Solovki Camp Museum, Vangengeim shared Florenskii's fate during his imprisonment.[164] He also sent his daughter many letters in which he describes the local plant life; some of the letters contain sketches or even dried leaves. Both Vangengeim and Florenskii's privileged position, however, lasted only while they were on the Solovki archipelago and did not spare them from capital punishment.[165]

Daller's death written on the tomb was 2 February 1925, and not 1923. Neither the crosses on it, nor Daller's execution are reported by the author. See Boris Shiriaev, 'Syr', SO, 5–6 (1926), 3–14 (p. 5).

163 [Об имени для Васи и Наташи я не писал, потому что меня не спрашивали, а навязывать свое мнение не хочу. Очень трудно об этом вопросе говорить вообще, не конкретно. Ведь имя само по себе не дает хорошего или плохого человека, оно — лишь музыкальная форма, по которой можно написать произведение и плохое и хорошее. Имя можно сравнить с хрией, т. е. способом распределения и соотношения основных частей и элементов сочинения, но не именем создается тема сочинения или качество его.] Florenskii, *Pis'ma s Dal'nego Vostoka i Solovkov*, pp. 432–33.

164 He was also shot in 1937, during the Sandormokh massacre.

165 The letters were recently published in: Aleksei Vangengeim, *Vozvrashchenie imeni* (Moscow: Tablitsy Mendeleeva, 2005). Through Vangengeim's letters it is possible to reconstruct daily life on the Solovki in the last years of the camp. They are extremely valuable, because they show how, even if the prisoners' life conditions worsened in the 1930s, the intellectual activities continued to be pursued up until 1937, when most of the intellectuals were shot. In his letters, Vangengeim explains how he holds seminars (letter dated 18 May 1934, p. 32), how he goes to the theatre (letter dated 8 August 1935, p. 40), and he also describes the museum in 1936 (pp. 49–50, letter dated 18 April 1936). More information about Vangengeim's letters can be found in the interview published in *Novaia gazeta* with Irina Ostrovskaia, archivist of Moscow Memorial. See Nikita Khlebnikov, 'Chernil'nyi pribor s Solovkov, ili Rasstrel za pogodu', *Novaia Gazeta*, 5/6/2008, <http://www.novayagazetadata/2008/40/37.html> [accessed 25 July 2014]. His letters have been used recently by Memorial in an exhibition entitled *Papiny Pis'ma* [Letters from Dad], and some of them have been published in the exhibition catalogue. See *Papiny pis'ma. Pis'ma ottsov iz GULAGa*, ed. by Alena Kozlova and others (Moscow: Agey Tomesh/WAM, Memorial, 2014), pp. 29–53. Vangengeim's story

FIG. 2.15. Avenir Vadbol'skii, ASM

Intellectuals were not the only ones who enjoyed privileged positions on the Solovki. At first engaged in forced labour, Aleksandr Dmitrievich Bulygin managed to rise up through the ranks thanks to his work as an accountant.[166] He led such a peaceful life at the camp that his memories are incredibly light-hearted when compared with other prisoners' writings. Hours spent with his classmates, jokes about accountancy, long walks — it was only his recurring anxiety about what was to happen after his release that darkened his memories. When he mentions violence it is always violence reported by other people, as Bulygin himself never experienced any during his period at the SLON.

Office or administrative positions, in themselves, did not guarantee happiness. In Bulygin's memoirs, two figures stand out from the rest. Avenir Vadbol'skii[167] and Mikhail Frolovskii,[168] who both worked for the camp administration, were not involved in the camp intellectual élite. A former prince and a poet, Vadbol'skii published only one poem in camp journals.[169] Frolovskii never published anything, and was totally traumatized by his experience on Solovki. In the journal-like letters he sent to his son while in exile after being freed from the SLON, letters which he certainly wrote under pressure,[170] the poet yields to his utter despair — the ultimate effect of imprisonment.

---

has inspired Olivier Rolin's *Stalin's Meteorologist: One Man's Untold Story of Love, Life and Death*; see Olivier Rolin, *Le météorologue* (Paris: Seuil, 2014).

166 It was not only working skills that were fundamental. Sometimes money helped too. Other than the episode quoted above (see 2.2.3), Professor Nikolai Antsiferov recalls how, when he arrived at Kem', he could afford private housing for a while. See Antsiferov, p. 341.

167 Bulygin, ll. 5–6.

168 Ibid., l. 19.

169 Vadbol'skii was shot in Moscow in 1930, two years after his release from SLON. See *Poeziia uznikov Gulaga*, p. 68. His published poem is: Avenir Vadbol'skii, 'Ekho', *SLON*, 6 (1924), 68.

170 Frolovskii wrote his notes during his forced exile in the Northern Urals after he was released. His last letter dates back to 20 October 1940. He was arrested after a few months, and died in the Karlag in 1943. Frolovskii felt that he was doomed, as testified by many meditations contained in his journal: he knew for sure that he would be arrested again, and the letters helped him create a dialogue with his newborn child, which would otherwise have been impossible. Mikhail Frolovskii, *Listki iz dnevnika, vedennogo v ssylke*, in *Kitezh: proza, poeziia, dramaturgiia, vospominaniia*, ed. by Vladimir Murav'ev (Moscow: Vozvrashchenie, 2006), pp. 302–12.

As suggested above, an analysis of memoirs provides a varied spectrum of narrated experience that is difficult to find in similar corpora. Schaufelberger's suffering and Shchegol'kov's shockingly dry account are diametrically opposed to Likhachev's and Bulygin's narratives. In Semen Vilenskii's view, the experimental nature of the SLON accounts for the chekists' unexpected permissiveness and for the strikingly varied lives prisoners led there.[171] However, if this explanation fits the first years of the SLON, it does not explain the experiences prisoners went through during the later years. Individual fates might well have depended upon mere chance: where they were assigned to work and the like are elements that ultimately proved fatal for the camp prisoners. Sometimes, money or flattery helped them survive in better conditions. In some cases, their professional skills saved their lives, as was the case for manual labourers. Finally, their contact with 'power groups' was of fundamental importance. Through these different paths writers, poets, actors, theatre directors, and other *intelligenty* were spared because the administration needed them in order to create educational and cultural activities whose final results, however, far exceeded the chekists' expectations.

171 Interview with Semen Samuilovich Vilenskii (Moscow, July 2010).

CHAPTER 3

❖

The Publishing System of the SLON and its Peculiarities

The *Solovetskie Ostrova* [...] could be bravely defined as the freest of the Russian journals published in that period in the USSR.

BORIS SHIRIAEV[1]

Reasons for the Existence of a Publishing System

A Solid Tradition

Of the many educational and cultural initiatives proposed by the camp administration, publishing was one of the leading activities of the SLON. In the 1920s and 1930s, many Soviet prisons and camps had a publishing system. This phenomenon had deep historical roots, both through the well-established publishing tradition of the Russian revolutionary movements of the late nineteenth century and through the theoretical basis of the Soviet prison system. Though merely theoretical, the notion that prisoners should be re-educated through labour — an alternative to the purely repressive character of Tsarist jails — informed the development of specific processes and phenomena, including prisons publications.

As N. Stogov explains in his previously mentioned article, prison publications first appeared in Europe and eventually spread across Russia. Whereas in Europe this type of publication was fully sanctioned, in Tsarist Russia it was usually the political prisoners who ran illegal newspapers and journals that escaped state control: exiled prisoners, in particular, took advantage of their inaccessible place of detention to launch powerful, though typically rudimentary, publishing systems. Handwritten or copied with a pantograph machine, prisoners' publications boasted a large circulation and were usually given rather bizarre titles, such as the Shlissel'burg-based *Vinegret i Pautinka*, the Moscow prison journal *Kamenshchik*, and the Odessa-based journal *Tiuremnyi Khokhot*.[2] Classic titles were also used: *Kariiskii Listok Ob''iavlenii* (based at the Kara penitentiary), *Butyrskii Vestnik* (based at the Butyrka prison in Moscow)[3] and *Vol'noe Slovo* are but a few examples.

---

1   [Соловецкие острова [...] мог быть смело названным самым свободным из русских журналов, выходивших в то время в СССР], Shiriaev, p. 135.

2   'Vinegret' and 'pautinka' are the names of two traditional salad recipes, 'kamenshchik' means 'bricklayer' and 'khokhot' means 'guffaw'.

3   The Butyrskaia prison (generally known as the 'Butyrka' or 'Butyrki') was one of the most

By contrast, official prison publications were an exception to the rule. In 1905, the first official journal for prisoners, the *Tiuremnaia Gazeta*, legally published its first issue in a prison in St Petersburg, but no further issues followed. According to Stogov, a second attempt was made more than ten years later, when the *Zerna* journal went to press at the Kresty prison in Petrograd.[4] The *Zerna*, a supplement of the *Tiuremnyi Vestnik* journal that was written by jurists and addressed prison-related questions, was also short-lived. Its publication was interrupted after a mere four months, following the collapse of the Tsarist regime in February 1917.

By and large, official prison publishing activity does not bear comparison with the clandestine press. On the one hand, Tsarist prison policies were not particularly aimed at the cultural development of prisoners;[5] on the other hand, revolutionary publishing activities proved altogether much more effective, based as they were on a deep-seated tradition.

Significantly enough, the development of Russian revolutionary groups had always been largely supported by clandestine publications. Russian revolutionary philosophy originally sprang from, and had hitherto developed through, questions first broached in debates in illegal political journals. Newspapers and journals were fertile ground for the seeds of anti-Tsarism: *Kolokol*, for example, led by Aleksandr Herzen, or *Narodnoe Delo*, an initiative of Mikhail Bakunin and Nikolai Zhukovskii. In addition to these publications, which were produced overseas, innumerable newspapers, journals, and manifestos were produced in Russia, but the *Okhrana*'s[6] stranglehold on them was so strong that they were generally doomed to extinction. Nonetheless, manifestos and cyclostyled documents continued to be one of the primary means of the dissemination of revolutionary thought, both in Russia and abroad.[7]

Coming from such a tradition, it is not surprising that the press played such an important role for the Soviet government. Once in power, the Bolsheviks did not hesitate to carry out a policy of centralization of the press and more generally of any material written for publication, by subjecting all publications to the kind of

---

important prisons in Moscow and in the Soviet Union. Moscow prisons included the Taganskaia and the Lefortovo ones. Several jails were set up in the environs of Moscow: e.g., the Sukhanovskaia prison, where Semen Vilenskii was interned. See Lidiia Golovkova, *Sukhanovskaia tiur'ma. Spetsob"ekt 110* (Moscow: Vozvrashchenie, 2009).

4   The most important prisons in the St Petersburg/Petrograd/Leningrad area were the Kresty prison, the Shpalernaia prison, and the fortress of St Peter and St Paul.

5   Stogov hints at the poor quality of the *Zerna*, which further testifies to the prison administration's limited attention to prison press. Stogov, p. 530.

6   Tsarist Political Police.

7   It is worth mentioning the role played by the document *K molodomu pokoleniiu* in the history of the revolutionary movement. Written by Nikolai Shelgunov with the help of Mikhail Mikhailov, the document was printed in London and circulated in St Petersburg. It proved crucial in the building of the notion of 'going to the People' — a key element of Russian revolutionary thought. See *Istoriia russkoi literatury*, ed. by Mikhail Alekseev and others, 10 vols (Moscow and Leningrad: AN SSSR, 1941–56), VII (1956), I, p. 34. Dostoevskii's *Besy* further confirms the importance of the press. On how the Bolsheviks used to smuggle *Iskra* into Russia from abroad, see Adam Ulam, *The Bolsheviks: The Intellectual and Political History of the Triumph of Communism in Russia* (New York: Mamillan, 1965), pp. 160–76.

preventive censorship that remained part of the Soviet publishing system until the advent of perestroika.[8] A strong effort (in both economic and human terms) was made by Soviet authorities above all in the early years after the Revolution in order to sponsor the creation of publications in Soviet prisons and camps. Thanks to their own pre-revolutionary experience of creating prison journals, and to their use of publications for ideological purposes, the Soviet authorities created a phenomenon that is unique if compared with the penitentiary systems of other countries of the time.

Publications of Soviet Prisons and Camps[9]

The first Soviet prison newspapers and journals were founded during the establishment of the Soviet state. Although Stogov maintains that the phenomenon of prison publications was created in 1921, some newspapers and journals had already been published, as the list of prison publications included in Alla Gorcheva's book shows.[10]

The urge to publish was closely connected to the strong official position on the allegedly innovative character of the Soviet prison system. As a matter of fact, the Soviet theoretical programme for dealing with prisoners did not foreshadow the bloodshed that eventually took place across the Soviet Union. Theoretically, the primary objective of the Bolsheviks was not to punish but to re-educate prisoners through labour. This objective sprang from one crucial deviation from Marxist sociology which lay at the core of Soviet Communism: that of 'genetic categorization'. From the Bolshevik perspective, the very notion of crime was transferred from practical to theoretical categories — from behaviour to class membership and ultimately from acting to being — in the early years of the Soviet state. The criminal was consequently considered either a representative of a social class that opposed the Revolution or a potential enemy of Revolution.[11] Redemption was only ensured by Socialist re-education, which was the only means to turn the prisoner into a 'socially close' rather than a 'socially dangerous' individual.[12]

The newly born Soviet institutions set to work strictly along the lines indicated above, and did not underestimate the cultural aspect of the question. The early post-revolutionary years saw the publication of prison newspapers and journals, mostly

---

8   It was mainly controlled by the Glavlit, an institution founded in 1922. Glavlit's extended name was *Glavnoe upravlenie po delam literatury i izdatel'stv* ('Main Administration for Literary and Publishing Affairs'). Glavlit was only officially dismantled as late as 1991.

9   Part of this paragraph was published in Gullotta, 'A New Perspective for Gulag Literature Studies'.

10   Gorcheva, *Pressa GULAGa (1918–1955)*, pp. 113–63.

11   See the SLON's code quoted above, p. 46.

12   This distinction was crucial to the Soviet prison and camp system as a whole. 'Socially close' elements (thieves, murderers, and common criminals) often enjoyed privileges, high-ranking positions and freedom of action within prisons and camps. All of these were forbidden to 'socially dangerous' criminals ('counter revolutionaries' and 'political criminals'), a category that gradually came to include all those who were sentenced to prison or camps following the notorious 58th article of the Penal Code.

written by prisoners, which supposedly testified to the success of re-education. As time went by, however, the number of publications grew dramatically. In his 1978 article, N. Stogov lists as many as 176 journals and newspapers published between 1921 and 1935.[13] In the appendix to Gorcheva's updated version of *Pressa GULAGa* (2009), publications reached a vertiginous 487 between 1918 and 1955, 251 of which published between 1918 and 1935.[14]

In order to explain why so much energy was being expended on these activities, it is important to point out how Communist theories resulted in the establishment of executive agencies. GUMZ (*Glavnoe Upravlenie Mestami Zakliucheniia*, 'Main Administration of Places of Confinement') was the most important of these organizations. A department of the NKVD, GUMZ was founded in 1922 to super-vise the whole network of places of imprisonment.[15] It was eventually replaced by the GULag administration, which marked the transition to a national camp system aimed at territorial and industrial expansion. The GUMZ's focus on re-education surfaces quite clearly in the 4042 collection of the State Archive of the Russian Federation.[16] Remarkable efforts were made to fulfil the 'educational' objective of the GUMZ, testifying to the centrality of culture in the management of places of imprisonment, where the publication of newspapers and journals was but one of many concrete activities.

First and foremost, re-education also meant education. One of the GUMZ's favourite watchwords was the *likvidatsiia negramotnosti* ('liquidation of illiteracy'):[17] Soviet prison officials accordingly started to create schools and libraries within the prisons. The schools regularly sent reports on the prisoners' educational level to the GUMZ. Libraries too were carefully established and managed. GUMZ provided funds for their establishment together with lists of banned and recommended books. Moreover, Moscow sent proposals to Soviet prisons for workshops to be held there.[18] Significantly, GUMZ provided prisoners with a practical rather than exclusively theoretical education. All of them, especially the youngest inmates (the *besprizorniki* in particular), were offered professional training and the opportunity to work in a *trudkommuna*.[19]

13   Stogov, pp. 562–79.
14   It is worth underlining that Gorcheva possessed more sources than Stogov/Dubkin.
15   See Dundovich, Gori, Guercetti, *Reflections*, p. 7. Jakobson defines it a 'subagency' of the NKVD, see Michael Jakobson, *Origins Of The Gulag: The Soviet Prison Camp System, 1917–1934* (Lexington: University Press of Kentucky, 2015), p. 111. I am here using quotations from the most recent edition of the book.
16   See Moscow, GARF, f. 4042, 'Glavnoe Upravlenie Mestami Zakliucheniia'.
17   In the SLON press, this kind of activity was labelled *likbez* (from the words *Likvidatsiia bezgramotnosti*).
18   To present-day readers these kind of documents are very similar to the commercial advertisements of artists on tour, and therefore look quite bizarre. On 9 May 1924, GUMZ sent all Soviet prisons a proposal for a series of two-ruble lessons on the creation of the world by comrade Lavrov-Sokolov. See Moscow, GARF, f. 4042, op. 4, d. 63, l. 79, 'Postanovleniia Sovnarkoma RSFSR i Vneukrainskogo tsentral'nogo ispolkoma i Sovnarkoma Ukrainskoi SSR, doklady gubernskikh inspektsii mest zakliucheniia i perepiska s nimi ob izdanii gazety *Golos zakliuchennogo*, ob uvolnenii sotrudnikov, o periodicheskikh izdaniiakh (9.5.1924)'.
19   In the history of the Gulag, the *trudovye kommuny* were labour camps for underage inmates. The

Theatre companies comprised of prisoners were likewise founded. It was up to GUMZ to select both the subject for a performance and the ways the *mise-en-scène* was to be done. A special permit was required to start producing plays. It was quite difficult to obtain the permit, as the GUMZ's directives were quite strict. Some scenes, for example, were categorically forbidden. The 17 May 1924 newsletter required the following:

> Thereby it is necessary to take into consideration that types of entertainment that are permissible for common citizens like, for instance, films that depict adventurous escapades, shows with scenes of murders or violence, entertainment of light genre, farcical comedies and so on are ABSOLUTELY FORBIDDEN IN PLACES OF DETENTION, where shows are one of the means of corrective action on criminals.[20]

Another newsletter stated more specifically: 'The programme of every type of amusement needs to correspond with the tasks of communist instruction and education'.[21]

As shown by the documents referred to above, Soviet institutions strenuously carried out re-educational cultural activities — whenever they stumbled into unauthorised performances or plays containing forbidden scenes, prison commanders were required to personally account for the crime.[22]

Largely supported by forced labour and by oppressive practices, cultural re-education was so insistently pursued by the new government that a 'methodological' commission was created within GUMZ. The commission's function was to issue directives on the educational and re-educational activities to be performed in Soviet places of detention. The newsletters provided by the methodological commission were quite detailed and even included specific instructions for stage settings.[23] Prison and camp directors had to brief the GUMZ about all the cultural activities performed within their jurisdiction and regularly reported the results of re-education to GUMZ. One of the most important entries concerned the prisoners' newspapers and journals.

---

most famous was the Bolshevo commune.

20   [При этом необходимо принять во внимание, что зрелища вполне допустимые для граждан вообще, как, напр. киноленты изображающие авантюристические похождения, спектакли со сценами убийств, насилий, зрелища легкого жанра, комедии фарсового характера и т.д. СОВЕРШЕННО НЕДОПУСТИМЫ В МЕСТАХ ЗАКЛЮЧЕНИЯ, где зрелища являются одним из средств исправительного воздействия на преступников] GARF, f. 4042, op. 4, d. 63, l. 118.

21   [Программа каждого развлечения должна соответствовать задачам коммунистического просвещения и воспитания] Moscow, GARF, f. 4042, op. 4, d. 65, l. 9, 'Polozhenie ob upravlenii mestami zakliucheniia pri rabochei chasti, tsirkuliary GUMZ i instruktsii po uchebno-vospitatel'noi chasti v mestakh zakliucheniia Respubliki'. GUMZ also issued a list of banned and recommended books, which unfortunately is not included in the dossier.

22   GARF, f. 4042, op. 4, d. 63, l. 125.

23   See Moscow, GARF, f. 4042, op. 4, d. 64, 'Protokoly №№ 1–16 zasedanii metodicheskoi komissii pri kul'turno-vospitatel'noi chasti GUMZ za oktiabr'–dekabr' 1924 g. i ianvar'-mai 1925 g. (podlinniki i prilozheniia k nim)'.

As mentioned above, the publication of prisoners' journals and newspapers started immediately after the Revolution, and boomed in the aftermath of the Civil War when publications were flourishing all over the prisons and camps of the Soviet Union. A letter sent by GUMZ to Glavlit on 9 August 1926 perfectly sums up the guidelines that informed such profuse growth (re-education, distance from the Tsarist prison regime, juridical basis):

> Among the means of educational impact on prisoners, the Corrective Labour Code of the RSFSR allows for the publication of journals, newspapers, collections of texts and so on by the prisoners themselves. Actually, as our experience has shown, 'their own words', the words they read in 'their' journal, 'their' newspaper, in which they are active collaborators, has a much stronger educational impact on prisoners than the normal periodical press. This phenomenon, noted long ago by Soviet pedagogues, induces GUMZ and its local organs to use more extensively the publication of wall newspapers and journals with the aim of awakening the prisoners' independent action in the task of their own correction, and in the task of fighting the remains of the old prison way of life.[24]

The passage hints at the *stengazety*[25] or wall newspapers, which represented one of the most widespread forms of publication in the Soviet prison world. Wall newspapers offered the latest news from the camp (or prison), articles written by the prisoners and by the guards, poetry and satirical vignettes. Thanks to their low production costs and circulation potential, the *stengazety* were successful from the very start. The administration would put them up on gangways (aisles, canteens, and meeting places), where prisoners were only too eager to read them.

Technically and economically well-equipped places of imprisonment published not only *stengazety*, but also newspapers (*gazety*) and journals (*zhurnaly*). Newspapers (which contained only basic information) were more widespread than journals, since the latter were much more demanding and consequently required a number of literate and professional prisoners which most prisons could not supply. *Stengazety*, newspapers, and journals typically lacked continuity and expired after a few issues. Some of them did not even survive the first opening issue due to lack of funds or paper, or even commanders' whims.

The fate of publications, in fact, was closely linked to the fate of the prison/camp directors. How many publications a prison or labour camp produced, and the quality of these publications, often depended on the extent to which individual

---

24   [В числе средств воспитательного воздействия на заключенных, Исправительно-Трудовой Кодекс РСФСР предусматривает издание самими заключенными журналов, газет, сборников и т.д. и, действительно, как показывает опыт, на заключенных «свое слово», слово, прочтенное в «своем» журнале, в «своей» газете, активными сотрудниками которых они состоят, оказывает гораздо сильнее воспитательное воздействие, чем общая периодическая печать. Это явление, уже давно подмеченное советскими педагогами, побуждает главное управление м.з. и его местные органы широко использовать издание стенных газет и журналов в целях пробуждения самодеятельности заключенных в деле их собственного исправления, в деле борьбы с пережитками старого тюремного быта] Moscow, GARF, f. 4042, op. 4, d. 126, l. 53, 'Perepiska s gubernskimi ispravitel'no-trudovym domami o vypuske zhurnalov, izdavaemykh zakliuchennymi, ob assignovanii sredstv na izdanie (3.10.1925–16.12.1926)'.
25   *Stennaia gazeta*: literally, 'Wall newspaper'.

commanders were in control of cultural re-education, and on their interpretations of this concept. For example, the Viatka-based journal *Za Zheleznoi Reshetkoi*[26] (the most 'celebrated' newspaper of the first phase of Soviet prison publishing) owed its success to its promoter, Iurii Bekhterev. Believing in the re-educational potential of Soviet prisons, Bekhterev worked hard to pursue his goal, both as a director of the Viatka prison and inspector for GUMZ in Viatka, and in 1924, when he started his career in Moscow at GUMZ.

What were the specific features of camp or prison press? The camp or prison administration typically appeared as the official publisher. The quality of publications depended on the administration's funds. Some texts were handwritten; some newspapers or journals were copied using pantograph machines; most of the publications, however, were typewritten using high-quality machines. Directors and members of the editorial board were usually chosen from among management officers. At times prisoners were assigned the task of making editorial decisions and consequently played a major role in writing the articles. While the chekists and the guards often wrote editorials and ideologically charged articles, prisoners were also given the task of working as reporters. They covered a wide range of subjects, from camp/prison news to special issues and cultural columns that typically included poetry and prose submissions by other prisoners. Several newspapers and journals gave significant space to prisoners' memoirs, which included reflections on the Russian Civil War or the October Revolution as well as past meetings with important people. Prisoners were sometimes also responsible for the further, crucial task of selling their newspapers or journals in nearby towns.[27] In fact, the scope of the *tiuremnaia pechat'* varied. Whereas several newspapers typically addressed those who lived within the camp, other newspapers or journals were also sold outside the camp in order to create some profit for the administration. Nevertheless, they typically ended up in the hands of the prisoners, who often made great sacrifices in order to be able to buy a copy. The analysis of a Soviet camp journal might give us interesting insights into the *tiuremnaia pechat'* (prison publications).

The front cover of the third 1925 issue of the *Golos Zakliuchennogo*,[28] the journal of the Gomel' Ispravtruddom,[29] has several lines of poetry framed by flowers and two keys at the bottom. The second page is entirely occupied by advertisements, an important part of prison publications which enabled the administration to raise funds through sales revenue to invest in more publications. The first texts of the *Golos Zakliuchennogo* are devoted to politics: in particular, an article on May Day,

26   Munich, CBSB, 'Za zheleznoi reshetkoi — Zhurnal zakliuchennykh viatskago ispravtruddoma', Film P 2000.673 n° 024, 025, 050, 051. More information on *Za Zheleznoi Reshetkoi* can be found in Gorcheva, p. 30. The same name was given to other publications in Soviet places of imprisonment. The Viatka one was the most important among the journals which had this title, and it was the only one (together with the *Solovetskie Ostrova*) that could be found abroad. See Gorcheva, p. 29.
27   Gorcheva, p. 28.
28   The number quoted is included in the collection of *lagernaia pressa* at the Bayerische Staatsbibliothek in Munich, see Munich, CBSB, 'Golos zakliuchennogo — Zhurnal zakliuchennykh gomel'skogo ispravtruddoma, 3 (1925)', Film P 2000.673 n° 002.
29   *Ispravitel'no-trudovoi dom*, 'Institute for the Re-education through Labour'.

an appeal to 'tovarishchi zakliuchennye' (comrade prisoners),[30] and a long essay on the Soviet fight against criminality. Page 6 is devoted to foreign politics, notably an important detail, since that was often the only way prisoners were informed about what was happening in the wider world.[31] On the following page there is a report on the cultural and educational work of the Gomel' camp, and a little poem at the bottom of the page. A short essay closes the following page, where the memoirs of a prisoner are also published. Pages 9 and 10 are devoted to prisoners — photographs are followed by an essay on prisoners' appeals and a study of prison jargon.

The interest in prison habits, jargon, and 'folklore' represents a further, typical subject of the Soviet prison press. More poems, a feuilleton, and a text framed by drawings of crying women can be found in the pages that precede what the management deemed to be an important part of the journal, the résumé of the activities of the camp's school and of radio programmes. The same page advertises a workshop on the liquidation of illiteracy, while the last pages are devoted to interviews, legal advice for prisoners, and letters sent to the editorial board.

The camp publishing activities were strictly controlled by camp or prison censors. From the end of 1924 onwards, 'regionalism' was finally overcome and GUMZ started to control the prison press across the country. On 30 September, the Chief Administration of Places of Confinement sent a newsletter to all regional departments as part of an investigation into prison publications. All prisons and camps had to provide information about the newspapers and journals published by them between 1918 and 1924, the price and the number of issues of any publications, the typewriting machines used, the reading public targeted by publications, the names of the director and of the editorial board, and the number of regular contributors.[32]

In November 1925, this first request was followed by a request to send GUMZ copies of any journal issue.[33] GUMZ's requests met a number of requirements: firstly, the need to centralise re-education across the Soviet Union; secondly, the need to control re-educational activities by either approving or correcting the choices of editorial boards; thirdly, the need to prevent any intervention from Glavlit, thus trying to resist the ever increasing (and threatening) interest of the central Soviet censorship institution in the prison press.

From 1926 onwards, Glavlit's grip tightened. Camp and prison publications could not exceed 100 copies, a policy that led to the shutting down of a remarkable number of newspapers and journals.[34] The new rule practically made publishing impossible, since production costs were impossible to cover with such a small circulation.

30   In later years, prisoners would eventually be denied the epithet *tovarishch* (comrade). When, at the end of their sentence, they were addressed again as comrades, this signalled their reintegration into society.
31   Outdoor newspapers and radio bulletins were further sources of information for the prisoners. Not all of the prisons, however, had a radio.
32   GARF, f. 4042, op. 4, d. 63, l. 200.
33   The request was sent to all the places of detention on 19 November 1925. See GARF, f. 4042, op. 4, d. 126, l. 16.
34   GARF, f. 4042, op. 4, d. 126, l. 50.

GUMZ reacted fiercely against Glavlit's instructions and supported many camp directors who also objected to them. Following Bekhterev's advice, GUMZ wrote a document carefully listing all the advantages of the *tiuremnaia pechat'*, thus defending many places of imprisonment which had opposed Glavlit's decision.[35]

Bekhterev's harsh reaction had no effect. Glavlit rejected GUMZ's initiative without further explanation.[36] It was a sign of the times. The first phase of publishing in the camps, the establishment of prison newspapers and journals and the government's relatively liberal attitude towards them, was on the wane. Its decline coincided with the rise of Stalinism and with the tightening of the government's grip on social and cultural activities. The following phase — the glorification of the 'Great Construction Projects of Communism' — would see the subjugation of the *tiuremnaia pechat'* to the Party's directives and to the 'Stalinization' of the Soviet Union.[37] The camp press would thus rapidly be reduced to nothing more than a mouthpiece of Communism and its successes, created through the deaths of thousands of prisoners who worked at the building sites of the White Sea–Baltic Sea Canal, Moscow-Volga Canal, and the BAM.[38]

The development of publishing in the SLON ran in parallel to what has been described so far. Though grounded on the same ideological basis as any Soviet camp publishing operation, the distinctive independence of the SLON from GUMZ meant that it could develop without external interference. The SLON was the very first camp to be entirely run by the OGPU, whose jurisdiction (and power) extended to practically every aspect of the camp, including re-education. A further, more substantial peculiarity of the SLON was that its status as a 'special purpose' camp allowed for its population to be comprised of a large number of artists and intellectuals. These prisoners, under specific circumstances, made it possible for the camp to produce cultural and artistic work of the highest quality, and placed the SLON in a unique position in the cultural history of Soviet labour camps.

The First Period of SLON Publications (1923–1926)

The SLON press was established while the camp was still being set up. On 29 October 1923, that is, no later than six days after the Central Committee's establishment of the Solovki camp, the Party cell of the local, ninety-fifth division of the OGPU published its first *stengazeta*, the *Ostrovok*.[39] Unfortunately, no information about the contents of the newspaper has reached us. The copies were all lost and the later articles that mention it do not provide any clues to its content. The only official piece of evidence is a short note dating back to December 1924

---

35   GARF, f. 4042, op. 4, d. 126, l. 53. Regarding the dispute between GUMZ and Glavlit, see Fischer von Weikersthal, pp. 167–69.

36   GARF, f. 4042, op. 4, d. 126, l. 54.

37   My chronology follows Gorcheva's paradigm: *Tiuremnaia pressa* (1918–27), *Pechat' velikikh stroek kommunizma* (1928–34), *Lagernaia pressa* (1935–55).

38   More building sites were created after the foundation of the BBK, though the above-mentioned were by far the largest ones. BAM was an acronym for *Baikalo-Amurskaia Magistral'*, one of the biggest railway networks in the Soviet Union.

39   Shenberg, p. 77 and Driakhlitsyn, p. 128.

in which the administration congratulated the editorial board on the brilliant layout of the *Ostrovok*.[40] Its contributors, chosen from both the prisoners and the *krasnoarmeitsy*,[41] aimed to appeal to an audience that included both groups. The reviewer was harsher on another *stengazeta*, the *Severnyi Pioner*, which was the official organ of the Marxist circle of the 5th SLON office based on the island of Kond. In the author's view, its editorials were politically ineffective, its scientific column was poor, and its caricatures and drawings were weak in their content.[42]

The rapid establishment of a publishing system in the camp is indicative of the administration's interest in it. This interest was, of course, ideologically grounded, but it was probably also fuelled by the effort made by the administration in proposing a new communist Solovki to rival that of the monastery and, simultaneously, 'overwriting' the cultural tradition of the monastery where the camp had been set up. The *Solovetskii monastyr'* had been a flourishing cultural centre where important manuscripts, chronicles, and *Zhitiia* (lives of saints) had been handwritten for centuries. However, the 1923 fire had destroyed most of them along with the monastery's typolithography.[43] The lack of typewriting machines persuaded the administration to look for machines and tools, so that the camp's print culture might flourish.[44]

The Journal SLON-Solovetskie Ostrova

While waiting for the delivery of professional machines, the management opted for the tentative launch of a monthly journal, which was also called *SLON*. The first issue required a huge effort. The secretary of the editorial board, Shenpolenskii, worked for three days around the clock to get it to press.[45] Typographical work was performed by Isaac Slepian, who had been imprisoned for forgery and who had thus some skill in the use of typewriting machines, even rudimentary ones.[46]

The first issue came out in March 1925. It was quite a rough copy, typewritten and interspersed with photographs glued to the pages.[47] Owing to the lack of

40   'Bibliografiia', *SLON*, 9–10 (1924), p. 110.

41   A common epithet for party guards or guards who were also members of the OGPU. It means 'Red Army soldier'.

42   'Bibliografiia', *SLON*, 9–10 (1924), p. 110. For a more detailed description of the *stengazety* see Fischer von Weikersthal, pp. 179–84.

43   At the beginning, all that the SLON typographers could use was a lithographic stone. Driakhlitsyn, p. 128.

44   Even when typewriting machines arrived and the SLON publishing system was fully operational, the chekists did not give up their traditional camp *stengazety*. Though the list of internal press organs provided by Gorcheva does not include publications issued on the Solovki islands, Kiselev-Gromov talks about the chekists' *stengazety* in his memoir, however he does not specify any name or title.

45   See Shenberg, p. 67.

46   As Felicitas Fischer von Weikersthal recalls in her monograph, Slepian in the SLON press was described as a skilled lithographer (Fischer von Weikersthal, p. 225). However, at the beginning of the chapter devoted to the SLON press Shiriaev explains how his work as a typographer was a cover for his criminal activity, see Shiriaev, pp. 129–30. One thing does not exclude the other.

47   Copies of the *SLON* were available in the GARF in the period 2008–2010. As noted in the introduction (p. 12), when I tried to work on them in 2013 and 2014, I was told they had been moved

FIG. 3.1. Isaac Slepian. From the DVD *Solovetskaia Pechat'*

materials, only fifteen copies were printed. In the opening editorial, an anonymous member of the *Kul'turno-Vospitatel'naia Chast'* (known as KVCh, Cultural and Educational Department), which was officially indicated as being the publisher,[48] maintains that the objective of the journal is to 'hold up a mirror to the Solovki islands and to their inhabitants'. Besides, he hints at the willingness to represent life on the Solovki as something new, opposed to the life at the monastery, which had by then been relegated to the *'oblast' istorii'*.

> The Solovki are no longer the former Solovki. The monastery and the monks
> are part of history. The Solovki prison camp is the present, the hope for the
> future. [...] And so the purpose of our journal is to cast light on this new life of
> the Solovki islands, to introduce its creators and participants.[49]

to another office, but no one from the State Archive could tell me where they were. I hope these rare documents will be made available soon to researchers.

48   The real publisher was, in fact, the Vospitatel'naia-Trudovaia Chast', but the office changed its name so many times that throughout the present research it will be referred to as the KVCh — an acronym for *Kul'turno-Vospitatel'naia Chast'*, a term which is commonly used in the history of the Gulag.

49   [Соловки перестают быть прежними Соловками; монастырь, монахи — область истории; Соловецкие лагеря — действительность, надежда на будущее. [...] И вот осветить эту новую жизнь Соловецких островов познакомить о ее созидателями и участниками и

Rather poor in both form and contents, the first issue of *SLON* raises some questions about the KVCh's hasty move. If, on the one hand, the KVCh badly needed to show its achievements, on the other hand, it is hard to say why the first issue was not postponed — new printing equipment was about to arrive and it would immediately improve the layout and quality of the journal. The KVCh's impatience might only be explained by the parallel development of new, non-orthodox camp cultural activities — in particular the establishment of a camp theatre.

In fact, the Solovki theatre was created well before the official establishment of the camp. Its first performance, a play by Miasnitskii, was staged at the SLON on 23 September 1923.[50] The theatre was an initiative of G. I. Nikitin, an amateur actor who had been formally allowed to set up a company.[51] Nikitin was eventually supported by other amateurs, until Sergei Armanov[52] took over, injecting much needed life into the company. Shiriaev describes Armanov as a man without talent who was nevertheless extremely passionate about drama.[53] Though the history of the Solovki theatre in *Neugasimaia lampada* is rather fictionalized, Armanov's crucial role in the implementation of theatre activities, described in Shiriaev's book, is confirmed by other sources.

The first SLON actors worked in rather extreme conditions. They were allowed to use the sacristy of the Assumption Cathedral, one of the few places that had survived the May 1923 fire. Actors would meet in the evening after a day (that is, ten to twelve hours) of forced labour. Rather than going to bed, they would rehearse and then wake up, exhausted, the next morning only to start working again. For this reason, many of them were so worn out that they finally gave up. What helped those who endured this exhausting routine was the opportunity to give their detention a cultural meaning and to escape from everyday life at the camp. They were also willing to take the edge off their fellow inmates' misery. When they were told that the management would be their only audience, some of the performers were about to give up the stage.[54] The theatre directors consequently went to the camp commanders, and prisoners were finally admitted to watch the plays, which included Miasnitskii's works as well as turn-of-the-century plays and melodramas.[55]

The theatre was therefore launched long before the establishment of the KVCh. While the camp's official re-educational and cultural section was being set up, the company was already working on its pre-revolutionary repertoire and was powerful enough to get the administration's permission to have prisoners as an audience. This situation probably accounts both for the rapid establishment of the *SLON* journal

является целью нашего журнала]. 'Ot redaktsii', *SLON*, 3 (1924), p. 2.

50   Kuziakina, p. 48. Miasnitskii was the stage name of the playwright Ivan Baryshev (1854–1911).
51   Unfortunately, there is no more biographical information on Nikitin.
52   Real name: Ivan Andreevich Armanov.
53   Shiriaev, p. 63.
54   The episode is mentioned by Shiriaev (p. 64). However, as seen above, he tended to fictionalize facts, so the information might not be fully accurate.
55   Chekhov's *Uncle Vania* and Ostrovskii's *The Storm* were the most performed plays. See Kuziakina, pp. 49–50.

FIG. 3.2. The cover of the *SLON* designed by Lendvai. From the DVD *Solovetskaia Pechat'*

and for its underlying ideological rigour — an aspect which affected its readability, despite the director's apparent effort to improve it in the following issues.

By the time the second issue of the *SLON* came out (April–May 1924), the available technology had improved and circulation rose to fifty copies. When a competition was announced for the cover image, prisoners flooded into the newly established editorial office with quite bizarre drawings, most of which represented elephants.[56] The winner was a drawing by the *'plakatnyi master'* Lendvai,[57] showing sheaves of wheat with a sickle and hammer, a pile of books at the bottom of the page and a luminous sun in the background. Lendvai's use of obvious symbols represents the editorial line of the *SLON*, which exploited well-established Communist ideals of labour and culture as the path to a 'bright future'.

Both chekists and prisoners took part in the writing and editing of the *SLON*. As happened in the contemporary camp or prison press, the former usually wrote the editorials and the ideological articles, whereas the latter performed journalistic activities, although this was not a strict rule. The journal was divided into different sections (*otdely*). The general section (*Obshchii otdel*) and the socio-political section generally hosted 'ideological preaching'. Their regular contributors were the KVCh head Vas'kov, whom both Shiriaev and other memoir writers depict as a rough man,[58] A. F. Nedzvetskii, and, most significantly, Tiberius Tver'e. He was the only prisoner allowed to write ideological articles — and ultimately an ungifted prose writer. The *krasnoarmeitsy* normally contributed also very long and very tedious reports on camp labour, which occupied the largest section of the journal.

The journal included other, far more interesting, sections, among which were sections run by the *uzniki* (prisoners), such as the literary section (*literaturnyi otdel*). One of the KVCh's primary goals was to promote the education and re-education of 'criminal elements', who would, it was hoped, become the new 'socially close *intelligentsiia*'. 'Converted' elements consequently had to be opposed to the bourgeois *intelligentsiia*, whose theatre activities earned its members privileged positions.[59]

In the summer of 1924 Makar Borin, a famous actor whose reputation had spread across the southern region of the Soviet Union, was sent to the Solovki. Borin took up the reins of the camp theatre, which in the meantime had broadened its repertoire to include musical intermezzos, dances, and comedy sketches. After some months, actors, costume designers, set designers, and make-up artists were exempted from work requirements. The SLON theatre thus rapidly became a real and well-grounded theatre, with professionals who were fully committed to drama. As a consequence, the quality of its performances increased dramatically. The company welcomed new actors and theatre professionals coming from Moscow, Leningrad, and other cities in the Soviet Union, as well as common criminals (*ugolovniki*) and even former prostitutes.

---

56   In Russian the word 'slon' means 'elephant'.
57   Driakhlitsyn, p. 129.
58   Shiriaev, p. 39.
59   The term 'bourgeois' is somewhat misleading, but it was widely used in the camp press and consequently it will be adopted here.

Theatre activities obviously forced the KVCh to make the re-education of prisoners more visible through the use of the camp press. To some extent, the 'bourgeois-*intelligentsiia*' theatre productions were actually carrying out a sort of 'spontaneous re-education' — while performing classics from the Russian theatre repertoire — which the audience, including the administrative directors,[60] could witness every day. As a consequence, the KVCh editorial board tried hard to suggest ideologically charged repertoires which celebrated 're-educational values'. However, artistic quality and the fulfilment of explicitly re-educational tasks were shown to be incompatible by the low quality of much of the material published in the *SLON* journal. Only the representatives of the *intelligentsiia* were able to lend the journal new depth. Foremost was Nikolai Litvin, who published the first passages of his novel *General'skii grekh* (The General's Sin)[61] in it, and who gradually became the most prominent representative of the Solovki journalists. Additionally, an extremely well-educated prisoner, professor Vladimir Krivosh-Nemanich, published his translations of Chinese and Persian love epigrams[62] and contributed several articles to the scientific-popular section (*Nauchno-populiarnyi otdel*), of which he was in charge.[63]

The chekists generally controlled the organization of the economic section as well as the section devoted to camp life, where the prisoners' habits and their activities, including educational activities, were investigated. Judging by their contents, two columns were apparently controlled by the chekists: *Krasnaia doska* (Red Board) and *Chernaia doska* (Black Board). Despite the light implications of the title, both represented the dark side of camp life. The 'good vs. bad' game divided prisoners into the 'good' workers listed in the *Krasnaia doska*, who were skilful enough to earn prizes or sometimes even remission of sentence, and the 'bad' workers listed in the *Chernaia doska*, who were punished and sometimes even sentenced to death. A passage from the 6th issue (August) reads:

> For beating prisoner BERENBAUM Aaron and for causing him severe physical injuries, the Solovki prison camp prisoners: MUSEYKO I.A., SUSLIK I.K., KUCHEROVSKY M.M., PINSKY M.A., PINSKY I.A., BELOUSOV A.P. and LIMAREV I.M. are condemned by the OGPU board following the 18 August 1924 resolution to EXECUTION. The sentence was carried out on the Solovki islands on 1 September of the current year.[64]

Parallel to this section were comic pieces and satirical sketches, which foreshadowed

---

60   The former had the privilege of sitting in the front row, whereas prisoners who managed to attend the *postanovki* normally sat in the back row.

61   Litvin published it in the number 7–8 of *SLON*. Unfortunately, I was not able to find this issue. The report about his publication is in Driakhlitsyn's article.

62   Vladimir Krivosh-Nemanich, 'Proiskhozhdenie pis'ma', *SLON*, 4 (1924), 47–48 (p. 47).

63   See Fischer von Weikersthal, p. 205.

64   [За избиение заключенного БЕРЕНБАУМА Аарона и нанесение ему тяжелых телесных повреждений — заключенные Соллагерей: МУСЕЙКО И.А., СУСЛИК И.К., КУЧЕРОВСКИЙ М.М., ПИНСКИЙ М.А., ПИНСКИЙ И.А., БЕЛОУСОВ А.П. и ЛИМАРЕВ И.М. — приговорены коллегию ОГПУ — постановлением от 18-го августа 1924 года к РАССТРЕЛУ. Приговор приведен в исполнение на Соловецких островах 1-го сентября с.г.]. 'Krasnaia i chernaia doska', *SLON*, 5 (1924), 54.

the acts of 'cultural resistance' that prisoners organized by using their only weapon — ink. Whereas some texts and vignettes were quite innocuous, others were explicitly critical of the camp management. In his *Encyclopaedic dictionary of Solovki humour*, Tiberii (a pseudonym of Tiberius Tver'e), who was generally close to the camp administration, gave vent to 'black humour' about the abuses and vexations prisoners had to endure:

> RECIDIVIST THIEF — A prisoner with solid professional education and practical experience.
> [...]
> MOSQUITO — One of the Solovki internal enemies; it occupies the fourth place after the *kaery*, xxx[65] and the cook.
> KAER[66] — A prisoner who was sent to the red islands in the White Sea for his black deeds.
> [...]
> INFORMANT — [...] Therapy: a trip to Kond Island.[67]

This brief entry mentions some of the tortures the commanders inflicted and takes issue with the distinctions drawn between 'socially close' and 'socially dangerous' prisoners. Moreover, it speaks about the existence of informers among the prisoners. Whereas most probably Tiberius did not deliberately mean to expose the dramatic episodes of camp life, satirical vignettes conveyed criticism much more openly. A vignette entitled *Na balanakh. Nashi udarniki*,[68] for example, depicts the average working day of labourers engaged in logging.

In the first frame to the left, a guard in chekist guise rather rudely wakes a prisoner up at 5 a.m.; the right-hand frame depicts the roll-call, which takes place from 6 a.m. to 8 a.m. In the central, larger frames two prisoners are seen carrying heavy logs on their backs and crawling back to the camp, totally exhausted. In this way, just a few scenes conjure up the lives prisoners had to lead: they were harshly treated from the very moment they woke up, they were forced to stand for two hours in the freezing cold morning and were subjected to hard labour for hours, after which they were so tired that they would find it difficult to go back on foot.

Another 'comical' vignette published in the same issue evokes the harsh fate that awaited the SLON prisoners, some of whom are seen walking along a thin rope between a tower of the Solovki monastery and the Sun of Future and Freedom. A big fish, seemingly a shark, observes them (a rather bizarre detail considering the latitude, it clearly conceals a hidden meaning). In the sea are some rocks on which

---

65   The word is illegible in the copy I have consulted.
66   See list of abbreviations.
67   [ВОР-РЕЦИДИВИСТ — Заключенный, имеющий солидное профессиональное образование и практический стаж.[...]КОМАР — Один из Соловецких внутренних врагов; занимает четвертое место после каэров, xxx и повара.КАЭР — Заключенный, попавший за черные дела на красный остров в Белом море.[...] СТУКАЧ — [...] Лечение: командировка на Кондостров.] Tiberii, 'Solovetskaia entsiklopediia (prodolzhenie)', *SLON*, 4 (1924), 60. Kond Island is in the White Sea. It became one of the Solovki camp departments. *Stukach* means 'spy, informant'. See Rossi, pp. 396–99.
68   Published in the sixth 1924 number of *SLON*. The expression *udarniki* refers to 'shock workers', whose food rations increased depending on the amount of work they did.

FIG. 3.3. The vignette *Na balanakh. Nashi udarniki*. AAS

the words 'Sekirka', 'solitary confinement', and 'sentence extension' are visible. The vignette depicts four prisoners: two of them are falling into the sea, a third prisoner has just begun his walk along the tightrope, and the fourth is on the tightrope, close to the end. The perspective is skilfully realised. In the foreground, a prisoner has just started walking, while in the background a prisoner has almost reached the end of the rope. The focus is all on the prisoner who just started. He is trembling. By contrast, the prisoner we see walking towards the Sun of Freedom is far away from his fellow inmates. Most significantly, nobody has reached the tower of freedom. This use of perspective highlights the conditions experienced by the prisoners who fell[69] there by the hundreds; the image is charged with symbolic significance, and might be a case of Aesopian use of text and image.

While the journal *SLON* went through difficulties, the increasing success of the camp theatre far exceeded expectations. Theatre activities were flourishing. The repertoire had developed a wide range that included works which had officially been blacklisted by Glavlit, works which referred back to pre-revolutionary years, such as Ostrovskii's, Gogol''s, and Andreev's plays, and even abridged versions of Dostoevskii's *The Idiot*. Moreover, theatre activities were enjoyed by the

---

69   As in other languages, the Russian for 'to fall' (*past'*) is also a synonym for 'to die'.

FIG. 3.4. The vignette *Iz nashikh aforizmov*. AAS

administration's cadres and by the overseers, for whom the plays — together with heavy drinking, card games and other vices — relieved the hard winter nights.

Because it had to meet the requirements imposed on camp publications, the *SLON* journal was not able to meet its objective of 'holding up a mirror to camp life'. Driakhlitsyn mentions a debate in which the members of the camp administration recognized that their plans to re-forge 'proletarian' culture by re-educating criminals had failed. As a result, they expressed their misgivings about the future development of the journal, which seemed clearly inadequate.[70]

A radical change coincided with the arrival in December 1924 of what in Solovki camp jargon was called the *amerikanka*, i.e. a top-quality American typographic machine. The machine had long been needed by the USLON, and it was assigned to the expertise of Slepian, who had personally chosen it. The circulation of the 9/10 1924 issue of *SLON* rose to unprecedented levels[71] and its quality was impressive. Now that the typographic machine was available, the camp directors decided to turn over a new leaf and changed the journal's name to *Solovetskie Ostrova*.

Change was by no means limited to the title. The very first issue of the *Solovetskie Ostrova* was remarkably different from the *SLON*. The *Chernaia doska* section had been deleted and the *Krasnaia doska* was reduced to a short page (only two prisoners are mentioned, without the typical photographs and portraits that had been included until then). Vignettes and caricatures had both disappeared. Interestingly, the editorial of the first 1925 number of the *Solovetskie Ostrova* does not even refer to the title change and insists on referring to the journal as the *SLON*.[72] After celebrating the fortunes of the previous journal, the editorial mentions the increased

70   Driakhlitsyn, p. 129.
71   That is, about 200 copies. Driakhlitsyn, p. 130.
72   'Ot redaktsii', *SO*, 1 (1925), 3.

FIG. 3.5. The typography of the SLON. AMM

'Marxistization' of the contents which is, in fact, nowhere to be found, since the new journal actually includes fewer political texts and more literary or cultural articles.

These first signs of change in respect to the experience of the *SLON* were followed by that of the second issue, which probably contains the editorial that should have been published in the previous number, as shown by the hints at the title change and at the different organization of the sections.[73] In it, no mention is made of 'Marxistization'; in fact, the author explicitly asks the prisoners to cooperate with the editorial board. This shows that a total change in perspective had taken place, from the Marxist propaganda provided by the chekists to the editors' appeal to the prisoners to collaborate in greater numbers in the journal's production.

The March 1925 issue of the *Solovetskie Ostrova* introduced a completely new way of organizing the different sections. In the first place, the journal opened with the literary section which ran for up to twenty pages.[74] In the second place, the political section ran for no more than fifteen pages, while the scientific section had more space than before, and centred on the technical-scientific aspects of the SLON economy. Finally, Nedzvetskii was totally downgraded: his serial article *Politicheskoe obozrenie* (Political Overview), which used to be one of the main articles of the *SLON*, was transferred to the back page of the new journal.

---

73   'Bez nazvaniia', *SO*, 2 (1925), 3.
74   It is worth noticing that the last issue of the *SLON* included 17 literary pages out of a total of 111. In the March 1925 issue of the *Solovetskie Ostrova* the ratio was 20:85.

The new look of the *Solovetskie Ostrova* and its new editorial line was fully confirmed in the 4/5 issue of 1925. The opening *literaturny otdel* was coupled with the creation of an 'ethnographic' section that included all the scientific articles ranging from economy to biology and history. This new ethnographic section became by far the largest section of the journal. By contrast, the socio-political section included only two strictly political articles, while the remaining contributions described prisoners' life in the camp. Articles ranged from an analysis of the *shpana* songs[75] to reflections on prisoners' poetry.[76] Nedzvetskii's column had disappeared, and only Tiberii survived the reshuffling of the editorial board, although his article was not at all influential.[77] Foreshadowed by the eloquent deletion of the *Krasnaia doska* in previous issues, a purge of the editorial board of the *SLON* had taken place.

Why did the substance of the official camp publication change so much? Early in 1925, cultural turmoil inside the camp once more reached its peak. The theatre had experienced such unexpected demand that the rooms which usually hosted the plays could no longer hold the audience. This led to the creation of a new building for the performances in 1926.[78] Moreover, several 'artistic trends' had been established — a most extraordinary fact, considering the living and working conditions of prisoners. The '*KhLAM kollektiv*',[79] born from a former section of the 'Theatre of the first Department',[80] was founded by representatives of the *intelligentsiia*. Its promoters wanted to introduce 'new' plays and staged performances that looked back at different, otherwise declining cultural models, such as Western dances. *KhLAM* was so successful that the KVCh immediately battened down the hatches by supporting a new *kollektiv* formed by common criminals, called the '*Svoi*'.[81] Although they were enthusiastically performed and directed by rather talented individuals like Ivan Panin and Aleksei Chekmazov, the *Svoi* plays would never bear comparison with the *KhLAM*.

In addition to founding *KhLAM*, the camp *intelligenty* played a major role in other cultural initiatives. A library was opened in 1924, in which some of them were steadily employed and which boasted officially censored books.[82] Early in 1925,

75   Boris Glubokovskii, 'Pesni shpany', *SO*, 4–5 (1925), 57–60. The expression 'shpana' usually referred to prisoners charged with common crimes, especially violence; more generally, it was the common phrase for 'gang'.

76   A. Akarevich, 'Poeziia zakliuchennykh', *SO*, 4–5 (1925), 45–47. A. Akarevich was one of Shiriaev's pseudonyms.

77   Tiberii, 'Byt zakliuchennykh', *SO*, 4–5 (1925), 47–49.

78   This theatre had a capacity of 700–800. See Rozanov, *Solovetskii kontslager' v monastyre*, II, 17.

79   The expression, which literally means 'trash', is, in fact an acronym for *Khudozhniki, Literatory, Artisty, Muzykanty* ['Painters, Writers, Artists, Musicians'].

80   Several theatres were set up at the SLON. Most of them were amateur theatres. The 'Theatre of the First Department' was the most important among them.

81   In criminal camp jargon, the expression refers to thieves, though in Russian *svoi* means 'trustworthy people'. For a more detailed description of how the *Svoi* collective was created by the KVCh, see later in this chapter, p. 119.

82   On libraries in Soviet concentration camps, see Ikka Mäkinen, 'Libraries in Hell: Cultural Activities in Soviet Prisons and Labor Camps from the 1930s to the 1950s', *Libraries and Culture*, 28 (1993), 117–42.

FIG. 3.6. Aleksandr Ivanov during the profanation of the relics of
St. Savvatii and St. Zosima for the Antireligious museum. AMM

a museum was soon to be established.[83] Officially regarded as an 'anti-religious'
institution (it was run by the chekist Vas'kov),[84] it was always controlled by
the *intelligenty* who, while formally supporting antireligious propaganda, saved
numerous religious finds from sure destruction.

Despite its distinctive character, the success of the SLON 'bourgeois' culture has
never been thoroughly investigated. The very creation of camp culture was the result
of insufficient control by the organs that had been established to promote it. The
theatre was founded well before the establishment of the KVCh and immediately
developed beyond all expectations. It seems likely that prisoners and camp guards
shared a common interest in the theatre's success, although there is little evidence
of such complicity. Both groups took part in the selection of the repertoire, which
maintained a balance between pro-Communist work and classical theatre works:
on the shores of Prosperity Bay,[85] Gor'kii and Lermontov went arm in arm.[86]

83   On 19 July 1925 two departments of the Ethnographic society (see below, p. 108) were founded
to direct both the botanic garden and the museum. The *SLON* refers to a pre-existing botanic
garden, while the museum was a novelty on the Solovki islands (see '19 Iiulia 1925', *NS*, 28 (1925),
4). In 1925, the relics of St Zosima and St Savvatii were profaned.
84   The most famous member of museum staff was Aleksandr Ivanov, whose antireligious activity
won him a none too flattering nickname, *antireligioznaia batsilla* ('antireligious germ').
85   'Prosperity Bay' was the name of the bay onto which the monastery looks; it was also the name
of the harbour on the main island.
86   Performances confirmed a balance between the classics (e.g. Lermontov's *Masquerade*) and
ideologically committed works (e.g. Gor'kii's *The Lower Depths*).

The high quality of the plays and of the actors themselves probably persuaded the SLON directors to turn a blind eye to the theatre programme, therefore allowing non-ideologically committed plays to be produced. The Solteatr plays were as good as Leningrad or Moscow-based performance. When people from elsewhere visited the SLON year after year during official visits, the performances they attended were often by no means in tune with the principles of Communist re-education. What the Solteatr offered was, instead, the *intelligenty*'s selection of song, dance, cabaret, performance, and symphonic sessions. So proud were the camp's administrators of the SLON theatre company, that they did nothing to change the repertoire.

In the end, any attempt to tip the scales in favour of ideological 'purism' failed. The journal *SLON* did not live up to its promoters' expectations and the *Svoi* finally gave way to *KhLAM*. How was this situation possible? The surprising hardships of the 'purists', as well as the outstanding development of *intelligent* culture within the camp, were caused by the actions of Fedor Eikhmans, the highest-ranking patron of the *intelligenty*, who was supported by some members of the KVCh.

Eikhmans's role and character are quite difficult to define. Some depict the Latvian rifleman as a pitiless criminal; others describe him as a mild and understanding chekist. Eikhmans did take an active part in various criminal actions, such as the 19 December 1923 shooting, and he was deliberately silent about all the tortures and the violence that guards inflicted on the camp prisoners throughout his career at the SLON. Nonetheless, his gradual, growing appreciation of and support for the camp *intelligentsiia*'s cultural commitment is confirmed by documents.

Born into a peasant family, Eikhmans was a diligent student who managed to pass university exams even though he had only attended an agricultural school. He was working as a typographer when the First World War broke out. Though weakened during the war years — i.e. when he embraced a political career — Eikhmans's natural affinity for culture resurfaced during his stay at the Solovki camp. We can only assume that he protected 'bourgeois' culture from the founding of the SLON theatre up to 1924. We are indeed sure of his active role in promoting the unique culture of the camp after 1925, thanks to thorough documentation. A first clue to Eikhmans's role is the creation of the SOK (*Solovetskoe Obshchestvo Kraevedeniia*, 'Society of Ethnography of the Solovki'),[87] which he personally directed. He hired professionals to collaborate with him[88] in order to meet both production objectives and to start original research — as was the case of prisoners' studies of the history of the monastery.

Moreover, Eikhmans succeeded remarkably well in striking a balance between the official re-educational façade of the camp and the effective support he gave to the *intelligentsiia*, as can be seen from an article published in the 4/5 1925 issue of

---

87   This was originally a department of the Society of Ethnography of Arkhangelsk. Its acronym was 'SOAOK' (*Solovetskoe Otdelenie Arkhangel'skogo Obshchestva Kraevedeniia*, 'Solovki Department of the Society of Ethnography of Arkhangel'sk').

88   In *Neugasimaia lampada*, Shiriaev says Eikhmans assigned the *intelligenty* different jobs, depending on their education. Shiriaev, pp. 121–22.

the *Solovetskie Ostrova*. The changes the SLON press had undergone, and which Eikhmans himself might have planned as head of the editorial board of all camp publications,[89] most probably caused immense dissatisfaction among the chekists and, in particular, among the disempowered members of the KVCh. Eikhmans decided to write a short, brilliant theoretical essay that defined the SLON future editorial line. His article, 'K voprosu o lagernoi obshchestvennosti' ('On the question of public opinion in the camp'),[90] was a vindication of the *intelligentsiia* disguised as Marxist propaganda.

Using language and tropes drawn from Marxist essay-writing, Eikhmans's article offers an in-depth analysis of the Solovki society, which he compares to an equally extraordinary social situation — that created by War Communism. In a place where social classes are virtually non-existent, he writes, three classes exist *de facto*: the criminals (labourers), the *intelligenty* (educated professionals), and the chekists (commanders and guards). The chekists, he continues, are at the top of the hierarchy; the *intelligenty* are in the middle; and the criminals represent the proletariat. Endowed with distinctive class features and a specific class vision, each class can be seen struggling against the others — a dynamic that perfectly fits Marxist dialectics. Eikhmans does not question the role played by the chekists; nonetheless, he recognizes the *intelligenty*'s superiority over the 'camp proletariat'. He regards this as a merely temporary phase. In 1925, he stated, a battle between different ideas, classes, and opinions was going on at the SLON, one that would eventually culminate in the proletariat's victory. Until then, the *intelligenty* would always be 'superior' to the common criminals.

In his essay Eikhmans further discusses the question of the SLON press, whose role in his view is essentially to mould public opinion. He maintains that the press 'has been feared, ignored, criticized', but he defends it rather passionately by comparing it to the contemporary Soviet press:

> It is clear to all, that the press is the main barometer of social and economic life, that the press exercises an influence on its readers, that its opinion expresses the opinions of the proletarian state.
>
> The Soviet press's criticism is the watchful eye of the revolution. The Soviet press rejects formal optimism, self-satisfied complacency. Indeed, it promotes the necessity of healthy Marxist analysis.
>
> What is the situation then with the expression of the opinions of our public in our press? It is feared, disparaged, ignored, seen as the desire to 'cheat, harm someone'. Work is seen as being undermined by criticism, and everyone tries to escape from it by all possible means.
>
> Yes, criticism for the sake of criticism is useless, it is meaningless noise. But if the press with its critical thought is necessary on the mainland, outside, where socially-dangerous elements are dispersed and the proletarian masses are clearly in the majority, then it is even more necessary here, in the camps, where the prevalent intellectual force in our society belongs to the bourgeois *intelligentsiia* and the *kaerovshchina*.[91]

89   A. Akarevich, 'My. Literaturnye nabroski', *SO*, 3 (1925), 23–31 (p. 23).
90   F. Eikhmans, 'K voprosu o lagernoi obshchestvennosti', *SO*, 4–5 (1925), 38–40.
91   [Всем известно, что пресса — главный барометр общественной и хозяйственной жизни,

Eikhmans's belief in the need for a camp press paved the way for his challenging vindication of the *intelligentsiia*, the very group he claimed to be attacking:

> And only when on our ideological front all the Marxist armies are mobilized, only when sound Marxist analysis will touch every moment of our life, only then we can be reassured that our public will not be under the influence of bourgeois-philistine ideological decay and tinted in unhealthy shades.
>
> Regardless of the relatively high position that the *kaerovshchina* occupies in the hierarchy of the prisoners, regardless of the ideological pressure exerted by the objective conditions of our life, regardless of its famous hardiness, the *kaerovshchina* will be ideologically and administratively constrained.
>
> This is why the watchful Marxist eye and healthy Marxist criticism are more necessary than ever, as they dismantle the prisoners' class system and define the role that the *kaerovshchina* plays in our public opinion, i.e. that of a technically qualified force. Only then it will be possible for us to develop a healthy public opinion.[92]

The watchful Marxist, Eikhmans concludes, must keep an eye on the *intelligentsiia*, which at the end of the ongoing dialectical process will turn into a *tekhnicheskaia intelligentsiia* — a class which society will exploit in order to carry out research on the administrative, economic, and technological life of the camp. As Eikhmans implicitly suggests, until then the *intelligentsiia* will go on playing a major role, and to pursue its 'bohemian lifestyle'[93] within the camp.

что к прессе прислушиваются, что ее мнение является выразителем мнения пролетарского государства. Критика советской прессы — зоркий глаз революции. Советская пресса отвергает казенный оптимизм, самовлюбленное успокоение, а, наоборот, выдвигает необходимость здорового марксистского анализа. Как же обстоит дело с выражением мнения нашей общественности в нашей прессе? Его боятся, его третируют, игнорируют, видят желание „подкузьмить, насолить кому то", видят в критике подрыв работы и всячески стараются избавиться от нее. Да, критика ради критики — ненужна, она пустой звук. Но если на материке, на воле, где социально-вредные элементы рассеяны, а пролетарские массы составляют явное большинство, — пресса и ее критическая мысль необходима, то тем более она необходима у нас, в лагерях, где фактически превалирующей интеллектуальной силой в наших общественных слоях является буржуазная интеллигенция и каэровщина.] Eikhmans, p. 40. The term '*kaerovshina*' refers in general to the *kaery*, i.e. the so-called 'counter-revolutionaries'.

92   [И только тогда, когда на нашем идеологическом фронте будут мобилизованы все марксистские силы, только тогда, когда здоровый марксистский анализ коснется всех пор нашей жизни, только тогда мы можем быть обеспечены, что наша общественность не будет под влиянием идейного буржуазно-мещанского разложения, окрашена в нездоровые тона.Несмотря на сравнительно высокую ступень, которую каэровщина занимает на иерархической лестнице заключенных, несмотря на оказываемое по объективным условиям нашей жизни идеологическое давление, несмотря на известную устойчивость, — она тогда идеологически будет так же ограничена, как и административно.Вот почему, разобрав классовые прослойки заключенных, определив ту роль, которую „каэровщина" — как техническая квалифицированная сила — играет в нашей общественности, необходим, повторяем еще более, чем когда-нибудь, зоркий марксистский глаз, здоровая марксистская критика. Только тогда у нас возможно будет развитие здоровой общественности.] Eikhmans, p. 40.

93   *Bogema* ['Bohème'] is the term referred in the camp press to the intellectuals' relatively easy life at the SLON.

Eikhmans's scheme theoretically culminated in the victory of the 'camp proletariat'. For all practical purposes, it entailed the disempowerment of the KVCh in its role of department devoted to Communist re-education. In fact, Eikhmans justified the *intelligenty*'s cultural prominence and ensured their privileged role in the publishing administration, a role that he further assured with the creation of the SOK and his consequent use in it of the *tekhnicheskaia intelligentsiia* that he personally promoted.

In the same 4/5 issue of the journal, Eikhmans's line of thought was confirmed by a second political article. This one was signed by I. S. Kamenogradskii,[94] who supported the thesis of the USLON director by foreshadowing a process through which the cultural legacy would be gradually handed down to the 'working masses' through the bourgeois *intelligentsiia*'s teaching.

Eikhmans was by no means alone in his actions. Memoirs testify to the active role played by some KVCh leaders in the cultural policies that he started. For instance, Shiriaev maintains that D. Ia. Koganov[95] was the life and soul of the KVCh during the years he spent at Solovki, while the KVCh's official director (the coarse-mannered and violent Vas'kov) was only a puppet in the hands of its 'ideological purist' members.[96] In *Neugasimaia lampada*, Shiriaev described Koganov as a well-educated chekist who actively promoted the activities of the *intelligenty*. Koganov also turned out to be the intellectuals' favourite interlocutor because he was the only guard who grasped the importance and the quality of their ideas, despite his firm commitment to Communist doctrines.[97] Among other supporters mentioned by Shiriaev is Pavel Aleksandrovich Petriaev, the director of the *Biuro Pechati*, whom the writer describes as a connoisseur of literature and at the same time as a careerist — an aspect of Petriaev's personality which Shiriaev also identifies: 'We did not even know if he was a communist or a *kaer*'.[98]

Petriaev's and Koganov's roles were not, however, influential when compared to Eikhmans's much more prominent role. He was responsible for a further range of initiatives aimed at the development of bourgeois culture in the camp. His words are remembered by Shiriaev, who described the cultural élite of the first period of the SLON at greater length than any other memoir writer: 'At Solovki I can find any specialist'.[99] Narrative reliability might be reasonably questioned, but facts largely testify to the substance of Shiriaev's version of Eikhmans: in his role as head of camp administration and cultural patron, Eikhmans created the SOK and hired Krivosh-Nemanich as a meteorologist; promoted the establishment of the *Biosad* ('Botanical garden'); finally, he accepted Koganov's resolution and provided

94   I. S. Kamenogradskii, 'O solovetskoi obshchestvennosti', *SO*, 4–5 (1925), 41–44.
95   Shiriaev calls him Kogan. He most probably confused him with the notorious chekist Lazar' Kogan (1889–1939).
96   Shiriaev, p. 92.
97   In Shiriaev's view, Koganov was a former Communist thinker, well-known among Russian intellectuals. He had been sent to the SLON following disputes with other Party members. We do not have biographical details to support this information. Shiriaev, pp. 69–70.
98   [Мы не знали даже, коммунист он или каэр] Shiriaev, p. 131.
99   [У меня на Соловках любой специалист найдется] Shiriaev, p. 121.

FIG. 3.7. Fedor Eikhmans

the Solovki library with books that had been seized from arrested people's private libraries in Moscow — just to give the Solovki inhabitants the opportunity to read high-quality books.[100]

Another episode quoted in Shiriaev's memoirs explicitly testifies to Eikhmans's role, as well as to Koganov's connivance and to the complaints of the 'purist' members of the KVCh. During a *KhLAM* performance, camp overseers felt insulted by the satirical misrepresentation of their group:

> The supervisors of the labour forces [...] gave Eikhmans an official declaration, accusing the author of the sketch of having undermined their authority. They asked for the author to be severely punished and the piece to be forbidden. Eikhmans ripped up that document. So then they started to systematically harass me and the actors who played the role of the supervisors, giving us the heaviest labour. This harassment was interrupted by Eikhmans himself, after Kogan informed him about their actions.[101]

As revealed by Rozanov's works and Likhachev's notes,[102] Shiriaev's memoirs should not be treated as completely historically accurate because some episodes in the book might have been distorted and are therefore unreliable. Yet Eikhmans's

---

100 Rozanov, *Solovetskii kontslager' v monastyre*, p. 27.

101 [Надсмотрщики рабсилы [...] подали Эйхмансу официальное заявление, обвиняя автора скетча в подрыве их служебного авторитета, и требовали строгого его наказания и запрещения пьесы. Эйхманс порвал этот рапорт. Тогда они начали систематическую травлю меня и изображавших их на сцене актеров, назначая нас на самые тяжелые работы. Эта травля была прекращена тем же Эйхмансом, которому Коган доложил об их действиях.] Shiriaev, p. 98.

102 The St Petersburg 'Fond Likhacheva' contains Likhachev's own copy of *Neugasimaia lampada* on which he wrote notes about unreliable passages in the novel. It is available at the following link: http://likhachev.lfond.spb.ru/Images/avtograf/lampada.htm [Accessed: 24 November 2014].

personality in the book is sharply outlined. Shiriaev further maintains that:

> To Eikhmans's credit, it is necessary to point out that before the establishment of the system of socialist concentration camp slavery by N. A. Frenkel' (before 1926/27), he easily granted everyone who wanted to or was able to work the possibility of developing their initiatives in every sphere of working life.[103]

Konstantin Gurskii's words confirm Shiriaev's impressions. Though he was a SLON prisoner only for a short time, Gurskii first met Eikhmans during the Vaigach expedition and soon realized Eikhmans's interest in cultural activities. Eikhmans tried to create a cultural village even in the midst of a ghastly, frozen desert.[104] Gurskii states:

> Based on the views of the former Solovki prisoners, you could judge him in two different ways, as opinions on him were ambiguous. As is well known, in the twenties, the years when Eikhmans was there, the Solovki were subjected to an unprecedented and bloody outrage and terror. Some of the witnesses refer to Eikhmans as to one of the active participants in imposing arbitrary rule; others (the majority) refute this, speaking of him as a humane and just man, often interceding for the victims of persecution by the Solovki *oprichniki*. Besides, they remembered his strong disagreements with the head of the SLON [...] Nogtev, a particularly violent monster. [...] But in my period at Vaigach, I never heard a bad word about him from any of the prisoners in the group that I happened to go round with. On the contrary, they said that he was an honest and fair commander who never set himself apart from the prisoners...[105]

While memoirs are inevitably partial, it is worth pointing out that Eikhmans's activities are described in several documents, such as the above-mentioned article in the 4/5 1925 issue of the *Solovetskie Ostrova* and in a letter that will be analysed later on. Of course, Eikhmans was quite a controversial man, but his plea for culture and for the role of the *intelligenty* is well-documented. One can argue about the reasons why he behaved like that. However, the sources quoted have to be taken into account: Eikhmans cannot be considered on the same level as figures like Nogtev or Frenkel'.

---

103 [К чести Эйхманса надо сказать, что до оформления Н. А. Френкелем системы социалистического концлагерного рабства (до 1926/27 гг.) он легко предоставлял всем желавшим и умевшим работать возможность развития их инициативы в любой области труда.] Shiriaev, p. 121

104 Vaigach is an island located in the extreme North of Russia, close to Novaia Zemlia. Its winter temperature averages −20° C.

105 [По отзывам бывших соловецких узников, о нем можно судить двойственно из-за разноречивости. Как известно, в эти двадцатые годы, годы пребывания Эйхманса на Соловках, там царил небывалый кровавый беспредел и террор. Одни, свидетели и очевидцы, отзываются об Эйхмансе, как об активном пособнике произвола, иные — большинство, это опровергают, отзываясь о нем, как человеке гуманном и справедливом, часто заступавшегося за подвергающихся преследованию со стороны соловецких опричников, при чем припоминали случай его острых разногласий с начальником 'СЛОНа' [...], — Ногтева, особо жестокого выродка. [...] Но в бытность мою на Вайгаче, я ни от о[д]ного заключенного, в массе которых мне приходилось вращаться, я ничего плохого о нем не слышал. Наоборот говорили, что он честный и справедливый начальник, не чуравшийся заключенных...] AMM, f. 2, op. 3, dd. 15–18, p. 70.

The sixth issue for 1925 of the *Solovetskie Ostrova* adhered quite strictly to Eikhmans's 'official' directives. The section with the most articles was the ethnographic one, which was the realm of the *tekhnicheskaia intelligentsiia*. The political section re-appeared, maybe to placate the most ideologically committed faction of the KVCh; and the literary section was drastically reduced. Even the cover image changed, portraying an impressive red column formed by a hand holding a torch and backed by the dark outlines of the monastery. The drawing was eventually replaced by the red-coloured portrait of a worker throwing coals into a boiler, a locomotive (a reference to the SLON railway network), and the unmistakable Sun of the Future — all recognisable Communist symbols.

In the political section of the sixth issue, T. Kovenskii returned to the question of public opinion, appealing to Eikhmans's reflections on the promotion of Communist re-education and the *Svoi*'s plays as opposed to *KhLAM*'s bourgeois art. Kovenskii did not understand that Eikhmans's article was nothing but a bluff. In fact, the rest of the 1925 issues of the journal would eventually fit the 'hierarchy/pyramid' that the USLON director had previously described, presenting first the literary section, then the ethnographic one, and lastly the socio-political section. Moreover, the first two sections would now be far more comprehensive than the third one, which was reduced. By browsing the journal issues, it is clear to see that, at this point, the ethnographic section was becoming more and more specific and was focusing on the new SLON industrial areas, as the camp expanded into the mainland, into the neighbourhood of Kem', and Karelia.[106] The literary section gained momentum thanks to its excellent contributors and to the feuilleton. Significantly enough, from the December issue onwards the very adjective '*politicheskii*' disappeared from the headlines, and the 'political section' was replaced by a *sotsial'no-obshchestvennyi otdel*, a section that would gradually lose its allocated space.

At this point, some exasperated KVCh leader probably sent a complaint to Moscow. Though this episode is not documented, something of the kind might have taken place because GUMZ, which had always ignored SLON publications because they were subjected to the OGPU jurisdiction, suddenly started to require information about the camp's publications. A short note sent by Vas'kov and Petriaev to the GUMZ on 21 November 1925 reads:

> Confirming with gratitude to have received from you the note on the periodical publications in places of detention, we inform you that from 1 October 1925 we have been sending you one copy of each number of the weekly newspaper *Novye Solovki* and, from 15 January next year, following your request, three copies. Moreover, we will send you from January of the next year the monthly literary-popular, economical and socio-cultural journal *Solovetskie Ostrova*.[107]

---

106 The *Solovetskie Ostrova* started to publish several articles about Karelia or the economic-productive potential of the Russian Northern regions, into which the SLON would soon expand.

107 [Подтверждая с благодарностью получение от Вас справки о периодических изданиях мест заключения, сообщаем, что с 1 октября 1925 г. Вам высылалось по одному экземпляру еженедельной газеты «Новые Соловки» и с 15 января с/г., согласно Вашей просьбе, по три экземпляра. Кроме того, Вам будет высылаться, начиная с января с/г., ежемесячный литературно-бытовой, экономический и социально-общественный журнал «Соловецкие

FIG. 3.8. The cover of the sixth 1925 issue of the *Solovetskie Ostrova*.
From the DVD *Solovetskaia Pechat'*

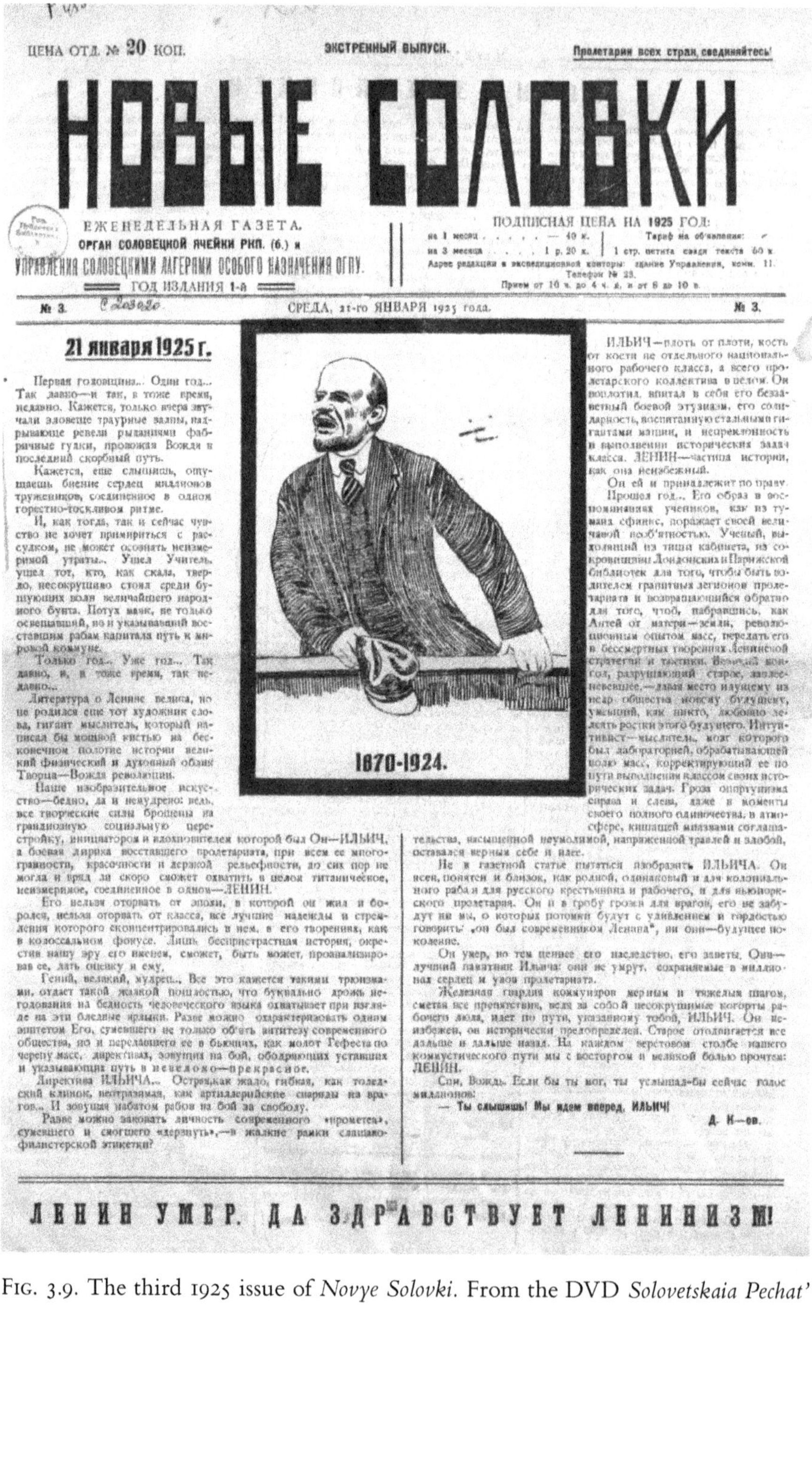

ЦЕНА ОТД. № 20 КОП. ЭКСТРЕННЫЙ ВЫПУСК. Пролетарии всех стран, соединяйтесь!

НОВЫЕ СОЛОВКИ

ЕЖЕНЕДЕЛЬНАЯ ГАЗЕТА.
ОРГАН СОЛОВЕЦКОЙ ЯЧЕЙКИ РКП. (б.) и
УПРАВЛЕНИЯ СОЛОВЕЦКИМИ ЛАГЕРЯМИ ОСОБОГО НАЗНАЧЕНИЯ ОГПУ.
ГОД ИЗДАНИЯ 1-й

ПОДПИСНАЯ ЦЕНА НА 1925 ГОД:
на 1 месяц . . . . . . — 40 к. | Тариф на об'явления:
на 3 месяца . . . . . 1 р. 20 к. | 1 стр. петита сзади текста 60 к.
Адрес редакции и экспедиционной конторы: здание Управления, комн. 11.
Телефон № 23.
Прием от 10 ч. до 4 ч. д. и от 6 до 10 в.

№ 3. СРЕДА, 21-го ЯНВАРЯ 1925 года. № 3.

21 января 1925 г.

Первая годовщина... Один год... Так давно—и так, в тоже время, недавно. Кажется, только вчера звучали зловеще траурные залпы, надрывающе ревели рыданиями фабричные гудки, провожая Вождя в последний скорбный путь.

Кажется, еще слышишь, ощущаешь биение сердец миллионов тружеников, соединенное в одном горестно-тоскливом ритме.

И, как тогда, так и сейчас чувство не хочет примириться с рассудком, не может осознать неизмеримой утраты... Ушел Учитель, ушел тот, кто, как скала, твердо, несокрушимо стоял среди бушующих волн величайшего народного бунта. Потух маяк, не только освещавший, но и указывавший восставшим рабам капитала путь к мировой коммуне.

Только год... Уже год... Так давно, и, в тоже время, так недавно...

Литература о Ленине велика, но не родился еще тот художник слова, гигант мыслитель, который написал бы мощной кистью на бесконечном полотне истории великий физический и духовный облик Творца—Вождя революции.

Наше изобразительное искусство—бедно, да и немудрено: ведь, все творческие силы брошены на грандиозную социальную перестройку, инициатором и вдохновителем которой был Он—ИЛЬИЧ, а боевая лирика восставшего пролетариата, при всем ее многогранности, красочности и дерзкой рельефности, до сих пор не могла и вряд ли скоро сможет охватить в целом титаническое, неизмеримое, соединенное в одном—ЛЕНИН.

Его нельзя оторвать от эпохи, в которой он жил и боролся, нельзя оторвать от класса, все лучшие надежды и стремления которого сконцентрировались в нем, в его творениях, как в колоссальном фокусе. Лишь беспристрастная история, окрестив нашу эру его именем, сможет, быть может, проанализировав ее, дать оценку и ему.

Гений, великий, мудрец... Все это кажется такими трюизмами, отдает такой жалкой пошлостью, что буквально дрожь негодования на бедность человеческого языка охватывает при взгляде на эти бледные ярлыки. Разве можно охарактеризовать одним эпитетом Его, сумевшего не только об'ять антитезу современного общества, но и передавшего ее в бьющих, как молот Гефеста по черепу масс, директивах, зовущих на бой, ободряющих уставших и указывающих путь в неведомо—прекрасное.

Директива ИЛЬИЧА... Острая, как жало, гибкая, как толедский клинок, неотразимая, как артиллерийские снаряды на врагов... И зовущая набатом рабов на бой за свободу.

Разве можно заковать личность современного «прометея», сумевшего и смогшего «дерзнуть»,—в жалкие рамки слащаво-филистерской этикетки?

ИЛЬИЧ—плоть от плоти, кость от кости не отдельного национального рабочего класса, а всего пролетарского коллектива в целом. Он воплотил, впитал в себя его беззаветный боевой энтузиазм, его солидарность, воспитанную стальными гигантами машин, и непреклонность в выполнении исторических задач класса. ЛЕНИН—частица истории, как она неизбежный.

Он ей и принадлежит по праву.

Прошел год... Его образ в воспоминаниях учеников, как из тумана сфинкс, поражает своей величавой необ'ятностью. Ученый, выходящий из тиши кабинета, из сокровищницы Лондонских и Парижской библиотек для того, чтобы быть водителем гранитных легионов пролетариата и возвращающийся обратно для того, чтоб, набравшись, как Антей от матери—земли, революционным опытом масс, передать его в бессмертных творениях Ленинской стратегии и тактики. Великий вождь, разрушающий старое, заплесневевшее,—давая место идущему из недр общества новому будущему, умевший, как никто, любовно лелеять ростки этого будущего. Интуитивист—мыслитель, мозг которого был лабораторией, обрабатывающей волю масс, корректирующий ее по пути выполнения классом своих исторических задач. Гроза оппортунизма справа и слева, даже в моменты своего полного одиночества, в атмосфере, кишащей миазмами соглашательства, насыщенной неумолимой, напряженной травлей и злобой, оставался верным себе и масс.

Не в газетной статье пытаться изобразить ИЛЬИЧА. Он всем понятен и близок, как родной, одинаковый и для колониального раба и для русского крестьянина и рабочего, и для ньюоркского пролетария. Он и в гробу грозен для врагов, его не забудут ни мы, о которых потомки будут с удивлением и гордостью говорить: „он был современником Ленина", ни они—будущее поколение.

Он умер, но тем ценнее его наследство, его заветы. Они—лучший памятник Ильича: они не умрут, сохраняемые в миллионах сердец и умов пролетариата.

Железная гвардия коммунаров мерным и тяжелым шагом, сметая все препятствия, ведя за собой несокрушимые когорты рабочего люда, идет по пути, указанному тобой, ИЛЬИЧ. Он неизбежен, он исторически предопределен. Старое отодвигается все дальше и дальше назад. На каждом верстовом столбе нашего коммунистического пути мы с восторгом и великой болью прочтем: ЛЕНИН.

Спи, Вождь. Если бы ты мог, ты услышал-бы сейчас голос миллионов:

— Ты слышишь! Мы идем вперед, ИЛЬИЧ!

Д. К—ов.

1870-1924.

ЛЕНИН УМЕР. ДА ЗДРАВСТВУЕТ ЛЕНИНИЗМ!

FIG. 3.9. The third 1925 issue of *Novye Solovki*. From the DVD *Solovetskaia Pechat'*

This means that GUMZ's request for information about publishing in Soviet camps, written in 1924 and mentioned earlier,[108] was forwarded to the SLON only in the following year. Until that time, the Solovki camp had never been mentioned, not even in the inquiries and communications that GUMZ sent to the Arkhangel'sk province, to which the Solovki islands then belonged administratively.

Rather significantly, in the note Vas'kov and Petriaev sent back to GUMZ, neither the *Solovetskie Ostrova* nor the *Novye Solovki* were defined as 'political publications'. This detail may have played an important role in the ongoing battle around the Solovki camp press, which the second publication mentioned in the note, the weekly newspaper *Novye Solovki*, made more urgent.

The Newspaper Novye Solovki

The early months of 1925 saw the publication of another important camp publication, the mass-circulation weekly *Novye Solovki*. The creation of *Novye Solovki* was apparently due to the presence of intellectuals who could cope with that undertaking. In Shiriaev's view, it was Litvin himself, i.e. the most prominent contributor to the SLON publications, who first suggested the launch of a newspaper as a way to counter the *Solovetskie Ostrova*, which had gradually turned into a *tolstyi zhurnal*.[109] The newspaper soon became the KVCh's 'purist' faction's favourite corner, the place where 'traditional' re-education could be safely pursued — the kind of re-education that the *Solovetskie Ostrova* editorial board formally praised but ignored in practice on its pages. If the opening of the *Novye Solovki* was a part of Eikhmans's strategy to let the 're-educators' give vent to their passions, his plan ultimately proved a mistake: the journal provided the 'purists' with the very arena from where they launched the political struggle which ultimately crushed all of them.

The release date of the *Novye Solovki* was 10 January 1925. The third number coincided with the first anniversary of Lenin's death, on 21 January 1925. The eight-page A3 format issue was therefore devoted to the leader of the Bolshevik revolution with contributors chosen from among the most prominent representatives of the camp administration and featuring photographs of Lenin. The Solovki islands were mentioned only in passing on the back page, where the SLON tribute to Lenin was advertised.

In the fourth issue (25 January 1925), the newspaper started to develop its most distinctive and recognisable features. The front page was devoted to important national and international news; the central pages were devoted to the political

Острова».] GARF, f. 4042, op. 4, d. 126, l. 16. The graphic quality of the document was far better than the average quality of notes sent to GUMZ from places of imprisonment. This testifies to the quality of SLON typography.

108 See above, p. 94.

109 The *tolstye zhurnaly* ('Thick journals') were almanacs which played a major role in the establishment of literary and cultural trends in both Tsarist and Soviet times. The adjective '*tolstyi*' referred to their remarkable size: although the camp journal *Solovetskie Ostrova* was not thick, it played the same role as the *tolstye zhurnaly* did in the outside world.

and working conditions in the camp; the back page chronicled the SLON cultural activities and sports.

In the first seventeen issues, the front page included an important column (*Telegrammy*) which — as in other Soviet camp bulletins — focused on both national and international news. Thanks to this, prisoners were constantly informed about developments in a world from which they were excluded. News reported in the *Telegrammy* column ranged from the West's failure to recognize the Soviet Union to the rise of Mussolini, from crime news to the reports of the 'achievements' of the newly-born Soviet State. As part of the camp's re-educational 'mission', the bulletin was regularly buttressed by general political articles.

As mentioned above, the *Novye Solovki* editorial board put an emphasis on political questions. Prisoners' re-education through labour and culture was a prominent topic. The average issue included at least one article in which the tasks, aims, and results of Communism at both the national and international level (and, of course, at a local, camp-related level) were widely illustrated. Regular in-depth columns in the central pages were then devoted to the camp, to its economic output and its political life. News ranged from the results of peat extraction to timber production, from Party activities to the work of the Red Army soldiers.

The back page was a comprehensive introduction to SLON cultural activities. Every issue offered weekly theatre programmes, theatre reviews, suggestions about forthcoming plays, comments on and reviews of concerts, workshops and other occasional cultural events, such as important anniversaries or events connected to the development of the Party. Special emphasis was given to the cinema that occasionally appeared at the camp. Concerts and workshops were typically hosted by the camp club. Regular reports on the fourth page advertised official club activities, including chess tournaments and debates. A sports diary was also included. It listed innumerable activities which took place on the island, from wrestling tournaments to football matches, from track-and-field events to winter sports such as skiing or ice-skating. Accurate weather reports by Krivosh-Nemanich appeared on the back page. In the first issues, the *Poslednee radio* (Last Radio News) column included various news items coming from the latest radio bulletins.

The outside world, however, was gradually set aside. *Poslednee radio* soon disappeared, while *Telegrammy* was downgraded to the third page and finally replaced by the *Mezhdunarodnoe obozrenie* (International Survey), directed by T. Gorskii rather than by Nedzvetskii.[110] Media attention rapidly turned to camp news, where the ideological struggle between the *intelligenty* and the *ugolovniki* was raging, as was the subliminal struggle between the factions within the camp administration which supported the former and the latter.

The foundation of the *Novye Solovki* in 1925 coincided with a peak in tension. Most of the KVCh members were still smarting over the closure of the *SLON*, which had lost its role as the camp's official journal. The success of *Solovetskie Ostrova*, moreover, was *per se* ominous, considering the gradual impoverishment

---

110 The length of the column *Telegrammy* depended on the accessibility of the central newspapers like *Pravda* and *Izvestiia* at the SLON (Fischer von Weikersthal, p. 307).

of its political columns, which were replaced by columns run by the *intelligenty*. Furthermore, in February, the KVCh suffered a double setback. Firstly, *KhLAM*, which the 'purist' upholders of re-education considered to be an act of defiance, was founded. Secondly, and even more seriously, KVCh's ideologically committed journalists were officially disempowered. From the second issue on, the former 'organ of the educational-working section' *Solovetskie Ostrova* became the 'organ of the SLON administration' and the KVCh lost its role in the journal's activities. This exclusion was, *de facto*, a *casus belli* — the almost immediate reaction of the 'purist' faction of KVCh signalled the beginning of a harsh struggle.

The seventh issue of the *Novye Solovki* came out on 15 February — that is, soon after the KVCh had been deprived of its editorial authority over *Solovetskie Ostrova*. A long article dedicated to the recruitment of new *lagkory* (or 'camp correspondents')[111] pointed out the prisoners' duty to serve the Party, even as correspondents — a role which the Party badly needed. A precise strategy underlay that apparently innocuous article. The KVCh members actually wanted to increase the number of both *ugolovniki* and re-educated criminals involved in contributing to the newspaper in order to counteract the increasingly powerful *intelligenty*.

While waiting for recruitment of *lagkory* to be completed, the authors whom the *Solovetskie Ostrova* had pushed into the background and who were instead immediately welcomed at the *Novye Solovki* moved in to attack. Amongst them was Tiberii, who directly attacked the *KhLAM* in the tenth issue of the newspaper (8 March) by defining it as 'ideologically unfit', even though he recognised the quality of its artistic achievements.[112] The article had the desired effect — *KhLAM* immediately came under attack by the administration and the always ambiguous Shiriaev abandoned the collective with a short yet fiery declaration. Published in the fifteenth issue of *Novye Solovki* (12 April), Shiriaev's note conveyed his intention to extricate himself from the debate — a reaction to 'dictatorial decisions' which tainted the activity of the whole *kollektiv*.[113] *KhLAM*, newly born and already under attack, decided to batten down the hatches by appointing a special commission which included Litvin and Shiriaev himself, as revealed in the following issue.[114]

In the meantime, it is more than likely that the KVCh's 'purist' faction decided to establish the *Svoi* in order to counter the creative efforts of the camp *intelligentsia*. Widely advertised in the *Novye Solovki*, the founding of *Svoi* was certainly ill-fated. The company found it very difficult to get going and to stage a show that might match the *KhLAM*'s widely appreciated productions. At the same time, the recruitment of *lagkory* went on so slowly that a further call for contributors was advertised in the twenty-first issue (24 May).[115]

At this point, reviews had turned into a most important arena for pursuing the struggle between *Novye Solovki* and the camp *intelligenty*. While generally

111 'Ugolok lagkora', *NS*, 7 (1925), 3. The expression *lagkor* ('lagernyi korrespondent', camp correspondent) was modelled on *rabkor* ('rabochyi korrespondent', worker correspondent).
112 Tiberii, 'O KhLAMe', *NS*, 10 (1925), 4.
113 B. Shiriaev-Akarskii, 'Zaiavlenie', *NS*, 15 (1925), 4.
114 'Bez nazvaniia', *NS*, 16 (1925), 4.
115 'Bez nazvaniia', *NS*, 21 (1925), 4.

recognizing the *intelligenty* as highly talented artists, the *Novye Solovki* contributors tried hard to cast almost all of their cultural activities in an unfavourable light. The representatives of the *intelligenty* immediately responded to their attacks. Litvin was the most productive *intelligent* reviewer, and he proved extremely impartial in judgement. Nonetheless, the attacks soon moved on to a different, higher level.

Eikhmans's passionate defence of the *intelligenty* in the April/May 1925 issue of the *Solovetskie Ostrova* was followed by a reply in the journal's rival publication. Starting from its twenty-fourth issue (14 June), the *Novye Solovki* launched a series of columns signed by 'Al'm.'[116] and devoted to the SLON art movements. The very first article focused on new artistic forms. Its beginning is quite indicative of the author's intention to undermine Eikhmans's vision:

> The work of the *kul'tprosvet*[117] on the Solovki, obviously, has to be part of Soviet cultural work in general.
> The *kul'tprosvet* is not aimed at amusing and comforting the prisoner, but at educating and creating a Soviet citizen. That's why *kul'tprosvet* is a window on freedom. [...] The importance of *kul'tprosvet* in concentration camps and prisons is huge.[118]

The author further declares the end of the old art, based on the 'market and bazaars', and the beginning of a new art — art as the expression of a collective stance. The author's hint at a 'collective stance', of course, betrays his partiality; unsurprisingly, the back page includes an enthusiastic review of the first performance of the *Svoi* group which had taken place on 6 June.[119]

Al'm.'s second article revolves around theatre in the camp. After criticizing the set chosen by the *KhLAM* and underlining the need for seriousness, the author attacks the very notion of drama which had been formulated by what he defines as *meshchanskie razgovory* (petty bourgeois conversations):

> What should the repertoire of the Solovki theatre be? I only hear voices saying that, obviously, theatre in the concentration camp has to make us happy, amuse us, make us forget the conditions around us etc.
> But let me disagree! I believe that it's precisely the camp conditions that we should never ever forget. Otherwise the reason for the existence of the camps would cease.[120]

As the author suggests, drama should not make prisoners forget their present

---

116 It is, obviously, a pseudonym, although it is impossible to know who used it.
117 Kul'tprosvet is one of the names by which the KVCh, i.e. *Kul'turno-Prosvetitel'naia Chast'* was known.
118 [Работа культпросвета в Соловках, конечно, должна быть частью советской культурной работы вообще.Культпросвет призван не позабавить и утешить заключенного, а воспитать и создать советского гражданина. Поэтому культпросвет — это окно на волю. [...] Значение культпросвет в концлагере и тюрьме огромна.] Al'm., 'Iskusstvo na ostrove', *NS*, 24 (1925), p. 2.
119 Zritel', 'Vecher kollektiva "Svoikh"', *NS*, 24 (1925), p. 4.
120 [Каков должен быть репертуар Соловецкого театра? Слышу одни голоса: — конечно, театр в концлагере должен развеселить нас, позабавить, заставить забыть нас окружающую обстановку и т.д. Но позвольте! Я полагаю, что именно эту концлагерную обстановку мы и не должны никогда забывать и забыть. Иначе бы пропал смысл трудовых лагерей.] Al'm., 'Iskusstvo na ostrove', *NS*, 25 (1925), 2.

FIG. 3.10. The crew of one of the companies of the SLON theatre. AMM

condition. A passage from Gennadii Andreev-Khomiakov's memoirs explains that the emotions of a spectator were in fact exactly the opposite:

> The bell jangles, the music falls silent, the lights go out: the curtain opens and you find in front of you another world. There, if you focus all your attention on the stage, if you immerse yourself in the play so much that you can feel as though you are one of the characters, you can forget about the Solovki and about the fact that you are a prisoner. As long as the stage is open, you can feel like a complete and real human being, living following his own dictates and intelligence.[121]

Al'm's third *ocherk* is on the front page and returns to the theme of exposing the shortcomings of theatre in the camp and, above all, to denounce the 'lack of discipline' of the SLON company and its alleged crisis, provoked by its *khlestakovshchina*.[122] The only solution, in the author's view, is the creation of

---

121 [Дребезжит звонок, умолкает музыка, гаснет свет: распахивается занавес и перед тобой другой мир. Вот тут, если все свое внимание сосредоточить на сцене, если вжиться в пьесу так, что бы почувствовать себя одним из ее действующих лиц — ты можешь забыть и о Соловках и о том, что ты заключенный. Пока открыта сцена, ты будешь ощущать себя полноценным, настоящим человеком, живущим по своему велению и разуму.] Gennadii Andreev, 'Solovetskie Ostrova', *Grani*, 216 (2005), 36–78 (p. 75). Andreev was a SLON prisoner in the years 1927–1929 and later between 1933 and 1935 (see below, p. 324), however there is no reason to doubt that the feelings the prisoner felt during the shows were similar to the ones described by Andreev.

122 A reference to Khlestakov, the main character in Gogol's *Revizor* ('The Inspector General'),

autonomous collectives such as *Svoi*, as well as the development of the *KhLAM*, which Al'm. seems to appreciate even though it is a '*neskol'ko inaia gruppirovka*' (a somewhat different group). It is the *Svoi* drama, however, that wins the author's acclaim. Two more articles by Al'm. focus on literature, as did his previous articles, and are likewise used to attack both the intellectuals and the journalists. Al'm. underlines the qualities of the *lagkor*, whose role is basically to serve the 'majority' (that is, the workers), and suggests a necessary distinction between journalists and writers. Al'm.'s implicit targets are obviously the most prolific authors of the SLON press, Litvin, Shiriaev, and Boris Glubokovskii — in particular Litvin who, when the article was published, was already the most active contributor to the *Novye Solovki* and the author of literary works published in the *Solovetskie Ostrova*.

In the last of his five articles, Al'm. delves deeply into the question broached in the conclusion of the preceding article. He tries to push his arguments on a stage further by suggesting a clear distinction between bourgeois intellectuals and proletarian intellectuals:

> The bourgeois poet is separated from the masses, he has lost his social link to the broad layers of the population, he is lonely, and in that powerful freedom, in that creative despotism, his class instincts find an expression. The elevation of the individual, isolation from society, the tragedy of loneliness: these are some of the basic motifs of bourgeois poetry. [...] The proletarian poet has different duties and conditions. He is fused with the masses by the tenacious concrete of production; he is part of a collective, and not a self-oriented individual, and his images and language are the images and the language that live among the workers, that he has been able to embody.[123]

Al'm.'s arguments are clearly aimed at questioning most of the *intelligenty*'s literary output. At the end of the series of his essays, the author therefore asks the intellectual to 'show the way to proletarian rebirth', thus definitively rejecting the artistic scene set up by the camp *intelligenty*.

Al'm.'s *ocherki* did not, however, result in the victory of the 're-educational' faction. Next to his last article was a short paragraph by one of the directors of the *Biuro pechati* (Press office), Sukhov, who drily recognises that the *Novye Solovki* is generally regarded as of little or no interest at all,[124] while the twenty-ninth issue (19 July) hosts a very positive review of the play *1881*, written by two members of the camp *intelligentsiia*, Borin and Glubokovskii.[125]

---

who is a dull young man who is mistaken for an inspector and revered by the local authorities of a corrupt small town. Other than criticizing the *intelligenty*, this allusion might be critical also of the camp administration.

123 [Поэт буржуазный оторван от масс, он утерял социальную связь с широкими слоями населения, он одинок, и в этой мощной свободе, в этом творческом произволе, сказываются его классовые инстинкты. Возвышение личности, отрешенность от общества, трагедия одиночества — вот некоторые основные мотивы буржуазной поэзии. [...] Иные задачи и иные условия у пролетарского поэта. Он спаян с массой цепким цементом производства, — он часть коллектива, а не самоценная личность и его образы и язык — это язык и образы, которые живут в среде рабочих, но которые он сумел воплотить.] Al'm., 'Iskusstvo na ostrove', *NS*, 28 (1925), 2.

124 I. Sukhov, 'Bez nazvaniia', *NS*, 28 (1925), 2.

125 'Bez nazvaniia', *NS*, 29 (1925), 4. It is one of the many plays written by an inmate, none of which

It is worth underlining that the skirmish had nothing to do with the terrible smear campaigns that were gradually becoming a distinctive feature of literary developments across the Soviet Union,[126] nor can it be compared to the contemporaneous, violent fight for power which involved Stalin, Kamenev, Zinov'ev, and Trotskii in the Central Committee.[127] The SLON press hosted both factions involved in the battle. As a matter of fact, both had their strengths and weaknesses. The 're-educational' faction relied on its strong ideological basis, but its theoretical tenets typically resulted in that rather depressing kind of art that even the administration despised, that had provoked Sukhov's dismissive comment and had also led to the failure of the journal *SLON*. The pro-*intelligenty* faction relied on the bourgeois intellectuals' high-quality cultural work, but it did not fit into the ideological framework underlying the development of the SLON and, more generally, of the Soviet Union. Battles, however, were waged in a relatively quiet way. The attacks were never too harsh and never really questioned the cultural policy which animated the SLON.

Though Party members apparently pulled the strings behind the scenes of this ideological battle, camp prisoners were, in fact, its real champions. As Shiriaev suggests, their loyalty to their fellow inmates made them respectful of the opposite faction even when antithetical artistic notions divided them.[128] Nevertheless, neither faction was spared from criticism. Thus the leading *Svoi* artist Chekmazov wrote an extremely caustic article which set the debate alight:

> Where is the public opinion in the press? 25 articles, 3–4 poems, 25 pseudonyms and, under twenty-five pseudonyms, five or six professional writers. And that's all. [...] If you yell that much about public opinion, then acknowledge that we are not outside of it, so give us space on the pages of the Solovki press![129]

Chekmazov's attack marks the beginning of a period when the *Svoi* (by then a professional company) started to dominate. The rise of the 'proletarian' collective was actually propelled by the results of the recruitment campaign. From their occasional column *Lagkorovskie zametki* (Notes of a Lagkor) in *Novye Solovki*, the *lagkory* launched a relentless promotion of proletarian art and Communist re-education, as the following passage reveals:

> I was feeling like everyone who has just arrived in the camp.
> Frightened, silent, I was scared of moving a step. It felt strange even to see on the Solovki concerts, soirees, etc.

have survived to date.

126 Just to quote an example, Zoshchenko had to endure defamation between the 1920s and the 1930s. He was attacked even more fiercely at the end of the Second World War.

127 See Robert Service, *Stalin: A Biography* (London: Macmillan, 2004), pp. 240–50.

128 Shiriaev, p. 105. Significantly enough, both factions were honest enough to recognise their opponents' qualities.

129 [Где же общественность в прессе? 25 статей, 3–4 стихотворения, 25 псевдонимов а под двадцатью пятью псевдонимами пять-шесть литераторов профессионалов. И только. [...] Если вы так много кричите об общественности, то мы не чужды ей, и дайте нам место на страницах соловецкой прессы!] A. Chekmazov, 'O solovetskom presse', *NS*, 30 (1925), 3.

> At one of these soirees, a man (who later turned out to be the secretary of
> the Military-Political Section) was sitting beside me.
> He talked to me about this and that, and then...
> — You, comrade, should write for our newspaper about camp life.
> — Me? — For the newspaper?!
> Nevertheless, I did write something. As a result, not only did they publish
> what I wrote, but they also gave me a copy of the newspaper as a reward.
> I started feeling differently, I have understood what camp opinion means.
> I started writing more.
> And I am still writing now.[130]

Holding the monopoly on the *Solovetskie Ostrova*, the *intelligenty* defended themselves
in the *Novye Solovki* through Litvin's feuilletons and invitations to their plays. They
even organised a 'press party' which gave their opponents the opportunity to attack
them once more. In the thirty-seventh issue of *Novye Solovki* (13 September 1925),
they were overtly mocked in Tiberii's feuilleton, while Kovenskii defined them as
'the soft *intelligenty*' whom the Solovki press 'does not really need'.[131] Kovenskii also
insisted on the recruitment of the *lagkory* — a detail which reveals that, in fact, the
recruitment campaign was still not really that effective.

Kovenskii's appeal was apparently successful. Starting from the thirty-ninth issue
of *Novye Solovki* (27 September) the *lagkory* had their own regular column, the
Stranichka lagkorov (Lagkors' Page), which came to include texts written by the *Svoi*
representatives, who later were given a proper space, a regular 'nook' (*Ugolok*).

By the end of 1925 the storm was finally over. The *KhLAM* closed down or
was closed down,[132] and the power relations in the newspaper's editorial board
consequently became more balanced. The omnipresent short 'proletarian' *lagkory*
columns were counterbalanced by Litvin's feuilleton on the front page, which
certainly fulfilled its goal: Litvin was honest enough to defend the *intelligenty* in a
sober and elegant way, alternately admiring or criticizing them quite objectively.
His skills surface in a short essay with a title, 'Seven Days that Shook the Solovki',
that refers to Reed's famous book.[133] The article was published in the forty-fourth
issue, which celebrated the anniversary of the October Revolution, and speaks
about the different ways prisoners were treated:

> Stepanov, Brike, Lepesha and Madame Krauze were at the opera house on
> the other side of the little bridge. They had been waiting for this day all year,

---

130 [Была, как все в лагере только приехавшие.Испуганная, молчаливая, боялась шаг лишний
сделать. Странно даже казалось видеть в Соловках концерты, вечера и т.д.На одном из таких
вечеров сидел рядом со мной человек (секретарем ВПО после оказался).Говорил со мной и про
то и про это, а потом... — Вы, товарищ, в газету нашу пишите о жизни лагерной. — Я? — В
газету?! Однако, написала и в результате не только напечатали, а еще газету в премию дали.
По другому я себя чувствовать стала, поняла что такое лагерная общественность значит.
Больше писать начала. — И теперь] Lagkorka M., 'Kak ia stala lagkorkoi!', *NS*, 44 (1925), 3.
131 M. Kovenskii, 'Lagkory za rabotu', *NS*, 37 (1925), 1.
132 Unfortunately, it has not been possible to determine when, and for what precise reasons,
KhLAM was closed down, since the episode was not mentioned in the contemporary camp press, but
the *KhLAM* productions and shows were no longer mentioned in the Solovki camp publications.
133 See John Reed, *Ten Days That Shook the World* (New York: International Publishers, 1919).

and now the day had arrived: Stepanov, Brike and Lepesha were submitting their declaration to the revision commission...

Stepanov started up well:

— Taking into consideration my services to the revolution.

Brike shyly observed: The word is they consider not the services rendered to the revolution, but those during the war.

— Nonsense! The question is all in the form. They will never take these minutiae into consideration!

Brike wrote more modestly:

— Being of proletarian origin by birth...

— I would be more careful: you don't have a proletarian surname.

— That's fine, I'll add something about my calloused hands.

Lepesha wrote perfectly modestly:

— Being the son of an actress and being born, one might say, in a restroom, and being currently in the *kul'tprosvet*...

Stepanov, Brike and Lepesha write. They wait. They pack.

Madame Krauze in the *zhenbarak* also writes. Waits. Packs.

[...]

An uncontrollable, impetuous life was going on all around. In those days, Solovki lived a-là Meierkhol'd. In the administration corridors, the doors would bang. The typewriting clerks were clattering with their typewriters and tongues.

Even those who had been on Solovki for a long time could not remember days like these.

Suddenly, the tension of the atmosphere eased. In the productive areas, the productive excitement settled as a placid dew on projects and schemes:

— They've added fresh forces. Now they are 138. There will be more. The productive plan will not be interrupted.

Stepanov and Lepesha can rest. It's someone else's turn.[134]

---

134 [— И Степанов, и Брике, и Лепеша, и мадам Краузе в лирическом доме за мостиком — целый год ждали этого дня. Теперь время настало: | Степанов, Брике и Лепеша подали заявления в разгрузочную комиссию... У Степанова здорово запущено: | — Принимая во внимание мои заслуги перед революцией. | Брике робко заметил: | — Говорят, те заслуги засчитываются, которые были не перед революцией, а во время войны. | — Ерунда. Дело в форме. Станут они на такие мелочи обращать внимание! | Брике писал скромнее: | — Будучи от роду пролетарского происхождения... | — Осторожнее-бы надо: фамилия у тебя не пролетарская. | — Ничего, я насчет мозолистых рук прибавлю. | Лепеша писал совсем скромно: | — Будучи сыном актрисы и родившись, можно сказать, в уборной, и занимаясь в настоящее время культпросветом... | Степанов, Брике и Лепеша пишут. Ждут. Укладываются. | Мадам Краузе в женбараке тоже пишет. Ждет. Укладывается. | [...] | Кругом катилась неудержимая, буйная жизнь. Соловки в эти дни жили по Мейерхольду. В управленческих коридорах хлопали дверями. Машинистки трещали машинками и языками. | Других дней, похожих на эти, не помнят даже старожилы. | Внезапно напряженность атмосферы разрядилась. В производственных комнатах производственное волнение спокойной росой осело на проектах и чертежах: | Подсыпали свеженьких. Пока 138. Будет еще. Производственный план не будет нарушен. | Степанов и Лепеша могут отдохнуть. Очередь за другими.] En. Li., 'Sem' dnei, kotorye potriasli Solovki', *NS*, 44 (1925), 1. 'En. Li.' is one of the many ways in which Litvin used to sign his articles. The revision commission visited the camp in October 1924. This gave some prisoners the possibility of having their sentence shortened. Mal'sagov maintains that only the common criminals had any benefits from the commission, see Mal'sagov, 'Adksie ostrova', p. 69. For more on the revision commission, see Aleksandr Plekhanov, *VChK — OGPU v gody novoi ekonomicheskoi politiki, 1921–1928* (Moscow: Kuchkovo pole, 2006), p. 144.

As if to seal the official truce between the 'proletarian' faction and the *intelligentsiia*, Tiberii and Armanov (representatives of, respectively, the former and the latter) left the island. Tiberii's departure was ironically celebrated by Litvin in his feuilleton: 'Now Tiberii has been freed from Solovki and I of Tiberii'.[135]

At the end of 1925 Litvin lost his front-page feuilleton, although it is not clear why. The journalist was in disgrace. Sukhov's long acknowledgements at the end of the first 1926 issue — which celebrated the first anniversary of the *Novye Solovki* and which included intellectuals such as Shiriaev — do not mention Litvin.[136] The writer was also excluded from the 'drama commission' which was responsible for discussing and 'filtering' the company's repertoire, and which included both Shiriaev and Boris Glubokovskii.

Glubokovskii, in the meantime, had become a regular contributor to the *Novye Solovki*, where he published his typically accommodating articles. In the early months of 1926, the writer took a keener interest in the *ugolovniki*, in their traditions, language, and habits.[137] His articles reconciled the 're-educative' faction, who regarded him as an upholder of the proletarian cause,[138] and Eikhmans's faction, who regarded him as the perfect spokesman of the *intelligentsiia* — the intellectuals who, in Eikhmans's view as it emerged from his previously mentioned article, were crucial to the intermediate stage leading to the empowerment of the proletariat.

Several articles published in the *Novye Solovki* explained that, in fact, the proletariat was not yet ready to lead the camp's publications. Reviews of the *Svoi* plays were typically rife with harsh criticism, sometimes even when written by the *Svoi*'s own supporters. Contributors often complained about the *lagkory*'s ignorance — a question that had contributed to the closure of the *SLON*.[139] Here is an example of text from a *lagkor*:

> Day. The corridor of the medical centre. The weak light of two little windows barely lights up the ends of the corridor. And in the middle it's as black as pitch. And in this darkness, like spirits, people prowl and hurry, to the tenth company, to the working section, to the medical centre, to the warehouse.
>
> — Hey, brothers, where's room 51? — someone's voice asks god knows who in midair.
>
> By the door, a figure, resting its forehead against the wall, its hasty hands looking for the door, sends into the darkness roars of joyous swearing.
>
> Suddenly, not far away, a frantic female voice goes:
>
> — Oi! ... Ai! ...

135 [Теперь — Тиберий освободился из Соловков, я — от Тиберия] N. Litvin, 'Malen'kii feleton', *NS*, 46 (1925), 1.

136 Sukhov, 'V den' pervoi godovshchiny', *NS*, 2 (1926), 1.

137 Glubokovskii showed his interest in this subject earlier on the *Solovetskie Ostrova*. See below, p. 183.

138 Similar actions were undertaken elsewhere in Soviet camps: the annual instructions from GUMZ to directors of places of imprisonment required that investigations about camp folklore be carried out. Glubokovskii's initiative was thus perfectly attuned to the directive.

139 One of the authors, 'Lagkor Zorkii' ('The watchful *lagkor*'), often complains about this aspect by underlining how poor the education was for 'common criminals'. See Lagkor Zorkii, 'Bez nazvaniia', *NS*, 37 (1925), 4.

And as an accompaniment there is an incomprehensible sound of
knocking:

— Boom! ... Boom! ...

After a one minute long pause, in the darkness the 'collective declamation'
of the same type of Russian heavy swearing hangs in the air.

— Don't despair, *madame*, things go wrong in the dark — a young man
from the tenth company, picking up from the floor the 'jug' with the spilled
hot water, apologizes in a calm and cold way, surely not for the first time.

— You'll get over it. What a pity, though, about the hot water! ...[140]

What lends the passage its comical implications for the SLON reader is certainly
its sub-textual reference to rape, which in the SLON was an everyday practice.
This sort of deficiency had its consequences. Both the *Solovetskie Ostrova* and the
Novye Solovki were regularly sold outside the camp. Readers could even subscribe
to the publications, which could be found in city kiosks. Above all, expatriates and
prisoners' relatives regularly subscribed to them from abroad. These publications
therefore represented a sort of manifesto, used by the camp administration to show
that criticism of the terrible living conditions of prisoners was ill-founded.[141] This
is probably why Eikhmans supported the *intelligenty* in the first place — to demonstrate that camp prisoners enjoyed intellectual freedom and that the horrible camp
conditions denounced by the world did not exist.[142] The above-mentioned passage
and similar articles (such as that published in the forty-sixth 1925 issue,[143] which
dealt with prisoners' self-mutilation) seriously undermined Eikhmans's objective.

The debates regularly published in the *Novye Solovki* also contributed to the
notoriety of the SLON. In particular, the creation of several theatre collectives (the

140 [День. Корридор околодка. Слабый свет двух маленьких окошек, едва освещает концы
корридора. А посредине его — тьма кромешная. И в этой тьме словно духи, шныряют,
торопятся люди, — в 10 роту, отдел труда, околодок, вещкаптерку. | — Эй, братцы, где здесь
51-ая комната? — неизвестно у кого спрашивает в воздушном пространстве чей-то голос. |
Возле двери, упершись в стену лбом фигура, шарят в поисках двери, ея торопливые руки,
а сама она посылает в темноту раскаты мажорнаго мата. | Невдалеке, вдруг, неистовый
женский голос: | — Ой!.. Ай!.. | И в аккорд ему непонятный стук: | Бум!.. Бум!.. | Минутная
пауза и в темноте повисла 'коллективная декламация' того-же русского забористого мата.
| — Не отчаиваетесь мадам, здесь не то впотьмах случается, — неторопясь, холодно,
видимо не первый раз, извиняется юноша из 10-й роты, поднимая с пола 'жбан' с пролитым
кипятком. | — Обойдется. Только жаль вот, кипяточка!..] Lagkor 'Ike', '- Oi!.. Ai!.. — Bum!..
Bum!..', *NS*, 41 (1925), 3.
141 Fischer von Weikersthal has described in detail both the distribution of the SLON press outside
of the camp (pp. 262–70) and the apologetic content of the articles (pp. 315–19).
142 This was suggested by Irina Flige, who believes that mainly political and professional
motivations led Eikhmans to support the cultural development of the SLON. See interview with
Irina Flige (St Petersburg, June 2009). In a later interview (St Petersburg, September 2013) she hinted
at the fact that Eikhmans was not only educated, but also in love with a prisoner, and this might have
softened his behaviour. She took this idea from the daughter of Eikhmans, whom Flige interviewed.
The record of the interview is kept in the archive of Memorial in St Petersburg, see St Petersburg,
AMSPB, 'Interv'iu s El'viroi Fedorovnoi Eikhmans (28.11.1993, Moscow)'. Curiously enough, it was
Eikhmans's love story that inspired Zakhar Prilepin's novel, see: Evgenii Dodolev, *'Obitel'* Zakhara
Prilepina', http://top.oprf.ru/blogs/176/14803.html [accessed 9 November 2014].
143 Sochuvstvuiu, 'Nuzhny ekstrennye mery', *NS*, 46 (1925), p. 2.

Ukraintsy, the *Belorusskie*, and the *KKhP*)[144] raised a furore. In the meantime, the Solovki school of drama was again on the rise. Theatres were being set up all over the archipelago. The brick factory had its own theatre, as did the island of Anzer — and even the terrible 'Golgotha'.

This sudden creative boom intensified the political-cultural debate to such an extent that one of the directors of the *Biuro pechati*, Sukhov, raised his voice. In the fifth issue (31 January 1926)[145] he demanded that debates should end, and in the following issue he suggested the creation of a new series of commissions which were to eventually screen all cultural activities.[146]

Other Publications

In the meantime, the number of camp publications was increasing dramatically. The administration set up more publications in order to meet the requests of a wide and varied reader network. In particular, the idea of creating some newsletters to publish humorous sketches first surfaced in 1924. Though they were forced to endure torture and violence, prisoners actually created songs and jokes that soon fuelled the unwritten cultural reservoir of the *lagernyi byt* ('Camp everyday life'). A first attempt was made in the autumn of 1924, when a magazine of humour and satire, the *Stukach*, was published. The *Stukach*, however, did not go further than the first issue, probably because the administration did not appreciate its articles and texts.

After the launch and the sudden success of the *Novye Solovki*, the camp press needed to diversify its output. Three supplements were consequently added to three separate issues of the *Novye Solovki*, in order to appeal to the tastes of its various readers. The *Solovetskii Bezbozhnik* covered 'antireligious subjects'; the *Radio Solovki* was a bulletin that collected news from the outside world (by then totally excluded from both the *Solovetskie Ostrova* and the *Novye Solovki*); and, finally, the *Solovetskii Krokodil* was a satirical magazine whose title was borrowed from the famous Soviet journal *Krokodil*. Like its forerunner the *Stukach*, however, the 'crocodile' was not appreciated by the administration, which closed it down after the first issue.[147]

Apart from the publication of supplements, the mid-1920s saw a sudden, vigorous proliferation of the *stengazety*, the founding and editorial activity of which were regularly advertised in the *Novye Solovki*. Dozens of *stengazety* were being published across the archipelago, among which were the *Trudovoi Kond* (Kond island), the *Krasnyi Anzer* (Anzer island), the *Muravei* (Kremlin), the *Kustar'*, and the *Muskolomets* (Muksalma island).[148] Each department, too, had its own wall newspaper, such as the *Krasnyi Kirpich* for the brick factory, the *Pervye Shagi* for the women's department. The *Nash Trud* was published by timber labourers; the

---

144 'Kollektiv Khudozhestvennoi Propagandy' [Collective for Art Propaganda].
145 'Ot redaktsii', *NS*, 5 (1926), 2.
146 I. Sukhov, 'Novyi etap', *NS*, 6 (1926), 2–3.
147 In his article on the SLON press, Shenberg states this clearly. See Shenberg, p. 87.
148 The 'o' in *Muskolomets* comes from one of the two variants of the place-name (Muksalma and Muksolma).

FIG. 3.11. The *Solovetskii Krokodil*. AMSPB

tanneries published the *Gashpil'*. The Kemperpunkt was also well equipped and its labourers published the *Na Peresylke*.

Not all of the *stengazety* were typewritten. Many of them were handwritten by prisoners, who did the writing and the drawing. The *stengazety* represented camp life from a privileged perspective. Had they survived, they would have provided most original insights into the history of the Solovki islands and their inhabitants — especially considering that some *intelligenty* who did not participate in the cultural élite were used in general work and probably contributed to the *stengazety* as well.[149]

Of all the SLON publications, the books published by the SOK were the most impressive in terms of quality. From 1926 onwards, the Society of Ethnography started to publish books (especially monographs) dealing with a wide range of questions. The *Materialy Solovetskogo Otdeleniia Arkhangel'skogo Obshchestva Krae-vedeniia* contains works that are still considered remarkably relevant to their respective areas of research. According to some staff of the Solovki Museum, for example, the prisoners' studies of the pre-historical labyrinths of the Zaiatskie island paved the way for further studies of this type of ritual site. Prisoners' research on the flora and fauna of the islands, its water resources, and the climate of the archipelago are still read today. The SOK also published essays on the history of the monastery and on its manuscripts, and numerous, always interesting, works edited by the Krimkab.[150]

To provide a comprehensive account of SLON publications, it is worth mentioning the only book written by a single author ever published by the SLON. This was *49*,[151] a text written by Boris Glubokovskii based on his full-length study of common criminals, in which the multifarious aspects of the criminals' lives are so carefully depicted that the book still represents a most valuable source for both sociologists and Gulag historians.

Too Much of an Open Debate: Eikhmans's Defence and the Closure of SLON Publications

As seen above, GUMZ did not fully realise the extent of this cultural revival until well into 1925. After requesting that the USLON publications[152] be sent to their headquarters, the Moscow officials received some copies of the two prominent

---

149 This is why the editors of anthologies erroneously maintain that some of the poems were originally published in the *Solovetskie Ostrova* or in the *Novye Solovki*. Prisoners would probably connect those poems to the most important camp journals, though they were probably first published in the *stengazety*.

150 Some of the Krimkab works addressed camp press or camp literature (in particular Shenberg's article) and have thus been a valuable source for the present research.

151 Boris Glubokovskii, *49* (o. Solovki: Biuro pechati USLON, 1926), see: Moscow, CRSL, Shrift W333/544 C/A 8510. *49* was the number of the 'Penalty for general crimes' article in the Soviet Penal Code.

152 That is, the *Solovetskie Ostrova* and the *Novye Solovki*. It was actually the SLON administration that edited both journals since 1925. To avoid confusion, the phrase 'SLON publications' has been used to refer to both throughout the present study.

camp journals, the contents of which most probably annoyed them immensely. They were so different from anything that was being published in other Soviet prisons and camps that GUMZ almost certainly demanded an explanation. Of course, that such a developed public opinion should exist was, per se, dangerous and suspicious for Moscow; but that a 'bourgeois intellectual citadel' should be set up in the very 'special purpose camp' created to re-educate 'anti-social elements' far exceeded their imagination and could not be overlooked.

The document in which the GUMZ asked the SLON directors to justify the editorial line of the SLON press has never been found; it is probably part of the camp archive that to date cannot be traced. This is not, of course, mere speculation. We know the document existed because the Moscow officials received a letter from Eikhmans dated 25 March 1926, in which the SLON director took up the cudgels on behalf of the SLON cultural, and more specifically publishing, policies. Apart from Eikhmans, no other prison or camp directors dared to write this kind of letter. Most simply, they wrote short messages, as Petriaev and Vas'kov did in the above-mentioned message dated November 1925. Moreover, the very fact that Eikhmans's plea was written four months after the above-mentioned letter shows in my opinion that his was a reply to a precise question, as the undertone of his note reveals:

> The administration of the Solovki Special Purpose Camps for Corrective Labour of the OGPU publishes the weekly newspaper *Novye Solovki* (second year of publication) and the monthly journal *Solovetskie Ostrova* (third year of publication). Without remarking on the fact that both its literary and technical-publishing work is performed by the prisoners, we consider necessary to draw the attention of the workers of the corrective organs towards the publications of the USLON. The corrective labour policy of the Solovki camps; the educational and enlightenment work, as a method of this policy, consistently pursued in the conditions of the far north including the nearly six month-long period when the Solovki islands are cut off from the mainland; the contemporary Solovki economy, its achievements and incessant growth; the considerable work on the study of the region (and of the Solovki's antiquities) — all of these questions find appropriate coverage in the pages of our newspaper and journal. Both in the newspaper and in the journal a special place and particular attention are devoted to the current life of Solovki. Among the focuses of our publications are prisoners' everyday lives, the different categories of prisoners, the social and journalistic study of their previous lives and the paths that have brought today's forced labourers to Solovki. The prisoners' understanding of the necessity and inevitability of their isolation and the opposite 'non-comprehension' in all its multifaceted manifestations are analysed and represented, in one form or another, both in the newspaper and in the journal. The composition of the prisoners of the Solovki camps is very diverse: from former members of our secret police, to counter-revolutionaries of all kinds and degrees (from ministers of all possible governments to Kornilov's cadets and Cossack bandits) and ending with the so-called 'shpana' — *sorokadeviatniki*[153] — criminal recidivists

153 That is, the prisoners arrested for the 49th article of the penal code. The Chernavins maintain that they were usually sent to work in the forests, although, as seen, some of them enjoyed privileges. See Vladimir Chernavin and Tat'iana Chernavin, *Zapiski 'vreditelia': Pobeg iz GULAGa* (St Petersburg: Kanon, 1999), p. 219.

and prostitutes, sent here under the 49th article of the Penal Code as socially harmful. The variety of those who make up the body of forced labourers, of the observations and sometimes even of the investigative materials relating to them, which portray their behaviour on the Solovki, is covered as fully as possible in the newspaper and in the journal and makes us confident that our newspaper and journal not only represent a body of distinctive penitentiary-criminological informative material, but may satisfy and attract any worker who has to carry out a punitive policy and deal with similar living material. The terms of subscriptions to the publications of the USLON are overleaf.

25 March 1926
Head of the Administration of the USLON
Eikhmans — Deputy Head of the *Biuro Pechati*.[154]

After pointing out the qualities of the SLON press, Eikhmans clearly explains that the status quo is not in danger. The liberal façade hides, in fact, the sound walls of real imprisonment. Eikhmans further underlines the SLON's unique blend of different social classes as well as of socially, culturally, and ideologically different personalities — a universe which in his view needs to be supported rather than criticized. As a result of Eikhmans's argument, what might have been weaknesses turn out to be strengths. At the end of the document, the SLON director seems unable to conceal his pride. The SLON press becomes, in his words, a model for other places of imprisonment and a point of reference for all readers, both in the Soviet Union and (as the last sentence suggests) abroad.

---

154 [Упр.Сол.Лаг. прин.раб.Ос.Наз. ОГПУ издает еженедельную газету «Новые Соловки» (2-ый год издания) и ежемесячный журнал «Соловецкие Острова» (3-ый год издания). Не касаясь того факта, что как литературная, так и техническо-издательская работа выполняются силами заключенных, считаем необходимым обратить внимание работников карательных органов на издания УСЛОН. Исправительно трудовая политика Соловецких лагерей, воспитательная-просветительная работа, как метод этой политики, неуклонно проводимой в условиях крайнего севера и почти полугодовой оторванности Соловецких островов от материка, современное соловецкое хозяйство, его достижения и непрестанный рост, большая работа по изучению края (и Соловецкой старины) — все эти вопросы находят себе должное освещение на страницах н/газеты и журнала. Как в газете, так и в журнале особое место и внимание уделяется текущей жизни Соловков. Быт заключенных, разнообразность категорий, социально-публицистическое освещение прошлого и путей приведших на Соловки нынешних принудиловцев — входят в задачи наших издания. Восприятие принудиловцами необходимости и неизбежности их изоляции, «невосприятие» в его многогранном проявлении является предметом разбора и отображения в той или иной форме, как в газете, так и журнале. Состав заключенных Соллагерей весьма разнообразен: начиная от б. сотрудников наших карательных органов, контрреволюции всех рангов и оттенков (от министров всевозможных правительств до корниловских юнкеров и казачьих бандитов) и кончая, так называемой, «шпаной»-сорокадевятниками-уголовными рецидивистами и проститутками, высланными по 49 ст. УК и как социально вредные. Разнообразие состава принудиловцев, наблюдений над ними а порой и следственных материалов, рисующих поведение их на Соловках, находит возможно полное освещение в газете и журнале и создают нам уверенность, что наши газета и журнал не только представляют собою своеобразный пенитенциарно-криминологический справочный материал, но могут удовлетворить и заинтересовать всякого работника, которому приходится проводить карательную политику и сталкиваться с подобным живым материалом. Условия подписки на издания УСЛОН изложены на обороте. | 25 марта 1926 г. | Начальник Управления СЛОН | Эйхманс — замзав. Бюро Печати.] GARF, f. 4042, op. 4, d. 126, l. 28.

Well-founded though it was, Eikhmans's defence was not unassailable. It did not mention re-education, and instead tackled the question of 'corrective labour policies' in general terms without further explanations of the 'bourgeois' contents of the SLON publications. It underlined the isolation of the Northern camps, only to admit that SLON publications were also sent by mail and sold outside the camp — a question that must have been of major interest to GUMZ, as they most probably asked specifically about the distribution of publications outside the camp, hence Eikhmans's precise answer about the subscription terms. Above all, it did not condemn counter-revolutionary prisoners, but suggested that they should be regarded as useful, not dangerous, individuals — quite a daring suggestion.

Eikhmans chose the worst moment to take this sort of risk. As already suggested, the irresistible rise of Frenkel', who by 1925 had become the head of the Economic Department of the camp and whose theories were already rather successful, was changing the direction of the SLON.[155] What is more, in 1926 Frenkel''s name reached Moscow for the first time, and, on 1 February, the Commission for Qualification of the Central Committee issued a protocol in which they expressed their positive judgement of the former prisoner: 'In the camp he proved to be an exceptional, outstanding worker. Thanks to this, he has earned the confidence and authority of the administration of the USLON. He constantly carries out most responsible work.'[156]

Thanks to this note, Frenkel' had his sentence halved in May 1926. When Eikhmans wrote his report, Frenkel''s rise had already commenced, as testified by the increasing number of articles that the press dedicated to the SLON's economic expansion into the Russian continent — a move that was first proposed by the former merchant's 1925 article. The general guidelines of Frenkel''s economic project have already been underlined. It basically revolved around the elimination of unproductive activities among which were, of course, cultural activities and, more specifically, the camp press with its higher production costs than, say, the theatre. This was soon to have a big impact on the SLON press.

The early 1926 issues of both the *Solovetskie Ostrova* and the *Novye Solovki* reiterated well-established clichés. The former was dominated by literary and scientific essays, while the latter was mostly based on camp-related news, though both were a remarkable arena for internal debates over the class struggle between intellectuals and common criminals. Debates were rekindled by the feuilletons and by the articles of a writer who was particularly harsh towards the *intelligenty*. Writing under a pseudonym (Tsvibelfish'),[157] this author aimed to incite hatred towards the members of the camp *intelligentsiia*, whom he calls 'bisons' or 'idlers' — the useless

---

155 Frenkel''s article in the *Novye Solovki* (see p. 49 n. 52) was published on 7 June 1925.

156 [В лагере проявил себя как исключительный, выдающийся работник, благодаря чего пользуется большим доверием и авторитетом администрации УСЛОН. Работает все время на весьма ответственной работе.] St Petersburg, AMSPB, 'Lichnoe delo Naftalia Aronovicha Frenkelia'.

157 'Zwiebelfisch' is the German word for typographic anomalies in a text or characters printed in the wrong font.

targets of camp re-education:

> The Solovki bisons are a real *Société*. If you have an inherited or acquired gout, if you hope for the liquefaction of the brain, if you are *siusiukaia*[158] and can give many colours[159] to your 'frensh'[160] sentences with proverbs and sayings, if, finally, you do manicures and you sigh about how good the past was, you are welcome to this *Société*.
>
> [...]
>
> If at the Kul'tprosvet there's a historical play, the *Société* comes to look at the 'costumes'.
>
> [...]
>
> They have a 'note':
>
> — Exempted from physical work.
>
> I would suggest that medical board should add:
>
> — Exempted from physical and intellectual work.[161]

The dispute, however, was drawing to a close. The July 1926 issue of the *Solovetskie Ostrova* was its last. Though the reasons are still obscure, the decision to shut down the journal was quite unexpected, as showed by Glubokovskii's tale *Puteshestvie iz Moskvy v Solovki*,[162] which was published in instalments and remained unfinished. Additionally, the *Novye Solovki* continued to publish advertisements for subscriptions to the *Solovetskie Ostrova* when the latter had already been closed. Finally, *Novye Solovki* included articles that revealed their editors' intention to go on publishing and even to improve the printing presses.[163] The closure of the journal is even more difficult to explain when reading the article Mikhail Kol'tsov[164] published in *Pravda* (2 April 1926), an enthusiastic feuilleton on the Solovki press:

> For an ELEPHANT, writing would be an inappropriate activity. The real elephanty[165] thing is to supply ivory from Africa, or, at worst, to devour French bread in a zoological garden. However, our SOVIET ELEPHANT writes, in the truest sense of the word. And even prints. Publishes and distributes a monthly journal! What an incredible country. Here, everything is possible.

158   This onomatopoeic phrase ironically refers to the habit of the camp *intelligentsiia* of speaking French.

159   The author uses a neologism, *opestriat'*, from the Russian *pestryi*: 'multicoloured', 'pied'.

160   The author uses an incorrect spelling of the word 'French' in an ironical way: *fransusskimi* instead of *frantsuzskimi*.

161   [Соловецкие зубры — это настоящее сосьетэ. Если у вас наследственная или благоприобретенная подагра, надежда на разжижение мозга, если Вы, сюсюкая, сможете опестрять свои фразочки 'франсусскими' пословицами и поговорками, если Вы, наконец, делаете маникюр и вздыхаете о хорошем прошлом, — Вы желанный гость такого сосьетэ. | [...] | Если в Культпросвете идет пьеса историческая, сосьетэ отправляется смотреть 'костюмы'. | [...] | У них 'бумажка': | — Освобожден от физических работ. | Я бы предложил Медкомиссии добавить: | — Освобожден от физических и умственных работ.] Tsvibelfish', 'Zubry', *NS*, 8 (1926), 1.

162   Boris Glubokovskii, 'Puteshestvie iz Moskvy v Solovki', *SO*, 7 (1926), 60–73.

163   I. Slepian, 'Bez nazvaniia', *NS*, 29 (1926), 4.

164   Mikhail Efimovich Kol'tsov (1898–1940) was one of the most remarkable journalists in the Soviet Union. He wrote for *Pravda* for almost twenty years. Arrested during the years of the Great Terror, he was shot in 1940.

165   The author utilizes a neologism, *sloniach'e*, 'of the elephant'.

> Who says that in Russia there have never been elephants since the ice
> age! The inexhaustible Bolshevik creativity [...] gave birth to a SOVIET
> ELEPHANT. And such a terrible one...
>   — An ELEPHANT? Oh, my God! It's the Solovki Special Purpose Prison
> Camp...[166]

Several factors may have led to the interruption of the *Solovetskie Ostrova*. The limited circulation (100 copies) imposed by Glavlit on prison publications,[167] Frenkel''s rise, and, last but not least, Moscow's interest in the SLON press and in its circulation may have been crucial.

It is probable that Eikhmans tried to oppose the closure of the *Solovetskie Ostrova*, but his efforts, like so many events in the history of the SLON, are not documented. A close reading of the *Novye Solovki*, in which nobody hints at the episode, might nonetheless provide some interesting clues to what really happened. Instructions to close down the journal were probably given between mid-July and mid-August. In the thirty-fourth issue (22 August) of the *Novye Solovki*, an article hints at the reorganization of the *Biuro Pechati* (Press office).[168] In the following issue, the front page includes a short, anonymous article announcing the publication of phenological studies in the forthcoming issue of the *Solovetskie Ostrova*. The issue is not, however, referred to as *sleduiushchii* (next), but as *blizhaishii* (forthcoming). The difference is slight but revealing, since the former usually refers to regular issues, while the latter more vaguely refers to a journal issue that may be published within a short time.

In the thirty-seventh issue (12 September) of the *Novye Solovki*, the front page included an article about Petriaev's speech at a *Tsentral'noe Biuro Kraevedeniia* conference in Leningrad, where he read a report on the successful activities of the SLON Society of Ethnography.[169] On the third page, Mikhail Nikolaevich Gernet,[170] a jurist who owed his fame to his books on Tsarist prisons and on the Soviet prison press, thanked the editorial board for sending him copies of both the *Novye Solovki* and the *Solovetskie Ostrova*. This might have been part of a strategy to inform the cadres of the latest results of re-education at the SLON, and ultimately to make them reconsider their decision. The very fact that Gernet thanked the *Novye Solovki*[171]

---

166 [Неподходящее как будто для СЛОНА занятие — писать. Настоящее слонячье дело — это поставлять слоновую кость из Африки или, на худой конец, жрать французские булки в зоологическом саду. Однако наш СОВЕТСКИЙ СЛОН в самом прямом смысле слова пишет. И даже печатает. Издает и распространяет ежемесячный журнал! Невероятная страна. Здесь все возможно. | Что с того, что в России со времен ледникового периода никогда не водились слоны! Нескончаемая большевистская изобретательность [...] породила и СОВЕТСКОГО СЛОНА. Да еще какого страшного... | — СЛОН? Ох, господи! Так ведь это же Соловецкий лагерь Особого Назначения...] Mikhail Kol'tsov, 'SLON pishet', *Pravda*, 7 (1926), 1.

167 See p. 94.

168 'Bez nazvaniia', *NS*, 34 (1926), 4.

169 'Bez nazvaniia', *NS*, 37 (1926), 1.

170 Mikhail Gernet (1874–1953) was one of the most highly regarded jurists of the Soviet Union. Professor at the Moscow University from 1918 to 1931, in 1947 Gernet received the Stalin Prize.

171 'M. N. Gernet o Solovkakh', *NS*, 37 (1926), 3.

shows that initiatives had started from there — which is hardly surprising. It is very likely that the closure of the *Solovetskie Ostrova* was a warning to the editorial board of the newspaper, which, following the departure of many of its contributors, was undergoing a crisis. In fact, most of the *Novye Solovki* contributors had actually been sentenced to three years, and consequently left the islands between 1926 and 1927. Among them were leading figures of the SLON cultural scene (Borin, the stand-up comedian George Leon, and Ivan Panin) and several other journalists. By the end of 1926, even Litvin and Shiriaev, together with the typographer Slepian, had left the archipelago.

With the general turmoil and the farewell parties at the club, nobody noticed that the camp was bidding farewell also to its newspaper. Again quite unexpectedly, in the middle of the 1927 subscription campaign, the *Novye Solovki* failed to appear. Yet when the fiftieth and ultimately last issue appeared (12 December 1926), nobody had hinted at its imminent closure.

The reasons for the closure of the *Novye Solovki* are likewise obscure. Shiriaev, who provided the most accurate memoir of the cultural epic which ran from 1923 to 1926, does not linger over the closure of the SLON publishing system, which he simply ascribes to Frenkel''s directives. Other memoir writers are also silent about the episode, which took place in the middle of the international scandal provoked by the publication of memoirs by Mal'sagov,[172] who undermined the myth of freedom within the Soviet camps.

Whatever the reasons for the sudden move, it is undeniable that the end of the *Novye Solovki* represented the silencing of the *intelligenty* as well as the end of all the controversies that had stimulated internal debate at the camp. The information formerly provided by the *Novye Solovki* was transmitted daily in the form of a radio bulletin and the *Solovetskie Ostrova* was absorbed by the Leningrad-based journal *Karelo-Murmanskii Krai*. An analysis of the issues of the *Karelo-Murmanskii Krai* from 1926 onwards shows that, in all reality, the *Solovetskie Ostrova* was closed: former SLON contributors made only occasional interventions and the new publication rarely broached any of the questions that had raised such a furore at the time of the SLON press. SOK documents were only published until the end of 1927, while the fates of the other publications of the SLON are still a mystery.

The Second Period of SLON Publications (1929–1930)

Cultural life at the SLON did not end with the closure of its publications in 1926: in the late 1920s the SLON theatres were still working, as were the museum and the SOK. Quite unexpectedly, in 1929 typographic activities started again, as feverishly as before. Both SLON main publications reappeared in the August of 1929. After

---

172 Mal'sagov's book is often historically inaccurate. Mal'sagov never visited the Solovki camp, since he managed to escape during his stay at the Kemperpunkt. His depiction of the SLON cultural scene is typically inaccurate: Mal'sagov maintains that the *kaery* were excluded from it, while in fact they played a major role in its development. See Mal'sagov, *Adskie ostrova*, p. 66.

a short interruption in 1927, even the SOK's series of monographs began to be published again.

There was no apparent reason why the SLON press should have restarted its activity. After suppressing the voices of camp prisoners, the SLON authorities suddenly brought them back to life at a time when the SLON was undergoing violent and repressive change. Publishing in the SLON restarted at a time when Stalinism was already beginning to take hold, when changes proposed by Frenkel' were already being implemented, and in a year marked by summary trials, shootings, and epidemics on the archipelago. While the resumption of publishing can be explained, as Felicitas Fischer von Weikersthal does, by the OGPU's victory over the People's Commissariat of Justice and by the necessity of using the press as a tool for motivating the prisoners for the purposes of the *Stalinskii perelom*,[173] the fact that the editorial line that had first allowed the exceptional development of SLON press was reconfirmed for the *Solovetskie Ostrova* is harder to explain.

Maksim Gor'kii's Visit

Apart from the resumption of publishing activities in the camp, another decisive moment for SLON cultural history happened in 1929. This was Maksim Gor'kii's visit, an important literary event and a truly extraordinary episode that has fuelled debate ever since. It could not have been any other way. Gor'kii's visit to the Solovki camp was one of the most important episodes in the history of his return to the Soviet Union and resulted in a book still widely debated today. Even more significantly, it marked a crucial turn in the story of Soviet literature and culture and can consequently be regarded as one of the moments that paved the way to the formation of a new artistic canon based on Socialist Realism, which became a hand-maiden to the regime. Gor'kii's oath of fidelity to one of the most bloodthirsty dictators in history was one of the most remarkable of all Stalin's personal successes. A writer who had been building his success on the protection of the weakest gave his moral assent to a pitiless repressive system; in this sense, the Solovki visit was the first visible manifestation of the decline of Gor'kii's image. As Vitalii Shentalinskii puts it, it was the moment when the former 'defender and inspirer of the oppressed' gave way to the 'defender and inspirer of the oppressors'.[174]

Accounts of Gor'kii's visit and the very circumstances under which it took place have always been suffused with ambiguity and vagueness.[175] It has alternately been used by detractors or apologists as a means either to discredit or to protect the reputation of the writer, therefore debate has typically been rather lacking in objectivity. Gor'kii has been variously described as a calculating, monstrous, sadistic admirer of Soviet camps, or as a naive hero who dared to criticize Stalinism and

173 Fischer von Weikersthal, p. 145; pp. 185–86.
174 Vitalii Shentalinskii, *Raby svobody: v literaturnykh arkhivakh KGB* (Moscow: Parus, 1995), p. 328.
175 Recently Il'ia Veniavkin has proposed an interesting and user-friendly recollection of some of the points debated about Gor'kii's visit on the website of the project Arzamas. See Il'ia Veniavkin, *Solovki: chto Gor'kii videl i chto skryl*, http://arzamas.academy/materials/316 [accessed 29 April 2016].

whom the chekists (sent by Stalin) betrayed. Considering its relevance to the life of the SLON and to the administration's choices about the SLON press, it is necessary to provide a thorough assessment of Gor'kii's stay at the SLON — the starting point being, of course, Gor'kii's own reasons for visiting the Solovki islands, which date back to some years before his visit.

Gor'kii left the Soviet Union in 1921, following his rift with Lenin. Their story is similar to the story of a love affair gone bad. At first close friends, they gradually became more and more radically estranged. The turning point was the October Revolution. Gor'kii, who bore with Lenin's innumerable and sudden twists with difficulty, tried hard to oppose the ongoing violence against intellectuals that Lenin himself supported. Their relationship was marked by increasing tension; they finally ended their friendship immediately after Gumilev's execution, against which Gor'kii had protested. As tensions grew to a climax, Lenin suggested that Gor'kii leave the Soviet Union. His letter included threats of arrest:

> Your nerves are clearly not holding... You come to the 'conclusion' that a revolution cannot be made without the *intelligentsiia*. Your mind is completely sick... You do not deal with politics and with the observation of our work of political construction, but with a special profession, which surrounds you with embittered bourgeois *intelligentsiia*... It is clear that you've made yourself ill. You write that you find life not only difficult, but also 'totally repugnant'. Of course! You are sick of life, 'your divergence' with communism 'deepens'... I do not want to impose any advice, but I can't help saying: change radically your situation and environment, and place of residence, and occupation, or you may be sick of life irrevocably.[176]

Once abroad, Gor'kii found himself in great trouble. The most famous left-wing writer in the world, he had been, in fact, excluded from the Bolshevik Revolution. Russian émigrés, who were animated by a profound anti-Bolshevism, sometimes welcomed Gor'kii rather warmly, sometimes distrusted him. Some did not forgive his sympathy for Socialist ideas. Others, on the contrary, appreciated his intellectual honesty, which had provoked his estrangement from Lenin because of Gor'kii's relentless defence of intellectuals. Gor'kii himself, in the early years of his second exile, did not hide his disappointment with the Russian Revolution, as shown by the letters he sent to Anatole France[177] and to Aleksei Rykov[178] in 1922:

176 [Нервы у Вас явно не выдерживают... Вы договариваетесь до «вывода», что революцию нельзя делать без интеллигенции. Это — сплошь больная психика... Занимаетесь Вы не политикой и не наблюдением работы политического строительства, а особой профессией, которая Вас окружает озлобленной буржуазной интеллигенцией... Понятно, что довели себя до болезни: жить Вам, Вы пишете, не только тяжело, но и «весьма противно». Еще бы!.. Жизнь опротивела, «углубляется расхождение» с коммунизмом... Не хочу навязываться с советами, а не могу не сказать: радикально измените обстановку и среду, и местожительство, и занятие, иначе опротиветь может жизнь окончательно.] Shentalinskii, p. 306. In a letter to Gor'kii, Lenin had pronounced the following, famous words: 'The educated classes, the lackeys of capital, consider themselves the brains of the nation. In fact they are not its brains, but its sh.t' [интеллигентиков, лакеев капитала, мнящих себя мозгом нации. На деле это не мозг, а г..но]. Lenin's comment is indicative of his attitude towards the *intelligentsiia*. See ibid., p. 307.

177 Anatole France (1844–1924), who was awarded the Nobel Prize for Literature in 1921, sided with the Bolsheviks and became a supporter of the Revolution in the West.

178 Aleksei Ivanovich Rykov (1881–1938) was one of the most prominent Bolsheviks. He was the

Honourable Anatole France!

The trial against the Socialist-Revolutionaries took on the character of public preparations for the murder of people who sincerely served the cause of the liberation of the Russian people. I urgently ask you: please contact the Soviet government once again and state that this crime is unacceptable. Maybe your powerful voice will save the valuable lives of the socialists. I hereby inform you of a letter I sent to one of the representatives of Soviet power. Cordial greetings!

3 July,   Maksim Gor'kii

To A. I. Rykov. Moscow.

Aleksei Ivanovich!

If the trial of Socialist Revolutionaries ends in murder, it will be a premeditated murder, a vile murder. I ask you to inform L. D. Trotskii and others about this opinion of mine. I hope it will not surprise you, since during the entire period of the revolution, I pointed out a thousand times to the Soviet power the senselessness and criminality of the extermination of the *intelligentsiia* in our illiterate and uncultured country. Now I am convinced that if the *esery* are killed, this crime will cause a moral blockade against Russia by socialist Europe.

3 July   Maksim Gor'kii[179]

Gor'kii's idyll among the émigrés did not last long, since their differences were too great. A crucial moment in their relationship was Gor'kii's experience with the *Beseda* journal, the foundation of which alienated many members of the expatriate *intelligentsiia*. Gor'kii's new home in Sorrento where he bought a villa was far from the centres of Russian emigration, Berlin and Paris. He knew the surrounding area well, having spent his first exile there.[180] Gor'kii's decision to live in Italy was primarily motivated by his poor health, but it was also a strategy to escape from a world that he increasingly resented or even despised.

When Gor'kii's relations with Russian expatriate circles began to deteriorate, he started to reconsider his relationship with his homeland with increasing anxiety. Lenin's death brought about a first, tangible sign of Gor'kii's rapprochement with

first director of the NKVD and the Sovnarkom president (1924–30). He was tried with Bukharin at the great Moscow Show Trial, and was shot with his fellow defendants.

179 [Достопочтенный Анатоль Франс! | Суд над социалистами-революционерами принял характер публичного приготовления к убийству людей, искренне служивших делу освобождения русского народа. Убедительно прошу Вас: обратитесь еще раз к Советской власти с указанием на недопустимость преступления: может быть, Ваше веское слово сохранит ценные жизни социалистов. Сообщаю Вам письмо, посланное мною одному из представителей Советской власти. | Сердечный привет! | 3 июля | Максим Горький | А. И. Рыкову. Москва. || Алексей Иванович! | Если процесс социалистов-революционеров будет закончен убийством — это будет убийство с заранее обдуманным намерением, гнусное убийство. Я прошу Вас сообщить Л.Д. Троцкому и другим это мое мнение. Надеюсь, оно не удивит Вас, ибо за все время революции я тысячекратно указывал Советской власти на бессмыслие и преступность истребления интеллигенции в нашей безграмотной и некультурной стране. Ныне я убежден, что если эсеры будут убиты, — это преступление вызовет со стороны социалистической Европы моральную блокаду России. | 3 июля Максим Горький] Shentalinskii, p. 317.

180 During his first exile (1906–13), Gor'kii spent most of the time in Capri.

Russia. Far from considering his possible return to the Soviet Union, he swore loyalty to the Soviet authorities and wrote an apology of his former enemy-and-friend. Russian émigrés were not, of course, indifferent to these actions. Gor'kii's break from them took place over the 'tomb' of the journal *Beseda*, which closed in 1925. On that occasion, Gor'kii was not able to honour his previous arrangements with many authors, most of whom were exiled intellectuals who lived in extreme poverty. They did not forgive the writer for that.

Gor'kii had financial problems of his own. Although he was better off than most of the representatives of the Russian emigration at the time, his monthly budget turned out to be inadequate. In *Arkhipelag GULAG*, Solzhenitsyn makes some bitter remarks concerning Gor'kii's return to the Soviet Union. He actually suggests that the writer came back because he was not successful abroad and because of his financial troubles.[181] This, in fact, was only partially true. Whereas Gor'kii was not as successful abroad as he had expected (some biographers state that in those years he expected to be awarded the Nobel Prize, which never arrived), he was certainly never indigent. He spent about a thousand dollars every month. The monthly honorarium he received from his publishers was about 320 dollars, to which he could add further income: his short stories and novels were translated and sold everywhere, his plays were regularly performed.[182] His very name, in fact, attracted foreign audiences. His major work as an émigré, *Delo Artamonovykh*, was translated into Spanish, Italian, German, and French in the course of just four years. Money was not, in fact, the primary reason why he returned to the Soviet Union.

Vitalii Shentalinskii investigates both Gor'kii's rift with the Russian émigrés and his late, profound personal crisis, which played a major role in the events that followed. At the age of almost seventy, Shentalinskii states, feeling the closeness of death, an old and weak Gor'kii started to think about his possible return. Already in 1927 he was beginning to think about going back on a trip to his homeland in order to find out more about the achievements of the Revolution. Although his family was around him, Gor'kii felt lonely in his Italian golden cage. His vulnerability caused him to go constantly from elation to sadness, from intense enthusiasm to sheer apathy. This internal turmoil made him change his mind about his past ideological beliefs — in particular, his attitude towards the role of the *intelligentsiia*. In a letter quoted by Shentalinskii, he overtly takes sides against some representatives of the Russian emigration.[183] At the same time, he seemed to be eager to reconsider the Soviet experience and took keener interest in the 'remoulding' of the individual and in the system of re-education through labour.

Gor'kii's radical change of heart has been variously explained. First of all, the writer was growing physically and psychologically old. The strong-willed man who had dared to criticise Lenin had slowly given way to a weaker man. In the letters he wrote from 1925 to 1932, he often complained pathetically, as two letters he sent to the writer Vsevolod Ivanov between 1927 and 1928 show:

181 Solzhenitsyn, II, 48.
182 Pavel Basinskii, *Gor'kii* (Moscow: Molodaia gvardia, 2006), p. 368.
183 Shentalinskii, p. 324.

Only yesterday was I able to get up and write, but a few days ago for the first time I felt how close to a person is that unpleasant little thing called 'death'. I am filled with camphor, with which I have been injected five times, camphor and another sort of liquid. I feel horrible... I shake your hand!
8 September 1927   A. Peshkov[184]

Yes, I will come in May and, it seems, I will not see you: why are the devils taking you to Tashkent? And why did you sent the second volume without sending the first? I love reading you, please send it.

With this jubilee I'm starting to feel famous as Mary Pickford, and I'm already afraid that I will receive a proposal to enter into legal marriage with Serafimovich...[185]

In October 1928, Gor'kii sent Ol'ga Loshakova-Ivina[186] a note pervaded by the same bitter tone:

Dear Ol'ga Fominishna, — I do not like my private life and do not like to remember it in any other way than as literary material; it should be clear from my books that this is true. In them I participate as a figure who observes, narrates, but rarely acts. By this I do not mean that I did not visit O\<l'ga\> Iu\<l'evna\> and you out of my unwillingness to 'immerse myself' in the past: by this I only say that, in general, the past for me is a material I do not much like, since I have treated it very badly.[187]

Stalin and the OGPU[188] perfectly understood Gor'kii's vulnerable state of mind and started to court him, artfully playing on his weaknesses. A spider's web was rapidly spun around the writer, who became ensnared in it almost wilfully. His villa

---

184 [Только вчера встал на ноги и могу писать, а несколько дней тому назад впервые почувствовал, как близка человеку неприятная штучка, именуемая «смертью». Налит камфарой, которую вспрыскивали мне раз пять, камфарой и еще какой-то жидкостью. Чувствую себя отвратительно... Крепко жму руку! | 8 сентября 1927 г. | А. Пешков] Ibid., pp. 326–27.

185 [Да, в мае приеду и, кажется, не увижу Вас: почему черти несут Вас в Ташкент? И почему Вы прислали 2-й том, не прислав первого? Я очень люблю читать Вас, пришлите. | С этим юбилеем я начинаю чувствовать себя знаменитым, как Мери Пикфорд, и уже боюсь, что мне предложат вступить в законный брак с Серафимовичем...] Ibid., p. 327. In the second letter, a resentful Gor'kii hints ironically about his return to Russia.

186 Ol'ga Fominichna Loshakova (1883–1979) was the daughter of Gor'kii's first wife. She was an actress (her stage name was Ivina) and she wrote a memoir about her step-father, see Ol'ga Ivina-Loshakova, 'Moi vospominaniia ob Aleksee Maksimoviche', in Aleksei Eliseev, ed., *A.M. Gor'kii nizhegorodskikh let: Vospominaniia* (Gor'kii: Volgo-Viatskoe knizhnoe izdatel'stvo, 1978), pp. 51–85.

187 [Милая Ольга Фоминишна, — я не люблю мою личную жизнь и не люблю вспоминать о ней иначе, как о литературном материале; что это — правда, это должно быть видно из моих книг, в которых я участвую как лицо наблюдающее, рассказывающее, но — мало действующее. Этим я вовсе не хочу сказать, что не посетил О\<льгу\> Ю\<льевну\> и Вас из нежелании «окунуться» в прошлое, — этим я говорю только то, что прошлое для меня вообще — материал мало приятный, ибо он крайне плохо обработан мною.] Gor'kii's letter to Ol'ga Loshakova-Ivina, 27 December 1928, in: Ol'ga Bystrova, *Gor'kii i ego korrespondenty* (Moscow: IMLI-RAN, 2005), pp. 342–43.

188 Iagoda and other OGPU officials were the go-betweens between Stalin and Gor'kii. Gor'kii's personal secretary, Petr Kriuchkov, probably played a major role in Stalin's plan, too. Although existing documents only refer to Kriuchkov's cooperation with Iagoda after Gor'kii's return to Russia, their relationship might have started in the last years of Gor'kii's exile.

in Sorrento was visited by an increasing number of Soviet writers who would extol the achievements of the Soviet Union — especially its literary achievements. He read similar reports in the Soviet newspapers and journals (the only press he read)[189] as well as in the (censored) private letters which Gor'kii regularly received from ordinary citizens, letters that dealt with the successes of the Soviet people.[190]

Gor'kii was particularly moved by the letters he received from the Kuriazh working commune for underage inmates, which was named in Gor'kii's honour and which had been set up in the neighbourhoods of Khar'kov. The Kuriazh was a replica of the Bolshevo commune that the OGPU established in 1924 to house *besprizorniki*. Gor'kii replied to the children's letters with care and enthusiasm, as the following passage taken from the above-mentioned letter to Vsevolod Ivanov reveals:

> Listen to this: it's already six years since a colony of 'socially dangerous' children was established near Khar'kov, and I am its patron. Its organization, position, and life are surprisingly interesting. I correspond with the children, and for every letter of mine they reply with 22 letters, that is the number of the directors of the various working groups. It's enormously interesting to see such a passion. Do you have in the *Kr<asnaia> N<ov'>* a man who would go there and describe the colony? It's worth it.[191]

One of the *ocherki*[192] included in the book Gor'kii wrote after visiting the commune, *Po soiuzu sovetov*, widely testifies to the writer's growing interest in the re-educational experiment that was being carried out in Kuriazh. Gor'kii's visit took place on 8 July 1928, during his first return journey to the Soviet Union:

> The head of the Baku labour colony (I forgot his surname) and A. S. Makarenko, the organizer of a colony near Khar'kov, in Kuriazh — all of these 'liquidators of *besprizornost''* are neither dreamers, nor visionaries. They must be a new type of pedagogue; they are people who burn in the fire of an active love for children: above all, they are people who, I think, are well aware of their responsibilities towards the children. The countless tragedies of our century, which arose in the volcanic soil of irreconcilable class contradictions, tell the children rather convincingly the story of the bloody mistakes of their fathers. This should have aroused the fathers' sense of responsibility towards their children; it should have, and it's high time![193]

189 Gor'kii totally distrusted the 'bourgeois press', see Spiridonova, p. 224.
190 Several citizens sent Gor'kii letters about the real situation in Russia. These letters were usually censored and their authors were often repressed. Shentalinskii discusses the episode in more detail. See Shentalinskii, pp. 331–33.
191 [Вот что: под Харьковом существует уже 6-й год колония «социально опасных» детей, я состою шефом ее. Организация, положение, жизнь ее — удивительно интересны. С детьми я переписываюсь, и на каждое мое письмо они отвечают 22 письмами, по числу начальников различных рабочих отрядов. Любопытно — страсть как. | Нет ли у Вас — в «Кр<асной> Н<ови>» — человека, который бы съездил туда и описал колонию? Стоит.] Ibid., pp. 327–28.
192 The word *ocherk* ('essay') is quite misleading. Gor'kii's *Po soiuzu sovetov* is a travelogue, not a collection of essays. The expression, however, is commonly used to address the works contained in *Po soiuzu sovetov*; therefore it will be used here too.
193 [Заведующий Бакинской трудовой колонией, — я забыл его фамилию, — и А.С.Макаренко, организатор колонии под Харьковом, в Куряже, — все эти «ликвидаторы беспризорности» не мечтатели, не фантазеры, это, должно быть, новый тип педагогов, это люди, сгорающие в

Gor'kii most likely grew enthusiastic about the notion of 'remoulding' the Soviet people, and about Communist re-education of the individual after visiting the colony. His sincere support for the Soviet repressive system — which he regarded essentially as a re-educational system — sprang from that first experience.

From 1928 onwards, Gor'kii started to draw closer and closer to Leopol'd Averbakh.[194] At first, they simply exchanged letters. Averbakh, whom Gor'kii initially distrusted, eventually managed to gain the writer's trust and even went to visit him in his Italian villa. Averbakh's role, of course, had been carefully planned in advance by the Moscow leaders. As Bystrova suggests, Iagoda used him as a sort of intermediary to cajole Gor'kii into going back to the Soviet Union.[195] At the same time, Gor'kii was materially courted with expensive gifts and generous rewards; they were meant to make him understand that, once he was back in the Soviet Union, money would no longer be a nagging worry.

The strategy to get the proletarian writer out of his safe refuge in Fascist Italy and back to Communist Russia soon had the desired effect. Gor'kii had grown tired of his life abroad. His rift with the Russian émigrés was irreversible; he missed his country terribly, his country wanted him back; and he was starting to have some problems with the Fascist regime, which authorized a police search of his translator's room in his villa in Sorrento.[196]

In May 1928, Gor'kii returned to the Soviet Union for the first time in almost seven years. Though the journey did not mark his final return, it certainly sanctioned his official, renewed relations with the Soviet regime and made him realise what his future in the Soviet Union might well be like. On his first trip to Moscow, he plunged into crowds of admirers. He was warmly fêted every time the train stopped in Soviet cities along the journey and celebrations turned into something little short of an apotheosis at the Belorusskaia station in Moscow. Gor'kii was given a luxurious flat (which Stalin himself had chosen) within walking distance of the Kremlin[197] and two dachas, one in Crimea, one in Podmoskov'e. Moreover, he was officially invited to set out on a journey across the Soviet Union — an endless *pokazukha*[198] of the achievements of Socialism, including Kuriazh.

огне действенной любви к детям, а прежде всего — это люди, которые, мне кажется, хорошо сознают и чувствуют свою ответственность пред лицом детей. Бесчисленные трагедии нашего века, возникнув на вулканической почве непримиримых классовых противоречий, достаточно убедительно рассказывают детям историю кровавых ошибок отцов. Это должно бы возбудить у отцов чувство ответственности пред детьми; должно бы, — пора!] Gor'kii, 'Po soiuzu sovetov', p. 159.

194 Leopol'd Averbakh (1903–37) was a literary critic. The leading representative of RAPP (Rossiiskaia Assotsiatsiia Proletarskikh Pisatelei), he regarded the journal of the association, *Na literaturnom postu*, as a sort of arena where he would typically attack non-aligned writers (in particular, though not exclusively, the *poputchiki*). He was a victim of Stalin's Terror.

195 Bystrova, pp. 568–71.

196 Paola Cioni, 'Gor'kii v Italii (po dokumentam Tsentral'nogo arkhiva Italii)', *Novaia i noveiishaia istoriia*, 5 (2010), 205–09.

197 Gor'kii's flat was in Malaia Nikitskaia street. Westerman describes it in detail in his book; see Westerman, pp. 9–11.

198 This term refers to a situation staged with the aim of hiding the real situation from an observer.

Back in Italy in October 1928, Gor'kii believed that he would not reject Stalin's proposal, which promised Gor'kii a prominent role in the literary life of the Soviet Union.[199] He was, however, fully aware of the consequences of his return. He knew Stalin very well, and he knew his return would mean that he would have to give up any disagreements he might have with the dictator.[200] It was a price Gor'kii was willing to pay, since his journey back to Italy and his meeting with hostile Russian émigrés had proved particularly wearisome after his triumph in the Soviet Union.

In Sorrento, Gor'kii set out to write his first impressions after the journey. He first wrote the *ocherki* which he eventually collected into *Po soiuzu sovetov*, a book he had planned to write as early as 1927. He began his first essay in October, and started his second essay in November. He worked with much enthusiasm, being most willing to celebrate the Soviet achievements he had seen for himself.

In the summer of 1929, Gor'kii was back in the Soviet Union for his second return journey. On this occasion, he visited the SLON. As the editors of *Polnoe sobranie sochinenii* point out, Gor'kii never mentions his intention to visit the labour camps (or more specifically, the Solovki islands) in the letters he wrote before setting out for the journey, whereas the intention to visit the children's colony was explicit in his previous letters:

> During his stay in Sorrento, Gor'kii followed life in the Soviet Union with great interest and had an extensive correspondence with people of various professions. 'What interesting people — he wrote to P. M. Kerzhentsev on 21 March 1927 — everything in them boils and burns! Amazing!' (G-30, t. 17, p. 482). And added: 'I am a man greedy for people and, of course, after my arrival in Russia I will not stop working, but I will go, look and talk. And I would like to go to all the places that I know: the Volga, the Caucasus, the Ukraine, Crimea, on the Oka, and to all the former pits, and potholes' (ibid.).
> In a letter to A.B. Khalatov written on 10 October that same year he wrote: 'I want to write a book about the new Russia. I have already accumulated a lot of interesting material for it. I will need to go — unseen — to the factories, clubs, villages, pubs, construction sites, to the Komsomol members, university students, to lessons in schools, to colonies for socially dangerous children, to the workers' and village correspondents, to the women-delegates, to the Muslim women etc., etc. It is an incredibly serious affair. When I think about this, my hair bristles with excitement' (Archive, GC, Vol. 1, page 91).[201]

See Leonid Roizenzon, 'Zametki po russkoi leksikografii. Pokazukha', *Etimologicheskie issledovaniia po russkomu iazyku*, v (Moscow: Izdatel'stvo MGU, 1966), pp. 104–10.

199 One of Gor'kii's most recent biographers, Pavel Basinskii, maintains that Gor'kii set specific conditions for his return to Stalin's Soviet Union — above all freedom to move and travel abroad. Gor'kii's final return in 1932 coincided with the launch of the plan to build a new Soviet literature. This eventually led to the creation of Socialist Realism and of a new literary canon, which constructed a list of writers (and texts) who were presented as the predecessors of Socialist Realism. Up to his definitive return to the Soviet Union, Gor'kii continued to live in Italy, though he often visited the Soviet Union. Once in Moscow, he became a 'prisoner' of Stalin. See Basinskii, p. 379.

200 Ibid., p. 389.

201 [В период своего пребывания в Сорренто Горький с огромным интересом следил за жизнью в Советском Союзе и вёл обширную переписку с людьми самых различных профессий. «Какие интересные люди, — писал он П. М. Керженцеву 21 марта 1927 г., — как всё у них кипит и горит! Славно!» (Г-30, т. 17, стр. 482). И добавлял: «Я — человек жадный

Why did Gor'kii visit the SLON? The scholar Lidiia Spiridonova suggests that he decided to visit the labour camps because human misfortunes moved him and because he hoped he could help the *besprizorniki*, for whom, as noted above, a special community had been set up at the camp.[202] This version is plausible yet not documented. The widespread belief that Gor'kii's decision was a response to a specific request of the OGPU is indeed more persuasive.

Among the 'rumours' which offer an explanation for Gor'kii's visit to Solovki is Bykov's assertion that Iagoda himself talked Gor'kii into setting out on the journey in an attempt to solve the international crisis unleashed by publications by former SLON prisoners in the West.[203] Though it does not mention Iagoda, the reconstruction of the events by the editors of Gor'kii's 1974 *Polnoe sobranie sochinenii* appears to confirm Bykov's version. It also significantly hints at the 500th anniversary of the monastery as well as the anti-Soviet campaign the Vatican launched at the time as causes for the trip — a circumstance that Reznikov confirms.[204] Whatever Gor'kii's real reasons were, the following words, which Gor'kii presumably uttered and which are reported in P. Moroz's *vospominaniia*, seem to reveal that the writer's journey was not his own decision: 'I was put under such conditions that I could have not done anything but go'.[205]

Unfortunately, the documents and memoirs available to us are not sufficiently reliable to reveal whether Gor'kii's journey was part of a well-planned strategy or the consequence of a sudden political move. The SLON memoir writers who mention the episode describe the preparations at the camp for Gor'kii's arrival, but they do not specify how long they went on prior to his arrival: it is therefore impossible to assume if Gor'kii's visit was planned well in advance or not. Some departments were freshly painted; trees were planted outside the barracks so that they would not look so gloomy; and all the places Gor'kii was to visit were carefully rearranged. The SLON officials were waiting for his arrival and the prisoners were looking forward to that moment, too — after all, they regarded Gor'kii as a fierce defender of their rights.

на людей и, разумеется, по приезде на Русь работать не стану, а буду ходить, смотреть и говорить. И поехал бы во все места, которые знаю: на Волгу, на Кавказ, на Украину, в Крым, на Оку, и — по всем бывшим ямам, по ухабам» (там же). | В письме А. Б. Халатову от 10 октября т.г. он сообщал: «Мне хочется написать книгу о новой России. Я уже накопил для нее много интереснейшего материала. Мне необходимо побывать — невидимкой — на фабриках, в клубах, в деревнях, в пивных, на стройках, у комсомольцев, вузовцев, в школах на уроках, в колониях для социально опасных детей, у рабкоров и селькоров, посмотреть на женщин-делегаток, на мусульманок и т. д. и т. д. Это — серьезнейшее дело. Когда я об этой думаю, у меня волосы на голове шевелятся от волнения» (Архив, ГХ, кн. 1, стр. 91).] Maksim Gor'kii, 'Solovki', *Polnoe sobranie sochineniia v 25 t.* (Moscow: Nauka, 1974), xx, 571–72.

202 Spiridonova, p. 226.

203 Dmitrii Bykov, *Byl li Gor'kii?* (Moscow: AST-Astrel, 2009), p. 284. Bykov only refers to Mal'sagov, but there were indeed other former SLON prisoners whose books were published in the West, as seen in chapter 1, p. 22. Bykov adds that Gor'kii himself was moved also by the desire to see the 'laboratory' where the new man was being formed, see Bykov, p. ivi.

204 Leonid Reznikov, *Gor'kii izvestnyi i neizvestnyi* (Petrozavodsk: A/O Amitie, 1996), p. 222.

205 ['Я был поставлен в такие условия, при которых я не мог не приехать.'] David Shub, *Politicheskie deiateli Rossii (1850-kh–1920-kh gg.). Sbornik statei* (New York: Izdanie 'Novogo zhurnala', 1969), p. 343.

FIG. 3.12. Maksim Gor'kii (centre) with Gleb Bokii (left)
during his visit at the SLON. AMM

After visiting the transit camp in Kem', Gor'kii boarded the 'Gleb Bokii' in the
company of the man after whom the boat was named. He was also accompanied
by his son Maksim, his daughter-in-law, Nogtev, his 'orderly' Arvid Iakovlevich
Martinelli, and several chekists. Gor'kii's stay on the Solovki islands lasted two days.
He visited all the manufacturing areas, from the forest to the peat deposits and the
farms. He even visited the Sekirka in a coach. He was taken to the hospital and the
library. On his first night there, he attended a show at the Solteatr. He was, of course,
strictly supervised by the chekists, who had carefully re-arranged the 'Potemkin
village'[206] and who made sure that no more encounters took place between Gor'kii
and the SLON prisoners than those they had planned themselves.

Some meetings were actually planned in advance by the camp administration.
They made sure that Gor'kii met a drunk monk on his journey to and back from
the islands;[207] that he visited a colony of *besprizorniki*; that he met an old thief, a
former robber, some prisoners who were working at the stables, and more prisoners

---

206 The term refers to what the authorities want important guests to see. Grigorii Potemkin was the
prince who, during Empress Catherine II's visit to Crimea in 1787, had villages built from scratch to
hide the dire condition of the Russian countryside.

207 The dossier containing Gor'kii's manuscript kept in Gor'kii's archive at the IMLI RAN
includes the letter that religious representatives wrote to the administration in order to ask for
alcohol. Mentioned in Gor'kii's *ocherk*, the letter was either a fake or a document that was misleading
in its implications of the religious community's vices. See Moscow, AG, KhPG-41–13–6, Maksim
Gor'kii, *Solovki*, rukopis'.

who knew very well what they could and could not say. However, the SLON prisoners, who had been told not to address the writer, tried hard to demystify the chekists' fabrications. As Nikonov suggests, some of them managed to give Gor'kii notes asking for his intercession or revealing their real living and working conditions.[208] Gor'kii found his pockets full of prisoners' notes in the middle of the show he was attending in the evening. Other prisoners tried to get in contact with him later on. Brodskii, for example, quotes from the letter Vadim Chekhovskii sent to Gor'kii:

> Answer me, Aleksei Maskimovich. To you, an old man whom I would like to respect, I dedicate this testimony. I heard many different things about you. You are for me a symbol of the GPU, of the party and of the power — a symbol of the Sphinx. And I ask this Sphinx: 'Sphinx, who are you? An executioner, a malefactor, a gang of rapists, liars and careerists, or the severe Guardian of the Threshold,[209] smashing the shortcomings before a new and bright era for mankind?'
>
> From prisons to concentration camps — all the time I've seen outrageous injustice. More than half of the prisoners sentenced under Article 58 do not know what they have been punished for. And what about the people deported to other camps? To Siberia? To prisons? Four to five million people deported out of a population of a hundred and forty million... And what about the people who return to Solovki with a second term under their previous conviction? And those who got a second term without a break just for their resoluteness or for their honest convictions? What about the *lesozagotovki* (timber felling), what about the frostbitten people, people without proper clothing, the self-mutilators, the ones who were shot, the fugitives? And the shooting of the political prisoners? And what about the 47-day-long hunger strike of the Musavatists?[210] What about the beatings? What about the swearing? What about the informers, so often using false accusations and not always punished? And there is much, much more, without end...
>
> [...] A lot of injustice, Aleksei Maksimovich, a lot more than you think, should be corrected. [...] You cannot hide the obvious. And you cannot conceal the destruction of prisoners either.
>
> Vadim Chekhovskii
> 14 September 1929[211]

208 Nikonov-Smorodin, pp. 179–81.

209 Chekovskii here refers to the famous character of Edward Bulwer-Lytton's *Zanoni*, although Chekovskii might have taken it from the drama *The Guardian of the Threshold* by Rudolf Steiner, whose influence in some circles of the *intelligentsiia* was strong.

210 Musavat was the name of a nationalist party in Azerbaijan which underwent repression after the October Revolution. See Michael G. Smith, 'Anatomy of a Rumour: Murder Scandal, the Musavat Party and Narratives of the Russian Revolution in Baku, 1917–1920', *Journal of Contemporary History*, 36 (2001), 211–40.

211 [Ответьте мне, Алексей Максимович, Вам, старику, которого я хотел бы уважать, посвящаю я эти показания. Много разного слышал о Вас. Вы для меня символ ГПУ, партии и власти — символ Сфинкса. И этого Сфинкса я вопрошаю; «Сфинкс, кто ты? Палач, злодей, шайка насильников, лжецов и карьеристов или суровый страж Порога, разящий недостатки перед новой и светлой эрой человечества?» | С тюрьмы и до концлагерей — все время я видел вопиющие несправедливости. Более половины осужденных по 58-й статье не знают, за что они подвергнуты наказанию. А сосланные в другие лагеря? Сибирь?

During Gor'kii's visit, prisoners tried their best to make him understand that everything he was being shown was a fake. In the library, Gor'kii met several prisoners who were cunningly reading newspapers upside-down. Likhachev says that Gor'kii even turned round one of the newspapers.[212] Nikonov also says that some prisoners managed to evade the vigilant chekists and move the writer to tears.[213] Finally, several memoir writers mention the following episode: a boy of roughly fourteen asked Gor'kii whether he really wanted to know the truth about the camp; Gor'kii consented, and the boy took him aside for some minutes. Gor'kii came back with his eyes full of tears, since the boy had revealed to him all the atrocities prisoners endured. Once Gor'kii had left, the boy was immediately shot or, as other writers suggest, the chekists handed him over to professional criminals who had been told to 'take care' of him.

There is insufficient documentation to allow us to assess the reliability of the above-mentioned episodes. While some of them are supported by historical documents (such as Chekhovskii's letter), others seem legendary rather than historical, even though many memoir writers mention them. For example, Gor'kii's well-known 'chance encounter' with the young inmate is still a mystery. Although witnesses agree about and even swear on the most widespread version of the meeting,[214] it is surprising that nobody mentions the boy's name or his physical appearance — how could it be that nobody recognized him? Is it possible that none of his *rota* fellows remembered the name of that bold child-hero? In his report, Gor'kii talks about a boy in the *besprizorniki* colony who gave him a note and was consequently insulted by his fellow inmates, who treated him as a spy. Applebaum is probably right in suggesting that the episode rings a bell with the episode narrated by memoir writers.[215] The meeting probably took place this way and was the source of widespread rumours among the prisoners — a *parasha*[216] which the memoir writers would eventually re-tell.

Whatever the truth was, this episode became the historical-literary nemesis of the famous '*a byl li mal'chik*', and it backfired on its creator.[217] In the background

Тюрьмы? Четыре-пять миллионов высланных из ста сорока миллионов населения... А люди, возвращающиеся в Соловки со вторым сроком по прежнему делу? А получившие второй срок без перерыва за одну твердость и честность убеждений? А лесозаготовки — обмороженные, раздетые, саморубы, расстрелянные, беглецы? А расстрел политических заключенных? А сорокасемидневная голодовка мусаватистов? А побои? А мат? А стукачество, столь часто лживое и не всегда наказуемое? И многое, многое без конца... [...] Много несправедливости, Алексей Максимович, много больше, чем Вы думаете, надлежит исправить. [...] Шила в мешке не утаишь. Уничтожения заключенных — тоже не скроешь... | Вадим Чеховский | 14 сентября 1929 года.] Brodskii, pp. 328–29. Brodskii found this letter among the documents of the trial that led to the shooting of Chekhovskii, on 29 October 1929: it most probably cost the author his life.

212   Likhachev, *Izbrannoe: Vospominaniia*, pp. 187–88.

213   Nikonov-Smorodin, p. 180.

214   For example, Likhachev maintains that he was there when Gor'kii came back crying. Likhachev, *Izbrannoe: Vospominaniia*, p. 187.

215   Applebaum, pp. 60–61.

216   See above, p. 25 n. 36.

217   This is a quotation from Gor'kii's novel *Klim Samgin*. The sentence ('But was there a boy at all?')

of this event, there remains an incontrovertible truth confirmed even by Gor'kii's most strenuous defenders, such as Reznikov: Gor'kii must have realized that everything he saw was staged.[218]

Late that October, Gor'kii finished his *ocherk*, *Solovki*, which was published in the journal *Nashi Dostizheniia*. The underlying tone of Gor'kii's essay was appreciative. The SLON seemed to be a model and Gor'kii praised the SLON commanders and guards as well as the notion of positive re-education. Toward the end of the report, he wrote the words that have tainted his reputation ever since: 'It seems to me, that the conclusion is clear: such camps as Solovki, and such *trudkommuny* as Bolshevo are necessary... Specifically, by this method the state will achieve one of its purposes: the destruction of prisons.'[219]

Gor'kii's *ocherk* was rapidly published all over the West. As the Soviet leadership had foreseen, the proletarian writer, whom the whole world regarded as the defender of the oppressed, had finally turned into an apologist for Soviet re-educational policies. Apart from its obvious effects, Gor'kii's book had a much more meaningful, if subliminal, effect. The writer publicly justified the Soviet regime, as well as the endless bloodshed that that regime provoked. Even more surprisingly, he glorified the perpetrators of mass murder in the Soviet Union. The conclusion seems clear — Gor'kii had finally surrendered to Stalin.

There are, however, researchers who do not share this interpretation. As Reznikov points out, Moroz stated that Gor'kii himself dissented from the text that was published under his name:

> The memoirs of P. Moroz (which are completely unknown here in Russia) about the conversations he had with Gor'kii in the summer of 1930 are particularly important, since they shed additional light on some of the publications of the writer, not only the one published in 1929. Moroz asked Gor'kii:
> — How could you write such a one-sided article as 'Solovki'? (The question itself suggests that in 1930 there were people who knew more about the reality than they could have found out from the official press).
> Gor'kii replied that in the *ocherk* on the Solovki islands, published in *Izvestiia*,[220] 'the only thing the pencil of the editor left untouched was my signature; everything else is COMPLETELY THE OPPOSITE OF WHAT I WROTE, AND UNRECOGNIZABLE'.[221]

---

has become a *krylataia fraza* (i.e. a literary quote that enters common use), and it perfectly testifies to the importance of lies in Gor'kii's works. Seeing his young rival falling through the ice of the lake he was skating on, young Klim Samgin wonders whether the episode he had just seen really took place or not. Bykov's book takes its title from this sentence: it means 'but was there Gor'kii at all?'.

218 The only exception is Oleg Volkov, who thought that Gor'kii saw only what others wanted him to see and did not pay attention to anything else. See Volkov, p. 175.

219 [Мне кажется — вывод ясен: необходимы такие лагеря, как Соловки, и такие трудкоммуны, как Болшево. Именно этим путем государство быстро достигнет одной из своих целей: уничтожить тюрьмы.] Gor'kii, *Po soiuzu sovetov*, p. 231.

220 The *ocherk* was published also in *Izvestiia*.

221 [Воспоминания П. Мороза (у нас совершенно неизвестные) о разговорах с Горьким летом 1930 года особенно важны потому, что они проливают дополнительный свет на некоторые публикации писателя не только 1929 года. Мороз спросил Горького: | — Как вы могли написать такую одностороннюю статью, как «Соловки»? (Сам вопрос свидетельствует

Spiridonova and Reznikov add further details — although the former's suggestions are more well-documented than the latter's. In their version, Gor'kii's suitcase containing his private notes was stolen. Spiridonova's comments on the episode are confirmed by the recollection of Gor'kii's daughter-in-law (and fellow traveller), which Spiridonova quotes:

> The same thing happened during the trip in the summer of 1929, when Gor'kii went to Leningrad, Murmansk, Stalingrad, Astrakhan, Sukhumi, Tbilisi, Vladikavkaz, etc. This time he was able to see not only the *sovkhoz* 'Gigant', but also the Solovki islands. All this time he was accompanied by the same kind and helpful people who were keenly watching every move of his. Did Gor'kii understand that they did not show him the real achievements, but 'Potemkin villages'? That the porters on the wharves of the Volga do not wear Dutch sailors' hats every day, that the peasants do not drink cocoa, and that the prisoners on Solovki do not sleep on clean sheets and do not read newspapers? This question could have been answered by the notes that Gor'kii wrote during the trip. But, strangely, two of his suitcases were stolen, and the manuscripts confiscated. N. A. Peshkova, who accompanied the writer, recalled: '... one beautiful day, when he was not at home or sleeping, the suitcase with his manuscripts disappeared, and two months later, this case was sent back. Some boots were in it, but the box which had contained his manuscripts was full of ash. And Iagoda explained that the swindlers, when found, realized that these papers were Gor'kii's manuscripts, got scared and, it seems, burnt these manuscripts. And there were a lot of notes'.
> What were those strange 'swindlers' scared of, if Gor'kii's impressions were only positive and could not damage the prestige of the authorities? Evidently, in those notes — that Gor'kii could have published in the West — there was not only 'euphoria'. The nature of the burnt papers can be judged by a small note which remained by chance in the possession of N. A. Peshkova: 'You used to shoot and hang with indifference, we shoot with disgust'. A significant declaration by one of the masters of the Gulag![222]

о том, что и в 1930 году были люди, которые знали действительность более основательно, чем о ней сообщала официальная пресса). | Горький ответил, что в очерке о Соловецких островах, опубликованном в «Известиях», «карандаш редактора не коснулся только моей подписи, — все остальное СОВЕРШЕННО ПРОТИВОПОЛОЖНО ТОМУ, ЧТО Я НАПИСАЛ, И НЕУЗНАВАЕМО».] Reznikov, p. 223.

222 [То же самое повторилось во время поездки летом 1929 года, когда Горький побывал в Ленинграде, Мурманске, Сталинграде, Астрахани, Сухуми, Тбилиси, Владикавказе и др. На сей раз ему удалось повидать не только совхоз 'Гигант', но и Соловки, все в том же сопровождении любезных и услужливых людей, которые зорко следили за каждым его шагом. Понимал ли Горький, что ему показывают не реальные достижения, а "потемкинские деревни"? Что грузчики на волжских пристанях не ходят каждый день в шляпах голландских моряков, что мужики не пьют какао, а заключенные в Соловках не спят на чистом белье и не читают газеты? На этот вопрос могли бы ответить горьковские записи, которые он вел во время поездки, но странным образом два его чемодана были похищены, а рукописи изъяты. Сопровождавшая писателя Н.А. Пешкова вспоминала: '...в один прекрасный день, когда его не было дома, или он спал, чемодан с его рукописями исчез, а месяца через два чемодан этот был прислан обратно, там были какие-то сапоги вложены, но коробка, где были его рукописи, была с пеплом. И Ягода объяснил, что когда они обнаружили жуликов, и когда те увидели, что это рукописи Горького, они перепугались и будто бы эти рукописи сожгли. А записей там было много'. | Чего же перепугались странные "жулики", если впечатления

Spiridonova also quotes from a short letter Gor'kii sent to Iagoda in January 1930, in which he apologized for his report on the Solovki camp.[223] It is worth underlining that, had the writer meant to tell the whole truth about the SLON, they would not have allowed him to do so — especially considering how strictly scrutinized both the writer and his books were. Still, Gor'kii might have disowned the book once he was back in Italy — losing any opportunity to go back to the Soviet Union, giving up the parades, the laurels, and the crowds. He did not do so. While abroad, he never disowned his 'essays'. Finally, his later attitude — in particular the leading role he played in the publication of the encomiastic book about the Belomorkanal — testifies to his loyalty to the Soviet cause.

In the summer of 1929, Gor'kii's loyalty was still being tested. The visit to the SLON could have been the main test that Stalin had arranged for Gor'kii. Although in his own mind he had already accepted Stalin's proposal about his return to the Soviet Union, Gor'kii was probably torn by inner conflict. He strongly believed that re-education was necessary and he clung to this belief in order to overcome his moral qualms during his journey. The man who visited the Solovki islands was by no means happy. Photographs show him looking annoyed, and he barely smiles. In fact, Gor'kii's troubled conscience seems to surface both in his gloomy depiction of nature, which in June was probably most luxuriant,[224] and in his untypically unrefined style.[225] Gor'kii probably decided to do his duty but soon repented rather bitterly — unless, of course, he had been lying to Moroz and had acted in bad faith.

That Gor'kii did not lie to his friend is confirmed by the original manuscript of his *ocherk*, which is contained in the *Institut Mirovoi Literatury* archive of the Russian Academy of Sciences in Moscow. However, if Gor'kii was right about the fact that Soviet censors sifted meticulously through his 'essays', in his words to Moroz he might have been referring to stylistic aspects, because the ideas expressed in the essay were by no means affected by the censors. In fact, although Gor'kii's draft is full of erasures and corrections (which make reading difficult in places), the famous sentence about the necessity of the Gulag is neatly formulated in words Gor'kii chose and which the censors did not change.[226] Moreover, the readable passages share a similar underlying tone, which is perfectly in tune with the published book and which informs all the *ocherki* included in *Nashi Dostizheniia*. The whole book is pervaded by Gor'kii's celebration of the achievements of Socialism, weighed

Горького были лишь положительного характера и никак не могли повредить престижу официальных властей? Видимо, не только 'эйфория' отражалась в этих записях, которые Горький мог бы опубликовать на Западе. О характере сожженных бумаг можно судить по маленькой заметке, случайно оставшейся у Н.А. Пешковой: 'Вы расстреливали и вешали равнодушно, мы расстреливаем с отвращением'. Выразительное признание одного из хозяев ГУЛАГа!] Spiridonova, p. 220.

223 Ibid.

224 I wish to express my thanks to Elena Rafaelovna Matevosian, who suggested this to me.

225 Including extremely clumsy passages, such as the description of the pigs bred at the SLON, which Gor'kii compares to the capitalists. Gor'kii, *Po soiuzu sovetov*, pp. 219–20.

226 AG, KhPG-41-13-6.

against his trenchant (and often unrefined from a literary point of view) critique of the Capitalist world.

Literary critics and historians have sometimes depicted Gor'kii as a highly skilled diplomat who sacrificed his reputation and determination to pursue his lifelong defence of intellectuals and of the 'weakest' even towards the end of his life. It is undeniable that Gor'kii was wholeheartedly committed to the establishment of a 'Soviet National Literature' when he was unofficially appointed director of the project in 1932.[227] While Gor'kii did not help all writers and sometimes ignored requests for help from endangered authors, once he started to direct the Union of Soviet Writers, Gor'kii managed to support fellow writers and help intellectuals in need — sometimes also former prisoners, whom he hired as translators.[228] He did intercede on behalf of some of his friends, as happened when he helped Iuliia Danzas (an old friend and a former SLON inmate) to emigrate.[229] Nonetheless, it is absurd to consider him as a 'rescuer of souls' — especially in regard to his second visit to the Soviet Union.

There are no documents which show, for example, that Gor'kii interceded with the SLON authorities on behalf of the SLON prisoners. Spiridonova says that Gor'kii was responsible for the removal of the *besprizorniki* colony as well as for the establishment of the Shanin commission and the subsequent internal purges: however, in addition to camp guards, prisoners were also among the victims of the purges (in fact, the months that followed Gor'kii's visit saw a peak in shootings), and this testifies against this hypothesis.

Restarting Publications

It is impossible to say whether Gor'kii played a direct role in the re-opening of the SLON publications. Since the SLON press was re-established immediately after the writer's visit, it is highly probable that he did. It is also possible that, despite the underlying argument of *Nashi Dostizheniia*, he complained about the closure of the camp publications.[230] However, his private library, kept at the Gor'kii Archive at IMLI in Moscow, did not include any copies of the SLON journals and Gor'kii did not personally meet any SLON intellectuals.[231] His role in the revival of the press

227 The correspondence between Stalin and Gor'kii often shows Stalin's intention to have Gor'kii leading the process. Once the novelist arrived in Moscow, in 1932, Stalin went to Gor'kii's home several times and organized there some meetings with writers which Gor'kii himself chaired. See Roi Medvedev and Zhores Medvedev, *Neizvestnyi Stalin* (Moscow: Vremia, 2011), p. 275. Gor'kii then became the first president of the Union of Soviet Writers, in 1934.

228 As was the case with Boris Leitin, who asked Gor'kii for some translation work. See Moscow, AG, KG-P 44–11-X, Boris Leitin, 'Pis'ma M. Gor'komu'.

229 Moscow, AG, KG-R3I 1–136, Iuliia Danzas, 'Perepiska s M. Gor'kim'.

230 In his *ocherk*, Gor'kii wrote about the interruption of the *Novye Solovki*, but stated that the journal was still being published. 'On the island ethnographic studies are conducted, a journal is published, and a newspaper used to be issued, but its publication is temporarily interrupted' [Ведется на острове краеведческая работа, печатается журнал, издавалась газета, но издание ее на время прекращено]. See Gor'kii, *Po soiuzu sovetov*, p. 226.

231 That Gor'kii interceded on behalf of the SLON prisoners whom he knew is false, apart from his only acquaintance among the SLON prisoners, i.e. the aforementioned Iuliia Danzas. For more

was probably indirect. In fact, the reopening of the SLON publications might have been part of the Soviet propaganda campaign associated with Gor'kii's visit.[232] The words of his *ocherk* might actually have been better supported by the existence of journals that were sold overseas and could be bought by subscription. Again, this is merely hypothetical.[233]

It can be guessed that inspiration came either from Gor'kii's straightforward request or from the OGPU, which might have made a decision during or after Gor'kii's visit. There is, however, a third hypothesis, one which involves, once again, Fedor Eikhmans. Eikhmans had been relocated to Moscow before Gor'kii's visit (in May 1929) and had become one of the cadres. He directed the Third Special Office of the OGPU, to which the SLON administration had to report from the very beginning. It is possible that Eikhmans took advantage of Gor'kii's visit to publish journals in the camp once more. This hypothesis is supported by another coincidence — Eikhmans, who later became for a very short time the first director of the newly-born GULag in 1930, was removed from his position precisely when the two main publications of the SLON press were replaced by publications that were typical of prison camp press elsewhere in the Gulag.[234] It is, however, difficult to substantiate Eikhmans's actions from Moscow.

Since no documents explain the real reason for this sudden turn in the history of the SLON press, it is only possible to formulate hypotheses. What we know for sure is that both the relaunched *Solovetskie Ostrova* and the *Novye Solovki* underwent some radical changes when compared to the early phase of the SLON publications.

The *Solovetskie Ostrova* was the first to come out. Its first issue (August 1929) opened with a short message by the editorial board announcing the reopening of the journal by tracing its history since the beginning of the SLON press and referring to other camp publications. The article pinpointed the primary objective of the SLON press, that is to say, 'to describe everyday life in the camp, to celebrate its achievements, and to underline its flaws'.[235] More objectives followed; the very

on Danzas, see Giovanna Parravicini, *Julija Danzas* (Milan: La casa di Matriona, 2001).

232 This would chime with the thesis formulated by some researchers, including Irina Flige (see Interview with Irina Flige, September 2010). Flige maintains that the reopening of the camp press was part of a strategy aimed at undermining increasing rumours about the violence inflicted on the SLON prisoners; presumably Gor'kii's visit was a key part in the strategy to counter rumours about the mistreatment of prisoners. The writer's journey was to be followed by the opening of journals, which he mentioned in his *ocherk*.

233 Kuziakina, quoting Chukhin, maintains that the reopening of the camp press was part of a preventative strategy: the British 'Thompson mission', appointed by the British Parliament, had by then started its journey across the Soviet Union to monitor human rights in the Gulag. It visited the SLON in 1929 but could not reach the Solovki due to some well-planned (i.e. by the OGPU) accidents. This explanation, however, accounts neither for the duration of the 'second season' of the camp press nor for the fact that the *Novye Solovki* was published four months after the *Solovetskie Ostrova*. See Kuziakina, p. 90.

234 Eikhmans became the director of the GULag on 25 April 1930. On 16 June, he began to organize the Vaigach expedition, and therefore left his position. The last issue of the *Solovetskie Ostrova* came out in May, immediately after Eikhmans had left his post at the Third Office of the OGPU. The last issue of *Novye Solovki* came out on 25 July.

235 'Ot redaktsii', *SO*, 1 (1929), 3.

last was 'to channel camp prisoners' creative potential',[236] which in fact would turn out to be the major achievement of the new *Solovetskie Ostrova*.

From the very beginning, the journal looked like a literary almanac. Apart from the message from the editorial board, the first issue included two full-page politics columns (on the revival of publishing activities in the camp and on the anniversary of the First World War, seen as the beginning of the October Revolution) and three sections devoted, respectively, to the economy, daily life, and general work. These sections were followed by prisoners' poems and short stories, which could also be found at the bottom of the previous pages. It was quite a large section: forty-eight pages of the newly-born journal, whose cover image showed the Solovki seagull,[237] were interspersed with eighteen literary texts.

The front cover and the literary section were not the only novelty. More space was actually devoted to engravings, drawings, and sketches — which significantly improved the graphic quality of the journal. The first issue, of course, included several epigrams and celebratory poems dedicated to Gor'kii, and a portrait of the writer was placed among poems by prisoners.

The literary section of the journal was further improved in the second issue. Pages three to twenty-two were devoted to camp prisoners' poems and short stories, whose quality was largely rewarding. When the SLON press was reopened, contributors included several relatively talented poets and writers. Some of them were already professional writers; others had been inspired by the extraordinary, feverish cultural life of the camp. Far from marking a decline in intellectual activities, the interruption of the SLON press ultimately coincided with a creative climax.

Meanwhile, the SLON theatre company had been working without interruption and was now directed by Boris Glubokovskii, the only artist who had remained after the 'first season' of camp publications. It is difficult to say why Glubokovskii served his entire sentence at the camp: in any case, in 1929 he was the director of the *Biuro Pechati*, and he consequently played a most prominent role in the intellectual life of the camp. As a result, he could afford elegant clothes that set him apart from other prisoners. This is how Likhachev describes him:

> In the years of my stay on Solovki, the soul of the Solteatr and of the journal *Solovki*[238] was Boris Glubokovskii — an actor of Tairov's Chamber Theatre, the son of a well-known (in his time) theologian and church historian Nikolai Nikanorovich Glubokovskii, whose correspondence with V. V. Rozanov has recently been published.[239]
>
> I knew Boris Glubokovskii well, not as a close friend, but rather as a very prominent personality, who did much for the camp *intelligentsiia*. Basically

---

236 Ibid.

237 The seagull plays a significant role in the imagery of the SLON. A large number of memoir writers remember the seagull's cries as a torture (curiously enough, Gor'kii perceived the seagull's cries as a torture too, as he wrote in his report). In that place of imprisonment and suffering, the seagulls were also 'guilty' of being free. There was, however, one more detail. The seagull was depicted on the stage of the SLON theatre. It was a replica of the symbol of the Art Theatre in Moscow, where some of the actors and directors working at Solteatr used to play. See Kuziakina, p. 49.

238 Likhachev here clearly means the *Solovetskie Ostrova*.

239 Here again Likhachev makes a mistake: Glubokovskii's father was one Aleksandr Glubokovskii, his patronymic being 'Aleksandrovich'.

FIG. 3.13. The entrance of the main theatre of the SLON. AMM

everyone knew him. It is a pity that no photographs of him have survived to date.[240] He was a tall, slender, beautiful, lively man, with good manners. He was dressed following the Solovki fashion, available only to the few people who were admitted to Pomof (the sewing workshop, which would provide clothing for the wives of the few free workers and most of the criminal prisoners): a black short coat with a sash, black breeches, high boots, a cap slightly askew. His talent was versatile. It was said that he took part in the bohemian circles around Esenin. He was charged for participating in some conspiracy called the 'White Centre'. Of course, he could have been accused of that, but I highly doubt that he would have risked it, since by character he had quite a selfish nature.[241]

By the time the camp press reopened, the SLON museum and the SOK were also well-established institutions. Other institutions, such as the botanical garden and

---

240 In fact, at least one photograph of Glubokovskii *has* survived: see Chapter 4 below.

241 [В годы моего пребывания на Соловках душой Солтеатра, как и журнала «Соловки», был Борис Глубоковский — актер Камерного театра Таирова, сын известного в свое время богослова и историка церкви Николая Никаноровича Глубоковского, переписка которого с В. В. Розановым не так давно опубликована. Бориса Николаевича Глубоковского я хорошо знал, но не как близкого знакомого, а как чрезвычайно видную и много сделавшую для лагерной интеллигенции личность. Его, по существу, знали все. Жаль, что не сохранилось его фотографии. Это был высокого роста человек, стройный, красивый, живой, с хорошими манерами. Одет он был по соловецкой моде немногих людей, которым был доступен Помоф (пошивочная мастерская, одевавшая жен немногих вольнонаемных и наиболее блатных из заключенных): черное полупальто с кушаком, черные галифе, высокие сапоги, кепка чуть набекрень. | Он был разносторонне одарен. Ему приписывалось участие в богемном окружении Есенина. Обвинялся за участие в каком-то заговоре «Белого центра». Обвиняться он, конечно, мог, но вряд ли бы он стал рисковать по свойствам своей несколько эгоистической натуры.] Likhachev, *Izbrannoe: Vospominaniia*, p. 212.

the library, were fully operational. Two more elements contributed to the camp's prominent cultural status. On the one hand, the administration was more than ever committed to the 'liquidation of illiteracy', a goal that it carried out through a network of new schools and training centres. On the other hand, a *Kriminologicheskii kabinet* was set up as a special department of the SOK. The unit was entirely run by prisoner-intellectuals and investigated the cultural output of criminals and of ordinary prisoners.

The number of *intelligenty* among camp inmates was rapidly increasing. Some of them were prominent intellectuals; for example, prisoners involved in the Meier affair (some of whom enjoyed fame on a national scale)[242] were sent to the Solovki islands and eventually became part of the camp administration and cultural activities. In general, the SLON started to host an increasing number of writers and intellectuals who were sentenced to imprisonment and who formed a group of mutually supportive and mutually encouraging minds. Several of them had desk jobs and consequently managed to save their acquaintances by offering them office jobs. Solidarity and intimate closeness lay at the core of a particularly lively cultural system. Poetry readings and philosophical debates regularly took place in the camp's dimly lit barracks. Cultural meetings were clandestinely arranged and held at the administration headquarters, where the *intelligenty* even managed to organise some literary debates. Wholeheartedly committed to *likbez*, the camp directors actively promoted workshops and lectures on a wide range of cultural topics. Well-known academics and young intellectuals (rather than Party officers and chekists, as was the case in most camps) mounted the stage of the Solteatr or of the club, which regularly hosted this kind of event.

This remarkable cultural vigour poured out onto the pages of the *Solovetskie Ostrova*. The most prominent figures of this second period were Vladimir Sveshnikov-Kemetskii,[243] Aleksandr Peshkovskii,[244] and Iurii Kazarnovskii, who turned out to be a real 'joker', playing the same role as Nikolai Litvin had done a few years before. Unlike Litvin, Kazarnovskii was also a gifted poet and a talented humourist. He wrote poems and light-hearted articles which perfectly blended the literary and the economic-scientific depths of the *Solovetskie Ostrova*.

While the economic-scientific section of the journal was published in the second issue, it covered cultural themes such as re-education, reading, and the editing of old manuscripts contained in the Solovki library. In addition, a poetry column was published on the back page of the second issue and became a regular column of the journal.

---

242 Apart from Meier, new SLON inmates included the scholar Nikolai Antsiferov (who wrote pioneering studies on urban space and other famous books, as *The Soul of Petersburg*, written in 1922, see Nikolai Antsiferov, *Dusha Peterburga* (Leningrad: Lenizdat, 1991)), the historian Nina Pigulevskaia, and the *Mir Iskusstva* painter Pavel Smotritskii.
243 Kemetskii was the poet who published most frequently, as shall be seen in the following chapter.
244 Peshkovskii, who was the vice-director of the Krimkab, published literary works. Moreover, he was a *lagkor*, who often published articles about the *likbez*. His role was prominent as a mediator between the two aspects of SLON literary culture, the ideological and the *intelligentnyi*.

The 3/4 issue of the *Solovetskie Ostrova* (October–November) continued with the same layout used in the first issue. It included a short politics column (2 pages), a large literary section (23 pages), a series of scientific, economic, and cultural articles, and lastly prisoners' poems. Recurring references to Germany — identified as 'the most corrupt Capitalist nation' — explain the presence of plates by the painter Pavel Smotritskii attached to poems describing that country. Some of the poems were by intellectuals like Kemetskii, who had spent several years in Berlin and had been sentenced to prison on his return to the Soviet Union.[245]

The October–November issue also included two remarkable cultural essays. The first was by the composer Aleksandr Kenel', who described the SLON concerts, and the second was by Nikolai Vinogradov, who wrote about the history of the monastery.[246] Vinogradov was, to some extent, an ambiguous man, but the role he played as a scholar and as a defender of the intellectuals in the camp is undeniable. Likhachev — the memoir writer who devoted most of his reflections to cultural life at the time of the press revival — writes that Vinogradov managed to save many *intelligenty* thanks to his connections to high-ranking officers:

> In her memoirs, written in France, Iuliia Nikolaevna Danzas speaks in an extremely harsh way about the museum, calling it 'anti-religious', and also about N. N. Vinogradov and his staff, claiming that she firmly refused to conduct anti-religious guided tours. Vinogradov would hardly have made her lead these guided tours: for this he had a handy villain, A. B. Ivanov. On the contrary, Vinogradov would help members of the *intelligentsiia* in any way he could and never forced anyone to do anything. He saved Iuliia Nikolaevna herself from 'general' (physical) work, before she went to work at the Krimkab. [...] Before my arrival on the Solovki, Vinogradov had the famous painter Osip Emmanuilovich Braz working at the museum, after providing him with paper and watercolours, and after acquiring permission for him to paint watercolours freely beyond the walls of the Kremlin, allegedly to 'make immortal the remarkable achievements of re-education'. O. E. Braz painted dozens of beautiful landscapes which were later exhibited in the well illuminated choir of the Annunciation Church. I was later told that these watercolours were in the Kazan' Cathedral, in the Museum of Religion and Atheism of the Academy of Sciences of the USSR. I do not know where they went afterwards.
>
> When two students from Ukrainian art schools came to Solovki — one from Kiev, the other from Chernigov — Petrash, and Vovk, N. N. Vinogradov gave them watercolours and paper. N. N. Vinogradov was a good judge of character, and knew who was worth helping.[247]

---

245 Having lived abroad was typically considered evidence of spying activities.

246 A. Kenel', 'Muzykal'noe oformlenie v Solovetskom teatre', *SO*, 3–4 (1929), 26–28 (p. 26); N. Vinogradov, 'K istorii Solovetskogo monastyria', *SO*, 3–4 (1929), 40.

247 [Юлия Николаевна Данзас в своих воспоминаниях, написанных во Франции, чрезвычайно резко отзывается о Музее, называя его «антирелигиозным», а также о самом Н. Н. Виноградове и о его сотрудниках, заявляя при этом, что она решительно отказалась водить антирелигиозные экскурсии. Вряд ли Н. Н. Виноградов заставлял ее водить такие экскурсии: для этого у него был сподручный негодяй — А. Б. Иванов. Напротив, Н. Н. Виноградов всячески спасал интеллигенцию и никого ни к чему не принуждал. Спас он от «общих» (физических) работ и саму Юлию Николаевну, прежде, чем она перешла потом на работу в Криминологический кабинет. [...] Еще до моего приезда на Соловки Виноградов

Fig. 3.14. Pavel Smotritskii's engraving on Germany. AMSPB

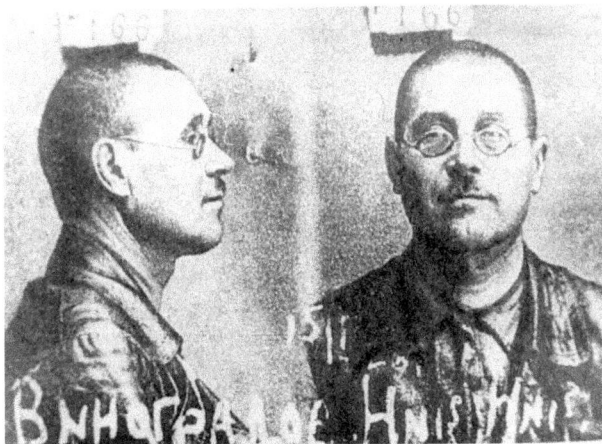

FIG. 3.15. Nikolai Vinogradov. AMM

Vinogradov also managed to save (at least temporarily) some valuable icons from the incinerator. He also wrote several important books, including the above-mentioned survey of the pre-historical labyrinths on the Zaiatskie islands.

Rather surprisingly, the fifth issue of the *Solovetskie Ostrova* (December) did not come out, probably because of the definitive relocation of the camp administration to Kem', which according to Kuziakina took place in December 1929, while the printing equipment had already been moved on 22 September 1929.[248] The fact that a typhus epidemic was raging across the SLON might further account for the interruption. Figures in Chukhin's book reveal that typhus is estimated to have killed about 44% of the SLON population.[249] By the early months of 1930, however, the SLON press was operational again, marked by the reopening of the camp newspaper, the *Novye Solovki*. The first 1930 issue (5 January) had a typical four-page format, but its contents were totally new, as the first editorial announced:

> The days when the *gazeta* served as a distraction for unoccupied people, when the *gazeta* allowed 'canards',[250] invented sensational news, provided 'entertaining' but meaningless reading, have gone. Now the press, in the hands of the working class, has acquired a different direction.[251]

устроил работать в музее известного художника Осипа Эммануиловича Браза, добыв ему бумагу и акварельные краски и получив на него разрешение свободно писать акварели за пределами Кремля, якобы «для увековечения замечательного достижения перевоспитания». О. Э. Браз нарисовал несколько десятков прекрасных пейзажей, выставленных затем на хорошо освещенных хорах Благовещенской церкви. Впоследствии мне говорили, что акварели эти находились в Казанском соборе — «Музее религии и атеизма Академии наук СССР». Куда они делись затем, — не знаю. | Когда на Соловки прибыло два студента украинских художественных училищ — один из Киева, а другой из Чернигова — Петраш и Вовк, Н. Н. Виноградов и их снабдил акварелью и бумагой. Н. Н. Виноградов разбирался в людях и знал, кому следует помогать.] Likhachev, *Izbrannoe: Vospominaniia*, p. 206.

248 M. Malchanov, 'Tipografiia USLON', *NS*, 3 (1930), 3.

249 Kuziakina, p. 88.

250 Journalistic term for 'fake news'.

251 [Прошло то время, когда газета служила развлечением бездельным людям, когда газета

Тов. И. В. СТАЛИН

FIG. 3.16. The portrait of Stalin on 2/3 1930 issue of the *Solovetskie Ostrova*

The author plainly points out the need to cut ties with the past. The new *Novye Solovki* would essentially be a tool of camp re-education and, unlike its predecessor, would not include any references to camp entertainments. In fact, the first issues still contained some hints at the SLON theatres. Kazarnovskii's genius was typically responsible for this, as shown by the epigrams he dedicated to the actors of a SLON performance:

1. И.Д. КАЛУГИН
(К... надцотому[sic!] чтению «Гармони»)

Опять! — вопит гармонь в испуге —
Нет отдыха ни на момент!
Пора бы, гражданин Калугин,
Переменить вам... инструмент!

2. А.С. МОСКВИН
(К песенке «Пионер»)

Вот детства милого пример
Поет... И нежно розовеет:
Ведь сам почти что пионер —
Всего три года лишь имеет. *)

*) Примечание: Правда, не по метрике, а по Коллегии, но это не важно.[252]

Kazarnovskii's epigrams were, however, merely an exception. The new issues of *Novye Solovki* adhered quite strictly to the directives announced by the opening editorial because the editorial board was now in Kem'.[253] On the Solovki islands, a new journal, the *Solovetskii Listok*, was rapidly founded (unfortunately, no copies have survived to date). Its distance from the archipelago and the cultural turmoil of the Solovki, and its closeness to the innumerable building sites of Soviet Karelia, affected the editorial board of the *Novye Solovki* rather profoundly. The legacy represented by the early issues of the journal and by its cultural debate was lost forever. Short, sporadic articles were devoted to the SLON theatre companies, whereas politics and 'production achievements' of the mainland departments of the SLON were given the spotlight.

Only Kazarnovskii brightened up the grey landscape of the *Novye Solovki* with

пускала «утки», выдумывала сенсации, давала «занимательное», но бессодержательное чтение; теперь в руках рабочего класса печать получила иную устремленность] 'Pechat' i proizvodstvo', *NS*, 1 (1930), 1.
252 [1. I.D. KALUGIN | (To the ... umpteenth recital 'The Accordion') || Again! — The accordion wails in terror — | There is no rest, not even for a moment! | It's time for you, o citizen Kalugin, | To change... your instrument! || 2. A.S. MOSKVIN | (For the song 'The Pioneer') || Here is an example of sweet childhood | He sings... And gently blushes: | After all, he is almost a pioneer — | He is only three. *) ||*) Note: Actually, not from his birth certificate, but according to the tribunal, but it does not matter.] Iu. Kazarnovskii, 'Druzheskie epigrammy k kontsertu № 3', *NS*, 1 (1930), 4. Poems will be produced in Russian in the text with their English translation in the footnote. This is to show the original graphic arrangement of the poems, which sometimes were laid on the page in a particular way, as will be seen later.
253 Although the editorial board was now in Kem', a number of former contributors, among whom was Kazarnovskii, were still living in the Solovki islands.

his distinctively creative touch. Of all the original *Solovetskie Ostrova* contributors, Kazarnovskii was the only one who managed to write a regular column in the reborn *gazeta* as well. He published his poems, his light-hearted quatrains, and his 'friendly epigrams' in both the *Solovetskie Ostrova* and the *Novye Solovki*. The latter, starting from its second issue (12 January 1930),[254] allowed him to edit his own feuilleton. Kazarnovskii cunningly used the column to publish either poetry or prose pieces that were pervaded by his distinctive humour:

> Above all, Kem' is not a carefree city.
> Unlike the other insubstantial cities, here people do not come for 'two or three days'. It is not that type of city.
> They come here directly for three, five, ten years.
> [...]
> The landlady, waving her plump hands, told me with conviction:
> — And please tell me what, just what does this apartment not have?
> She is right — said the tenant bitterly.
>
> What does my apartment not have? No electricity, no beds, no toilet, no sink.
> And, having lost count, he muttered:
> — And the landlady's character, what a pain in the neck!
> And, not wanting to say only negative things, he guiltily added:
> — But there are cockroaches...[255]

Kazarnovskii's unique brio was the only concession that the *Novye Solovki* made to feed its readers' desire for entertainment. This is, however, hardly surprising. The reopening of the SLON press coincided with a crucial moment in the history of the camp and the Soviet Union. It occurred in the middle of the first *piatiletka* (five-year plan), which affected the *Novye Solovki*, now filled with party slogans. Some excerpts from the newspaper explicitly reflect common themes of the years of Stalinization:

> Being participants in the implementation of the five-year plan in one of the most serious and important parts of cultural construction — the participation of socially dangerous elements in cultural re-education through labour, — we must use all possibilities, all means for the development and improvement of our work, in order to achieve the maximum success in it.[256]

---

254 Iu. Kazarnovskii, 'Fel'eton', *NS*, 2 (1930), 1.
255 [Кемь город, прежде всего, не легкомысленный. | Не в пример прочим несолидным городам, сюда не едут «денька на два-на три». Не такой это город. | Едут сюда уж сразу на годика на три, на пять, на десять. | [...] | Хозяйка квартиры, размахивая полными руками, убежденно мне говорила: | — И чего, чего только у меня в квартире нет. | Она права — горько сказал квартирант. | Чего, чего только нет: электричества нет, рам нет, уборной нет, умывальника нет. | И сбившись с перечисления, пробурчал: | — А характер у хозяйки, что конская щетка. | И, не желая все только отрицать, виновато добавил: | — Тараканы есть...] Iu. Kazarnovskii, 'Sobstvenno govoria, v Kemi ... (zametki iz Blok-nota)', *NS*, 10 (1930), 2.
256 [Являясь участниками реализации пятилетнего плана на одном из серьезных и важных участках культурного строительства, — участие культурно-трудового перевоспитания социально-опасного элемента, — мы должны употребить все возможности, все средства для развертывания и улучшения нашей работы, для достижения в ней максимальных успехов.] 'Vyzovy na sotsialisticheskoe sorevnovanie', *NS*, 2 (1930), 1.

Paradoxical though this might seem, no mention of such radical change was made in the *Solovetskie Ostrova*. Its first 1930 issue, in fact, shows a preponderance of literary and cultural essays. Out of its sixty-four pages, only twenty were devoted to other topics. Significantly enough, this issue included the first in a series of Kazarnovskii's literary parodies, which were greatly appreciated by the camp prisoners. Moreover, this issue also coincided with Dmitrii Likhachev's first-ever published article, a study of camp card games.[257] The 2/3 issue of *Solovetskie Ostrova* did not include any political editorials, even though a drawing of Stalin strikingly appears immediately after the table of contents. The page devoted to a portrait of the *Vozhd'* was followed by eighty pages containing not only scientific articles but also a copy of a speech by Nogtev, then director of the camp after Eikhmans's departure to Moscow. Apart from those pages, literary texts dominated the issue.

In the meantime, *Novye Solovki* finally achieved one of its lifelong goals: the recruitment of *lagkory*. Through its constant focus on re-education, the journal was promoting a number of initiatives to implement re-educational activities and to highlight the achievements of *perevospitanie* and of *likbez*. The thirteenth issue (6 April 1930) of *Novye Solovki* thus ran a new competition for the best camp *stengazeta*[258] and the thirtieth issue (5 July 1930) advertised a competition[259] for the best article and the best camp short story, to be eventually published in *Solovetskie Ostrova*. The results, however, were never published.

The End of the Main Publications of the SLON Press

The results of the competition for the best article and short story were not published because, shortly after the announcement of the competition, the *Solovetskie Ostrova* was closed down once more, this time for ever. The journal's fourth issue for 1930 had confirmed its distinctive trend: thirty-eight literary pages vs ten pages devoted to economic news. The last issue (May 1930) proposed a long-forgotten balance between literary works and political-scientific ones.

On 25 July 1930, the last issue of the *Novye Solovki* was published. In the preceding months, fewer and fewer pages had been devoted to culture, whereas the editorial board paid greater attention to current affairs. Theatre-focused columns had by then almost disappeared and Kazarnovskii had lost his feuilleton to a writer whose pseudonym was 'Ovod'. In the meantime, some of the former *Solovetskie Ostrova* contributors, like Maks Kiunert, had started their careers as *lagkory*, while Kemetskii published his poetry in the *Novye Solovki* after the closure of the journal. Finally, a larger number of columns focused on topics such as poor-quality food, poor services, and sanitary emergencies.[260]

---

257 Since no copies of the *Solovetskii Listok* have survived to date, it is impossible for researchers to read Likhachev's review of drama performances as well as his first (and unique) literary experiments. See Dmitrii Likhachev, 'Kartezhnye igry ugolovnikov' (iz rabot krim. kabineta), SO, 1 (1930), 35–37.
258 'Bez nazvaniia', NS, 13 (1930), 4. The *stengazety* continued to be published even after 1926.
259 'Bez nazvaniia', NS, 30 (1930), 2.
260 Once again, the press never hinted at typhus. Only scurvy was mentioned.

The closure of both *Novye Solovki* and *Solovetskie Ostrova* came unexpectedly. Ongoing competitions actually indicated the editorial board's intention to go on publishing both journals and the subscription campaign went on in the pages of the *gazeta* until its last issue. It is therefore hard to say why the main organs of the SLON press were shut down. The closure seems even more surprising considering the success of the SLON press: the *Novye Solovki* had a circulation of 5,000 copies (all of which were sold inside the camp), whereas the *Solovetskie Ostrova* reached a circulation of 3,000 copies, hundreds of which were sold by subscription. A convincing explanation can be found in the reorganization of the camp, which in these years became part of the USIKMITL,[261] although it is difficult to understand why the interruption came so abruptly if the main organs of the SLON press were either enjoying success outside the camp, or meeting the requirements of propaganda. Trying to follow the hypotheses outlined above about the revival of these two publications, we might assume that their closure had to do either with weaker international pressure on the SLON (with the withdrawal of the West's threat to stop all timber imports from the Soviet Union), or with the fact that Eikhmans no longer held a position which allowed him to influence the situation or, ultimately, with Gor'kii's absence from the Soviet Union in the summer of 1930. The only hint we have is a short text published by the KVCH in May 1930 requesting proposals for all publications needed in 1930–31, as suggested in a decree (no. 174). We do not know who asked for this, but presumably the decree suggested some reorganisation in publishing activities which resulted in the closure of the main publications.[262]

Finally, the definitive closure of the main organs of the SLON press can be regarded as a first step towards the creation of the 'Press for the Great Construction of Communism'. The 1930 season of *Novye Solovki* was a worthy father of this kind of camp publication, which was first experimented with on the Solovki islands. The newspaper *Perekovka*[263] was actually founded in the SLON in the October 1930. It rapidly turned into the most notorious instrument of Soviet propaganda and agitation on the Baltic-White Sea Canal, where censorship control was stricter.

Censorship and its Oversights: 'Freer than the Free'

One of the most surprising aspects of the SLON press is that its contributors enjoyed an unparalleled degree of freedom of speech. This peculiar phenomenon cannot be ascribed simply to Eikhmans's protection. That prisoners of a camp devoted to the repression — or, at least, the re-education — of counter revolutionary elements should enjoy the freedom of speech denied to Soviet citizens is totally bewildering.

It is, however, worth considering how censorship worked on the Solovki islands. In the early years, censorship was primarily local and did not rely on external

---

261 See p. 51 and Fischer von Weikersthal, pp. 186–87.
262 'Bez nazvaniia', NS, 21 (1930), 4.
263 The SLON press now included also the *Trudovik* newspaper. Unfortunately, no copies of it have survived to date. Only a photograph of a front page exists. The same applies to the last SLON journal, the *Golos Perekovki*, which first came out in 1935.

support. No Glavlit officers or general censors entered the SLON, where the KVCh selected and censored the SLON publications. As far as the first period of publications is concerned, Shiriaev's memoirs show that the KVCh had no special censorship department and it was Sukhov — one of the three KVCh members of the editorial board — who controlled the SLON press. Sukhov was an authorized representative of the Karlit (Karelian Glavlit).[264] Shiriaev described the workings of the administration's editorial board, which Eikhmans directed from 1925, thus:

> A weekly printed newspaper was permitted. There were no signatures of editors or publishers on it, but in practice P. A. Petriaev was appointed as editor, Tver'e as secretary, and as censor Sukhov, *komissar* of the Solovki special regiment. Each of them was typical of the Solovki of those times. [...] Official censorship did not incommode Petriaev, since the real censor was Sukhov, a long-service sergeant-major of the cavalry, who had been through some *sovpartshkola*.[265] The communist treatment was however not good enough to erase the strong principles laid down in it by the training regimen of the Imperial Army from the soul of that pen-pusher. On the Solovki the former sergeant-major Sukhov was military commissar of the regiment, while Petriaev, the former captain of the guard and a revolutionary commander, was a convict. But, in Sukhov's unconscious mind, Petriaev remained the captain of the guard. And although he was a revolutionary captain, he was still a sort of army commander, or general. The officer of the special regiment was evidently timid in his dealings with the convict, and unconditionally signed off all the proofs presented by Petriaev, sometimes without even reading them. Even after a careful reading, he was clearly not able to make sense of many of them.[266]

Tver'e, who was soon demoted and replaced by Shenberg, a much more yielding and indulgent person, was the only person depicted rather negatively by Shiriaev:

> The captious, suspicious Tver'e (real surname: Tveros) was the black sheep of the editorial board. Fortunately, he did not stay in it for long, because he

---

264 Fischer von Wiekersthal, p. 249.

265 Sovetskaia partiinaia shkola, a school dedicated to the political education of party members in the 1920s and 1930s.

266 [Еженедельная печатная газета была разрешена. На ней не стояло подписей ни редактора, ни издателя, но фактическим редактором был назначен П. А. Петряев, секретарем Тверье, цензором комиссар Соловецкого особого полка Сухов. Каждый из них был колоритен для Соловков того Времени. [...] Официальная цензура не стесняла Петряева, ведь цензором был Сухов из сверхсрочных вахмистров, прошедший какую-то совпартшколу. Коммунистическая обработка не могла вытравить в душе этого служаки крепких устоев, заложенных в нее учебной командой полка императорской армии. Теперь на Соловках бывший вахмистр Сухов был военкомом полка, а Петряев, бывший капитан гвардии и революционный командарм, — каторжником, но в подсознании Сухова Петряев оставался гвардии капитаном, да еще, как-никак хоть и революционным, но все же командармом, генералом. Военком охраны явно робел перед каторжником и безоговорочно подписывал к печати все предложенные Петряевым корректуры, иногда даже не читая их. Но и при внимательном чтении разобраться во многом ему явно было не по силам.] Shiriaev, pp. 130–31. A. Akarevich/Shiriaev's *My* describes the team and the work of the editorial board as per March 1925: Eikhmans (Head of the Editorial Board), N. V. Neverov (Vice Head of the Editorial Board), Tver'e, Koganov, Shiriaev, Berezin, Nedzvedstkii (members of the Editorial Board). See A. Akarevich, 'My'.

was moved to the guard squad in Kem'. After his transfer, Petriaev reduced the position of secretary to a purely technical role, and hired for it the exact opposite of Tver'e: the nice, friendly and accommodating Shenberg.[267]

The trio formed by Petriaev, Sukhov, and Shenberg — which would eventually become the staff of the *Biuro pechati* — generally proved to be understanding.[268] At the beginning, the result of the censors' work appeared in *Pochtovyi iashchik*, a column on the back page of the *SLON* journal, in which comments on submissions, whether rejected or approved, were published. This is an excerpt from the 9–10 1924 issue of the journal:

> To A. Trifil'ev. — Your travel notes of a naturalist, 'Kond and Onega', will not be published. There is little scientific material, while the literary aspect suffers from excessive subjectivity and is abundantly garnished with clichéd and sugary anachronisms. In response to your letter, the editorial board informs you that your reference to longstanding literary activity, to Slavophile-populist orientation (oh my, what liberalism!), as well as to your long night-time work, cannot serve as a reason for your manuscripts to escape the editorial board's rubbish bin, if they deserve it. Draw your own conclusions!
>
> N. P. — Your article 'The Chemical Industry in Relation to the Defense of the State' will be published in the January number.
>
> c. Glagolev. — For technical reasons, your article about geological research on the Kond islands will be published in the January number.
>
> c. Krivosh-Nemanich. — Your notes on the hydro-meteorological station and your poem 'New Year on Solovki' will not be published. We have already used part of the other texts, part we will use in the future.
>
> Dal'nevostochnyi. — Your note 'Our Landlords in the Forest' needs to be checked. Please come to the editorial board office.
>
> c. Leikin. — Your note 'Sukharevka No. 2' will not be published. Many of the things that you write about are already out of date. Try to set out the facts in a more objective way.[269]

267 [Придирчивый, подозрительный Тверье (подлинная фамилия Тверос) был темным пятном редакции. К счастью, он оставался в ней недолго, т. к. был переведен в команду охраны в Кемь. После его перевода Петряев свел должность секретаря к чисто технической работе и взял на нее полную противоположность Тверье — милого, приветливого и услужливого Шенберга.] Ibid., p. 132.

268 This much can be gathered from Shiriaev's book (ibid., pp. 129–41). Articles were, however, pre-selected by the prisoners who belonged to the editorial board of each journal, and the articles chosen by the editorial boards were subject to the final decision of the *Biuro Pechati*.

269 [А. Трифильеву. — Ваши путевые заметки натуралиста „Конд и Онега" помещены не будут. Научного материала в них мало, беллетристическая сторона их страдает излишней суб'ективностью и обильно уснащена трафаретно-слащавыми анахронизмами. В ответ на Ваше письмо, редакция ставит Вас в известность, что Ваши ссылки на долголетнюю литературную деятельность, славянофильско-народническую ориентацию (подумаешь, какой либерализм!), равно как и на длительную работу в ночную пору — не могут служить мотивом для того, чтобы Ваши рукописи избегли редакционной корзины, если они этого заслуживают. | Выводы делайте сами! | Н. П. — Ваша статья „Химическая промышленность в связи с обороной страны" будет помещена в январском номере. | т. Глаголеву. — По техническим условиям Ваша статья о геологическом исследовании Конд-Острова будет помещена в январском номере. | т. Кривош — Неманич. — Ваши заметка о

FIG. 3.17. The crew of the SLON typography. ASM

Whereas in the cases of Glagolev and others, the text hints at editorial activities, the author's reply to Trifil'ev and, in particular his trenchant remark on Trifil'ev's professional past, has political overtones.[270] The column eventually disappeared from both *Solovetskie Ostrova* and *Novye Solovki*,[271] as did any text related to publishing activity.

This silence might have been imposed by external censorship. As censorship

гидро-метеорологической станции и стихотворение „Новогоднее на Соловках" помещены не будут. Остальное частью использовали, частью используем. | Дальневосточному. — Ваша заметка „Наши помещики в лесу" — требует проверки. Заходите в редакцию. | т. Лейкину. — Ваша заметка „Сухаревка № 2" помешена не будет. Многое, о чем вы пишите — сейчас уже изжито. Постарайтесь более об'ективно излагать факты.] 'Pochtovyi iashchik', SLON, 9–10 (1924), 111. Like many of the *SLON* contributions, the text is grammatically inaccurate. Moreover, the soft sign, ь, is represented by an apostrophe. Here and throughout I have left the writing as it appears in the original source.

270 Trifil'ev was a former priest in the Church of St Nikolai in Rostov on Don. He was victim of a campaign in the SLON press throughout 1924 and in the beginning of 1925. See Il'ia Ershov, *'Bogema' i ugolovniki: Solovetskii teatr 1920-kh godov. Boris Glubokovskii*, Shkol'nyi konkurs 'Chelovek v istorii. Rossiia — XX vek' 1999–2000, http://urokiistorii.ru/node/209 [accessed 24 November 2014].

271 It disappeared from *Novye Solovki* much later and gradually became similar to a list of the decisions made by an editorial board.

scholar Nikolai Klepikov[272] points out, camp censorship was gradually transferred to Glavlit's regional departments. This occurred when the *SLON* was replaced by the *Solovetskie Ostrova*, which from the first 1925 issue to the seventh 1926 issue (the final issue before the first interruption) was published with the Karlit's imprimatur. The Karlit intervened also in the *Novye Solovki*, but its intervention was felt only from the seventeenth issue of 1925 (26 April) onwards. In the meantime, the Arkhangel'sk region party committee regularly requested copies of SLON publications. In the second period (starting from 1930), the Karlit was replaced by the Railit, the regional headquarters of the Glavlit in Arkhangel'sk. During the whole period of existence of the SLON publishing system, publications were therefore doubly sifted by the editorial board and by the Karlit (or the Railit). Nevertheless, SLON publications showed traces of preventive censorship or self-censorship only in the very first period of the publications (up until 1925). They appear to be completely free of it only from 1926 onwards — whereas both mechanisms were typical of the contemporary Soviet press. Moreover, those traces in Shiriaev's or even in Litvin's works seem to be part of a diplomatic strategy rather than the effect of self-censorship, since both writers also published freer pieces. In an attempt to explain this kind of freedom, Klepikov maintains, supporting Shiriaev's view, that the rejection of preventive censorship was basically the result of a deliberate political strategy:

> Nevertheless, in spite of some easing of censorship on the part of the camp administration, it is hardly worth exaggerating the degree of freedom of thought and action in the Solovki prison camp. The purpose of the *gazeta* and journal was subjected to the purely pragmatic interests of the OGPU leadership, according to which it regulated both the nature and the subject of the material published. In this regard, it is possible to agree with B. N. Shiriaev, one of the Solovki camp prisoners: 'I now understand the reasons for that freedom. The journal gave the OGPU undoubted benefits, firstly by providing information on [...] the state of minds of some circles of the *intelligentsiia*; secondly, it was an advertising trump card in the hands of that institution as a proof of the humanity of the Solovki regime in the eyes of the foreigners and, most importantly, of the higher levels of the party, in which, at that time, a strong opposition was active'.[273]

Though Klepikov might be right, this does not quite account for the trenchant criticisms concerning the Soviet leadership or the contents and forms of literary

272 Klepikov, pp. 120–21. See also Fischer von Weikersthal, pp. 249–50.
273 [Тем не менее, несмотря на некоторые цензурные послабления со стороны лагерной администрации, вряд ли стоит преувеличивать степень свободы в мыслях и действиях в Соловецком лагере. Цель издания газеты и журнала была подчинена сугубо прагматичным интересам руководства ОГПУ, в зависимости от которых оно регулировало тематику и характер публикуемых материалов. В данной связи можно согласиться с Б.Н. Ширяевым — одним из заключенных Соловецкого лагеря: «Теперь мне понятны причины этой свободы. Журнал приносил ОГПУ несомненную пользу, во-первых, осведомляя [...]. о настроениях некоторых кругов интеллигенции; во-вторых, был рекламным козырем в руках того же учреждения как доказательство гуманности соловецкого режима перед иностранцами, а главное — перед высшими слоями своей же партии, где в это время была сильная оппозиция».] Klepikov, p. 118 (the quotation from *Neugasimaia lampada* is in Shiriaev, p. 135).

works that were published in the SLON press.[274] Moreover, Klepikov seems to underestimate two important aspects of SLON literature.[275] Firstly, the author mentioned that some of the SLON journals were sold across the Soviet Union. Their readership thus included non-inmates who could compare the 'free' Soviet press to camp press. It also included the inmates' families and Party members, who could not help noticing the relative freedom that SLON contributors enjoyed. While internal disputes in 1925–26 might account for this anomaly (similar disputes on the intellectual activities held by *intelligenty* do not feature in the publications of other Soviet camps), by the time the SLON press reopened (the 1929–30), most of Stalin's opponents had already been purged or defeated. Secondly, the official press was becoming more and more monolithic. Freedom of speech was thus an exception in a regime whose leaders had paid great attention to official publications from the very start. The control of the press was established by one of Lenin's first decrees on 27 October 1917 and had gradually become more systematic. Glavlit[276] was eventually set up to filter all publications and was already operational when the SLON publishing system was created.

The degree of freedom that SLON intellectuals enjoyed might, to some extent, be explained by the publishing censorship's slip-ups and, more specifically, by the cultural chasm that existed between the writers and the censors (Shiriaev maintains that writers would escape censorship by playing on ambiguity).[277] A remarkable factor was the censors' neglectful attitude, which basically depended on their distrust of 're-education'[278] — and finally, on their superficiality, which the censors shared with analogous institutions both in the SLON and outside it.

The censors' excessively relaxed attitude was only one of the many anomalies of the SLON. The situation of the Solovki camp prisoners was truly unique, and so exceptional that one of the most prominent Soviet censorship experts, Arlen Viktorovich Blium, could not help commenting: 'They were freer than the free'![279]

---

274 As, for instance, the poetic tribute to Sergei Esenin published in *Solovetskie Ostrova*, which will be discussed in Chapter 4. See p. 204.

275 It is fundamental to stress that Klepikov's work does not only address the SLON. His work is about the phenomenon of censorship in the Northern regions of Soviet Russia. The case of the Solovki islands is thus one of several episodes covered in it.

276 Zalambani provides a short and excellent survey of Soviet censorship institutions in her book: Maria Zalambani, *Censura, istituzioni e politica letteraria in URSS (1964–1985)* (Florence: Firenze University Press, 2009), pp. 53–71. Glavlit censors were completely effective throughout the Stalin years, but eventually lost their determination and power.

277 Shiriaev, p. 136.

278 Ibid.

279 Interview with Arlen Viktorovich Blium (St Petersburg, July 2009). Blium wrote several books and articles on Soviet censorship, including *Za kulisami 'Ministerstva Pravdy': tainaia istoriia sovetskoi tsenzury 1917–1929* (St Petersburg: Akademicheskii proekt, 1994), *Sovetskaia tsenzura v epokhu total'nogo terrora. 1929–1953* (St Petersburg: Akademicheskii proekt, 2000) and *Zapreshchennye knigi russkikh pisatelei i literaturovedov, 1917–1991: indeks sovetskoi tsenzury s kommentariiami* (St Petersburg: Sankt-Peterburgskii gosudarstvennyi universitet kul'tury i iskusstv, 2003).

FIG. 3.18. Dmitrii Likhachev. ASM

The SLON Publishing System as an Expression of *Intelligentsia* Culture

Archival documents, memoirs, and publications indicate that there was an extremely stimulating cultural environment in the 'first Gulag'. Against the background of terrible violence and abuses, an extraordinary cultural system flourished. Originally sent to the Solovki islands in order to be isolated, re-educated, or eliminated, the *intelligenty* managed to set up an unbelievable cultural citadel — at times supported, at times ignored by the administration. In practice, re-education became the object of derision. The camp publications that were founded in order to show the results of *perevospitanie* — a newspaper around which revolved a lively cultural debate and a 'bourgeois' journal (which Shiriaev defined as 'the freest journal in the whole Soviet Union')[280] — were and still are crucial examples of cultural resistance within the Gulag. The closure of *Novye Solovki* and, even more so, of *Solovetskie Ostrova* marked the disappearance of pre-revolutionary culture from the official press in the Soviet Union. In the years that saw the venomous polemics of the RAPP's leaders, Maiakovskii's suicide and the first (but still implicit) steps towards the canonization of Socialist Realism, the last flame of 'Old Russia' was still alight in the camp which had been set up to extinguish it.

Philosophers and university professors, post-Romantic poets, witty playwrights and actors, clergymen and students were the real protagonists of that extreme resistance. Originally caught up in the general enthusiasm for theatre companies and clever enough to win the camp commanders' trust, the *intelligenty* managed

280 Shiriaev, p. 135.

to create a strong community that gained otherwise unthinkable privileges and that saved other intellectuals from certain death. As reliable workers for the camp administration, they soon became a necessary presence for the Soviet officials who on the one hand used them and on the other hand allowed them to enjoy more intellectual freedom than they would have enjoyed in the rest of the Soviet Union. As Likhachev says, the Krimkab was a place where people read books, wrote literary texts, and discussed the Logos and the Act.[281] In the barracks, prisoners read poetry and engaged in endless cultural discussions; theatre companies performed classic pre-revolutionary plays as well as contemporary ones; workshops on social psychology, the history of music, and Shakespearean drama were organized in the Solteatr;[282] the club (and camp theatres) hosted events, concerts, and chess tournaments; the camp library boasted several 'European and banned books';[283] and, finally, the museum, the botanical garden, and the Society of Ethnography worked to their full capacity to preserve traditional icons, to promote research on the local plant life, and to encourage further research into the pre-historical labyrinths on the Zaiatskie islands.

The intellectuals who belonged to the SLON cultural élite enjoyed a different kind of freedom. They could go for long walks,[284] they could listen to Western radio stations,[285] and they could cook for themselves or for their relatives. Above all, they were exempt from the forced labour that the other prisoners had to endure, including the intellectuals who did not belong to that highly exclusive circle.

The privileged did not only enjoy their special status, but managed to wage a cultural war through their ideas and literary work, whereby they attacked the very system which gave them a unique stage on which to perform their final act — with scenery provided by one of the most glorious monasteries in Russian and Orthodox history, an archipelago alive with luxuriant nature, and an excessively horrible prison camp. While the echoes of innumerable shootings and of prisoners' suffering reached them, the *intelligenty* succeeded in building a half-oneiric *intelligentny gorod*.

Their dream was violently interrupted by the consolidation of Stalinism. When the huge building sites of the White Sea–Baltic Canal were opened, the *intelligenty* were transferred to the mainland, into the Karelian woods. There they managed to re-create (at least in part) the intense cultural atmosphere of the SLON,[286] but were deprived of the possibility to express it in print. The uniqueness of their activities consequently went officially unrecorded. In the meantime, the imagery imposed

281 Likhachev, *Izbrannoe: Vospominaniia*, p. 228.
282 Ibid., p. 184.
283 Rozanov, *Solovetskii kontslager' v monastyre*, p. 28. In Rolin's film it is possible to see some European books among the titles coming from the SLON collections and kept in Ertsevo's library.
284 Several literary and philosophical discussions began during these walks, see Likhachev, *Izbrannoe: Vospominaniia*, p. 228.
285 Ibid.
286 While going from Leningrad to Medvezh'ia Gora, Meier told Antisferov: 'We are now going to the capital of the Russian *intelligentsiia*' [Мы теперь едем в столицу русской интеллигенции]. I would like to thank Professor Karl Schlögel for this reference. See Antsiferov, *Iz dum o bylom*, p. 386.

by Stalinist propaganda was making its way into the Gulag press, which had no space left for 'Solovki art'.[287] The Belomorkanal press and cultural events, including theatre performances, lacked the liveliness of those to be found in the SLON. On the Solovki islands, then, the 'cultural miracle' faded out in a few years. After the final closure of the *Solovetskie Ostrova* and the *Novye Solovki* in 1930, the SOK too was closed in 1934, as were the SLON theatre and museum three years later: their last years had seen the development of propaganda themes and writing, but also the involvement of prominent personalities, such as the Ukrainian theatre director Aleksandr Kurbas.[288]

Scientific activities and museum-related events were also on the wane. Although personalities such as Pavel Florenskii and Aleksei Vangengeim were still active, they could not speak out. As soon as the SLON was closed, the library too was closed.[289] Eventually brought into line with the contemporary cultural scene of other camps, the SLON saw its last days.

Its publications were the last words of a vigorous yet endangered human species — the 'bourgeois' *intelligentsiia*, and the final statement of its values, of a creativity which would disappear from the Soviet scene. The émigrés' strenuous efforts to keep that original core of intellectual energies alive outside the Soviet Union did not manage to preserve the pre-Revolutionary intellectual framework.

The only way to provide a thorough assessment of the SLON intellectuals' unique achievements is to examine their individual works in some detail. Their literary works still appeal to us as the voices of those who witnessed the last solitary cry of the *intelligentsiia*, and who registered in their texts the pride, the frailty, the vitality, the despair, and the enthusiasm that resounded in them.

---

287 Most of the above-mentioned intellectuals were murdered during Stalin's Terror. See biographies, p. 311.
288 Kuziakina's works provide an extensive account of Kurbas's life and activity; see Kuziakina, pp. 31–45. The Moscow archives of Memorial include a file on the Ukrainian director (Moscow, AMM, f. 1, op. 1, d. 2576, 'Kurbas, Aleksandr Stepanovich'). Apart from Kurbas, several Ukrainian intellectuals ended up at the SLON, including the poet and novelist Andrei Stepanovich Panov (Moscow, AMM, f. 1, op. 1, d. 3503) and the novelist Evgenii Pavlovich Pliuzhnik (Moscow, AMM, f. 1, op. 4, d. 4312). Like most of the Ukrainian prisoners, they were all shot in 1937.
289 See above, p. 58.

CHAPTER 4

❖

SLON Literature

The camp also had its own publication, the journal *Solovetskie Ostrova*. In it the prisoners wrote elegies and romantic legends based on themes from medieval times, fairy tales... Many miracles happened in a concentration camp in the twenties!

NIKOLAI ANTSIFEROV[1]

The literary image of the Solovki islands before 1917 was closely linked to the history of the monastery. The *Solovetskii monastyr'* was a crucial centre for the production of manuscripts. Its monks wrote several *zhitiia*[2] and, most importantly, the *Letopisets Solovetskii*, which chronicled the history of the monastery through the centuries.[3] Whereas the monastery's early literary output sprang from a tightly knit web of genre conventions, a distinctive literary tradition developed after the reign of Peter the Great — a tradition that was eventually fuelled by many important figures of Russian literature.

An early eminent contributor was the eighteenth-century writer Mikhail Lomonosov — a poet who pioneered and theorized Russian verse, a scientist, an eclectic intellectual and the founder of the University of Moscow. In his unfinished long poem *Petr Velikii* Lomonosov sang of the heroic deeds of Peter the Great, including his 1694 journey to Arkhangel'sk and to the Solovki islands. In this first poetic depiction of the Solovki islands, which is included in the first of the two *pesni* Lomonosov wrote in honour of Peter the Great's journey, the walls and the prison of the monastery stand out against an extremely dark landscape.[4] The whole passage devoted to Solovki was aimed at celebrating the heroic deeds of Peter and his heroic

---

1   [Был и свой орган, журнал «Соловецкие острова». В нем заключенные писали элегии и романтические легенды на темы средних веков, сказки... Много чудес было в концлагере в конце 20-х годов!»] Antsiferov, p. 341.

2   German's as well as Savvatii's and Zosima's *zhitiia* were written between the fifteenth and the sixteenth centuries. Miracle books, *skazaniia* and *povesti* on the history of the monastery were written in the following centuries. An important contribution to early Solovki literature is the *Solovetskii Paterik*, which was written in the late nineteenth century and which, together with the Volokalamsk book and manuscript of the Kiev-based Pecherskii monastery, form the only *Lives of the Fathers* books written in Russia. See Alda Giambelluca Kossova, *All'alba della Cultura Russa. La Rus' kieviana (862–1240)* (Rome: Edizioni Studium, 1996), p. 166.

3   The handwritten *Chronicle* spans events from the second half of the seventeenth century to 1762, whereas a typeset *Chronicle* extends as far as 1847.

4   Mikhail Lomonosov, 'Petr Velikii', *Polnoe sobranie sochinenii: Poeziia, oratorskaia proza, nadpisi (1732–1764)*, 11 vols (Moscow: Academiia nauk SSSR, 1959), VIII, 705.

Fig. 4.1. Nikolai Antsiferov. ASM

virtues; as a result, Peter's character and warlike virtues are in the foreground, rather than the Solovki archipelago itself.[5]

More writers followed in Lomonosov's footsteps, including Aleksandr Pushkin. In 1833, Pushkin began to write a chronicle, the *History of Peter the Great*, which was never completed. Borrowing from documented biographies of the Tsar, the poet recorded the dates of the Tsar's journeys to Arkhangel'sk and the Solovki islands. The relevance of the Solovki archipelago to the work of Pushkin goes well beyond his mere annotation. In a letter he sent in 1824 to a friend, the poet Vasilii Zhukovskii, Pushkin says that exile at the Solovki monastery would be better than his exile in the South: 'Save me even by sending me to a fortress, even to the Solovki monastery'.[6] Shortly after writing the letter, Pushkin depicted the monastery as a prison in a scene of his play Boris Godunov, written in 1825.[7] As was the case with Lomonosov, Pushkin ultimately evoked images of the archipelago by focusing on the monastery's prison.

Later, Lev Tolstoi devoted one of his many short stories to the archipelago, undermining the well-established negative image of Solovki. Written in 1885, his short story *Tri Startsa*[8] can rightly be regarded as the epitome of Tolstoi's popular

---

5   Ibid., p. 706.

6   ['Спаси меня хоть крепостью, хоть Соловецким монастырем], see Georgii Chulkov, *Zhizn' Pushkina* (Moscow: Terra, 2008), p. 145.

7   Aleksandr Pushkin, 'Boris Godunov', in *Lirika, poemy, povesti, dramaticheskie proizvedeniia, Evgenii Onegin* (Moscow: Astrel', 2003), pp. 251–346 (p. 269).

8   Lev Tolstoi, 'Tri startsa', *Sobranie sochinenii v 22-kh tomakh*, xx (Moscow: Khudozhestvennaia literatura, 1982), 342–47.

fiction, through which the writer gave the Russian people a literary corpus that had little in common with traditional popular fiction — a genre that combined 'romance and sexually offensive novellas'.[9] The leading characters included not only the three *startsy* of the title and one *arkhierei*, but the people themselves, whom Tolstoi depicted on a pilgrimage to the Solovki monastery. Tolstoi is thus the first modern writer to charge the Solovki landscape with spiritual overtones by sympathetically depicting the hopes and the burning faith of the peasant pilgrims travelling to the sacred islands.

The 1916 short poem 'Za Solovkami' by the 1933 Nobel Prize winner Ivan Bunin takes its cue from Tolstoi's short story.[10] A slight trace of the ominous feeling of the 'end-of-Russia' pervading Bunin's pre-revolutionary output runs throughout *Za Solovkami*, which impressively invokes details of the imagery related to the Solovki archipelago, such as its 'white nights' and its seagulls, without the author ever having been there.

Other writers and poets devoted literary works to the Solovki before the Revolution, from Vasilii Nemirovich-Danchenko to Nikolai Kliuev, Aleksei Ganin and Sergei Esenin.[11] Their descriptions conjured up a world of rich imagery and were deeply rooted in the Solovki landscape, rendering the literary image of the Solovki as a kind of of mystical corner of heaven on earth.

The revolution radically affected the literary representation of the Solovki archipelago. On the one hand, the *lagernye Solovki* were celebrated both by Gor'kii and Mikhail Prishvin;[12] on the other hand, the ideologically free literary output of Russian writers provided a 'more faithful' depiction of the Solovki camp, as was the case in Mikhail Bulgakov's *The Master and Margarita*. The novel's opening dialogue. written between 1929 and 1930, evokes through the words of the poet Ivan Bezdomnyi the image of the Solovki islands in the late 1920s as a place where 'political criminals' were eliminated.[13] This is no surprise: by the 1920s and 1930s

9   Marija Pljuchanova, 'Tolstoj', in *Storia della civiltà letteraria russa*, ed. by Michele Colucci and Riccardo Picchio, 2 vols (Torino: UTET, 1997), I, 717.

10   Ivan Bunin, 'Za Solovkami', *Sobranie sochinenii v shesti tomakh: Stikhotvoreniia 1888–1952* (Moscow: Khudozhestvennaia literatura, 1987), I, 318. Also in 1916 Teffi visited the Solovki monastery: she published a story entitled Solovki in 1921, and dedicated it to Bunin: Teffi, 'Solovki', *Zhar-ptitsa*, I (1921), 7–15. The story will be included, in a translation by Robert Chandler, in an anthology of Russian women writers edited by Natasha Perova and provisionally titled *Slav Sisters*, to be published in late 2017 by Dedalus.

11   Nemirovich-Danchenko; Nikolai Kliuev, 'Pogorel'shchina', in *Stikhotvoreniia i poemy* (Moscow: Sovetskii pisatel', 1991), pp. 124 and 322; Sergei Esenin, 'Otchar'', in *Sobranie sochinenii v shesti tomakh* (Moscow: Khudozhestvennaia literatura, 1978), I, 297; Sergei Esenin, 'Nebo li takoe beloe', ibid., IV, 138; Aleksei Ganin, 'Rusalka', in *Stikhotvoreniia. Poemy. Roman* (Arkhangel'sk: Severo-Zapadnoe knizhnoe izdantel'stvo, 1991), p. 50. Kliuev was mentioned by Litvin, see N. Litvin, 'Na Bab-gube', *SO*, 7 (1926), 10.

12   See Mikhail Prishvin, 'Puteshestvie', *Solovetskoe more*, 4 (2005), 164–66. Also a young Aleksandr Tvardovskii celebrated Solovki in relation to the *raskulachivanie* in his poem *Strana Muraviia*, see Aleksandr Tvardovskii, 'Strana Muraviia', in *Sobranie sochinenii* (Moscow: Khudozhestvennaia literatura, 1976), I, 232–33.

13   Mikhail Bulgakov, 'Master i Margarita', in *Sobranie sochinenii v vos'mi tomakh* (Moscow: Tsentrpoligraf, 2004), VI, 129–30. Other than the literary works quoted above, there is also a poem

the Solovki were widely known across the Soviet Union as a place of detention. But few knew that, inside the camp, the re-education of the prisoners was leading to unexpected results.

The First Period of Publications: Literature and Theatre

The unique SLON literary scene developed gradually, reflecting the progress and achievements of the cultural life discussed in chapter 3; at the core of this development lies its relationship with the SLON theatre. As was the case with a number of aspects of culture inside the SLON, literature was also propelled by the rather unexpected success of playwrights and actors. The fact that some of the promoters of the literary scene were also key personalities in the SLON theatre created a powerful creative exchange between literature and drama, although this did not have much influence on the texts prisoners wrote.

Until 1925, the SLON literary output was by no means different from 'typical Soviet labour camp literature'. This mostly resulted from the unremarkable achievements of the SLON's leading journal, *SLON*. Interspersed with propaganda pieces written by untalented writers, *SLON* was artistically unsatisfactory, as a quatrain signed by a certain 'Utka'[14] in the third (March) 1924 issue shows:

> За горами, за лесами,
> меж водой и небесами
> в Белом море остров тот
> и на нем труда оплот.[15]

Stylistically and thematically unrefined, these lines could not even be compared to those to be found in contemporary camp publications elsewhere, where prisoners wrote much more accomplished poems centred on the same themes. For example, the 1923 issue of *Novaia Zhizn' Domzaka*, a journal published in the Maikop prison, included the following (and more refined) celebration:

> Не надо нам ни храмов, ни попов,
> Ни грубо сделанных малеванных богов!
> Нам надо храмы строить без идолов-кумиров,
> Без золота, сиянии и сапфиров!
> [...]
> Нам нужен храм искусств и мудрость знаний
> О вечности миров и мироздании!
> Не надо больше нам ни богов,
> Ни звона колокольного попов![16]

by Sofia Parnok written in 1925, where two lines refer to the Solovki camp and are ambiguous in their attitude towards repression: 'Oh well, they took away the riches | They exiled them to Solovki' [Но что ж, богатства отняли, | Сослали в Соловки], Sofia Parnok, 'Nalei mne, drug, iskristogo moroznogo vina', in *Sobranie stikhotvorenii* (St Petersburg: Inapress, 1998), p. 373.

14   In Russian this word means 'duck' but also, as seen above, 'fake news'.

15   [Beyond the mountains, beyond the forests, | Between the water and the heavens | In the White Sea is that island | And in it Labour is a stronghold.] Utka, 'Ostrov chudes', *SLON*, 3 (1924), 74.

16   [We do not need churches or priests, | Nor roughly made painted gods! | We need to build temples without idols and fetish, | Without gold, radiance and sapphires! [...] We need a temple of

A slightly more successful attempt to combine propaganda with artistic skill was made by a SLON contributor, Ivan Mikhailov. In the fourth (April) 1924 issue of *SLON*, Mikhailov published a verse play entitled *Erkopiia*. Stylistically ineffective yet quite expressive, the poem focuses on the thwarted relationship between Kaeriia (a counterrevolutionary) and a character called 'GPU'. The other *dramatis personae* are the USSR ('SSSR'), and the Russian Communist party ('Erkopiia').[17] Despite his use of deplorable didacticism, Mikhailov managed to create a tense situation and to hint quite subtly at the camp experience, such as when Kaeriia, who is afraid of the GPU's love, is threatened by the SSSR's reprimand:

> Каэрия — Твоя любовь мне страх наводит,
> она бессмыслицей полна.
> СССР — С тебя очей ОГПУ не сводит,
> и чашу счастья пьет до дна.[18]

Naive though it was, Mikhailov's attempt proved nonetheless original in its willingness to depart from the lifeless 'celebratory poems' published in the *SLON* journal. Other poets tried to disentangle themselves from the snares of ideology. This, however, should be understood in relation to a well-established literary convention of the early years (*c.* 1918–25) of the Soviet prison and camp press: writers were able to distance themselves from Soviet ideology because the censors controlling prison camp publications were willing to accept an apolitical approach in certain kinds of texts. These texts were aimed either at foregrounding the prisoners' sad recognition of their conditions — and consequently their regret — or at depicting their confinement in a light-hearted way. The poems published in the above-mentioned journal *Novaia Zhizn' Domzaka* are examples of this trend:

> Как вихрем буйным жалкую былинку,
> судьба меня в объятьях закрутила,
> и все страданья были мне в новинку...
> Не говори, что молодость сгубила.[19]

At the SLON, the literary representation of prisoners' lives became the specific task of the first 're-educated *ugolovniki*', amongst whom was the former pickpocket Ivan Panin. Together with Aleksei Chekmazov and Vladimir Bedrut, Panin was to become one of the leaders of the *Svoi* company. The author of *chastushki*, *kuplety* and an eclectic playwright,[20] Panin managed to publish a few quatrains in

arts and wisdom of knowledge | About the eternity of worlds and the universe! | We no longer need any gods, | Nor priests ringing bells!] V. Neroslev, 'Ne nado nam ni khramov, ni popov', *Novaia zhizn' domzaka*, 1 (1923), 6.

17   The name, Erkopiia, is based on the acronym of the Communist Party, the 'Rossiiskaia Kommunisticheskaia Partiia' (RKP).

18   [Kaeriia — Your love frightens me, | It is full of nonsense. | USSR — From you the OGPU will not take off its eyes, | And will drain to the dregs the cup of happiness.] I. Mikhailov, 'Erkopiia', *SLON*, 4 (1924), 23.

19   [Like a pathetic blade of grass shaken by violent whirlwind, | Fate twisted me in its embrace, | And all the sufferings were new to me... | Do not say that youth has destroyed me.] G. Pannenkov, 'Ne govori, chto molodost' sgubila', *Novaia zhizn' domzaka*, 1 (1923), 10.

20   The little biographical information we have about Ivan Panin comes from Glubokovskii's 1926

SLON. His rather unmusical poetry proved nonetheless effective in its depiction of imprisonment and of a prisoner's need to survive his hard fate by accepting it:

> Молчи, мое бедное сердце,
> Довольно. Не стоит грустить,
> слезами несчастного в жизни
> навряд ли возможно выжить.[21]

While Panin's lines were more in tune with *blatnoi* folklore, Vladimir Krivosh-Nemanich's more intellectually refined works paved the way for the development of a distinctive SLON literature. The role played by the Serbian scholar and his translations of Chinese love epigrams has already been mentioned. However, Krivosh-Nemanich also published short poetic sketches that, despite their poor conceptual elaboration, were thoroughly independent of ideological or camp-related themes compared to the average *SLON* literature. In his *Moon* poem, Krivosh-Nemanich played on internal assonances ('menia/luna'; 'ona/nocham') and succeeded in lending his unimpressive poetry a certain brio:

> «Скажи меня, почему улыбается луна»,
> «Ну как же, посуди ты сам. Хитро не
> улыбаться ей,
> Когда, глядя на землю с высоты своей,
> всем тем любуется она, что здесь творится по ночам».[22]

Panin's and Krivosh-Nemanich's works were but the first seeds of the development of SLON literature. A real turning point came with the arrival of several intellectuals who changed the quality of the SLON press quite radically, creating an atmosphere where literature might flourish.

Litvin, Glubokovskii, and Shiriaev between Intellectual Autonomy and Flattery

Nikolai Kirillovich Litvin was certainly the first and the most important among the intellectuals who contributed to SLON literature. Born in Mogilev in 1890, Litvin started his career as a journalist in pre-revolutionary Ukraine and eventually joined the White Guard as a war correspondent covering the Civil War. After spending a

---

tribute to the actor, who had finally been released. Panin had been repeatedly arrested and had committed himself to drama with enthusiasm, thus becoming one of the leaders of the SLON's dramatic output. He had already written some light-hearted and relatively successful *kuplety* when he was an inmate at the Butyrskaia prison, in Moscow. In 1921 he founded the Moscow-based Ordynskii camp theatre, and in 1922 the Gorardom ('*Gorodskoi Arestantskii Dom*') theatre, also in Moscow. During his 'career' as a prison theatre actor he played hundreds of parts. Glubokovskii's note reads, 'His biography is a page of the history of prison theatre' [Его биография — страница истории тюремного театра]. B. Glubokovskii, 'Ivan Panin', *NS*, 21 (1926), 5–6.

21   [Be quiet, poor heart of mine, | Enough. There's no point being sad, | With tears I doubt that the unhappy | Could manage to survive.] I. Panin, 'Uznik', *SLON*, 3 (1924), 31.

22   ['Tell me, why does the moon smile?' | 'Well, you judge for yourself. She cannot smile | Cunningly | When, looking to the earth from her altitude, | She admires all that happens here overnight'.] Vladimir Krivosh-Nemanich, 'Stikhi (Luna)', *SLON*, 4 (1924), 19.

few years abroad (where, according to Shiriaev, he adhered to the *smenovekhovstvo*),[23] he returned to Russia in 1923, taking advantage of the Soviet government's promised amnesty for all former officials and White Guard supporters.[24] Like many of those who relied on the government's promise of amnesty, he was arrested upon his arrival in Moscow. He was later tried, found guilty, and sentenced to imprisonment on the Solovki islands, where he arrived in June 1924.

Litvin took part in the activities of the SLON press from the very beginning, publishing passages from his novel *General'skii grekh*[25] and his short story *Po vekham*[26] in *SLON*. Litvin's short story is particularly interesting. It sprang from his memories of the Civil War, which Litvin rendered in a style that foreshadowed his typical artistic choices — simple diction, a plain style, and extensive use of dialogues. His writing was most effective when representing strong feelings, as in the following passage:

> We were expelled to the Bosphorus. Then we were carried off to Europe. Hungry Russian men were surrounded by poor Turks. [...] And, strange as it was, we — who just yesterday were marching under the banner of Vrangel' — were baptized in Europe with an unexpected nickname:
> — Bolsheviks.
> And it was not Europe, not yesterday's allies who injected white camphor into our staggering bodies, but we ourselves while still in Rostov and in Crimea began to understand: we were not the same. Why were we not the same? The poor devastated White intellect could hardly answer. [...] What were we doing? Were we doing the right thing? And one of the White leaders, who had raised a mad rebellion in the southern Russian steppes, found the courage to understand:
> — No, we are not right. We went on the wrong path, and Russia will not forgive us for that...[27]

Litvin's text (and most of his prose writing) contained a typical feature of the *intelligenty*'s literary output in the early years, which I will call *locus fidelitatis*. In

23   The *smenovekhovstvo* movement was organized in the Russian emigration immediately after the October Revolution. It was named after a journal, *Smena vekh*, which was published in 1921. The *smenovekhovtsy* supporters promoted the émigrés' reconciliation and possible cooperation with the Soviet leadership. In their view, Soviet Communism was a natural stage in the development of Russian national history and, therefore, should be accepted.

24   The amnesty was declared on 3 November 1921. The whole text of the amnesty can be read on the website of the Krasnoiarsk section of Memorial, see http://www.memorial.krsk.ru/ DOKUMENT/USSR/211103.htm [accessed 30 June 2016].

25   See chapter 3, p. 101.

26   N. Litvin, 'Po vekham', *SLON*, 9–10 (1924), 30–36.

27   [Нас выкинуло на Босфор. Потом — понесло в Европу. Голодных русских обступили бедные турки. [...] И, как это не странно было, но нас, только вчера еще шедших под флагом Врангеля, — в Европе уже окрестили нежданным прозвищем: — Большевики. | И не Европа, не вчерашние союзники, впрыскивавшие в наше шатавшееся тело белую камфару, мы сами, еще в Ростове и Крыму стали понимать: Мы — уже не те. Почему не те — на это с трудом мог ответить бедный, выдвинувшийся белый ум. [...] Что мы делаем? Так-ли мы делаем? И один из белых вождей, поднявших безумный бунт в южно русских степях, — нашел в себе мужество понять: — Нет, мы не правы. Ложным путем пошли мы, и этого не простит нам Россия...] Ibid., p. 32.

those years, writers had to render their texts suitable from an ideological point of view, turning them into overt evidence of their loyalty. All authors, whether they supported Soviet power or not, found it necessary to include in their work some visible sign — such as ideologically charged or celebratory sentences, passages, and ideas — of their adherence to Soviet power. It is impossible to say whether the SLON authorities imposed the *locus fidelitatis* or if the writers adopted this strategy spontaneously, imposing a sort of self-censorship and thus mitigating works that were inappropriate from a political point of view. In any case, the *locus fidelitatis* became a leitmotiv of early SLON output, with only a few exceptions. Its use tended to vary from writer to writer. Litvin, for example, aptly used it to justify his fiction by carefully fitting ideologically orthodox passages into his original text, as can be seen in *Po vekham*. After describing the defeat of the White Guard and the soldiers' dismay at the end of the 'old' Russia in rather dramatic tones, the narrator concludes with a passage that justified the establishment of the Solovki camp:

> This article was written on the Solovki. This is just a superficial overview of well-known feelings. All of this is part of the past. But these feelings were so characteristic that they can and should be written down in the final pages of the end of the Whites. [...] But we know that the Solovki are also a stage. And for us it is a stage of enormous importance. The Solovki for us are the gateway of the life that we accepted while still abroad. [...] We no longer need milestones or tiresome examination: the RSFSR adopted us.[28]

Litvin was overtly ambiguous. He extolled the prison-like system of the new Soviet Russia precisely after declaring that the Whites would never survive the Soviet age. This ambivalence was deliberate, since the 'orthodox' ideological frame allowed writers to write about every sort of topic, even a description — such as Litvin's — of the tragic collapse of Tsarist Russia from the perspective of its very defenders, alarmed lest the violent Soviet tidal wave should crush them for good. By exploiting the strategy of *locus fidelitatis*, Litvin managed to address unexpected topics. His own *Letopis' solovetskaia*[29] (a very long narrative of the history of the monastery) was published in instalments after a long, ideological introduction that was in fact aimed at concealing the author's subtle sympathy for the monastic tradition. Litvin's sympathy was, in fact, so evident that Tiberii accused him of writing 'ecclesiastical hymns' in an article that conveyed his trenchant critique of the *intelligenty*.

Elsewhere Litvin used subtle camouflage as a compromise between ideologically committed texts and *locus fidelitatis*. In this kind of literature, the ideological frame was simply assumed while, in fact, the writer explored quite 'unconventional'

---

28 [Эта статья написана в Соловках. Это — только поверхностный обзор известных настроений. Все это — уже пережитое. Но настроения эти были настолько характерны, что могут и должны быть отмеченными на заключительных страницах белого конца. [...] Но мы знаем, что Соловки — тоже этап. И для нас — этап колоссального значения. Соловки для нас — порог той жизни, которую мы приняли еще там, за рубежом. [...] Больше не надо вех, не надо томительного прощупывания: РСФСР принял нас.] Ibid., pp. 35–36. The word 'вехи' is a clear reference to the *smenovekhovstvo*.

29 N. Litvin, 'Letopis' Solovetskaia', SO, 1 (1925), 39–46; 2 (1925), 37–48; 3 (1925), 9–13; 4–5 (1925), 53–56.

'Іаен редакционной коллегии Н. К. ЛИТВИН.

FIG. 4.2. Nikolai Litvin portrayed on the *Solovetskie Ostrova*

themes — a strategy to which he resorted because it enabled him to draw on his narrative skills. Litvin's early training as a journalist proved crucial; his work often focused on SLON life seen from a whole range of different angles. The scenes sketched in *Po ostrovam solovetskim*,[30] in particular, were extremely compelling, since they evoked a series of walks and visits Litvin made while he was a 'special correspondent' of *Solovetskie Ostrova*. Camouflage is evident in the first short story, devoted to the Muksalma island:

> Along the lake I slowly wandered up to the forest. I looked back from the ceremonial gates. It is nice to look at the Solovki Kremlin under the setting sun. [...] The siren sounded, the working day was over. Things might seem to be fine, but then my torments were only just beginning. [...] I walked past a little house by a lake. A little birch avenue marks the way to the house. A professor, a friend, loved to walk as far as this avenue. [...] Clusters of white rowan tree flowers hang above the lakes. Even the Solovki monks approved of this fruit. [...] But about six versts away you can see a completely different fruit in great abundance. And who on Solovki does not know this fruit! And how much of it is dumped along the road of Muksolma (and don't even think of comrade Frenkel'!). This fruit, my brothers, is the *balany*, something that every company of the Solovki knows very well.[31]

30 N. Litvin, 'Po ostrovam Solovetskim', *SO*, 6 (1925), 57–63; 7 (1925), 5–14; 8 (1925), 15–22.

31 [Вдоль озера потихоньку доплелся я до самого леса. От красных ворот оглянулся — хорошо на Кремль соловецкий смотреть под уходящее солнышко. [...] Гудок заревел — день рабочий кончился. Будто хорошо, а тут-то муки мои только и начинаются. [...] Прошел домик над озером. Аллейка к нему березовая просвечивает. Профессор, знакомый, любил,

A light-hearted description of the house on the lake is followed by Litvin's ironic description of the woods and hints at the SLON timber-felling operations — which are evoked through his ironic definition of the *balany* as the 'offshoot' of the SLON and through his mention of Frenkel' in a sentence in which he mentions his torments.

Far from drawing upon sheer imagination, Litvin's plain prose was well-rooted in reality. All the texts he published in the SLON press described real episodes filtered through the author's literary perspective. In addition to his not particularly distinguished literary achievements, Litvin was fundamental to the launch of the SLON press. He explored new narrative paths and readjusted contemporary narrative clichés, all the while striking a balance between his loyalty to the Soviet leadership and his vindication of intellectual independence. Litvin paved the way for the development of SLON literature, which would be further shaped by a new arrival: Boris Aleksandrovich Glubokovskii.

A famous actor from Moscow and a budding writer, Glubokovskii arrived at the SLON in May 1925, bringing with him the turmoil of the Moscow literary scene. A notorious bohemian, he was quite well known in Moscow. His brilliant performances at the Tairov theatre, in particular, had earned him a place in the private circle of Sergei Esenin and Aleksei Ganin. On 1 November 1924, however, the OGPU put an end to his bohemian life. He was arrested during an operation aimed at flushing out the 'Order of Russian Fascists', an allegedly violent terrorist group that planned to overthrow the Communist regime. The supposed group, in fact, was formed by Glubokovskii's friends, among whom was Ganin. At the end of a show trial, Ganin was found guilty of plotting against the regime and was consequently shot along with five others also found guilty of the same charges on 30 May 1925, while Glubokovskii was sentenced to ten years at the SLON.

From the very moment he arrived at the camp, Glubokovskii was absorbed into its cultural life, where he found a vent for his energy and his overwhelming enthusiasm, which persisted despite the trauma of detention. He arrived at a moment when Eikhmans's action on SLON culture was being implemented — he had become the head of the editorial board early in 1925 — and most probably found himself to be the right man at the right time. At the SLON, Glubokovskii somehow managed to re-create the *bohème* he had left behind in Moscow. He became one of the theatre's leading actors and directors; he promoted cultural evening meetings at the club; he contributed to *KhLAM* activities; he wrote both for *Novye Solovki* and *Solovetskie Ostrova*; and he managed to win the sympathy of camp commanders. The descriptions of Glubokovskii offered by Shiriaev and Likhachev vary slightly.[32] Yet

---

бывало, до этой аллейки доходить. [...] Рябина гроздьями белыми цветочными висит над озерами. Этот фрукт даже отцы соловецкие одобряли. [...] А вот примерно за шестой верстой, совершенно другой фрукт в большом обилии встречается. И кто его только не знает на Соловках, этого фрукта. И сколько его вдоль дороги муксоломской навалено — и самому товарищу Френкелю не перечесть! Это, братцы мои, баланы, значит, те самые, которые каждой роте соловецкой весьма знакомы.] Litvin, 'Po ostrovam Solovetskim', p. 58.

32   See Shiriaev, pp. 80–85; Likhachev, *Izbrannoe: Vospominaniia*, pp. 212–14. Part of Likhachev's

Fig. 4.3. Boris Glubokovskii. AAS

both of them make a point of mentioning his bold, unscrupulous determination — by which he earned remarkable privileges. Though according to the memoirists' accounts Glubokovskii's moral integrity might be debatable, the role he played in the cultural development of the SLON is undeniable.

Glubokovskii's distinctive voice pervaded the articles he published in the SLON press. He made his debut as a journalist soon after his arrival. The 4/5 1925 issue of the *Solovetskie Ostrova* (April–May) (i.e. the same where Eikhmans's article 'K voprosu o lagernoi obshchestvennosti' was published), for example, included his review of the songs of the criminals. His essay provided stimulating insights and impressed readers with its nonchalant tone. The beginning of the *ocherk* reads:

> A song is a sacred thing. A song is a confession. Tell me what you sing and I shall tell you who you are. Therefore the songs of the streets, of the factories, of the villages are most interesting historical documents.[33]

The end of the essay shows Glubokovskii's use of the *locus fidelitatis*. Unlike Litvin, however, Glubokovskii was able to be sincerely sympathetic to the Communist cause. When he first arrived at the Solovki as an *uznik*, Glubokovskii had just published a play that celebrated communist youth, *Kak Fediushka pionerom stal*.[34] It was a one-act play full of witty dialogue that revolved around the arrival of a young orphan, Fedia, in a pioneers' 'Communist family'. This was by no means an exception in the playwright's career. Kuziakina maintains that, between 1921 and 1922, Glubokovskii had already written propaganda literature, while directing his plays in suburban theatres.[35] Although his motivations might be disputed, Glubokovskii was one of the few SLON writers who showed some interest in

---

description was quoted above, p. 154.

33   [Песня — это заветные думы. Песня — это исповедь. Скажи мне, что ты поешь и я скажу тебе, кто ты. Поэтому песни улицы, песни фабрик, песни деревни — интереснейшие исторические документы.] Glubokovskii, 'Pesni shpany', p. 57.

34   Boris Glubokovskii, *Kak Fediushka pionerom stal. P'esa dlia detei v dvukh deistviiakh* (Moscow and Leningrad: Molodaia gvardiia, 1925) (CNLR, Shrift 39/770a).

35   Kuziakina, p. 39.

Communism before being arrested. Nonetheless, this did not prevent him from transforming the SLON cultural scene rather radically. His activity as a journalist within the camp helped other writers to rid themselves of their previously celebratory and reverential attitude to Soviet ideology and to discover a truer form of art that would soon show its face.

In his second article for the *Solovetskie Ostrova*, Glubokovskii launched an attack on panegyric poetry:

> It feels as though on Solovki the struggle between the past and the present is more intense than anywhere else. Nowhere in the Soviet Union is that fight as evident as here.
>
> Indeed. We see the monuments of the past: the smell of incense and prayers and the powerful hand of the present, as it raises up a new life on Solovki. This is something external, but it is good material for lyrical sketches and for epic poems. But the opportunities that Solovki provides are far from being exhausted by works of this kind. [...] But here is a world full of man's struggle with himself, his habits, attitudes, and so on. The poetry of Solovki could offer vivid pages about this internal struggle. If only... If only the Solovki poets did not relate to their poetry in a purely formal way.[36]

Here Glubokovskii quotes *Moskva-Solovki*, a poem by S. Akar/Shiriaev, after which he writes:

> Well, are they not just empty words that snap like toasted sunflower seeds? But alas! [...] Of course, these verses are very literary, but why are they so vainly elegant?[37]

He went on to accuse other authors of insincerity: he maintained that they did not thoroughly represent the theme of 'man's internal conflict' as experienced by Solovki prisoners; he also bitterly rejected their slogans and their empty words; he made fun of the celebratory mood of a number of poems, and he legitimized poetry's independence from ideology.

> Solovki poetry should be free from its formal relationships to the tasks posed by the camp...[38]

This is the first, 'official' step towards the establishment of a unique literary scene at the SLON, as well as a writer's first, firm stand on the controversial issue of non-

---

36 [Кажется нигде так ярко прошлое не борется с настоящим, нигде в СССР в наши дни так не показательна эта борьба, как здесь, в Соловках. В самом деле. Мы видим памятники прошлого: запах ладана и молитвословия и энергичную цепкую руку настоящего, воздвигающую новую соловецкую жизнь. Это внешнее, но это материал и для лирических эскизов и для эпических поэм. Но этим далеко и далеко не используются соловецкие возможности. [...] Но здесь мир, полный борьбы человека с самим собой, своими привычками, взглядами и т. д. Соловецкая поэзия могла бы дать яркие страницы этой внутренней борьбы. Если бы ... Если б соловецкие поэты не отнеслись к своим стихам чисто формально] B. Glubokovskii, 'Solovki v poezii solovchan', *SO*, 6 (1925), 38–40.

37 [Ну, разве это не пустые слова, которые щелкают, как жареные семячки, но увы! [...] Конечно, эти стихи очень литературны, но зачем они так фатовски нарядны.] Ibid.

38 [Соловецкая поэзия должна освободиться от формального отношения к задачам, поставленным лагерем...] Ibid.

ideological poetry. Glubokovskii eventually took a second stand through the theme of one of his articles, *Dokhlyi byt* (Sickly everyday life), which was published in the August 1925 issue of the *Solovetskie Ostrova*. The target of Glubokovskii's critique was now the '*shpana*' literature — a particularly important question that the author had already raised in his very first article. *Dokhlyi byt* focused on writers coming from among the *ugolovniki*: Aleksei Chekmazov, Vladimir Bedrut, and Guliaev.[39] While recognizing the literary value of some poems (in particular those by Bedrut), Glubokovskii exposed their basic insincerity:

> So here is his tale *Untitled*. The tale is about 'prison' life. An extremely interesting theme, but unfortunately Chekmazov represents only a very little of what a real prison is.
>
> So here is a morning in prison, 'a winter's morning. Patterns lit up by electric light shine on the glass of the prison windows. A bell rang mournfully, inviting the prisoners to work. Human figures in grey jackets and goatskin coats blossomed in the prison yard. The working life started to seethe in the workshops. The machines began to clatter, the sewing machines to hum, the shuttles of the loom started to run, the saws squeaked cutting thick logs, the iron began to clang, scattering fiery spray under the blows of the heavy hammer'.
>
> Such is the picture of a Soviet prison written by the pen of a prisoner. Chekmazov is a poet, his descriptions are lively and expressive, but its plot and characters are made of cardboard, they are not alive and are stilted.[40]

The importance of sincerity in art had always been a prominent feature of Glubokovskii's criticism in the SLON press, which seems to foreshadow Vladimir Pomerantsev's 1953 theses.[41] The writer used it both to undermine the reliability of encomiastic poetry and to expose the living conditions of camp prisoners. By denying the very substance of contemporary eulogy, he thus began to wage a cultural war that immediately showed its effects. His articles might consequently be regarded as a watershed between early SLON literature (i.e the years when the *SLON* journal was published and the early 1925 issues of the *Solovetskie Ostrova*) and later SLON literature. While the early stage was characterized by ideological

39   Glubokovskii does not mention Guliaev's first name. This was the only instance of Guliaev's name that I have found in the SLON press, but he might have been writing for publications which have not come down to us.

40   [Вот, она его повесть «Без заглавия». Повесть о «тюремной» жизни. Тема исключительно интересная, — но, к несчастью, Чекмазов настоящей тюрьмы дал очень немного.Вот, утро тюрьмы, «зимнее утро. Блестят на стеклах тюремных окон освещенные электрическим светом узоры. Уныло прозвучал удар колокола, приглашая заключенных на работы. Запестрели на тюремном дворе человеческие фигуры из серых бушлатах, козловых полушубках. Закипела рабочая жизнь в мастерских. Застучали станки, затрещали швейные машины, забегали в ткацких станках челноки, запищали пилы, разрезая толстые бревна, зазвенело железо, рассыпая огненные брызги под ударами тяжелого молота».Такова картина советской тюрьмы, картина, написанная пером заолоченного. Чекмазов — поэт, его описания живы и выразительны, но его фабула и герои — картонные, не жизненны и ходульны.] В. Glubokovskii, 'Dokhlyi byt', *SO*, 8 (1925), 7.

41   After Stalin's death, Vladimir Pomerantsev published an article in *Novyi Mir* entitled 'On sincerity in literature', which is still regarded as one of the first steps towards the literature of the 'Thaw', see Vladimir Pomerantsev, 'Ob iskrennosti v literature', *Novyi Mir*, 12 (1953), 218–45.

Член редакционной коллегии Б. Н. ШИРЯЕВ

Fig. 4.4. Boris Shiriaev portrayed on the *Solovetskie Ostrova*

literature and only occasional 'free' texts, the later stage was dominated by 'uncommitted' literature interspersed with rare encomiastic pieces.

The pages of the SLON press offer considerable evidence of the long-term effects of this 'cultural revolution', as does the development of the SLON writers' distinctive poetics. Some of them were so motivated by Glubokovskii's initiative that they committed themselves to increasingly more spontaneous and 'sincere' writing, changing the very mood of their texts.

A third prominent figure in the history of SLON literature is Boris Nikolaevich Shiriaev, who was one of the most active intellectuals during the first period of SLON publications. Even though some moments of his biography are rather obscure, we know that Shiriaev, born in Moscow in 1889, was a former *rotmistr* (Cavalry Captain) in the Tsarist army. He joined the White Guard during the Russian Civil War, and was then arrested and sentenced to death in two different trials. On both occasions he managed to avoid execution. The second time, he had the sentence commuted to ten years in a labour camp. He arrived at the Solovki islands as early as June 1923, yet his integration into the cultural life of the SLON was by no means smooth. From the 9/10 1924 issue onwards, he became a regular contributor to the *SLON* under the pseudonym 'S. Akar'.[42] This was hardly a *début*; the former *rotmistr* had already published a short collection of poems in 1917,

---

42   Shiriaev typically used pseudonyms such as S. Akar, A. Akarevich, and S. Akarskii, as seen above.

and his stay at the SLON gave him the possibility to pursue his literary activity. As soon as the *Solovetskie Ostrova* and the *Novye Solovki* were founded, Shiriaev joined Litvin and Glubokovskii. The three of them eventually became the early promoters of the Solovki press scene but, unlike his fellow journalists, Shiriaev was an anti-Bolshevik writer, a former White officer and a practising Orthodox believer, who suddenly started to write pro-Communist poems, articles, and short stories. Considering his contribution to SLON literature, it is hardly surprising that he was the target of Glubokovskii's critique of 'false, celebratory' poems. In his short poem of 1924, *Moskva-Solovki*, quoted in Glubokovskii's above-mentioned article *Solovki v poezii solovchan*, Shiriaev describes his life in a Moscow prison and his subsequent confinement on the Solovki islands. His attitude towards the *popy* is almost sarcastic:

> Но, как с трудом? Попы немного
> Надеялись на милость бога,
> Но сила веры их слабела
> По мере приближения дела.[43]

In the following issue of the *Solovetskie Ostrova* (the first 1925 issue), he published a text (*Davnee*) which was pervaded by satisfaction at the closure of the Solovki monastery:

> Седатые старцы пели:
> «Будь радостен, новый Сион»...
> и чем-то из меда и прели
> пахло от палых сосен.
>
> Звучали по-детски протяжно
> Седые псалмов слова.
> На тощей березе важно
> Круглила зеленки сова.
>
> И море, и берег строгий,
> И бледных озер затон,
> Дремали под ветхий, убогий
> Первых иноков древний звон.[44]

Even though Shiriaev's quatrains in alternate rhyme did not fully exploit his poetic potential, they certainly foreshadow the mood and distinctive traits of his typical output. Although apparently committed to communist ideology, his lines nonetheless carried a certain degree of conceptual ambiguity, as is the case in the last quatrain quoted above, where the adjective *ubogii* carries a twofold meaning,

---

43 [But what to do about work? The priests | Were hoping a bit for God's mercy, | But the power of their faith grew weak | As action came closer] S. Akar, 'Moskva-Solovki (putevka), stikhi', *SLON*, 9–10 (1924), 52.

44 [White-haired old men were singing: | 'You be joyous, New Zion'... | And a smell of honey and decay | Came out from fallen pines. || The hoary words of Psalms | Sounded childish like singsong | Majestically on a thin birch | There circled an owl above the foliage. || Both the sea, and the austere shore, | And the morass of dull lakes | Slumbered beneath the decrepit and miserable | Ancient bell-ringing of the first monks.] B. Shiriaev, 'Stikhi. Iz tsikla 'Solovki'. 1) Davnee', *SO*, 1 (1925), 37.

'morally miserable' and 'materially miserable' (or poor), with the implication that sanctity somehow still looms over the place as well as over its transformation into a place of socialist re-education. Shiriaev introduces a double, antithetical perspective which can change the meaning of the whole poem. If we accept the meaning of 'poor', and the use of words to convey a hidden meaning, then the smell of decay can become physical, the lullaby rhythm of the song can tenderly (*po-detski*) recall a past long gone, and the owl soaring above the birches can be not so much an omen as a sign of the potential harmony between man and nature in the years before the forests were felled for timber. The poem may therefore be a case of Aesopian literature.

Ambiguity is no doubt a prominent feature in Shiriaev's writing: he continued to be torn between his deepest lyrical instincts and the need to win the chekists' esteem. Both his literary texts and his critical articles appeal to the *topoi* of the Soviet cultural imagination that informed SLON political literature: scorn for the past, visions of a brighter future, the anti-religious struggle, the Communists' heroic actions as opposed to the meanness of counter-revolutionaries, the correct and just policies pursued by the Soviet prison system, the Communist project to 'remould' reality, and so on. Yet a secret strength underlies Shiriaev's writings — a sort of 'repressed consciousness' that resisted flattery and brought critical elements to the fore by drawing from a sort of Aesopian wisdom. In a passage of the article *Iz dnevnika* marking Lenin's death, which he published in the first issue of the *Solovetskie Ostrova*, he wrote:

> And today, here, during the evening roll-call on the Solovki, I stood with the coalminers from Donetsk, the mineworkers from the Ural, the textile workers from Ivanovo; I was with all the working world in the same line, with one mind, and one heartbeat, and the future was roaring at us with its millions of factories, horns, sirens...[45]

No matter how hard Shiriaev tried to juxtapose the image of a 'choral heart' beating to the sad landscape of a mourning Moscow, described in the early lines of the text, his words implicitly seem to maintain that the classes that are 'socially close' to the Soviet leadership are, in fact, together with him, in the camp.[46] This hints at one of the crucial topoi of Gulag culture, i.e. that of the 'zone', as described in the introduction to this book, i.e. at the fact that the prison camps (the 'zone') and the rest of the Soviet Union (the 'bigger zone') had much in common.

---

45 [И сегодня, здесь, в час вечерней проверки на Соловках, я стоял с донецкими шахтерами, уральскими горняками, ивановскими текстильщиками, со всем трудовым миром в едином строю, с единой мыслью, и единым биением сердец, а грядущее ревело нам миллионами фабрик, заводов, гудков, сирен...] B. Sh., 'Iz dnevnika', *SO*, 1 (1925), 16.

46 In the seventh 1925 issue of *Solovetskie Ostrova*, Shiriaev included a quite similar scene. In *Solovetskaia Moskva*, his description of Moscow was a lyrical reflection on his native city and on its inhabitants, thus implicitly conveying the writer's nostalgic re-evocation of the pre-revolutionary world. Shiriaev was later to declare that the same people that he wrote about were with him at the camp, thus meaning that all the representatives of the pre-revolutionary Russian elite were said to be condemned to imprisonment.

The first issue of the *Solovetskie Ostrova* also included Shiriaev's review of the poetry of several *ugolovniki*, i.e. on the same topic (and one of the same writers, Chekmazov) that Glubokovskii would write about some months later. Unlike Glubokovskii, Shiriaev adopted a radically different perspective: his text *Literaturnye popytki*, in fact, was actually an essay on the art of celebration.[47]

Shiriaev's inner conflict became quite interesting in the following issue of *Solovetskie Ostrova*, which includes two formally and thematically contrasting texts by the author. A specimen of Shiriaev's skilful use of techniques and a proof that he shared the sensibilities of his time,[48] the poem *Inochii minuet* was also, despite its title, an eloquent example of contemporary non-ideological literature:

> Замело поземкой
> Снег, след.
> Желтою каемкой
> Слеп свет.
> Замерла вечерня,
> Скит спит.
> В заморозке двери
> Стих скрип.
> Ризою узорной
> Лег шаг.
> Тишью от собора
> Став так.
> Теплота лампадок,
> Лик. Блик.
> В золоченых складках
> Спит, стих.
> Замело поземкой
> Снег, след.
> Желтою каемкой
> Слеп свет.[49]

The alternation of couplets and their spondee-based closure lends Shiriaev's minuet its musical drift by echoing the very three-beat rhythm, sealed by a concluding pause typical of the minuet in music. The couplets thus become fully developed

---

47 B. Shiriaev, 'Literaturnye popytki', *SO*, 1 (1925), 90.

48 As Massimo Maurizio arguably suggested in a recent conversation, the use of such short forms was typical of the Silver Age (for instance, the sonnet *Pokhorony*, written by Vladislav Khodasevich in 1928, is made only of monosyllables, see Vladislav Khodasevich, *Sobranie sochinenii*, 2 vols (Ann Arbor, MI: Ardis, 1983), I, 213). Moreover, the use of couplets consisting of one longer line followed by a shorter line was typical of poets such as Briusov or Annenskii. See, for instance, the poem *Na ulitse* by Valerii Briusov, *Sobranie sochinenii v semi tomakh* (Moscow: Khudozhestvennaia literatura, 1973–75), I, 413. I would like to thank Massimo Maurizio for his precious contribution to the present chapter.

49 [The gale swept away | The snow, the trace. | With a yellow margin | The light becomes dull. | The vespers fell silent, | The hermitage is asleep. | In the frost of a door | A poem creaks. | Like a patterned garment | Lay the footsteps. | Through the silence of the cathedral | Becoming so. | The heat of the icon lamps, | The face of Christ. A patch of light. | In gilded folds | Sleeps a poem. | The gale swept away | The snow, the trace. | With a yellow margin | The light becomes dull.] B. Shiriaev, 'Inochii minuet. Stikh', *SO*, 2 (1925), 34.

musical phrases.[50] Though the censors read the poem as an ironic commentary on the monks, Shiriaev managed to convey in it his anguished apprehension of the end of monastic life, which was barely sublimated by the image of the 'dull light' that is first used in the fourth line and on which the poem significantly ends. Again, Shiriaev's poem is ultimately ambiguous. Shiriaev's ambiguity is further enhanced by the publication of a rather different text in the same issue of the journal — one of the most openly mystifying articles ever published in the SLON press, *Eli solovetskie*:

> The forest stands. But the monks are not there any more. They have scattered. [...] Other people came... Hurried, noisy, expert... [...] The master had arrived. [...] And it was wonderful and frightening for the forest, and it was strange to hear songs unheard, incomprehensible hoots through the crackling of icy needles which were scattered over his branch-paws. The master had arrived.[51]

Shiriaev's unique achievement ultimately lies in the very tension between flattery and the aspiration for sincerity that breaks through his words, probably as an expression of subconscious needs. The writer seemed to be constantly torn between 'sycophancy' (when, for example, he turned his back on the *KhLAM*)[52] and the need to break through his unfathomable reticence and let spontaneous, inner rebellion finally emerge.

Litvin's independence, Glubokovskii's enthusiasm, and Shiriaev's unconscious revolt proved crucial to the creation of the SLON literary scene.

Celebration and Rebellion

Significantly enough, Shiriaev did not give up his propensity for encomiastic-ideological poetry. Though his writing became increasingly experimental and challenging, he continued for a long time to privilege themes and concepts that were in tune with the need to 'celebrate' or which complied with the political direction of the camp administration. His poems generally hinged on a visible hiatus between his use of technique and the basically monotonous themes he chose, as is the case in *Mai*:

> Тише машины!
> Сегодня уймите
> Гул свой до сотой процента.
> Первое Мая — всесветный митинг
> Фабрик,
> Заводов,
> Промцентров.

---

50   I wish to express my gratitude to Francesca Lazzarin, who helped me to detect the analogies between the poem's progression and the musical structure of the minuet.

51   [Стоит лес. А монахов уже нет. Рассеялись. [...] Иные люди пришли.. Торопливые, шумные, деловитые... [...] Пришел хозяин. [...] И чудно лесу и боязно, и любопытно слушать песни неслыханные, гудки непонятные, сквозь похруст иголочек льдистых ветви-лапы его усыпавших. Пришел хозяин.] В. Shiriaev, 'Eli Solovetskie (vpechatleniia s lesorazrabotok)', *SO*, 2 (1925), 94.

52   See chapter 3, p. 119.

[...]
Сотворят беспримерные сдвиги
Те,
Кто с нами наш Май познал,
И в столетий расчетной книге
Впишут
Свои имена.[53]

Shiriaev here plays with rhythmic variation: he breaks and remoulds lines as he chooses and masters them using his distinctive play with enjambment. As time passed, Shiriaev started to grow more and more interested in modernism and in early twentieth-century avant-garde writing. He also implemented for the SLON press several typical experimental forms (such as the *lesenka*),[54] as his poem *Buntar'* published in the eighth issue of the *Solovetskie Ostrova* (1925) shows:

В каменном сердце
    Глухо.
Толп неподвижен строй.
    Городу спруту
        В ухо:
На бой!
    На бой!
        На бой![55]

Shiriaev's debt to the avant-garde and to Futurism in particular became more and more evident as time went by. Shiriaev himself made this explicit in *Oktiabr'*, a poem he wrote in 1925 to celebrate the October Revolution. In the poem, the poet played on the recurring isolation of words and concepts to lend them a higher degree of semantic force, while images become increasingly powerful — thus reminding readers of the formal ruptures of the avant-garde.

Не поэт я
Между поэтами
    Я
Топота толп рупор.
Нет у меня панихиды поэтому
Над ветхой России
    Трупом.
[...]
На Театральной
    Окоп
Рот открывал среди скверика.

53 [Hush machines! | Today settle down | Your noise up to hundred per cent. | The first of May is the universal rally of | Factories, | Plants, | Industrial Centres. | [...] | Together will create unprecedented changes | Those | Who with us experienced our May, | And in the pay-book of the centuries | Will write | Their names.] B. Shiriaev, 'Mai', *SO*, 4–5 (1925), 5.

54 The *lesenka* is a stylistic device that was widely used by modern Russian poetry. It appears often in Belyi's and Maiakovskii's works.

55 [In the heart of stone | It's hollow. | Is still the formation of the masses. | Comes to the city-octopus's | Ear: | To the battle! | To the battle! | To the battle!] B. Shiriaev, 'Buntar'', *SO*, 8 (1925), 3.

> Пилась
> Печатнику в медный лоб
> С Лубянки
> Пулеметов истерика.[56]

Though Shiriaev was not alone in developing this line of encomiastic poetry, he was no doubt the most talented of its representatives. Other writers tried their hands at explicitly ideological poems and works, while never reaching the aesthetic standards of the Moscow poet. Celebration was first attempted by Tiberii,[57] who was, however, an arguably untalented writer who mostly played a political role. His essays against the *intelligenty*'s culture were pervaded by a certain degree of resentment. Sergei Kargopol'skii (or the man who hid behind what may have been a pseudonym)[58] was one of the leading 'encomiastic' poets, yet his poems were always unremarkable. Despite his modest qualities, Kargopol'skii wrote poems that show some recurring themes and features of the SLON panegyric lyrical tradition.

> Умер вождь, чье имя будет вечно
> 21-го туман висел соленый...
> Намахровелся под высью бесконечной
> наш октябрьский флаг окровавленный...[59]
>
> Что же, что ни север строгий,
> Путь наш тяжел и крут.
> Нас укрепит в дороге
> Честный, свободный труд.[60]

As Kargopol'skii's poem shows, celebratory poetry was sometimes based on long lines — it almost resembled prose ending in rhymes. Writers such as Kargopol'skii, Tiulen',[61] B.B.,[62] and My[63] could not, however, stand up to comparison with

---

56   [I'm not a poet | Among poets | I | Am the megaphone of the tread of the masses. | I therefore have no requiem | For Russia's decrepit | Corpse. [...] On Theatre Square | A trench | Opened its mouth among a garden. || The typographer | With a copper forehead | From the Lubyanka | Wanted to drink the hysterics of the machine-guns.] B. Shiriaev, 'Oktiabr'', *SO*, 10–11 (1925), 17.

57   Tiberius Tverie, mentioned in chapter 3.

58   Kargopol' is the name of a town in Russia. The author could have been someone who was born there.

59   [The leader died, whose name will be forever | On the 21st there was a salty fog... | Under an infinite height got soaked | Our blood-stained October flag] S. Kargopol'skii, 'Pamiati V.I. Lenina', *SO*, 1 (1925), 10.

60   [So what, is not the north tough? | Our path is heavy and whirly. | On our way we'll be reinforced | By honest, free labour.] S. K., 'Pressa na sever', *SO*, 3 (1925), 18.

61   The writer who wrote under this pseudonym — *Tiulen'* means 'seal' — was also the author of a short lyrical poem, *Ran'she i teper'*, whose strength lies in its graphic layout. The poem is actually structured as six quatrains that illustrate the history of the Solovki islands. The three quatrains of the 'before' are shown on the left, the three of the 'after' are on the right. See Tiulen', 'Ran'she i teper', stikhi', *SLON*, 9–10 (1924), 58.

62   The writer who wrote under this pseudonym published an antireligious poem accusing the monks of sodomy and sexual perversion in the third issue of 1925. See B. B., 'Soblazny', *SO*, 3 (1925), 14.

63   This was a typical stage-name for the *Svoi* members. It was meant to underline the collective spirit of their group (*my* in Russian means 'we'). See My, 'Rifmy lagkora', *NS*, 27 (1925), 3.

one of the *Svoi* leaders, Aleksei Chekmazov, whose style was more refined. A former Cossack of the Don region, Chekmazov became a bandit during the Civil War. He was arrested and started to read and study while in prison. At the SLON, Chekmazov became the life and soul of the *ugolovniki* collective, where he co-operated with Panin. A former criminal and a man fond of poetry and drama, he was the only 're-educated' prisoner whom the KVCh could use in publications as a counterweight to the cultural leadership of the *intelligenty*. His poems were generally laudatory in mood, and they firmly supported the *ugolovniki*'s artistic output. Chekmazov was a contributor to *Novye Solovki*, in which he published his poems:

> Пусть в этот день наполнится земля
> Вселенским гимном Интернационала.
> Пусть в этот день от Красного Кремля
> Союза мощь дойдет до капитала.[64]

Chekmazov's most important collaborator was Vladimir Bedrut, one of the leading figures of the *Svoi* group. The son of a Moscow doctor, Bedrut had gone astray in the war years and had eventually become part of the local underworld. Arrested for theft, he was sent to the SLON, where he became a member of the *ugolovniki* despite his 'non-proletarian' origins. In the camp, he started to write encomiastic (and utterly unrefined) poetry:

> Рос обман слюнявый —
> Первый плод Февраля,
> Грянул Октябрь алый
> Ленин стал у руля.[65]

Both Chekmazov and Bedrut, however, were most successful whenever they dropped the mask of ideological alignment. Chekmazov wrote *Solovetskii nabrosok*, a short story in verse in which the main character is a seal giving birth on the shores of the archipelago and which concludes with the following lines:

> Не хотел расстаться с красотой.
> Солнце — сила, но сильней испуг,
> Глубоколюбимый и простой
> Моей музы мимолетный друг.[66]

Bedrut wrote poems pervaded by a gloomy sense of life spent in jail — as in the lines quoted by Glubokovskii in one of his articles, *Dokhlyi byt*.

---

64 [Let today the earth be filled | By the universal hymn of the International. | Let today from the Red Kremlin | The might of the union reach the capitalists.] A. Chekmazov, 'Pust' v etot den'', *SO*, 10–11 (1925), 4.

65 [The slobbery deceit grew, | The first fruit of February. | Scarlet October came like a crash of thunder | Lenin took the helm.] V. Bedrut, 'Stal'nye slova', *SO*, 10–11 (1925), 3.

66 [I didn't want to part from beauty | The sun is a strength, but fear is stronger, | This deeply loved and simple | Fleeting friend of my muse.] A. Chekmazov, 'Solovetskii nabrosok', *SO*, 8 (1925), p. 4.

Сердце тревогу ударами бьет
              Тихо.
Медленно стрелка часов подвигается,
              Скрипнула дверь
                   Вот!
       Идет!
       Светел, спокоен,
       Только в глаза мне не может взглянуть.
              „Я ухожу не надолго,
       Может, совсем ночевать не вернусь".
              Встала невольно.
       Горло сжимают стальные тиски,
              Жутко и больно, больно,
       На сердце камень тоски.
                   [...]
       Пусто, тоскливо,
              Все мне постыло,
              Я не хочу больше жить.[67]

As these short passages suggest, non-celebratory poetry seemed a much more fertile ground for both writers than politically committed verse. Quite the same might be said of another prominent figure of early SLON literature: Boris Evreinov. Born in Moscow, Evreinov — a relative of the famous theatre director Nikolai Nikolaevich Evreinov[68] — was sent to the Solovki islands in 1924 and started to publish his poems in the 9/10 issue of *SLON*. His early work owes much to 'ideologically orthodox' SLON literary conventions. His very first poem, *Palomnichestvo*,[69] focused on the poetic comparison between the journey of the pilgrims to the monastery and that of the prisoners to the camp. After this unoriginal and unremarkable poem, Evreinov offered a sonnet, *Solovki*:

       Кремля воинственные стены,
       Замшенных башен строгий ряд, —
       Хранят столетий перемены
       И молча о былом твердят.

       Знакомы смуты им, измены
       И святотатственный разлад.
       И в бури — злобный зов сирены.
       И цепь томительных осад.

       А средь озер завороженных,

---

67 [The heart sounds the alarm with its beats | Silently. | Slowly moves the pointer on the clock | A door shouted | Here! | It comes! | Bright, Tranquil, | Only he doesn't want to look me in the eyes. | 'I am going away not for long, | Maybe I won't come back for the night'. | She stood up involuntarily. | The throat is pressed by a steel vice | Terribly and painfully, | On my heart there's a stone of anguish. | [...] | It's empty, sad, | Everything is nauseating to me, | I do not want to live anymore.] Quoted in Glubokovskii, 'Dokhlyi byt', p. 8.

68 Nikolai Nikolaevich Evreinov (1879–1953) was a theatre director and dramatist who was profoundly influenced by Russian symbolism. In 1923 Evreinov moved to France, where he lived until the end of his life, becoming one of the most appreciated dramatists of the world.

69 B. Evreinov, 'Palomnichestvo. Stikhi', SLON, 9–10 (1924), 43.

FIG. 4.5. Boris Evreinov, AAS

Укрытых, в дрему погруженных,
Скиты разбросаны в лесах.

И где-то в дебрях соловецких
Героев сказок наших детских
Курганы спрятали в потьмах.[70]

With this sonnet Evreinov wrote an apparently anti-religious poem that is nonetheless infused with the author's unmistakable sympathy for the monastery. The *smuty*, the cries of the sirens, and the sieges are images that hint at the monks' disloyalty in relation to the Schism while in fact conjuring up the more recent traumatic experience of the Soviet takeover of the Solovki islands. In these first published works, Evreinov was still cautious with his aesthetic output. In fact, his third contribution to the 9/10 1924 issue of *SLON* was a rather weak short story, *Zabludshee radio*,[71] in which a radio bulletin announcing Charlie Chaplin's prospective wedding provoked the author's violent attack against the capitalist West. *Zabludshee radio* was, per se, a *locus fidelitatis*.

In his next published piece, which appeared in the first issue of *Solovetskie Ostrova*), Evreinov dared to disentangle himself from the snares of ideology and celebration, thus paving the way for a totally liberated poetry and for Glubokovskii's future change of direction. He consistently chose to be daring in his poems. In the first

---

70 [The bellicose walls of the Kremlin | The severe line of towers covered in moss | Keep the changes of centuries | And, silently proclaim the past. || They are familiar with disorders, treasons | And sacrilegious discord. | And in storms they hear the spiteful call of the siren. | And a succession of exhausting sieges. || But among the enchanted lakes, | Hidden, surrounded by sleep, | Hermitages are dispersed in the forests. || And somewhere in the thick Solovki woods | The *kurgany* hid in the dark | The heroes of our childhoods' fairy tales.] B. Evreinov, 'Solovki. Stikhi', *SLON*, 9–10 (1924), 43. The *kurgany* are prehistoric burial mounds; the Solovki archipelago has several.

71   B. Evreinov, 'Zabludhsee radio', *SLON*, 9–10 (1924), 57–58.

poem he published in the *Solovetskie Ostrova*, *Byl'e karel'skoe*,[72] which sets a stylistic standard for Evreinov's subsequent poems (quatrains with alternate rhyme), the poet uses a different, more elevated tone and register, as well as lexically daring choices. The second poem, *Zarei okhotnich'ei*, is again a specimen of Evreinov's effective depiction of nature:

> Зари еще не вспыхнул плат
> И лес задернут дымкой сизой...
> Еще огни Кремля горят
> И тает небо звездной ризой.
>
> Под лыжей наст хрустит тугой.
> Мороз бодрит и подгоняет...
> Снег лапы елей гнет дугой...
> — За льдами медленно светает.[73]

Evreinov's landscapes are typically animated and vibrant. The use of prosopopeia, in particular, gives nature a primary role in the description of hunting, and Evreinov managed to hint at the stifling, violent atmosphere of the camp by probably identifying himself as the hunted animal, as the lines below seem to suggest:

> Тревожит выстрел снежный бор
> И эхо долго в елях бродит...
> А день, крадя часы, как вор
> Тропой валежною уходит.[74]

The echo heard among the trees seems to turn into the desperate cry of the prisoners who, as has already been suggested, were shot in the forest and whose deaths were often recorded as 'escape attempts'. This is what the writer seems to suggest in the concluding evocation of felled trees — the ultimate trademark landscape of forced labour in the SLON.

A possibly more challenging move was Evreinov's publication of *Smiatennost'* in the second 1925 issue of the *Solovetskie Ostrova*. The anxiety of imprisonment is articulated in a succession of eight quatrains, in which Evreinov's more conventional use of literary tropes lends his poetry depth, while his use of archaisms becomes more evident:

> Мне пути заказаны далеко —
> Ограничен островом мой круг.
> И в пределах кованого срока
> Задержать стараюсь сердца стук.
>
> Дни несутся быстрым ураганом,
> То как дроги похорон ползут...

---

72   B. Evreinov, 'Stikhi. 1) Byl'e karel'skoe, 2) Zarei okhotnich'ei', *SO*, 1 (1925), 35–36.

73   [The headscarf of the dawn has not yet been lit | And the forest is wrapped by a bluish haze... | The Kremlin lights still burn | And the sky melts in a starry icon frame. || Under the skis the hard icy crust crunches. | The frost invigorates and spurs... | The snow bends the firs' branches in an arc... | Beyond the ice day slowly dawns.] Ibid.

74   [A shot disturbs the snowy pine forest | And the echo wanders for a long time among the firs... | But the day, stealing the hours like a thief, | Moves off along a trail of dead branches] Ibid.

Я о прошлом думать не устану
И о тех, кто стал дороже тут.

Ураган ревет и бьется в плаче.
Заснеженных стен причудлив крап.
Этими ль стенами обозначен
Мой последний жизненный этап?

Что потом? В каком найду притоне
Для тоски губительный исход?
Иль бродяжнический дух погонит,
Закружив, как льдину в ледоход?

Впереди туман и мгла.
Колючий, Как вот этот рвущий ураган.
Да иль нет?.. Шагаю через кучи.
Да иль нет?.. Я ураганом пьян.[75]

The prisoner's anguished apprehension of life, his sense of impending death, his fear of an indefinite future are highlighted by the poet's more elaborate technique: his use of chiasmus throws some points into sharper relief, regular alliteration sets lines into a different, relaxed pattern and the anaphora crucially seals a long series of questions. The poet's subject-matter here is more daring than his style: Evreinov broke through the conventional limits of thematic freedom in a moment when most SLON publications (the only exception being Litvin's work) were clearly encomiastic. For this reason, Evreinov, who did not even bother to resort to the *locus fidelitatis*, was forbidden to publish for a long time. He had gone too far.

In the two issues of the journal that followed Evreinov's expulsion, the *Solovetskie Ostrova* was again dominated by 'aligned' writers, including not only the above-mentioned trio (Shiriaev, Tiberii, and Kargopol'skii) but also Sergei Solovkov and Nim.[76] It is, however, during this 'return to ideology' that the journal started its radical departure from the policies it had pursued hitherto. The layout and format of the journal underwent extensive changes — starting with the prominence of

---

75   [Paths are closed to me for miles around | My circle is limited by an island. | And within the boundaries of the iron-bound prison term | I try to contain the beat of my heart. || The days rush by like a fast hurricane | Sometimes they crawl like a hearse... | I won't stop thinking of the past | And of those who have become dearer here. || The hurricane roars and writhes in mourning. | The snow-covered walls make a peculiar pattern. | Do these walls define | The last stage of my life? || What comes afterwards? In what dent will I find | A fatal end for my anguish? | Or will a vagabond spirit drive me, | Spinning like a block of ice in an ice drift? || Ahead there's fog and darkness. | The fog bites like this tearing hurricane. | Yes or no?.. I step through the drift. | Yes or no?.. I'm drunk on the hurricane.] B. Evreinov, 'Smiatennost'. Stikh', *SO*, 2 (1925), 33. Other than the old form of 'if' ('*il*' instead of '*ili*'), it's worth noting the use of the verb '*zakazat*' in its old sense of 'to forbid'. See Vladimir Dal', *Tolkovyj slovar' zhivago velikoruskago jazyka*, 4 vols (Moscow and St Petersburg: Izdanie tipografa M. O. Vul'fa, 1881), I, 581. I would like to thank Igor' Loshchilov for helping me with this point.
76   It is still difficult to say for sure who wrote under the pseudonym of 'Nim'. 'Sergei Solovkov' might instead be a stage name of Kargopol'skii: it means 'Sergei of the Solovki', and Kargopol'skii was the only encomiastic author with this name.

the literary section over the politics columns. Moreover, in those months (i.e. early 1925) the *KhLAM* group was founded within the SLON, thus launching a most lively cultural season. The 4/5 issue, in this sense, already marked a departure from the literary image of the *lagernye Solovki* that had been pursued up to that moment. This issue, in fact, was the one which included Eikhmans's article 'O lagernoi obshchestvennosti' and Glubokovskii's first article on criminal songs; yet it was the following issue, in which Glubokovskii published his article on SLON poetry, that transformed the history of SLON literature for good.

Signs of this change were already apparent in the seventh 1925 issue, but they become most prominent in the eighth issue, in which a poet, Boris Emel'ianov started to publish more interesting poems than had previously appeared under his name. Although Shiriaev provides a detailed portrait of Emel'ianov as a real person in *Neugasimaia lampada*,[77] there is hardly any doubt that the name designated Glubokovskii's poetic alter-ego. 'Emel'ianov' actually became a regular contributor to the SLON press as soon as the Moscow actor started to appear in it. Moreover, his work showed clear affinities with Glubokovskii's criticism and his biography. After his début in the seventh issue of the *Solovetskie Ostrova* — in which he published *Vesna v Solovkakh*,[78] a poem which disregarded the typical use of *locus fidelitatis* — Emel'ianov published two poems in the eighth issue, *V dvenadtsat' dnia*[79] and *Pered utrom*, both of which addressed some of Evreinov's recurring motifs, such as the overlapping between the poet's lyrical thoughts and the surrounding natural world of the archipelago, the image of the stones of the Kremlin, a tone of resignation.

> Поют о снах суровых, мшистых стен
> Мои стихи у колоколен острых...
> Я полюбил тебя, могучий плен,
> Я полюбил тебя, зеленый остров.
>
> Мне любы здесь озера и поля,
> В сосновый лес бегут, рифмуясь, строчки,
> С ними я иду от стен кремля,
> Иду один, считая пни и кочки.[80]

Emel'ianov's poem has several features which appeared in Evreinov's *Smiatennost'*: the reiteration of anaphoric sequences, the all-pervading sense of the prisoner's anxiety, and the use of words and images such as the hills, the stumps, lines of poetry ushered among the trees. The similarity between the two poems is further strengthened by Emel'ianov's final evocation of a natural world that is almost epic:

---

77   Shiriaev, p. 84.
78   B. Emel'ianov, 'Vesna v Solovkakh (stikh.)', *SO*, 7 (1925), 3.
79   B. Emel'ianov, 'V dvenadtsat' dnia', *SO*, 8 (1925), 5.
80   [They sing about the harsh dreams of mossy walls | My poems composed by the sharp bell towers... | I fell in love with you, mighty captivity, | I fell in love with you, green island. || Lakes and fields here are dear to me, | In the pine wood run, rhyming, my lines, | With them I go from the Kremlin's walls, | I go alone, counting stumps and tussocks.] Emel'ianov, 'V dvenadtsat' dnia'.

> А через миг в мозолистой руке,
> Перо пойдет привычно по бумаге,
>
> Ловя в прибойчатой, заморевой тоске,
> Призывы вдаль и северные саги.[81]

Even though various coincidences relating to imagery and form might lead one to identify Emel'ianov with Evreinov, this hypothesis proves altogether unsatisfactory: Emel'ianov rapidly became a successful author of musical intermezzos, whereas no mention was made of Boris Evreinov's activity in the theatrical life of the camp. It was Emel'ianov, for example, who wrote the famous song *More beloe — vodnaia shir'*, which soon became a classic Gulag song and from which comes the following, well-known specimen of camp humour:

> Всех, кто наградил нас Соловками,
> Просим, приезжайте сюда сами,
> Посидите здесь годочков три иль пять —
> Будете с восторгом вспоминать.[82]

The song was included in the first part of a play written by Glubokovskii to welcome one of the Moscow OGPU-appointed commissions. In fact, the song revealed the bold character of Glubokovskii — its irony proved prophetic: three of the people who attended the show (Bokii, Eikhmans, and Martinelli) were eventually shot, while Nogtev endured five years of detention in the Gulag.[83] Some memoir writers who mention the play ascribe the song to Glubokovskii:[84] among them is Likhachev,[85] who told the songwriter Aleksei Grigor'evich Iatskovskii that 'Boris Emel'ianov' was only one of Glubokovskii's pseudonyms.[86]

Emel'ianov's poetry is very much in line with Glubokovskii's 'manifesto' for sincere poetry within the camp. After rejecting panegyric poetry in his essay *Solovki v poezii solovchan*, Emel'ianov/Glubokovskii first published two 'free' poems (*Vesna v Solovkakh* and *V dvenadtsat' dnia*), then used *Pered utrom* to promote freedom for poetry and its disengagement from ideology:

---

81   [And in a moment in the calloused hand | The pen will move as usual across the paper, | Fishing in the waves of longing beyond the sea | For the summons to far away and northern sagas.] Ibid.

82   [To all who sentenced us to Solovki, | We say: please, feel free to come here, | Stay here three years or even five | You'll remember this with delight.] Svetlana Tiukina, 'Teper' vy v Solovkakh (lirika vremen SLONa)', *Solovetskoe more*, 2 (2003), 181.

83   During his imprisonment, the former director of the SLON became the author of poems pervaded by a strong sense of resignation.

84   This hypothesis has been further confirmed by a recent *Children's Encyclopaedia*, in the 'Sovetskie lageria i tiur'my. Solovetskii zhurnal' section. See *Entsiklopediia dlia detei*, ed. by Svetlana Ismailova (Moscow: Avanta+, 1993–96), V (1996), 461.

85   Likhachev, *Izbrannoe: Vospominaniia*, p. 215.

86   I received this information in an email exchange with Iatskovskii. Reading the description which Shiriaev gives of Emel'ianov in his book, I mistakenly indicated that Emel'ianov was a real person in the article: Andrea Gullotta, 'The "Cultural Village" of the Solovki Prison Camp: A Case of Alternative Culture', *Studies in Slavic Cultures*, 9 (2010), 9–25 (p. 21). Iatskovskii was right: I thank him here for his observation. E-mail dated 19 February 2010.

> Я стихи не пишу для редакций
> Лишь для тех, кто поймет строчек рать...
> Мне на золото тысячи акций
> В эту синюю ночь наплевать![87]

In addition to its contributors' individual achievements, the eighth issue of the journal was thoroughly 'revolutionary': Chekmazov published his previously mentioned apolitical sketch; and, even more significantly, Sof'ia Okerman published her second short story, which was totally deprived of ideological overtones, as the writer concentrated on a love story.[88]

The following three issues of the *Solovetskie Ostrova* were far less 'overtly committed' than the previous issues — a fact that was enhanced by the need to celebrate the anniversary of the October Revolution. In that period, the SLON was also the background for an important literary event. The camp *gazeta*, *Novye Solovki*, which had been publishing *lagernaia poeziia* and ideological poetry in its previous forty-four issues, included for the first time a totally 'free' poem, *Rybaki*, signed by 'K'.[89] Despite its lack of elaboration and unremarkable style, the poem opened a new phase in the development of SLON literature in which more poets would contribute their work without being forced to express political commitment.

The new year coincided with a turn in the poetic quality of the *Solovetskie Ostrova*. Thanks to burgeoning, so-called 'bourgeois' cultural activities, to the animated cultural debate on camp art, and to the strategic moves of Glubokovskii and (above all) Eikhmans, the liberation of literary language from the snares of ideology had finally been achieved.

The first 1926 issue of the *Solovetskie Ostrova* included both a poetic tribute to Lenin (which Litvin probably wrote in an attempt to mend his rift with the SLON administration and to make up for his subsequent exclusion from the official acknowledgements of the editorial board)[90] and several passages taken from a poem by Emel'ianov. Excerpts from the poem opened with a ringing dedication to the *kaery*, who were regarded as no different from the chekists and the guards:

> Посвящаю... ребятам с Хитрова,[91]
> Всем каэрам, чекистам и ментам.
> Кто виноват, что поэма хитрая
> Стала историческим документом.[92]

---

87   [I do not write poems for editorial boards | Only for those who will understand the assembled ranks of my lines... | For the gold of thousands of shares | I care nothing, in this blue night!] Emel'ianov, 'Pered utrom', *SO*, 8 (1925), 5.

88   See below, p. 213.

89   K., 'Rybaki', *NS*, 45 (1925), 2. It is impossible to know the author's real name.

90   See chapter 3, p. 126.

91   The name refers to Khitrovskaia Square, which was the favourite area of the Moscow 'bohemian *intelligentsiia*' despite being one of the most ill-famed neighbourhoods. Gor'kii's successful play *Na dne*, which was originally set in Nizhnyi Novgorod, was 'transferred' there in the MKhAT representation of the play. The Khitrovka started thus to be associated with Gor'kii and it was eventually named after the author, turning into 'Ploshchad' Maksima Gor'kogo'.

92   [Dedicated to... the guys from Khitrova, | To all the *kaery*, the chekists and cops. | Who is to blame, if a shrewd poem | Has become a historical document.] B. Emel'ianov, 'Otryvki iz poemy',

As the poem progressed through its several, intertwined quatrains, readers might have detected hints at the possible identity of Glubokovskii/Emel'ianov (я давно забыл о фокстроте),[93] several *loci fidelitatis*, and above all a new, daring vindication of the writer's intellectual freedom:

> Буду всегда поэтом
> Я, не согнувший плечи.[94]

The first 1926 issue also marked the literary début of Boris Rado, who published his poem *Nochnoi inei*. Boris Rado was most probably a pseudonym; to date, no information about his life has been found. *Nochnoi inei* reminded readers of the themes that led to Evreinov's exclusion from the SLON literary scene. The tone, in particular, is as dramatic as in Evreinov's poems:

> Лес и снег, и узенькие тропы
> И уходит вдаль олений след,
> Завиваю дней замерзших строфы,
> Запеваю дни заковных лет.
> Хрустнул хруст трусливый еле-еле
> Засмеялась белая сова,
> В эту ночь рассказывали ели
> Мне свои кудрявые слова.
> [...]
> Шаг — быстрей, коричневая тропка
> Уходя слилася с старым пнем,
> Как же мне не оглянуться робко
> Если я с моим вчерашним днем.
> [...]
> Если все кругом очертенело,
> Если нет загадки бытия...
> И хрустит тропинкой иней белый,
> И назад гляжу с испугом я.
>
> Слез? — Глаза мои пустая пачка
> Крикнуть — спазмы тяжелее слег,
> Нет недаром в эту ночь запачкал
> Я моих тропинок белый снег.[95]

SO, 1 (1926), 43. The poet plays with the toponym 'Khitrova' and the adjective *khitraia*, 'shrewd'.

93   'I have long forgotten the foxtrot.' The reference to the foxtrot is deliberate: Glubokovskii's group of 'bourgeois' intellectuals, who were accused of organizing the SLON 'Bohème', were usually called '*fokstrotisty*'.

94   [I will always be a poet | I, who haven't bowed my shoulders.] Emel'ianov, 'Otryvki'.

95   [Forest and snow and narrow footpaths | And the deer's footprints are visible in the distance, | I weave the stanzas of the frozen days, | I sing the days of my enchained years. || A coward crackle barely crackled | A white owl laughed, | In this night the pines told | Me their curly words. [...] My step is faster, the brown trail | In the distance merged with an old stump, | How could I not look back shyly | If I'm with my yesterday. [...] If everything around has become wearisome, | If there are no mysteries of existence... | And the white frost crunches like a footpath, | And I look back in fear. || Tears? My eyes are an empty parcel | If I shout the spasms are heavier than wooden beams, | No, not by chance in this night I befouled | The white snow of my paths.] B. Rado, 'Nochnoi inei', *SO*, 1 (1926), 96.

The recurrent use of disquietingly questioning anaphoras and the use of the concluding, dramatic climax — which contains two allusions to the Solovki context, i.e. the parcels and the wooden beam, with its implicit reference to timber felling — that at the close brings us back to the image of footsteps in the snow, heightens its all-pervading, embittered resemblance to Evreinov's poetry. This sensation is supported by the poem's use of images similar to those of the *Zarei okhotnich'ei* and by the insistent use of alliteration. 'Rado' might have well been influenced by, or even be a pseudonym of Evreinov, who was once again admitted to be one of the journal contributors starting from the 2/3 1926 issue of the *Solovetskie Ostrova*. The two poems share an affinity for rural landscapes and the outspokenness that caused Evreinov's exclusion. In the first poem published by Evreinov in the 2/3 1926 issue, which contains a suggestive and gloomy depiction of the *izby*,[96] there is a lamentation for the Russian countryside and the peasants' resistance. Its symbol is a cross that is still standing after many furious hurricanes — an image which might allude to the onslaught of communism, as the poem subtly suggests:

> У двух избушек старый крест,
> Скривившийся и обомшелый,
> Плетня разрушенного шест
> И моря переплеск несмелый.
> В избушке пусто. Косари
> Давно ушли в места иные,
> И ветер шалый до зари
> Бьет дверью в косяки дверные.
> [...]
> Вблизи болото. Дальний лес
> Укутан пеленой тумана.
>
> Скрипит под ветром жуткий крест —
> Свидетель многих ураганов.[97]

Evreinov's topical perception of the indissoluble bond between man and nature runs throughout *Zakat*; this privileged relationship is again set against the background of harsh imprisonment.

As was the case with Rado's work, Evreinov's poem was not influenced by Soviet ideology. This was a sign that times had already changed and that the 'Solovki Muse' was freer. Beginning with the 2/3 1926 issue of the *Solovetskie Ostrova*, writers dropped the *locus fidelitatis* strategy completely and published almost exclusively literary works which made no concessions to ideological demands. In that issue of the journal, free poetry was epitomized by the literary début of Georgii Rusakov. Rusakov had been imprisoned in Moscow during the Russian Civil War and spent

---

96   The *izba* is a Russian peasant's hut or cottage.

97   [Beside two peasant huts is an old cross, | Crooked and covered in moss, | The post of a destroyed fence | And the sea's timid lapping. || The hut is empty. The mowers | Have long gone to other places, | And the wind, furious before dawn | Beats the door against the door jambs. [...] Nearby there is a swamp. The distant forest | Is swathed in a veil of fog. || The dreadful cross creaks in the wind, | Witness of many hurricanes.] B. Evreinov, 'Stikhi (U dvukh izbushek)', *SO*, 2–3 (1926), 38.

some time in the Taganka prison. The poems he published there in 1921 in the prison journal *Tiur'ma* went well beyond the topical description of prisoners' dismay at their condition and tried instead to resist the repressive regime that Rusakov had to endure:

> Да я умру. Но в тихом птичьем свисте,
> в осеннем золоте уже опавших листьев,
> и в изумрудных всходах ячменя —
> Я буду жить! И, мыслью той пленя,
> Покой души загадочно инертен:
> Я чувствую — я знаю — я бессмертен.[98]

This feeling informed Rusakov's publications in the SLON press from the very beginning. His *Venok sonetov* is devoted to the history of the monastery. Its dedication to Litvin (who, as seen above, at that moment was still the victim of the KVCh's retaliation, having lost his feuilleton and his predominant role in the SLON publications)[99] was a very courageous act. Rusakov's crown of sonnets progressed through the internal repetitions that tie the last line of a sonnet with the first line of the following one. This stanzaic progression then leads into the creation of the madrigal, which is made up of the first lines of all the sonnets. Rusakov's madrigal celebrates the fortunes of the monastery:

> Молитвой до кровавых капель пота
> Смиряя страсти бешеные сны,
> Нагромождала черная пехота
> Столетиями седые валуны.
>
> Бойницами надежного оплота
> От бесов и врагов ограждены,
> Спасались старцы. И была забота:
> Царя и церкви блудные сыны.
>
> Ни ржа цепей, ни сырость подземелья
> Не изживали мрачного похмелья
> И буйной дерзости в еретиках.
>
> Два мира шли на подвиг, на мученье.
> О твердости, упорстве и терпеньи
> Вещает каждый камень в Соловках.[100]

---

98 [Yes, I will die. But in the quiet whistle of a bird, | In the autumn gold of the already fallen leaves, | And in the emerald sprouts of barley | I will live! And, being enchanted by that thought, | The peace of the soul is mysteriously inert: | I feel — I know — I am immortal.] G. Rusakov, 'Iz nashego al'boma', *Tiur'ma*, 3 (1921), 75.

99 See above, p. 126.

100 [With a prayer so intense that they sweated blood | Subduing mad dreams of passion, | The black infantry heaped up | Grey boulders for centuries. || By the loopholes of a secure stronghold, | They were protected from demons and enemies, | The elders survived. And they had a concern: | The prodigal sons of the Tsar and of the Church. || Neither the rust of the chains, nor the dampness of the dungeon | could overcome the dark hangover | And the wild audacity of the heretics. || Two worlds set out for feats of heroism, for torment. | About their steadiness, perseverance and patience | Speaks every stone on Solovki.] G. Rusakov, 'Solovki. Venok sonetov', *SO*, 2–3 (1926), 3–16 (p. 3).

In the other sonnets, Rusakov managed to trace the history of the monastery back to its origins by highlighting moments of suffering and violence and by subtly evoking the impending threat of 'Communist occupation' that would eventually take place.

The final literary contribution to this issue of the journal is Boris Rado's poem, *A.Z.*, which was an attempt to freely address the theme of eroticism in poetry:

> Две буквы в Соловках я ставлю над „люблю”,
> Совсем по новому продумав наши встречи,
> И белых льдин взрывающий салют
> Привет вам шлет, целуя ваши плечи.
> Сегодня, как вчера, в каком-то бурном скетче
> Я не могу сказать — мне кажется я сплю, —
> Две буквы в Соловках я ставлю над „люблю”,
> Совсем по новому продумав наши встречи.[101]

Though it certainly does not represent a climax in the SLON literary output, Rado's crucial and straightforward representation of love is almost unique in the panorama of the *tiuremnaia pechat'*. It is also part of the first-ever publication of the SLON press where no literary text is subjected to the demands of ideology.

An example of writing which entirely ignores ideological demands is to be found in the journal's following issue, the fourth 1926 issue, which included 'purely literary' prose pieces. It also introduced two important new features, such as Shiriaev's disengaged and totally non-encomiastic tale (*1237 strok*)[102] and equally non-celebratory poems by Litvin. Litvin's sonnet *Kudeiar* and his poem *Po gradu Kitezhu*[103] were nonetheless indicative of Litvin's (not always remarkable) creative attempts, focused on different experiences rather than life at the labour camp.

As well as including two more poems (one by Evreinov and the other by Emel'ianov),[104] the fourth 1926 issue of the *Solovetskie Ostrova* also crucially conveyed some writers' overt condemnation of the Soviet state. The journal was published soon after prisoners learned about Sergei Esenin's suicide. This event affected the intellectual circles of the camp and raised a furore, especially among prisoners who had met the poet personally. Among them was Boris Glubokovskii, who immediately started to organize commemorative soirées, published an article in the *Novye Solovki*,[105] and 'directed' mourning events at the SLON. At the same time, the *Solovetskie Ostrova* included a short section called *Pamiati Sergeia Esenina* which

---

101 [Two letters on the Solovki I put above 'I love' | Having thought of our meetings in a totally new way, | And the exploding fireworks of white ice floes | Send you greetings, kissing your shoulders. | Today, as yesterday, in some turbulent sketch | I cannot tell — it seems to me that I'm dreaming — | Two letters on the Solovki I put above 'I love' | Having thought of our meetings in a totally new way.] B. Rado, 'A. Z. (Stikhi)', *SO*, 2–3 (1926), 38.

102 B. Shiriaev, '1237 strok', *SO*, 4 (1926), 19.

103 N. Litvin, 'Kudeiar. Po kraiu Kitezhu', *SO*, 4 (1926), 74–75.

104 Emel'ianov's poem was actually the lyric of a song, 'Chasha solovetskaia', written (as 'More beloe — vodnaia shir'') for one of Glubokovskii's plays. It later also became a classic of *lagernaia pesnia*. See B. Emel'ianov, 'Chasha solovetskaia', *SO*, 4 (1926), 77.

105 B. Glubokovskii, 'Esenin', *NS*, 6 (1926), 2.

FIG. 4.6. A winter photograph of the SLON. AMM

consisted of two poems. The first poem, by Emel'ianov, was a poetic dialogue between Esenin and the author, composed of an interplay between Esenin's couplets and his own couplets:

> Не увидеть старушке-маме
> В захлестнувшей веревке Мессии,
> Веревке обернувшей шею в кровавый след,
>
> «Что если б вы понимали,
> Что сын ваш в России
> Самый лучший поэт».[106]

The second poem was, on the other hand, a full-blown invective by the 'unbridled' Georgii Rusakov. Speaking from the SLON literary arena, Rusakov accused the Soviet authorities of sacrificing a poet such as Esenin on the altar of ideology:

> Не сберегли кудрявого Сережу,
> И он ушел в непредрешенный день...
> Придет — да поздно! — к брошенному ложу
> Печаль осиротевших деревень.[107]

106 [The old mother will not be able to see | In the rope that is tied around the Messiah | The rope which has circled his neck with a bloody trace || 'What if you understood | That your son in Russia | Is the best poet'.] B. Emel'ianov, 'Tsitaty', SO, 4 (1926), 72.
107 [They have not spared Serezha and his curls, | And he ran away suddenly... | Too late the abandoned bed will be reached | By the sadness of the orphaned villages.] G. Rusakov, 'Ne sberegli',

Rusakov's overflowing rage would be echoed by *Chernoe ozero*, a poem Rado
published in the following issue of the *Solovetskie Ostrova* (5/6). The poem was
centred on an impressively strong and straightforward image:

> Вот-вот у кованых ворот,
> Склонив точено-острый профиль,
> Скривив красноармейский рот,
> Вслед захохочет Мефистофель.[108]

Mephistopheles with the mouth of a Red Army soldier — this image reveals that
the Solovki Muse's freedom had by then turned into pure rebellion. Rebellion
pervaded both Rado's and Rusakov's poems. The subtle connections between these
poems suggest that they could have been written by the same person (instead of
being Evreinov's pseudonym, 'Rado' might have been a pen name for Rusakov:
Evreinov never dared to be so overtly polemical). What the two authors shared
was a bitter rage, the kind of intimate revolt that led Rusakov to write a poem,
'Solovetskoi vesnoi', where the *intelligentsiia* is infected by the violent Pecheneg
tribesmen, the communist-barbarians.

> И вижу я: прорвав столетий бег,
> В вас, литераторы, бухгалтеры, и снобы
> Проснулся он, жестокий печенег.
> Для грубых радостей и темной злобы.[109]

Another connection between the two is to be found at a stylistic level. The sonnet
entitled *Mai* includes both an image found in Rado's poems (ice breaking, as in
Nochnoi inei: 'Хрустнул хруст трусливый еле-еле' [A cowardly crackle barely
crackled]) and the intensive use of alliteration:

> Журчат ручьи, ворча парчей текучей,
> По вечерам хрустален робкий хруст.
> Из под сугроба брызнул быстрый куст
> И лавина расплавилась под кручей.[110]

Finally, Rado and Rusakov, as has been already suggested, appeared almost at
the same time on the SLON scene (though Rado's début also coincides with
Evreinov's return). It is therefore impossible to say exactly who was hiding
behind the pseudonym of 'Rado'. Evreinov himself, after being cast out from the
Solovetskie Ostrova for a year, became a regular guest of the journal. A poem of his
was printed in the 5/6 issue, which also features poems by Emel'ianov (a not too

---

SO, 4 (1926), 73.

108 [In a moment by the wrought-iron gates, | Bowing his chiselled and sharp profile, | Making a
wry-Red-Army-soldier mouth | Mephistopheles will then guffaw.] B. Rado, 'Chernoe ozero', *SO*,
5–6 (1926), 25.

109 [And I see: having broken through the run of centuries, | In you, writers, accountants, and
snobs | He woke up, the cruel Pecheneg | For rough joys and dark rage.] G. Rusakov, 'Solovetskoi
vesnoi', *SO*, 5–6 (1926), 28.

110 [The streams murmur, grumbling like flowing brocade, | In the evening the timid crackle is
crystal-clear. | From beneath a snowdrift a quick bush sprang | And the avalanche melted under the
steep slope.] G. Rusakov, 'Mai', *SO*, 5–6 (1926), 29.

remarkable reply to Rusakov's *venok*)[111] and by Shiriaev. It must be mentioned that this moment coincided with the final stage of Shiriaev's metamorphosis. His long poem *Turkestanskie stikhi*[112] was totally apolitical. Less constrained by ideological requirements, Shiriaev opted at this point for plain poetry, leaving behind all experimentation — the *lesenki* and the avant-garde techniques.

The last issue of the first period of the *Solovetskie Ostrova* was a synthesis of the various unique traits of SLON poetry. Emel'ianov published a poem on the *ugolovniki* à la Glubokovskii and also *Noch'*, in which the cry of independent poetry managed to carve out a place for itself — in the night, realm of the poet:

> Время, когда горизонт сутул,
> Наше время. Поэтов![113]

Emel'ianov's poem, which was dedicated to Esenin, is interspersed with suggestive images, such as the monastery-sphinx ('монастырь-сфинкс') and the dawn-caged sun ('а гулящее солнце не спит, мечется в заре-клети'). It also dared to announce the poet's irreversible freedom from having to celebrate Soviet Russia:

> Но ведь я не собака-поэт,
> да поэт Руси бездорожной.[114]

Emel'ianov's deliberate use of the word *Rus'* instead of *Rossiia* sheds some light on the poet's feeling for ancestral Russia — something that was a prominent feature in 'New Peasant' verse and, more generally, the work of many poets — especially in Leningrad, like for instance Vaginov — who drew a contrast between the return to an ancestral purity and the evolution of poetry under the Soviets.[115] Emel'ianov was not alone in his celebration of boundless conceptual freedom. Besides publishing a second love poem, 'Rado' published other poems that lament the deaths of fellow prisoners shot in the woods; in them, he did not even attempt to disguise his real intentions and adopted instead a kind of heart-felt lyricism. He even evoked the spurting blood, the farewells to the fellow-inmates who lie dying in the bushes or elsewhere on the archipelago, and the prisoners' fruitless efforts to survive by harmonizing these images through the use of the rhythm created by recurring alliteration and polysyndetons that emphasise the tragedy of the episode:

> В тумане чей-то тонкий профиль —
> За льдами тот, кто слишком строг,
> В бреду расхлябанности строфик
> Я в сумерках чужих дорог.
>
> Гляжу в отверстия ущелий —
> Земли раскосые глаза.
> Одно из тысячи прощений

111 Rusakov, 'Solovki. Venok sonetov'; B. Emel'ianov, 'Berdysh', *SO*, 5–6 (1926), 23–24.

112 B. Shiriaev, 'Turkestanskie stikhi', *SO*, 5–6 (1926), 42.

113 [The time when the horizon is bowed | Is our time. The time of poets!] B. Emel'ianov, 'Stikhi (Noch')', *SO*, 7 (1926), 29.

114 [But I am not a dog-poet, | but the poet of the roadless Rus'.] Ibid.

115 See, for instance, Konstantin Vaginov, 'Do belykh barkhanov tvoikh', *Sobranie stikhotvorenii* (Munich: Otto Sagner, 1982), p. 93.

Оплакала вчера слеза.

И сгустками покрыта рана
Кровавых потемневших брызг,
И в клочьях белого тумана
Торосов белые бугры.

Иду один, иду шатаясь,
И ночь склонилась на плечо,
И даль попрежнему пустая
Целует в губы горячо.

И в ней, голубовато синей,
Торжественной, как прошлый век,
В бесплодных судоргах усилий
Потерян мною человек.

И в шорохе замерзшем края,
Сбирая крохи прежних крох,
Ищу „потерянного рая‟ —
Я в сумерках чужих дорог.[116]

Rado's poem represents by no means the acme of the SLON poets' intellectual freedom. Boris Evreinov's poem *Voskresnym dnem*, pervaded by the unmistakable religious feelings evoked by the title, was one of the highest manifestations of the poetic freedom of *lagernaia poeziia*. The poem's 'Aesopian' epigraph, borrowed from Aleksei Lozina-Lozinskii[117] ('Теперь мне все равно, | Где молодость моя проходит') was only apparently at odds with the rest of the poem. In fact, it is possible that it secretly referred to the priest and poet Vladimir Lozina-Lozinskii, who, as we shall see later, composed several clandestine religious poems. The religious meaning that runs throughout the poem is made fairly explicit in the following image:

И выйдя к морю, стершему все грани,
Где на песке следы от неводов,

Прилечь под солнцем, грезя без желаний,
И слушать волн напевный часослов.[118]

116 [In the mist there's someone's slim profile | Beyond the ice is the one who is too severe, | In the delirium of the unseemliness of the stanzas | I am in the twilight of someone else's roads. || I look at the opening of the ravines — | The almond-shaped eyes of the earth. | One of a thousand farewells | A tear yesterday mourned. || And the wound is covered with clots | Of bloodied darkened splashes, | And in the shreds of a white fog | Are white mounds of ice-packs. || I go alone, I go reeling, | And the night bent over on my shoulder, | And the distance, empty as before, | Kisses my lips passionately. || And in the distance, bluish blue, | Solemn as the last century, | In the fruitless convulsions of effort | Is the person I lost. || And in the freezing rustle of the border, | Harvesting the crumbs of old crumbs, | Looking for the "paradise lost" — | I am in the twilight of someone else's roads.] B. Rado, 'Iskaniia', *SO*, 7 (1926), 37.

117 Aleksei Lozina-Lozinskii (1886–1916) was a poet whose ideas about suicide traumatized pre-revolutionary Russia. His diaries written during his stay in Italy have been published thanks to the work of Simone Guagnelli, see Aleksei Lozina-Lozinskii, *Solitudine. Capri e Napoli (appunti di un girovago)* (Rome: Scienza e Lettere, 2010). The quotation from Aleksei Lozina-Lozinskii reads: 'Now for me it makes no difference/ Where I live my youth.'

118 [And going towards the sea, which erases all the margins | Where on the sand are the traces

The waves sing the prayers from a Book of Hours while the sea erases all boundaries. This image probably hints at a gentle hypostasis of death, and the tracks on the sand — i.e. destined to be washed off by the sea or blown away by the wind — as well as the supine position of the speaker, add further power to the metaphorical reading of the poem.

The above poems marked the end of the first season of the journal *Solovetskie Ostrova*. It was also the end of SLON poetry's 'first season'. Once the journal was closed down, most of its poets started to publish elsewhere, especially in the *Novye Solovki*, which, while adhering quite strictly to the line of 'encomiastic poetry' until the end of 1926, opened itself up to different trends. As a consequence, Rusakov published a couple of poems there and Rado published his 'poetic reflections' on the SLON. Evreinov, on the other hand, disappeared completely. Shiriaev, Glubokovskii, and Litvin exploited their creative energies to publish several essays, meditations, and feuilletons. Significantly, at the end of 1926 Emel'ianov — who since 1925 had been the most outstanding contributor of all of the poets to the *Novye Solovki* and in the *Solovetskie Ostrova* had pushed poetry beyond all tolerated thematic limits — seemed to reconsider his actions, as suggested by his extensive use of *locus fidelitatis* and celebratory poetry. His very last poems owed much to the early production of Shiriaev, including several *lesenki* and encomiastic lines clearly inspired by him.

This sudden change in Emel'ianov's poetic output was probably caused by the release of many intellectuals, as has already been suggested. In 1926, several prisoner-authors had served their sentences and were allowed to leave the Solovki islands. Yet the only writer who had his sentence significantly reduced was Shiriaev. Emel'ianov (or rather Glubokovskii, whose sentence was the same as Shiriaev's) eventually tried to imitate Shiriaev. Probably Glubokovskii hoped the authorities would also reduce his sentence and release him, but his attempts were in vain. He remained at the SLON and therefore 'bridged' the early and the later periods of the SLON literature. However, Glubokovskii eventually refused to write poetry in the second period — thus also 'eliminating' Emel'ianov. Well aware of what the future had in store for him, Emel'ianov/Glubokovskii bid readers farewell with a last, 'entirely free' poem, once again marked by an archaism, '*mety*', which refers to the traces left on the wood, symbolically short-lived:

> Вы видали хвост у кометы,
> когда снежный туман позади?
> Вот такие же яркие меты
> На пахучей сосновой груди.[119]

of the drag-nets, | Lie down in the sun, day-dreaming without desires, | And listen to the waves' melodious Book of Hours.] B. Evreinov, 'Voskresnym dnem', *SO*, 7 (1926), 33.

119 [Have you seen the tail of the comet, | when the snowy fog was behind it? | Just as bright are the marks | On the fragrant chest of the pine.] B. Emel'ianov, 'Vy vidali khvost u monety', *NS*, 50 (1926), 3.

Prose: Irony and Boldness

Despite its relative paucity and lack of substantial thematic or stylistic innovation, prose fiction was an important element of SLON publications during its first stage. Whereas writers' essays and poems (from a theoretical and practical perspective respectively) were the very engine of SLON literary development, fiction too contributed in a way, although it always remained in the background.

The fiction that was published in the *SLON* and in the *Solovetskie Ostrova* before Glubokovskii's arrival had very similar features to the poetry of the same period — as the previous analysis of Litvin's prose writing has shown. A landmark of this period was the writers' absolute devotion to the *lagernaia tema*. Their works almost invariably included episodes, characters, and situations that were typical of SLON life. Not only essays and literary portraits, but purely fictional pieces were deeply rooted in their authors' experience of the SLON or of other prisons. For example, Tiberii's series of short stories *Solovetskie siluety*[120] was aimed at making fun of the representatives of *kaerovshchina* (with descriptions such as the 'inter-individualist Communist' who takes up stealing, the 'political burglar-prisoner', and so on) and paid little or no attention to literary form. The author who wrote under the pseudonym 'Tot' was relatively more successful. His *Solovetskie zarisovki*,[121] while maintaining its propaganda features and didacticism, experimented with different narrative techniques.

With the exception of Tot, Litvin, and Shiriaev, SLON fiction did not improve on its early, poor results. A radical change coincided with the arrival of Glubokovskii and — as was the case with poetry — with the launch of the 'campaign for the liberation of literary word' within the SLON. Prose works started to free themselves from ideology and create better-quality offshoots while retaining the theme of 'camp life'.

Most prominent among the writers of SLON prose fiction was Glubokovskii, who published a short and altogether unremarkable *lagernaia tema* short story (*Pet'ka*)[122] in the seventh 1925 issue of the journal and a second short story (*Solovetskaia psisha*, the story of Marusia, a prisoner turned actress)[123] in the ninth issue. The tenth issue included the first instalment of Glubokovskii's story *Puteshestvie iz Moskvy v Solovki*, which is by far the most extensive work ever published in the SLON press.[124] Its 129 pages, published in instalments, conjured up the post-revolutionary years by focusing on the excesses and the peculiarities of that period. Interestingly, Glubokovskii used some features of 'autofiction' to tell his story: his alter-ego/hero had the same name as the author (Boris) and the story was based on the author's own experiences, which were fictionalized in order to lend the story more intensity

---

120 Tiberii, 'Solovetskie siluety', *SLON*, 9–10 (1924), 47–50.
121 Tot, 'Solovetskie zarisovki', *SO*, 6 (1925), 54–56; 7 (1925), 30–31; 8 (1925), 12–14; 9 (1925), 29–30; 10–11 (1925), 34–35.
122 B. Glubokovskii, 'Pet'ka', *SO*, 7 (1925), 15–21.
123 B. Glubokovskii, 'Solovetskaia psisha', *SO*, 9 (1925), pp. 9–16.
124 B. Glubokovskii, 'Puteshestvie iz Moskvy v Solovki', *SO*, 10–11 (1925), 5–16; 12 (1925), 3–9; 1 (1926), 24–42; 2–3 (1926), 41–71; 4 (1926), 80–101; 5–6 (1926), 46–69; 7 (1926), 60–73.

and depth.[125] Kuziakina, quoting Glubokovskii, states that the objective of this short story was 'to show bohemianism as a kind of internal emigration (the Solovki, indeed, are conceived by the author as an image of redemption) — a purpose which, apparently, determined the starkly sarcastic, vicious characterization and apparent coolness of presentation'.[126] In my view, Glubokovskii went far beyond this 'official' justification, which is nothing more than a *locus fidelitatis*. His assumed ideological motivation might ultimately be simply a mask for the novelist eager to restart his narrative production after his arrest.

Glubokovskii, in fact, had made his literary debut as both playwright and prose writer. With a still-unattributed pamphlet as the only exception,[127] he started to write short stories in 1918 under the pseudonym of Boris Veev. 'Boris Veev' was a contributor to *Gostinitsa dlia puteshestvuiushchikh v prekrasnom*, a journal published between 1922 and 1924 that included essays and short stories written by pioneering Russian Imagists, along with works by Esenin and Mandel'shtam.[128]

The early output of Glubokovskii/Veev included unexpected themes and distinctively challenging stylistic choices. His *Uezdnyi Oskar Ual'd*,[129] for example, tackled the question of homosexuality, a theme raised in Russian literature at the same time by Mikhail Kuzmin's work. It created a deliberate conceptual confusion that springs from the juxtaposition of aestheticism and homosexuality while lending the argument a remarkable narrative edge. Though the story of Zametkin 'the aesthete' and his eventual repentance through his marriage may not exploit Glubokovskii's full potential, it is nonetheless a lively narrative incorporating vivacious and original dialogues.

Narrative rhythm and lively dialogues are also distinctive features of the *Puteshestvie*, in which the main character, Boris, progresses through a series of original situations and equally original dialogues that occur, for instance, when he follows the pattern of the speeches by the representatives of Futurism during the October Revolution and incites others to destroy theatres during a public debate, thus finding his aspirations ironically fulfilled:

> I was called by the chair of the meeting. We went aside to have a word.

125 Rather significantly, the title is derived from *Puteshestvie iz Peterburga v Moskvu* by Aleksandr Radishchev, who took his cue from a nobleman's journey across the Russian countryside to denounce the living conditions of peasants under Catherine II's reign. Considering the fact that Radishchev was eventually sent into exile in Siberia, it is possible to suggest that Glubokovskii identified with him.

126 Kuziakina, p. 38.

127 I am referring to *Proklyatyi vopros Rossii*, a short essay on international politics that was presumably written by Glubokovskii in 1914 but which is clearly distant from the author's subsequent output. Both its theme and style seem a little too precocious for a twenty-year-old Glubokovskii. See B. Glubokovskii, *Proklyatyi vopros Rossii (Vostochnyi vorpos)* (Moscow: Knigoizdatel'stvo 'Obshchee delo', 1914/1915) (CNLR, Shrift Z. 37, Sh. 80, R. 4, n. 215).

128 See Vladimir Markov, 'Gostinitsa dlia puteshestvuiushchikh v prekrasnom; iz knigi "Ocherk istorii ruskogo imazhinizma"', *Zvezda*, 2 (2005), 211–19.

129 Moscow, RGALI, f. 1345, op. 1, ed. khr. 141, 'Boris Glubokovskii (psevd. Boris Veev), Uezdnyi Oskar Ual'd. Rasskaz'. The standard transliteration of Oscar Wilde's name in Russian is 'Uail'd'.

'We don't know each other' — he started off quite rudely — 'My name is
Kolia Kirasov, I'm a partisan and I want to speak with you'
'Nice to meet you' — I replied.
'When are we going to wreck the theatre? Tomorrow, or the day after? Well!
That'll be fun burning down the abomination!'
I looked at him to see whether he was joking, but no, he was deadly
serious.
'What do you mean — burn down the theatre?' — I wondered, shocked.
'But didn't you say so yourself? We must go tomorrow; I'll fetch the boys
and off we'll go.'
He was resolute. I understood that there was no way he could be dissuaded.
I moved the conversation onto another topic.[130]

Glubokovskii's ironic treatment of the gullibility of the revolutionaries is crystal-
clear. Irony was, of course, one of the most powerful (and legitimate) weapons of
Glubokovskii's prose during the 'SLON season', as the actor and playwright ofter
resorted to irony in the texts he wrote for the theatre, such as his (i.e. Emel'ianov's)
previously mentioned song *More beloe — Vodnaia shir'*.

Привезли нам надежд полный куль
Бокий, Фельдман, Филиппов и Вуль.
А назад повезет Катанян
Только грустный напев соловчан.[131]

His strong link with the theatre appears also in other episodes of the *Puteshestvie*, as
in the one quoted below, where characters are portrayed through their speech in a
scene that seems taken from a theatre script rather than from a tale:

Leshchilov woke me up. You couldn't understand whether it was the
morning or the evening. No, it was the morning — out there, in a cold light,
the nearby, transparent blue-grey scaly stream was turning pink, and out there
below back of the steppe, which was turning green, were the immaculately
white chalk mountains.
'We've arrived', — said Leschilov quietly.
'We're already near to our destination' — already near to our destination?!
— Sergei was alarmed and surprised, and turned pale.
'There is the Don' — pointed out Leschilov — 'you see, it's a tiny river.
This is the great Don, and over there — beyond these forests — there is the
Hetmanate'.

130 [Меня отозвал председатель. Отошли в сторонку. — Мы с тобой незнакомы, —
грубовато просто начал он: Я Коля Кирасов — партизан, вот поговорить с тобой хочу. —
Очень рад, — ответил я. — Когда мы пойдем театр-то громить? Завтра или после завтра? Ох,
и с удовольствием сожгу я его, анафему! Я глянул на него: не смеется-ли? — нет, серьезен.
— Как сжечь театр? — удивился отчаянно я. — А как-же, сам ведь говорил? Нужно идти
завтра, вот соберу ребят и пойдем. Он был решителен. Я понял, что переубедить его нельзя.
Я перевел разговор на другую тему.] B. Glubokovskii, 'Puteshestvie', *SO*, 4 (1926), p. 100. This
passage is also quoted in Kuziakina's book (see Kuziakina, pp. 38–39). Part of this translation is taken
from Kuziakina's book.
131 [They brought us a sack full of hope | Bokii, Fel'dman, Filippov and Vul'. | And Katanian will
carry back | Just the sad melody of the Solovki people] Svetlana Tiukina, 'Teper' vy v Solovkakh…',
Status-kvo, 30/06/2009, http://www.statusquo.ru/ [Accessed 23 January 2015].

'When will we go?' — asked Sergei.

'Tomorrow at dawn. During the day we have to sniff around. We have to check out the map. Pretend you've come here for flour. Well, we're almost there. Shut up. Shh...'

The rolling wheels creaked under the brake, someone shouted not too loudly:

'The station! The station!'

And the wagon suddenly came to life.

'There it is, the Ukraine, finally!' Loudly, just as if he hadn't just been asleep, a guy in a cap yelled happily. 'Oh, my dear one, and beautiful as well!'

'The Ukraine is good, but the hetman is a bitch' — a sailor muttered indifferently.

'Brothers, don't get off while we're moving, there will be a search. Chicks, don't shout!' — one man ordered, energetically.

His girlfriend looked at him with warm and sparkling eyes.[132]

Whereas Glubokovskii's work mostly hinged on irony, other writers pushed the limits of art even further. One of the SLON's few women writers, Sof'ia Okerman, managed to carve out a space for herself in the camp press. Her first short story, *V Solovki*,[133] was published in the seventh 1925 issue of the *Solovetskie Ostrova*, that is, after the publication of Glubokovskii's essay *Solovki v poezii solovchan*. It strictly obeyed the conventions of ideological camp prose. Okerman was, however, encouraged by the development of cultural debate at the SLON and she subsequently published a rather original text in the eighth issue of the journal. Looking back on Krivosh-Nemanich's love epigrams, her *Koe-chto o liubvi solovetskoi*[134] raises the question of eroticism by narrating the love story between a *polkovnik* and a 'brunette'. The story, which anticipates the later advent of Boris Rado's erotic lyric poetry, was set in the camp and still reminds readers of the comments by Rosalind Marsh on turn-of-the-century women Realists, who 'while providing general insights into contemporary society, are often particularly successful at depicting female characters and raising issues of interest to women'.[135]

---

132 [Разбудил Лещилов. Не поймешь, утро ли, вечер. Нет, утро — вон розовеет холодным светом прозрачная голубень-серая чешуйчатая реченка недалече, а там из-под обзеленевшей степной спины непорочно белые меловые горы. Приехали, — сказал Лещилов тихо. Уже у цели, — уже у цели?! — Встревоженно удивился Сережа и побледнел. Вон там Дон, — указал пальцем Лещилов: видите — речушка. Это великий Дон, а вон там — за этими лесами — там Гетманство. Когда же мы пойдем? — спросил Сережа. Завтра на рассвете. Днем разнюхать надо. Свериться по карте. Делайте вид, будто вы за мукой приехали. Ну, под'езжаем. Молчите. Тссс... Заскрипели под уздой тормоза, раскатившиеся колеса, кто-то полугромко выкрикнул: — Станция! Станция! И теплушка ожила вмиг. Вот она, Украина-то! — громко, точно и не-спал он, весело заорал парень в картузе. Эх, матушка, и красавица же! Украина-то хороша, да гетман сука, — равнодушно процедил матрос. Братишки, не слезай на ходу, обыск будет. Бабы, не ори! — лихо командовал парень. Молодуха глядела на него теплыми и сочными глазами.] В. Glubokovskii, 'Puteshestvie', *SO*, 2–3 (1926), p. 43.

133 S. Okerman, 'V Solovki', *SO*, 7 (1925), 27.

134 S. Okerman, 'Koe-chto o liubvi solovetskoi', *SO*, 8 (1925), 10.

135 Rosalind Marsh, 'Realist Prose Writers 1881–1929', in *A History of Women's Writing in Russia*, ed. by Adele Marie Barker and Jehanne M. Gheith (Cambridge: Cambridge University Press, 2002), pp. 175–206 (p. 175).

This focus on issues related particularly to women is demonstrated by the author's explicit sympathy for her female protagonists which, starting from the second short story, leads Okerman to unexpected daring. The twelfth 1925 issue of the journal includes her *Siluety zhenbaraka*, the story of Niunichka, a representative of the *intelligentsiia* who is arrested and sent to the Solovki islands. Working at the camp laundry, Niunichka decides to improve her life through the help she obtains by courting one of the customers of the laundry, a soldier working as a camp guard. This enables her to leave her previous job and become a theatre actress. Niunichka continues to act until she gets sick of having to work too much as an actress and decides to find another protector within the theatre:

> In the theatre work is in full swing. There's one play after another. All the 'new' directors stage a play. And also Niunichka wants to understand. But she can't.
> — It's a bad thing — thinks Niunichka — one 'protector' is not enough, it is necessary to find a second.
> And Niunichka, who has hated women her whole life... wants to start a friendship with a woman.
> — What a mind, what talent, what beauty — Niunichka makes flattering remarks to the leading lady.
> [...]
> In the small cell all is quiet. Everyone has got up to go to work and Niunia still lolls in bed.
> She gets up, pour herself two bowls of soup and half a dozen river sprats, then gets back into bed, lying on her side.
> It is not life, but a carnival.[136]

The end of the story is pitiless. After realizing that her 'connection' is no longer able to protect here (we guess from the text that has died), Niunichka is left alone with her own anger:

> The Kremlin walls shuddered. The sad news spread through the Solovki.
> — He was a good man, but he got tangled up with a useless girl.
> — *Cherchez la femme!* — the *kaery* explain.
> Niunichka shudders too. She doesn't see the familiar military cap, she can't hear his pleasant voice.
> Niunia buries her nose in the pillow and snivels the whole night through until the morning.
> — It's all over, oh — oh — oh, damned Solovki![137]

136 [В театре работа кипит. Пьеса за пьесой идет. Все „новые" какие-то постановки делают. И хочет понять и Нюничка. А не может. — Плохо дело, думает Нюничка, одного „блата" мало, надо второй завести. И Нюничка, всю жизнь ненавидя женщину... с женщиной дружбу завести хочет. — Вот ум, вот талант, вот красота — ластится к примадонне Нюничка. [...] В маленькой камере тихо. Все на работу стали, а Нюня еще в постели нежится. Встанет, выхлещет миски две супу, да селедочек с полдюжины, потом опять на боковую. Не жизнь, а масляница.] S. Okerman, 'Siluety zhenbaraka', *SO*, 12 (1925), 14–15 (p. 14).

137 [Содрогнулись Кремлевские стены. Печальная весть Соловки облетела. — Хороший был человек, да с непутевой бабой спутался. — Cherchez la femme! — об'ясняют каэры. Нюничка тоже содрагается. Не видно знакомой фуражки, не слышно приятного голоса.

'Damned Solovki' is a sentence that is heard twice (in fact the damnation resounds three times, if we consider the beginning of the story, when Niunichka is in the Butyrki prison). The second time Niunichka utters it, her words bring the story to a close. Niunichka's words echo throughout the three-page story, in which a woman's tragedy is deftly disguised as an ideological text. While she seems to condemn the protagonist for being both an unscrupulous aristocrat and a person who does not want to work, Okerman used the awkward experience of a counter-revolutionary to bring to light the kind of degradation woman prisoners have to endure. This is supported by several clues as to the tragic situations that marked the history of the SLON: the common prisoners' abuse of the *kaery* is mentioned (the narrator speaks of an 'offence through an action' by the criminal prisoners, most probably a reference to a rape), only to be eventually forgotten. Niunichka's downfall hints at the real sexual slavery that women prisoners had to endure. All this is implied by that crucial echo: *Solovki prokliatye!*[138]

What can be regarded as the most interesting specimen of SLON fiction is a short story written by Boris Shiriaev. An exception to the mediocre standards of pre-Glubokovskii prose, Shiriaev managed to write a short yet impressive text. His was the first thematically experimental prose piece, the very first short story that registered the influence of Modernist fiction. It was the first to cross genre boundaries and adopt cinematographic techniques; most crucially, it represented an incredible case of 'parallel writing'. *Opyt Professora Kal'*[139] can be seen as something like the 'non-identical twin' to Bulgakov's *Sobach'e serdtse*:[140] Shiriaev shared Bulgakov's inspiration but adjusted it to suit a labour camp-inspired setting. His story starts with the arrival of a new SLON prisoner, Professor Kal', whose reputation as a renowned scientist is soon destroyed by his experiment. Supported by a fellow scientist, Professor Ognivtsev, he conducts an experiment and — as in *Heart of a Dog* — implants parts of the brain (in this case, brain cells) from one organism to another, though in his case both are human beings. Kal''s motivation is also different from that suggested by Bulgakov, since Shiriaev's character wants to eliminate criminality by forging a prototype of the 'average man'.

> The world is saved. There are no mental deformities. The forms of life are now healthy. The average psychic type has been worked out. Genius is allowed as an exception from the plan that has been agreed in advance. The injection of brain cells discovered by me, Professor Kal', on the Solovki, will strengthen this shattered world. Equilibrium has been restored. Requirements and specifics have been normalized.[141]

Зарывается Нюня носом в подушку и нюнит всю ночь на пролет до утра. — Все кончено, у — у- у, Соловки проклятые!-] Ibid., p. 15.

138 In the last short story she published at the SLON, Okerman included a final, depressing portrait of a woman prisoner: S. Okerman, 'V strokakh i mezhdu strok', *SO*, 7 (1926), 24–28.

139 A. Akarevich, 'Opyt professora Kal'', *SO*, 3 (1925), 15–18.

140 Mikhail Bulgakov, *Sobach'e serdtse: povesti, rasskazy, fel'etony, ocherki: 1925–1927* (Moscow: Tsentrpoligraf, 2004).

141 [— Мир спасен. Нет психического уродства. Формы жизни оздоровлены. Разработан средний психический тип. Гениальность допускается как исключение по заранее утвержденному плану. Ин'екции психической клетки, открытой мною, профессором Калем,

The experiment involves a clergyman and a criminal: the former is the old, chaste Father Ferapont while the latter is the rough pickpocket Vas'ka Buzyga. The experiment proves quite successful, as the two scientists observe all the changes that the two 'guinea-pigs' undergo. These, however — as also happens in Bulgakov's story — are not up to the scientists' expectations and ultimately result in grotesque situations. The conclusion of the short story, which is written as a cinema script and interspersed with notes about the scenery, is more dramatic than the end of *Sobach'e serdtse*. Both Vas'ka and Father Ferapont end up in prison, the former pickpocket for his extremely explicit faith, the former priest because he is found guilty of living off immoral earnings. In the last scene of the story, *Konets opyta*, the two disappear in silence:

> For the last time Vas'ka Buzyga pulled his priest-like beard, got up from the floor and crossed himself.
> — In thy glory, o Lord, take me, a sinner.
> And serenely went ahead of the officer to the isolation cell. But the grey-haired little priest, spitting through his lips, was weeping tears and swearing oaths at the same time. And swearing foully at the officer at intervals. So the three of them walked on a warm spring night, along a road that was well known to each of them.
> Priest Ferapont was being punished because of a woman.
> Vas'ka Buzyga because of the church.
> The officer accompanied them because it was his job. And entering the silence of the isolation cell, each spoke from his soul. Buzyga, lifting up his eyes, called on the Lord to look on his innocent suffering, and the priest, also remembering God through the Holy Mother, started smoking a cigarette he had hidden from a search.[142]

Though their deaths are only implied, the author seems to suggest that the two are destined to die in jail.

Despite obvious differences from Bulgakov's short story, Shiriaev's *Opyt Professora Kal'* presents several analogies with it. What makes these analogies even more surprising is the fact that most probably the two writers had never met. This fact seems to hint at an even more suggestive scenario, that of a pure coincidence that made possible the creation of 'twin tales'. In his autobiographical texts, Shiriaev never mentioned the Kiev author and, considering Bulgakov's relative fame in the 1930s, it is hard to believe that Shiriaev deliberately failed to refer to him. After all, he spoke openly of his other more famous acquaintances and, in fact, tended to boast of them, as was the case in his account of his alleged meeting with the

---

на Соловках, укрепят расшатанный мир. Равновесие восстановлено. Запросы и подробности нормализированы.] Akarevich, 'Opyt', p. 15.

142 [Дернул в последний раз за бороденку попову Васька Вузыга, с попа слез, перекрестился. — Во славу твою, Господи, окаянного. И смиренно пошел впереди дежурного к изолятору. А попик то седенький, через губу поплевывая, то плачем плакал, то клятвой клялся — в переслойку. А между делом дежурного матом поругивая. Так шли они трое в ночь теплую, весеннюю, путем известным каждому. Поп Ферапонт за бабу. Васька Бузыга за церковь. А дежурный сопровождал по должности. И войдя в затишно карцерное, каждый изрек от души своей. Бузыга, очи горе возведя, Господа призвал на безвинное поношение взглянуть, а батя тоже про бога через родительницу вспомнив, закурил спрятанную от обыска папиросу.] Ibid., p. 18.

painter Nesterov.[143] Taking into account all of the above, it is surprising that the two writers wrote two parallel short stories, considering the huge spatial distance between them. Even more impressively, they did it almost at the same time. Bulgakov wrote *Heart of a Dog* from January to March 1925,[144] whereas Shiriaev published *Opyt Professora Kal'* in the March 1925 issue of the *Solovetskie Ostrova*. It is therefore probable that the two had the same intuition and a shared source of inspiration, H. G. Wells's *Island of Dr. Moreau*. It is acknowledged that Bulgakov read Wells's science-fiction and that he took the 'climax' of his short story from him. It is likewise probable that Shiriaev read Wells's short story in the SLON library, which included some banned books, amongst which were books in their original language. It is important to underline that evolutionary biology and 'Soviet eugenics' were part of the literary discussion of the times.[145] Both writers wove their stories into the great arabesque of Russian literature, using almost the same allegories while charging them with different meaning. Unlike Bulgakov's tale, which took a long time to be published but eventually became part of the Russian literary tradition, Shiriaev's *Opyt Professora Kal'* was almost obliterated, thus hiding away from researchers' attention this rare case of parallel writing.

The Second Period of Publications: The Triumph of Poetry

The SLON writers left the stage as soon as the *Solovetskie Ostrova* merged with the *Karelo-Murmanskii Krai*. The main contributors to *Karelo-Murmanskii Krai* were a group of chekists; the editorial board permitted the publication of just two literary works by SLON prisoners in the period between the closure and the reopening of the SLON publications. Evreinov published a very odd poem in the second 1927 issue (February) of the journal, in which he borrowed largely from *Byl'e Karel'skoe* (published in the first 1925 issue of the *Solovetskie Ostrova*) and simply turned Karelian place-names into Lapp names.[146] Boris Emel'ianov's last poem, a quite unremarkable attempt to explore Karelian mythology by readjusting the recurrent motif of local folklore that underlay most of the issues of the journal, was published in the ninth issue of *Karelo-Murmanskii krai*.[147]

---

143 Shiriaev dedicated *Neugasimaia lampada* to the Russian painter Mikhail Nesterov who, after Shiriaev's sentence was pronounced, told him: 'Don't fear the Solovki. There, Christ is nearer' [Не бойтесь Соловков, там Христос близко]. This is, however, not likely to have happened. In reality, prisoners were not allowed to have contacts with people outside the camp or the prison and Nesterov was not in prison in 1923. See Shiriaev, p. 21. Rozanov wrote about Shiriaev that 'he knew everyone, especially the famous people' [он знал всех, тем более известных], see Rozanov, *Solovetskii kontslager' v monastyre*, II, 19.

144 I would like to thank Maria Isola for helping me reconstruct the simultaneous writing of the two texts.

145 See Muireann Maguire. 'Post-Lamarckian Prodigies: Evolutionary Biology in Soviet Science Fiction', *New Zealand Slavonic Journal*, 43 (2009), 23–53.

146 Boris Evreinov, 'Byl'e loparskoe', *Karelo-Murmanskii krai*, 2 (1927), 17.

147 Boris Emel'ianov, 'O rozovom kamnem i novykh liudiakh', *Karelo-Murmanskii krai*, 9 (1927), 18.

When the SLON press resumed its activities in 1929, the literary scene in the camp had radically changed. A new group of authors had taken over from the journal's former contributors. As was suggested above, the only 'survivor' was Glubokovskii, who stayed on the archipelago and who still took part in the cultural life of the camp. In 1929 Glubokovskii worked full time at the SLON theatre, where he was still a leading personality; his contribution to the SLON press was therefore much less prominent than it had been in 1925–26. The 'turnover' entailed several changes. While the 'new writers' were in tune with their predecessors' longing for intellectual independence, their literary attempts were less daring. Fiction and prose writers lost prominence and gradually gave way to a much more important and well-organized breed of poets.

Changes in publishing dynamics provoked further disruption. The *Solovetskie Ostrova* in 1929 was finally independent of ideological conventions and its contributors no longer needed to fight for a free space in the journal. There was now a relatively small number of talented authors[148] — mostly professionals who had entered the circle of the *lagernaia intelligentsiia*. Many among them had met beforehand, like the poets Iuri Kazarnovskii, Aleksandr Pankratov, and Aleksandr Peshkovskii, who had been arrested during a raid in Rostov-on-Don.[149] Some of them met for the first time in the camp as soon as they entered the cultural circles of the SLON, as happened to Vladimir Kemetskii, Boris Leitin, and Maks Kiunert. There is no documentation on how other writers, such as Aleksandr Iaroslavskii or N. Orlov, entered the SLON press. All these authors sang hymns to Soviet power only when they had to do so — which, in fact, happened very rarely.[150] Apart from N. Orlov, there was no longer a place for the authors of encomiastic poetry or for writers who, like Kargopol'skii or Tiberii, were ideologues rather than poets. The very mood of encomiastic poetry had changed radically, as the laudatory poems written for Maksim Gor'kii show.

148 Other writers took part in the second phase of the SLON press (A. Sh., A. Makedonskii, Kseniia Shtamm, Ia. Shironin). Since their works seem not altogether remarkable, they will not be discussed in the present chapter. Likhachev maintained that two other poet-inmates, Lada Mogilianskaia and Dmitrii Shipchinskii, published in the SLON press (Likhachev, *Izbrannoe: Vospominaniia*, p. 240). However, I could not find any trace of their work in the material I analysed, apart from an altogether unremarkable poem under the signature 'D. Sh.'. I found poems by Lada Mogilianskaia in the Beltbaltlag press, see Lada Mogilianskaia, 'Burevestnik surovyi', *Na shturm trassy*, 7 (1936), 8 (CBSB, Film P 2000.673 n° 110). Another poet whose work allegedly appeared in the SLON publications is Nikolai Berner: while Andrei Ustinov, quoting Shiriaev (Shiriaev, pp. 129–30), maintains that he was an author of poems for the *Solovetskie Ostrova*, there is no trace of him in the journal. He might have been writing under a pseudonym, as might have been the case with Shipchinskii and Mogilianskaia. See Andrei Ustinov, 'Dve zhizni Nikolaia Bernera', in *Litsa: Biograficheskii al'manakh* (St Petersburg: Feniks, 2002), pp. 5–64 (p. 39).

149 Antonina Soshina, 'Podstrelennye na vzlete (molodezh' v lagere na Solovkakh)', *Solovetskoe more*, 8 (2009), 118–28 (pp. 121–22).

150 The few encomiastic poems were usually published in *Novye Solovki*. The only moments when they were published in *Solovetskie Ostrova* were after Gor'kii's visit and on the anniversary of Lenin's death.

Odes to Gor'kii

The 'second season' of the SLON press opened with the first 1929 issue (August) of the *Solovetskie Ostrova*, which was published immediately after Gor'kii's visit. As has already been pointed out, Gor'kii had no personal meetings with the camp prisoners. Except for his long-term acquaintance with Iuliia Nikolaevna Danzas (who published some short stories in the *Solovetskie Ostrova* under the pseudonym of Iurii Nikolaev),[151] the only connection between Gor'kii and the Solovki prisoners were the letters they sent him, which the censors carefully and regularly sifted through. However, it is hard to say whether those letters ever reached Gor'kii. One of the prisoners who tried to make contact with Gor'kii was Iurii Kazarnovskii, who sent him a letter in 1928. Kazarnovskii had just been arrested, and he wrote to Gor'kii to complain about his unjust sentence. The letter reads:

> Who benefits? The state sends to his death a man sincerely devoted to it and completely innocent. [...] It is very painful to die in such a useless, pathetic, and shameful way at 23, when I have done nothing yet, but have conceived so much and have so much that I want to do. After all, there is still so much to see, to write and to read.[152]

Kazarnovskii and two fellow poets, Vladimir Kemetskii and Aleksandr Pankratov, published poems that paid tribute to Gor'kii in the first 1929 issue of the *Solovetskie Ostrova*. A portrait of Gor'kii by Iv. Nedrit[153] was followed by a sonnet by Kemetskii, entitled *Maksimu Gorkomu* and which was highly indicative of the new mood of encomiastic verse:

> Кто доверялся песне и мечте,
> Кто не страшился странствия земного,
> Кто падал от усталости и снова
> Бродяжничал. Кто в очи нищете
>
> Умел глядеть с улыбкой, — знают те,
> Какую радость возвести готово
> Подчас простое, человеческое слово,
> Иль возглас чайки в бледной высоте...
>
> И ты напрасно вкрадчиво и тихо
> Нашепчиваешь, горестное Лихо.
> Прочь, одноглазое, доколе нить
>
> Годов моих прядется, укоризне
> Бесплодной не продам я жизни,
> Не разучусь смеяться и любить.[154]

151 Iu. Nikolaev, 'Staraia kniga na Solovkakh', *SO*, 2 (1929), 30–32; Iu. Nikolaev, 'Solovetskii abeliar', *SO*, 3–4 (1929), 16–20; *SO*, 1 (1930), 13–15.

152 [Кому это нужно — государство посылает человека на гибель, искренно ему преданного, ни в чем не виноватого. [...] очень больно так бесполезно, жалко и позорно гибнуть в 23 года, когда еще ничего не сделано, но столько задумано и столько хочется сделать. Ведь вперед еще столько невиданного, непрочитанного и ненаписанного.] Soshina, 'Podstrelennye', p. 121.

153 They were the initials of Ivan Petrovich Nedrit, a Latvian graphic artist who was active at the SLON as an illustrator. See Eva Krasnova and Anatolii Drozdovskii, 'Solovki — zhemchuzhina Belogo moria', *Debirasovskaia — Reshil'evskaia*, 45 (2011), 15–24.

154 [Who trusted in songs and dreams | Who was not afraid of being an earthly pilgrim, | Who

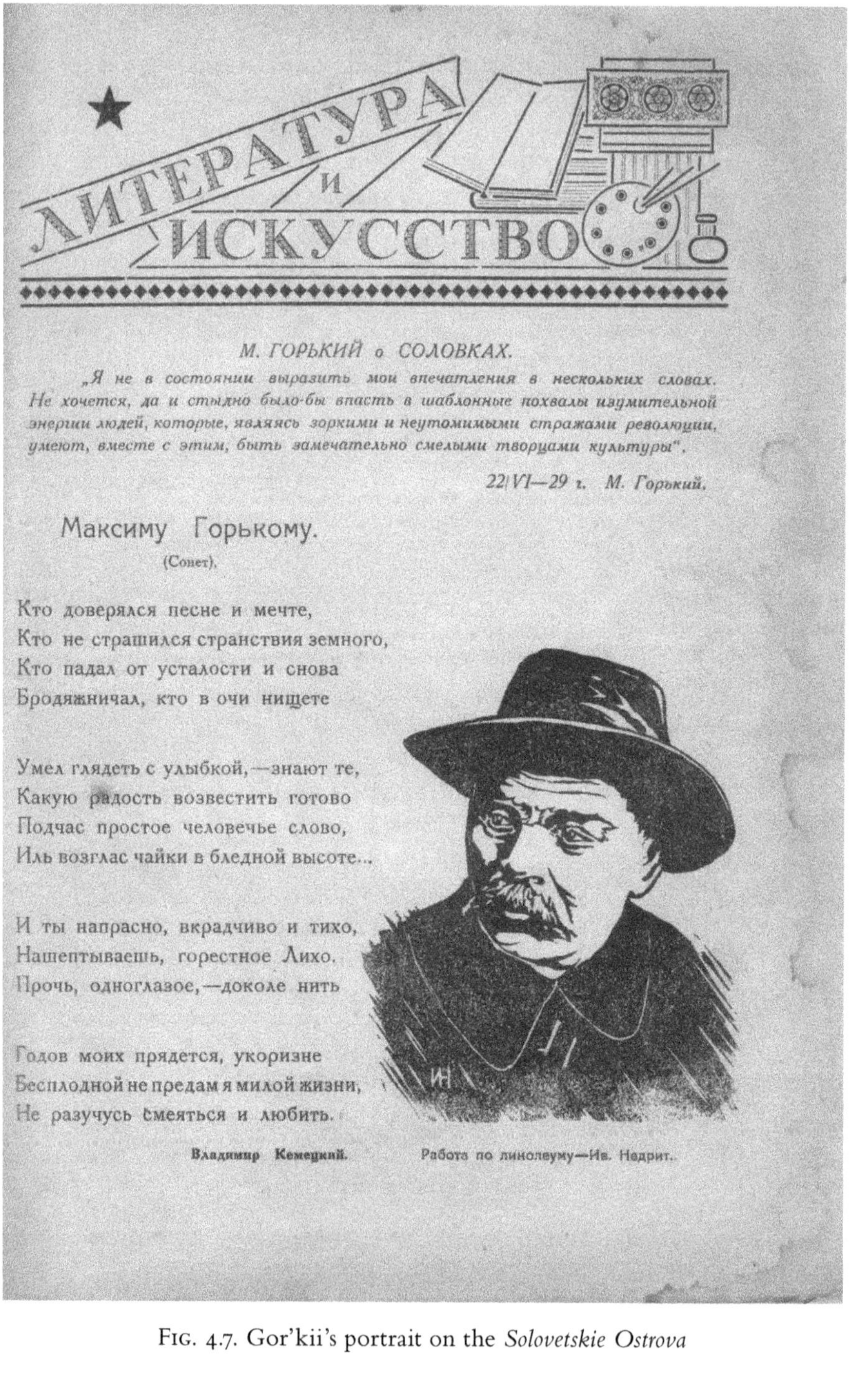

ЛИТЕРАТУРА и ИСКУССТВО

М. ГОРЬКИЙ о СОЛОВКАХ.

„Я не в состоянии выразить мои впечатления в нескольких словах. Не хочется, да и стыдно было-бы впасть в шаблонные похвалы изумительной энергии людей, которые, являясь зоркими и неутомимыми стражами революции, умеют, вместе с этим, быть замечательно смелыми творцами культуры".

22|VI—29 г.   М. Горький.

Максиму Горькому.

(Сонет).

Кто доверялся песне и мечте,
Кто не страшился странствия земного,
Кто падал от усталости и снова
Бродяжничал, кто в очи нищете

Умел глядеть с улыбкой,—знают те,
Какую радость возвестить готово
Подчас простое человечье слово,
Иль возглас чайки в бледной высоте...

И ты напрасно, вкрадчиво и тихо,
Нашептываешь, горестное Лихо.
Прочь, одноглазое,—доколе нить

Годов моих прядется, укоризне
Бесплодной не предам я милой жизни,
Не разучусь смеяться и любить.

Владимир Кемецкий.

Работа по линолеуму—Ив. Надрит.

Fig. 4.7. Gor'kii's portrait on the *Solovetskie Ostrova*

Unlike the dry and sterile laudatory tones of the first period of the SLON press, Kemetskii's poem developed through his command of imagery and form (interstanzaic enjambement, anastrophe, anaphora, chiasmus, and synaloepha). The melody and stylistic elegance of the sonnet, the absence of routine rhymes which rely on yoking together key elements of ideologically charged vocabulary (such as those used by Kargopol'skii as previously mentioned) highlighted the author's independence from ideological conventions. Even more surprisingly, the poem sounded extremely vague, with the first tercet containing a reference to the Evil fate, and no ideologically determined conclusion in the final tercet. The sonnet therefore seems deliberately suspended between panegyric poetry and irony.

Pankratov's poem to Gor'kii was also unconventional. In *Dva ostrova* the Solovki islands are juxtaposed with Capri (the two islands are respectively evoked in the first five and the second five couplets). Unlike Kemetskii's, Pankratov's poem is apparently more ideologically committed; yet Pankratov depicts Capri in a surprising way. In fact, the evocation of its bright landscape is at odds with the dark-tinged and gloomy description of the White Sea archipelago: the dichotomy of the West/Soviet Union ends in the prominence of the former over the latter.

> «Капри»
> Светлой Авзонии остров, любезная сердцу Капрея,
> Ты, что приняла любовь, все благотворно в тебе;
> [...]
> «Соловки»
> Остров угрюмый встает среди волн неприветного моря,
> Смутны изгибы его в серой завесе дождя.[155]

The third poem was one of Kazarnovskii's typically comical epigrams. As was the case with the epigrams mentioned in the previous chapter, Kazarnovskii's tribute to Gor'kii was also structured in short lines with alternating rhyme, followed by a comical coda. The poem's humorous overtones were wittily meant to question (or to ridicule) Gor'kii's visit to the SLON:

> Писатель, трепетно любимый,
> Зачем такой тяжелый путь, —
> Полотен бег неизмерымый,

fell from exhaustion and again | Wandered. Who into the eyes of poverty || Managed to look with a smile — they know | What joy is ready to generate | The sometimes simple human word, | Or the cry of the seagull in the pale heights... || And you in vain softly and quietly | Are whispering, o woeful Likho. | Go away, you one-eyed creature, until the thread || Of my years is spun, I will | not give my life to useless reproach | I will not unlearn how to laugh and love.] V. Kemetskii, 'Maksimu Gor'komu (sonet)', *SO*, 1 (1929), 3. Kemetskii here refers to Likho, a mythological figure typical of many Slavonic cultures, which is often represented as a one-eyed woman. It embodies evil fate.
155 ['Capri' | Island of the bright Ausonia, o Kapreia, dear to the heart, | You, who accepted love, everything in you is beneficial; || [...] || 'Solovki' | The gloomy island rises among the waves of an unfriendly sea, | Its shadowy curves are in a grey curtain of rain.] A. Pankratov, 'Dva ostrova (Maksimu Gor'komu). Kapri, Solovki', *SO*, 1 (1929), 4. Pankratov shows that he is well informed about Italian culture: he mentions Ausonia, i.e. the old name of a part of the Campania region which was used in Classical poetry to identify Italy; and Kapreia, i.e. the legendary island where the sirens used to live, which was usually identified with Capri.

> Туман болот, давящий грудь
> Не лучше ль было, в самом деле,
> Себя в пути не утомить,
> А нас, всей шумною артелью,
> К себе Вам в гости пригласить.[156]

Kazarnovskii's disrespectful attitude, Pankratov's ambivalent descriptions, and Kemetskii's ambiguous closing lines all mark these poets' distance from the kind of panegyric poetry common in the early stages of SLON literature, in which Shiriaev's challenging style was the only disruptive element in an otherwise monotonous landscape. Change surfaced also in Kazarnovskii's epigram to Gleb Bokii (which appeared next to Gor'kii's tribute).[157] The piece closed the ideological/encomiastic section of the first 1929 issue of the *Solovetskie Ostrova*, after which only ideology-free poetry was published.

These changes marked the *Solovetskie Ostrova*'s ultimate editorial line during the second stage of the SLON press — years that saw the emergence of several gifted poets, among whom the most talented was arguably Vladimir Kemetskii.

The Unlucky Fate of Vladimir Kemetskii

Vladimir Kemetskii was only 25 years old when he first came to the SLON. His life had not been easy. While abroad, his enthusiasm for radical ideals created traumatic rifts with his family (and also within a few intellectual émigré circles). Everything for which he had fought, in the end, turned against him, and his efforts were repaid on his return to the Soviet Union with imprisonment and extremely harsh living conditions. By the time he was sent to the Solovki islands, Kemetskii was devastated. He realized that his mistakes were irreversible and that a hard fate awaited him. Poetry was his only source of release at the time; it was this intimate bond that helped him to reach artistic maturity. His experiences at the SLON helped him develop his potential. To the *Solovetskie Ostrova* he contributed the poems of his maturity, which were also the last ones he published.[158]

Kemetskii was born Vladimir Sergeevich Sveshnikov in St Petersburg in 1902, but his family emigrated to Turkey in 1920, only to reach France a few months later. His father was a former Tsarist officer who had joined the White Guard. The father's relationship with his son, who was instead a radical, pro-Soviet intellectual, deteriorated during the years spent in emigration. In Paris, young Vladimir Sveshnikov joined the cultural circles of Russian migrants, like that of Zinaida

---

156 [Oh beloved and cherished writer, | Why did you accomplish such a difficult journey? | The immeasurable racing of the railroads, | The fog of the marshes crushes the chest | Would it not have been better, after all | Not to tire yourself on the road | And instead to invite us all, | As one noisy team, to your place?] Iu. Kazarnovskii, 'M. Gor'komu (druzheskaia epigramma)', *SO*, 1 (1929), 4.

157 Iu. Kazarnovskii, 'G. I. Bokii (druzheskaia epigramma)', *SO*, 1 (1929), 4.

158 More information about Kemetskii's life can be found in Mikhail Rogachev, 'Vladimir Sveshnikov', in *Pokaianie. Komi respublikanskii martirolog zhertv massovykh politicheskikh repressii*, ed. by Mikhail Rogachev, 11 vols (Syktyvkar: Komi knizhnoe izdatel'stvo, 1998–2011), VII (2007), pp. 207–13.

Gippius and Dmitrii Merezhkovskii. He joined the poetic circle *Cherez*, among whom was Boris Poplavskii, who wrote a prophetic poem dedicated to him:

> Мой бедный друг, живи на четверть жизни.
> Достаточно и четверти надежд.
> За преступленье четверть укоризны
> И четверть страха пред закрытьем вежд.[159]

However, Sveshnikov did not waver from his intention to return to the Soviet Union. He became a leftist political activist, which is probably why he was forced to migrate again with his family. They moved to Berlin. There, his relationship with his father grew so sour that Sveshnikov decided to adopt his mother's family name as his pen name. In Berlin, Sveshnikov-Kemetskii pursued his political activities (he enrolled in the 'Jugendbund', the German 'Komsomol') as well as his commitment to poetry. There he published his first important poems, in particular three sonnets that were included in the renowned almanac *Nedra*.[160]

Kemetskii's stay in Germany further sharpened his pro-Soviet sympathies. In his opinion, bourgeois society was nightmarish and hypocritical. While his early Paris-based poems were centred on unappealing depictions of city life, his Berlin-based poems were pervaded with rage. Kemetskii poured his indignation at false Western social conventions into sonnets that dig into the abyss of suburban life, from which he draws his most frequently recurring subjects — prostitutes, pimps, and drunkards who populate a rather drab and squalid underworld.

Kemetskii's dream came true; however his return to the Soviet Union resulted in his arrest in 1927 and in a sentence to imprisonment in the camps. After his first publications, for five years (1924–29) Kemetskii led a virtual existence as a writer, never publishing. His name would eventually resurface in the SLON press, where Kemetskii published some of the poems he had written between 1920 and 1925 during his stay abroad. His early output was locked into literary clichés, but brightened by his natural musical skills and by inspired images. In *Pamiatnik Russo*, for example, Paris becomes a stage on which a curtain of fog falls and where time has turned into a statue:

> Как холоден тяжелый Пантеон...
> Как неподвижен занавес тумана...
> Последний лист продрогшего платана
> Дождем ночным к асфальту пригвожден.
> [...]
> И льется дождь на бронзовые веки,
> И равнодушны тучные дома.[161]

---

159 [My poor friend, you live one quarter of a life. | And one quarter of hopes is enough. | One quarter of reproach for your misdeed | And one quarter of terror before you close your eyelids.] Boris Poplavskii, 'Dozhd', in *Sobranie sochinenii v 3-kh tomakh*, I (Moscow: Knizhnitsa, Russkii put', Soglasie, 2009), p. 71.

160 Vladimir Kemetskii, 'Liubliu ia restoranchik uglovoi, zelenyi stol...'; 'Sutulykh spin bugry...'; 'U kassy stuk i zviakan'e monet', in *Literaturno-khudozhestvennye sborniki 'Nedra'*, III (Moscow: Novaia Moskva, 1924), 129–31.

161 [How cold is the heavy Pantheon... | How still is the curtain of fog... | The last leaf of the

Kemetskii wrote a number of Berlin 'snapshots'. His poems were interspersed with inspired images, such as the 'black glue' that makes the clouds over the Brandenburg Gate stick to the city in *Berlinskii peizazh* (Седые Бранденбургские ворота | И тучи, вязкие, как черный клей...),[162] or the delicate image of 'Ophelia' strolling about in Berlin:

> Подобны двум чернеющим воронкам
> Широкие зрачки. И ни следа
> Румянца, но улыбка иногда
> Мелькает на лице больном и тонком.
>
> Поет: «В ту пору я была ребенком
> Минуло мне пятнадцать лет». Куда
> Ты, девочка? Безмолвствует вода.
> Молчанье на мосту пустом и звонком.[163]

Most of Kemetskii's early output was, however, still immature. It was limited to occasional and superficial social sketches (e.g. the city underworld depicted in *Vedding*)[164] or clichéd portraits (the pimp in *Ryzhyi Frants, Gerr Miuller* who beats his prostitutes).[165] These works' strength lies only in the poetic depiction of Germany's post-war disillusionment about the greatness of the German Empire.

Compared with what he wrote during his emigration, Kemetskii's poems published in the *Novye Solovki* and especially those in the *Solovetskie Ostrova* have quite a different depth. Since the very moment of his arrest (and particularly during the year 1928), Kemetskii wrote several poems, giving voice to his feelings.[166] He finally selected and eventually published the best of his work in the SLON press.

The first two poems he published in the SLON press, together with his tribute to Gor'kii, epitomise Kemetskii's new inspiration, propelled by the chill blast of the Northern winds. 'Ispei vina sozvezdii' is an example of his more mature production both on a thematic and on a stylistic level, with its muffled rage against his fate and indirectly against Soviet power, and in its use of neologisms and challenging metaphors, which verge on synaesthesia, underlined by a strong use of alliteration:

chilled plane tree | Has been nailed to the asphalt by the rain overnight. | [...] | And the rain flows on bronze eyelids, | And indifferent are the corpulent homes.] V. Kemetskii, 'Tri soneta (Luksorskii oberlisk, Pamiatnik Russo, Verlen)', *SO*, 2 (1929), 3.

162 [The Brandenburg Gates are grey-haired | And the clouds are viscous, like black glue...] V. Kemetskii, 'Sonety o Germanskoi respublike', SO, 3–4 (1929), 14.

163 [Like two blackened craters | Are the wide pupils. And not a trace | Of a blush, but at times a smile | Flashes on her sick and thin face. || She sings: 'At that time I was a child | I'm more than fifteen'. Where | Are you going, girl? The water keeps its silence | It is silent on the empty and sonorous bridge.] Ibid.

164 Wedding is a district of Berlin.

165 All the poems about Germany quoted in the text were published in the *Solovetskie ostrova*, 50, 3–4 (1929), 11–15.

166 Kemetskii's poems were handed down to us by the poet Aleksandr Pankratov. At first, Kemetskii's work was published in samizdat, as seen in chapter 1. Part of it was eventually published by the publishing house 'Vozvrashchenie'. Finally, Kemetskii's friend Dmitrii Likhachev included the poems in one of the editions of his *Vospominaniia*. See Svetlana Tiukina, '"Krome, kak v USLONe, nigde ne khochu sidet'". Mirovaia i russkaia literatury v solovetskoi lagernoi poezii', *Solovetskoe more*, 4 (2005), 167.

Испей вина созвездий и лучей,
Цветов и трав. И радостно спокоен
Да будешь ты, как неистомный воин
В бушующем скрещении мечей.[167]

'Belaia noch'', the second Kemetskii poem published in the first 1929 issue of the *Solovetskie Ostrova*, was a milestone in the poet's career in the SLON. The author's resigned attitude to his fate was brought to the forefront:

Двух бледных зорь немая встреча.
И крылья чайки, и залив...
Всю ночь не умирает вечер,
С часами утренними слит.

Плывут в изменчивом движеньи
Вдоль искривленных берегов
Расплывчатые отраженья
Зеленоватых облаков.

И так томителен над нами
Двойной зари двуличный свет...
Обманчивое упованье —
Забытой страсти мертвый след.[168]

Two nights, two suns dawning on two worlds that are radically divided — this image measures the unfathomable distance between two physically and conceptually different dimensions. 'Beforehand' and 'now', 'here' and there' thus emerge as a twin conceptual pair. The poet's hope to regain what he has lost and forgotten is underlined dramatically by the image of the dead trace of a forgotten passion, which might be identified with the fervent radicalism of his youth.

Whereas resignation pervaded 'Belaia noch'', a sense of controlled dismay bears down on the reader in a later poem, 'Nad snegom vozdukh', which clearly refers to the poetry of Zinaida Gippius and Valerii Briusov:

Над снегом воздух тих и мглист
Вечерний. Солнце напоследки
Похоже на потухший лист,
Едва держащийся на ветке.

Своих лишенная красот,
Земля узнала — темный ветер
Сей лист поблекший оторвет
И звезды горькие засветит.[169]

167 [Taste the wine of constellations and rays, | Of flowers and grass. And joyously calm | You will be, like a tireless warrior | In the tempestuous crossing of swords.] V. Kemetskii, 'Sonet (Ispei vina)', *SO*, 1 (1929), 8.

168 [The mute meeting of two pale dawns. | And the wings of the seagulls, and the gulf... | All night long the evening does not die, | Fused with the morning hours. || In variable movements float | Along the twisted shore | The blurred reflections | Of the greenish clouds. || And so wearisome above us is | The two-faced light of a double dawn... | A deceptive expectation — | The dead trace of a forgotten passion.] V. Kemetskii, 'Belaia noch'', *SO*, 1 (1929), 46.

169 [Above the snow is the quiet and dark | Evening air. The sun ultimately | Resembles a dead

After lingering on the sea — one of Kemetskii's leitmotifs — in the following stanza, and after conjuring up images of the sea, the poem ends by mentioning a quite unexpected 'guest':

> О, Муза, не печалься ты,
> И не страшись угрозы рока, —
> Прекрасны белые цветы,
> На стеклах выросшие окон.
>
> Ты поселись в моем углу
> С гремящим холодом в соседстве,
> И наступающую мглу
> Вином и песнями приветствуй.[170]

The poet's intimacy with his true partner, the Muse, is further made explicit in *Moei muze*, where the poet recognises how the brightest inspiration coincides with one of the more painful periods of his life:

> То струн ли отдаленных переборы,
> То ль ветра стон — иль милый голос твой?
> Веду опять, прелестная, с тобой
> Воображаемые разговоры.
>
> Не раз ко мне, гонимому судьбой,
> Задумчивые покидая горы,
> Слетала ты. Твои движенья скоры,
> А в волосах дыханье влажных хвой.
>
> Звук узнаю негромкого напева —
> Ты вновь со мною, солнечная дева,
> Посланница парнасских гулких скал...[171]

The sonnet's straightforward, terrifying yet touching final image can be rightfully regarded as one of the most powerful images of SLON literature:

> Позволь же, гостья, за твое здоровье
> Наполненный незримых гроздьев кровью
> Поднять воображаемый бокал.[172]

This blood-drenched toast tied Kemetskii to his muse from 1927 (when the sonnet

leaf, | Barely holding on to a branch. || Deprived of her beauties | The land realized that the dark wind | Will tear off this faded leaf | And will illuminate the bitter stars.] V. Kemetskii, 'Nad snegom vozdukh tikh i mglist. Stikhi', *SO*, 2–3 (1930), 10.

170 [Oh, Muse, do not be sad, | And do not fear the menaces of fate, | Beautiful white flowers, | Have grown over the glass of the windows. || You come and settle in my corner | Close to the reverberating cold, | And hail the advancing darkness | With wine and songs.] Ibid.

171 [Is it the sound of distant strings, | Or the moaning of the wind, or your dear voice? | I have again, charming one, with you | Imaginary conversations. || Often to me, persecuted by destiny, | Abandoning the meditative mountains, | You flew. Your movements are fast, | And in your damp hair there's the breath of pine-needles. || I recognize the sound of your soft melody | You are again with me, virgin of the sun, | Ambassadress of the resounding cliffs of Parnassus...] V. Kemetskii, 'Moei Muze (stikhi)', *SO*, 4 (1930), 23.

172 [Allow me, o visitor, to raise | the imaginary goblet | filled with the blood of invisible grapes, | to your health.] Ibid.

was written) to the end of his life. Throughout this period, other Muses appeared in his poetry — but they were less idealized. One 'material' muse was the dedicatee of Kemetskii's large-scale project, the *Saga ob Erike, syne Ial'mara, i o poslednem iz ego potomkov*.[173]

Kemetskii's *Saga* developed through a series of five cantos, in which the poet took inspiration from the story of his family (allegedly descended from legendary Scandinavian stock) to link this theme to the present life of the poet in the Solovki camp. The first two cantos evoke the arrival of the Vikings in a succession of images (the boat surfacing on the 'convex plain' of the sea and the howling horns). The initial stanzaic progression brings to the foreground the role both of Kemetskii's ancestor — the Viking 'epic' warrior Erik — and Kemetskii himself, who, from the Solovki islands, can hear him calling. The third canto introduces instead a quite unexpected turn: it is entirely devoted to silence, which the poet eroticizes and with which the poet engages in dialogue by implicitly putting aside his family's heroic past and the chaotic present of the *lagernye Solovki*:

> Нежная, покорными глазами
> Княжишь ты, бездумна и ясна,
> Сладости безмолвные лобзанья,
> Невзначайной ласки тишина.
>
> Твой призывный, ветрами звучащий
> Голос древние приносит сны,
> Тихий шорох непробудной чащи,
> Плеск прозрачной ильменской волны.
>
> А когда нежданными слезами
> Затуманится твой светлый взор,
> Восстают забытые сказанья,
> Затаенные на дне озер.
>
> Помнишь, слушая, как вьюга злится
> И терзает чахлые поля,
> Ты в своей бревенчатой светлице
> Пряжу до полуночи ткала.[174]

Silence becomes the bearer of sad truths. Miles away from his ancestor's heroic deeds, Kemetskii could rely only on his personal, distinctive weapon — poetry. Looking back to his ancestor in a final attempt to evoke him, the poet suggests an arresting hypostasis of his own death. Erik leads him to Valhalla, releasing him from his suffering to eternal life:

---

173 V. Kemetskii, 'Saga ob Erike, syne Ial'mara, i o poslednem iz ego potomkov', *SO*, 1 (1930), 16–20.

174 [O gentle one, with docile eyes | You rule, thoughtless and bright, | Your silent kisses of sweetness, | O silence of unexpected affection. || Your summoning voice, that resounds in the winds | Brings ancient dreams, | The quiet rustle of a virgin thicket, | The lapping of the waves of the transparent Il'men'. || And when by unexpected tears | Your bright eyes will be clouded, | Forgotten legends will rise up, | Which have been hidden at the bottom of lakes. || You remember, listening to the angry blizzard | Tormenting the barren fields | You in your wooden parlour | Spun the yarn until midnight.] Ibid., p. 18.

За ладьей моей веселой стаей
Волны-псы не гонятся, ворча,
И рука моя не обнимает
Кованую рукоять меча.
Ветер, песни, сны, воспоминанья,
Тихий отзвук жизни вековой,
Лишь закат, как боевое знамя,
Развевается над головой.
[...]
Рухнет шумная волна на берег,
И, сверкая взора синевой,
Из тумана прародитель Эрик
Царственно возникнет предо мной.
Мощью, равной ясеню иль буку,
Встанет он, кольчугою звеня,
И протянет жилистую руку,
И в ладью свою возьмет меня.
[...]
И, взойдя на облачные скалы,
В синем блеске ледяных лучей
Я вступлю в высокую Валгаллу
Под бряцанье арф и лязг мечей.[175]

At the poem's close Kemetskii introduced his 'earthly Muse':

Слушай тихие повествованья,
Дочь страны озерной и лесной,
Слушай эти смутные сказанья,
Для тебя лишь сложенные мной.[176]

The 'daughter of the lakes and the trees of the Solovki islands' is the metaphorical representation of a member of the *intelligentsiia* who in the SLON became the wife of a camp employee. She worshipped Kemetskii's poems and used to send him food and tobacco.[177] Kemetskii later managed to create a literary image based on his relationship with this woman by connecting her to the roots of St Petersburg Symbolism. His 'earthly Muse' became a *prekrasnaia neznakomka*,[178] to whom he devoted some lines in the fourth issue of the *Solovetskie Ostrova*. The poem relied on poetic images such as the *neznakomka* becoming a 'hyperborean Aphrodite'.

---

175 [Following my boat in a merry pack | The grumbling wave-dogs do not chase, | And my hand does not embrace | The forged handle of the sword. || Wind, songs, dreams, memories, | The quiet echo of a life that has lasted for centuries, | Only the sunset, like a battle flag, | Is fluttering over my head. | [...] | The noisy wave breaks upon the shore, | And, with his glittering blue gaze, | Out of the mist my ancestor Erik | Will regally rise in front of me. || With mightiness similar to an ash tree or a beech, | He will stand, his chain mail ringing, | And will stretch out his sinewy hand, | And will take me into his boat. | [...] |And, climbing up onto the rocks of clouds, | In the blue glare of icy rays | I will enter into high Valhalla | Under the music of harps and the clang of swords.] Ibid., pp. 19–20.

176 [Listen to these quiet tales, | Daughter of the country of lakes and forests, | Listen to these troubled legends, | Which I have created just for you.] Ibid., p. 20.

177 Likhachev, *Izbrannoe: Vospominaniia*, p. 242.

178 V. Kemetskii, 'Prekrasnoi neznakomke (stikhi)', *SO*, 4 (1930), 28.

In another (altogether unremarkable) canto dedicated to the New Year, the poet recollected the mirrors in the free world that 'still preserve the images of the prisoners'. However, it was by focusing on sheer pain that Kemetskii found inspiration, sublimating it into the depiction of nature — that silent godmother of his poetry. Snow-capped fields triggered the poet's nostalgia for a world that is 'frolicking' elsewhere. The poet's belief in his eventual freedom, which in *Belaia noch'* was 'deceptive', becomes in *Pered navigatsiei* 'ill-founded', since the poet knew it would never be realized:

> В иных краях безумствует земля,
> И руки девушек полны цветами,
> И солнце льется щедрыми струями
> На зеленеющие тополя...
>
> Еще бесплодный снег мертвит поля,
> Расстаться море не спешит со льдами,
> И ветер ходит резкими шагами
> Вдоль ржавых стен угрюмого кремля.
>
> Непродолжительною, но бессонной
> Бледно-зеленой ночью сколько раз
> Готов был слух, молчаньем истомленный,
>
> Гудок желанный услыхать для нас
> О воле приносящий весть, быть может...
> Но все молчит. Лишь чайка мглу тревожит.[179]

In the last issue of the *Solovetskie Ostrova* Kemetskii published an intense poem, *Pesn' o vozvrashchenii*.[180] In this poem, man's hope to find freedom and love with an anonymous beloved one can be conveyed only through poetry. Resignation is depicted delicately: the first lines, for example, juxtapose a tormented landscape with the faint hope of a future meeting:

> Разбиваются в море льды,
> Вдоль тропы прорастает трава,
> Острый запах соленой воды
> Обволакивает острова.
>
> Разбиваются льды, звеня,
> Хриплый ветер кричит, смеясь...
> Ты едва ли узнаешь меня
> В нашей встречи вечерний час.[181]

179 [In other regions the world frolics | And the hands of the girls are full of flowers, | And the sun pours his munificent rays, | Over the greening poplar trees... || The unfruitful snow still makes the fields lifeless, | The sea is in no hurry to part from the ice, | And the wind goes with brusque strides | Along the rusty walls of the gloomy Kremlin. || In the brief, but sleepless | Pale-green night how many times | My ear, exhausted by the silence, was ready || To hear the long-awaited signal for us | Bringing news of freedom, maybe... | But all is silent. Only a seagull disturbs the darkness.] V. Kemetskii, 'Pered navigatsiei (sonet)', *SO*, 2–3 (1930), 54.

180 Apart from two minor poems published in the *Novye Solovki*, it was his last poem published during his lifetime.

181 [The ice cracks on the sea, | Along the paths the grass is growing, | The pungent smell of salty

The poet's vision seems to come true in the description of the meeting, when Kemetskii brings to his beloved's home the very smells of the camp and tells her about the prisoners' dignity and their desperate living conditions, hiding them behind some 'people of these unfriendly places', whom the poet, confined in the camp, had never met:

> Я приду — и внесу в твой дом
> Запах водорослей и смолы,
> Я приду поведать о том,
> Что узнал у замшелой скалы.
>
> И прочту я тебе стихи
> О стране, где не пахнут цветы,
> Не поют по утрам петухи,
> Не шуршат по весне листы.
>
> Расскажу тебе про народ
> Неприветливых этих мест —
> Он отважно и просто живет,
> Бьет тюленей и рубит лес.[182]

Using a device typical for Kemetskii's work, the poem's close brings a sudden return to harsh reality which puts an end to the poet's hopes:

> Замолчу. Оборву рассказ.
> Попрошу для трубки огня.
> Может быть, хоть на этот раз
> Ты сумеешь услышать меня.[183]

Restraint and dismay, despair and the longing for an impossible relationship were the ingredients of Kemetskii's final tribute to the Solovki islands. Kemetskii's last poems drew to a close the tragic yet epic career of a poet who, disentangling himself from ideology, managed to dignify the anguished cry of so many prisoners and so carried out, with elegance, Glubokovskii's 1925 manifesto of 'sincere poetry'. Kemetskii's election into the camp élite was due only to his aesthetic achievements and his original artistic inspiration. A shy, fragile, and nervous man, Kemetskii was perennially destitute. It was in a delirious dialogue with his Muse that he, 'grumbling', composed his poems — as Likhachev puts it in his portrayal of the poet. His poetic gift persuaded other *intelligenty* to protect him. He found a job in the camp library so that he could be exempt from general work. In exchange, Kemetskii recited his poems in the barrack rooms, evoking his Scandinavian

water | Envelops the islands. || The ice cracks, resounding, | The hoarse wind screams, laughing... | You will barely recognize me | In the evening hour of our meeting.] V. Kemetskii, 'Pesn' o vozvrashchenii', SO, 5 (1930), 1.

182 [I will come, and I will bring to your home | The smell of seaweed and tar, | I will come to tell you what | I learned beside the mossy cliffs. || And I will read you the lines | About the country where the flowers have no scent | Where roosters do not sing in the morning, | And in the spring the leaves do not rustle. || I will tell you about the people | Of these unfriendly places | They live with courage and simplicity | They club seals and cut wood...] Ibid.

183 [I will fall silent, I will break off my story | I will ask for a light for my pipe... | Maybe, at least this time | You will be able to hear me.] Ibid.

Fig. 4.8. A portrait of Vladimir Kemetskii
by Dmitrii Likhachev. AAS

ancestors and the sadness of imprisonment, thus paying his benefactors back with a gift rarely found in a concentration camp: beauty.

Kiunert, Leitin, Pankratov: Exotic Verses and Prison Themes

Several other poets, in addition to Kemetskii, tried to lend the SLON cultural scene more depth, and some of them succeeded in doing so. Though they went through different experiences and pursued distinctive careers, Maks Kiunert, Boris Leitin, and Aleksandr Pankratov all shared a double-edged attitude to poetry. While they never yielded to the flattering, encomiastic tones of the SLON's first poetic wave (1924–26), they nonetheless managed to intertwine free poetry with prison-related themes, something the administration had always supported.

When he arrived at the SLON, Maks Nikolaevich Gintsenberg had already published two poetry collections under the pseudonym of 'Maks Kiunert' — a reminder of his German origins. His first collection, which was supposed to be his début in 1924, had been withdrawn by the Soviet censors. His two privately published collections, *Chudesnoe kol'tso*[184] and *Zheltaia siren'*[185] (both published in 1926), had secured him a place among the so-called ego-Futurists, an affiliation the poet himself stated.[186] Unfortunately, the movement had gradually disappeared after Igor' Severianin's flight to Estonia in 1918 and had been neutralized by the Petrograd chekists in 1922, when the *organy* put an end to the actions of the 'Ring of poets' (*Kol'tso poetov*, a literary group which according to Krusanov looked back to the legacy of the Ego-Futurists).[187] Kiunert would pay dearly for his artistic sympathies for a group that had been targeted by the *organy*. His first collection (*Chudesnoe kol'tso*, composed of poems that probably dated back to his youth) was clearly inspired by Severianin's strong egocentrism, by the theme of the poet as a challenge

184 Maks Kiunert, *Chudesnoe kol'tso. Poezii* (Moscow: Izdanie avtora, 1926) (CNLR, Shrift 34/594).

185 Maks Kiunert, *Zheltaia Siren'* (Moscow: Izdanie avtora, 1926) (CNLR, Shrift 41/2215).

186 Boris Koz'min, *Pisateli sovremennoi epokhi. Bio-bibliograficheskii slovar' russkikh pisatelei XX veka* (Moscow: DEM, 1992), I, 158–59. Koz'min's book was originally published in 1928.

187 Andrei Krusanov, *Russkii avangard. 1907–1932. Istoricheskii obzor v trekh tomakh*, 3 vols (Moscow: Novoe literaturnoe obozrenie, 1996), I, 284–85.

to the world, and by the use of half rhymes.[188] His second collection (*Zheltaia siren'*) included more lyrical and heart-felt poems, which clearly foreshadowed the author's anxiety over his own fate, as the poem *Skol'ko raz* shows:

> Сколько раз по знакомой дороге
> Возвращаясь из клуба домой
> Я просил Вас, жестокие боги,
> Не шутить так жестоко со мной.[189]

Kiunert's premonition became a reality. He was arrested on 2 April 1929 and condemned to serve three years at the SLON.[190] As soon as he arrived on the Solovki, Gintsenberg/Kiunert started to write for the SLON press. Two of his poems, *Ne tsenish' zvezd* and *Aliaska*, were published in the first 1929 issue of the *Solovetskie Ostrova*.[191] Both are indicative of the strengths and weaknesses of the poet. The first, short poem is thematically and stylistically marked by a lack of originality — a trait that mars his previous collections, where remarkable poetic ideas are played out against rather drab passages. Its underlying theme is old-fashioned, if not clichéd — the entire poem is related to the prisoner's gaze at the starry sky. His second poem is more interesting. The title is borrowed from an earlier poem Kiunert published in *Chudesnoe kol'tso*,[192] in which the poet describes the American state in almost mythological terms. His vision in this poem was largely inspired by Jack London's Alaska-based short stories, written after the North American writer's short stay in the North. However, Kiunert's new tribute to *Aliaska* evokes a totally different mood from the one he had desribed some years before:

> Аляска... Джек Лондон... И золота звон...
> И виски... И вьюга... И ветер...
> О, юношеский увлекательный сон
> за книгой, при ласковой свете...
> О, юношеский увлекательный бред!
> Желание скитаний, лишений и странствий,
> [...]
> Какая наивнейшая мечта.
> Что Север? — Лишенья, борьба да удача...[193]

---

188 See for instance the use of half rhymes in the poem 'Na reke Forelevoi': *gubernii/vechernie, osinovke/malinovki* etc. See Igor' Severianin, 'Na reke Forelevoi', in *Stikhotvoreniia* (Leningrad: Sovetskii pisatel', 1975), p. 168.

189 [How many times along the familiar road | Returning home from the club | I asked you, cruel gods, | Not to joke with me so cruelly.] Maks Kiunert, 'Skol'ko raz', in Kiunert, *Zheltaia*, p. 5.

190 See the document about some SLON prisoners sent by the regional Petrozavodsk office of the MVD in response to a request of mine forwarded by the president of the Karelian office of Memorial, Viktor Paaso: 'Pis'mo ot ITs MVD RK predsedateliu Pravleniia KROU NITs 'Memorial' Paaso V.T. (27.02.2012)'.

191 M. Kiunert, 'Stikhi (Ne tsenish' zvezd. Aliaska)', *SO*, 2 (1929), 17.

192 Maks Kiunert, 'Aliaska', in Kiunert, *Chudesnoe*, p. 10.

193 [Alaska... Jack London... and the jingling of gold... | And whisky... And the blizzard... And wind... | Oh, fascinating juvenile dream | By a book, with a gentle light... || Oh, juvenile amusing delirium! | The desire for wandering, deprivations and hardships, | [...] | What a naive dream. | What is the North? Deprivations, struggle and luck...] M. Kiunert, 'Stikhi', p. 17.

Kiunert takes his cue from the poet's juvenile recurrent dream of escaping north-wards; this vision, which lost its early elegiac implications and turned tragically true, takes on mocking, bitterly self-ironic overtones in the poem. The poet's youthful dream thus becomes 'delirious' and the North appears as the destination of his relentless inner conflict. In the poem's close Kiunert might have hidden a message about his own change of literary direction, i.e. the repudiation of Jack London (meaning the type of poetry that led to Kiunert's arrest) in favour of Dickens:

> Джек Лондон и пережит и перечтен
> Мечтаю о Диккенсе, лампе и кресле.[194]

Choosing another author permitted by the Soviet authorities, Kiunert hints at a domestic setting, thus finding another way of expressing his desire for freedom and, overall, for a calm life.[195]

Aliaska brings to the fore Kiunert's self-ironizing mask, which he uses to keep the very source of his poetry alive, by preserving his fascination for exotic settings (in particular, those borrowed from Anglophone writers). This had been an ingredient of his art since *Zheltaia siren'* and one that he would further develop through his contribution to the SLON press. While the poem *Severnyi polius*[196] largely draws upon the Northern landscapes that the poet had abandoned in *Aliaska*, Kiunert's short story *Nochnaia smena*[197] foregrounded and registered the sense of freedom inspired by the chance the poet had to listen to Celtic music while at the SLON.

Thanks to his experience as a *lagkor* for the *Novye Solovki*, the poet also managed to address more conventional prison-related themes. He published *Liubimye*,[198] a sonnet (composed as a reply to Kazarnovskii's short tale *Svidanie*)[199] about the prisoners' heart-breaking separation from their beloved ones, and, later on, the poem *Kanun Oktiabria*.[200] Departing from previous encomiastic poetry, the poet introduced a canto on Red October that is centred on the day before the Revolution rather than on the day of the October Revolution itself. In this poem, Kiunert avoided flattery by refusing to celebrate the Revolution and focusing instead on the turmoil that preceded the 'Storming of the Winter Palace'. *Kanun Oktiabria* thus ultimately rejected any positive evaluation of the Russian Revolution.[201]

---

194 [Jack London has been outgrown and read to the end | I dream about Dickens, a lamp and an armchair] Ibid.

195 Dickens was one of the main authors Gor'kii wanted to propose when he started his publishing house 'Vsemirnaia literatura' in the years following the October revolution. Among the many sources, see the recent: Michael Hollington, *The Reception of Charles Dickens in Europe* (London: Bloomsbury, 2013), p. 107.

196 M. Kiunert, 'Severnyi polius (stikhi)', *SO*, 1 (1930), 4.

197 M. Kiunert, 'Nochnaia smena (ocherk)', *SO*, 1 (1930), 29–35.

198 M. Kiunert, 'Liubimye (stikhi)', *SO*, 1 (1930), 61.

199 Iu. Kazarnovskii, 'Svidanie', *SO*, 3–4 (1929), 6–10.

200 M. Kiunert, 'Kanun Oktiabria', *SO*, 3–4 (1929), 3.

201 The name of Maks Kiunert/Gintsenberg appears in recent publications; see for instance Molodiakov's quotation of Kiunert's article on Briusov (M. Kiunert, 'Valerii Briusov', *SO*, 3–4 (1929), 23–26). See Vasilii Molodiakov, *Valerii Briusov v poezii ego sovremennikov* (Moscow: Volodei, 2013), p. 213.

FIG. 4.9. A portrait of Lenin on the *Solovetskie Ostrova*.
From the DVD *Solovetskaia Pechat'*

Unlike Kiunert, Boris Leitin foregrounds the condition of women, a theme that had hitherto been largely ignored by SLON writers, except for Sof'ia Okerman's short stories and other occasional pieces. Leitin rejected encomiastic verse by choosing to develop prison-related literature, focusing particularly on women prisoners. He managed to portray some of his fellow prisoners and their tragic lives. *Meshchanka*, for example, is the story of a noblewoman who ended up in the camp and whose life had turned into 'mourning'. The woman's passage from the life she led before her arrest to the life that followed is rendered by the syntactic structure of the first line devoted to her life before the camp which is then mirrored by the structure of the first line devoted to her life in the camp.

Окно. Левкой. Тюль и занавески...
Застенчивый и розовый уют.
[...]
Тюрьма. Этап. И желтый женбарак
Тебя принял под кров гостеприимный.
Ты в трауре: мечта лишь, облак дымный —
Ушедших лет веселый кавардак.

О нем звенят, поют в ушах подвески,
В окне ж — ромашка, тюль и занавески.[202]

In another poem, *Torfushka*, the work on the extraction of peat within the camp is suffused with the aura of the Ukrainian countryside. Its main character is a young peasant girl who, as the poem draws to its close, finds a lover:

И в ласках краденых, в лесу иль в травах,
Ты вновь познаешь просто, нелукаво[203]
Нехитрую крестьянскую любовь.[204]

Leitin never allowed his poetry to depart from real life. The beginning of *Torfushka* links past and contemporary events by mentioning events related to the dekulakization in the Ukraine:

От поля, что устало зеленеть,
От брошенных, ненужных больше грабель
В голодный год ты к тем, кто крал и грабил,
Пришла кудрями цвета ржи звенеть.[205]

---

202 [Window. Gillyflowers. Tulle and curtains... | A modest and pink comfort. | [...] | Jail. Transfer. And the yellow women's barrack | Welcomed you under its hospitable roof. | You're in mourning: it's only a dream, a cloud of smoke — | The happy jumble of bygone years. || The earrings in your ears sing of those times, | And in the window there are daisies, tulle and curtains.] B. Leitin, 'Meshchanka (stikhi)', *SO*, 4 (1930), 36.

203 The use of this term may hint at love in opposition to sexual abuse. Other than 'cunningly', 'crafty' the word 'lukavo' is used in a religious context to indicate evil. The word 'lukavyi' is often used to refer to the devil.

204 [And in the stolen caresses, in the forest or in the grass, | You will find again simply and without cunning | Guileless peasant love.] B. Leitin, 'Torfushka (sonet)', *SO*, 2–3 (1930), 20.

205 [From the fields, that are tired of being green, | From the abandoned rakes that are no longer needed | In the year of the famine to those who stole and plundered you | Came with your ringing curls the colour of rye.] Ibid.

FIG. 4.10. Women extracting peat at the SLON. AMM

Leitin developed his interest in contemporary events in later poems. *Komandirsha zhenskoi roty*, for example, foregrounded a dangerous theme by using a mannered language (as indicated, for example, by the archaism 'nits', used not only for stylistic, but also for rhyming necessity). It is the story of a woman whose strong, uncompromising personality helps her become the commander of the women's community at the camp, underlining the woman's courage in not denouncing her first husband, thus 'defending' a type of virtue (failure to denounce) that, in the following years, would have been swept away by Stalinism and, indeed, became a criminal offence.

> Твой статный муж охранником и хватом
> Был для других. Но преклонялся ниц
> Он перед твоим воинственным ухватом,
> Пред гневом глаз, пред манием ресниц.
>
> Ты счет вела его карманным тратам,
> Ежовых не снимая рукавиц,
> И, в ужасе пред окриком крылатым,
> Детишки жались стайкой робких птиц.
>
> Но в час, когда очаг твой разметала
> Двух революций пенная волна,
> Ты на допросах — стойкая жена —
>
> О прошлом мужа говорить не стала.

И теша здесь характер непреклонный,
Ведешь ты женщин узкие колонны.[206]

Leitin proved to possess other qualities. One of his poems included an explicit appeal to 'Misfortune', whom he asks to leave him in peace — in a highly personal variation on Kemetskii's theme:

Рука тверда и голос звонок.
И черна еще борода —
Ты в глубины чертовских воронок
Не затянешь меня, беда![207]

Most significantly, Leitin paved the way for the representation of a particular kind of exotic landscape, like the one depicted in his *Vesna* sonnet, published in the second to last issue of the *Solovetskie Ostrova*. In this poem, the Solovki islands and Venice are superimposed, thus creating a compelling interplay of perspectives and sensations:

Весна. И голуби воркуют жарко.
Венеция приснилась в Соловках.
Венеция. Сверкающий Сан-Марко.
Видения, застывшие в веках.

Но синь небес так трогательно марка —
Взгляни: уже пятнится, в облаках.
Какой безумец — Данте ли, Петрарка
Расцвет, любовь размерит здесь в строках,

Нет! Лишь на миг мечте поэта просто,
Игрой пленившись нежной голубей,
Взнестись в лазурь, что выше, голубей,
Забыть дыханье жгучее норд-оста.

Чу! Севера пронзительный язык —
То будит к жизни чайки резкий вскрик.[208]

206 [Your noble husband was a guard and a dashing fellow | For others. But he bowed in worship | Before your bellicose oven fork, | Before the anger of the eyes, before the flicker of your eyelashes. || You kept the bills of his expenses, | Without removing your iron gloves, | And, terrified by your fierce shouts, | The children huddled like a flock of timid birds. || But in the moment when your hearth was swept away | By the foamy wave of two revolutions | You, under interrogation — o steadfast wife — || Did not speak about the past of your husband. | And here, to gratify your inflexible character, | You lead the narrow columns of women.] B. Leitin, 'Komandirsha zhenskoi roty', *SO*, 3–4 (1929), 58. The *ukhvat* is a utensil used for moving cooking pots which have no handle of their own.
207 [My hand is firm and my voice is clear. | And my beard is still black — | Into the depths of hellish craters | You will not draw me, o misfortune!] B. Leitin, 'Otryvok iz poemy', *SO*, 1 (1929), 10.
208 [Spring. And the pigeons coo intensely. | Venice appeared in a dream on the Solovki. | Venice. The sparkling San Marco. | Visions which have been preserved for centuries. || But the blue skies are so touchingly delicate — | Look: it is already becoming patchy, in the clouds. | What madman — Dante maybe, or Petrarch | Here measures out the blossoming or love in his lines? || No! Only for an instant is it simple for the dream of the poet, | Captivated by the doves' gentle game, | To rise up in the azure, which is higher, bluer, | To forget the searing breath of the Northeast. || Hark!

The interplay between the Solovki monastery and St. Mark's Basilica in Venice, although derived from a very popular cliché of the Silver Age era,[209] is totally unexpected. It is also at odds with the typical poetic depiction of the Solovki landscape realized by writers from Lomonosov onwards. The poem gradually fades away (an effect created also by the 'fake anaphora' of the first four lines) from the central image, which imperceptibly blurs out of focus until the mirage fades away and reality returns. In the very last couplet, the notorious cries of the Solovki seagulls replace the cooing of Venetian pigeons. Towards the end of the poem, the poet's dramatic recognition is further triggered by the last, equivocal rhyme, which de-semanticizes (or 'trans-semanticizes') the noun *golub'* (pigeon) by playing on the homonymic superlative of *goluboi* (blue), thus lending the very image of seagulls a more vivid and concrete character.

Exoticism surfaces also in the work of Aleksandr Pankratov. Arrested in connection with the same case as Aleksandr Peshkovskii and Iurii Kazarnovskii, the poet (born in 1902) proved himself one of the most talented and well-educated authors of SLON literature. Pankratov promoted the publication of translations of both classic and contemporary writers, following in the footsteps of Krivosh-Nemanich. It is not by chance, then, that his exoticism is time-specific rather than place-specific. His exotic poetry drew from classical mythology and conjured up a most original poetic representation of imprisonment. The refined diction and the pseudo-Hellenistic echoes in *Ukroshchennyi kentavr*[210] do not show the writer's subtler intentions. They emerge, however, quite plainly in his free-verse poem *Plach Odisseia*. Through his juxtaposition of Ulysses and himself, Pankratov used the classical age as a filter through which to interpret contemporary events. His imprisonment is thus compared to Ulysses' stay in Ogygia.

> Словно сказание, мерно текут мои дни здесь у моря,
> Грозно вздымаясь, волна рвется на скользкий утес.
> Где-то далеко бегут корабли по неверной пучине,
> Ветра могучая грудь дышит, свистя в паруса.[211]

At the beginning of the poem, the writer is amazed and confused at the situation he has to endure; he is then 'seen' looking at the sea and at the ships that move there, heading towards unknown destinations. Later on, he writes from his 'imposed' shelter:

The shrill language of the north | It is the sharp cry of a seagull that reawakens me to life.] B. Leitin, 'Vesna', SO, 4 (1930), 3.

209 Many poets during the Silver Age devoted their art to Venice, e.g. Aleksandr Blok and Dmitrii Merezhkovskii, see Aleksandr Blok, 'Venetsiia', in *Sobranie Sochinenii*, 8 vols (Moscow and Leningrad: Khudozhestvennaia Literatura, 1960–63), III, 102–04; Dmitrii Merezhkovskii, 'Venetsiia', in *Stikhotvoreniia i poemy* (St Petersburg: Novaia Biblioteka Poeta, 2000), p. 501. Curiously enough, in a later poem written in 1957, Nikolai Zabolotskii used the same rhyme (*San Marko/zharko*) as does Leitin, see Nikolai Zabolotskii, 'Venetsiia', in *Stolbtsy i poemy, 1926–1933; Stikhotvoreniia, 1932–1958; Stikhotvoreniia raznykh let; Proza* (Moscow: Khudozhestvennaia literatura, 1983), p. 434.

210 A. Pan., 'Ukroshchennyi kentavr', SO, 1 (1929), 9.

211 [Like a legend, rhythmically flow my days here by the sea, | Threateningly surging, the wave breaks on a slippery cliff. | Somewhere far away the ships run across the treacherous deep | The mighty chest of the wind breathes, whistling in the sails.] A. Pankratov, 'Plach Odisseia (stikhi)', SO, 1 (1930), 61.

Странником был я в морях. Вот обломок ладьи на прибрежье,
Ныне на этой земле встретил невольный приют.
Пищу имею и кров, от стужи хранят одеянья.
Многострадальному, мне полный оказан почет.

Страстью к себе приклонить нежеланная хочет царица,
Юности вечной дары мне, обещая взамен.
Ах, но тоскует душа по милой далекой Итаке,
Где Пенелопа прядет, все поджидая меня!

Долгие годы текут, похищая и силы и бодрость...
В горестно сладком плену держит меня Калипсо.[212]

The metaphor of Calypso, who embodies the Soviet leadership and who offers the poet eternal youth, was one of the most sophisticated images of SLON poetry. Pankratov, of course, hinted at untimely death as one of the adventures a camp prisoner might face. The image of the poet's potential loss of strength and pride while living at the camp was the last image offered by a very elegant representative of Gulag literature.

Apart from writing (as he does in his short poem *Posle izvestiia o smerti Lenina*)[213] more conventionally encomiastic poetry than his fellow writers of the second SLON generation, Pankratov also wrote a number of poems à la Kemetskii, in which the ordeal of imprisonment is depicted through compelling perspectival shifts. *Chto, esli* focused once more on the way camp prisoners lost their strength by evoking the image of a poet who is physically unable to jump on to life's *troika*, which passes by with its bells jingling. The theme of the loss of both physical and moral strength, central to some of the most outstanding works of Gulag literature (e.g. Shalamov, Demidov, Solzhenitsyn) but not to SLON literature, testifies to the deep sensitivity of Pankratov, the only author capable of understanding the connection between the two phenomena:

Что, если жизнь веселой тройкою,
Бубенчиками звеня,
С разгульной песней, рысью бойкою,
Промчится около меня.
[...]
Схвачу ли я рукой уверенной
Пылающих лошадей.
И полечу, в степи затерянный,
К далекой радости моей?

Или останусь робко... Тройкою,
Бубенчиками звеня,

---

212 [I was a wanderer on the seas. Here's the wreckage of a ship on the coast, | Now, in this land I have found imposed shelter. | I have food and a roof, my clothes protect me from the cold. | After long suffering, I am given complete respect. || The undesired queen wants to attract me to herself with passion | Promising me gifts of eternal youth in return. | Ah, but my soul yearns for dear, distant Ithaca, | Where Penelope spins, waiting for me! || Long years pass, stealing both strength and courage... | Calypso keeps me in bitterly sweet captivity.] Ibid.

213 A. Pankratov, 'Posle izvestiia o smerti Lenina (stikhi)', *SO*, 1 (1930), 3.

> Жизнь огневая, рысью бойкою,
> Промчится около меня.[214]

Khochu odno shows instead Pankratov's impatience with the Solovki Northern landscape, often snow-capped and blown by frosty winds. The poet's departure from the firmly established representation of the islands was remarkable; in the poem, the natural world of Solovki loses its conventional, magical connotations to turn into a 'dead' body:

> Хочу одно: увидеть луг
> С простыми пестрыми цветами,
> И рожь с родными васильками,
> И неба светло-синий круг.
> [...]
> Такая, видно, полоса.
> Но тяжелей мне год от года —
> Реки бесплодная коса,
> Задернутые небеса —
> Вся эта мертвая природа.[215]

Finally, *Mne grusto pet' o Solovkakh* is indicative of the poet's resistance not only to the Northern landscape but to the very nature of his art. As the poem suggests, he had grown tired of his role as a SLON poet and had realized the ultimate uselessness of poetry when man has to endure such extreme conditions:

> Мне грустно петь о Соловках,
> О высоте твердынь кремлевских,
> О ветре, дующем в лесах,
> Кочующем на перекрестках.
>
> И скучно думой измерять
> Нас поглотившее пространство,
> Иль соловецких зим убранство
> В стихах беспечных прославлять.[216]

Through his ultimate demystification of poetry aimed at 'celebrating' the Solovki winter, Pankratov seemed to have come full circle in SLON literature. He had returned to the same point from which Glubokovskii had departed in 1925. Poetry finally doubted itself.

---

214 [What if life, like a happy troika, | With its bells jingling, | With a wild song, at a lively trot | Rushes past me? | [...] | Will I seize with a confident hand | The fiery horses? | And will I fly towards my distant joy, lost in the steppe? || Or will I remain behind timidly... Like a troika, | With its jingling bells, | Life, fiery, at a lively trot | Will rush past me.] A. Pankratov, 'Stikhi (Chto esli, igraet solntse)', *SO*, 1 (1929), 45.

215 [I want one thing: to see the meadow | With simple, colourful flowers, | And the rye with its cornflowers, | And the clear blue circle of the sky. | [...] | Evidently, this is what the region here is like. | But every year it is harder for me — | The barren sandbank of the river, | The covered skies | — All this dead nature.] A. Pankratov, 'Khochu odno (stikhi)', *SO*, 4 (1930), 1.

216 [I am sad to sing about Solovki, | About the height of the strongholds of the Kremlin, | About the wind blowing in the woods, | Wandering at the crossroads. || And it is boring to measure with thoughts | The space that devours us | Or the ornaments of the Solovki winter | In careless poems to praise.] A. Pankratov, 'Mne grustno pet' o Solovkakh (stikhi)', *SO*, 2–3 (1930), 26.

The Satirical and Poetic Talent of Iurii Kazarnovskii

Iurii Kazarnovskii's steadfast commitment to poetry throughout the second period of SLON publications was remarkable. He had first met Pankratov at the 'Vremennik' literature circle; both of them were eventually arrested with Aleksandr Peshkovskii in 1927. Kazarnovskii's arrest put an end to his promising career, which began when he was only seventeen and had already earned him the esteem of Evgenii Zamiatin, among others.[217]

Before his arrest Kazarnovskii was a budding prose writer. In the SLON, he distinguished himself mostly as a satirical poet. Brilliant and gifted, with a witty and elegant sense of humour, Kazarnovskii became, as much as Kemetskii, the 'lord' of the second period of the SLON press. Kazarnovskii, however, published much more than the St Petersburg poet. Other than publishing in the *Solovetskie Ostrova*, he was in great demand as a poet because his lines lent a light-hearted tone to the strictly ideological contents of the camp newspaper, the *Novye Solovki*. He contributed to almost every issue of both the *Solovetskie Ostrova* and the *Novye Solovki*.

Though Kazarnovskii's SLON-related output was considerable, it certainly lacked variety. The poet never managed to drop his mask as the camp's jester and clung to comic poetry without addressing more serious issues. One of his rare attempts at writing prose tempted him into raising the difficult question of a prisoner's life at the SLON and finally to choose to tackle the theme seriously. His short story *Svidanie*,[218] which focused on the tragic story of two distant lovers, a SLON prisoner and his wife, was published in the 3/4 1929 issue of the *Solovetskie Ostrova*. Their story is shaped by the only moments when the two are allowed to meet once a year. It focuses on the woman's experience during her journeys to the Solovki islands and her traumatic meetings with her husband, who is withering away day by day. In the story, their love does not withstand the test of time. Kazarnovskii's story was the only one in which he devoted himself to a serious theme. He touched on such a painful topic that Kiunert replied to him with the above-mentioned poem *Liubimye*.

The strength of the poem *Vynuzhdennoe priznanie* lay in Kazarnovskii's half-serious, half-ironic representation of imprisonment. This short poem takes its cue from a violent debate between the poet and his reflection on the surface of a lake in the Solovki archipelago. Kazarnovskii's decision to represent his alter ego in the slightly frothy water rather than in a mirror had far deeper implications than the poet's ironic, humorous mask might suggest at first sight:

> Стою у озера в смиреньи...
> И, чуть колеблемо волной,
> В воде темнеет отраженье
> Мое — пришедшее со мной.
> [...]
> И вдруг пискляво и сердито
> Мне отраженье говорит:

217 Soshina, 'Podstrelennye', p. 121.
218 Kazarnovskii, 'Svidanie'. See footnote 199 above, p. 233.

Довольно северного спорта!
Чужда мне мерзлая вода!
И, вообще, какого черта,
Вы привезли меня сюда?..

Вы совершили преступленье
Бродя как кислое вино,
Но я — я ваше отраженье
За что же я сидеть должно?[219]

Except for *Svidanie* and *Vynuzhdennoe priznanie*, Kazarnovskii's work was typically cheerful — which is hardly surprising, if we give credit to Likhachev's portrait of the poet in his memoirs:

> Among the poets on Solovki, Iu. A. Kazarnovskii, who was still quite young, distinguished himself. We all called him simply Iurka, not only because he was young, but also because dealing with him was simple. He did not have a poetic face, like, say, Volodia Kemetskii-Sveshnikov. He was superficial, but wrote poems with extraordinary, surprising ease and wit. In one of the issues of the *Solovetskie Ostrova* it is possible to find his parodies of Maiakovskii, Blok, Severianin... In another, his comic aphorisms. And all of them were related to life in the Solovki camp. He had an inexhaustible memory for poetry. He knew almost all Gumilev, the Mandel'shtam of those years, Belyi. He had a taste for real poetry, which he appreciated. He constantly tried to share his poetic pleasures. He did not have a shadow of envy: people would ask him to read his poems, and he would read someone else's he liked.[220]

Likhachev also describes Kazarnovskii as 'a great prankster, as far as that was possible in a camp'.[221] Kazarnovskii's harsh fate and imprisonment did not destroy his innate optimism. It is worth highlighting some unique features of Kazarnovskii's pieces by analysing his literary parodies, which were by far his most successful work and brought him fame within the camp.

---

219 [I was standing by the lake in resignation... | And, shaken slightly by a wave, | In the water I saw a dark reflection | My own, which had come here together with me. | [...] | And suddenly, shrilly and angrily, | The reflection tells me: || Enough of this northern sport! | This freezing water is alien to me! | And, in general, what the hell | Did you bring me here for?.. | You have committed a crime | Fermenting like sour wine, | But I — I, your reflection | What I should I be imprisoned for?] Iu. Kazarnovskii, 'Vynuzhdennoe priznanie (stikhi)', *SO*, 4 (1930), 18.

220 [Среди поэтов на Соловках выделялся тогда еще совсем молодой Ю. А. Казарновский, которого мы все звали просто Юркой — не только по его молодости, но и по простоте, с которой можно было с ним обращаться. У него не было своего поэтического лица, как, скажем, у Володи Кемецкого-Свешникова. Он был поверхностен, но стихи писал с необычайной, поражающей легкостью и остроумием. В одном из номеров «Соловецких островов» можно найти его пародии на Маяковского, Блока, Северянина... В другом его шуточные афоризмы. И все это на темы соловецкого быта. У него была неиссякаемая память на стихи. Он знал чуть ли не всего Гумилева, тогдашнего Мандельштама, Белого. Вкус у него был, настоящую поэзию ценил и постоянно стремился поделиться своими поэтическими радостями. Ни тени зависти. Просили его почитать его стихи, а он читал кого-то другого, понравившегося ему.] Likhachev, *Izbrannoe: Vospominaniia*, p. 254.

221 ['...великий озорник. Насколько это было возможно в лагерных условиях.'] Dmitrii Likhachev, '"Na Solovkakh ia ponial, chto kazhdyi chelovek — chelovek". Zametki i nabliudeniia', *Pravoslavie i mir*, 30/09/2014 <http://www.pravmir.ru/na-solovkax-ya-ponyal-chto-kazhdyj-chelovek-chelovek/> [accessed 23 January 2015].

As Likhachev suggests, Kazarnovskii had an excellent knowledge of Russian poetry, from which he drew from mainly by filtering it through his sense of humour. Through his review and parody of the leitmotifs of a number of famous Russian authors who were committed to a purely imaginary imprisonment at the SLON,[222] Kazarnovskii managed to address a wide range of urgent and even controversial camp-related topics, lending a comical edge to dramatic situations. His parody of Aleksandr Blok thus became a strategy to show the camp commanders' drinking problems and their violent behaviour through the image of the head of a company of prisoners. Kazarnovskii saw the prison camp in terms of the dissolute urban atmosphere in Blok's depiction of St Petersburg in *Ante Lucem* and *Gorod*:

> По вечерам над соловчанами
> Весенний воздух мглист и сыр.
> И правит окриками пьяными
> Суровый ротный командир.[223]

Juxtaposition was a recurring trait in these parodies. The letter Kazarnovskii's 'Esenin' writes to his 'mother' is a perfect specimen of literary mimesis, being very closely modelled on Esenin's 1924 poem *Pis'mo materi*.[224] Kazarnovskii superimposed life at the SLON camp with Esenin's bohemian life and indulged in deliberate wordplay while producing puns:

> Ты еще жива, моя старушка.
> Жив и я. Привет тебе, привет...
> Получил в посылке я подушку
> И цилиндр с парою штиблет.
> [...]
> Ничего, родная, успокойся...
> Не грусти на дальнем берегу.
> Я, хотя отчаянный пропойца.
> Но без водки — спиться не могу.
>
> Я по-прежнему такой же нежный,
> И мечта одна лишь в сердце есть:
> Чтоб скорей от этой вьюги снежной
> Возвратиться к нам — на минус шесть.[225]

222 The title of the series was 'What would some poets write if they arrived at Solovki???' [Кто что из поэтов написал бы по прибытии в Соловки???']. This, again, was typical of those years: in the 1920s a group of poets based in Kiev published a book, *Parnas dybom*, which contained parodies of famous poets and writers such as Blok, Esenin, and Maiakovskii, but also Dante, Shakespeare, and Homer. Thus — but also in fake translations — poets dared to say what they could not officially say in their poems. See Ester Palernaia, Aleksandr Rozenberg, and Aleksandr Finkel', *Parnas dybom: Pro kozlov, sobak i Veverleev* (Moscow: Khudozhestvennaia Literatura, 1990). The book (first published in Khar'kov in 1927) was very popular: maybe Kazarnovskii (who, it might be worth remembering, was living in the Ukraine when he was arrested in December 1927) drew from this the idea of his parodies.
223 [In the evenings above the Solovki inhabitants | The spring air is dark and humid. | And rules with drunken shouts | The strict company commander.] Iu. Kazarnovskii, 'Iumor. Literaturnye parodii', *SO*, 2–3 (1930), 72. The first line is a parody of Blok's poem *Neznakomka*: See Blok, II, 185.
224 Sergei Esenin, 'Pis'mo materi', in *Polnoe sobranie sochinenii v 7 tomakh* (Moscow: Nauka, Golos, 1995–2002), I, 179–80.
225 [You are still alive, my old woman. | I'm alive too. My greetings to you... | I received the parcel

While supposedly referring to the outdoor temperature, the expression 'minus six' hints in fact at restrictions on prisoners, who were usually not allowed to live in the six biggest cities of the Soviet Union after being released.[226] The poem is interspersed with this kind of wordplay, which makes the poet's parody of Esenin and his sophistication highly amusing. For instance, throughout Kazarnovskii's poem 'Esenin' is worried lest his mother, who is willing to 'visit often' the prosecutor to talk him into interceding on the poet's behalf, should dress up and discard her old *shushun* (an outer female garment similar to a little coat, typical of Northern and Central Russia). In Esenin's original poem, the old coat that the mother wears is the symbol of her despair and anxious attitude.[227]

While Kazarnovskii's caricature of Esenin is nifty, his portrait of the leader of Russian Futurism Maiakovskii is quite caustic. The self-centred attitude of the Futurist poet — who was still alive when the poem was published in the first (January) 1930 issue of the *Solovetskie Ostrova* — is transfigured so that 'Kazarnovskii's Maiakovskii' becomes a vile, greedy and selfish individual:

> Мой лозунг:
> — «От жизни
> Все берите».
> Но все
> Я
> Брать не готов:
> Это вам —
> Не какой-нибудь
> Толстый критик —
> А 10 лет Соловков!
> СЛОН высок,
> Но и я высокий.
> Мы оба —
> Пара из пар.
> Ненавижу
> Всяческие сроки!

with the pillow | And a top hat with a pair of gaiters. | [...] | Don't worry, dear, take comfort | Don't be saddened on the faraway shore. | Although I am a desperate drunkard, | I can't get drunk without vodka. || I am as tender as I was before | And I have just one dream in my heart: | That as soon as possible, from this snowstorm | I can return home — to minus six.] Iu. Kazarnovskii, 'Iumor. Literaturnye parodii', *SO*, 1 (1930), 64–66 (p. 64). The original middle quatrain in Esenin's poem is instead: 'Ничего, родная! Успокойся. | Это только тягостная бредь. | Не такой уж горький я пропойца, | Чтоб, тебя не видя, умереть.' [Don't worry, mother, take comfort | It's only a foolish fancy. | I'm not such a bitter drunkard, | To die without seeing you again]. See Esenin, 'Pis'mo materi'.

226 Similarly, if prisoners were banned from ten cities, they would talk about 'minus ten' (*minus desiat'*) and so on. In Gulag jargon, this was referred to simply as 'minus'. See Rossi, pp. 220–21.

227 Esenin's lines ('Пишут мне, что ты, тая тревогу, | Загрустила шибко обо мне, | Что ты часто ходишь на дорогу | В старомодном ветхом шушуне' [I am told in letters that you, hiding your worries, | Saddened hugely because of me, | That you often go around the street | In your old-fashioned, worn-out *shushun*) are thus modified by Kazarnovskii: 'Слышал я: тая тоску во взоре. | Ты взгрустнула шибко обо мне. | Ты так часто ходишь к прокурору | В старомодном ветхом шушуне'.

— Обожаю
Всяческий гонорар![228]

By drawing on the *lesenka*, Kazarnovskii makes fun of Maiakovskii's main themes
through his wordplay. The second part of the poem reveals Kazarnovskii's ironic
attitude to everyday life in the camp. Unfortunately, part of the meaning of his
irony is lost on modern readers.[229] Sometimes, however, it is possible to understand
the puns, and appreciate their wit, as is the case in Kazarnovskii's parody of another
Futurist poet, Igor' Severianin. Highlighting Severianin's sympathy for the West (as
a typical trait of the *kaerovshchina*), Kazarnovskii revelled in the grotesque depiction
of characters as well as in the use of neologisms (*usloneiut*, *kaeriat*, *val'sit*) and of
misspelt foreign words that exemplify the poet's comic brio:

Среди красот полярного бомонда,
В десерте экзотической тоски,
Бросая тень, как черная ротонда,
Галантно услонеют Соловки.

Ах, здесь изыск страны коллегиальной,
Здесь все сидят — не ходят, — а сидят.
Но срок идет во фраке триумфальном,
И я ищу, пардон, читатель, blat.

Полярит даль бушлат демимонденки,
Вальсит грезер, балан искрит печаль,
Каэрят дамы — в сплетнях все оттенки —
И пьет эстет душистый вежеталь.[230]

228 [My slogan is | 'Take everything | from life'. | But | I | am not ready to take everything: | I
leave you | Not some kind of | Fat literary critic | but ten years in the Solovki! || The elephant is
tall | But I am tall too. | We both are | The couple of all couples. | I hate | All kinds of deadlines!
|| I adore | Any kind of honorarium.] Kazarnovskii, 'Iumor. Literaturnye parodii', p. 65. Here
Kazarnovskii plays with the meaning of the words 'slon' (elephant, but also the acronym of the
Solovki camp) and 'srok' (prison term or sentence, but also deadline).
229 Puns which are now impossible to understand usually referred to unidentifiable addressees.
It was Likhachev who underlined this aspect of the SLON poetry when, after the publication of
a Kazarnovskii poem in the journal *Ogonek*, revealed to the readers an episode which is indicative
of this problem: 'Успенский однажды сказал Казарновскому и Шипчинскому [...], что нужно
написать лозунг к Октябрьской революции, к празднику, мол, на Соловках все делается для
рабочих и крестьян. И тогда кто-то из них — я не знаю, кто — быстро выпалил: «Соловки
— рабочим и крестьянам!» Успенский сказал: «Во здорово! Вот это нам и нужно!». Написали
на плакате лозунг и повесили над входом в лагерь [...]. И только потом кто-то указал, что
это неприлично, и лозунг сняли.' [Uspenskii once told Kazarnovskii and Shipchinskii [...] that it
was necessary to write a slogan for the October Revolution from which it would be clear that all
was done for the workers and the peasants. And one of them — I can't remember who — quickly
blurted: 'The Solovki for the workers and the peasants!' Uspenskii said: 'Well done! That's exactly
what we need!' They wrote the slogan on a poster and put it on the camp's entrance. [...] And only
later someone pointed out that it was improper, and they took it off.]. This episode, out of context,
would have been difficult ro recognise for today's readers as a truly exhilarating moment of wit. See
Likhachev, 'Ne tak davno ...'.
230 [Among the beauties of the polar *beau-monde*, | In the dessert of exotic anguish, | Casting a
shadow, like a black rotunda | Gallantly the Solovki uslonate. || Ah, here you find the cream of the
world of colleges, | Here they all sit — they don't walk, they sit. | But the term wears a triumphant

There are numerous instances of puns and moments of irony in these three stanzas: the play between 'dessert' and 'desert'; the reference to the rotunda, connected to the elephants' (i.e. the camp's) mightiness; the use of the invented verbs 'uslonet" (i.e. they do the USLON) or 'kaerit" (to do the kaer); the reference to the nobility, which was educated in colleges and ended up in the Solovki camp; the wordplay linked to the verb 'sidet" which means both 'to sit' and 'to serve a term'; the play on the verb 'idti' (to walk) in regard to the specific use of 'srok idet' (i.e. the term is being served'); the use of Latin letters for a Russian word, while the whole text is based on erroneous spellings in Russian of French and Italian words. More are to be found in the following stanzas.

A further element of Kazarnovskii's poetry that is possible to see in this parody, which is most probably also a key to his successful literary career in the SLON, is the poem's typically straightforward address to the reader. Kazarnovskii's device was aimed specifically at involving the public. It proved very effective in the restricted setting of the camp, as happened with his pastiche of the first stanza of Pushkin's *Evgenii Onegin*, in which Kazarnovskii went so far as to imitate Pushkin's language and style. The pastiche is a way of recalling Pushkin's uncle Pavel Isaakovich Gannibal, who had been a prisoner at the Solovki monastery from 1827 to 1832[231] and who 'reappears' at the SLON, surrounded by *komroty* and *balany*.

> Мой дядя самых честных правил,
> Когда внезапно "занемог",
> Москву он тотчас же оставил
> Чтоб в Соловках отбыть свой срок.
> Он был помещик. Правил гладко,
> Любил беспечное житье,
> Читатель рифмы ждет: десятка —
> Так вот она — возьми ее!
> Ему не милы те широты,
> И вид Кремля ему не мил,
> Сперва за ним ходил комроты,
> Потом рукраб его сменил.
> [...]
> В бушлат УСЛОНовский одет,
> Мой дядюшка невзвидел свет.[232]

Iurii Kazarnovskii's remarkable gift for poetry ultimately made him the only satirical writer in the SLON camp who was appreciated by the camp administration. Others

tail-coat, | And I'm looking for, begging your pardon, dear reader, a favour. || The distance of the jackets of the demi-mondaines is polar, | The gréser waltzs, the balan makes sadness sparkle | The ladies kaerate — in all shades of gossip — | And the aesthete drinks a perfumed hair lotion.] Kazarnovskii, 'Iumor. Literaturnye parodii', p. 66.

231 I. Blinov, 'Pavel Isaakovich Gannibal, diadia A. S. Pushkina', *Russkaia starina* (1899), 9.

232 [My uncle was a man of most honest principles, | When he suddenly 'fell ill' | He immediately left Moscow | To serve his sentence on the Solovki. || He was a landowner. He ruled smoothly, | He loved a carefree way of life, | The reader is waiting for a rhyme: ten years | So here it is — take it! | He did not enjoy these latitudes, | Nor the view of the Kremlin, | First the company commander used to walk behind him, | Then he was replaced by the head of works. || [...] | Dressed in the USLON jacket | My uncle grew weary of the world.] Iu., 'Literaturnye parodii', *SO*, 4 (1930), 47.

who had tried their hand at humour or satire (Tiberii, and the contributors of the *Stukach* and the *Solovetskii Krokodil*) had all been forbidden to continue composing satirical works. Kazarnovskii instead became the most prominent of the SLON press contributors. Even the camp administration recognized his craft, his witty elegance and his shrewdness.

Orlov and Peshkovskii: The Avant-Garde at the SLON

Unlike most of the writers mentioned so far, the literary output of N. Orlov and Aleksandr Peshkovskii was not particularly successful. Though he was a regular contributor to the SLON press in the second phase of the camp's cultural life, Peshkovskii has never been included in the poetry collections about SLON published after the advent of perestroika. This is hardly surprising. Born in 1905, Peshkovskii was a truly untalented poet. His rhymes were rather trivial; he was never daring enough; and his lines lacked musicality and were tediously flat, as these lines taken from one of his poems, *Pust' solovetskie lesa* demonstrate:

> Пусть наши дни грубы и колки,
> Пусть жизнь тоской омрачена,
> Я знаю, знаю в комсомолке
> Играет хмельная весна.[233]

Although his lines were intrinsically deprived of musicality, Peshkovskii (whose brilliant academic career had been interrupted by his arrest in 1927) wrote several enjoyable prose pieces. Only Peshkovskii's eventual adherence to the experimentalism of the avant-garde marked a turn in his artistic development. Likhachev curiously associated the poet's transformation with the neurological disease that affected him and caused his early release in 1933:

> He was extremely active and 'mobile'. Mobile not only because he was always procuring or arranging something (for himself, first and foremost, and sometimes for us), but he was also mobile because he was affected by some form of chorea: he would jerk his leg (wearing plus-fours and pointy-toed fashionable 'Jimmy' shoes), he would twist his shoulders, wiggle his head, an words would erupt in a very particular way (some of the words he was thinking about would always burst out, especially when he was writing). On the basis of the individual words that escaped him when he was writing — for example, an application for clemency — we would clearly imagine this 'document' as full of humiliations and exaggerations. [...] Arturych tried to write poetry and prose. His 'masterpiece' was *Kuzma's widow*.[234] Arturych published in the *Solovetskie Ostrova*, highlighting in his works a few words in large print, and this seemed somehow to be a continuation of his strange illness.[235]

233 [Although our days be rough and bitter, | Although life be marred by sadness, | I know, I know that in the Komsomol-girl | The lush spring is at play.] A. Peshkovskii, 'Stikhi (Pust' Solovetskie lesa)', *SO*, 1 (1929), 10.

234 A. Peshkovskii, 'Kuz'ma vdova', *SO*, 4 (1930), 3–10; 5 (1930), 3–12.

235 [Он был чрезвычайно активен и «подвижен». Подвижен не только потому, что вечно что-нибудь добывал и устраивал (для себя, в первую очередь, — иногда и для нас), но и потому подвижен, что был болен какой-то формой хореи: дрыгал ножками (в гольфах и

In fact, Peshkovskii's great achievement was to introduce the graphic experimental
perspectives of the avant-garde into SLON literature, somewhat following Shiriaev's
first stylistic experiments inspired by the avant-garde movements. Peshkovskii's
poem *Veter*, published in the second 1929 issue of the *Solovetskie Ostrova*, perfectly
epitomized the interplay between semantics and layout that was typical of Futurist
art. His stanzas created the impression of being wind-blown by the way the words
were arranged on the page:

> Ветер, в полинялый полдень
> Закрутись, завертись в буран,
> В блесках снежных молний
> Разгуляйся, весел и пьян.
> > Ночи и дни,
> > Иди, лети.
> > Искры, ОГНИ
> > > Размети,
> > > Разгони!
>
> В прорывах мятели
> Беснуйся в ущельи,
> Чтоб скалы запели
> Об иглах твоих —
> Иглах любви.
> > Живи,
> > > Лови,
> > > > Беги,
> > > > > Жги!²³⁶

The use of the imperative mood at the end of the second stanza gave the lines their
frantic rhythm, thus reminding the reader of the verse experiments of the Russian
avant-garde. These literary and visual echoes can be found even in more traditional
texts, as in the short-story *Kirpich*:

остроносых модных туфлях «джимми»), крутил плечами, ерзал головкой и как-то особенно
прорывался словами (из того, что он думал, вечно вырывались какие-то слова, особенно
когда писал). Из отдельных слов, которые вырывались у него, когда он писал, например,
заявление с просьбой о помиловании, мы отлично представляли себе этот «документ»,
полный унижения и преувеличений. [...] Артурыч пытался писать стихи, прозу — его
«шедевр» «Кузьма вдова». Печатался Артурыч в «Соловецких островах», выделяя в своих
произведениях отдельные слова крупным шрифтом, и это казалось каким-то продолжением
его странной болезни.] Likhachev, *Izbrannoe: Vospominaniia*, pp. 243–44. Likhachev probably
did not own any copies of the *Solovetskie ostrova* when he formulated this bizarre hypothesis. His
recollection of Peshkovskii's experimentation was rather confused (or he might have been speaking
ironically about the author, whom he did not seem to appreciate from a human point of view).
236 [O wind, in the faded noon | Twist, spin until you become a storm, | In snowy blazes of
lightning | Go wild, happy and drunk. | Nights and days, | Go, fly. | Sparks, FLAMES | Sweep
them away, | Disperse them! || In the outbreaks of the snowstorm | Rage in the gorge, | So that
the rocks sing | About your needles | The needles of love. | Live, | Catch, | Run, | burn!] A.
Peshkovskii, 'Veter', *SO*, 2 (1929), 20–22.

вспомогательных заведений, как на том. Главное, не было канавы. Но зато имелись:

ДОМАШНИЕ НОМЕРА
„РЕДКОСТЬ"
А·Р·У·Т·Ю·Н·О·В·А

И ◆ подвал

ВЕРСАЛЬ

а к тому же **Андроник** умел заливать калоши, чего не умел делать **Семеон.** Одно восполнялось другим, и оба были довольны как своей работой, так и своими местами.

Оба они жили в одном доме, **оба** были холосты и оба занимали углы у одного общего хозяина—многосемейного **Айсора.**

Жизнь обоих молодых айсоров, а они еще были молоды, каждому из них не исполнилось тридцати лет, протекала, наполненная их айсорскими радостями и печалями. Братья жили дружно, и возможно, что дружба эта никогда бы не нарушилась, если бы...

Первой жертвой пал **Семеон.**

Сердце его растаяло с той минуты, когда „маленьким ножкам" Мани опустилась на подставку ящика. Руки бегали с меньшей проворностью, нежели обычно, губы шептали:

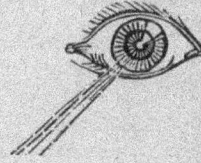

— Миленьким барышням, туфелькам настоящим зеркалам делать будим.

Но зеркала на этот раз не получилось, так как Семеон, забыв все и вся, в волнении, вместо желтого крема, мазнул черным.

Маня топнула „туфелькам" и сказала, что за такую чистку надо отправить в милицию и лишить патента, на что Семеон, разводя руками, робко возражал:

— Что будишь делать! таким ножкам, таким ножкам, первый раз таким ножкам красивый видим.. Прасти пажалиста, за нашим ашибкам десять разов чистить даром будим.. Черный крем снимаем, желтый накладаем, красивым барышням ублажаем...

Перспектива десятикратного бесплатного использования щеток Семеона примирила с ним Маню, и она милостиво разрешила довести начатое **дело до** благополучного **конца.**

Приятнейшее ощущение, оставшееся у Семеона от прикосновеня к тонкой и теплой ткани чулка своей клиентки, долго еще волновало его и заставило сухо и коротко бросить: „Не чистим!" франтоватому малому в узких и длинных шимми.

Fig. 4.11. Aleksandr Pehskovskii's story *Kirpich*. From the DVD *Solovetskaia Pechat'*

4   Соловецкие Острова   № 3—4

ШТОРМ

I.

Мы плыли морем третьи сутки.
И вдруг волнение.....
          „Ей, братва!
сегодня...
Радио...
НЕ шутки??"
Приносит ветер радости слова
„Царя
    на шкендель."
          „Ай-ай-ай!"
    „Тащи на бак!"
          „За борт плесни!"
    „Эй, слышишь, море,
          Принимай!
Подарок матросни."
Не захлебнуться-бы,
          Сидишь, как в шлюпке.
Захлестывает грудь шальная весть.
    „Перемените курс". Опять на рубке.
„Норд-вест"
    „в РОССИЮ"

          „Полный"

    „ЕСТЬ"

II.

„Товарищи!"
    Оратор в кепке
На капитанском мостике—
          такой простой.
„Товарищи!"
    И ромом крепким
Пьянят слова:
    „Вперед!"
          „На бой!"
И мы под орудийный грохот
Кровавую месили хлябь
    В огне,
          В ДЫМУ,
              Под конский т
Рождался яростный **Октябр**

FIG. 4.12. Orlov's poem *Shtorm*. AMSPB

The unknown poet N. Orlov, one of the few panegyric poets of the second SLON season, was also a promoter of experimentation. After publishing his long poem *Tak prosto* (a love story abetted by the silence of a guard, set in the Solovki woods)[237] and an altogether unremarkable poem (*Ne pereskazhesh' eto*),[238] Orlov published *Shtorm* in the 3/4 1929 issue of the *Solovetskie Ostrova*. The poem intertwines encomiastic accents and formal features associated with the avant-garde:

> Мы плыли морем третьи сутки
> И вдруг волнение...
>   ...„Эй, братва!
> Сегодня...
>   Радио...
>   Не шутки??"
> Приносит ветер радости слова
> „Царя
>   на шкендель".[239]

The poem's layout consistently uses Futuristic poetic devices.

The presence of avant-garde at the SLON was not limited to these instances. Whereas Orlov and Peshkovskii carried out their experimentation and contributed to the development of the SLON avant-garde, the poet Aleksandr Iaroslavskii went through a radically different poetic experience. He abandoned his early participation in a minor current of the Russian avant-garde movement and embraced a different poetics, choosing a basically bare, unadorned style for the poems he published in the SLON press.

A Complex Figure: Aleksandr Iaroslavskii[240]

Iaroslavskii started out as a writer at the age of sixteen in the far-eastern city of Vladivostok. Since his début, his restless, vigorous, and poetically audacious personality proved quite noteworthy. It was in the Russian Far East that young Iaroslavskii privately published his first collection, *Plevok v beskonechnost'* (1917).[241] Well supported by the poet's impressive imagery, as reflected in his choice of title, *Plevok v beskonechnost'* delved deep into immortality, one of his central themes. After spending two years in prison while the region was under the control of the White Army because of his pro-Revolutionary sympathies, Iaroslavskii started to wander across Russia, publishing books that showed his confident use of poetic language:

> Попробую праздничные яства.
> Долго ел я всякую гадость.
> Говорят, что лучшее лекарство
> Собаке и человеку
> Радость!

---

237 N. Orlov, 'Tak prosto', *SO*, 1 (1929), 31.
238 N. Orlov, '*** (Ne pereskazhesh' eto)', *SO*, 2–3 (1929), 13.
239 [We sailed the sea for three days | And suddenly, the excitement. . | ...'Hey, brothers! | Today... | The radio... | Was it not a joke??' | The wind brings the joy of the word | 'The Tsar | is on the gallows'.] N. Orlov, 'Shtorm', *SO*, 3–4 (1929), 4.
240 A full and detailed description of Iaroslavskii's life and work is in Genis, pp. 378–439.
241 Aleksandr Iaroslavskii, *Plevok v beskonechnost'* (Vladivostok: Izd. Dal'nevostochnogo soiuza profsoiuzov, 1917).

В огне мечты крамольной, —
Гигантского роста, —
Вот стоит он свободный и вольный —
Человек просто.[242]

Iaroslavskii reached Moscow in the late spring of 1922. There, he immediately found fertile ground for his poetry. His meeting with the poet Aleksandr Sviatogor[243] and with other young writers who belonged to the new poetic trend of 'biocosmism' was to play a crucial role in his literary career. Biocosmism was one of the many avant-garde literary movements born in Russia after the revolution. The biocosmists followed Nikolai Fedorov's ideas, which influenced various authors, including Andrei Platonov. The biocosmists' 1922 literary manifesto stated that their three main aims were 'the realization of space flight, the realization of personal immortality and the resurrection of the dead'.[244] Iaroslavskii shared with the biocosmist poets the yearning for immortality, which their fascination with science and science-fiction made more expressive.[245] The application of scientific concepts such as anabiosis and cryonics to philosophical-aesthetic reflection proved extremely fertile. The intellectual atmosphere of the biocosmist circles was electric. The poet became a leading personality of the movement, though this soon led to a rift between him and Sviatogor. Iaroslavskii eventually moved to Petrograd, where that same year he founded a parallel biocosmic faction.

During one of the *biokosmisty*'s meetings in Petrograd, Iaroslavskii met Evgeniia Isaakovna Markon, a young intellectual whom he married soon afterwards.[246] His literary activity, in the meantime, became quite hectic. In 1922, he founded *Bessmertie*, a short-lived journal for biocosmist poets. Meanwhile, Iaroslavskii had his first troubles with the Soviet censors, who closed the journal because of its allegedly 'pornographic' contents.[247] Iaroslavskii did not lose hope and continued

242 [I'll try festive delicacies. | For a long time I ate all kinds of filth. | The word is that the best medicine | For dogs and humans | Is happiness! | In the fire of a seditious dream — | High as a giant — | There he is, free and autonomous | A man, simply.] Aleksandr Iaroslavskii, 'Anarkhiia', *Slova i piatna* (1921), 22.

243 Pseudonym of Aleksandr Agienko.

244 Aleksandr Sviatogor, 'Biokosmicheskaia poetika', in Stanislav Dzhimbulov, *Literaturnye manifesty ot simvolizma do nashikh dnei* (Moscow: Soglasie, 2000), pp. 305–14. The English translation is in Veronica Shapovalov, *Remembering the Darkness: Women in Soviet Prisons* (Lanham: Rowman & Littlefield, 2001), p. 66.

245 Information about the Biocosmic movement can be found in Krusanov, II, 387–93, and in the recent volume by Groys on Russian cosmism: Boris Groys, *Russkii kosmizm* (Moscow: Ad Marginem, 2015). Iaroslavskii was quite renowned during his biocosmic period. Some of his poems were translated into Italian by Ettore Lo Gatto, see Alessandro Iaroslavskii, 'La preghiera della terra. Ai nuovi venuti. Versi di Alessandro Iaroslavskii (1918)', *Russia: rivista di letteratura, storia e filosofia*, 2 (1920), 96–99. The biocosmic movement has been recently studied more thoroughly both in Russia and abroad. One of the most recent works is: Nikolai Krementsov, *Revolutionary Experiments: The Quest for Immortality in Bolshevik Science and Fiction* (Oxford: Oxford University Press, 2014), pp. 29–30 and 89–90.

246 On Evgeniia Markon, see Shapovalov, pp. 23–69. The same book includes the biographies of other three women prisoners of the SLON, i.e. Anna Skripnikova (pp. 71–86), Iuliia Danzas (pp. 97–106), and Ol'ga Vtorova-Iafa (pp. 253–61).

247 A. Sherman, 'Aleksandr Iaroslavskii. Biograficheskii ocherk', in Aleksandr Iaroslavskii, *Argonaty*

to publish both biocosmist anthologies and his own poetry collections, choosing bizarre titles such as *Svoloch' Moskva*,[248] *Sviataia bestial'*,[249] and *Argonavty vselennoi*.[250] These early collections show a gradual development in his view on immortality, which shifts from an individual to a cosmic level:

> Усвоив глупую привычку
> Умирать —
> Мы и животных ею заразили:
> Какой-нибудь прекрасный
> Серый
> Кис,
> Которому бы жить
> И жить
> Беспутно
> На радость кошкам
> И на страх мышам, —
> Вдруг умирал внезапно и нежданно.[251]

Although the poet's prosodic and stylistic preferences were far from those of the Russian avant-garde — in the above-quoted lines it is possible to recognise the broken verse which Shershenevich typically used, while Iaroslavskii's violent imagery, his use of neologisms, and the impact of science on his poetry are all features derived from the turn-of-the-century Russian poetry:

> В небесах, между звезд многоточий,
> Не растеряется звездочет. —
> Но и здесь ведь каждый рабочий
> Знает боли свои на перечет. —
> И, если думает о том он,
> Что еще не пора отдыхать,
> И что, может быть, красный гомон
> Загорланит в мире опять, —
> То тогда и ты заалеешь, —
> Старая старуха Москва,
> И о прошлом не пожалеешь,
> Новое восприняв едва![252]

vselennoi (n.p.: Salamandra, 2013), pp. 238–39. The censors wrongly ascribed to the journal the title of one of Iaroslavskii's books of poems, *Sviataia bestial'*. Iaroslavskii made some ironic comments in relation to this mistake, see Genis, p. 387.

248 Aleksandr Iaroslavskii, *Svoloch' Moskva* (Moscow: Suradiny, 1922) (CRSL, Shrift w300/72).

249 Aleksandr Iaroslavskii, *Sviataia Bestial'* (Petrograd: Komitet poezii Biokosmistov-immoralistov (Severnoi gruppy), 1922) (CNLR, Shrift 3.37, Ш.62, P.2, H° 268a).

250 Iaroslavskii, *Argonavty vselennoi*.

251 [Having adopted the silly habit | Of dying — | We have infected the animals with it too: | Some wonderful | Grey | Tomcat, | Who should have lived, | And lived | Dissolutely, | To the delight of female cats | And to the fear of mice, | Has suddenly died, abruptly and unexpectedly.] See L. L., 'Leteiskaia biblioteka — 44', *Kommersant Weekend*, 37 (2009), 63. The author of the quoted article is Luka Leidenskii.

252 [In the skies, among dots of stars, | The astrologer doesn't get lost. | But also here each worker | Knows his troubles as an inventory. | And, if he thinks about | The fact that it's not yet time to rest, | And that, maybe, the red hubbub | Will start raging in the world again, | Then even you

In the 1920s, the poet and his wife travelled across Russia, until a serious railway accident forced Evgeniia Iaroslavskaia-Markon to have both feet amputated and to use prostheses and crutches for the rest of her life. During one of their last journeys before the accident occurred, the couple visited Kem', which had already become a *lagernyi gorod* — a 'prison-camp city'. The town was described in such a way as to evoke its boredom rather than its tragic aura:

> А жизнь кругом безрадостно скользит
> По склизким тротуарам
> Скучной Кеми...[253]

The poem ultimately proved ominously prophetic:

> — Эй, сочинитель бог —
> Наверно ты
> Нарочно нас сюда забросил.[254]

The poem *Kem'* was included in Iaroslavskii's 1926 collection *Koren' iz IA*, which came out immediately after the reconciliation between the Moscow and Leningrad biocosmist factions. Later that year, Iaroslavskii and his wife went abroad; first to Berlin, where they arrived in late September, then to Paris, where they lived for three months. The couple naïvely attracted the attentions of Soviet informers abroad.[255] At a lecture in Berlin which he organized, Iaroslavskii uttered audacious comments on contemporary life in the Soviet Union. As a reviewer put it:

> It was immediately evident that giving lectures had become his profession. Having travelled all over Russia, from Murmansk to Tbilisi and from Petersburg to Vladivostok with his lectures on literature and atheism, the lecturer gave the impression that the dominant mood in Russia [...] is that of uncontrolled and indeterminate fear. Not only the man in the street is frightened, yet more afraid and confused are the people who work for the Soviet authorities, trembling in front of each other in hierarchical order...[256]

If her husband felt free to speak at that time, Evgeniia did the same in a later meeting. Additionally, Iaroslavskii published in the Russian émigré press, including

---

will start to redden, | You old lady Moscow, | And you won't complain about the past, | Barely accepting the new condition.] Iaroslavskii, *Svoloch'*, p. 3.

253 [But all around life slips joylessly | On the slimy pavements | Of boring Kem'...] Aleksandr Iaroslavskii, *Koren' is IA* (St Petersburg and Moscow: Biokosmisty, 1926) (CPD, Shrift 84–10/47, инв. ¹ 27660), p. 98.

254 [— Hey, writer-God — | Perhaps you | Have thrown us here on purpose.] Ibid., p. 99. This way of calling god directly is typical of this period, see for instance Vladimir Maiakovskii, 'Oblako v shtanakh', in *Polnoe sobranie sochinenii*, 13 vols (Moscow: Khudozhestvennaia literatura, 1955–61), I, 194–95.

255 Vladimir Genis, who had access to the personal file of Aleksandr Iaroslavskii, found in it a full record of Iaroslavskii's lecture done by an OGPU agent abroad. See Genis, pp. 403–05.

256 [Сразу видно, что лекторство стало его профессией. Объехав всю Россию от Мурманска до Тифлиса и от Петербурга до Владивостока с лекциями по литературе и атеизму, лектор вынес впечатление, что доминирующее настроение в России [...] безотчетный неопределенный страх. Запуган не только обыватель, еще более боится и растерянно советское начальство, трепещущее друг перед другом в порядке иерархии...] 'V Berline. Lektsiia A.B. Iaroslavskogo', *Rul'*, 1802 (1927), p. 4.

Rul' and *Dni*, which were well known for their hostile attitude towards the Soviet leadership.[257] His most daring act was the open letter Iarsolavskii wrote to the Central Committee of the Communist Party of the Soviet Union and to the People's Commissar of Education Anatolii Lunacharskii, published in *Rul'*, where the poet declared his intention of leaving Russia because it was impossible for a poet to 'live and breathe' in the Soviet Union.[258] More dangerous statements followed in his collection *Moskva-Berlin* which was published in Berlin in 1927.[259] Iaroslavskii's tribute to Esenin, which describes the carrying of Esenin's coffin around Pushkin's statue during the poet's funeral procession, included a most controversial stanza:

> И не знали тусклые, пошлость взвеевая, [sic!]
> Что Есенин Пушкину
> Кинул сквозь гам: —
> — "Тебя пристрелили, мол,
> Александр Сергеевич,
> А я —
> Повесился сам!.."[260]

Although Iaroslavskii and his wife were well aware of the possible consequences of their actions, they decided to go back to Russia. Iaroslavskii, in particular, insisted that they should go back; as a poet, he could not live outside his country.[261] Although he was basically an anarchist, the poet had, in fact, supported the Revolution throughout his life. In the opening poem of his Berlin collection, *Boi. Byt. Plakat*, his beliefs are not too distant from the philosophy of the Soviet leadership. Iaroslavskii's radicalism was supported by his (rare) use of experimental forms apparently inspired by the Russian avant-garde and specifically by their search for a language which could break down conventional syntactic and semantic relations:

> — Ура-ра! –
> Бляди!
> — Кто железом сковал кулаки? —
> — Рука, — рука — на прикладе! —
> В штыки!
> — Ав-вв!
> Хр-р-р-ш-ш-!..
> — Шмяк! —
> Бац![262]

257 Aleksandr Iaroslavskii, 'Pis'mo v redaktsiiu', *Dni*, 31 October 1926; Aleksandr Iaroslavskii, 'Pis'mo v redaktsiiu', *Rul'*, 2 November 1926.

258 Aleksandr Iaroslavskii, 'Otrkytoe pis'mo tsentral'nomu komitetu kommunisticheskoi partii i narkomprosu Lunacharskomu', *Rul'*, 30 October 1926.

259 Aleksandr Iaroslavskii, *Moskva–Berlin* (Berlin: Biokosmisty, 1927) (CRSL, Shrift Rb 10/6654).

260 [And these dull people, lifting up vulgarity, didn't know | That Esenin to Pushkin | Said through the din: | 'They say they shot you, | Aleksandr Sergeevich, | But I | Hanged myself with my own hands!..'] Ibid., p. 30.

261 'Я — более поэт, чем анархист, и без России просто не могу жить' [I am more a poet than I am an anarchist, and without Russia I simply can't live.] See Genis, p. 415.

262 [— Hur-rah! — | Whores! | — Who forged its fists with iron? — | — The hand, the hand

Knowing the risk they were running, the Iaroslavskiis felt an absolute need to go back to the Soviet Union. Evgeniia Iaroslavskaia-Markon's memoirs included words uttered by the poet on their journey back to the Soviet Union: 'I am going to Russia to execute myself... And if the Bolsheviks won't execute me, then so much the better!'[263]

The Iaroslavskiis arrived in Leningrad in the winter of 1927. They then made their way to Moscow, where the poet continued his activity as a leader of the biocosmist movement. His deeds abroad eventually led to his arrest in May 1928. Iaroslavskii was charged with 'counter-revolutionary activity' and sentenced to five years' imprisonment. In a letter Evgeniia wrote to Ekaterina Peshkova after her husband's arrest, she maintained that his Berlin lectures and his contributions to the Russian émigré press had convinced the authorities of Iaroslavskii's guilt.[264]

Despite Evgeniia's attempts to intercede on behalf of her husband, Iaroslavskii was sent to the SLON in the autumn of 1928. His return to Kem' as a prisoner had unexpected consequences. At the Kemperpunkt he met Likhachev, whose words seem to cast a dark shadow over Iaroslavskii:

> At night [the next night] when by the light of lamps [of course, kerosene lamps, known as 'the bat'] all our company was copying down tattoos ['nakolki'] from the criminals on cards [as 'distinguishing marks']. [Involuntarily there] emerged a bossy tone (particularly from I[van] M[ihailovich Andreev]). So, we immediately took sides with the minority (as demanded by our platoon leader, a Pole). The poet Iaroslavskii arrived to copy tattoos. Iaroslavskii began to whisper something in his ear [to the platoon leader]. [The platoon leader menacingly banged his fist on the table and said]: 'You were secret, now you're secret no more'.[265]

Likhachev, who was one of the 227 people interviewed by Solzhenitsyn during his work on *Arkhipelag Gulag*, basically accused the poet of being one of the guards' informers. The episode was later included in Solzhenitsyn's work: most probably, the episode really happened, since it was first reported in the notes Likhachev kept during his SLON experience, notes that were found and published in full in 1995.[266] However, Likhachev apparently mistook Iaroslavskii for the well-known anti-

on the rifle butt! — | Fix bayonets! | Av-vv! | Khr-r-r-sh-sh-! . . | — Bang! — | Zap!] Ibid., p. 10.

263 [Еду в Россию расстреливаться... А если большевики меня не расстреляют, — тем лучше!] Evgeniia Iaroslavskaia-Markon, ' "Klianus' otomstit' slovom i krov'iu ..." ' (Publikatsiia i primechaniia Iriny Flige), *Zvezda*, 1 (2008), 127–59 (p. 132).

264 Moscow, GARF, f. 8409, op. 1, d. 372, l. 169 (Solovki, AAS, copy), 'Ekaterina Iaroslavskaia-Markon. Pis'mo Ekaterine Peshkovoi'.

265 [Ночью [на следующую ночь] при лампах [разумеется, керосиновых — «летучая мышь»] вся наша компания переписывала татуировки [«наколки»] на шпане на карточки [как приметы]. [Невольно у нас] появился начальственный тон (у И[вана] М[ихайловича Андреевского]). Итак, мы сразу стали на сторону меньшинства (как требовал от нас взводный-поляк). Полез переписывать татуировки поэт Ярославский. Ярославский стал что-то шептать на ухо [взводному]. [Взводный грозно стукнул по столу кулаком и сказал]: «Был тайным — станешь явным».] Likhachev, *Izbrannoe: Vospominaniia*, p. 403.

266 The square brackets in the quoted text are indicative of the reconstruction of the original text done by Likhachev.

religious journalist Emel'ian Mikhailovich Iaroslavskii, who was never arrested.[267] Moreover, as Nikonov-Smorodin showed us in his memoirs, Iaroslavskii's fate was not really that of a *seksot*.[268]

> In the half-darkness of the early morning our party went from the Kremlin to the brick factory past the snowy plains of the Holy Lake. We were going there to serve as horses, and therefore they called us 'Vridlo', that is those temporarily functioning as a horse. Each group of five people, harnessed to a sledge by rope straps, was assigned the task of one horse.
>
> The sleepy foreman showed us the stuff we had to carry: bricks. Our head of squad assigned the loads amongst us and we, having loaded up a sledge with a good amount for a horse, set off along a road I did not know.
>
> [...]
>
> We pull together harmoniously, and the sledge, creaking, creeps along a road that had not previously been travelled [since the latest fall of snow].
>
> — Oh, what a road! — grumbles the poet Iaroslavskii, on the right-hand side of the group.
>
> — You are not here to storm the universe — Petrashko laughs. — Here your root will be extracted according to all the rules.
>
> The author of a collection of poems entitled *The root from the I*, who in these poems stormed the universe and dosed the constellations with *salvarsan*, Iaroslavskii, a tall and solidly-built man, is silent, breathing heavily from the effort.
>
> On the second *verst* he begged:
>
> — Let's wait here for a little while. My legs won't move any more...
>
> — Why did you stop? — Yells the head of squad. — Come on, come on![269]

Why, after all, should an informer perform some of the most degrading tasks at the camp? Maybe Iaroslavskii had been punished for his lack of dissimulation, but

---

267 Likhachev wrote down also in his notes the following words: 'Предложение Ярославского [второй раз] стать антирел [игиозным] лектором и сексотом [мне кажется, что Ярославский — был тот самый]' [Proposal by Iaroslavskii [for the second time] of becoming an antirel[igious] lecturer and secret informer [I think that Iaroslavskii was that famous one]]. Likhachev, *Izbrannoe: Vospominaniia*, p. 406. Likhachev confirms Emel'ian Iaroslavskii's sensation that Aleksandr Iaroslavskii had created confusion among the public. For this reason, he tried his best to stop Aleksandr Iaroslavskii from lecturing in public. See Genis, pp. 396–402.

268 Acronym for '*Sekretnyi sotrudnik*', which officially referred to informers.

269 [В полусумраке раннего утра наша партия шла из Кремля к кирпичному заводу мимо снежной равнины Святого озера. Мы шли исполнять обязанности лошадей, а потому и называли нас «вридло», то есть временно исполняющий должность лошади. За каждой группой из пяти человек, впряженных в сани веревочными лямками, был урок одной лошади. Сонный десятник указал нам груз для перевозки — кирпич, наш старший сделал распределения груза и мы, нагрузив сани добрым лошадиным грузом, двинулись по незнакомой мне дороге. [...] Мы дружно тянем, и сани, поскрипывая, ползут по непроезженной дороге. — Ну, и дорога, — ворчит поэт Ярославский, идущий справа. — Это вам не вселенную штурмовать, — смеется Петрашко. — Тут корень из вас извлекут по всем правилам. Автор сборника стихов под названием «Корень из я», штурмующий в этих стихах вселенную и вливающий сальварсан созвездиям — Ярославский, высокий и плотный человек, молчит, сопя от усилий. На второй версте он взмолился: — Подождем здесь немного. Ноги не идут... — Что встали? — орет сзади старший. — Давай, давай!] Nikonov-Smorodin, p. 171. Salvarsan was the name of a substance used to treat syphilis.

it is also possible that Likhachev confused the writer with someone else.[270] Both hypotheses are plausible: however, it must be noted that no other memoirs recall this sensational discovery of an informer among the prisoners.

At the beginning of the second period of the SLON press, Iaroslavskii unexpectedly and immediately found a stage on which he would pursue his literary career. The first 1929 issue of the *Solovetskie Ostrova* included an essay[271] and a poem by the former biocosmist leader:

> На небе разостлали кисею,
> пронизанную холодом и светом.
> Чуть слышно облака вверху снуют,
> Как будто под большим ночным секретом.
>
> Глаза свои сиянью отдаю,
> Растаять я б хотел в сияньи этом,
> Но Север не берет чужих в семью,
> И северная прелесть под запретом.
>
> Ужель мои восторги были зря?
> Не погасай, Полночная заря!
> Все небо бледным [солнцем][272] горит,
>
> И нежный свет таинственно разбросан.
> И, чудится, негромко говорит
> Стихи свои [xxx][273] Ломоносов[274].[275]

Polnochnaia zaria was indicative of Iaroslavskii's departure from the dominant stylistic features of the poetry he had been writing as a free man. It is, in fact, his very first sonnet — which clearly shows how the SLON's cultural microcosm immediately affected him, passing on to him a fascination with a poetic form frequently used in SLON publications.

Unfortunately, apart from the above-quoted texts by Nikonov-Smorodin and Likhachev, we have no clues as to the kind of life Iaroslavskii led at the SLON. What is certain is that the poet did not play an active role in the cultural life of the

---

270 This is highly plausible, as Likhachev wrote: 'он вскоре был освобожден' [He was soon released]. As we shall see, his destiny turned out to be very different. See Likhachev, *Vospominaniia*, p. 406.

271 A. Ia., 'Na kanatnoi', *SO*, 1 (1929), 42–44.

272 The word is barely readable in my copy of the text.

273 The word is unreadable in my copy of the text.

274 This is not a reference to the poem that Lomonosov wrote on Peter the Great's trip to the Solovki (see above, p. 173), but to a philosophical poem in which Lomonosov analysed the phenomenon of aurora borealis by questioning the theories of Christian Wolf. The epigraph in Iaroslavskii's poem is one of Lomonosov's tercets: 'Как может быть, | Чтоб мерзлый пар | Среди зимы рождал пожар?' [How could it be, | That frozen steam | In the middle of winter created a fire]. See Mikhail Lomonosov, *Izbrannye proizvedeniia* (Leningrad: Sovetskii pisatel', 1986), p. 510.

275 [In the sky muslin is spread out, | Pierced by cold and light. | You can just hear the clouds above scurrying, | As if under a big nocturnal secret. || I will give my eyes to the gleam, | I would like to melt in this gleam, | But the North doesn't accept strangers into the family, | And the Northern beauty is forbidden. || Could it be that my enthusiasm was in vain? | Don't fade away, Midnight dawn! | All the sky burns with the pale [sun], || And a gentle light is mysteriously scattered. | And, I imagine, softly reciting | [xxx] his poems Lomonosov.] A. Ia., 'Polnochnaia zaria', *SO*, 1 (1929), 8.

camp. Whatever happened to Iaroslavskii after his literary début at the SLON, his second (and last) poem, included in the fifth and last 1930 issue of the *Solovetskie Ostrova*, revealed a totally different poet. Whereas *Polnochnaia zaria* implied only a change in the form used by the poet, in *Sluchainoi zhenshchine* the adoption of the sonnet form is coupled with Iaroslavskii's dramatic shift towards rather melancholy imagery and unadorned style.

> Весна.. Карелия... и струи рельс...
> И десять лет, распахнутые в вечность...
> И хрупкий смех, змеящийся беспечно
> Вдоль узких губ, вдоль глаз, где бродит хмель.
>
> Есть, вероятно, в этой жизни цель, —
> Она в любви и радости, конечно,
> Но разве можно так бесчеловечно
> Мне прямо в сердце выплеснуть апрель.
>
> На будущее жалобней взгляни
> Как вспугнутые кони, эти дни...
> Но в этих днях над дымкой сероватой,
>
> Сквозь скучный мрак болот и острых скал,
> Лица очаровательный овал
> И лишь улыбка, как письмо без даты.[276]

The bold biocosmist, the fearless avant-garde leader of the Leningrad faction, and the courageous rebel has suddenly been replaced by a soft-hearted lover, who delicately hints at his beloved (in the image of railway tracks) and to a disillusioned man who calmly broods over his situation. The lexical shift is impressive and the prosodic harmony of this second sonnet testifies to Iaroslavskii's renewed inspiration.

The sonnet might have been inspired by Evgeniia's letters. After his arrest, Iaroslavskii's wife tirelessly tried to have him released; but she soon found herself without any money and had to sell newspapers to survive. When she was caught stealing, she was sent into exile in Siberia, where she managed to escape despite her disability. She travelled to the Solovki islands in an extreme attempt to save her husband, probably sending him letters or notes to inform him of her coming. That is perhaps why Iaroslavskii mentioned the letters in his sonnet; that could explain why he wrote about the future using the metaphor of the bolting horses; finally, that might be the reason why his poem was pervaded by a sincere and lucid pessimism. His clear perception of reality, which had accompanied him throughout his journey back to Russia, had not faded away. The poet feared the worst. And the worst, in fact, was awaiting him.

---

276 [Spring... Karelia... And the rail of the streams... | And ten years, wide open to eternity... | And a brittle laugh, winding nonchalantly | Along narrow lips, along the eyes, where intoxication wanders. || There is, probably, a purpose in this life, | It is in love and joy, of course, | But is it possible to so heartlessly | Fling April right into my heart. || Look at the future more mournfully, | These days are like bolting horses... | But in these days above a greyish haze, || Through the dull gloom of marshes and sharp rocks, | The charming oval of your face | And just a smile, like a letter without a date.] A. Iaroslavskii, 'Sluchainoi zhenshchine', *SO*, 5 (1930), 2.

Evgeniia Iaroslavskaia-Markon's desperate flight was interrupted in Kem', where she was arrested in August 1930. She was tried, sentenced to three years, and sent to the Solovki islands. At the SLON, she was sent to the isolation cell at the *zhenskii shtrafizoliator*, on the isle of Bol'shoi Zaiatskii. In the meantime, Aleksandr Iaroslavskii was tried for 'an escape attempt' and sentenced to death. Iaroslavskii was executed on 12 December 1930, the only SLON writer who was shot in the camp about whom we have detailed information. Evgeniia, after learning of her husband's sentence, tried to commit suicide. Having failed, and full of rage, she then attempted to take revenge. On 11 November, she waited for the then SLON's director Uspenskii's visit and, when he arrived, she tried to kill him with a rock she had kept for this purpose. Charged with 'terrorist actions', she was shot on 20 June 1931. According to Irina Flige, Uspenskii insisted on shooting her personally.[277]

The Clandestine Poems

The story of SLON literature went beyond the story of the SLON press. Poets other than those who contributed to the SLON publications were active between 1923 and 1930. Though their works were never officially published, prisoners made sure their poems circulated among other prisoners. These works were read during the night in the barracks or during the prisoners' cultural debates. Prisoners often learned these poems by heart, so that they might write them down once they had left the camp.

The reasons why these poets were not published were various. Some writers did not play an active role in the cultural life of the camp or did not belong to the élite of the camp *intelligentsiia*. Others did not want their works to be published, since publication entailed (to some extent) cooperation with the very regime that had sent them to the camp. Finally, some chose not to publish in order to preserve their freedom of speech.

Total freedom of expression was actually the main feature of the SLON clandestine literary output. Moving outside the scope of censorship institutions and of the chekists' 'watchful gaze', writers felt free to convey their feelings, and did not need to resort to the *loci fidelitatis* or other stratagems. A recurring motif in 'free' literature was, unsurprisingly, religion.

The Orthodox priest Vladimir Lozina-Lozinskii, who had been sent to the Solovki islands at the time of the 'delo litseistov',[278] was one of the most prolific writers. His poems, which almost invariably used iambic or trochaic tetrameters, were pervaded with the poet's impressive spiritual serenity. In a poem he wrote on 19 November 1926, *Solovetskoe*, bright representations of nature are juxtaposed with the image of the monastery — a silent witness to contemporary barbarity:

---

277 Iaroslavskaia-Markon, p. 135.
278 The famous Aleksandrovskii Litsei in Tsarskoe Selo hosted a traditional service in memory of dead students in 1924. Lozina-Lozinskii held the service and prayed for the Tsars as well. All the participants were arrested in February 1925 after witnesses informed the authorities about the events.

Старых башен острых вышек
Еле видный силуэт...
Море дышит и не дышит...
Монастырь молчит в ответ...

Купола его высокий
Не возносят в небо крест,
Только ветер одинокий
Помнит святость этих мест.[279]

Lozina-Lozinskii's poetry, which was characterized by the use of religious and archaic terms and phrases, was imbued with the poet's trust in 'God's final victory' and his belief that the anti-religious massacre which had already killed thousands of innocent people would come to an end. The poem dedicated to Archbishop Ilarion, who died in prison in 1929,[280] clearly shows this tendency:

Настанет день, и в час расплаты
За годы крови и тревог
Когда-то на земле распятый
На землю снова снидет Бог.

С крестом, как с символом спасенья,
Он воззовет и рай и ад:
И, се, расторгнутся каменья,
Се, бездны тайны возвестят.[281]

Ilarion's death was also marked by another poem, written by an anonymous Subdeacon who happened to share his imprisonment with the Archbishop:

Тебе я хвалился стиховой обновой,
Из песенных ульев ты черпал мой мед.
О, белые ночи, о, лов окуневый,
Морошковый праздник — убранство болот.[282]

Bishop Serafim, originally called Mikhail Aleksandrovich Pozdeev, was among the clergymen interested in literature and writing. His story has been recounted in several versions, some of them particularly bizarre.[283] He was described as the last

279 [The old towers' sharp turrets' | Silhouette is barely visible... | The sea breathes and does not breathe... | The monastery is silent in response... || Its high domes | Do not raise up the cross into the sky, | Only the wind, lonely, | Remembers the sanctity of these places.] Vladimir Lozina-Lozinskii, 'Solovetskoe', in Vilenskii, *Poeziia uznikov Gulaga*, p. 57.

280 Archbishop Ilarion (Vladimir Alekseevich Troitskii) was arrested three times — the third time was in 1923. He spent three years at the Solovki islands and he was sentenced to an additional three years just before being released. When he was finally allowed to leave the island, he was sent into exile, but he soon fell ill and died at the hospital of the Leningrad prison.

281 [The day will come, and in the hour of reckoning | For years of blood and worries | Once crucified on earth | God will descend to earth once more. || With a cross as a symbol of salvation, | He will raise both heaven and hell: | And then, behold, the stones will crumble, | Then, behold, the depths will proclaim their mysteries.] Vladimir Lozina-Lozinskii, 'Posviashchaetsia Arkhiepiskopu Ilarionu', in Vilenskii, *Poeziia uznikov Gulaga*, p. 59.

282 [I praised you with a poetic novelty, | From the beehives of my songs you drew my honey. | Oh, white nights, oh, fishing for perch, | The festival of cloudberries, adornment of the marshes.] Ipodiakon, 'Pamiati Arkhiepiskopa Vereiskogo Ilariona', in Vilenskii, *Poeziia uznikov Gulaga*, p. 73.

283 See Arkhiepiskop Ioann, *Solovki — Vtoraia Golgofa. Solovki v istorii Rossii* (Moscow: Pravoslavnaia

member of the Romanov family in disguise. Sent to the SLON towards the mid-1920s, Serafim wrote a series of 'bitter songs', in which the poet's simple and plain language evokes a state of peace attained by the author through suffering.

> Я и так много лет
> Безутешно страдал,
> Много бед и скорбей
> С юных лет испытал.
>
> Я теперь не боюсь
> Ни судьбы, ни людей
> И о прошлом молюсь
> В бедной келье своей.[284]

Religious poetry, however, was not the sole prerogative of priests and monks. One of the major writers in the SLON, who never published any of his works there, was Mikhail Nikolaevich Frolovskii. His poems were pervaded by an intense religious feeling, one of the main characteristics of his works. Frolovskii gave the tragic stories of men and women an unexpected light-heartedness. A former Tsarist officer, he sided with the Red Army during the Civil War. The OGPU caught up with him in 1925 and eventually sent him to the Solovki islands.[285] Frolovskii did not give up poetry even after his arrest. In fact, he managed to use it to address urgent, controversial themes, such as the proud defence of the 'condemned generation', which the poet uttered in his sonnet 'Solovki':

> Упорно шли на север поколенья
> Безмолвною борьбой утомлены,
> Измучены, но не побеждены,
> Победы предвкушая наслажденья.[286]

Frolovskii envisioned a future where the 'exhausted but still undefeated' generations would triumph. His faith in the final defeat of the oppressors, which God himself would support, ran throughout his work. In what can be considered the poet's finest contribution to Solovki literature, *Tiazhelo sdavili svody*, the image of the monastery as a silent witness to events, already used by other religious poets, was

tserkov' Bozhiei Materi Derzhavaia, 2002) and Arkhiepiskop Ioann, *Solovetskii sad* (Moscow: Sofiia press, 2003). As Irina Reznikova (Flige) states, these recollections pertain more to the realm of mythology than to reality (see Reznikova, *Pravoslavie na Solovkakh*, p. 182). Pozdeev is not to be confused with another Episkop Serafim, Aleksandr Alekseevich Protopopov (1894–1937), who eventually became Arkhiepiskop Serafim. Ibid., pp. 183–84.

284 [For so many years I | Inconsolably suffered, | Many troubles and afflictions | Since my youth I have experienced. || Now I'm not afraid | Neither of fate nor people | And I pray for the past | In my poor monastic cell.] Mikhail Pozdeev, 'Ty ne poi solovei', in Vilenskii, *Poeziia uznikov Gulaga*, p. 61.

285 Frolovskii was the main organizer of the service that caused the '*delo litseistov*'. That was the reason for his arrest. More details about Frolovskii's biography can be found in Anna Mozhanskaia, 'Po prochtenii Sinodika M. F. Andreeva', *Vestnik PSTGU*, 2 (2010), 63–64 and Vladimir Murav'ev, *Sviataia doroga: Nikol'skaia ulitsa, Lubianka, Sretenka, Prospekt Mira, Iaroslavskoe Shosse* (Moscow: Algoritm, 2007), p. 131.

286 [Stubbornly to the north went generations | Worn out by a silent battle, | Exhausted, but not defeated, | Foretasting the delights of victory.] Mikhail Frolovskii, 'Solovki', in Murav'ev, *Solovetskaia muza*, p. 9.

Fig. 4.13. Mikhail Frolovskii. ASM

further developed and imbued with new strength. The stones hand down their role as witnesses to God. In addition, a sort of apocalyptic mystique (but deprived of the aestheticizing implications of a Rozanov or a Blok poem) runs throughout the poem. It is instead well-grounded in a reassuring sort of quietness — the result of the poet's faith.

> Тяжело сдавили своды,
> Тяжело гнетет тюрьма,
> Мутным призраком свободы
> За решеткой дразнит тьма.
>
> Спит тюрьма и трудно дышит.
> Каждый вздох — тоска и стон,
> Только мертвый камень слышит,
> Ничего не скажет он.
> [...]
> И когда последний пламень
> Опалит и свет, и тьму,
> Все расскажет мертвый камень,
> Камень, сложенный в тюрьму.

> Спит тюрьма и тяжко дышит.
> Каждый вздох — тоска и стон,
> Неподкупный камень слышит,
> Богу все расскажет он.[287]

Frolovskii's faith did not lead to a complete lack of interest in earthly life. The prisoners' suffering was a recurring theme in his poems, which occasionally tackled the question of his own 'passion'. The poet seemed to focus on irreversibility, on the very impossibility of going back. The day of his arrest becomes, therefore, an insurmountable barrier separating him from the life he had been leading so far which becomes a sheer utopia, leaving no room to hope for the possibility of restoring the past conditions of his life. The poet's bright, prophetic vision (which foreshadows his real ordeal) was supported by his powerful depiction in another poem he wrote at the SLON, *Ia khochu k tebe vernut'sia prezhnim*. This is a truly delicate love poem dominated by the author's disillusionment, which seems to reflect on the changes that the experience of the camp can have on the individual.[288]

> Я хочу к тебе вернуться прежним,
> Прежним быть, как много лет назад.
> Не гляди, что время неизбежно
> Заостряет мой спокойный взгляд.
>
> Стал смелее, тише и суровей,
> Стал суровей, может быть, добрей.
> Слишком много потеряло крови
> Мое сердце в этой смуте дней.
>
> Но зато по-новому быть нежным,
> Нежным быть могу — но не с тобой,
> Я с тобой хочу остаться прежним
> Мальчиком с большою головой.[289]

A large number of SLON poets continued to write well after 1930. Although it could no longer be published inside the camp, SLON (and STON) poetry continued to circulate illegally. Its tone and mood chimed with the general traits of clandestine Gulag poetry, which typically focused on the prisoners' lives, love, and

---

287 [The vaults pressed down heavily, | The prison heavily oppresses, | Like a blurred ghost of freedom | Beyond the bars the darkness taunts us. || The prison sleeps and breathes with difficulty. | Every breath is filled with yearning and groans, | Only the dead stone hears, | It will not tell anything. | [...] | And when the last flame | Will scorch both the light and the darkness, | The dead stone will tell all | The stone piled up to make the prison. || The prison sleeps and breathes heavily. | Every breath is filled with yearning and groans, | The incorruptible stone hears, | It will tell God everything.] Mikhail Frolovskii, 'Tiazhelo sdavili svody', in Vilenskii, *Poeziia uznikov Gulaga*, p. 63.
288 The poem somewhat echoes the Pushkin's *Ia Vas liubil*, see Aleksandr Pushkin, *Lirika, poemy, povesti, dramaticheskie proizvedeniia, Evgenii Onegin* (Moscow: Astrel', 2003), p. 18.
289 [I want to come back to you as I was, | To be the same as many years ago. | Pay no attention to the way that time will inevitably have | Sharpened my serene look. || I have become bolder, quieter and more severe, | I became more severe, and maybe kinder. | Too much blood has been lost | By my heart in this turmoil of days. || But I can be gentle in a new way, | I can be gentle — but not with you, | With you I want to remain as I was | The boy with a big head.] Mikhail Frolovskii, 'Ia khochu k tebe vernut'sia prezhnym', in Vilenskii, *Poeziia uznikov Gulaga*, p. 65.

religion, impregnating its lines with the increasing suffering of those years. Though many poets composed interesting works in the SLON,[290] a poem not written by a professional was nonetheless was one of the most impressive. Its author was Viktor Kharodchinskii,[291] who was born in 1913, the grandson of the Menshevik leader Iulii Martov. One of the last representatives of the left-wing political movement, Kharodchinskii was imprisoned at the age of sixteen and remained at the SLON from 1932 to 1937. His confinement was repeatedly interrupted by periods of isolation at the Sekirka, to which he was sent because of his political protests, as Chirkov tells us in his memoirs.[292] Well aware of what life had in store for him, Kharodchinskii wrote a poem in which he gave voice to his feelings in a lucid and proud way. Death is brutally evoked from the very beginning, where he described the firing squad:

И меня расстреляют.
Печален, спокоен.
Я пройду сквозь тюремную сизую муть.
Пред взводом поставят.
И точен и строен
Ряд винтовок поднимется, целя мне в грудь.
Мимолетно припомню судьбу Гумилева,
Лица милых расстрелянных где-то друзей.[293]

By identifying with Gumilev, Kharodchinskii passed proud, bitter judgement on the perpetrators, whom the poet's gaze challenges just before he is shot:

На солдат посмотрю —
Будут странно суровы
И угрюмо-бездушны глаза палачей.
И спешащим вдогонку годам отгремевшим
Будет страшен секунд утомительный бег.
Залпа я не услышу.
Лицом побледневшим
Вдруг уткнусь в окровавленный
Колющий снег.[294]

Kharodchinskii shared Iaroslavskii's prophetic stance. He was actually shot on 5 October 1937.

---

290 Amongst them are Iurii Chirkov, Ol'ga Adamova-Sliozberg, Ol'ga Vtorova-Iafa (whom I have already mentioned), Viktor Vasil'ev, Lev Martiukhin, and the Udmurt poet Kuzebai Gerd.

291 The author is usually referred to as Khorodchinskii. Antonina Soshina discovered that his real surname was indeed Kharodchinskii. See Soshina, 'Podstrelennye na vzlete', p. 119.

292 See above (p. 66 n. 107). More information about Kharodchinskii is in Tamara Popova (Tsederbaum), *Sud'ba rodnykh L. Martova v Rossii posle 1917 goda* (Moscow: Rossiia molodaia, 1996), pp. 47–52.

293 [And I will be shot too. | Sad, tranquil. | I will go through the grey haze of the prison. | I will be put in front of the platoon. | And precise and orderly | The line of rifles will rise, aiming at my chest. | I will fleetingly recall Gumilev's fate, | The faces of dear friends who were shot somewhere.] Viktor Khorodchinskii, 'Rasstrel', in Vilenskii, *Poeziia uznikov Gulaga*, p. 116.

294 [I will look at the soldiers: | Strangely severe | And gloomy and soulless will be the eyes of the executioners. | And to the years that passed, and now hurry to catch up | The exhausting race of seconds will be terrible. | I will not hear the gunshot. | With my face turned pale | Suddenly I will fall in the blood-stained | Searing snow.] Ibid.

Fig. 4.14. Viktor Kharodchinskii. AAS

Observations on SLON Literature

Throughout this book I have used the term 'SLON literature'. This term underlines the peculiarity of the literary works produced within the Solovki prison camp. The differences between the literature that appeared in prison publications elsewhere in the same period and between the literary works published in the SLON have already been highlighted in previous paragraphs. While a thorough analysis of SLON literature would probably require a separate monograph, it is worth dwelling on some aspects which make SLON literature unique with the aim of providing a base for future works, starting from some general considerations on the creative process inside the camp of Solovki.

First of all, it is important to analyse the context in which creative writing took place. Literary practice inside a concentration camp has in itself some 'atypical features', such as the difficulty of acquiring pen and paper, the risk of being persecuted by the guards/officers or betrayed by fellow prisoners who act as informers, the impossibility of being alone in the barracks, etc. At the SLON in the first years these difficulties were more nuanced owing to the cultural and social dynamics arising from the administration's conduct and to the subsequent cultural controversy that led to the creation of the peculiar literary scene in the SLON. Unfortunately, the sources at our disposal do not provide enough detail for a full analysis of literary practice within the Solovki prison camp. In fact, one of the biggest gaps in the history of the SLON concerns the participants in literary and cultural activities: except for Shiriaev, none of the main authors who wrote for the SLON press produced memoirs. Moreover, Shiriaev himself did not describe his experience as an author. Some memoirs were written by people who were quite close to the cultural milieu of the camp: however, not being prominent authors of the SLON press, they report only their impressions from the margins of the literary life of the camp. It is therefore only possible to offer hypotheses on the topic, relying as far as possible on the scarce sources at our disposal.

The main question that remains unanswered concerns the very act of creation. Except for rare cases, we have no information on how the works that were published in the SLON press were created. We know for sure that some of Kemetskii's texts were composed prior to his arrival on the camp and then printed in SLON publications, and this may have happened with other authors. However, it is clear from the content of the literary works that most of them were created within the camp; it is therefore important to understand how the creative act was realized within the SLON.

Judging from the texts, it is possible to recognize three different situations in which literary works were created. The first, 'regular' type concerns some authors (e.g. Shiriaev himself, but also Litvin, Glubokovskii, Kazarnovskii, etc.) who had the privilege of being prominent figures of the camp press and were therefore able to devote themselves totally to their writing or, in general, to the cultural activities of the camp, working with or at the KVCh. In some cases it is easy to figure out how these authors went about their creative work: it is for example possible to 'see' Litvin wandering around the archipelago collecting ideas for his writing, then going back to the KVCh office and writing his text.

The second type of situation in which authors created their works was similar: the *lagkory* and other people were not constantly pursuing creative activity, but were nonetheless given pen and paper. For instance, prose writers were typically among the few prisoners who were given the opportunity to sit at a desk and write. These writers include, for example, Sof'ia Okerman, who started out as a *lagkorka* and was eventually allowed to publish her more ideologically free works, Iuliia Danzas and Aleksandr Pankratov, who were regularly hired to work at the library and at the krimkab. This, however, does not mean that all prisoners who were also employees in administrative roles could write. These first two examples of how authors could pursue their writing explain why some of these authors had the chance to publish prose works.[295]

The third situation in which authors created literary works is the most fascinating and it is also the one that has a stronger impact on the form of SLON literature: mental or oral composition. Apart from the cases mentioned above, no other prisoners were given desks, paper, or writing implements. Writing, therefore, was above all a mental process, transferred to paper only when the literary works were passed on to the editorial board of one of the SLON publications and eventually published.[296] In order to understand how this happened, one might recall the

---

295 See Akarevich, 'My', pp. 28–29.
296 Some employees sometimes wrote down their poems wherever they happened to be, attempting to hide from the guards (like Likhachev, who kept his notes, see above, p. 256). Others managed to smuggle pens from the offices and wrote poems on cigarette paper or on available newspaper, so that their works could be handed down to other prisoners. This is how Vasilii Ivanovich Smirnov ultimately salvaged several poems by Aleksei Alekseevich Zolotarev. See Moscow, AMM, f. 2, op.

image of the poetry reading in the barracks, recorded in prisoners' memoirs. As already mentioned, sometimes the authors' mnemonic ability was remarkable. Other than Kazarnovskii, Kemetskii, for example, could recite all of his poems by heart — including those he had published abroad some years before. This is a typical feature of Russian culture, which has an impact on the nature of the literary works produced.

The memorization of poetry has been studied effectively by Mikhail Gronas in the article 'Why Did Free Verse Catch on in the West, but not in Russia? On the Social Uses of Memorized Poetry', and later in his monograph *Cognitive Poetics and Cultural Memory: Russian Literary Mnemonics*.[297] Gronas explains in detail — drawing on theories from the field of cognitive poetics — the cultural roots of the Russian tradition of memorization of poetry and the influence of this tradition on Russian verse. The author links this to the limited spread of free verse — 'free' intended here to indicate a particular feature of versification, i.e. the rejection of regular metre — in Russian poetry. In the final part of his article, Gronas focuses on Gulag poetry, explaining the mechanisms by which the memorization of poems becomes crucial for individuals in their daily struggle against the horror of life in the camps. Gronas mentions repetition, one of the key structures of rote learning, which, as explained in another section of his article, has a decisive influence on the moment of composition:

> And it is one of the central theses of the mnemocentric approach that in a mnemonic literary culture, the composition of poetry belongs to the same chain of practices — a mnemonic poet's mind is filled with pre-existing poetic utterances that serve as material or background for the ones being newly created.[298]

In the light of these observations, it is therefore possible to hypothesize that most of the SLON poets created their works without writing them down. This hypothesis is supported by the extensive use of fixed rhyming schemes and the modest length of most of the poems published in the SLON press: moreover, SLON poetry is characterized by the abundance of the alternate rhyming quatrain, which is much easier to learn by heart than other patterns.[299]

It must be noted that oral creation is a typical trait of Gulag literature. Archives, both public and private, contain a massive amount of poetic texts composed orally during detention and later put down on paper by the poets or by what I call the

2, d. 83, l. 103, Lidiia Kititsyna, 'Materialy dlia biografii Vasiliia Smirnova (1882–1941)'.

297 Mikhail Gronas, 'Why Did Free Verse Catch on in the West, but not in Russia? On the Social Uses of Memorized Poetry', *Toronto Slavic Quarterly*, 33 (2010), pp. 166–213; the article was published also in Russian, in a special section of the journal *Novoe Literaturnoe Obozrenie* devoted entirely to the question of mnemonization in Russian culture: see Mikhail Gronas, 'Naizust': o mnemonicheskom bytovanii stikha', *Novoe Literaturnoe Obozrenie*, 114 (2012); idem, *Cognitive Poetics and Cultural Memory: Russian Literary Mnemonics* (New York: Routledge, 2010).

298 Gronas, 'Why Did Free Verse', p. 202.

299 'The alternating rhyme generates two halves of identical structure in the quatrain: their structure is relatively "simple", they tend to stand out clearly, as relatively independent entities'. Reuven Tsur, *Toward a Theory of Cognitive Poetics* (Amsterdam: North-Holland, 1992), p. 129.

'living books' (i.e. people who undertook the task of storing poems in their mind with the hope that they would put them down on paper once freed).[300] The main difference between 'common oral Gulag poetry' and 'SLON oral Gulag poetry' is that the SLON authors had the opportunity to publish their works immediately, sometimes — as seen above — avoiding the intervention of the censors. They most probably had the opportunity to revise their texts before having them appear in print, a privilege which other oral poets of the Gulag did not have and which probably accounts for the overall better quality of SLON poetry when compared to oral Gulag poetry. However, while it is easy to understand why one author would prefer to produce short poems rather than long poems or prose when composing orally within the Gulag, the question becomes more complex in the context of a camp where a poem, even if it had been created orally, could have been put down on paper and printed in one of the camp's publications. Other publications of Soviet camps and prisons in these years are filled mainly with prose rather than poetry. SLON literature is instead mainly comprised of poems, and this fact cannot be explained only by the prisoners' living and writing conditions within the camp.

There is another explanation which goes to the very roots of the creative process, and that is the 'literary pedigree' of the SLON authors. The intellectual education of the SLON prisoners, as well as the official débuts as writers of those who had the chance to publish their work before their arrest, dated back to the first decade of the twentieth century — a decade that saw the absolute predominance of poetry over prose. As a consequence, most of them had been affected by the dominant literary trends of the time. This had a direct effect on both the content (as seen above) and form of SLON literature. One of the most privileged poetic forms — or, to use Gronas's term, 'poetic utterances' — by SLON authors, the sonnet, had been made fashionable by the Symbolists and had been widely used throughout the so-called Modernist or Silver Age. Rusakov's crown of sonnets was a typical product of the sonnet revival that had taken place at the turn of the century and that had brought many poets to the challenge of composing a *venok sonetov*.[301] Far from being merely a source of stylistic influence, Symbolism also affected the SLON authors' thematic preferences. A clear example is given by the motif of the *prekrasnaia dama* or the *neznakomka*, which was part of Symbolist imagery.

An analysis of this poetic image is helpful in deciphering an extremely interesting aspect of poetic creation in SLON, i.e. how these poetic images and structures found their place within a repressive context. In other words: what meaning does the image of a beautiful unknown lady convey within a prison camp? This poetic image, outside its original context, loses its character and acquires a new semantic connotation. In order to explain one of the mechanisms by which this effect is caused, I would rely on Roland Barthes's concept of referential illusion, used by

---

300 See Andrea Gullotta, 'Gulag Poetry: A Mostly Unexplored Research Field', in (Hi-)Stories of the Gulag. Fiction and Reality, ed. by Felicitas Fischer von Weikersthal and Karoline Thaidigsmann (Heidelberg: Universitätsverlag Winter, 2016), pp. 175–92 (p. 183).

301 Among the authors who wrote crowns of sonnets, the most remarkable was Valerii Briusov. See, for instance, Valerii Briusov, 'Chetyrnadtsat' imen nazvat' mne nado...', in Sobranie sochinenii v semi tomakh (Moscow: Khudozhestvennaia literatura, 1974), II, 303.

the French philosopher in order to explain how the 'reality effect' is created in literature. As Barthes explains, 'eliminated from the realist speech-act as a signified of denotation, the "real" returns to it as a signified of connotation; for just when these details are reputed to *denote* the real directly, all they do — without saying so — is *signify* it'.[302] I would like to take the liberty of using this concept not in regard to the question of realism and reality, but to convey a specific literary concept, in this case Blok's image of the *prekrasnaia dama* and its use by Kemetskii. The *prekrasnaia dama* is an important concept within the Russian literary context of the time: it is a 'cultural object' that carries a 'load of significance' that was clear to every reader of the SLON — just like every reader who is familiar with Dante's *Divine Comedy* knows that the Limbo is not just a literary metaphor, but carries other meanings. The choice of the *prekrasnaia dama* by Kemetskii activates a series of meanings that are codified by the SLON reader through a common semiotic system of references. However, by his use of a typical image of Russian Symbolism — i.e. the unfathomable being which the Symbolist poet sees as a magical creature — in the context of the prison camp, Kemetskii denotes a specific 'cultural object' which is signified in a different way, being set in a specific context; this way it breaks away from its previous semantic connotations and creates new ones. Kemetskii's *prekrasnaia dama* is therefore a peculiar case of iconism:[303] it functions on the basis of a referential illusion which has particular characteristics and which I would define as 'metareferential illusion'. As we have already seen, Kemetskii's *prekrasnaia neznakomka* was the well-educated wife of a camp employee. The image therefore has a triple reference: a real one (the concrete woman, i.e. the wife of the camp employee), a referential one (the Symbolist poetic figure of the *prekrasnaia dama*), and a 'metareferential' one (the poetic figure of the *prekrasnaia dama* within its specific and 'concrete' context, i.e. the Solovki prison camp). This triple referentiality is further enhanced by the metaphor which Kemetskii uses in order to identify her — i.e. Aphrodite, the goddess of love and fertility. Kemetskii's choice is therefore deliberate because, together with the image of the *prekrasnaia dama*, it unleashes a hurricane of meanings which give extreme poetic power to the image. The double action of the metareferential icon and its metaphor causes a 'semantic explosion': the unknown lady becomes a tender lover, a prostitute, a goddess, a saviour, the guarantor of fecundity (maybe a symbol of the poet's life), etc.

This process of 'resemantization' or, I would say, 'plurisemantization' through a semiotic shift happens in other literary works. Just to cite one case, Kazarnovskii's literary parodies are based on this same process. Their comic effect is due mainly to this: in his parodies, this 'semiotic shift' can be considered a literary device aimed at stimulating laughter. The literary parody, based on a highly qualitative stylistic mimesis, resemantizes an existing literary text. Just like Kemetskii's *prekrasnaia neznakomka*, the literary parody in this peculiar cultural context works like a patch

302 Roland Barthes, *The Rustle of Language* (New York: Hill and Wang, 1986), pp. 147–48. The words in italics are reproduced as they are in the original. See also Roland Barthes, 'Introduction to the Structural Analysis of Narrative', *New Literary History*, 6 (1975), 237–72.
303 On iconism, see the monograph: Fabrizio Podda, *L'iconicità, la lirica. Immagini, teorie e pratiche poetiche da Leopardi a Zanzotto* (Bologna: I libri di Emil, 2012).

taken from a dress (i.e. Russian literature) and attached to another (i.e. the SLON): it changes both the colour and the 'harmony' of the context, providing it with a specific system of references.

Such operations have a direct effect on the question of literary reception. They also bring to the foreground the question of the particular semiotic dimension of the camp. In fact, the 'immediate public' of the SLON authors was comprised of their fellow prisoners. What I described above as the 'cultural citadel' of the SLON allowed poets to express themselves, keeping in mind the fact that their immediate public was extremely cultured. Their texts were designed also for this peculiar public, with which they created a dialogue through their literary works. Moreover, the readers in the SLON were completely familiar with the nuances of the reality of life in the camp, in a way which is not available to us now — using Leona Toker's words, they had a high semiotic proficiency in relation to the reality of the camp.[304] The above-mentioned 'semantic hurricane' unleashed by Kemetskii's *prekrasnaia neznakomka* was probably clearly interpreted by SLON readers at first glance, while today we need to put in significant effort in order to understand the meaning of this image, and most probably achieve only a partial understanding of it. It is possible (I would say even probable) that these ulterior meanings remained obscure to the camp censors and, in general, to the less cultured strata of the SLON public. This might be another reason why these 'literary patches' (i.e. citations and parodies) were frequently and effectively used by SLON authors, whose awareness of their readers' ability to detect and decode subliminal meanings allowed them to implement this sort of Aesopian use of the word. It guaranteed that the authors of SLON and the intellectuals who read their works would have at their disposal a parallel language which was difficult for the censors and the directors of the camp to decipher.

The question of Aesopian language in itself is rather difficult to resolve, as it is not easy to say whether some of the cases analysed previously in this chapter can actually be considered Aesopian in their nature. I am referring to works such as, for instance, Shiriaev's *Davnee*: it would be difficult to prove that the poet's use of language (e.g. the use of the adjective 'ubogii' for the Solovki monks, which, as seen above, can refer both to them being 'miserable' human beings in moral terms, and to their living in poverty like the saints)[305] was aimed at creating a parallel discourse and a dialogue with the readers. In those years, the 'SLON public' was still being formed, and these texts might have been either an attempt to obtain freedom of expression (in accordance with the use of the *locus fidelitatis*) or simply literary texts that did not have any particular function. Nevertheless the 'fluid' situation of the SLON reading public might be a decisive factor in the analysis of such a question, and may help to support the interpretation of a deliberate use of language in its Aesopian function as something needed to prevent the intervention of the censors and therefore avoid punishment by camp administrators.[306]

304 See Leona Toker, 'Rereading Varlam Shalamov's Stories *June* and *May*. Four Kinds of Knowledge', in Thaidigsmann and Fischer von Weikersthal, pp. 193–203.
305 See above, p. 187.
306 On Aesopian language in the Soviet context, see Irina Sandomirskaia, '"Bez stali i leni":

In fact, it should not be forgotten that while today we know for sure that none of the authors of the SLON press was killed (apart from Iaroslavskii, who was sentenced for a specific reason not connected with his writing, i.e. his attempted escape), tortured, or punished physically for their activity for the camp press, those who wrote had no reason to believe that their texts would not be used against them. Therefore, above all in the first period of SLON publishing, they were aware that every single word they published could potentially be used against them. In addition to that, most of the texts written by the *Svoi* collective or, in general, by the 'ideological' part of the camp administration against the 'camp bohème' were filled with accusations against them which could have led to terrible consequences. Finally, while the contents of the texts published in the press were often frivolous, the authors of the SLON press were well aware of what was happening around them. This is why the *loci fidelitatis* or some ambiguous texts (above all those devoted to the monastery) might have been aspects of a hidden communication code used in times when these authors were not yet free to express their opinions openly, as happened later after Glubokovskii's 'intellectual campaign'. It must be said that Shiraev's silence about this aspect of writing within the SLON in his *Neugasimaia lampada* seems to prove the contrary as far as his texts were concerned — although Shiriaev himself, as seen above, was one of the authors who most flattered the authorities, and this might have led him to be silent about his activity as a contributor to SLON publications.

The same cannot be said about other texts of the first period of press activity in the camp. When considered in relation to the repressive context in which these authors carried out their creative work, some initiatives by SLON authors are indeed surprising for their courage. When Glubokovskii started writing for the SLON press and inaugurated his campaign to eliminate literature that proclaimed its loyalty to the regime, was he aware of how dangerous his words were for him? The same applies to Georgii Rusakov's *J'accuse* about Esenin and Boris Rado's description of Mephistopheles with the mouth of a Red Army Soldier. It is possible to hypothesize that the authors were reassured by the administrators (or by certain individuals among them, e.g. Eikhmans) that their words would not have had any consequences for them. In any case, even if this hypothesis proves correct, the SLON authors were already taking a major risk by trusting the word of the chekists within a Soviet prison camp.

All these considerations of the creative process within a repressive context become even more complicated when taking into account the fact that some authors wrote under a pseudonym. The author who hid behind the pseudonym Boris Rado surely knew that the camp censors and administrators were aware of his identity. Nevertheless, he or she published under a pseudonym. Was there a reason behind the use of pseudonyms? Most of the researchers with whom I talked about this topic (e.g. Ol'ga Bochkareva, Irina Flige, Antonina Soshina) were convinced that it was a specific choice by camp administrators, who needed to show to the 'external public'

Aesopian Language and Legitimacy', in *Power and Legitimacy: Challenges from Russia*, ed. by Per-Arne Bodin, Stefan Hedlund, and Elena Namli (New York: Routledge, 2013), pp. 188–98.

that the authors who wrote for the SLON press were many, and in any case more numerous than was actually the case. This is a convincing reply, as Chekmazov's polemic about the use of pseudonyms[307] unveiled this hypothetical strategy of the administration to the readers (as seen above, his article was part of the 'battle' between the 'ideological' and 'liberal' forces of the camp). However, I believe there is another possible explanation for this. What reason did the administrators have to 'create' authors, if the SLON was full of intellectuals who could have been recruited at any time? Also, some authors — such as Iuliia Danzas or Maks Ginstenberg — decided to publish their texts in the SLON press using the same pseudonym they had used for their literary activity before their arrest, i.e. Iurii Nikolaev and Maks Kiunert. This, in my view, proves that the use of pseudonyms was not only the result of deliberate political actions by the administration of the camp.

This choice made by Iuliia Danzas — and probably by other authors who wrote under a pseudonym — was therefore a conscious one, triggered by other needs. As far as Danzas is concerned, it seems that her decision was motivated by purely aesthetic needs: Iurii Nikolaev was the same pseudonym she used for some texts published before the October Revolution.[308] The same can be said about Maks Gintsenberg/Kiunert. Glubokovskii, on the contrary, once in the camp decided to reject the literary pseudonym he used before his arrest, Boris Veev. Analysing these three authors, and in particular their literary activity before and during detention, it is possible to say that their choice of pseudonym was influenced by aesthetic, personal, and finally political reasons which are tightly linked to the representation of the self.

As a matter of fact, in many cases the choice to use a pseudonym is linked to the question of identity. The author decides to use a *nom de plume* and, with this specific gesture, claims his existence as 'authorial creature' separate from the concrete person who writes the literary texts. His gesture denotes a strong self-consciousness as author: it is almost a divine, mythopoeic action. There are other reasons behind the decision to use a pseudonym, as Max Saunders explains: it might be for intimate reasons (e.g. the author does not want to reveal private information: 'Pseudonymity can provide a protective disguise. White may not have wanted all his acquaintances and neighbours to know of his spiritual doubts')[309] or for promotional needs ('Publishing a book under a pseudonym is one thing. If the name on the title page is unfamiliar, we are likely to assume it belongs to a new writer, or a little-known one').[310] Most probably Danzas, Gintsenberg, and Glubokovskii followed these needs when they used their pseudonyms before their arrest. Once in the camp, their attitudes were different. As seen above, Glubokovskii became one of the 'builders' of SLON culture. He dismissed his old pseudonym Veev and adopted a new one (Emel'ianov), while at the same time, possibly, he used

307 See chapter 3, p. 123.
308 See for instance Iurii Nikolaev, *V poiskakh za bozhestvom: ocherki iz istorii gnostitsizma* (St Petersburg: tip. A. S. Suvorina, 1913).
309 Max Saunders, *Self Impression: Life-Writing, Autobiografiction and the Forms of Modern Literature* (Oxford: Oxford University Press, 2010), p. 112.
310 Ibid., p. 113.

other pseudonyms too. What is more interesting is that Glubokovskii wrote what can be defined as a 'proto-autofiction', *Puteshestvie iz Moskvy v Solovki*, where the author and the main character share the same name and biographical details. His choice is therefore a clear attempt to abandon his artistic past in favour of a new authorial self. Born inside the SLON, Glubokovskii's new authorial self is not only multifaceted, but also projected towards the future, as it recalls the author's own past as a claim for its ideological suitability to be a contributor to the camp press. In a way, Glubokovskii's attitude fits pefectly within Jochen Hellbeck's studies on life-writing during Stalinism, as self-oriented texts often provide testimony of a shared belief in the Soviet experience, even in spite of an individual's own experience of persecution. Individuals' writing is often marked by the need to provide evidence that the author fits into the Soviet ideological framework, thus indicating the interplay between private and political.[311] In Glubokovskii's case, and in the absence of earlier or later self-oriented texts by the author, his career as a cultural activist within the SLON can be seen as an attempt to have a different, proactive approach to his context. It is not by chance that Boris Emel'ianov 'dies' after the closure of the press in 1926 and the release of most of his fellow writers. Once his hopes for liberation and, maybe, for a future artistic career outside the SLON have been frustrated, Glubokovskii's 'multiple selves' lose all their significance and vanish.[312]

Gintsenberg and Danzas's choice of pseudonyms seems to be the exact opposite to Glubokovskii's. When given the opportunity to publish once again within the SLON, they decide to utilize the *nom de plume* they used before arrest. This choice seems to be an identity claim: the person Maks Gintsenberg, or better, the detainee Maks Ginstenberg, presents himself as an author, as Maks Kiunert, and thus affirms his own self-awareness as a poet. And not just a poet, but a poet whose views on life eventually led to his arrest: unlike Glubokovskii, his choice is a result of a statement made 'in the present' on the basis of the author's past. It is, in itself, an act of cultural resistance, just like Iuliia Danzas's and Vladimir Sveshnikov/ Kemetskii's. However, it is probably worth emphasizing that Glubokovskii's main activity was not related to writing even before his arrest: this might suggest that Danzas/Nikolaev's, Ginstenberg/Kiunert's, and Sveshnikov/Kemetskii's choices are related to their stronger self-awareness as writers. In any case, all these authors make deliberate choices in regard to what Irina Paperno calls 'connecting the I and history' in reference to memoirist and diary writers:

311 See Jochen Hellbeck, 'Writing the Self in the Time of Terror: Alexander Afinogenov's Diary of 1937', in *Self and Story in Russian History*, ed. by Laura Engelstein and Stephanie Sandier (Ithaca and London: Cornell University Press, 2000), pp. 69–93; Jochen Hellbeck, 'Working, Struggling, Becoming: Stalin-Era Autobiographical Texts', *The Russian Review*, 60 (2001), 340–59; Jochen Hellbeck, *Revolution on My Mind: Writing a Diary under Stalin* (Cambridge and London: Harvard University Press, 2006).

312 I use the term 'multiple selves' by reference to Suzanne Nalbantian's theory on aesthetic autobiography which, as explained by Claudia Criveller, can be fruitfully applied to self-oriented aesthetic texts in repressive contexts. See Suzanne Nalbantian, *Aesthetic Autobiography: From Life to Art in Marcel Proust, James Joyce, Virginia Woolf and Anaïs Nin* (New York: St. Martin's Press, 1994) and Claudia Criveller, '"Io sono il padrone del mio sogno". Evgenij Charitonov e la letteratura del sottosuolo come costruzione dell'io', *eSamizdat*, 8 (2010–2011), 119–33.

a memoirist tells a story of self forcibly embedded in history: the 'I' confined to a prison barrack; the 'I' in the womb of the mother wandering through occupied territory: the 'I' born of an illicit wartime affair and named after a lover lost in the camps. By tracing one's origins or one's authorship to such formative moments, a memoirist makes a claim to personal selfhood and to authorial legitimacy.[313]

In this context, Iaroslavskii's case is unique. While keeping his name, he changed his literary output enormously. As the cases of Shiriaev, N. Orlov, and Peshkovskii have shown, Iaroslavskii could easily have pursued his formal experiments within the camp. A possible explanation of this can be found by looking at Iaroslavskii in the broader context of Gulag poetry. As is well known, Gulag literature does not contain many formal experiments. On the contrary, it is marked by conventional forms and stylistic features. This can be an effect of the contingencies of the creative process: for instance, a poet who composes orally will not choose experimental forms or avant-garde features, as they are not appropriate for memorization.[314] However, Iaroslavskii's case and that of most authors who wrote literary texts after their liberation seem to suggest that the act of writing trauma cannot be done in innovative and experimental ways. The narration of traumatic events in works of prose is often rendered by realism. Iaroslavskii's experience seems to show how the absence of hope can bring about the end of literary experimentation, just as was the case for Glubokovskii's literary alter ego, Boris Emel'ianov. In Glubokovskii's case, we can only construct this hypothesis on the basis of the silence that followed the phase when the author had an 'experimental self' triggered by his proactive approach to his new situation as a prisoner. Iaroslavskii's poems resemble instead a body of evidence. This might widen the horizon of the long-discussed topic of man's need for art, as stated for instance by Iurii Lotman in the foreword to his *Struktura khudozhestvennogo teksta*.[315] The question of the need for art might therefore be followed by the question of what type of art man needs under extreme conditions and under trauma.[316]

Returning to the question of the scarcity of avant-garde features in the SLON press: avant-garde movements usually reject the past and put themselves forward as an aesthetic tool for the construction of a new culture. Analysing the publications

313 See Irina Paperno, *Stories of the Soviet Experience: Memoirs, Diaries, Dreams* (Ithaca: Cornell University Press, 2009), p. 17.

314 Semen Vilenskii suggested this idea during an interview he gave me on 10 September 2013.

315 Iurii Lotman, *Ob iskusstve: Struktura khudozhestvennogo teksta; Semiotika kino i problemy kinoestetiki; Stat'i; Zametki; Vystupleniia (1962–1993)* (St Petersburg: Iskusstvo-SPB, 1998), pp. 14–19.

316 One should not forget Nina Gagen-Torn's explanation of the need for poetry in a repressive context: 'Poetry in prison is a necessity: it harmonizes consciousness in time. [...] Man escapes from prison, seizing time as if it was space. [...] Those who dig into their consciousness to the very depth of rhythm and give themselves up to it, do not lose their minds. Even the snowflakes dance rhythmically under the light, white against a black sky... The conquest of rhythm is liberation'. [Стих в тюрьме — необходимость: он гармонизирует сознание во времени. [...] Человек выныривает из тюрьмы, овладевая временем, как пространством. [...] Те, кто разроет свое сознание до ритма, — не сойдут с ума... Снежинки в луче тоже танцуют ритмически... Белые на черном небе... Овладение ритмом — освобождение.] Nina Gagen-Torn, *Memoria* (Moscow: Vozvrashchenie, 1994), p. 102.

of the Soviet camps, it is possible to note that avant-garde stylistic features (and sometimes even contents) are typical of the more ideologically charged publications, i.e. those that were more controlled or devoted more effort to celebrating state power, praising a state destined at birth to destroy the past and to construct a new future. This was the case in publications dealing with the 'great construction projects of communism', such as the Belomorkanal. If applied to single literary works, this tendency was confirmed in the SLON press: out of all the authors, the most 'avant-gardist' were Shiriaev in his apologetic phase and Orlov, the most celebratory poet of the second phase of SLON publications. Shiriaev's experience is in this regard emblematic: as long as he celebrates power, he uses avant-garde stylistic features extensively (e.g. *lesenki* and innovative syntax), but, as the literary scene is cleared of ideological constraints, he abandons the avant-garde and utilizes other forms.

Freed from ideological art, the SLON authors tried to defend their world (its values, its cultural references, their strongholds which had been destroyed by the revolution), which was in danger. They did so through the constant reference to social practices and aesthetic models which were typical of the life they had led before their arrest. In this context, the aesthetic references to literary movements that emerged in the period in which these authors were formed are *per se* a mark of cultural resistance. The presence of Europe — where the word Europe identifies a cultural landmark, e.g. in Pankratov's digressions in classical mythology, Leitin's Venice, Kemetskii's Vikings — is a constant feature of the literature of the second period of publications. It is a subliminal sign of the authors' resistance to the new culture that they were forced to accept through re-education in a camp, as were all similar actions, e.g. the academic discussions in the barracks and the oral composition and dissemination of ideology-free poetry.

There are many more features that could be analysed, but two in particular are worth mentioning. The first regards those prose works which, as has been shown, were well-grounded in local, contemporary events and typically privileged camp-related topics. However, even if this is a feature common to all Gulag publications, when realized in the peculiar cultural context of the Solovki prison camp it had an original hallmark, i.e. the predominance of *skaz* — a dominant feature in Litvin's work — which writers felt would fit settings where characters from different classes happened to be described. This device was scarcely used in contemporary Gulag publications; the extensive use of *skaz* was, perhaps, triggered by the outstanding success of theatre in the camp: the readers of the SLON press were at the same time the audience of Solteatr. Litvin might have been aware of this and might have promoted the use of *skaz* in order to render a livelier, almost theatrical depiction of the situations he described.

Secondly, as far as the recurring motifs of SLON literary works are concerned, it is worth emphasizing that the image of traces — traces in the snow, traces in the sand, traces in the ice — are all about traces destined not to remain visible for long. This clearly testifies to the prisoners' urgent need to leave behind a 'trace' of the lives they were leading so far away from the rest of the world, while being aware that any such trace would be shortlived.[317] Also, the presence of terms taken from camp life in the literary works produced in the SLON deserves to be mentioned for one specific reason: as is well known, most of the literary works about the Gulag make extensive use of camp-related terms, making it a constant feature of almost all Gulag literature works. The texts published in the SLON press from 1925 onwards differ substantially from the other works of *lagernaia literatura* and also from the literary works published in the Gulag press of the same years. The use of camp-related terms is mainly limited to works by *lagkory*, with two fundamental exceptions: some prose works (e.g. Litvin's and Shiriaev's texts about the camp) and the humorous poems by Kazarnovskii, where they are used mainly in order to trigger puns. As for the SLON press published before 1925, there the use of *lagernyi leksikon* is quite extensive, as it is in most of the Gulag press.

317 Their fellow prisoners felt the same need and tried to leave their 'trace' visible as long as possible. I have already mentioned Likhachev's effort to keep Kemetskii's literary works alive. Some prisoners copied down in notebooks the literary works that had been published within the camp and handed them to people who could keep them with the hope of salvaging their memory. One such case is the notebook that Sergei Shchegol'kov gave to Aleksandr Solzhenitsyn and that is now kept in the Aleksandr Solzhenitsyn House of Russian Emigration. In this notebook dozens of literary works published in the SLON press are transcribed and sometimes equipped with commentaries. See Moscow, ADRZ, f. 1, op. 1, d. r-377, 'Stikhotvoreniia poetov-uznikov solovetskoi tiur'my'. The same archive holds material on Kemetskii which has been made available to the public in recent times, see Moscow, ADRZ, f. 61, op. 1, dd. 1–22, 'Kemetskii (Sveshnikov) Vladimir Sergeevich'. I have been able to consult the outstanding material kept in it — including the poet's autographs — in May 2017, i.e. when this book was already in its latest stages. I will make use of this material — which helps to contextualize and put into perspective the information outlined in this book on Kemetskii — in further publications.

CONCLUSION

❖

SLON Literature and Twentieth-Century Russian Literature

Russia has been living thirty years in jail
On the Solovki, or in Kolyma,
And only on Kolyma and Solovki
Is the Russia that will forever live...

GEORGII IVANOV[1]

The SLON intellectuals' resistance eventually ended in a movement back to a restoration of Soviet cultural norms. The closure of the press and the removal of typographical equipment to the mainland marked the end of the *intelligenty's* literature in Russia for a long time. Its representatives were wiped out in the years that followed. Some of the authors of SLON literature (Rusakov, Litvin, Evreinov, Peshkovskii, Bedrut) vanished into thin air, some were shot (Kemetskii, Kiunert, Lozina-Lozinskii) or died in the Gulag (Frolovskii). Some were marked for ever by the experience of the Gulag (Kazarnovskii, Glubokovskii, Pankratov). Leitin was once more arrested and found some measure of peace only after the Second World War. Shiriaev managed to emigrate after surviving many difficult years,[2] whereas Likhachev was the only one who was never re-arrested. Chekmazov, who had ended up at the Belomorkanal, was released thanks to the intercession of the chekists because of his political commitment,[3] but disappeared soon afterwards. Other than Chekmazov, who published in the BBK press, only Kazarnovskii succeeded in publishing again. In 1936 a collection of his panegyric poetry was published that completely lacked the splendour of the poems he had written as a SLON prisoner.[4]

---

1   [Россия тридцать лет живет в тюрьме | На Соловках или на Колыме | И лишь на Колыме и Соловках |Россия та, что будет жить в веках...] Georgii Ivanov, 'Rossiia tridtsat' let zhivet v tiur'me', in *Izbrannye stikhi* (Paris: Lev, 1980), p. 105.

2   Once abroad, Shiriaev managed to publish several other books. For a brief survey of his works, see Mikhail Dunaev, *Pravoslavie i russkaia literatura* (Moscow: Khristianskaia literatura, 2000), pp. 515–20.

3   Moscow, GARF, f. 3316, op. 64, d. 1200, 'Vypiski iz protokolov zasedanii Prezidiuma TsIK SSSR o khodataistve OGPU o pomilovanii i sniatii sudimosti s Anisimova K.A., Chekmazova A.M. i dr. s prilozheniem (6.6–25.12.1931)'.

4   Iurii Kazarnovskii, *Stikhi* (Moscow: Goslitizdat, 1936) (CPD, Shrift 1936и/601).

Regardless of the fact that all of them disappeared from the literary scene, leaving unanswered the question about what they would have written after their release (in other words, we will never find out if any of them was a 'potential Dostoevskii'), SLON writers managed to affect the representation of the Solovki and mediated between earlier, pre-revolutionary representations of the Solovki archipelago and later, post-camp images of it. The first and probably most intense representation ever of the Solovki after the closure of the prison camp in a literary work by a Russian writer was produced by an émigré poet. The lines which stand as an epigraph to this section are taken from one of Georgii Ivanov's short poems written in 1949. They hint at the Solovki islands and at the Kolyma as the custodians of a 'real Russia' — a Russia that is doomed to die in the camps.

Ivanov referred to the islands as the epitome of a world of moral values that was forever lost. The SLON was actually lost from view for a while by official writers: its return to the literary scene took place during perestroika. Other than Aleksandr Solzhenitsyn, who in his *The Gulag Archipelago* used the Solovki as a metaphor for the phenomenon of the Gulag as a whole, the SLON also featured in samizdat and *magnitizdat*, in texts by Iurii Aikhenval'd, Aleksandr Galich, and Iulii Kim,[5] where it is always cited in song-poems devoted to Soviet repression, and — this time in official literature — by Iurii Nagibin.[6] But it was in the 1990s that the SLON became more prominent in Russia.

Other than memoirs by former inmates, numerous examples of which — as shown above — became available to Russian readers at this time, in the early 1990s the Solovki are alluded to in various works, such as Iulii Kim's verse drama *Moskovskie Kukhni*, Viktor Astaf'ev's *Tsar'-ryba*,[7] and Evgenii Evtushenko's *Ballada o Mandel'shtame*, where the poet names the Solovki in a text which places Mandel'shtam's poetic revolt in opposition to Maiakovskii's attitude towards the Soviet regime, as well as Pasternak's silent fear of it. Evtushenko does not mention the camp as such, but his reference to the Solovki seems deliberate.[8]

The echo of the SLON intellectuals' deeds appeared from the first time in Russia at the end of the 1990s. In *Moskovskaia saga* (1999) Vasilii Aksenov mentioned the SLON (and the SLON *intelligentsiia*) twice in his characters' words:

> — Probably they will send me to the Solovki — he thought — People say that it is possible to survive there, there are plenty of educated people...[9]

5   See the 1961 song lyrics 'Slava geroiam', written by Gennadii Shpalikov, to which Galich added a stanza on repression, the last word of which is 'Solovki': Aleksandr Galich, 'U loshadi byla grudnaia zhaba', in *Kogda ia vernus': polnoe sobranie stikhov i pesen* (Frankfurt am Main: Posev, 1981), p. 223; the song 'Predosterezhenie', Aleksandr Galich, 'Predosterezhenie', ibid., p. 66; Iulii Kim, 'Moroz treshchit, kak pulemet', in *Pesni Russkikh bardov* (Paris: YMCA Press, 1977), 3, p. 58; Iurii Aikhenval'd, 'Gamlet v 1937 g.', *Po grani ostroi...: proza i stikhi* (Munich: Ekho, 1972), p. 151.

6   Iurii Nagibin, *Poezdka na ostrova* (Moscow: Molodaia gvardiia, 1987).

7   Iulii Kim, *Tvorcheskii vecher: Proizvedeniia raznykh let* (Moscow: Knizhnaia palata, 1990), p. 258; Viktor Astaf'ev, *Tsar'-Ryba* (Krasnoiarsk: Ofset, 1997), p. 94.

8   Quoted in Natal'ia Kravchenko, *Angely ada: stat'i, esse, zametki* (Saratov: Privolzhskoe knizhnoe izdatel'stvo, 2004), p. 101.

9   [— Наверное, отправят в Соловки, — думал он [...] — Там, говорят, можно уцелеть, много интеллигентных людей...] Vasilii Aksenov, *Moskovskaia saga: trilogiia* (Moscow: Izograf,

[...]

— To the Solovki, monsieur! All the respectable people are now taking their holidays on the Solovki. It will clearly be my next address in the near future — the poet replied.[10]

However, the literary work which completely changed perceptions of the Solovki camp was Zakhar Prilepin's *The Cloister*. A popular prose writer, Prilepin spent more than three years composing his novel, which was published in 2014 and gained great success. For the first time after perestroika, the public's attention was directed towards the history of SLON. Prilepin's novel was the first one in post-Soviet Russian literature to be set in its entirety in the Solovki camp. All in all, while making a contribution to preserving the memory of the SLON, Prilepin's postmemorial text[11] had the effect of offering for the first time in Russia a new narrative of the history of the Solovki camp.

In April 2016 another literary work that dealt with the history of the SLON was published. The novelist Evgenii Vodolazkin, who in 2011 had already published a collection of memoirs and photographs on the Solovki and the SLON, wrote the novel *Aviator*, which is partially set at the SLON.[12] It is impossible to evaluate the impact of *Aviator* on the Russian public so soon after its publication, but it is possible to assume that, given the popularity of Vodolazkin, the novel will leave yet another mark on the cultural memory of the camp.

All these works testify that the SLON has become part not only of Russian history and culture, but also of Russian literature. SLON literature is, however, still largely unknown, although it is a truly unique phenomenon in the long history of Russian literature.

The period between 1923 and 1930 marks the progressive expansion of state control over intellectual freedom, and specifically over literature. This process began with the establishment of the Soviet state and continued with the annihilation of Gumilev and the silent death of Blok in 1921, and the increasingly insistent pressure on intellectuals, who were attacked, threatened, and arrested in their hundreds. Many of them chose to emigrate, while others were forced to leave the country. The 1920s were also marked by the shocking suicide of Esenin and were symbolically closed by the suicide of Maiakovskii on the eve of the new decade, which was to be a decade of terror and death. This period saw the ambivalent behaviour of the state which, on the one hand, seemed to be more tolerant towards non-aligned writers (e.g. the 'poputchiki' or fellow-travellers) but, on the other

---

1999), p. 72.

10   [— В Соловки, мусье! Все приличные люди отдыхают сейчас в Соловках, очевидно, это будет и мой адрес на ближайшее будущее, — ответствовал поэт.] ibid., p. 120.

11   On the concept of 'postmemory', see Marianne Hirsch, *Family Frames: Photography, Narrative and Postmemory* (Cambridge, MA and London: Harvard University Press, 1997) and Marianne Hirsch, *The Generation of Postmemory: Writing and Visual Culture after the Holocaust* (New York: Columbia University Press, 2012).

12   Evgenii Vodolazkin, *Chast' sushi, okruzhennaia nebom: Solovetskie teksty i obrazy* (St Petersburg: Logos, 2011); Evgenii Vodolazkin, *Aviator* (Moscow: AST, 2016).

hand, showed a massive interest in bringing intellectual freedom under control or, at least, in establishing effective supervision of the literary world. The end of the decade saw a decisive turn towards state supervision and control. The events of the 1920s foreshadowed what was to come in the 1930s, when literature was finally turned into the handmaiden of the state and played a major role in the 'creation of the Soviet reader' and in the construction of Stalinist 'total art',[13] while many writers became victims of repression.

On the Solovki archipelago the situation was radically different. The birth of a theatre in the camp started an uncontrollable dynamic within the SLON. In the rest of the Soviet Union, the evolution of culture followed state directives aimed at gradually eliminating from society (and therefore from literature) all traces of the old Tsarist world in order to construct a Soviet literature (which would be implemented thanks to Gor'kii in the 1930s); but in the Northern archipelago the political culture was strongly affected by the success of the camp *intelligentsiia* which, thanks to the support of Eikhmans and of his fellow chekists, played a leading role in the cultural activities in the SLON. Isolated on a faraway archipelago, unable to leave the islands during the winter months, the Solovki authorities did not pay enough attention to the need to re-educate the inmates who offered them stunning theatre performances, an extremely interesting press, and other 'cultural services'. Taking advantage of the necessity of showing to the outside world the freedom of the inmates of the SLON, they allowed the *intelligentsiia* to run their '*intelligentnyi gorod*'. The final result of this dynamic was more than surprising. The SLON writers often enjoyed more creative freedom than their colleagues in Moscow or in Leningrad. They reached their goal after a cultural battle that left its traces in the camp's publications. After the first, sporadic manifestations of intellectual freedom on the pages of the *SLON*, the first weapon used in this battle was the pen of Litvin, who did his best to balance expressions of support for the regime with the promotion of an idea of culture that rejected any control over an author's thinking. Shiriaev followed a similar path, though in a more ambiguous way. Their caution proved well-founded, as their fellow inmate Evreinov, who dared to express creative freedom, was excluded from publishing activities. The arrival of Glubokovskii radically changed the position of the *intelligenty*. His essays questioned the very need for encomiastic art that was restricting the potential of SLON literature. Meanwhile, the camp theatre had already shown the achievements and benefits that free art could provide. Following Glubokovskii's action, and with the decisive support of Eikhmans, the SLON authors became increasingly audacious. Shiriaev's literary output was fundamental to the flourishing of the Solovki camp literature. His move from the subtle unconscious rebellion shown in his earlier texts to the full creative freedom of his later literary works inspired other authors such as Evreinov who, when he was finally allowed to publish, wrote poems — some of which were full of religious pathos — without facing further sanctions. In the

---

13   See Boris Groys, *The Total Art of Stalinism* (Princeton: Princeton University Press, 1992) and Evgeny Dobrenko, *The Making of the State Reader: Social and Aesthetic Contexts of the Reception of Soviet Literature* (Stanford: Stanford University Press, 1997).

meantime, the poems published by Rusakov and the works by Rado, Okerman, and Emel'ianov/Glubokovskii were inspired by an incredibly free impulse.

When institutions in Moscow learned about the level of freedom of expression in the SLON, the press was closed down and some of its activities transferred to a minor local journal, despite Eikhmans's attempt to keep it active. Significantly enough, the theatres in the camp, which were by definition restricted to the SLON and its departments on the mainland, kept on producing performances and shows, entertaining the Solovki authorities. When, in 1929, publications were allowed to restart, the rebirth of the two main press organs of the camp presented a polarized picture of Solovki culture. If the *Novye Solovki* followed the trend of the contemporary press and literature of the majority of Soviet camps, the *Solovetskie Ostrova* moved in quite the opposite direction, mostly presenting completely free literary works. Poets like Kemetskii, Pankratov or Leitin could write about harsh imprisonment by adopting stylistic and thematic choices in total freedom, while Kazarnovskii could fully express his humour and creative talent. This happened once again in contrast to the contemporary development of Russian literature within Soviet borders. The literature produced within the Solovki prison camp was tightly linked to the stylistic features of the Silver Age and of the first post-revolutionary years. In this way, one might say that it followed a 'parallel timeline' just as was the case within the circles of the first wave of Russian emigration, developing forms of art that in the meantime had vanished from the main stage of contemporary Russian literature.

The way in which Russian literature developed in the twentieth century has usually been understood in terms of a dichotomy between the literature that developed within the Soviet Union and that which developed in a unique way outside its borders. Soviet literature has also been often divided between an official literature and that which some scholars call 'internal emigration', i.e. works that were not aligned with state ideology and, consequently, not published until perestroika. Within the framework of this subdivision into three different categories (émigré, official, and unofficial Russian literature), SLON literature distinguished itself as a sort of 'literary enclave' which developed within a 'cultural enclave'. SLON literature offers a strange cultural mix of elements that derived from inside the Soviet Union (inescapably part of the 'hidden' world of the Gulag) and outside/ beyond the Soviet Union (through its preservation of Silver Age culture). To use Tynianov's words, SLON literature represented a separate 'series'. In his famous 1929 essay[14] Tynianov described literature as a complex system, a 'series', where all elements and functions were closely connected. Therefore, Tynianov suggested, the study of the evolution of literature needs to be implemented through the study of the 'literary series' and its interaction with other 'series' (e.g. social, political, intellectual, etc.). SLON literature therefore appears as a single, unique, and anomalous 'literary series', isolated from the 'literary series' that were developing in the rest of the country and outside it. Within this 'anomalous series', the functions

14   Iurii Tynianov, *Arkhaisty i novatory* (Leningrad: Priboi, 1929), pp. 30–47 ('O literaturnoi evoliutsii').

of literature, its motifs, and its stylistic features were influenced by the interaction of the peculiar 'political' and 'cultural' series of the camp. Being rooted in a cultural system that was imbued with pre-revolutionary values, SLON literature contains the last traces of pre-revolutionary literature (and in particular of the Silver Age) on Russian soil. This is what makes SLON literature unique within the context of the history of Russian literature.

If Gulag literature has not yet been thoroughly assessed, then the literature produced inside the camps themselves has been almost entirely ignored. Among the most recurrent and recognizable traits of literature published inside other camps is its ideological consistency and the writers' exclusive focus on the theme of imprisonment. The laudatory depiction and the enthusiastic celebration of the camp, together with the fictionalized accounts of prisoners' lives, hardly left any space for other themes. Whenever writers raised more controversial issues, their actions were only temporary. Within the SLON, the exception was the rule. The *Solovetskaia lagernaia literatura* was not so much part of the literature produced within the Gulag. It was a specific form of Gulag literature.

I firmly believe it is time to reconsider Gulag literature from a new perspective, as some scholars are proposing.[15] As the uniqueness of SLON literature shows, the study of 'internal Gulag literature' can bring to light unexpected findings. My hope is that this study will contribute by fostering future research in this field.

---

15   Anne Hartmann, 'Erschöpft und usurpiert. Plädoyer für ein erweitertes Konzept von Gulag-Literatur', in *(Hi-)Stories of the Gulag. Fiction and Reality*, ed. by Felicitas Fischer von Weikersthal, Karoline Thaidigsmann (Heidelberg: Universitätsverlag Winter, 2016), pp. 159–74.

APPENDIX 1

❖

Contents of Selected SLON Publications

I.I. Scheme of publications

Period	Events in the history of the SLON	Publications of the SLON	Publications of the press of the Gulag
1918-27	1923: Foundation of the camp 1925: Frenkel''s promotion and expansion of the activities at an industrial level	1923: *Ostrovok* 1924: *SLON* 1925: *Solovetskie Ostrova* 1926: *Solovetskie Ostrova, Novye Solovki* and the *Materialy SOK* 1927: *Materialy SOK* During this entire period, wall newspapers (*stengazety*) were also published	Period of the *Tiuremnaia pressa* Quoted publications: 1921: *Tiur'ma* (Moscow) 1923: *Za zheleznoi Reshetkoi* (Viatka) 1925: *Golos Zakliuchennogo* (Gomel')
1928-34	1929: Gor'kii's visit 1930: Transfer of the administration to Kem' 1931: Mass movement of prisoners, cadres and technical equipment to the Belomorkanal	1929: *Solovetskie Ostrova* and the *Materialy SOK* 1930: *Solovetskie Ostrova, Novye Solovki, Perekovka* 1931: *Solovetskii Listok* During this entire period, wall newspapers (*stengazety*) were also published	Period of the *Pechat' velikikh stroek kommunizma* Quoted publications: 1930-1932: *Perekovka* (Belbaltlag)
1935-55	1937: the SLON becomes STON 1937: mass shootings. 1939: closure of the camp	No publications	Period of the *lagernaia pressa*

1.2. *SLON*. List of Contents

СЛОН. № 3, 1924.

СЛОН. № 4, 1924.

СЛОН. № 5, 1924.

СЛОН. № 6, 1924.

СЛОН. № 9–10, 1924.

Общественно-политический отдел

Литературный Отдел

Лагерная жизнь

а) Партийная жизнь

   б) Красноармейская жизнь

   в) Лагерные торжества

1.3. *Solovetskie Ostrova*. List of Contents

Соловецкие Острова. № 2, 1925.

Соловецкие Острова. № 3, 1925.

Соловецкие Острова. № 6, 1925.

Соловецкие Острова. № 8, 1925.

Соловецкие Острова. № 1, 1926.

Соловецкие Острова. № 2–3, 1926.

Соловецкие Острова. № 1, 1929.

Соловецкие Острова. № 1, 1930.

Соловецкие Острова. № 2–3, 1930.

Соловецкие Острова. № 4, 1930.

Соловецкие Острова. № 5, 1930.

1.4. *Novye Solovki*. List of Contents (incomplete)

1925.

№ 7 (15/2/1925)
  Уголок лагкора, с. 3.
№ 10 (8/3/1925)
  ТИБЕРИЙ, О хламе, с. 4.
№ 15 (12/4/1925)
  Б. ШИРЯЕВ-АКАРСКИЙ, Заявление, с. 4.
№ 16 (19/4/1925)
  Б/т, с. 4.
№ 21 (24/5/1925)
  Б/т, с. 4.
№ 24 (14/6/1925)
  АЛЬМ., Искусство на острове, с. 2.
№ 25 (22/6/1925)
  АЛЬМ., Искусство на острове, с. 2.
№ 27 (5/7/1925)
  МЫ, Рифмы лагкора, с. 3.
№ 28 (12/7/1925)
  АЛЬМ., Искусство на острове, с. 2.
19 Июля 1925, с. 4.
  И. СУХОВ, б/т, с. 2.
№ 29 (19/7/1925)
  Б/т, с. 4.
№ 30 (26/7/1925)
  А. ЧЕКМАЗОВ, О соловецком прессе, с. 3.
№ 37 (13/9/1925)
  М. КОВЕНСКИЙ, Лагкоры за работу, с. 1.
  ЛАГКОР ЗОРКИЙ, б/т, с.4
№ 44 (1/11/1925)
  ЭН. ЛИ., Семь дней, которые потрясли Соловки, с. 1.
  ЛАГКОРКА М., Как я стала лагкоркой!, с. 3.
  ЛАГКОР 'ИКЕ', — Ой!.. Ай!.. — Бум!.. Бум!.., с. 3.
№ 45 (7/11/1925)
  К., Рыбаки, с. 2.
№ 46 (15/11/1925)
  Н. ЛИТВИН, Маленький Фельетон, с. 1.
  СОЧУВСТВУЮ, Нужны экстренные меры, с. 2.

1926.

№ 2 (10/1/1926)
  СУХОВ, В день первой годовщины, с. 1.
№ 5 (31/1/1926)
  От редацкии, с. 2.

№ 6 (14/2/1926)
    Б. ГЛУБОКОВСКИЙ, Есенин, с. 2.
№ 8 (21/2/1926)
    ЦВИБЕЛФИШЬ, Зубры, с. 1.
№ 21 (23/5/1926)
    Б. ГЛУБОКОВСКИЙ, Иван Панин, с. 5–6.
№ 29 (18/7/1926)
    И. СЛЕПЯН, б/т, с. 4.
№ 34 (22/8/1926)
    Б/т, с. 4.
№ 37 (12/9/1926)
    Б/т, с. 1.
    М.Н. Гернет о Соловках, с. 3.
№ 50 (12/12/1926)
    Б. ЕМЕЛЬЯНОВ, Вы видали хвост у кометы, с. 3.

1930.

№ 1 (5/1/1930)
    Печать и производство, с. 1.
    Ю. КАЗАРНОВСКИЙ, Дружеские эпиграммы к концерту № 3, с. 1.
№ 2 (12/1/1930)
    Ю. КАЗАРНОВСКИЙ, Фельетон, с. 1.
    Вызовы на социалистическое соревнование, с. 1.
№ 3 (15/2/1930)
    М. МАЛЧАНОВ, Типография УСЛОН, с. 3.
№ 10 (23/3/1930)
    Ю. КАЗАРНОВСКИЙ, Собственно говоря, в Кеми (заметки из Блок-нота), с. 2.
№ 13 (6/4/1930)
    Б/т, с. 4.
№ 30 (5/7/1930)
    Б/т, с. 2.

1.5 *Solovetskii Bezbozhnik*. List of Contents (incomplete)

№ 4. (27/9/1925)
    М. Капустин, Гимн безбожник, с. 1.
    Случай в музее, с. 2
№ 7. (7/11/1925)
    То было восемь лет назад, с. 1.
    Отец Венямин — игумен Соловецкий, с. 2.
    Старче Симеон катается, с. 3.

1.6 *Perekovka*. List of Contents (incomplete)

№ 1 (22/10/1930)
    Лапов, Ударникам, с. 2.
№ 2 (2910/1930)
    No literature works published.

APPENDIX 2

❖

Biographies

2.1. Leading SLON Writers and Intellectuals

Bedrut, Vladimir (?–?).
Very limited biographical information on Vladimir Bedrut is found in Shiriaev's book *Neugasimaia lampada*. The author describes Bedrut as the son of a bourgeois family from Moscow (his father was a doctor and his position granted his son the benefit of private study) who, following the tragic events of the Civil War, fell in with gangs of young Muscovites. Arrested for theft, he was transported to the SLON in 1925. No further biographical information is available.

Chekmazov, Aleksei (?–?).
A former Don Cossack, Aleksei Chekmazov dedicated himself to criminal activity during the Civil War and was consequently arrested for the first time in 1921. He was detained in the Sokol'niki prison of Moscow, in Vologda, and in Kargopol' between 1921 and 1922. He was released, but in 1924 his presence is recorded in an *ispravtruddom* (House of Corrective Labour) in Vitebsk. Soon after his arrival at the SLON he started publishing poems. Later he played the principal role in the activities of the *Svoi* collective. Poet, playwright, actor, and critic, Chekmazov led the entire collective right until it was liquidated. After the Solovki he was transferred to the BBK where he earned the good will of the administrators who interceded to obtain his release before the end of his sentence. In 1931 he was released but decided to remain in Medvezh'egorsk as chief editor of the propaganda newspapers of the White Sea–Baltic Canal. When this construction project finished he became the director of a musical instrument factory. No further biographical information is available.

Emel'ianov, Boris (?–?).
There is no documented biographical information on Boris Emel'ianov. Shiriaev, in *Neugasimaia lampada*, represented Emel'ianov as one of the active protagonists of the Solovki camp life. However, Emel'ianov was almost certainly a pseudonym. Most probably, Boris Emel'ianov was the poetic alter ego of Boris Glubokovskii. This is supported by a comparison of the contents and stylistic features of both Emel'ianov's and Glubokovskii's published works. It is unlikely that this was a pseudonym of Boris Evreinov, although this hypothesis cannot be excluded. The least plausible hypothesis is that Boris Emel'ianov was a real person.

Evreinov, Boris Sergeevich (?–?).

Information about Boris Sergeevich Evreinov is very limited. Sources describe his personality as that of a representative of the *intelligentsiia*. He was a poet and a relative of the famous playwright Nikolai Nikolaevich. Evreinov was arrested 4 April 1924 and sentenced to three years of detention on the Solovki. At the end of his period of imprisonment he was again sentenced to three years but this time as an exile to the city of Kerensk in Siberia. He lived in extreme poverty due to the fact that he was never able to find employment. According to Dmitrii Likhachev, Evreinov was shot in Siberia. There is no other documentation from other sources that confirm this.

Florenskii, Pavel Aleksandrovich (1882–1937)

Born in 1882 in Azerbaijan, Pavel Aleksandrovich Florenskii studied Mathematics at the University of Moscow. Later, he joined the Ecclesiastical Academy of the Monastery of Sergiev Posad, where he taught History of Philosophy at the end of his studies. Well appreciated for his immense knowledge of philosophy, mathematics, theology, and physics, Florenskii joined the Russian intellectual elite. He published his first work, *Stolp i utverzhdenie istiny: opyt pravoslavnoi feodichei v dvenadtsati pis'makh*, in 1914, after his ordination as a priest in 1911. His seminars on theology and philosophy were followed by some of the most important figures of Russian culture, such as the writers Andrei Belyi, Vasilii Rozanov, and Viacheslav Ivanov, or the philosopher Sergei Bulgakov. After the revolution, Florenskii continued to teach Mathematics and Theology. In 1918 the plan to publish all of his works in thirty-six volumes was cancelled. In those years his range of interest widened to Electrotechnics and Practical Sciences, turning Florenskii into an inventor. In 1921 he entered the Glavenergo of the Supreme Soviet of the National Economy and simultaneously started teaching at the Vkhutemas (Higher Art and Technical Studios). In 1927 he became the director of the Tekhnicheskaia Entsiklopediia. In 1928 Florenskii was arrested for his religious beliefs. Released after the intervention of Ekaterina Peshkova, he was arrested for a second time on 26 February 1933 and condemned to ten years' imprisonment in SLON. During his stay at the Solovki camp, he continued his research, without being able to publish his findings. In 1937 Florenskii was included in the list of prisoners to be shot following a personal request by the Commissar of NKVD, Nikolai Ezhov. Condemned to the death penalty by an NKVD troika on 25 November 1937, he was executed in Levashovo on 8 December 1937.

Frolovskii, Mikhail Nikolaevich (1905–43).

Mikhail Nikolaevich Frolovskii was born in St Petersburg in 1905 into a noble family (his father was a Tsarist official). In 1914, he was employed by a wealthy family migrating to the United States of America. In 1916 he returned to Russia where he finished his studies in the prestigious Aleksandrovskii Litsei at Tsarskoe Selo. During the Civil War he enlisted with the Red Army and fought between 1919 and 1921. Afterwards he returned to Petrograd, where he found work in the library of the Russian Academy of Sciences. In 1925 he was one of those arrested in the 'delo litseistov', for organizing the traditional mass in the Aleksandrovskii Litsei of Tsarskoe Selo in memory of deceased students. On 23 June he was condemned to three years' imprisonment in the Solovki. In the SLON was assigned to administrative work, but nevertheless remained traumatized by the experience. He wrote poems that were never published in the camp journals. He was released on 19 May 1928 and sent to exile in Sverdlovsk. Here began his life in extreme poverty in exile. He lived in Kem', then in Kudymkar (Perm' region), where he worked as a manual labourer, mainly on road works. On 22 May 1932 he was reunited with his family (his wife Rakhil Afanas'eva, daughter of an exiled minister and his son Nikolai, born that same year) in Briansk. They lived together in extreme poverty, as Frolovskii was unable to find work due to his past as a prisoner in the camp. Nevertheless, he decided to enrol in a correspondence course at the University of Moscow, obtaining a degree in engineering in 1940. He finally found work as an agricultural construction engineer. Arrested again on 24 June 1941, Frolovskii died of pellagra at the Karlag in 1943, without ever publishing his poems.

Glubokovskii, Boris Aleksandrovich (1894–?).
Boris Aleksandrovich Glubokovskii was born in Moscow in 1894. In his youth he took an interest in theatre and began acting in the popular 'Fedor Korsh' theatre. After obtaining a law degree, he dedicated himself entirely to acting. He acted at the prestigious Kamernyi teatr led by Aleksandr Tairov before the revolution. Thanks to his work in Tairov's theatre, he entered the capital city's foremost intellectual and cultural circles. He became an established member of the Moscow bohème. After the revolution he began to publish literary texts in various magazines. From 1918 onwards he was involved in many theatre companies, even moving to the Ukraine for work. In 1922 he returned to the Tairov theatre in Moscow and entered into the circle of Sergei Esenin and Aleksei Ganin, with whom he became close friends. On 1 November 1924 he was arrested together with Ganin and twelve others, and accused of participating in the alleged counter-revolutionary group 'Orden Russkikh fashistov' and for plotting against Soviet power. Due to these accusations he was sentenced on 27 March 1925 by an OGPU college to ten years' imprisonment in the SLON, while Ganin and five other members of the alleged subversive group were executed. Glubokovskii arrived on the Solovki in May 1925 and immediately became one of the principal cultural figures of the camp, dedicating himself to both the theatre and the publishing activity of the SLON. From the moment of his release after his transfer to the Belbaltlag, information on Glubokovskii become obscure. According to most sources, the actor and director returned to Moscow, where he died in 1935, most probably from drug abuse. Other oral sources, however, have stated that he committed suicide in 1932. One last version is that the suicide took place in 1937 while he was in exile in Siberia.

Iaroslavskii, Aleksandr Borisovich (1891–1930).
Aleksandr Borisovich Iaroslavskii was born in Tomsk in 1891. His family moved to Vladivostok immediately afterwards. Iaroslavskii spent his childhood in the

extreme East of Russia and in 1912 he published his first poems. He finished High School in Vladivostok in 1914, and began his university studies one year later in Petrograd. At the same time, he attempted to enrol in aviation school, but was never accepted. Having difficulties with his studies and unable to establish his career as a poet, he returned to the Far East of Russia in 1917; that same year he self-funded the publication of his first collection, *Plevok v bezkonechnost'*. It was the beginning of his literary career and of relative success: over the course of the next few years, Iaroslavskii published numerous collections, all in the Far East of Russia, becoming one of the main poets of that region thanks to his artistic ideas and radical political position. After his arrest by the White Guard during the Civil War for revolutionary acts and after almost two years in prison, he eventually moved to Moscow in 1922 where his artistic ideas allowed him to join the avant-garde group of *Biokosmisty*. Iaroslavskii became the leader of the Petrograd Biocosmist group and the director of the magazine *Bessmertie*, which was soon banned because of its 'pornographic' content. After meeting and marrying Evgeniia Markon, he made a series of trips around Russia, and continued with his poetic activity that led to numerous publications. In 1926 he went abroad together with his wife. They lived in Paris and Berlin, where Iaroslavskii participated in conferences and submitted articles and poems to émigré publications. At the beginning of 1927, the couple decided to return to Russia, well aware of the consequences their actions might have. On 27 June 1928 Aleksandr Iaroslavskii was arrested in connection with the texts he had published abroad. 1 October that same year he was condemned to five years of imprisonment in the Solovki. In the SLON he published sporadically. On 17 August 1930 Evgeniia Iaroslavskaia-Markon made her way to the Solovki in an attempt to help her husband escape. She was arrested and Iaroslavskii was charged with attempting to escape. He was found guilty and on 10 December that same year he was shot. His wife was subjected to the same fate and was executed on 20 June 1931 at the Sekirka.

Kazarnovskii, Iurii Alekseevich (1905–60?).
Iurii Alekseevich Kazarnovskii was born in 1905 in Rostov-on-Don. He started writing at the age of twelve. His first tales were published in 1922 in the journal *Iskra*. Soon afterwards, Kazarnovskii started to work for literary journals and magazines, publishing tales that gained him the respect of the writer Evgenii Zamiatin. On 19 December 1927 he was arrested together with Aleksandr Pankratov, Aleksandr Peshkovskii, and nine other students, part of the literary circle 'Vremennik'. During one of their meetings, one of the students spoke in favour of the Tsar. For this, after an informer told the authorities, all of the students were arrested and condemned to the Gulag. Kazarnovskii, sentenced to five years, wrote a letter to Gor'kii, but received no help. He arrived at the Solovki islands in 1928. When the camp's publications began to appear once more, Kazarnovskii became one of their main contributors. Transferred to the Belomorkanal in 1931, he published in the canal press (some of his poems have been collected in the anthology *Stikhi na Belmorstroe*). Released in 1932, Kazarnovskii

published in 1936 a collection of celebratory poems. In 1937 he was arrested again and condemned to ten years in Kolyma. In December 1938 he was in the transit camp Vtoraia Rechka, becoming allegedly one of the last people to see the poet Osip Mandel'shtam before his death on 27 December 1938. Kazarnovskii was completely traumatized by his experiences in Kolyma. In 1944 he lived in Tashkent, begging and sleeping at the station. Drug addicted, mutilated (he lost all his toes to frostbite), and psychologically unstable, Kazarnovskii was unable to give Nadezhda Mandel'shtam information about her husband when they met shortly after the Second World War. Rehabilitated in 1955, Kazarnovskii moved to Moscow. The last evidence of his life is a letter written from a hospital in Moscow on 25 December 1959, where he wrote to Il'ia Sel'vinskii about his severe health conditions. It is more than probable that he died soon afterwards.

Kemetskii (Sveshnikov), Vladimir Sergeevich (1902–38).
Vladimir Sergeevich Kemetskii (real name Sveshnikov), son of a Tsarist official, was born in Petersburg in 1902. In 1920 his family emigrated. After some months spent in Constantinople, the Sveshnikov family moved to Paris, where Vladimir's poetic talent began to emerge. He joined the poetic group 'Cherez' (one member of which, Boris Poplavskii, dedicated some of his poetry to the young Kemetskii), and frequented the literary salon of the Merezhkovskiis. His political inclinations became more and more radical and he was soon forced to emigrate with all his family. In 1923 he arrived in Berlin, where he passed many turbulent months. Indigence and arguments with his father marked this period. It was after this that the poet decided to publish his poems under his mother's maiden name. After publishing in the Russian émigré press also in Berlin, he decided to return to the Soviet Union, a natural move after he had joined the Jugendbund, the German Komsomol.
He arrived in Moscow in 1926, then moved to Tbilisi where he worked as a journalist for a year until, on 13 September 1927, he was arrested on the charge of espionage and was sentenced to three years' imprisonment. He arrived at the SLON in 1928 and in the second year of his stay he became the most-published author alongside Iurii Kazarnovskii. On 23 March 1930 he was exiled to the region of Arkhangel'sk, then he established himself firstly in Voronezh and then in Orel. There, he was arrested again and exiled to Bashkiria for a further three years. In conditions of extreme poverty during his exile, Kemetskii lived in Ufa and finally in Kerch', in the Crimea region. Here he found work as a proofreader. On 22 August 1936 he was again arrested and sentenced to five years in the Ukhpechlag. On 23 November 1937 he was arrested inside the camp and condemned to capital punishment for 'counter-revolutionary agitation'. He was executed 29 January 1938 in Novaia Ukhtarka in the Republic of Komi, together with poet Nikolai Aleksandrovich Bruni.

Kiunert (Gintsenberg), Maks Nikolaevich (1906–38).
Maks Nikolaevich Kiunert (real name Gintsenberg) was born into a German family in 1906 in Moscow, where his father was an inventor of security systems. He never completed his studies, constantly changing educational institutions

in Moscow and Nizhnii Novgorod between 1915 and 1919. He tried his hand at many different professions, from card dealer to cinematographer, driver to manual labourer. In 1919 he joined the Komsomol, but was expelled in 1921. He began to compose children's songs and in the 1920s he started to frequent the literary circles of the capital. After his first publications in Nizhnii Novgorod journals and work as a journalist for the *Molodaia Rat'* under the pseudonym 'Maks Moskovskii', he decided to publish his poems. In 1924 his first collection, *Goluboi slon* was blocked by the Glavlit. In 1926 Kiunert published his first two slim collections, *Zheltaia siren'* and *Chudesnoe kol'tso*, which showed the poet's declared affinity to the Ego-futurists' poetry. He was arrested on 2 April 1929, while he was preparing his fourth collection for publication, *Muza na vremia*. He was sentenced to three years imprisonment and sent to the SLON. After his release on 6 July 1931 he went to live in the region of Arkhangel'sk. He was re-arrested and sent to the Ukhtpechlag, where he lived in the nearby village of Madmas, which was part of the camp. In 8 December 1937 he was sentenced to death and was shot on 1 March 1938.

Leitin, Boris Natanovich (1893–1972).
Boris Natanovich Leitin was born in 1893 in Viatskoe, close to Iaroslavl'. He obtained a law degree at the Moscow Lomonosov University in 1918. He entered the arena of literature in 1919, publishing a collection of poems, *Vydumannaia liubov'*. With the start of the NEP, he joined a society run by a relative of his wife's. When the director was arrested in 1926, Leitin also finished up behind bars. He was given ten years on 31 May 1926. During his sentence Leitin passed through the Solovki, Kem', and Arkhangel'sk. In the camp he wrote poems that went on to be published in the SLON periodicals, learnt English, and worked on some translations. He was released from SLON on 10 April 1931 and sent into exile to Arkhangel'sk. He later decided to live in Aleksandrov, in the Vladimir region, baptized 'the capital of the one-hundred and first kilometre', meaning that it was the preferred place of residence of former prisoners due to the law that prohibited them from living no closer than one hundred kilometres to the capital and other important cities of the Soviet Union. In Aleksandrov, Leitin dedicated himself entirely to translating, working on Shakespeare and other classics such as Heine, Byron, Goethe, Longfellow, Shelley, Keats, and Hugo. He also translated works of Kyrgyz, Bashkir, Chuvasch, Lithuanian, Azeri, Ukrainian, and Jewish authors. At the beginning of the Second World War, he was treated as a suspicious person and was imprisoned once again, this time in the prison of Aleksandrov. Once released, he continued with his indefatigable translations that allowed him to translate poets from the Nations that signed the Warsaw Pact (Bulgaria, Czechoslovakia, and Romania). On Stalin's death Leitin was rehabilitated. His highly appreciated translations won him admission to the Union of Soviet Writers in 1961. Among his admirers was Kornei Chukovskii. He died in Aleksandrov in 1972. His translations are still being published today: his last translation was *Timon of Athens* by Shakespeare. The literary museum in honour of Marina Tsvetaeva in Aleksandrov houses a collection dedicated to Leitin.

Likhachev, Dmitrii Sergeevich (1906–99)

Born in 1906 in St Petersburg, Dmitrii Sergeevich Likhachev studied Romance and Germanic Literature at the University of Leningrad. On 8 February 1928 he was arrested because of his participation to the KAN (Kosmicheskaia Akademiia Nauk), a student association accused of being a counter-revolutionary organization. Sentenced to five years' detention in the Solovki camp, Likhachev arrived at the Kemperpunkt in October 1928. After being assigned to general work on the archipelago, he managed to be employed in the Krimkab, experiencing the cultural scene of the camp from the inside. During his stay, Likhachev managed to publish his first article in the SLON journal *Solovetskie Ostrova*. Transferred to the Belomorkanal, Likhachev was released on 8 August 1932 as '*udarnik stroitel'stva*' (shock-worker in construction). Between 1932 and 1938 he worked as a proofreader in a few publishing houses in Leningrad. In 1938 Likhachev started his collaboration with the 'Pushkinskii Dom', the Institute for Literature of the Soviet Academy of Sciences. During the Second World War, he survived the Leningrad siege. After the war, Likhachev published many studies of Old Russian Literature. He had a major influence on the study of Medieval Russian Literature, on the textual criticism of Ancient Russian Literature, and on Painting and Visual Art in Medieval Russia. His works gained him worldwide success. Likhachev received honorary doctorates from the University of Torun (1964), the University of Oxford (1967), and the University of Edinburgh (1970). His interests widened, to include the role of St Petersburg in Russian culture and the history of gardens in Russian culture. However, his most successful research is related to the stylistic and formal aspects of Old Russian literary works (especially the *Slovo o polku Igoreve*). His works, as well as gaining him many titles, modified for good the reception of Ancient Russian Literature within the international academic context. Likhachev's political commitment gained him fame amongst the dissidents especially after his official defence of Solzhenitsyn and Sakharov. After the collapse of the Soviet Union, Dmitrii Likhachev became one of the foremost public figures, receiving innumerable awards for his brilliant academic life. Likhachev continued his cultural and political activity until his death, on 30 September 1999.

Litvin, Nikolai Kirillovich (1890–?).

Nikolai Kirillovich Litvin (real name Evseev) was born in 1890 in Mogilev. When he was young his family moved to Odessa where he completed his studies. As a teenager he started journalistic activities that led to collaborations with magazines in Kiev, Rostov-on-Don, and Odessa. In 1913 his talent was displayed in a collection of poems called *Gody miatezhnye*, published thanks to the support of a relation in Novocherkassk. During the First World War he enrolled in the Tsarist troops and when the Civil War broke out he joined the White Army as a war correspondent. In 1920 he moved abroad, first to Turkey, then to Yugoslavia and Bulgaria, where Litvin worked as editor for the Russian emigration publication *Russkoe Delo*. Following a promise from the Soviet government to give amnesty to the supporters of the White Army if they returned to their homeland, Litvin moved to Moscow, where he was arrested on 13 September 1923. After a brief trial, during which the journalist started a hunger strike, he was sentenced to three years' detention for espionage and sent to the SLON. He arrived in Kem' on 3 May and docked on the Solovki on 6 June that same year. His independent spirit caused problems with the camp administration, which defined him as 'hard headed' and undisciplined. For this reason he was held on the island for another six months after his date of release. On 12 November 1926 he was given an additional three years of exile in Siberia. After receiving a 'minus six', he moved to Turkmenistan until 1933. There is no further record of the destiny of Nikolai Litvin.

Pankratov, Aleksandr Aleksandrovich (1903–47)
Aleksandr Aleksandrovich Pankratov was born 1903 near Nizhnii Novgorod. From 1924 he and his family moved to Rostov-on-Don, where he enrolled at the faculty of Philosophy and Literature, in the meantime publishing poems and working as a typist for various institutions. He joined a group of young intellectuals, among whom were Iurii Kazarnovskii and Aleksandr Peshkovskii. Together they were arrested on 19 December 1927. He was charged with being a member of a counter-revolutionary cell. On these grounds, he was sentenced to five years on the Solovki, where he arrived in 1928. On the island he published poems in the journal *Solovetskie Ostrova*. He was freed before the end of his term, on 20 May 1931. After his release there are no traces of him until the outbreak of the Second World War, when he enrolled on a special train for evacuation. He died suddenly in 1947 from causes undocumented.

Peshkovskii, Aleksandr Arturovich (1905–?)
Aleksandr Arturovich Peshkovskii was born 2 November 1905 in Vladikavkaz. Nephew of a famous professor of the University of Moscow, Peshkovskii started a brilliant academic career. On completion of his university studies in Rostov-on-Don in 1926, he gave seminars and lessons in Vladikavkaz. There he published his first poems. His arrest came before that of Kazarnovskii and Pankratov, on 27 September 1927. Peshkovskii was sentenced to ten years in the camp. On the Solovki he joined the Krimkab and became the right-hand man of the director Kolosov. In a short time he proved himself to be a prominent figure in the cultural scene of the camp. According to Likhachev, who left a curious description of him, Peshkovskii was the centre around which all the other poets who published in the *Solovetskie Ostrova* gravitated. He published both poems and prose in the camp periodicals, and in the *Novye Solovki* he worked as a *lagkor*. He was released before his sentence was completed due to a disorder of the nervous system, on 7 May 1931. He was exiled to Kotlas, where he worked as a journalist for the camp press. In the mid-1930s he went back to Leningrad, where he produced articles for various newspapers. He was rearrested on 16 September 1938, and was condemned to an eight-year sentence in 1939. There are no further traces of Aleksandr Peshkovskii.

Rado, Boris (?–?)

There are no biographical documents related to Boris Rado. In all probability it was a pseudonym. Some evidence points to Georgii Rusakov as the true author, other evidence indicates Boris Evreinov. There is no information that allows for a concrete hypothesis.

Rusakov, Georgii Sergeevich (?–?)

There is no document that indicates the date of birth of Georgii Sergeevich Rusakov. He was a student at the St Petersburg Polytechnical University. In the northern capital Rusakov tried to get in touch with the poet Mikhail Alekseevich Kuzmin by sending him some of his own poems, although he never received a reply. In 1921 he was in prison: he published some of his poems in *Tiur'ma*, a journal of the KVCh in the Taganka prison in Moscow. Arrested again on October 7, 1924, he was sentenced to 3 years in the SLON. He docked on the Solovki in 1925 where he published poems in the *Solovetskie Ostrova* and the *Novye Solovki*. On 30 March 1928 he was sentenced to three years' exile in Ioshkar-Ola. In holdings of the St Petersburg archives of the Academy of Science Institute of Russian Literature 'Pushkinskii dom' is a manuscript translation of the prologue to Schiller's tragedy *Kabale und Liebe* signed by a Georgii Rusakov and dated 1935. The manuscript was presented in Moscow to obtain authorization for publication in that same year. This could be a simple coincidence of names, but it could also be the last trace we have of Rusakov.

Shiriaev, Boris Nikolaevich (1889–1959)

Boris Aleksandrovich Shiriaev was born in Moscow in 1889. On the completion of his studies at the faculty of History at the University of Moscow, and after a period of study in Göttingen, he began to contribute to newspapers in the Russian capital. On the outbreak of the First World War, he enrolled as a volunteer in the Tsarist Army, gaining the rank of *rotmistr* (from the German *rittmeister*, i.e. cavalry officer). After taking sides with the White Army at the beginning of the Civil War, he was captured in 1918 but managed to escape. He was arrested again in 1920 and sentenced to death. This, however, was changed after the intervention of Frunze, who ordered him into forced labour for the Red Army. He returned to Moscow in 1922, where he was rearrested after a short period, because of his prior rank as an officer for the White Army. He was sentenced to death again and once again the sentence was commuted to ten years' imprisonment in the SLON. Once on the island he became one of the principal cultural figures of the camp. He was given an early release in 1927 and exiled to Central Asia, where he taught at the University of Tashkent, while also working for some local newspapers. On his return to Moscow, he was arrested for the fourth time in 1933 and exiled to the Rossosh' territory, in the oblast' of Voronezh, where he lived in extreme poverty. At the beginning of the Second World War, Shiriaev collaborated with the Germans and helped run different newspapers. Following the Nazi forces, he managed to emigrate with his family to Berlin. There he was sent to Belgrade and finally in Italy, to the Tolmezzo camp for Displaced Persons, where he ran the risk of being sent back to the Soviet Union. He managed to avoid returning to the Soviet Union and settled in Italy where he published the book *Panorama della letteratura russa contemporanea* [An Overview of Contemporary Russian Literature] using the pseudonym 'Aleksej Alimov'. At the same time, he contributed to Russian émigré publications. He moved to the region of Campania. There he finished his book *Neugasimaia lampada* (1925–50), which was published in New York in 1954. Thanks to its positive reception by the public, he finally escaped the poverty that had crippled him since he emigrated (poverty that had forced him to sell dolls made by his wife). He moved to Sanremo where he died in 1959.

2.2. Other Prisoners and Staff

Adamova-Sliozberg, Ol'ga L'vovna (1902–91)
  Born in Samara, Ol'ga Adamova-Sliozberg later moved to Moscow where she became an economist. After the arrest of her husband, in 1936, she was condemned to serve an eight-year sentence in the Solovki camp between 1936 and 1938. She was later transferred to Kolyma. Freed in 1946, she was arrested for the second time in 1949 and condemned to lifelong exile. After being rehabilitated in 1955, she finally moved to Moscow, where she died in 1991.

Antsiferov, Nikolai Pavlovich (1889–1958)
  Descendant of a noble family, after his graduation Antsiferov taught history and produced state-of-the-art research on the idea of urban space. Arrested in 1929 for his participation in the philosophical-religious circle 'Voskresenie', he was sent to the SLON until 1931, when he was transferred to the Belomorkanal. Freed in 1933, Antsiferov moved to Moscow where he was arrested again in 1937. Freed in 1939, he worked in the State Museum of Literature in Moscow until his death.

Armanov, Sergei (real name: Ivan Andreevich, 1885–?).
  Born in 1885, Armanov was arrested on 9 June 1923 and condemned to two years of imprisonment in a concentration camp. He served his term at the SLON, where he became a key figure in the establishment of theatre in the camp. The last information about him is his date of release, 16 November 1925.

Batser, David Mironovich (1905–87).
  David Batser joined a group of Social-Democrat students in 1921. The following year he was arrested. He spent the following periods in prisons, camps and in detention: 1923–33, 1941–47, and 1949–54. He then moved to Moscow, where he worked as an economist and published samizdat articles on the history of the Social-Democratic movement.

Bekhterev, Iurii Iur'evich (?–?)
  Little information is available on Bekhterev: he obtained a law degree at the University of Kazan and then moved to Petrograd until he became the director of the Viatka prison. In 1924 GUMZ (for which he already worked as an inspector in Viatka) moved him to Moscow. We know he worked there until 1928: no further traces of Bekhterev are available after that date.

Berner, Nikolai Fedorovich (1890–1969)

Born in Kiev in 1890. A poet strongly inspired by Symbolism, Berner lived mainly in Moscow. Arrested in Moscow in 1925, he was sentenced to five years' imprisonment. He served his term on the SLON, from which he departed in 1929. He later emigrated and continued his literary activity. Berner died in 1969 in France. He published mainly under the pseudonym 'Bozhidar'.

Bezsonov (Bessonov), Iurii Dmitrievich (1891–1959?).

Born in Petersburg into the family of an officer of the Tsarist army, Bezsonov followed in his father's footsteps and became an officer during the First World War. At the end of the war, he fought for the White Army. Arrested many times, he was finally sent to the SLON in 1925. While at Kemperpunkt, he managed to escape together with Soserko Mal'sagov and two other prisoners. After few months in Finland, he moved to Paris, where he lived until the end of his life.

Bogdanov, Boris Osipovich (1884–1960)

Born in Odessa, Bogdanov joined the revolutionary movement in 1904 and in 1906 joined the Social Democrats, becoming one of the leading figures in St Petersburg. After the revolution, he was arrested and sent to prisons and camps several times, spending most of his life in prison, until his liberation in 1955. Rehabilitated in 1956, he died in 1960.

Bokii, Gleb Ivanovich (1879–1937)

A communist since his youth, Bokii played an active role in the October Revolution in Petrograd, having been part of the Party Committee of Petrograd since April 1917. He was one of the main figures of the Cheka, as a member of the Central Committee of OGPU and later of the NKVD. He was arrested in 1937 together with Genrikh Iagoda and condemned to death. Bokii was shot in November 1937.

Borin, Makar Semenovich (1875–1936)

An actor, Borin worked in different companies, mainly in the Russian provinces. Arrested in 1924, he was condemned to three years' imprisonment, which he spent on the Solovki. There, he became a leading figure in camp theatre. Freed in 1926 or 1927, Borin died in 1936. He is buried in Ekaterinburg.

Braz, Osip Emmanuilovich (1873–1936)

Born in Odessa, Braz started painting at a young age, and travelled around Europe. From 1895 onwards he moved back to Russia, joining the 'Mir Iskusstva'. A leading Russian artist, Braz was arrested in 1924 for espionage and sent to the Solovki, where he continued his artistic activity. Released in 1926, he lived in emigration from 1928 to his death.

Bulygin, Aleksandr Dmitrievich (1902–86)

Accountant and son of an officer, Bulygin was arrested in 1925 and sent to the SLON, where he spent three years. After being freed, he was forced into exile for three more years. He is the author of mostly unpublished memoirs.

Chekhovskii, Vadim Karlovich (1902–29)

Born in a noble family, Vadim Chekhovskoi became a chemist. Arrested and sent to the SLON, he was one of the technicians employed at the meteorological station. He also provided his expertise for the construction of the railway on the archipelago. He was accused of attempting to escape and shot on 29 October 1929.

Chekhranov, Pavel Dmitrievich (1875–1961)

Chekhranov was the local priest at the Church of St Nikolai in Rostov-on-Don. Arrested in 1923 he was condemned to three years' imprisonment. After spending his term in the Solovki archipelago, he was freed but forced into exile. He served the Orthodox Church throughout his life.

Chirkov, Iurii Ivanovich (1919–88)

Arrested at the age of 15 as a student, Chirkov passed his sentence in the SLON from 1935 to 1938. After being sentenced to another five years, he was sent into isolation in Ukhtizhemlag until 1943. On his return to Moscow, he was arrested for a second time in 1951 and condemned to lifelong exile. After his rehabilitation in 1955 he moved to Moscow, where he became an influential geologist.

Danzas, Iuliia Nikolaevna (1879–1942)

Born in Athens, Danzas moved to Russia in 1889. After finishing her studies at the Sorbonne and becoming a member of the London Psychological Society, she became one of the ladies-in-waiting of the Empress Aleksandra Fedorovna. During the First World War Iuliia Danzas directed the Red Cross. After the war, she worked at the National Library in Petrograd and converted to Catholicism. Arrested in 1923 and sentenced to ten years' imprisonment in a camp, she arrived at the Solovki in 1928. Freed after the personal intercession of Maksim Gor'kii, she reached Germany in 1932. After living in Berlin and Paris, she settled in Rome, devoting herself to religion until her death.

Eikhmans, Fedor Ivanovich (1897–1938).

Eikhmans was a former Latvian rifleman, who entered the Cheka in 1918. In 1923 he became the head of the administration and vice-director of the SLON, maintaining this position until 1929 and even working as director for short periods. He was transferred to Moscow, where he became the head of the 3rd special office of the OGPU and then the first ever director of the GULag. He left the capital to organize the Vaigach expedition (1930–32). Arrested in 1937, Eikhmans was executed on 3 September 1938.

Frenkel', Naftalii Aronovich (1887–1960)

A merchant, Frenkel' was arrested in 1924 for attempting to cross the Soviet borders illegally to escape to Turkey and sentenced to ten years' detention in the Solovki. In the camp he managed to become the head of the economic office of the SLON and later was freed. His methods and theories on the industrial development of camps gained him a place in the cadres of OGPU. In 1928 Frenkel' was moved to Kem'. In 1931 became the site manager of the White Sea–Baltic Canal building site, and in 1933 director of Bamlag. After surviving the Terror, Frenkel' retired and died in 1960.

Gol'dgoer (Gol'tgoer, Gol'dgoeier), Zinaida Iavkovlevna (1880–?)

Born in Moscow as Zinaida Likhacheva, she married Konstantin Gol'dgoer, a general. Arrested in 1924 for making an illegal attempt to emigrate, she was sent to the SLON, where she became one of the most talented actresses of the Solteatr and joined the KhLAM collective. She later worked as a hairdresser both within the camp and in Novgorod, after her release. She was arrested once again in 1937 and condemned to ten years' imprisonment in Siberia. We have no further details on her life.

Gor'kii, Maksim (pen name of Aleksei Maksimovich Peshkov, 1868–1936)
After a turbulent youth Gor'kii published novels and short stories about the poorest social classes that gained him immediate universal success. Arrested in 1905, he lived in Capri until 1913, when he went back to Russia. Following his personal conflict with Lenin, Gor'kii emigrated again from 1921 until 1932, when the writer eventually agreed to work under Stalin constructing the new Soviet literature until his mysterious death in 1936.

Groisman, Anatolii L'vovich (1909–37)
Born in Rechitsia, a town near Kiev, Groisman was arrested on 16 April 1933 for his activity in the Jewish Socialist Union 'Gashomer-Gatsoir'. Condemned to three years' imprisonment, he was later rearrested and shot near Cheliabinsk on 10 October 1937.

Gurskii, Konstantin Petrovich (1911–2008)
After studying in the United States Gurskii was arrested in 1933 in Leningrad, accused of espionage, and sent to the SLON. He left the Solovki after a few months only to be transferred with a group of prisoners to Vaigach. Finally freed in 1955, he moved to Ialta, where he wrote his partly published memoirs.

Iudicheva, Serafima Grigor'evna (1897–1937)
Born in Kozlov, in the region of Tambov, Iudicheva joined the Socialist-Revolutionary Party. Arrested many times, she was finally arrested in Kudymkar (near Perm') in July 1937 and condemned to death for counter-revolutionary propaganda on 7 September 1937. She was shot the day after.

Ivanitskii (Ivanitskii-Vasilenko), Aleksandr Alekseevich (1884 or 1885–1937)
A Socialist-Revolutionary Party member, Ivanitskii worked as a journalist and specialist in the field of agriculture. Arrested many times, he lived in camps and exile for many years. He was shot during detention in a camp in Omsk.

Ivanov, Aleksandr Pavlovich (1886–?)
A former novice at the Pochaev Lavra, once in prison (he was arrested in 1924) Ivanov changed his political position, becoming one of the main antireligious activists, hence his nickname: 'antireligioznaia batsilla' (antireligious germ). He became the head of the historical-architectural office of the Solovki museum in 1925. Other than writing antireligious essays for the SLON press, he directed the profanation of the relics of St Savvatii and St Zosima. After the period he passed in the SLON, all traces of him disappear.

Katanian (Katan'ian), Ruben Pavlovich (1881–1966)
Ruben Katanian was one of the most influential jurists of the Soviet Union, in 1921 he was nominated head of the Soviet Foreign Intelligence Service and

later became a state prosecutor. Arrested in 1938 and condemned to seven years' detention in the Gulag, he passed ten years in the camps. The sentence was extended by five years, from 1950 to 1955.

Kedrov, Mikhail Sergeevich (1878–1941)

A member of revolutionary movements ever since 1899, Kedrov entered the Bolshevik party and, after the revolution, became one of the founding figures of the Cheka. He was given the task of closing down the Solovki monastery in 1920. Arrested in 1937, Kedrov was shot in 1941.

Kenel', Aleksandr Aleksandrovich (1898–1970)

Born in St Petersburg, Kenel' studied composition together with Dmitrii Shostakovich. He was arrested in 1927 for his alleged participation in a counter-revolutionary group and sentenced to three years' imprisonment at the SLON, where he composed music for the theatre. After his release he worked as composer in Khakassia, where he lived and composed for the rest of his life.

Kharodchinskii (Khorochinskii, Khorodchinskii), Viktor Fedorovich (1913–37)

Born in Vyborg in 1913, Kharodchinskii was arrested at the age of 16 for creating and leading a group of young counter-revolutionaries. Condemned to five years' imprisonment, he was later condemned to death and shot in 1937 near Cheliabinsk, five days before his friend Anatolii Groisman.

Khomiakov (Andreev), Gennadii Andreevich (1910–84)

Gennadii Khomiakov started his career as a journalist. He was arrested in 1927 and condemned to ten years' imprisonment. He spent the years 1927 to 1929 in the SLON. After planning an escape that was revealed in 1933 because of an informer, he was spared from capital punishment only thanks to his close friendship with the prosecutor. He remained in the Solovki camp until 1935. During the Second World War he managed to escape to Germany. He is the author of tales about the SLON and memoirs.

Kiselev-Gromov, Nikolai Ignat'evich (?–?)

A former White Guard officer, during his stay at the SLON (1928–30) Kiselev-Gromov collaborated with the OGPU guards. In 1930 he managed to escape to Finland. In 1936 he published his memoirs in Shanghai.

Klinger, Aleksandr (1878–1926)

An officer of the White Guard and a Finnish citizen, arrested and given a term in the Solovki camp, Klinger managed to escape in 1925. Once abroad, he published the book *Solovetskaia katorga: zapiski bezhavshego* in Berlin, just before his death.

Krasikov, Petr Ananevich (1870–1939)

A revolutionary ever since 1892, when he met Georgii Plekhanov, Krasikov entered the Bolshevik Party and, after the revolution, became an influential member of the Soviet establishment, becoming also the Procurator of the Supreme Court of the USSR. Krasikov escaped the purges.

Krivosh-Nemanich, Vladimir Ivanovich (1859 or 1862–1942)

Vladimir Krivosh was born in Serbia in 1859 or 1862. A scholar who had been trained as a linguist, Krivosh was arrested on 24 March 1923 and condemned to death. His sentence was commuted to ten years' imprisonment at the SLON, where he became a key figure for most of the scientific activities of the camp. From 1928, after his early release, he worked for the Soviet state until his death in 1942 while living in evacuation in Ufa.

Kuperman, Iakov (1899–after 1977)

Born into a Jewish Ukrainian family, Kuperman suffered persecution during the 1905 pogrom in the Ukraine. After finishing his studies in economics, he moved to Moscow in 1923, where he worked in the Narkomfin. Arrested in 1929, he was sent to Kem', where he became part of the staff of Frenkel', assisting him in his work at the White Sea Baltic Canal and BAM. He is the author of unpublished memoirs.

Kurbas, Aleksandr (Les') Stepanovich (1887–1937)

Born in Galitsia, Kurbas studied in L'vov and became soon the director of the Youth Theatre in Kiev. He was then the director for theatres in Khar'kov and Moscow. His career was interrupted by his arrest, on 26 December 1933. Sent to Solovki, Kurbas became the last director of the theatre of the Solovki camp. In 1937 he was shot in the mass shooting in Sandormokh.

Kurilko, Igor' (?–1930)

A former officer of the White Army, in the SLON Kurilko became one of the leaders of the overseers. After being nominated *komroty* of the Kemperpunkt, he was involved in the chistka of the Shanin commission following his arrival at the SLON. He was executed in 1930.

Lozina-Lozinskii, Vladimir Konstantinovich (1885–1937)

Born in Petersburg into a family of the *intelligentsiia*, Lozina-Lozinskii finished his studies as a lawyer but later decided to become a priest. Arrested in 1925, he was condemned to ten years' imprisonment in a camp. After spending three years in the SLON, he was freed thanks to an amnesty but was forced to live in exile. From 1934 onwards he lived in Novgorod. In 1937 he was arrested again and executed. He was canonized in 2000.

Mal'sagov, Sozerko Artaganovich (1893–1976)

Born into a noble family of Terek Cossacks, Mal'sagov fought in the First World War and in the Civil War, where he joined the White Guard. Arrested in 1923 and sent to the SLON in the early months of 1924, he managed to escape from Kemperpunkt in May 1925. Once abroad, Mal'sagov became the first former Soviet camp prisoner to publish a book of memoirs. From 1946 he lived in London, where he died in 1976.

Martinelli (Martyneli), Arvid Iakovlevich (1900–38)

Born in the oblast' of Kurlan, Martinelli was nominated Deputy Commander of the SLON. In the mid-1930s he became director of the Dallag (Dal'nevostochnyi lager') until 1937, when he was arrested. Condemned to death, he was shot in 1938.

Meier, Aleksandr Aleksandrovich (1875–1939)

A renowned philosopher, Meier was very active before and after the revolution in St Petersburg/Petrograd/Leningrad. After teaching philosophy in many different institutions, in 1909 he started to work at the Public Library, maintaining that position until his arrest, which came in 1928 with the accusation that he was the head of the religious-philosophical group 'Voskresenie'. He was condemned to death, but his sentence was then reduced. He was sent to the Solovki and then to the White Sea–Baltic Canal camp, Meier was released in 1934. He died in Leningrad in 1939.

Mel'nikova, Tsetsiliia Moiseevna (1923–)

Tsetsiliia Mel'nikova was born in a family of political activists. Her father was Moisei Izrailevich Babin, her mother Dar'ia Solomonovna Tsetlin. Both her parents were arrested and sent to Solovki. She followed them and lived there in the Savvat'evo commune. Afterwards she lived with them in exile in many different places in northern Russia until 1935, when her parents were arrested. She lived the rest of her life with relatives and later emigrated to Germany, where she now lives.

Mogilianskaia, Lada (Lidiia) Mikhailovna (1899–1937)

Daughter of a writer from Chernigov, Lada Mogilianskaia completed her studies in 1917 in Petrograd, where she started her career as a poet. She was arrested in 1929 and condemned to death. Her sentence was commuted to ten years' imprisonment on Solovki, where she remained for a few years before moving to the Belomorkanal and later to the Moscow–Volga canal. Arrested again in 1937, she was shot.

Nikonov (Smorodin), Mikhail Zakharovich (1889–1964)

Born Semen Vasil'evich Smorodin into a peasant family, he finished his studies in 1910, and became an agronomist. Leader of the peasant rebellion against the Soviets during the Civil War, he hid for years before being caught. Arrested in 1927, he was condemned to death. The sentence was commuted to ten years' imprisonment. He arrived at the SLON in 1928 and was later transferred to the Belomorkanal. Nikonov-Smorodin escaped to Finland in 1933. In 1938 he published his memoirs.

Nogtev, Aleksandr Petrovich (1892–1947)

Nogtev joined the Bolsheviks as early as 1918. He was a soldier of the Red Army during the Civil War, and became a member of the Political Police in 1921. Director of the SLON from 1923 to 1930 (but not continuously), Nogtev retired in 1930. In 1938 he was arrested and sent to the Norlag. Freed before the end of his term in 1944, he died of sarcoma in 1947.

Okerman, Sof'ia Aleksandrovna (1895–1973)

An actress, Okerman was born in Brest into a noble family. Arrested on 6 December 1924 together with her husband Viktor (who was shot in the SLON in 1926), she was condemned to three years' imprisonment on the Solovki islands, where she managed to publish tales in the SLON press and act for the theatre. After being released in 1929, she spent three years in exile in Tashkent. In 1935 she was arrested for a second time, in 1938 was arrested again and freed in 1940. She was rehabilitated in 1962.

Olitskaia, Ekaterina L'vovna (1899–1974)

After joining the Socialist Revolutionaries Olitskaia was arrested in 1924 and sent to the Solovki, where she joined the other *politiki* in the Savvat'evo hermitage. She was transferred in 1925 to Verkhneural'sk, and she was later arrested on various occasions until the Thaw. In the 1970s she gave the manuscript of her memoirs to Leonid Plyushch, who smuggled it into West Germany, where it was published. Ekaterina Olitskaia died in 1974 in the city of Uman, in the Ukraine.

Oshman, Arkadii Aleksandrovich (1869–1969?)

A well-known surgeon and specialist in orthopaedics, Oshman was also a professor at the Moscow Polyclinic. He was arrested on 26 April 1935 as a member of an alleged terrorist group and sent to the Solovki archipelago, where he worked as a surgeon in the hospital. Freed in 1942 after spending some years in Chkalov, Oshman supposedly died in 1969, although the sources on the date of his death might not be reliable.

Osorgin, Georgii Mikhailovich (1893–1929)

Born into an upper-class family, Osorgin enlisted to fight in the First World War and upon his return fought for the White Army. Arrested in 1925, was sent to the Solovki, where he was shot in 1929.

Ozerov, Ivan Khristoforovich (1869–1942)

An esteemed economist, Ozerov had published many books on economy and urban planning. A Member of the Russian Academy of Science since 1909, he became a member of the Directive Council of the Russian-Asian Bank in 1911. Ozerov spent a few years of detention in the SLON from 1930 onwards.

Peshkova, Ekaterina Pavlovna (1876–1965)

Ekaterina Peshkova was a leading figure of the Socialist Revolutionary movement, and the first wife of Maksim Gor'kii, married in 1896. Their marriage failed soon afterwards. She began to work in the Political Red Cross before the Revolution, and from 1918 onwards she became its leader, managing to help innumerable prisoners. After the closure of the Political Red Cross during the years of the Great Terror, she retired from public activity.

Petriaev, Pavel Aleksandrovich (1892–?)

Information on Petriaev is scarce. In 1920–21 he was in Moscow, leading the brigades of the Red Army. He was later on Solovki, where he directed the museum of SOAOK and was also vice-director of the newspaper *Novye Solovki*. After Solovki he worked as an agronomist.

Pigulevskaia, Nina Vikotorvna (1894–1970)

Born in a noble family, Nina Pigulevskaia worked in the National Library of Petrograd/Leningrad until her arrest in December 1928. Sent to Solovki, she remained on the archipelago until 1931, when she was moved to Arkhangel'sk because of her poor health. She later came back to Leningrad and became an established scholar in Oriental Studies.

Piskanovskii, Nikolai Akimovich (1887–1935)

Son of a priest, Nikolai Piskanovskii followed his father's path and became a priest in 1909. After the Revolution he was arrested several times and sent to different prisons and camps, including the Solovki camp. He died in 1935 during yet another arrest.

Pomerantsev, Nikolai Nikolaevich (1891–1986)

A famous art historian and restorer, Pomerantsev was sent to the Solovki monastery in 1922 and managed to save some of the treasures of the monastery from destruction. He then worked at the Kremlin Armoury in Moscow until his arrest in 1934. After being released he returned to Moscow, where he continued with his professional activity.

Rozanov, Mikhail Mikhailovich (1902–89)

Born in 1902, Mikhail Rozanov escaped to Manchuria in 1928 but suddenly decided to return. Rozanov was arrested and condemned to ten years' imprisonment. After sixteen months in the SLON, he asked to be transferred to the Ukhtpechlag, where he arrived in 1932. He was freed in 1941, and fought during the Second World War for the Soviets but, after being taken abroad as a prisoner of war, he decided to reside in the West. In West Germany (where he lived until 1970) he published his memoirs. During his stay in the United States (from the 1970s up to his death) he managed to publish the first research work on the Solovki prison camp, based on the comparison of the information reported in many different memoirs.

Rubinshtein, Vladimir Osipovich (1904–93)

A Social Democrat, Rubinshtein was arrested in 1923 and sent to the SLON with the first convoy of political prisoners. In 1925 he was transferred to Verkhneural'sk, where he stayed until 1926. After three years' exile in Narym, he moved to Novocherkassk.

Sapir, Boris Moiseevich (1902–89)

Born in Lodz, Sapir moved together with his family to Moscow in 1914. He joined the Mensheviks and, after the October Revolution, was arrested several times. In 1923 he was part of the group of prisoners who lived in the Savvat'evo hermitage. In 1925 Sapir managed to escape. He lived in Germany, Holland and in the USA.

Schaufel'berger, Arnol'd Sergius (1874–1938).

The second son of the Master of the Imperial porcelain factory in St Petersburg, after the revolution Schaufel'berger fled to the Caucasus, where he lived until 1921. He returned to Petrograd during the NEP after a personal invitation from Lenin. He was arrested in 1924 and sent to the Solovki camp. Thanks to the intercession of the German consulate, Schaufel'berger was freed in 1927 and expelled from Russia in 1928. After that, he lived in Berlin and in Switzerland, where he died in 1938.

Shanin, Aleksandr Mikhailovich (1894–1937)

Born into a peasant family, Shanin joined the Bolsheviks in 1918 and soon began an outstanding career in the VChK–OGPU, of which he became the secretary (from 1923 to 1931). Arrested in 1937, he was shot that same year.

Shchegol'kov, Sergei Vasil'evich (1915–2004)
Shchegol'kov was arrested at the age of 17 after being accused of attempting to take Stalin's life. He was sent to the Solovki camp in 1933, where he spent five hard years. After being freed in 1938, he went back to his work constantly waiting for a second arrest that never came.

Shchesnevskaia, Aleksandra Ippolitovna (1894–1930)
Together with her sister Ksenia Ippolitovna Kopytovskaia, Shchesnevskaia joined the Socialist-Revolutionary party before the revolution. Arrested many times, she died in 1930 in exile in the city of Chimkent (Shymkent) in Kazakhstan.

Shenberg, Pavel (?–?)
We have no official biographical information about Pavel Shenberg. The only biographical data about him are in Shiriaev's *Neugasimaia lampada*, where Shenberg is described as a Jew who lived in Paris and was a former official of the colonial French army. Returned to the Soviet Union, was arrested and sent to the SLON.

Smotritskii, Pavel Fomich (1876–1934)
Born in Khar'kov, Pavel Smotritskii moved to St Petersburg, where he started to work for the Mariinskii Theatre from 1914. He joined the 'Mir Iskusstva' and also found favour at court, compiling a catalogue of the collections in the Winter Palace. Arrested in 1928 and sent to the Solovki, he entered the 'camp bohème', but soon his severe ill health caused his move to the mainland, where he died in a camp hospital.

Solonevich, Ivan Luk'ianovich (1891–1953)
A journalist who fought for the White Guard, Solonevich was repeatedly persecuted as were all of his family members. For this reason, they tried twice to emigrate illegally and were all arrested both times. Upon his second arrest in 1933 Ivan Solonevich was sent to the Belomorkanal, where he managed to obtain good living conditions for himself and his son. They escaped (and so did Ivan's brother Boris) in 1934. Once abroad, Ivan Solonevich became one of the leaders of the monarchist movement among Russian émigrés.

Snegov (pen name: Shtein), Sergei Aleksandrovich (1910–94)
Born in Odessa, Snegov was arrested in 1936 and sent first to Solovki and then to Noril'sk. He spent nine years in the Gulag. Rehabilitated in 1955, he became a successful science-fiction writer. He also wrote two books on the Gulag, *Noril'skie rasskazy* and *Iazyk, kotoryi nenavidit*.

Solov'ev, Emel'ian Ivanovich (?–?)
We have very little biographical information about Emel'ian Solov'ev. A teacher living in Moscow, he was arrested in 1924 and, while on SLON, was kept in hospital and had to endure two surgical operations. He and his wife sought help from the Political Red Cross, but there is no record of an answer. No further information is available about him.

Titov, Leonid Timofeevich (1883–1938)
Titov was born in Moscow, where he lived, working as a doctor. He was arrested

several times (in 1919, in 1921) because of his religious beliefs. When he was preparing to become a priest, he was arrested in 1935 and sent to Solovki, where he worked in the hospital. In 1938 Titov was shot.

Trifil'ev, Aleksei Kirillovich (1872–?)

Born in the family of a priest, Trifil'ev himself became a priest in the church of Saint Nicholas in Rostov-on-Don. Arrested in 1923, he was sentenced to three years' imprisonment and sent to Solovki, where he wrote for the press and collaborated with SOK. After being freed, Trifil'ev was arrested again in 1927. Freed in 1928, he was sent to Kazakhstan and all traces of him disappear.

Uspenskii, Dmitrii Vladimirovich (1902–89)

Son of a deacon, Uspenskii was arrested and later became a collaborator of the Cheka. After the creation of USIKMITL he became director of the SLON from 1930 to 1931, then served in the administration of the building sites of the White Sea–Baltic and Moscow–Volga canals. Uspenskii survived the purges. In 1954 he was removed from the MVD. He died in Moscow in 1989.

Vadbol'skii, Avenir Avenirovich (1898–1930)

A poet, born into a noble family in St Petersburg, Vadbol'skii fought for the White Army during the Civil War. He was arrested in 1925 for counter-revolutionary acts, and was sent to the Solovki camp, where he worked as an accountant for the brick factory until his release in 1928. After two years of exile, he was arrested again and condemned to death. His execution took place on 18 November 1930.

Vangengeim, Aleksei Feodosevich (1881–1937)

Born in the province of Chernigov, Vangengeim became an outstanding meteorologist. His career turned in 1929, when he became the head of the Meteorology Committee of the USSR. In 1934 he was arrested and sent to Solovki, where he continued his activity, surrounded by other scholars. Vangengeim was shot in 1937 in Sandormokh.

Vas'kov (Vasko), Rodion Ivanovich (1891–1961)

Rodion Vas'kov joined the Cheka in 1918. He volunteered to work at Solovki since 1923, when he became vice director of the first section until 1926. He later became secretary of the USLON. After being vice-director of the Vishera ITL in 1932, he worked for years in the MGB. He was arrested in 1952 and sentenced to five years' imprisonment in a camp with the charge of having abused his power.

Vasil'ev, Viktor Georgievich (1916–2002)

Born in Moscow, Viktor Vasil'ev was arrested in 1932, when he was only 16. He was sent to the Solovki and then moved to other camps. He lived in the camps until 1950, when he was exiled to Ukhta. He finally moved back to Moscow in 1973. He wrote poems during his whole life.

Vinogradov, Nikolai Nikolaevich (1876–1938)

An ethnographer, Vinogradov worked in different institutions in Kostroma until 1926, when he was arrested and sent to Solovki. There he worked with SOK, of which he became the head from 1928 to 1932. After being freed, he settled in Petrozavodsk, where he pursued his scholarly activity until 1937, when he was arrested. He was shot in 1938.

Volkov, Oleg Vasil'evich (1900–96)

Born into a noble family from the region of Tver', Volkov worked as a translator at the end of the Civil War. In 1928 he was arrested and condemned to three years' imprisonment. He spent his entire sentence in the SLON. Freed, he was arrested another four times, spending in total twenty-seven years in different camps. After moving to Moscow and publishing his memoirs, he was awarded the Gor'kii State Prize of the Russian Federation in 1991. He died in Moscow in 1996.

Vtorova-Iafa, Ol'ga Viktorovna (1876–1959)

Vtorova-Iafa was born in St Petersburg, and was arrested in 1929 for her participation in the religious-philosophical group 'Voskresenie'. She was condemned to three years' detention and was sent along with her fellow-accused to the SLON. She was freed in 1931, and went back to Leningrad only in 1934. A survivor of the Siege of Leningrad, she wrote her memoirs in the 1950s.

Zaitsev, Ivan Matveevich (1879–1934)

A former Major General of the Tsarist Army, during the Civil War Zaitsev was arrested many times but always managed to escape. After emigrating, he returned to the Soviet Union in 1924 after the amnesty for former White Guard soldiers. Arrested in 1924 and sent to the Solovki, he was then forced to live in exile in the Komi Republic. He managed to travel until he reached the Chinese border in 1929. While in China, he committed suicide.

BIBLIOGRAPHY

❖

Archival material

Cologne, ATsM, Rubinshtein, Vladimir, *Vospominaniia*

Milan, AGFF, 'Dante Serpo'

Milan, AGFF, 'Luciano Visintini'

Milan, AGFF, 'Giorgio Perosio'

Moscow, ADRZ, f. 1, op. 1, d. r-377, 'Stikhotvoreniia poetov-uznikov solovetskoi tiur'my'

Moscow, ADRZ, f. 61, op. 1, dd. 1–22, 'Kemetskii (Sveshnikov) Vladimir Sergeevich'

Moscow, AG, KG-P 44–11-X, Boris Leitin, 'Pis'ma M. Gor'komu'

Moscow, AG, KG-R3I 1–136, Iuliia Danzas, 'Perepiska s M. Gor'kim'

Moscow, AG, KhPG-41–13-6, Maksim Gor'kii, *Solovki*, rukopis'

Moscow, AMM, f. 1, op. 1, d. 2576, 'Kurbas, Aleksandr Stepanovich'

Moscow, AMM, f. 1, op. 1, d. 3503, 'Panov, Andrei Stepanovich'

Moscow, AMM, f. 1, op. 4, d. 4312, 'Pliuzhnik, Evgenii Pavlovich'

Moscow, AMM, f. 2, op. 1, d. 77, Iakov Kuperman, *Piatdesiat' let 1927–1977 — vospominaniia.* Bez daty. Moskva. Mashinopis', bez podpisi

Moscow, AMM, f. 2, op. 1, d. 31, Aleksandr Bulygin, *Solovetskaia byl' — vospominaniia*, 1981, mashinopis', bez podpisi

Moscow, AMM, f. 2, op. 1, d. 127, Pavel Chekhranov, *Paskha 1926 goda. Vospominaniia*, Mashinopis'

Moscow, AMM, f. 2, op. 3, dd. 15–18, Konstantin Gurskii, *Po dorogam gulaga. Moi Vaigach.* Mashinopis'

Moscow, AMM, f. 2, op. 2, d. 83, Lidiia Kititsyna, 'Materialy dlia biografii Vasiliia Smirnova (1882–1941)'

Moscow, APRF, f. 3, op. 58, d. 212, ll. 55–78, 'Operativnyi prikaz narodnogo komissara vnutrennykh del soiuza S.S.R. № 00447 ob operatsii po repressirovaniiu byvshikh kulakov, ugolovnikov i dr. antisovetskikh elementov (30.7.1937)'

Moscow, GARF, f. 393, op. 43a, d. 487, 'Postanovleniia i vypiski iz protokolv zasedanii Malogo Soveta Narodnykh Komissarov RSFSR o rezul'tatakh proverki tserkovnogo imushchestva byvshego Solovetskogo monastyria (20.5–2.11.1924)'

Moscow, GARF, f. 1235, op. 71, d. 43, 'Delo o rassmotrenii i otklonenii khodataistva Arkhangel'skogo gubernskogo ispol'nitel'nogo komiteta o peredache territorii Solovetskikh Ostrovov iz sostava Arkhangel'skoi gubernii v sostav Karel'skoi SSR (16.12.26–22.3.27)'

Moscow, GARF, f. 1235, op. 95, d. 155, 'Perepiska s Narodnym komissariatom finansov RSFSR, redaktsiei gazety *Izvestiia*, Arkhangel'skoi gubernskim i Suzdal'skim uezdnym ispol'nitelnymi komitetami ob opublikovanii teksta privetstviia Suzdal'skogo uezdno-gorodskogo ispolkoma Vladimirskoi gubernii VTsIK v sviazi s postanovleniem o zamene prodovol'stvennoi razverstki prodnalogom, o peredache tsennostei Solovetskogo monastyria (30.12.20–8.4.21)'

Moscow, GARF, f. 1235, op. 125, d. 290, 'Delo po khodataistvu TsIK Karel'skoi ASSR o peredache Solovetskikh ostrovov iz Severnogo Kraia v sostav Karel'skoi ASSR (17.2–3.10.1930)'

Moscow, GARF, f. 2307(a), op. 2, d. 74, 'Delo o sozdanii gidrobiologicheskoi stantsii v Solovkakh (2.6.21–30.9.21)'

Moscow, GARF, f. 2307 (a), op. 2, d. 302, 'Doklad zaveduiushchego Arkhangel'skim gubernskim otdelom narodnogo obrazovaniia, dokladnye zapiski professora Livanova o rabote ekspeditsii po issledovaniiu Belogo Moria i o neobkhodimosti organizatsii Solovetskoi biologicheskoi stantsii (28.7–1.9.21)'

Moscow, GARF, f. 3316, op. 64, d. 86, 'Vypiska iz protokola zasedaniia Prezidiuma TsIK SSSR ob otmene postanovleniia TsIK Karel'skoi SSR po voprosu o nedopushchenii ispol'zovaniia rabochei sily Solovetskikh lagerei pri postroike mostov na territorii Karel'skoi SSR i perepiska po etomu voprosu, (21.4–11.5.25)'

Moscow, GARF, f. 3316, op. 64, d. 1200, 'Vypiski iz protokolov zasedanii Prezidiuma TsIK SSSR o khodataistve OGPU o pomilovanii i sniatii sudimosti s Anisimova K.A., Chekmazova A.M. id r. s priolozheniem (6.6–25.12.1931)'

Moscow, GARF, f. 4042, op. 4, d. 62, 'Svedeniia ob uchebno-vospitatel'noi rabote v mestakh zakliucheniia za dekabr' 1923 g.'

Moscow, GARF, f. 4042, op. 4, d. 63, 'Postanovleniia Sovnarkoma RSFSR i Vneukrainskogo tsentral'nogo ispolkoma i Sovnarkoma Ukrainskoi SSR, doklady gubernskikh inspektsii mest zakliucheniia i perepiska s nimi ob izdanii gazety *Golos zakliuchennogo*, ob uvolnenii sotrudnikov, o periodicheskikh izdaniiakh'

Moscow, GARF, f. 4042, op. 4, d. 64, 'Protokoly №№ 1–16 zasedanii metodicheskoi komissii pri kul'turno-vospitatel'noi chasti GUMZ za oktiabr'–dekabr' 1924 g. i ianvar'–mai 1925 g. (podlinniki i prilozheniia k nim)'

Moscow, GARF, f. 4042, op. 4, d. 65, 'Polozhenie ob upravlenii mestami zakliucheniia pri rabochei chasti, tsirkuliary GUMZ i instruktsii po uchebno-vospitatel'noi chasti v mestakh zakliucheniia Respubliki'

Moscow, GARF, f. 4042, op. 4, d. 68, 'Plan ispravitel'no-trudovogo kodeksa i instruktsiia dlia mest zakliucheniia i po uchebno-vospitatel'noi chasti v mestakh zakliucheniia RSFSR'

Moscow, GARF, f. 4042, op. 4, d. 126, l. 28, 'Pis'mo nachal'nika upravleniia SLON F.I. Eikhmansa Narkomvnudelu RSFSR Glavumzak (25.3.1926)'

Moscow, GARF, f. 4042, op. 4, d. 126, l. 53, 'Perepiska s gubernskimi ispravitel'no-trudovym domami o vypuske zhurnalov, izdavaemykh zakliuchennymi, ob assignovanii sredstv na izdanie (3.10.1925–16.12.1926)'

Moscow, GARF, f. 4042, op. 4, d. 128, 'Tsirkuliary GUMZ za 1926 g. I prilozhenie k nim'

Moscow, GARF, f. 4042, op. 4, d. 130, 'Tsirkuliar narkomata prosveshcheniia RSFSR ob ukazanii sodeistviia gubernskimi politprosvetami uchebnno-vospitatel'nym chastiam mest zakliucheniia, doklad kul'turno-prosvetitel'noi chasti GUMZ o ee deiatel'nosti za 1925/1926 gg. i perepiska s gubernskimi inspektsiiami'

Moscow, GARF, f. 4042, op. 4, d. 159, 'Perepiska s Glavnymi upravleniiami po delam literatury i izdatel'stv pri Narkomate prosveshcheniia RSFSR (Glavlit), s gubernskimi inspektsiiami i mestami zakliucheniia ob izdanii mestami zakliucheniia gazet i zhurnalov'

Moscow, GARF, f. 5446, op. 1, d. 2, l. 43, 'Postanovlenie SNK SSSR "Ob organizatsii Solovetskogo lageria prinuditel'nykh rabot" ot 13 oktiabria 1923 g.'

Moscow, GARF, f. 5446, op. 1; GARF, f. 5446, op. 1a; GARF, f. 5446, op. 2; GARF, f. 5446, op. 2a, 'Protokoly i postanovleniia Soveta Narodnykh Komissarov i Soveta Ministrov SSSR (podlinniki). 1923–1950 gg.'

Moscow, GARF, f. 5446, op. 5a, d. 558, 'Ob otpuske OGPU dlia Solovetskikh lagerei osobogo naznacheniia spirta (oktiabr' 1924 g.)'

Moscow, GARF, f. 5446, op. 5a, d. 720, 'Ob uvelichenii smety OGPU na 2-e polugodie na 600.000 rublei na pokrytie defitsita po soderzhaniiu sollagprinrabosnaz (mart-aprel' 1925 g.)'

Moscow, GARF, f. 5446, op. 7a, d. 537, 'Ob otpuske OGPU sredstv na pokrytie defitsita po soderzhaniiu Solovetskogo lageria prinuditel'nykh rabot osobogo naznacheniia i peresyl'no-raspredelitel'nogo punkta g. Kemi (May–iiul' 1926)'

Moscow, GARF, f. 5446, op. 8a, d. 365, 'Ob otpuske OGPU sredstv na raskhody po soderzhaniiu USLONa (iiun'-iiul' 1927)'

Moscow, GARF, f. 5446, op. 9a, d. 444, 'Ob ustanovlenii defitsita po smete Solovetskogo lageria OGPU osobogo naznacheniia/USLON/ s 1.VI.28 po iiun' 1929 g. (ma' 1928)'

Moscow, GARF, f. 8409, op. 1, d. 372, l. 169 (Solovki, AAS, copy), 'Ekaterina Iaroslavskaia-Markon. Pis'mo Ekaterine Peshkovoi'

Moscow, GARF, f. 8409, op. 1, d. 291, ll. 34–39 (Solovki, AAS, copy), 'Iuliia Nikolaevna Danzas. Pis'mo Ekaterine Peshkovoi'

Moscow, RGALI, f. 232, op. 1, ed. khr. 359, 'G. Ts. Rusakov. Pis'ma Kuzminu Mikhailu Alekseevichu'

Moscow, RGALI, f. 1185, op. 3, ed. khr. 83, 'Vypiski neustanovlennogo litsa iz pis'ma zakliuchennykh Solovetskikh lagerei v OGPU ob usloviiakh zhizni (26.9.1927–9.6.1928)'

Moscow, RGALI, f. 1345, op. 1, ed. khr. 141, 'Boris Glubokovskii (psevd. Boris Veev), Uezdnyi Oskar Ual'd. Rasskaz'

Moscow, TsA FSB ROSSII, f. 1, op. 6, d. 28, ll. 3–6, 'Zapiska upolnomochennogo po organizatsii i ustroistvu lagerei VChK Predsedateliu VChK F.E. Dzerzhinskomu ob ustroistve Severnykh kolonii VChK (24.1.1922)'

Moscow, TsA FSB ROSSII, f. 2, op. 8, d. 120, ll. 154–60, 'Iz materialov doklada zam. nachal'nika Administrativno-organizatsionnogo upravleniia OGPU A.M. Shanina zamestiteliu predsedatelia OGPU G.G. Iagode o proizvole i izdevatel'stvakh nad zakliuchennymi v Solovetskikh lageriakh (12.5.1930)'

Munich, CBSB, 'Golos zakliuchennogo — Zhurnal zakliuchennykh gomel'skogo ispravtruddoma, 3 (1925)', Film P 2000.673 n° 002

Munich, CBSB, 'Za zheleznoi reshetkoi — Zhurnal zakliuchennykh viatskago ispravtruddoma', Film P 2000.673 n° 024, 025, 050, 051

Saint Petersburg, AMSPB, 'Interv'iu s El'viroi Fedorovnoi Eikhmans (28.11.1993, Moscow)'

Saint Petersburg, AMSPB, 'Lichnoe delo Naftalia Aronovicha Frenkelia'

Saint Petersburg, AMSPB, Anna Petrovna Skripnikova, *Solovki: Vospominaniia*

Saint Petersburg, AMSPB, Ol'ga Vtorova-Iafa, *Vospominaniia*

Saint Petersburg, CPD, shrift 1935b/2d7, 'Georgii Rusakov. Prolog k tragedii Shillera *Kovarstvo i liubov''*, Mashinopis', Moskva 1935

Solovki, AAS, copy, 'Doklad o partrabote 15 maia 1926 goda' (Arkhangel'sk, GAOPDF — State Archive of Social and Political Movements and Formations in the Arkhangel'sk Region, f. 50115, op. 1, d. 9/a, l. 110)

Solovki, AAS, Antonina Alekseevna Soshina, *Biograficheskie ocherki ob avtorakh Solovetskogo lageria*

Solovki, AAS, Kemetskii, Vladimir, *Stikhi, Samizdatskaia kniga*

Solovki, AAS, Sergei Shchegol'kov, *Nebol'shoe povestvovanie o tom, kak sovetskaia vlast' i partiia VKP(b) sdelali menia 'gosudarstvennym prestupnikom-terroristom', kotoryi gotovil pokushenie na zhizn' tovarishcha Stalina*, Mashinopis's fotografiami i avtografami avtora

Solovki, ASM, copy, 'Plan na rasstrel' dlia Solovetskoi tiur'my, utverzhdennyi v Moskve 16 avgusta 1937 g.'

Solovki, ASM, copy, 'Postanovlenie № 1953–539ss SNK SSSR "O zakrytii Solovetskoi tiur'my i peredache Solovetskikh ostrovov v vedenie narkomvoenmorflota" (25.11.1939)'

Solovki, ASM, copy, 'Protokoly rasstreliannykh zakliuchennykh'

Articles and Literary Works Published in the SLON Press

'19 Iiulia 1925', *NS*, 28 (1925), 4

AKAR, S., 'Moskva-Solovki (putevka), stikhi', *SLON*, 9–10 (1924), 52

AKAREVICH, A., 'My. Literaturnye nabroski', *SO*, 3 (1925), 23–31

——'Opyt professora Kal'', *SO*, 3 (1925), 15–18

——'Poeziia zakliuchennykh', *SO*, 4–5 (1925), 45–47

AL'M., 'Iskusstvo na ostrove', *NS*, 24 (1925), 2

——'Iskusstvo na ostrove', *NS*, 25 (1925), 2

——'Iskusstvo na ostrove', *NS*, 28 (1925), 2

A. IA., 'Polnochnaia zaria', *SO*, 1 (1929), 8

——'Na kanatnoi', *SO*, 1 (1929), 42–44

B., B., 'Soblazny', *SO*, 3 (1925), 14

BEDRUT, V., 'Stal'nye slova', *SO*, 10–11 (1925), 3

'Bez nazvaniia', *NS*, 16 (1925), 4

'Bez nazvaniia', *NS*, 21 (1925), 4

'Bez nazvaniia', *NS*, 29 (1925), 4

'Bez nazvaniia', *NS*, 34 (1926), 4

'Bez nazvaniia', *NS*, 37 (1926), 1

'Bez nazvaniia', *NS*, 13 (1930), 4

'Bez nazvaniia', *NS*, 30 (1930), 2

'Bez nazvaniia', *SO*, 2 (1925), 3

'Bibliografiia', *SLON*, 9–10 (1924), 110

CHEKMAZOV, A., 'O solovetskom presse', *NS*, 30 (1925), 3

——'Pust' v etot den'', *SO*, 10–11 (1925), 4

——'Solovetskii nabrosok', *SO*, 8 (1925), 4

EIKHMANS, F., 'K voprosu o lagernoi obshchestvennosti', *SO*, 4–5 (1925), 38–40

EMEL'IANOV, B., 'Berdysh', *SO*, 5–6 (1926), 23–24

——'Chasha solovetskaia', *SO*, 4 (1926), 77

——'Otryvki iz poemy', *SO*, 1 (1926), 43

——'Pered utrom', *SO*, 8 (1925), 5

——'Stikhi (Noch')', *SO*, 7 (1926), 29

——'Tsitaty', *SO*, 4 (1926), 72

——'V dvenadtsat' dnia', *SO*, 8 (1925), 5

——'Vesna v Solovkakh (stikh.)', *SO*, 7 (1925), 3

——'Vy vidali khvost u monety', *NS*, 50 (1926), 3

EN. LI., 'Sem' dnei, kotorye potriasli Solovki', *NS*, 44 (1925), 1

EVREINOV, B., 'Palomnichestvo. Stikhi', *SLON*, 9–10 (1924), 43

——'Smiatennost'. Stikhi', *SO*, 2 (1925), 33

——'Solovki. Stikhi', *SLON*, 9–10 (1924), p. 43

——'Stikhi. 1) Byl'e karel'skoe, 2) Zarei okhotnich'ei', *SO*, 1 (1925), 35–36

——'Stikhi (U dvukh izbushek)', *SO*, 2–3 (1926), 38

——'Voskresnym dnem', *SO*, 7 (1926), 33

——'Zabludhsee radio', *SLON*, 9–10 (1924), 57–58

FRENKEL', NAFTALII, 'Eksploatatsionno-kommercheskie perspektivy Solovetskogo khoziaistva', *NS*, 23 (1925), 2
GLUBOKOVSKII, B., 'Dokhlyi byt', *SO*, 8 (1925), 7
—— 'Esenin', *NS*, 6 (1926), 2
—— 'Ivan Panin', *NS*, 21 (1926), 5–6
—— 'Pesni shpany', *SO*, 4–5 (1925), 57–60
—— 'Pet'ka', *SO*, 7 (1925), 15–21
—— 'Puteshestvie iz Moskvy v Solovki', *SO*, 10–11 (1925), 5–16; 12 (1925), 3–9; 1 (1926), 24–42; 2–3 (1926), 41–71; 4 (1926), 80–101; 5–6 (1926), 46–69; 7 (1926), 60–73
—— 'Solovetskaia psisha', *SO*, 9 (1925), 9–16
—— 'Solovki v poezii solovchan', *SO*, 6 (1925), 38–40
IAROSLAVSKII, A., 'Sluchainoi zhenshchine', *SO*, 5 (1930), 2
IU., 'Literaturnye parodii', *SO*, 4 (1930), 47
K., 'Rybaki', *NS*, 45 (1925), 2
K., S. 'Pressa na sever', *SO*, 3 (1925), 18
KAMENOGRADSKII, I. S., 'O solovetskoi obshchestvennosti', *SO*, 4–5 (1925), 41–44
KARGOPOL'SKII, S., 'Pamiati V.I. Lenina', *SO*, 1 (1925), 10
KAZARNOVSKII, IU., 'Druzheskie epigrammy k kontsertu № 3', *NS*, 1 (1930), 4
—— 'Fel'eton', *NS*, 2 (1930), 1
—— 'G. I. Bokii (druzheskaia epigramma)', *SO*, 1 (1929), 4
—— 'Iumor. Literaturnye parodii', *SO*, 1 (1930), 64–66
—— 'Iumor. Literaturnye parodii', *SO*, 2–3 (1930), 72
—— 'M. Gor'komu (druzheskaia epigramma)', *SO*, 1 (1929), 4
—— 'Sobstvenno govoria, v Kemi ... (zametki iz Blok-nota)', *NS*, 10 (1930), 2
—— 'Svidanie', *SO*, 3–4 (1929), 6–10
—— 'Vynuzhdennoe priznanie (stikhi)', *SO*, 4 (1930), 18
KEMETSKII, V., 'Belaia noch'', *SO*, 1 (1929), 46
—— 'Maksimu Gor'komu (sonet)', *SO*, 1 (1929), 3
—— 'Moei Muze (stikhi)', *SO*, 4 (1930), 23
—— 'Nad snegom vozdukh tikh i mglist. Stikhi', *SO*, 2–3 (1930), 10
—— 'Pered navigatsiei (sonet)', *SO*, 2–3 (1930), 54
—— 'Pesn' o vozvrashchenii', *SO*, 5 (1930), 1
—— 'Prekrasnoi neznakomke (stikhi)', *SO*, 4 (1930), 28
—— 'Saga ob Erike, syne Ial'mara, i o poslednem iz ego potomkov', *SO*, 1 (1930), 16–20
—— 'Sonet (Ispei vina)', *SO*, 1 (1929), 8
—— 'Sonety o Germanskoi respublike', *SO*, 3–4 (1929), 14
—— 'Tri soneta (Luksorskii obelisk, Pamiatnik Russo, Verlen)', *SO*, 2 (1929), 3
KENEL', A., 'Muzykal'noe oformlenie v Solovetskom teatre', *SO*, 3–4 (1929), 26–28
KIUNERT, M., 'Kanun Oktiabria', *SO*, 3–4 (1929), 3
—— 'Liubimye (stikhi)', *SO*, 1 (1930), 61
—— 'Nochnaia smena (ocherk)', *SO*, 1 (1930), 29–35
—— 'Severnyi polius (stikhi)', *SO*, 1 (1930), 4
—— 'Stikhi (Ne tsenish' zvezd. Aliaska)', *SO*, 2 (1929), 17
—— 'Valerii Briusov', *SO*, 3–4 (1929), 23–26
KOVENSKII, M., 'Lagkory za rabotu', *NS*, 37 (1925), 1
KRIVOSH-NEMANICH, VLADIMIR, 'Proiskhozhdenie pis'ma', *SLON*, 4 (1924), 47–48
—— 'Stikhi (Luna)', *SLON*, 4 (1924), 19
'Krasnaia i chernaia doska', *SLON*, 5 (1924), 54
LAGKOR, 'Ike', '- Oi! . . Ai! . . — Bum! . . Bum! . .', *NS*, 41 (1925), 3
LAGKOR, ZORKII, 'Bez nazvaniia', *NS*, 37 (1925), 4

LAGKORKA, M., 'Kak ia stala lagkorkoi!', *NS*, 44 (1925), 3
LEITIN, B., 'Komandirsha zhenskoi roty', *SO*, 3–4 (1929), 58
——'Meshchanka (stikhi)', *SO*, 4 (1930), 36
——'Otryvok iz poemii', *SO*, 1 (1929), 10
——'Torfushka (sonet)', *SO*, 2–3 (1930), 20
——'Vesna', *SO*, 4 (1930), 3
LITVIN, N., 'Kudeiar. Po kraiu Kitezhu', *SO*, 4 (1926), 74–75
——'Letopis' Solovetskaia', *SO*, 1 (1925), 39–46; 2 (1925), 37–48; 3 (1925), 9–13; 4–5 (1925),
    53–56.
——'Malen'kii feleton', *NS*, 46 (1925), 1
——'Na Bab-gube', *SO*, 7 (1926), 10
——'Po ostrovam Solovetskim', *SO*, 6 (1925), 57–63; 7 (1925), 5–14; 8 (1925), 15–22
——'Po vekham', *SLON*, 9–10 (1924), pp. 30–36
MALCHANOV, M., 'Tipografiia USLON', *NS*, 3 (1930), 3
MIKHAILOV, I., 'Erkopiia', *SLON*, 4 (1924), 23
'M.N. Gernet o Solovkakh', *NS*, 37 (1926), 3
MY, 'Rifmy lagkora', *NS*, 27 (1925), 3
NIKOLAEV, Iu., 'Solovetskii abeliar', *SO*, 3–4 (1929), 16–20; *SO*, 1 (1930), 13–15
——'Staraia kniga na Solovkakh', *SO*, 2 (1929), 30–32
OKERMAN, S., 'Koe-chto o liubvi solovetskoi', *SO*, 8 (1925), 10
——'Siluety zhenbaraka', *SO*, 12 (1925), 14–15
——'V Solovki', *SO*, 7 (1925), 27
——'V strokakh i mezhdu strok', *SO*, 7 (1926), 24–28
ORLOV, N., '★★★ (Ne pereskazhesh' eto)', *SO*, 2–3 (1929), 13
——'Shtorm', *SO*, 3–4 (1929), 4
——'Tak prosto', *SO*, 1 (1929), 31
'Ot redaktsii', *NS*, 5 (1926), 2
'Ot redaktsii', *SLON*, 3 (1924), 2
'Ot redaktsii', *SO*, 1 (1925), 3
'Ot redaktsii', *SO*, 1 (1929), 3
PAN., A., 'Ukroshchennyi kentavr', *SO*, 1 (1929), 9
PANIN, I., 'Uznik', *SLON*, 3 (1924), 31
PANKRATOV, A., 'Dva ostrova (Maksimu Gor'komu). Kapri, Solovki', *SO*, 1 (1929), 4
——'Khochu odno (stikhi)', *SO*, 4 (1930), 1
——'Mne grustno pet' o Solovkakh (stikhi)', *SO*, 2–3 (1930), 26
——'Plach Odisseia (stikhi)', *SO*, 1 (1930), 61
——'Posle izvestiia o smerti Lenina (stikhi)', *SO*, 1 (1930), 3
——'Stikhi (Chto esli, igraet solntse)', *SO*, 1 (1929), 45
'Pechat' i proizvodstvo', *NS*, 1 (1930), 1
PESHKOVSKII, A., 'Stikhi (Pust' Solovetskie lesa)', *SO*, 1 (1929), 10
——'Veter', *SO*, 2 (1929), 20–22
——'Kuz'ma vdova', *SO*, 4 (1930), 3–10; 5 (1930), 3–12
'Pochtovyi iashchik', SLON, 9–10 (1924), 111
RADO, B., 'A. Z. (Stikhi)', *SO*, 2–3 (1926), 38
——'Chernoe ozero', *SO*, 5–6 (1926), 25
——'Iskaniia', *SO*, 7 (1926), 37
——'Nochnoi inei', *SO*, 1 (1926), 96
RUSAKOV, G., 'Mai', *SO*, 5–6 (1926), 29
——'Ne sberegli', *SO*, 4 (1926), 73
——'Solovetskoi vesnoi', *SO*, 5–6 (1926), 28
——'Solovki. Venok sonetov', *SO*, 2–3 (1926), 3–16

SH., B., 'Iz dnevnika', *SO*, 1 (1925), 16

SHENBERG, PAVEL, 'Solovetskaia pechat'', *Materialy SOK*, 17 (1927), 65–91

SHIRIAEV-AKARSKII, B., 'Zaiavlenie', *NS*, 15 (1925), 4

SHIRIAEV, B., '1237 strok', *SO*, 4 (1926), 19

——'Buntar'', *SO*, 8 (1925), 3

——'Eli Solovetskie (vpechatleniia s lesorazrabotok)', *SO*, 2 (1925), 94

——'Inochii minuet. Stikh', *SO*, 2 (1925), 34

——'Literaturnye popytki', *SO*, 1 (1925), 90

——'Mai', *SO*, 4–5 (1925), 5

——'Oktiabr'', *SO*, 10–11 (1925), 17

——'Stikhi. Iz tsikla 'Solovki'. 1) Davnee', *SO*, 1 (1925), 37

——'Syr', *SO*, 5–6 (1926), 3–14

——'Turkestanskie stikhi', *SO*, 5–6 (1926), 42

SLEPIAN, I., 'Bez nazvaniia', *NS*, 29 (1926), 4

SOCHUVSTVUIU, INITIAL? 'Nuzhnyi ekstrennye mery', *NS*, 46 (1925), 2

SUKHOV, I., 'Bez nazvaniia', *NS*, 28 (1925), 2

——'Novyi etap', *NS*, 6 (1926), 2–3

——'V den' pervoi godovshchiny', *NS*, 2 (1926), 1

TIBERII, 'Byt zakliuchennykh', *SO*, 4–5 (1925), 47–49

——'O KhLAMe', *NS*, 10 (1925), 4

——'Solovetskaia entsiklopediia (prodolzhenie)', *SLON*, 4 (1924), 60

——'Solovetskie siluety', *SLON*, 9–10 (1924), 47–50

TIULEN', 'Ran'she i teper', stikhi', *SLON*, 9–10 (1924), 58

TOT, 'Solovetskie zarisovki', *SO*, 6 (1925), 54–56; *SO*, 7 (1925), 30–31; *SO*, 8 (1925), 12–14; *SO*, 9 (1925), 29–30; *SO*, 10–11 (1925), 34–35

TSVIBELFISH', 'Zubry', *NS*, 8 (1926), 1

'Ugolok lagkora', *NS*, 7 (1925), 3

UTKA, 'Ostrov chudes', *SLON*, 3 (1924), 74

VADBOL'SKII, AVENIR, 'Ekho', *SLON*, 6 (1924), 68

VINOGRADOV, N., 'K istorii Solovetskogo monastyria', *SO*, 3–4 (1929), 40

'Vyzovy na sotsialisticheskoe sorevnovanie', *NS*, 2 (1930), 1

ZRITEL', 'Vecher kollektiva "Svoikh"', *NS*, 24 (1925), 4

Print

ADAMOVA-SLIOZBERG, OL'GA, *Put'* (Moscow: Vozvrashchenie, 1993)

AIKHENVAL'D, IURII, *Po grani ostroi...: proza i stikhi* (Munich: Ekho, 1972)

AKHMATOVA, ANNA, *Sobranie sochinenii v shesti tomakh* (Moscow: Ellis Lak, 1998–2001)

AKSENOV, VASILII, *Moskovskaia saga: trilogiia* (Moscow: Izograf, 1999)

ALEKSEEV, MIKHAIL, OTHERS, eds, *Istoriia russkoi literatury* (Moscow and Leningrad: AN SSSR, 1941–56)

ALIMOV, ALEKSEI, *Panorama della letteratura russa contemporanea* (Milan and Venice: Montuoro, 1946)

ALPERT, ERIN, 'Reinventing Soviet Visual Memory: A Case Study of Marina Goldovskaya's Documentary *Solovki Power*', *Studies in Russian and Soviet Cinema*, 7/2 (2013), 207–26

ANDREEV, GENNADII, *Gor'kie vody* (Frankfurt am Main: Posev, 1954)

——'Pomilui Bog, my — Russkie', *Slovo*, 1 June 1992, pp. 56–57

——'Solovetskie ostrova', *Grani*, 216 (2005), 36–78

ANTSIFEROV, NIKOLAI, *Dusha Peterburga* (Leningrad: Lenizdat, 1991)

——*Iz dum o bylom: vospominaniia* (Moscow: Feniks, Kul'turnaia initsiativa, 1992)

APPLEBAUM, ANNE, *Gulag: A History* (New York: Doubleday, 2003)

ARKANOV, ARKADII, *Literaturnaia parodiia* (Moscow: Eskmo-Press, 2000)

ARKHIEPISKOP IOANN, *Solovki — Vtoraia Golgofa. Solovki v istorii Rossii* (Moscow: Pravoslavnaia tserkov' Bozhiei Materi Derzhavaia, 2002)

—— *Solovetskii sad* (Moscow: Sofiia press, 2003)

ARTIZOV, ANDREI and NAUMOV, OLEG, ed., *Vlast' i Khudozhestvennaia intelligentsiia. Dokumenty TsK RKP (B)–VKP (B), VChK-OGPU-NKVD o kul'turnoi politike. 1917–1953* (Moscow: Materik-Demokratiia, 2002)

ASCHER, ABRAHAM, 'The Solovki Prisoners, the Mensheviks and the Socialist International', *Slavonic and East European Review*, July (1969), 423–35

ASSMANN, ALEIDA, *Erinnerungsräume: Formen und Wandlungen des kulturellen Gedächtnisses* (Munich: C. H. Beck, 1999)

ASTAF'EV, VIKTOR, *Tsar'-Ryba* (Krasnoiarsk: Ofset, 1997)

BABICHEVA, MAIIA, *Pisateli vtoroi volny Russkoi emigratsii. Biobibliograficheskie ocherki* (Moscow: Pashkov dom, 2005)

BAKHTIN, VLADIMIR, PUTILOV, BORIS, ed., *Fol'klor i kul'turnaia sreda Gulaga* (Saint Petersburg: Fond 'Za razvitie i vyzhivanie chelovechestva', 1994)

BARKER, ADELE MARIE and GHEITH, JEHANNE M., eds, *A History of Women's Writing in Russia* (Cambridge: Cambridge University Press, 2002)

BARON, NICK, *Soviet Karelia: Politics, Planning and Terror in Stalin's Russia, 1920–1939* (London and New York: Routledge, 2009)

BARTHES, ROLAND, 'Introduction to the Structural Analysis of Narrative', *New Literary History*, 6 (1975), 237–72

—— *The Rustle of Language* (New York: Hill and Wang, 1986)

BASINSKII, PAVEL, *Gor'kii* (Moscow: Molodaia gvardia, 2006)

BATSER, DMITRII, 'Solovetskii iskhod', *Zven'ia*, 1 (1991), 288–98

BAUDIN, RODOLPHE, BERNARD-GRIFFITHS, SIMONE, CROISILLE, CHRISTIAN, and GRETCHANAIA, ELENA, eds, *Exil et épistolaire aux XVIIIe et XIXe siècles* (Clermont Ferrand: Presses Universitaires Blaise Pascal, 2007)

BEZSONOV, YOURI [IURII], *Mes 26 prisons et mon évasion de Solovki* (Paris: Payot, 1928)

—— *Dvadtsat' shest' tiurem i pobeg s Solovkov* (Paris: Impr. de Navarre, 1928)

BLINOV, I., 'Pavel Isaakovich Gannibal, diadia A. S. Pushkina', *Russkaia starina* (1899), 9

BLIUM, ARLEN, *Za kulisami 'Ministerstva Pravdy': tainaia istoriia sovetskoi tsenzury 1917–1929* (Saint Petersburg: Akademicheskii proekt, 1994)

—— *Sovetskaia tsenzura v epokhu total'nogo terrora. 1929–1953* (Saint Petersburg: Akademicheskii proekt, 2000)

—— *Zapreshchennye knigi russkikh pisatelei i literaturovedov, 1917–1991: indeks sovetskoi tsenzury s kommentariiami* (Saint Petersburg: Sankt-Peterburgskii gosudarstvennyi universitet kul'tury i iskusstv, 2003)

BLOK, ALEKSANDR, *Sobranie Sochinenii*, 8 vols (Moscow and Leningrad: Khudozhestvennaia Literatura, 1960–63)

BOCHKAREVA, OLGA, *Solovetskie lageria i tiur'ma 1920–1939. Materialy k istorii* (online publication on the website www.solovki.ca) <http://www.solovki.ca/gulag_solovki/karately_repressii.php> [accessed 22 October 2010)

BOGDANOVA, NATAL'IA, *Moi otets — Men'shevik* (Saint Petersburg: NITs Memorial, 1994)

BOGOMOLOVA, ZOIA, *Kak molniia v nochi: K. Gerd* (Izhevsk: Izd-vo Udmurtskogo universiteta, 1998)

BOIARSKII, PETR, LIUTYI, ALEKSANDR, and STOLIAROV, VIACHESLAV, eds, *Solovetskie ostrova: dukhovnoe, kul'turnoe i prirodnoe nasledie* (Moscow: Rossiiskii NII prirodnogo i kul'turnogo nasledia, 2005)

BONDARENKO, VLADIMIR, 'Arkhipelag Di-Pi', *Slovo*, 1 June 1992, pp. 48–50

——'Vozvrashchenie nevozvrashchentsev', *Slovo*, 1 June 1992, pp. 51–55

BORZENKO, VIKTOR, 'Psevdonimy donskikh zhurnalistov v rossiiskoi periodike XI — nachala XX vekov', *Relga*, 3, 20 February 2009, <http://www.relga.ru/Environ/ WebObjects/tgu-www.woa/wa/Main?textid=2334&level1=main&level2=articles> [accessed 11 November 2010]

BRIUSOV, VALERII, *Sobranie sochinenii v semi tomakh* (Moscow: Khudozhestvennaia literatura, 1973–75)

BRODSKII, IURII, *Solovki. Dvadtsat' let osobogo naznacheniia* (Moscow: Mir Iskusstv II, 2008)

——*Solovki. Le isole del martirio. Da monastero a primo lager sovietico* (Milan: La casa di Matriona, 1998)

BULGAKOV, MIKHAIL, *Sobach'e serdtse: povesti, rasskazy, fel'etony, ocherki: 1925–1927* (Moscow: Tsentrpoligraf, 2004)

——*Sobranie sochinenii v vos'mi tomakh* (Moscow: Tsentrpoligraf, 2004)

BUNIN, IVAN, *Sobranie sochinenii v shesti tomakh* (Moscow: Khudozhestvennaia literatura, 1987)

BYKOV, DMITRII, *Byl li Gor'kii?* (Moscow: AST-Astrel, 2009)

BYKOV, VLADIMIR, *Russkaia fenia* (Smolensk: Trast-Imakom, 1993)

BYSTROVA, OL'GA, *Gor'kii i ego korrespondenty* (Moscow: IMLI-RAN, 2005)

CHERNAVIN, VLADIMIR, 'Life in Concentration Camps in USSR', *Slavonic and East European Review*, 12 (1933/34), 387

CHERNAVIN, VLADIMIR and CHERNAVIN, TAT'IANA, *Zapiski 'vreditelia': Pobeg iz GULAGa* (Saint Petersburg: Kanon, 1999)

CERNOV, VITTORIO, ed., *La Ce-ka: il terrore bolscevico. Raccolta di testimonianze a cura di Vittorio Cernov* (Milan: La Promotrice, 1923)

CHIRKOV, IURII, *A bylo vse tak ...* (Moscow, Politizdat, 1991)

CHULKOV, GEORGII, *Zhizn' Pushkina* (Moscow: Terra, 2008)

CIAMPA, MAURIZIO, *L'epoca tremenda. Voci dal Gulag delle Solovki* (Brescia: Morcelliana, 2010)

CIONI, PAOLA, 'Gor'kii v Italii (po dokumentam Tsentral'nogo arkhiva Italii)', *Novaia i noveiishaia istoriia*, 5 (2010), 205–09

COEURÉ, SOPHIE, 'À propos de: Raymond Duguet, Un bagne en Russie rouge. — Walter Ruge, Prisonnier n° 8403', *Cahiers du monde russe*, 4 (2003), 748–50

COLOMBO, DUCCIO, 'Sbornik o Belomorkanale: velikaia stroika stalinskoi literatury', *Slavica Tergestina*, 10 (2002), 231–43

——*Scrittori, in fabbrica! Una lettura del romanzo industriale sovietico* (Ospedaletto: Pacini, 2008)

COLUCCI, MICHELE and PICCHIO, RICCARDO, eds, *Storia della civiltà letteraria russa*, 2 vols (Torino: UTET, 1997)

CONQUEST, ROBERT, *The Great Terror: A Reassessment* (Oxford and New York: Oxford University Press, 2008)

COOKE, OLGA M., 'Remembering Solovki: Gennady Andreev's *Solovetsky Islands*', *Gulag Studies*, 4 (2011), 91–120

CRIVELLER, CLAUDIA, 'Gli studi sui generi auto-biografici e memorialistici in Russia', *Avtobiografija*, 1 (2012), 21–48

——'"Io sono il padrone del mio sogno". Evgenij Charitonov e la letteratura del sottosuolo come costruzione dell'io', *eSamizdat*, 8 (2010–2011), 119–33

DAL', VLADIMIR, *Tolkovyi slovar' zhivago velikoruskago jazyka* (Moscow and Saint Petersburg: Izdanie tipografa M. O. Vul'fa, 1881)

DE LOTTO, CINZIA, 'Dostoevskij. Lettere dalla fortezza', in *'Le loro prigioni': scritture dal carcere*, ed. by Anna Maria Babbi and Tobia Zanon (Verona: Edizioni Fiorini, 2007), pp. 257–74

DE LOTTO, CINZIA and MINGATI, ADALGISA, ed., *Nei territori della slavistica. Percorsi e intersezioni* (Padova: Unipress, 2005)

DEMIDENKO, IULIIA, MAKOGONOVA, MARIA, ed., *Akademik D.S. Likhachev: dialog s XX vekom* (Saint Petersburg: GMI SPVB, 2006)

DICHAROV, ZAKHAR, ed., *Raspiatye* (Saint Petersburg: Severo-zapad, 1993)

DMITRIEV, IURII, *Belomorsko-Baltiiskii vodnyi put'. Ot zamyslov do voploshcheniia* (Petrozavodsk: Self publication, 2003)

DOBRENKO, EVGENY, *The Making of the State Reader: Social and Aesthetic Contexts of the Reception of Soviet Literature* (Stanford: Stanford University Press, 1997)

DOBROVOL'SKII, I., ed., *GULAG: ego stroiteli, obitateli i geroi* (Saint Petersburg: Norma, 1998)

DODOLEV, EVGENII, 'Obitel' Zakhara Prilepina', <http://top.oprf.ru/blogs/176/14803.html> [accessed 9 November 2014]

DOSTOEVSKII, FEDOR, *Besy: roman v trekh chastiakh* (Moscow: Soglasie, 1996)

DRASKOCZY, JULIE, *Belomor: Criminality and Creativity in Stalin's Gulag* (Brighton, MA: Academic Studies Press, 2014)

DRIAKHLITSYN, DMITRII, 'Periodicheskaia pechat' arkhipelaga', *Sever*, 9 (1990), 128–37

DUGUET, RAYMOND, *Un bagne en Russie rouge. Solovki: l'île de la faim, des supplices et de la mort* (Paris: J. Tallandier, 1927)

DUGIN, ALEKSANDR, *Neizvestnyi GULAG. Dokumenty i fakty* (Moscow: Nauka, 1999)

DUNAEV, MIKHAIL, *Pravoslavie i russkaia literatura* (Moscow: Khristianskaia literatura, 2000)

DUNDOVICH, ELENA, GORI, FRANCESCA, and GUERCETTI, ELEONORA, eds, *Reflections on the Gulag* (Milan, Feltrinelli, 2003)

——*Gulag: Storia e memoria* (Milan: Feltrinelli, 2004)

DZHIMBULOV, STANISLAV, *Literaturnye manifesty ot simvolizma do nashikh dnei* (Moscow: Soglasie, 2000)

EAKIN, JOHN PAUL, *Touching the World: Reference in Autobiography* (Princeton: Princeton University Press, 1992)

EFIMOV, EVGENII, 'Schastlivaia gor'kaia zhizn' Ivana Ozerova', *Boss*, 3 (2008) <http://www.bossmag.ru/archiv/2008/boss-03-2008-g/schastlivaya-gorkaya-zhizn-ivana-ozerova.html> [accessed 15 April 2015]

ELISEEV, ALEKSEI, ed., *A.M. Gor'kii nizhegorodskikh let: Vospominaniia* (Gor'kii: Volgo-Viatskoe knizhnoe izdatel'stvo, 1978)

EMEL'IANOV, BORIS, 'O rozovom kamnem i novykh liudiakh', *Karelo-Murmanskii krai*, 9 (1927), 18

ERSHOV, IL'IA, *'Bogema' i ugolovniki: Solovetskii teatr 1920-kh godov. Boris Glubokovskii*, Shkol'nyi konkurs 'Chelovek v istorii. Rossiia — XX vek' 1999–2000, <http://urokiistorii.ru/node/209> [accessed 24 November 2014]

ESENIN, SERGEI, *Polnoe sobranie sochinenii v 7 tomakh* (Moscow: Nauka, Golos, 1995–2002)

——*Sobranie sochinenii v shesti tomakh* (Moscow: Khudozhestvennaia literatura, 1978)

ETKIND, ALEXANDER, *Warped Mourning: Stories of the Undead in the Land of the Unburied* (Stanford: Stanford University Press, 2013)

ETKIND, EFIM, NIVAT, GEORGES, SERMAN, IL'IA and STRADA, VITTORIO, eds, *Storia della letteratura russa* (Turin: Einaudi, 1989)

EVREINOV, BORIS, 'Byl'e loparskoe', *Karelo-Murmanskii krai*, 2 (1927), 17

FABRE, GIORGIO, *Roma a Mosca: lo spionaggio fascista in URSS e il caso Guarnaschelli* (Bari: Dedalo, 1990)

FACCIOLI, ERICA, 'All'origine del modernismo teatrale ucraino: appunti su Les' Kurbas', *eSamizdat*, 5 (2007), 203–14

FERRETTI, MARIA, *La memoria mutilata: la Russia ricorda* (Milan: Corbaccio, 1993)

FISCHER VON WEIKERSTHAL, FELICITAS, *Die 'inhaftierte' Presse: Das Pressewesen sowjetischer Zwangsarbeitslager, 1923–1937* (Wiesbaden: Otto Harrassowitz, 2011)

FISCHER VON WEIKERSTHAL, FELICITAS, and THAIDIGSMANN, KAROLINE, eds, *(Hi-)Stories of the Gulag: Fiction and Reality* (Heidelberg: Universitätsverlag Winter, 2016)

FITZPATRICK, SHEILA, *Everyday Stalinism: Ordinary Life in Extraordinary Times* (New York: Oxford, 1999)

FLEISHMAN, LAZAR', HUGHES, ROBERT and RAEVSKAIA-HUGHES, OL'GA, eds, *Russkii Berlin 1921–1923* (Moscow: Russkii put', 2003)

FLORENSKII, PAVEL, *Detiam moim: Vospominaniia proshlykh dnei* (Moscow: Moskovskii rabochii, 1992)

——*Lagernaia pochta* (Moscow: Trudy MAKE, 1996)

——*Non dimenticatemi* (Milan: Mondadori, 2001)

——'Pis'ma iz Solovkov [1934–1937gg.]', *Nashe nasledie*, 4 (1988), 115–28

——'Pis'ma s Solovkov', *Vestnik Russkogo Khristianskogo Dvizheniia*, 160 (1990), 33–71

——*Sochineniia v chetyrekh tomakh* (Moscow: Mysl', 1998)

FLORENSKII, PAVEL, ed., *Prebyvaet vechno: pis'ma P. A. Florenskogo, R. N. Litvinova, N. Ia. Briantseva i A. F. Vangengeima iz Solovetskogo lageria osobogo naznacheniia v chetyrekh tomakh* (Moscow: Mezhdunarodnyi Tsentr Rerikhov-Master Bank, 2011–12)

FLORES, MARCELLO, *L'immagine dell'URSS* (Milan: Il saggiatore, 1990)

——'L'Occidente e il Gulag', in *Gulag. Il sistema dei lager in URSS*, ed. by Marcello Flores and Francesca Gori (Milan: Mazzotta, 1999), pp. 95–101

FLORES, MARCELLO and GORI, FRANCESCA, eds, *Gulag. Il sistema dei lager in URSS* (Milan: Mazzotta, 1999)

FROLOVSKII, MIKHAIL, *Severnaia vesna. Stikhi* (Moscow: Vozvrashchenie, 1992)

——*Listki iz dnevnika, vedennogo v ssylke*, in *Kitezh: proza, poeziia, dramaturgiia, vospominaniia*, ed. by Vladimir Murav'ev (Moscow: Vozvrashchenie, 2006), pp. 302–12

FRUMENKOV, GEORGII, *Solovetskii monastyr' i oborona Belomoria v XVI–XIX vv.* (Arkhangel'sk: Severo-Zapadnoe Knizhnoe Izdatel'stvo, 1975)

GAGEN-TORN, NINA, *Memoria* (Moscow: Vozvrashchenie, 1994)

GALICH, ALEKSANDR, *Kogda ia vernus': polnoe sobranie stikhov i pesen* (Frankfurt am Main: Posev, 1981)

GALL, ALFRED, *Schreiben und Extremerfahrung: Die polnische Gulag-Literatur in komparatistischer Perspektive* (Berlin: Lit Verlag, 2012)

GALMARINI, MARIA CRISTINA, 'Defending the Rights of Gulag Prisoners: The Story of the Political Red Cross, 1918–38', *The Russian Review*, 71.1 (2012), 6–29

GANIN, ALEKSEI, *Stikhotvoreniia. Poemy. Roman* (Arkhangel'sk: Severo-Zapadnoe knizhnoe izdatel'stvo, 1991)

GENIS, VLADIMIR, *Nevernye slugi rezhima. Pervye sovetskie nevozvrashchentsy (1920–1933). Opyt dokumental'nogo issledovaniia v 2-kh knigakh* (Moscow: no pub., 2009)

GHEITH, JEHANNE M., and JOLLUCK, KATHERINE R., *Gulag Voices: Oral Histories of Soviet Incarceration and Exile* (New York: Palgrave Macmillan, 2011)

GIAMBELLUCA KOSSOVA, ALDA, *All'alba della Cultura Russa. La Rus' kieviana (862–1240)* (Rome: Edizioni Studium, 1996)

GINZBURG, EVGENIIA, *Krutoi marshrut* (Frankfurt am Main: Posev, 1967)

GLUBOKOVSKII, BORIS, *49* (o. Solovki: Biuro pechati USLON, 1926)

——*Kak Fediushka pionerom stal. P'esa dlia detei v dvukh deistviiakh* (Moscow-Leningrad: Molodaia gvardiia, 1925) (CNLR, Shrift 39/770a)

——*Proklyatyi vopros Rossii (Vostochnyi vorpos)* (Moscow: Knigoizdatel'stvo 'Obshchee delo',

1914/1915) (CNLR, Shrift Z. 37, Sh. 80, R. 4, n. 215)

GOLDGOER, ALEKSANDR, 'Toska razluki', *Solovetskii vestnik*, 13.78 (1993), 3

GOLOVKOVA, LIDIIA, *Sukhanovskaia tiur'ma. Spetsob"ekt 110* (Moscow: Vozvrashchenie, 2009)

GORBAČËV, MICHAIL, *Riflessioni sulla rivoluzione d'Ottobre. Dal Palazzo d'Inverno alla perestrojka* (Rome: Editori riuniti, 1997)

GORCHEVA, ALLA, *Pressa GULAGa (1918–1955)* (Moscow: Izd-vo MGU, 1996)

—— *Pressa GULAGa. Spiski E. P. Peshkovoi* (Moscow, Izd-vo MGU, 2009)

GOR'KII, MAKSIM, *Neizdannaia perepiska s Bogdanovym, Leninym, Stalinym, Zinov'evym, Kamenevym, Korolenko* (Moscow: Nasledie, 1998)

—— 'Po Soiuzu Sovetov: Solovki', *Sobranie sochinenii v tridtsati tomakh* (Moscow: Khudozhestvennaia literatura, 1952) XVII, pp. 201–32

—— *Polnoe sobranie sochineniia v 25 t.* (Moscow: Nauka, 1974)

GOR'KII, MAKSIM, AVERBAKH, LEOPOL'D, and FIRIN, SEMEN, eds, *Belomorsko-Baltiiskii Kanal imeni Stalina: Istoriia Stroitel'stva* (Moscow: Gosudarstvennoe Izdatel'stvo 'Istoriia fabrik i zavodov', 1934)

GRACHEV, MIKHAIL, *Russkii zhargon: istoriko-etimologicheskii slovar'* (Moscow: AST-Press Kniga, 2008)

GRAZIOSI, ANDREA, *The Great Soviet Peasant War: Bolsheviks and Peasants, 1917–1933* (Cambridge, MA: Harvard University Press, 1996)

—— *L'Urss di Lenin e Stalin. Storia dell'Unione Sovietica. 1914–1945* (Bologna: Il Mulino, 2007)

GRONAS, MIKHAIL, *Cognitive Poetics and Cultural Memory: Russian Literary Mnemonics* (New York: Routledge, 2010)

—— 'Naizust': o mnemonicheskom bytovanii sticha', *Novoe Literaturnoe Obozrenie*, 114 (2012), <http://www.nlobooks.ru/node/2011> [accessed 14 January 2015]

—— 'Why Did Free Verse Catch on in the West, but not in Russia? On the Social Uses of Memorized Poetry', *Toronto Slavic Quarterly*, 33 (2010), 166–213

GROSSMAN, VASILII, *Zhizn' i sud'ba* (Ekaterinburg: U-Faktoriia, 2005)

GROYS, BORIS, *Russkii kosmizm* (Moscow: Ad Marginem, 2015)

—— *The Total Art of Stalinism* (Princeton: Princeton University Press, 1992)

GROYS, BORIS, and HAGEMEISTER, MICHAEL, eds, *Die Neue Menschheit. Biopolitische Utopien in Russland zu Beginn des 20. Jahrhunderts*(Frankfurt am Main: Suhrkamp Verlag, 2005)

GULLOTTA, ANDREA, 'The "Cultural Village" of the Solovki Prison Camp: A Case of Alternative Culture', *Studies in Slavic Cultures*, 9 (2010), 9–25

—— 'A New Perspective for Gulag Literature Studies: The Gulag Press', *Studi Slavistici*, 8 (2011), 95–111

HAIMSON, LEOPOLD H., GALILI Y GARCIA, ZIVA, and WORTMAN, RICHARD, *The Making of Three Russian Revolutionaries* (Cambridge: Cambridge University Press, 1987)

HELLBECK, JOCHEN, *Revolution on My Mind: Writing a Diary under Stalin* (Cambridge and London: Harvard University Press, 2006)

—— 'Working, Struggling, Becoming: Stalin-Era Autobiographical Texts', *The Russian Review*, 60 (2001), 340–59

—— 'Writing the Self in the Time of Terror: Alexander Afinogenov's Diary of 1937', in *Self and Story in Russian History*, ed. by Laura Engelstein and Stephanie Sandier (Ithaca and London: Cornell University Press, 2000), pp. 69–93

HIRSCH, MARIANNE, *Family Frames: Photography, Narrative and Postmemory* (Cambridge, MA and London: Harvard University Press, 1997)

—— *The Generation of Postmemory: Writing and Visual Culture after the Holocaust* (New York: Columbia University Press, 2012)

HOLLINGTON, MICHAEL, *The Reception of Charles Dickens in Europe* (London: Bloomsbury, 2013)

HOLMGREN, BETH, ed., *The Russian Memoir: History and Literature* (Evanston: Northwestern University Press, 2007)

IANOVSKAIA, LIDIIA, 'Vsem li memuaram verit'?', *Voprosy literatury*, 1 (2008), 54–72

IAROSLAVSKAIA-MARKON, EVGENIIA, '"Klianus' otomstit' slovom i krov'iu ..."' (Publikatsiia i primechaniia Iriny Flige), *Zvezda*, 1 (2008), 127–59

IAROSLAVSKII, ALEKSANDR, 'Anarkhiia', *Slova i piatna* (1921), 22

——*Argonavty vselennoi* (Moscow and Leningrad: Biokosmisty, 1926) (CRSL, Shrift i4/1435)

——*Argonavty vselennoi* (n.p.: Salamandra, 2013)

——*Koren' is IA* (Saint Petersburg-Moscow: Biokosmisty, 1926) (CPD, Shrift 84–10/47, инв. ¹ 27660)

——*Krov' i radost'* (Irkutsk, 1921) (CRSL, Shrift w301/489)

——*Moskva–Berlin* (Berlin: Biokosmisty, 1927) (CRSL, Shrift Rb 10/6654)

——'Otrkytoe pis'mo tsentral'nomu komitetu kommunisticheskoi partii i narkomprosu Lunacharskomu', *Rul'*, 30 October 1926

——'Pis'mo v redaktsiiu', *Dni*, 31 October 1926

——'Pis'mo v redaktsiiu', *Rul'*, 02 November 1926

——*Plevok v beskonechnost'* (Vladivostok: Izd. Dal'nevostochnogo soiuza profsoiuzov, 1917)

——*Sviataia Bestial'* (Petrograd: Komitet poezii Biokosmistov-immoralistov (Severnoi gruppy), 1922) (CNLR, Shrift 3.37, Ш.62, P.2, H° 268a)

——*Svoloch' Moskva* (Moscow: Suradiny, 1922) (CRSL, Shrift w300/72)

——'V Berline. Lektsiia A.B. Iaroslavskogo', *Rul'*, 1802 (1927), p. 4

IAROSLAVSKII, ALESSANDRO, 'La preghiera della terra. Ai nuovi venuti. Versi di Alessandro Iaroslavskii (1918)', *Russia: rivista di letteratura, storia e filosofia*, 2 (1920), 96–99

IGRUNOV, VIACHESLAV, BARBAKADZE, MARK, *Antologiia samizdata. Nepodtsenzurnaia literatura v SSSR. 1950–1980* (Moscow: Mezhdunarodnyi institut gumanitarno-politicheskikh issledovanii, 2005)

IOFE, VENIAMIN, 'Solovetskii rasstrel 1937 goda', in *Memorial'noe kladbishche Sandormokh. 1937, 27 oktiabria–4 noiabria (Solovetskii etap)*, ed. by Irina Flige (Reznikova) (Saint Petersburg: Izdanie NITs 'Memorial', 1997), pp. 160–63

ISMAILOVA, SVETLANA, ed., *Entsiklopediia dlia detei* (Moscow: Avanta+, 1993–96)

IVANOV, GEORGII, *Izbrannye stikhi* (Paris: Lev, 1980)

IVANOVA, GALINA, *Istoriia GULAGa, 1918–1958: Sotsial'no-ekonomicheskii i politiko-pravovoi aspekty* (Moscow: Nauka, 2006)

JAKOBSON, MICHAEL, *Origins Of The Gulag: The Soviet Prison Camp System, 1917–1934* (Lexington: University Press of Kentucky, 2015)

JAKOBSON, ROMAN, *Smert' Vladimira Maiakovskogo* (The Hague: Mouton, 1975)

JEANNELLE, JEAN-LOUIS, *Écrire ses Mémoires au XXe siècle: déclin et renouveau d'une tradition* (Paris: Gallimard, 2008)

JURGENSON, LUBA, *L'Expérience concentrationnaire est-elle indicible* (Monaco: Editions du rocher, 2003)

'K 70-letiiu kraevedcheskogo dvizheniia. Nikolai Pavlovich Antsiferov', *Solovetskii vestnik*, 9 (1993), p. 1

KALPASHNIKOV, ANDREI, *Prisoner of Trotsky's* (Garden city, NY: Doubleday, 1920)

KAPLAN, HÉLÈNE, 'The Bibliography of the Gulag Today', in *Reflections on the Gulag*, ed. by Elena Dundovich, Francesca Gori, and Emanuela Guercetti (Milan: Feltrinelli, 2003), pp. 225–46

KATAN'IAN, RUBEN, 'V Solovkakh u politicheskikh', *Izvestiia*, 7 October 1924

KAZARNOVSKII, IURII, *Stikhi* (Moscow: Goslitizdat, 1936) (CPD, Shrift 1936и/601)

KEMETSKII (Sveshnikov), Vladimir, *Belaia noch'. Stikhi* (Moscow: Vozvrashchenie, 1998)

—— 'Liubliu ia restoranchik uglovoi, zelenyi stol ...'; 'Sutulykh spin bugry ...'; 'U kassy stuk i zviakan'e monet', in *Literaturno-khudozhestvennye sborniki 'Nedra'*, III (Moscow: Novaia Moskva, 1924), pp. 129–31

KHLEVNIUK, OLEG, *1937-i: Stalin, NKVD i sovetskoe obshchestvo* (Moscow: Izdat. Respublika, 1992)

—— *The History of the Gulag: From Collectivization to the Great Terror* (New Haven: Yale University Press, 2004)

KHODASEVICH, VLADISLAV, *Sobranie sochinenii*, 2 vols (Ann Arbor, MI: Ardis, 1983)

KIM, IULII, *Tvorcheskii vecher: Proizvedeniia raznykh let* (Moscow: Knizhnaia palata, 1990)

KISELEV-GROMOV, NIKOLAI, *SLON: Solovetskii Les Osobogo Naznacheniia* (Arkhangel'sk: Tur, 2009)

KIUNERT, MAKS, *Chudesnoe kol'tso. Poezii* (Moscow: Izdanie avtora, 1926) (CNLR, Shrift 34/594)

—— *Zheltaia Siren'* (Moscow: Izdanie avtora, 1926) (CNLR, Shrift 41/2215)

KIZNY, TOMASZ, *Gulag: Life and Death inside the Soviet Concentration Camps* (Buffalo: Richmond Hill, 2004)

KHLEBNIKOV, NIKITA, 'Chernil'nyi pribor s Solovkov, ili Rasstrel za pogodu', *Novaia Gazeta*, 5/6/2008, <http://www.novayagazeta.ru/data/2008/40/37.html> [accessed 25 July 2014]

KINVIG, CLIFFORD, *Churchill's Crusade: The British Invasion of Russia 1918–1920* (London: Hambledon Continuum, 2006)

KLEPIKOV, NIKOLAI, 'Politicheskaia tsenzura na Evropeiskom Severe RSFSR/SSSR v 1920–1930-e gg.' (Unpublished doctoral dissertation, Pomorskii Lomonosov University of Arkhangel'sk, 2005)

KLINGER, ANTON, *Solovetskaia katorga: Zapiski bezhavshego* (Berlin: Publ. po: Arkhiv russkoi revoliutsii, 1928)

KLIUEV, NIKOLA, *Stikhotvoreniia i poemy* (Moscow: Sovetskii pisatel', 1991)

KNIAZEVSKAIA, TAT'IANA, ed., *Russkaia intelligentsiia. Istoriia i sud'ba* (Moscow: Nauka, 2000)

KOKURIN, ALEKSANDR and PETROV, NIKITA, eds, *Lubianka: Organy VChK-OGPU-NKVD-NKGB-MGB-MVD-KGB. 1917–1991. Spravochnik* (Moscow: Mezhdunarodnyi Fond Demokratiia, 2003)

—— *GULAG (Glavnoe Upravlenie Lagerei) 1918–1960* (Moscow: Materik-Demoktratiia, 2002)

KOKURIN, ALEKSANDR, *Stalinskie stroiki GULAGa. 1930–1953* (Moscow: Materik-Demo-kratiia, 2005)

KOL'TSOV, MIKHAIL, 'SLON pishet', *Pravda*, 7 (1926), 1

KOZLOVA, ALENA, and OTHERS, eds, *Papiny pis'ma. Pis'ma ottsov iz GULAGa* (Moscow: Agey Tomesh/WAM, Memorial, 2014)

KOZ'MIN, BORIS, *Pisateli sovremennoi epokhi. Bio-bibliograficheskii slovar' russkikh pisatelei XX veka* (Moscow: DEM, 1992)

KRASIKOV, PETR, 'Solovki', *Izvestiia*, 15 October 1924

KRASNOVA, EVA and DROZDOVSKII, ANATOLII, 'Solovki — zhemchuzhina Belogo moria', *Debirasovskaia — Reshil'evskaia*, 45 (2011), 15–24

KRAVCHENKO, NATAL'IA, *Angely ada: stat'i, esse, zametki* (Saratov: Privolzhskoe knizhnoe izdatel'stvo, 2004)

KREMENTSOV, NIKOLAI, *Revolutionary Experiments: The Quest for Immortality in Bolshevik Science and Fiction* (Oxford: Oxford University Press, 2014)

KRITSKII, IURII, 'Solovetskii monastyr' v 1917–1920 gg.', *Solovetskii vestnik*, 12 (1993), 1

KRUSANOV, ANDREI, *Russkii avangard. 1907–1932. Istoricheskii obzor v trekh tomakh*, 3 vols (Moscow: Novoe literaturnoe obozrenie, 1996)

KUSHLINA, OL'GA, *Russkaia literatura XX veka v zerkale parodii* (Moscow: Vyschaia shkola, 1993)

KUZIAKINA, NATALIA, *Theatre in the Solovki Prison Camp* (Luxembourg: Harwood Academy Publishers, 1995)

L. L., 'Leteiskaia biblioteka — 44', *Kommersant Weekend*, 37 (2009), 63

'Lagernye torzhestva i budni zimy 1924 goda', *Solovetskii vestnik*, 15 (1993), 1

LAR'KOV, SERGEI, ed., *Memuary o politicheskikh repressiiakh v SSSR, khraniashchiesia v arkhive obshchestva Memorial* (Moscow: Zvenia, 2007)

LEHNER, GIANCARLO, and BIGAZZI, FRANCESCO, eds, *La tragedia dei comunisti italiani. Le vittime del Pci in Unione Sovietica* (Milan: Mondadori, 2000)

LEJEUNE, PHILIPPE, *Le pacte autobiographique* (Paris: Seuil, 1975).

LENIN, *Che fare? Problemi scottanti del nostro movimento* (Rome: Newton Compton, 1976)

——*Sochineniia*, 35 vols (Leningrad: Gosudarstvennoe Izdatel'stvo Politicheskoi Literatury, 1948–50)

LEONT'EV, IAROSLAV, 'Politicheskii krasnyi krest v strane serpa i molota', *Obshchaia gazeta*, 42 (1996), <http://socialist.memo.ru/books/html/leont09.htm#y1> [accessed 29 April 2015]

LEVINE, ISAAC DON, ed., *Letters from Russian Prisons* (New York: Albert and Charles Boni, 1925)

LIECHTENHAN, FRANCINE D., *Le laboratoire du goulag 1918–1939* (Paris: Desclée de Brouwer, 2004)

——*Il laboratorio del Gulag* (Turin: Lindau, 2009)

LIKHACHEV, DMITRII, 'Karteznye Igry Ugolovnikov' (iz rabot krim. kabimeta)', 50, 1 (1930), 35–37

——'Ne tak davno ...', *Ogonek*, 28 (1988), 4–5

——*Ia vspominaiu* (Moscow: Progress, 1991)

——*Vospominaniia* (St Petersburg: Logos, 1995)

——'"Na Solovkakh ia ponial, chto kazhdyi chelovek — chelovek". Zametki i nabliudeniia', *Pravoslavie i mir*, 30/09/2014 <http://www.pravmir.ru/na-solovkax-ya-ponyal-chto-kazhdyj-chelovek-chelovek/> [accessed 23 January 2015]

LIVAK, LEONID, USTINOV, ANDREI, *Literaturnyi avangard russkogo Parizha. Istoriia, Khronika, Antologiia. Dokumenty* (Moscow: OGI, 2014)

LOMONOSOV, MIKHAIL, *Izbrannye proizvedeniia* (Leningrad: Sovetskii pisatel', 1986)

——'Petr Velikii', *Polnoe sobranie sochinenii: Poeziia, oratorskaia proza, nadpisi (1732–1764)*, 11 vols (Moscow: Academiia nauk SSSR, 1959)

LOTMAN, IURII, 'Literaturnaia biografiia v istoriko-kul'turnom kontekste (K tipologicheskomu sootnosheniiu teksta I lichnosti avtora)', *O russkoi literature* (Saint Petersburg: Isskustvo-SPB, 1997), pp. 804–16

——*Ob iskusstve: Struktura khudozhestvennogo teksta; Semiotika kino i problemy kinoestetiki; Stat'i; Zametki; Vystupleniia (1962–1993)* (Saint Petersburg: Iskusstvo-SPB, 1998)

LOZINA-LOZINSKII, ALEKSEI, *Solitudine. Capri e Napoli (appunti di un girovago)* (Rome: Scienza e Lettere, 2010)

MAGAROTTO, LUIGI, *La letteratura irreale: saggio sulle origini del realismo socialista* (Venice and Padua: Marsilio, 1980)

MAGUIRE, MUIREANN. 'Post-Lamarckian Prodigies: Evolutionary Biology in Soviet Science Fiction', *New Zealand Slavonic Journal*, 43 (2009), 23–53

MAIAKOVSKII, VLADIMIR, *Polnoe sobranie sochinenii* (Moscow: Khudozhestvennaia literatura, 1955–61)

Mäkinen, Ikka, 'Libraries in Hell: Cultural Activities in Soviet Prisons and Labor Camps from the 1930s to the 1950s', *Libraries and Culture*, 28 (1993), 117–42

Maksimenkov, Leonid, *Bol'shaia tsenzura. Pisateli i zhurnalisty v strane sovetov. 1917–1956* (Moscow: Materik-Demokratiia, 2005)

Mal'sagov, Sozerko, *Adskie ostrova: Sovetskaia tiur'ma na Dal'nem Severe* (Nal'chik: Izdat. tsentr 'El-fa', 1996)

——*An Island Hell: A Soviet Prison in the Far North* (London: A. M. Philpot, 1926

Manuil (Lemeshevskii), 'Solovetskii tsvetnik', *Dvkhovnyi Sobesednik*, 2.22 (2000), pp. 51-69.

Marie, Jean-Jacques, 'Quand l'histoire tombe au niveau du dépotoir ...', *Les Cahiers du mouvement ouvrier*, 23 (2004), 157–59

Markov, Vladimir, 'Gostinitsa dlia puteshestvuiushchikh v prekrasnom; iz knigi "Ocherk istorii ruskogo imazhinizma"', *Zvezda*, 2 (2005), 211–19

Martini, Mauro, *Oltre il disgelo: la letteratura russa dopo l'Urss* (Milan: Bruno Mondadori, 2002)

Medveded, Roi and Medvedev, Zhores, *Neizvestnyi Stalin* (Moscow: Vremia, 2011)

Mel'gunov, Sergei, *'Krasnyi terror' v Rossii 1918–1923* (Berlin: Vataga, 1924)

Mel'nik, Antonina, 'Razbivaiutsia v more l'dy ... Stikhi zakliuchennykh SLONa iz arkhiva A. V. Mel'nik', *Solovetskoe more*, 3 (2004), 177–81

Mel'nik, Antonina and Soshina, Antonina, eds, 'Zaiavleniia politzakliuchennykh Petrominska i Solovkov. 1923–1924 gg.', *Zven'ia. Istoricheskii al'manakh*, 1 (1991), 245–51

'Memorandum on the Russian Situation', *Slavonic and East European Review*, 9 (1930/31), 497–503.

Mengaldo, Pier Vittorio, *La vendetta è il racconto: testimonianze e riflessioni sulla Shoah* (Torino: Bollati Boringhieri, 2007)

Merezhkovskii, Dmitrii, *Stikhotvoreniia i poemy* (Saint Petersburg: Novaia Biblioteka Poeta, 2000)

Merridale, Catherine, *Night of Stone. Death and Memory in Twentieth Century Russia* (London: Granta Books, 2000)

Methwin, Eugene H., 'Isaac Don Levine: Herald of Free Russia', *Modern Age*, Spring (1995), 241–49

Mo, Ettore, *Gulag e altri inferni* (Milan: Rizzoli, 2001)

Mogilianskaia, Lada, 'Burevestnik surovyi', *Na shturm trassy*, 7 (1936), 8 (CBSB, Film P 2000.673 n° 110)

Molodiakov, Vasilii, *Valerii Briusov v poezii ego sovremennikov* (Moscow: Volodei, 2013)

Morozov, Konstantin, 'Fenomen subkul'tury rossiiskogo revoliutsionera nachala XX v.', in *Chelovek i lichnost' v istorii Rossii, konets XIX–XX vek. Materialy mezhdunarodnogo kollokviuma*, ed. by Marina Begletsova (Saint Petersburg: Nestor-Istoriia, 2012), pp. 134–48

Morshakova, Elena and Tutova, Tat'iana, 'Solovetskie sviatyni v Moskovskom Kremle', *Nashe nasledie*, 59–60 (2001), 108–21

Morukov, Iurii, 'Solovetskii lager' osobogo naznacheniia (1923–1933 gg.)', *Solovetskoe more*, 3 (2004), 122–29

Mozhanskaia, Anna, 'Po prochtenii Sinodika M. F. Andreeva', *Vestnik PSTGU*, 2 (2010), 63–64

Murav'ev, Vladimir, ed., *Solovetskaia muza. Stikhi i pesni zakliuchennykh SLONa* (Moscow: Vozvrashchenie, 1992)

——*Sred' drugikh imen* (Moscow: Moskovskii rabochii, 1990)

——*Sviataia doroga: Nikol'skaia ulitsa, Lubianka, Sretenka, Prospekt Mira, Iaroslavskoe Shosse* (Moscow: Algoritm, 2007)

Nagibin, Iurii, *Poezdka na ostrova* (Moscow: Molodaia gvardiia, 1987)

NALBANTIAN, SUZANNE, *Aesthetic Autobiography: From Life to Art in Marcel Proust, James Joyce, Virginia Woolf and Anaïs Nin* (New York: St. Martin's Press, 1994)

NEMIROVICH-DANCHENKO, VASILII, *Belomor'e i Solovki: vospominaniia i rasskazy* (Moscow: Izd. Gosudarstvennaia publichnaia istoricheskaia biblioteka Rossii, 2009)

NERLER, PAVEL, *Osip Mandel'shtam i ego solagerniki* (Moscow: AST, 2015)

NEROSLEV, V., 'Ne nado nam ni khramov, ni popov', *Novaia zhizn' domzaka*, 1 (1923), 6

NIKOLAEV, IURII, *V poiskakh za bozhestvom: ocherki iz istorii gnostitsizma* (Saint Petersburg: tip. A. S. Suvorina, 1913)

NIKONOV-SMORODIN, MIKHAIL, *Krasnaia katorga* (Sofia: Izd-vo N.T.S.N.P., 1938)

OBELOVA, TAT'IANA, 'Vospominaniia ob ottse', *Aleksandrov.ru*, 23/3/2007 www.aleksandrov. ru/mr_news_archive/53/40/1/4762 [accessed 6 December 2014]

OLITSKAIA, EKATERINA, *Moi vospominaniia* (Frankfurt am Main: Posev, 1971)

OLNEY, JAMES, ed., *Autobiography: Essays Theoretical and Critical* (Princeton, NJ: Princeton University Press, 1980)

OSIPENKO, MARINA, 'Khraniteli very. Bratiia Solovetskogo monastyria posle Oktiabr'skogo perevorota 1917 g.', *Sever*, 3–4 (2013), 31–59

PALERNAIA, ESTER, ROZENBERG, ALEKSANDR, and FINKEL', ALEKSANDR, *Parnas dybom: Pro kozlov, sobak i Veverleev* (Moscow: Khudozhestvennaia literatura, 1990)

PANCHENKOV, OLEG, FEDOTOVA, MARINA, FEDOROVA, IRINA, *Likhachev D. S.: Vospominania. Razdum'ia. Raboty raznykh let* (Saint Petersburg: ARS, 2006)

PANNENKOV, G., 'Ne govori, chto molodost' sgubila', *Novaia zhizn' domzaka*, 1 (1923), 10

PANTANO EDOARDO, 'Boris Cederholm, au pays du Nep et de la Tchéka', *Bibliografia Fascista*, 5–6 (1929), 47–50

PAPERNO, IRINA, *Stories of the Soviet Experience: Memoirs, Diaries, Dreams* (Ithaca: Cornell University Press, 2009)

PARNOK, SOFIA, *Sobranie stikhotvorenii* (Saint Petersburg: Inapress, 1998)

PARRAVICINI, GIOVANNA, *Julija Danzas* (Milan: La casa di Matriona, 2001)

PAVLOV, DMITRII, ' "Vyiavlena sistema proizvola i polnogo razlozheniia". Materialy komissii OGPU ob usloviiakh soderzhaniia zakliuchennykh v Solovetskom lagere osobogo naznacheniia. 1930 g.', *Istoricheskii arkhiv*, 5 (2005), 65–82

PAYNE, ROBERT, *Lenin* (Milan: Della Volpe Editore, 1967)

Pesni Russkikh bardov (Paris: YMCA Press, 1977)

PETROV, NIKITA and SKORKIN, KONSTANTIN, *Kto rukovodil NKVD. 1934–1941. Spravochnik* (Moscow: Zven'ia, 1999)

PIERALLI, CLAUDIA, 'The Poetry of Soviet Political Prisoners (1921–1939): An Historical-Typological Framework', in *Contributi italiani al XV Congresso Internazionale degli Slavisti*, ed. by Marcello Garzaniti, Alberto Alberti, Monica Perotto, and Bianca Sulpasso (Firenze: Firenze University Press, 2013), pp. 387–412

PIRETTO, GIAN PIERO, *Gli occhi di Stalin. La cultura visuale nell'era staliniana* (Milan: Raffaello Cortina Editore, 2010)

—— *Il radioso avvenire: mitologie culturali sovietiche* (Turin: Einaudi, 2001)

PLEKHANOV, ALEKSANDR, *VChK–OGPU v gody novoi ekonomicheskoi politiki, 1921–1928* (Moscow: Kuchkovo pole, 2006)

PLEKHANOV, ANDREI and PLEKHANOV, ALEKSANDR, eds, *F. E. Dzerzhinskii — predesedatel' VChK-OGPU. 1917–1926* (Moscow: Mezhdunarodnyi Fond Demokratiia, 2007)

PODDA, FABRIZIO, *L'iconicità, la lirica. Immagini, teorie e pratiche poetiche da Leopardi a Zanzotto* (Bologna: I libri di Emil, 2012)

POKROVSKII, NIKOLAI and PETROV, STANISLAV, eds, *Arkhivy Kremlia* (Moscow-Novosibirsk: ROSSPEN-Sibirskii khronograf, 1997)

POMERANTSEV, VLADIMIR, 'Ob iskrennosti v literature', *Novyi Mir*, 12 (1953), 218–45

POPLAVSKII, BORIS, *Sobranie sochinenii v 3-kh tomakh* (Moscow: Knizhnitsa, Russkii put', Soglasie, 2000–2009)

POPOVA (Tsederbaum), Tamara, *Sud'ba rodnykh L. Martova v Rossii posle 1917 goda* (Moscow: Rossiia molodaia, 1996)

PRILEPIN, ZAKHAR, *Obitel'* (Moscow: AST, 2014)

PRISHVIN, MIKHAIL, 'Puteshestvie', *Solovetskoe more*, 4 (2005), 164–66

PROTASOV, LEV, *Liudi Uchreditel'nogo sobraniia: portret v inter'ere epokhi* (Moscow: ROSSPEN, 2008)

PUSHKIN, ALEKSANDR, *Lirika, poemy, povesti, dramaticheskie proizvedeniia, Evgenii Onegin* (Moscow: Astrel', 2003)

REATI, FIORENZO, *Dio dirà l'ultima parola. La persecuzione della Chiesa cattolica in Russia in epoca sovietica* (Lavis: Arca, 2003)

REED, JOHN, *Ten Days That Shook the World* (New York: International Publishers, 1919)

REZNIKOV, LEONID, *Gor'kii izvestnyi i neizvestnyi* (Petrozavodsk: A/O Amitie, 1996)

REZNIKOVA, IRINA, 'Paskha v Solovetskom lagere', *Solovetskii vestnik*, 5 (1993), 1

—— 'Paskha v Solovetskom lagere', *Solovetskii vestnik*, 6 (1993), 1

—— 'Paskha v Solovetskom lagere', *Solovetskii vestnik*, 7 (1993), 1

—— 'Paskha v Solovetskom lagere', *Solovetskii vestnik*, 8 (1993), 1

—— *Pravoslavie na Solovkakh: Materialy po istorii Solovetskogo lageria* (Saint Petersburg: Memorial, 1994)

RITTERSPORN, GABOR, *Die undokumentierte Geschichte des Solovecker Lagers*, <http://www.solovki.org/de/files/Geschichte_des_SLON.pdf> [accessed 16 November 2010]

RIZZI, DANIELA, 'L'inafferabile Età d'Argento', *Europa Orientalis*, 2 (1996), 77–96

ROBSON, ROY, *Solovki: The Story of Russia Told through its Most Remarkable Islands* (New Haven: Yale University Press, 2004)

ROGACHEV, MIKHAIL, ed., *Pokaianie. Komi respublikanskii martirolog zhertv massovykh politicheskikh repressii*, 11 vols (Syktyvkar: Komi knizhnoe izdatel'stvo, 1998–2011)

ROLIN, OLIVIER, *Le météorologue* (Paris: Seuil, 2014)

ROSSI, ZHAK, *Spravochnik po GULAGu* (London: Overseas Publications Interchange, 1987)

ROZANOV, MIKHAIL, *Zavoevateli belykh piaten* (Munich: Posev1951)

—— *Solovetskii kontslager' v monastyre, 1922–1939 gody: fakty, domysly, 'parashi': obzor vospominanii solovchan solovchanami* (Printed in USA: Izdanie avtora, 1979)

ROIZENZON, LEONID, 'Zametki po russkoi leksikografii. Pokazukha', *Etimologicheskie issledovaniia po russkomu iazyku*, v (Moscow: Izdatel'stvo MGU, 1966), pp. 104–10

RUDER, CYNTHIA A., *Making History for Stalin: The Story of the Belomor Canal* (Gainesville, FL: University Press of Florida, 1998)

RUSAKOV, G., 'Iz nashego al'boma', *Tiur'ma*, 3 (1921), 75

RUSAKOV, GEORGII, 'Ostrova Georgiia Rusakova', *Solovetskoe more*, 10 (2011), 167–71

RUSAKOVA, ELENA, and FLIGE, IRINA, eds, 'Dobkin Aleksandr Iosifovich', *Enstiklopediia Sankt-Peterburga*, <http://www.encspb.ru/object/2805399823?lc=ru> [accessed 29 April 2015]

RYZHKOV, VLADIMIR, 'Putin's Distorted History', *The Moscow Times*, 18 November 2013 <http://www.themoscowtimes.com/opinion/article/putins-distorted-history/489799.htm> [accessed 25 July 2014]

ŠALAMOV, VARLAM, *I racconti di Kolyma*, 1 (Turin: Einaudi, 1999), pp. vii–xlii

SANDOMIRSKAIA, IRINA, ' "Bez stali i leni": Aesopian Language and Legitimacy', in *Power and Legitimacy: Challenges from Russia*, ed. by Per-Arne Bodin, Stefan Hedlund, and Elena Namli (New York: Routledge, 2013), pp. 188–98

SAUNDERS, MAX, *Self Impression: Life-Writing, Autobiografiction and the Forms of Modern Literature* (Oxford: Oxford University Press, 2010)

SCHLÖGEL, KARL, *Solowki — Laboratorium der Extreme*, <http://www.solovki.org/de/html/

Artikel_Schloegel_de.html> [accessed 16 April 2015]

SERVICE, ROBERT, *Lenin: A Biography* (London: Macmillan, 2000)

——*Stalin: A Biography* (London: Macmillan, 2004)

SEVERIANIN, IGOR', *Stikhotvoreniia* (Leningrad: Sovetskii pisatel', 1975)

SHAPOVALOV, VERONICA, *Remembering the Darkness: Women in Soviet Prisons* (Lanham: Rowman & Littlefield, 2001)

SHAUFEL'BERGER, ARNOL'D, 'Solovki — Vospominaniia', in *Leonard Shaufel'berger (10.1.1839– 19.2.1894)*, ed. by Elena Tarkhanova and Marcus Schütz (Saint Petersburg: Izd-vo Politekhnicheskogo Universiteta, 2009), pp. 58–103

SHENTALINSKII, VITALII, *Raby svobody: v literaturnykh arkhivakh KGB* (Moscow: Parus, 1995)

SHIRIAEV, BORIS, *Neugasimaia lampada* (New York: Izd-vo im. Chekhova, 1954)

——*Neugasimaia lampada* (Solovki: Spaso-Preobrazhenskii Solovetskii Stavropigial'nyi Muzhskoi Monastyr', 2013)

SHUB, DAVID, *Politicheskie deiateli Rossii (1850-kh–1920-kh gg.). Sbornik statei* (New York: Izdanie 'Novogo zhurnala', 1969)

SKOPIN, VLADIMIR, *Na Solovetskikh ostrovakh* (Moscow: Iskusstvo, 1991)

SMIRNOV, MIKHAIL, ed., *Sistema ispravitel'no-trudovykh lagerei v SSSR: 1923–1960. Spravochnik* (Moscow: Zven'ia, 1998)

SMIRNOVA, MARINA, ISTOMINA, ZINAIDA, RADIKAINEN, LIUBOV', *SLON-STON. Solovetskie lageria i tiur'ma osobogo naznacheniia (1923–1939): Rekomendatel'nyi ukazatel' literatury* (Arkhangel'sk: SGIAPMZ-AONB, 2003)

SMITH, MICHAEL G., 'Anatomy of a Rumour: Murder Scandal, the Musavat Party and Narratives of the Russian Revolution in Baku, 1917–1920', *Journal of Contemporary History*, 36 (2001), 211–40

SNEGOV (Shtein), Sergei, *Iazyk, kotoryi nenavidit* (Moscow: Prosvet, 1991)

——*Noril'skie rasskazy* (Moscow: Sovetskii pisatel', 1991)

SOLONEVICH, IVAN, 'Collectivisation in Practice', *Slavonic and East European Review*, 14 (1935–1936), 81

——*Rossiia v kontslagere* (Sofia: Izd. Natsional'no-trudovogo soiuza novogo pokoleniia, 1936)

Solovetskie lageria Osobogo Naznacheniia OGPU — Fotoletopis' (Saint Petersburg: Gosudarstvennyi muzei istorii Sankt-Peterburga, Muzei S. M. Kirova, Solovetskii gosudarstvennyi istoriko-arkhitekturnyi i prirodnyi muzei-zapovednik, 2004)

SOLZHENITSYN, ALEKSANDR, *Arkhipelag GULag, 1918–1956: opyt khudozhestvennogo issledovaniia*, 3 vols (Ekaterinburg: U-Faktoriia, 2006)

SOSHINA, ANTONINA, 'Materialy k istorii lageria i tiur'my na Solovkakh (1923–1939 gg.)', *Solovetskoe more*, 9 (2010), 122–34

——' "Mutnyi prizrak svobody" (o pobegakh s Solovkov v 1923–1939 gg.)', *Solovetskoe more*, 6 (2007), 127–35

——'Muzei Solovetskogo obshchestva kraevedeniia (1925–1937 gg.)', *Solovetskoe more*, 3 (2004), 130–42

——*Na Solovkakh protiv voli: sud'by i sroki 1923–1939* (Solovki: Spaso-Preobrazhenskii Solovetskii Stavropigial'nyi Muzhskoi Monastyr', 2014)

——'Podstrelennye na vzlete (molodezh' v lagere na Solovkakh)', *Solovetskoe more*, 8 (2009), 118–28

——'Repressirovannaia nauka. Uchenye v zakliuchenii na Solovkakh', *Solovetskoe more*, 10 (2011), 128–40

——'Solovetskii lager' osobogo naznacheniia: daty, tsifry, fakty', *Sm. vestnik*, spetsial'nyi vypusk (2001), 5

——'Tvorcheskaia intelligentsiia na Solovkakh', *Solovetskoe more*, 11 (2012), 104–18

SPIRIDONOVA, LIDIIA, *Gor'kii: dialog s istoriei* (Moscow: Nasledie — Nauka, 1994)

STERN, LUDMILA, *Western Intellectuals and the Soviet Union, 1920–1940* (London: Routledge, 2007)

STOGOV, N., 'Tiuremnaia pechat' 1921–1935 godov', *Pamiat'*, 1 (1978), 527–80

SVIRSKAIA, MINA, 'Iz vospominanii', *Minuvshee*, 7 (1992), 7–57

SYSOEV, NIKOLAI, 'General katorgi, ili kar'era riadovogo zeka', *Na boevom postu*, 11 (1996), 22–26

TAGANOV, LEONID, 'Potaennaia literatura: poeziia GULaga', in *Voprosy ontologicheskoi poetiki. Potaennaia Literatura. Issledovaniia i materialy*, ed. by Leonid Bykov (Ivanovo: Ivanovskii Gosudarstvennyi Universitet, 1998), pp. 80–87

TALALAI, MIKHAIL, *Boris Shiriaev. Di-Pi v Italii. Zapiski prodavtsa kukol* (Saint Petersburg: Ateleia, 2007)

TARTAKOVSKII, ANDREI, *Russkaia memuaristika i istoricheskoe soznanie XIX veka* (Moscow: Nauka, 1991)

TARTAKOVSKII, ANDREI, EMMONS, TERENCE and BUDNITSKII, OLEG, ed., *Rossiia i rossiiskaia emigratsiia v vospominaniiakh i dnevnikakh: annotirovannyi ukazatel' knig, zhurnal'nykh i gazetnykh publikatsii, izdannykh za rubezhom v 1917–1991 gg.* (Moscow: ROSSPEN, 2004)

TEFFI, 'Solovki', *Zhar-ptitsa*, 1 (1921), 7–15

THAIDIGSMANN, KAROLINE, *Lagererfahrung und Identität: Literarische Spiegelungen sowjetischer Lagerhaft in Texten von Varlam Šalamov, Lev Konson, Naum Nim und Andrej Sinjavskij* (Heidelberg: Universitätsverlag Winter, 2009)

TIUKINA, SVETLANA, '"Krome, kak v USLONe, nigde ne khochu sidet'". Mirovaia i russkaia literatury v solovetskoi lagernoi poezii', *Solovetskoe more*, 4 (2005), 167

——'Teper' vy v Solovkakh (lirika vremen SLONa)', *Solovetskoe more*, 2 (2003), 181

——'Teper' vy v Solovkakh ...', *Status-kvo*, 30 June 2009, <http://www.statusquo.ru/ 638/ article_835.html/> [accessed 23 January 2015]

TODOROV, TZVETAN, ed., *I formalisti russi* (Einaudi: Torino, 1968)

TOKER, LEONA, *Return from the Archipelago: Narratives of Gulag Survivors* (Bloomington: Indiana University Press, 2000)

TOLCZYK, DARIUSZ, *See No Evil: Literary Cover-ups and Discoveries of the Soviet Camp Experience* (Yale: Yale University Press, 1999)

TOLSTOI, LEV, *Sobranie sochinenii v 22-kh tomakh* (Moscow: Khudozhestvennaia Literatura, 1978–85)

TSUR, REUVEN, *Toward a Theory of Cognitive Poetics* (Amsterdam: North-Holland, 1992)

TSYGANKOV, ANATOLII, ed., *Ikh nazyvali KR: Repressii v Karelii v 20–30-kh godov* (Petrozavodsk: Kareliia, 1992)

TVARDOVSKII, ALEKSANDR, *Sobranie sochinenii* (Moscow: Khudozhestvennaia Literatura, 1976)

TYNIANOV, IURII, *Arkhaisty i novatory* (Leningrad: Priboi, 1929)

ULAM, ADAM, *The Bolsheviks: The Intellectual and Political History of the Triumph of Communism in Russia* (New York: Macmillan, 1965)

UDY, GILES, *Labour and the Gulag: Russia and the Seduction of the British Left* (London: Biteback Publishing, 2017)

UMNIAGIN, VIACHESLAV, ed., *Vospominaniia Solovetskikh uznikov*, 5 vols (Solovki: Spaso-Preobrazhenskii Solovetskii Stavropigial'nyi Muzhskoi Monastyr', 2013–17)

USTINOV, ANDREI, 'Dve zhizni Nikolaia Bernera', in *Litsa: Biograficheskii al'manakh* (Saint Petersburg: Feniks, 2002), pp. 5–64

VAGINOV, KONSTANTIN, *Sobranie stikhotvorenii* (Munich: Otto Sagner, 1982)

VANGENGEIM, ALEKSEI, *Vozvrashchenie imeni* (Moscow: Tablitsy Mendeleeva, 2005)

VASIL'EV, VIKTOR, *Spolokhi. Stikhi* (Moscow: Vozvrashchenie, 1992)

'V Berline. Lektsiia A.B. Iaroslavskogo', *Rul'*, 1802 (1927), 4

VENIAVKIN, IL'IA, *Solovki: chto Gor'kii videl i chto skryl*, <http://arzamas.academy/materials/316> [accessed 29 April 2016]

VILENSKII, SEMEN, ed., *Deti GULAGa. 1918–1956. Dokumenty* (Moscow: Rosspen, 2002)

——, ed., *Est' vsiudu svet … Chelovek v totalitarnom obshchestve* (Moscow: Vozvrashchenie, 2001)

——*Poeziia uznikov Gulaga* (Moscow: Materik Rossia. XX vek, 2005)

VITALE, SERENA, *A Mosca! A Mosca!* (Milan: Mondadori, 2010)

VODOLAZKIN, EVGENII, *Aviator* (Moscow: AST, 2016)

——*Chast' sushi, okruzhennaia nebom: Solovetskie teksty i obrazy* (Saint Petersburg: Logos, 2011)

VOLKOV, OLEG, *Pogruzhenie vo t'mu* (Moscow: Molodaia gvardiia, 1989)

VTOROVA-IAFA (Iasevich), Ol'ga, 'Iz vospominanii', *Pamiat'*, 1 (1978), 93–158

'V Suzdal'skom i Solovetskom lageriakh: Zakliuchennye v Suzdale i Solovkakh o svoem rezhime', *Izvestiia*, 30 September 1924

WESTERMAN, FRANK, *Engineers of the Soul: In the Footsteps of Stalin's Writers* (London: Harvill Secker, 2010)

WILK, MARIUSZ, *Wilczy notes* (Warsaw, Noir sur blanc, 2007)

ZABOLOTSKII, NIKOLAI, IN *Stolbtsy i poemy, 1926–1933; Stikhotvoreniia, 1932–1958; Stikhotvoreniia raznykh let; Proza* (Moscow: Khudozhestvennaia literatura, 1983)

ZAITSEV, IVAN, *Solovki. Kommunisticheskaia katorga ili mesto pytok i smerti. Iz lichnykh stradanii, perezhivanii, nabliudenii i vpechatlenii* (Shanghai: Slovo, 1931)

ZALAMBANI, MARIA, *Censura, istituzioni e politica letteraria in URSS (1964–1985)* (Florence: Firenze University Press, 2009)

ZUBOK, VLADISLAV, *The idea of Russia: The Life and Work of Dmitry Likhachev* (London: I.B. Tauris & Co. Ltd, 2017).

Websites and Other Sources

CDs and DVDs

GULAG. Das Lagersystem in der UdSSR (Berlin: Memorial Deutschland, 2006) [On DVD]

Solovetskaia pechat' (1924–1930) (Arkhangel'sk: Arkhangel'skaia oblastnaia nauchnaia biblioteka imeni N.A. Dobroliubova, 2007) [DVD-ROM]

Documents

'Federal Law "About Archive Activity in Russian Federation" and its Differences from Legislative Acts earlier Regulating Legal Relations about Archive Activity (22.10.2004)'

'Pis'mo ot ITs MVD RK predsedateliu Pravleniia KROU NITs 'Memorial' Paaso V.T (27.02.2012)'

Films

[Note: it was impossible to find the distributors of these movies apart from Lungin's and Rolin's. For the others I have indicated the country where they were filmed.]

Krepko tseluiu i liubliu, dir. by Anastasiia Cherkasova (Russia, 2006)

Ostrov, dir. by Pavel Lungin (Pavel Lungin's Studio, 2006)

Solovki — la Bibliothèque disparue, dir. by Olivier Rolin (ARTE France, 2014)

Solovki — Solovetskie lageria osobogo naznacheniia, dir. by Aleksei Cherkasov (USSR, 1928)

Vlast' Solovetskaia, dir. by Marina Goldovskaia (Russia, 1988)

Websites

<http://www.alexanderyakovlev.org/> [accessed 24 November 2014]
<http://www.anneapplebaum.com/Gulag-a-history/> [accessed 25 July 2014]
<http://antisoviet.narod.ru/>
<http://www.aonb.ru/ekb/solp/index.php> [accessed 24 November 2014]
<http://arch.iofe.center/?lc=ru>
<http://grani-tv.ru/entries/490/>
<http://gulaghistory.org/>
<http://www.gulag-italia.it/> [accessed 25 July 2014]
<http://gulagmuseum.org/start.do> [accessed 25 July 2014]
<http://imwerden.de/cat/modules.php?name=books>
<http://www.ktrv.ru/docs/history.doc>
<http://www.lastoriasiamonoi.rai.it/puntata.aspx?id=725http://leb.nlr.ru/> [accessed 25 July 2014]
<http://likhachev.lfond.spb.ru/Images/avtograf/lampada.htm> [accessed 24 November 2014]
<http://likhachev.lfond.spb.ru/Images/avtograf/solovky.htm>
<http://lists.memo.ru/> [accessed 24 November 2014]
<http://www.memo.ru/> [accessed 24 November 2014]
<http://www.memorialitalia.it/> [accessed 25 July 2014]
<http://www.memorial.krsk.ru/>
<http://www.nkvd.org/literature/solovki_literature.html>
<http://www.permgani.ru/repress/> [accessed 17 October 2014]
<http://www.perpetrator2004.narod.ru/>
<http://pkk.memo.ru/> [accessed 25 July 2014]
<http://psi.ece.jhu.edu/~kaplan/IRUSS/BUK/GBARC/buk.html>
<http://www.russinitalia.it/>
<http://www.sakharov-archive.ru/index.htm>
<http://www.sakharov-center.ru/asfcd/auth/> [accessed 24 November 2014]
<http://socialist.memo.ru/index.htm>
<http://www.solovki.ca> [accessed 25 July 2014]
<http://www.solovki.info/?action=topic&id=299> [accessed 20 January 2015]
<http://solovki-monastyr.ru/abbey/history/> [accessed 25 July 2014]
<http://www.solovki.org/>
<http://www.solovki.ru/history.html>
<http://www.solovky.ru/>
<http://www.unilib.neva.ru/dl/327/Theme_10/Sources/Soc_polit_life/Kremls_archievs.htm>
<http://vcisch2.narod.ru/> [accessed 24 November 2014]
<http://visz.nlr.ru/> [accessed 24 November 2014]

DVDROM

Zhertvy politicheskogo terrora v SSSR (Moscow: Obshchestvo Memorial, 2001)
Zhertvy politicheskogo terrora v SSSR, 2-e i dop. Izd. (Saint Petersburg: NIIPTs Memorial, 2002)

INDEX

❖